PROGRAMMING WITH
MICROSOFT® VISUAL BASIC® 2010

ONE WEEK LOAN

FIFTH EDITION

PROGRAMMING WITH MICROSOFT® VISUAL BASIC® 2010

DIANE ZAK

COURSE TECHNOLOGY
CENGAGE Learning·

Australia · Brazil · Japan · Korea · Mexico · Singapore · Spain · United Kingdom · United States

COURSE TECHNOLOGY
CENGAGE Learning

**Programming with Microsoft® Visual Basic®
2010, Fifth Edition, International Edition**

Diane Zak

Executive Editor: Marie Lee

Acquisitions Editor: Brandi Shailer

Freelance Product Manager: Tricia Coia

Associate Product Manager: Stephanie Lorenz

Marketing Manager: Shanna Shelton

Senior Content Project Manager: Jill Braiewa

Quality Assurance: Green Pen QA

Art Director: Faith Brosnan

Cover Designer: Cabbage Design Company

Text Designer: Shawn Girsberger

Print Buyer: Julio Esperas

Proofreader: Suzanne Huizenga

Indexer: Rich Carlson

Compositor: Integra Software Services

Library of Congress Control Number: 2011921828

International Edition:
ISBN-13: 978-1-111-57761-2
ISBN-10: 1-111-57761-7

Cengage Learning International Offices

Asia
www.cengageasia.com
tel: (65) 6410 1200

Australia/New Zealand
www.cengage.com.au
tel: (61) 3 9685 4111

Brazil
www.cengage.com.br
tel: (55) 11 3665 9900

India
www.cengage.co.in
tel: (91) 11 4364 1111

Latin America
www.cengage.com.mx
tel: (52) 55 1500 6000

UK/Europe/Middle East/Africa
www.cengage.co.uk
tel: (44) 0 1264 332 424

**Represented in Canada by
Nelson Education, Ltd.**
www. nelson.com
tel: (416) 752 9100 / (800) 668 0671

Cengage Learning is a leading provider of customized learning solutions with office locations around the globe, including Singapore, the United Kingdom, Australia, Mexico, Brazil and Japan. Locate your local office at **www.cengage.com/global**

For product information: **www.cengage.com/international**
Visit your local office: **www.cengage.com/global**
Visit our corporate website: **www.cengage.com**

AVAILABILITY OF RESOURCES MAY DIFFER BY REGION. Check with your local Cengage Learning representative for details.

Printed in the United States of America
1 2 3 4 5 6 7 17 16 15 14 13 12 11

Brief Contents

Preface . . . . **xviii**

Read This Before You Begin . . . . **xxiii**

OVERVIEW   An Introduction to Programming **1**

CHAPTER 1   An Introduction to Visual Basic 2010 . . . . **9**

CHAPTER 2   Designing Applications . . . . **.60**

CHAPTER 3   Using Variables and Constants **118**

CHAPTER 4   The Selection Structure **190**

CHAPTER 5   More on the Selection Structure **261**

CHAPTER 6   The Repetition Structure **327**

CHAPTER 7   Sub and Function Procedures **394**

CHAPTER 8   String Manipulation **446**

CHAPTER 9   Arrays **502**

CHAPTER 10   Structures and Sequential Access Files **562**

CHAPTER 11   Classes and Objects **615**

CHAPTER 12   Web Applications **681**

CHAPTER 13   Working with Access Databases and LINQ **740**

CHAPTER 14   Access Databases and SQL **796**

v

APPENDIX A   Locating Syntax and Logic Errors **848**

APPENDIX B   GUI Design Guidelines **858**

APPENDIX C   Visual Basic Conversion Functions **863**

APPENDIX D   Applications with Multiple Forms . . . . **Online**

Index **864**

Contents

Preface . . . . **xviii**

Read This Before You Begin. . . . . **xxiii**

OVERVIEW   An Introduction to Programming **1**

Programming a Computer 2
   The Programmer's Job 2
   Do You Have What It Takes to Be a Programmer? 2
   Employment Opportunities 3
Visual Basic 2010 4
   A Visual Basic 2010 Demonstration 4
Using the Chapters Effectively 6
Summary 7
Key Terms 8

CHAPTER 1   An Introduction to Visual Basic 2010. . . . . **9**

LESSON A   The Splash Screen Application **11**
   Managing the Windows in the IDE 15
   The Windows Form Designer Window. 16
   The Solution Explorer Window 17
   The Properties Window 18
Properties of a Windows Form 19
   The Name Property. 20
   The Text Property 21
   The StartPosition Property 21
   The Font Property 21
   The Size Property 22
Setting and Restoring a Property's Value. 22
Saving a Solution 23
Closing the Current Solution 23
Opening an Existing Solution 24
Exiting Visual Studio 2010 or Visual Basic 2010 Express 24
Lesson A Summary. 24
Lesson A Key Terms 26
Lesson A Review Questions 27
Lesson A Exercises 28

LESSON B   The Toolbox Window. **31**
The Label Tool. 32
   Setting the Text Property 34
   Setting the Location Property 34

Changing a Property for Multiple Controls 35
Using the Format Menu 35
The PictureBox Tool 36
The Button Tool 38
Starting and Ending an Application 38
The Code Editor Window 40
    The Me.Close() Instruction 42
Lesson B Summary 44
Lesson B Key Terms 45
Lesson B Review Questions 46
Lesson B Exercises 47

LESSON C   Using the Timer Tool **50**
Setting the FormBorderStyle Property 52
The MinimizeBox, MaximizeBox, and ControlBox Properties 53
Printing the Application's Code and Interface 54
Lesson C Summary 55
Lesson C Key Terms 56
Lesson C Review Questions 56
Lesson C Exercises 57

CHAPTER 2   Designing Applications **60**

LESSON A   Creating an Object-Oriented Application **63**
Planning an Object-Oriented Application 63
    Identifying the Application's Tasks 64
    Identifying the Objects 66
    Identifying the Events 67
    Drawing a Sketch of the User Interface 69
Lesson A Summary 71
Lesson A Key Terms 72
Lesson A Review Questions 72
Lesson A Exercises 73

LESSON B   Building the User Interface **75**
    Including Graphics in the User Interface 76
    Selecting Fonts for the Interface 77
    Adding Color to the Interface 77
    The BorderStyle and AutoSize Properties 78
    Adding a Text Box Control to the Form 80
Locking the Controls on a Form 80
Assigning Access Keys 81
Controlling the Tab Order 82
Lesson B Summary 86
Lesson B Key Terms 87
Lesson B Review Questions 87
Lesson B Exercises 88

LESSON C   Coding the Application **90**
    Using Pseudocode to Plan a Procedure 91
    Using a Flowchart to Plan a Procedure 92

Coding the btnClear Control's Click Event Procedure 93
   Assigning a Value to a Property During Run Time 94
   Using the Focus Method 96
   Internally Documenting the Program Code 96
Writing Arithmetic Expressions 98
Coding the Calculate Order Button. 100
   The Val Function 102
   The Format Function .103
Testing and Debugging the Application. 105
Assembling the Documentation 108
Lesson C Summary 109
Lesson C Key Terms 110
Lesson C Review Questions. 111
Lesson C Exercises 112

CHAPTER 3   **Using Variables and Constants** **118**

LESSON A   Using Variables to Store Information **121**
   Selecting a Data Type for a Variable 122
   Selecting a Name for a Variable 123
   Declaring a Variable 124
Assigning Data to an Existing Variable 125
   The TryParse Method .128
   The Convert Class 130
The Scope and Lifetime of a Variable 131
   Variables with Procedure Scope 132
   Variables with Class Scope 134
Static Variables 136
Named Constants 138
Option Explicit, Option Infer, and Option Strict 141
Lesson A Summary. 144
Lesson A Key Terms 146
Lesson A Review Questions .147
Lesson A Exercises 148

LESSON B   Modifying the Playtime Cellular Application. **152**
Modifying the Calculate Order Button's Code 153
Concatenating Strings 160
The InputBox Function 161
The ControlChars.NewLine Constant. 165
Designating a Default Button 166
Using the ToString Method to Format Numbers 167
Lesson B Summary 171
Lesson B Key Terms 171
Lesson B Review Questions. 172
Lesson B Exercises 174

LESSON C   Modifying the Load and Click Event Procedures. **178**
Coding the TextChanged Event Procedure 181
   Associating a Procedure with Different Objects and Events 182

x

Lesson C Summary 185
Lesson C Key Terms 186
Lesson C Review Questions. .186
Lesson C Exercises 187

CHAPTER 4   The Selection Structure **190**

LESSON A   Making Decisions in a Program **192**
Coding Single-Alternative and Dual-Alternative Selection Structures 198
Comparison Operators 199
   Using Comparison Operators: Swapping Numeric Values 201
   Using Comparison Operators: Displaying the Sum or Difference 204
Logical Operators 207
   Using the Truth Tables 210
   Using Logical Operators: Calculating Gross Pay. 211
Comparing Strings Containing Letters 213
Converting a String to Uppercase or Lowercase 215
   Using the ToUpper and ToLower Methods: Displaying a Message 216
Comparing Boolean Values 219
   Comparing Boolean Values: Determining Whether a String
   Can Be Converted to a Number 219
Summary of Operators 222
Lesson A Summary. 223
Lesson A Key Terms 223
Lesson A Review Questions. 225
Lesson A Exercises 227

LESSON B   Creating the Monthly Payment Calculator Application **231**
   Adding a Group Box to the Form. 231
Coding the Monthly Payment Calculator Application 233
   Coding the btnCalc Control's Click Event Procedure 234
Using the Financial.Pmt Method 236
The MessageBox.Show Method .238
Lesson B Summary 243
Lesson B Key Terms 244
Lesson B Review Questions. 244
Lesson B Exercises 245

LESSON C   Coding the KeyPress Event Procedures **248**
Coding the Enter Event Procedures 251
Lesson C Summary 254
Lesson C Key Terms 254
Lesson C Review Questions. 255
Lesson C Exercises 256

CHAPTER 5   More on the Selection Structure. **261**

LESSON A   Nested Selection Structures **264**
   The Voter Eligibility Application 265
Logic Errors in Selection Structures. 270
   Using a Compound Condition Rather than a Nested
   Selection Structure. 272
   Reversing the Primary and Secondary Decisions 273
   Using an Unnecessary Nested Selection Structure. 274

Multiple-Alternative Selection Structures 275
The Select Case Statement. 278
   Specifying a Range of Values in a Case Clause 280
Lesson A Summary. 282
Lesson A Key Terms 283
Lesson A Review Questions 283
Lesson A Exercises 286

LESSON B   Creating the Math Practice Application **290**
   Adding a Radio Button to the Form. 290
   Adding a Check Box to the Interface 292
Coding the Math Practice Application 294
Creating an Independent Sub Procedure 296
   Generating Random Integers .298
Coding the Grade Radio Buttons' Click Event Procedures 301
Coding the Operation Radio Buttons' Click Event Procedures. 303
Coding the Form's Load Event Procedure. 304
Lesson B Summary 306
Lesson B Key Terms 306
Lesson B Review Questions 307
Lesson B Exercises 309

LESSON C   Coding the Check Answer Button's Click Event Procedure **312**
Coding the Display Summary Check Box's
Click Event Procedure 315
Lesson C Summary 319
Lesson C Key Term 319
Lesson C Review Questions. 320
Lesson C Exercises 320

CHAPTER 6   **The Repetition Structure** **327**
LESSON A   Repeating Program Instructions. **329**
The Do . . . Loop Statement 333
   Coding the Modified Quarter of a Million Club Application 336
Counters and Accumulators. 339
   The Sales Express Company Application 340
Arithmetic Assignment Operators 347
The For . . . Next Statement 348
   The Monthly Payment Calculator Application 351
   Comparing the For . . . Next and Do . . . Loop Statements 354
Lesson A Summary. 355
Lesson A Key Terms 356
Lesson A Review Questions 357
Lesson A Exercises 361

LESSON B   Nested Repetition Structures. **365**
The Refresh and Sleep Methods. 366
Revisiting the Monthly Payment Calculator Application. 367
Lesson B Summary 371
Lesson B Key Terms 371
Lesson B Review Questions 371
Lesson B Exercises 372

LESSON C   Creating the Shoppers Haven Application **374**
Including a List Box in an Interface 375
   Adding Items to a List Box 375
   The Sorted Property 376
Coding the Shoppers Haven Application 377
   The SelectedItem and SelectedIndex Properties. 379
   The SelectedValueChanged and SelectedIndexChanged Events 381
   Coding the btnCalc Control's Click Event Procedure 381
Lesson C Summary 384
Lesson C Key Terms 385
Lesson C Review Questions 385
Lesson C Exercises 386

CHAPTER 7   Sub and Function Procedures **394**

LESSON A   More About Sub Procedures **396**
Passing Variables 397
   Passing Variables by Value 397
   Passing Variables by Reference 400
Function Procedures 405
Lesson A Summary. 409
Lesson A Key Terms 410
Lesson A Review Questions 410
Lesson A Exercises 414

LESSON B   Including a Combo Box in an Interface. **419**
Lesson B Summary 423
Lesson B Key Terms 424
Lesson B Review Questions. 424
Lesson B Exercises 425

LESSON C   Creating the Harvey Industries Application **427**
Coding the FormClosing Event Procedure 428
Coding the btnCalc Control's Click Event Procedure 430
   Creating the GetFwt Function 432
Completing the btnCalc Control's Click Event Procedure 436
Lesson C Summary 442
Lesson C Key Terms 442
Lesson C Review Questions. 443
Lesson C Exercises 443

CHAPTER 8   String Manipulation **446**

LESSON A   Working with Strings **449**
Determining the Number of Characters in a String 449
Removing Characters from a String 450
   The Product ID Application 451
Inserting Characters in a String 453
   Aligning the Characters in a String 453
   The Net Pay Application. 455
Searching a String 457
   The City and State Application 458
Accessing the Characters in a String 460
   The Rearrange Name Application 460

Using Pattern-Matching to Compare Strings 463
   Modifying the Product ID Application 465
Lesson A Summary. 467
Lesson A Key Terms 468
Lesson A Review Questions 468
Lesson A Exercises 471

LESSON B   Adding a Menu to a Form **476**
   Assigning Shortcut Keys to Menu Items 479
   Coding the Exit Menu Item 480
Lesson B Summary 481
Lesson B Key Terms 481
Lesson B Review Questions. .481
Lesson B Exercises 482

LESSON C   Completing the Hangman Game Application. **483**
   Coding the mnuFileNew Object's Click Event Procedure 484
Lesson C Summary 495
Lesson C Key Terms 496
Lesson C Review Questions 496
Lesson C Exercises 497

CHAPTER 9   Arrays **502**

LESSON A   Arrays. **504**
One-Dimensional Arrays 505
   Determining the Number of Elements and the Highest Subscript 508
   Traversing a One-Dimensional Array 509
The For Each...Next Statement 511
Calculating the Total and Average Values. 512
Finding the Highest Value. 515
Arrays and Collections 518
Accumulator and Counter Arrays 522
Sorting a One-Dimensional Array 525
Lesson A Summary. 529
Lesson A Key Terms 530
Lesson A Review Questions 530
Lesson A Exercises 534

LESSON B   Parallel One-Dimensional Arrays **539**
Lesson B Summary 543
Lesson B Key Term 543
Lesson B Review Questions. 543
Lesson B Exercises 543

LESSON C   Two-Dimensional Arrays **546**
   Traversing a Two-Dimensional Array 549
Totaling the Values Stored in a Two-Dimensional Array. 550
Searching a Two-Dimensional Array 552
Lesson C Summary 556
Lesson C Key Term 556
Lesson C Review Questions 556
Lesson C Exercises 558

CHAPTER 10   Structures and Sequential Access Files **562**

LESSON A   Structures **565**
Declaring and Using a Structure Variable. 566
    Passing a Structure Variable to a Procedure 567
    Creating an Array of Structure Variables 571
Lesson A Summary. 575
Lesson A Key Terms 576
Lesson A Review Questions 576
Lesson A Exercises 577

LESSON B   Sequential Access Files **581**
    Writing Data to a Sequential Access File 581
    Closing an Output Sequential Access File. 584
    Reading Data from a Sequential Access File 585
    Closing an Input Sequential Access File. 589
Lesson B Summary 592
Lesson B Key Terms 592
Lesson B Review Questions 593
Lesson B Exercises 594

LESSON C   Coding the CD Collection Application **598**
    Coding the Form's Load Event Procedure. 599
    Coding the btnAdd Control's Click Event Procedure 601
    Aligning Columns of Information 602
    Coding the btnRemove Control's Click Event Procedure 604
    Coding the Form's FormClosing Event Procedure 606
Lesson C Summary 609
Lesson C Key Terms 610
Lesson C Review Questions. 610
Lesson C Exercises 611

CHAPTER 11   Classes and Objects. **615**

LESSON A   Object-Oriented Programming Terminology **617**
Creating a Class. 618
Example 1—A Class that Contains Public Variables Only 620
Example 2—A Class that Contains Private Variables, Public Properties,
and Methods 624
    Private Variables and Property Procedures 625
    Constructors. 630
    Methods Other than Constructors 631
    Coding the Carpet Haven Application. 632
Example 3—A Class that Contains a Parameterized Constructor 636
Example 4—Reusing a Class 640
Lesson A Summary. 644
Lesson A Key Terms 645
Lesson A Review Questions 646
Lesson A Exercises 648

LESSON B   Example 5—A Class that Contains a ReadOnly Property **654**
Example 6—A Class that Contains Auto-Implemented Properties 658

Example 7—A Class that Contains Overloaded Methods 661
Lesson B Summary 667
Lesson B Key Terms 668
Lesson B Review Questions. 668
Lesson B Exercises 669

LESSON C   Example 8—Using a Base Class and a Derived Class **672**
Lesson C Summary 678
Lesson C Key Terms 678
Lesson C Review Questions. 679
Lesson C Exercises 679

CHAPTER 12   Web Applications **681**
LESSON A   Web Applications **684**
Creating a Web Application 687
Adding the Default.aspx Web Page to the Application 689
Customizing a Web Page 690
Adding Static Text to a Web Page 691
Viewing a Web Page in Full Screen View 693
Adding Another Web Page to the Application 693
Adding a Link Button Control to a Web Page 694
Starting a Web Application 696
Adding an Image to a Web Page. 698
Closing and Opening an Existing Web Application 700
Repositioning a Control on a Web Page 701
Lesson A Summary. 702
Lesson A Key Terms 704
Lesson A Review Questions. 704
Lesson A Exercises 705

LESSON B   Dynamic Web Pages. **708**
Coding the Submit Button's Click Event Procedure 712
Validating User Input 714
Lesson B Summary 716
Lesson B Key Term 717
Lesson B Review Questions. 717
Lesson B Exercises 718

LESSON C   Creating the DJ Tom Application **721**
Creating a Columnar Layout. .722
Using an ASP Table 724
Dragging Controls in Source View 727
Adding Items to a DropDownList Control 729
Coding DJ Tom's Web Page 730
Using the
 Tag 732
Lesson C Summary 734
Lesson C Key Terms 734
Lesson C Review Questions. 735
Lesson C Exercises 736

CHAPTER 13   Working with Access Databases and LINQ **740**

LESSON A   Database Terminology. **743**
Connecting an Application to a Microsoft Access Database 745
    Previewing the Contents of a Dataset 748
Binding the Objects in a Dataset 749
    Having the Computer Create a Bound Control 750
    The DataGridView Control .753
Visual Basic Code 756
    Handling Errors in the Code .757
The Copy to Output Directory Property. 760
Binding to an Existing Control. .762
    Coding the Next Record and Previous Record Buttons 764
Lesson A Summary. 767
Lesson A Key Terms 768
Lesson A Review Questions 769
Lesson A Exercises 771

LESSON B   Creating a Query **773**
Personalizing a BindingNavigator Control. 777
Using the LINQ Aggregate Operators 779
Lesson B Summary 782
Lesson B Key Terms 782
Lesson B Review Questions 783
Lesson B Exercises 785

LESSON C   Completing the Paradise Bookstore Application. **787**
Coding the Paradise Bookstore Application. 789
Lesson C Summary 792
Lesson C Key Terms 792
Lesson C Review Questions 792
Lesson C Exercises 793

CHAPTER 14   Access Databases and SQL. **796**

LESSON A   Adding Records to a Dataset. **799**
Sorting the Records in a Dataset 804
Deleting Records from a Dataset 805
Lesson A Summary. 810
Lesson A Key Terms 810
Lesson A Review Questions 811
Lesson A Exercises 812

LESSON B   Structured Query Language **815**
The SELECT Statement. 815
Creating a Query. 817
Lesson B Summary 823
Lesson B Key Terms 823
Lesson B Review Questions 824
Lesson B Exercises 826

LESSON C   Parameter Queries **828**
Saving a Query 831
Invoking a Query from Code. 833

The INSERT and DELETE Statements 836
Lesson C Summary 844
Lesson C Key Terms 844
Lesson C Review Questions 845
Lesson C Exercises .845

APPENDIX A   Locating Syntax and Logic Errors **848**

APPENDIX B   GUI Design Guidelines **858**

APPENDIX C   Visual Basic Conversion Functions **863**

APPENDIX D   Applications with Multiple Forms . . . . **Online**

Index **864**

Preface

Programming with Microsoft Visual Basic 2010, Fifth Edition uses Visual Basic 2010, an object-oriented language, to teach programming concepts. This book is designed for a beginning programming course. However, it assumes students are familiar with basic Windows skills and file management.

Organization and Coverage

Programming with Microsoft Visual Basic 2010, Fifth Edition contains an Overview and 14 chapters that present hands-on instruction; it also contains three appendices (A through C). An additional appendix (Appendix D) covering multiple-form applications and the FontDialog, ColorDialog, PrintForm, and TabControl tools is available online at *www.cengagebrain.com*. In the chapters, students with no previous programming experience learn how to plan and create their own interactive Windows applications. GUI design skills and OOP concepts are emphasized throughout the book. By the end of the book, students will have learned how to use TOE charts, pseudocode, and flowcharts to plan an application. They also will learn how to work with objects and write Visual Basic statements such as If...Then...Else, Select Case, Do...Loop, For...Next, and For Each...Next. Students also will learn how to create and manipulate variables, constants, strings, sequential access files, structures, classes, and arrays. Chapter 12 shows students how to create both static and dynamic Web applications. In Chapter 13, students learn how to connect an application to a Microsoft Access database, and then use Language Integrated Query (LINQ) to query the database. Chapter 14 continues the coverage of databases, introducing the student to more advanced concepts and Structured Query Language (SQL). Appendix A, which can be covered after Chapter 3, teaches students how to locate and correct errors in their code. The appendix shows students how to step through their code and also how to create breakpoints. Appendix B recaps the GUI design rules mentioned in the chapters, and Appendix C lists the Visual Basic conversion functions.

Approach

Programming with Microsoft Visual Basic 2010, Fifth Edition teaches programming concepts using a task-driven rather than a command-driven approach. By working through the chapters, which are each motivated by a realistic case, students learn how to develop applications they are likely to encounter in the workplace. This is much more effective than memorizing a list of commands out of context. The book motivates students by demonstrating why they need to learn the concepts and skills covered in each chapter.

Features

Programming with Microsoft Visual Basic 2010, Fifth Edition is an exceptional textbook because it also includes the following features:

READ THIS BEFORE YOU BEGIN This section is consistent with Course Technology's unequaled commitment to helping instructors introduce technology into the classroom. Technical considerations and assumptions about hardware, software, and default settings are listed in one place to help instructors save time and eliminate unnecessary aggravation.

VISUAL STUDIO 2010 METHODS The book focuses on Visual Studio 2010 methods rather than on Visual Basic functions. This is because the Visual Studio methods can be used in any .NET language, whereas the Visual Basic functions can be used only in Visual Basic. Exceptions to this are the Val and Format functions, which are introduced in Chapter 2. These functions are covered in the book simply because it is likely that students will encounter them in existing Visual Basic programs. However, in Chapter 3, the student is taught to use the TryParse method and the Convert class methods rather than the Val function. Also in Chapter 3, the Format function is replaced with the ToString method.

OPTION STATEMENTS All programs include the Option Explicit, Option Strict, and Option Infer statements.

FIGURES Figures that introduce new statements, functions, or methods contain both the syntax and examples of using the syntax. Including the syntax in the figures makes the examples more meaningful.

CHAPTER CASES Each chapter begins with a programming-related problem that students could reasonably expect to encounter in business, followed by a demonstration of an application that could be used to solve the problem. Showing the students the completed application before they learn how to create it is motivational and instructionally sound. By allowing the students to see the type of application they will be able to create after completing the chapter, the students will be more motivated to learn because they can see how the programming concepts they are about to learn can be used and, therefore, why the concepts are important.

LESSONS Each chapter is divided into three lessons—A, B, and C. Lesson A introduces the programming concepts that will be used in the completed application. The concepts are illustrated with code examples and sample applications. The user interface for each sample application is provided to the student. Also provided are tutorial-style steps that guide the student on coding, running, and testing the application. Each sample application allows the student to observe how the current concept can be used before the next concept is introduced. In Lessons B and/or C, the student creates the application required to solve the problem specified in the Chapter Case.

APPENDICES Appendix A, which can be covered after Chapter 3, teaches students how to locate and correct errors in their code. The appendix shows students how to step through their code and also how to create breakpoints. Appendix B summarizes the GUI design tips taught in the chapters, making it easier for the student to follow the guidelines when designing an application's interface. Appendix C lists the Visual Basic conversion functions. Appendix D, which is available online at *www.cengagebrain.com*, covers multiple-form applications and the FontDialog, ColorDialog, PrintForm, and TabControl tools.

xx

GUI DESIGN TIP BOXES The GUI DESIGN TIP boxes contain guidelines and recommendations for designing applications that follow Windows standards. Appendix B provides a summary of the GUI design guidelines covered in the chapters.

 TIP These notes provide additional information about the current concept. Examples include alternative ways of writing statements or performing tasks, as well as warnings about common mistakes made when using a particular command and reminders of related concepts learned in previous chapters.

SUMMARY Each lesson contains a Summary section that recaps the concepts covered in the lesson.

KEY TERMS Following the Summary section in each lesson is a listing of the key terms introduced throughout the lesson, along with their definitions.

REVIEW QUESTIONS Each lesson contains Review Questions designed to test a student's understanding of the lesson's concepts.

EXERCISES The Review Questions in each lesson are followed by Exercises, which provide students with additional practice of the skills and concepts they learned in the lesson. The Exercises are designated as INTRODUCTORY, INTERMEDIATE, ADVANCED, Discovery, and Swat The Bugs. The Discovery Exercises encourage students to challenge and independently develop their own programming skills while exploring the capabilities of Visual Basic 2010. The Swat The Bugs Exercises provide an opportunity for students to detect and correct errors in an application's code.

New to This Edition!

 VIDEOS These notes direct students to videos that accompany each chapter in the book. The videos explain and/or demonstrate one or more of the chapter's concepts.

YOU DO IT! BOXES These boxes provide simple applications that allow students to demonstrate their understanding of a concept before moving on to the next concept. The YOU DO IT! boxes are located almost exclusively in Lesson A of each chapter.

COURSE NOTES QUICK REFERENCE CARD This card shows the syntax of each command covered in the book and provides a quick reference for students.

START HERE ▶ **START HERE ARROWS** These arrows indicate the beginning of a tutorial steps section in the book.

DATABASES, LINQ, AND SQL The book now includes two chapters (Chapters 13 and 14) on databases. LINQ is covered in Chapter 13. SQL is covered in Chapter 14.

LINE CONTINUATION CHARACTER In Chapter 3, the students learn how to split a line of code without using a line continuation character.

ARITHMETIC ASSIGNMENT OPERATORS These operators are covered along with the repetition structure in Chapter 6.

CHAPTERS 4 AND 5 (THE SELECTION STRUCTURE AND MORE ON THE SELECTION STRUCTURE) Both chapters now refer to the different forms of the selection structure as single-alternative, dual-alternative, and multiple-alternative.

CHAPTERS 6 (THE REPETITION STRUCTURE) Lesson A was revised to include the following terms: looping condition and loop exit condition.

CHAPTER 8 (STRING MANIPULATION) The Insert and Remove methods are now covered in Lesson A. The Replace method and Mid statements are no longer covered in Lesson A; however, they are covered in Discovery Exercises at the end of the lesson. Also covered in Lesson A's Discovery Exercises are the StartsWith, EndsWith, TrimStart, and TrimEnd methods. Lesson A also contains a Discovery Exercise that shows students how to use the Trim method to remove characters other than spaces.

CHAPTER 9 (ARRAYS) The Arrays chapter has been revised.

CHAPTER 11 (CLASSES AND OBJECTS) Parameterized constructors are now covered in Lesson A. Coverage of auto-implemented properties was added to Lesson B.

CHAPTER 12 (WEB APPLICATIONS) Lesson A now shows students how to create a Web application that contains two Web pages. It also covers the LinkButton tool.

APPENDIX D (APPLICATIONS WITH MULTIPLE FORMS) This appendix is available online at *www.cengagebrain.com*. The appendix covers multiple-form applications and the FontDialog, ColorDialog, PrintForm, and TabControl tools.

Instructor Resources and Supplements

All of the resources available with this book are provided to the instructor on a single CD-ROM. Many also can be found at *www.cengagebrain.com*. At the CengageBrain.com home page, search for the ISBN of your title (from the back cover of your book) using the search box at the top of the page. This will take you to the product page where free companion resources can be found.

ELECTRONIC INSTRUCTOR'S MANUAL The Instructor's Manual that accompanies this textbook includes additional instructional material to assist in class preparation, including items such as Sample Syllabi, Chapter Outlines, Technical Notes, Lecture Notes, Quick Quizzes, Teaching Tips, Discussion Topics, and Additional Case Projects.

EXAMVIEW® This textbook is accompanied by ExamView, a powerful testing software package that allows instructors to create and administer printed, computer (LAN-based), and Internet exams. ExamView includes hundreds of questions that correspond to the topics covered in this text, enabling students to generate detailed study guides that include page references for further review. The computer-based and Internet testing components allow students to take exams at their computers, and also save the instructor time by grading each exam automatically.

POWERPOINT PRESENTATIONS This book offers Microsoft PowerPoint slides for each chapter. These are included as a teaching aid for classroom presentation, to make available to students on the network for chapter review, or to be printed for classroom distribution. Instructors can add their own slides for additional topics they introduce to the class.

DATA FILES Data Files are necessary for completing the computer activities in this book. The Data Files are provided on the Instructor Resources CD-ROM and also may be found at *www.cengagebrain.com*.

SOLUTION FILES Solutions to the Lesson applications and the end-of-lesson Review Questions and Exercises are provided on the Instructor Resources CD-ROM and also may be found at *www.cengagebrain.com*. The solutions are password protected.

DISTANCE LEARNING Course Technology offers online WebCT, Blackboard, and Angel courses for this text to provide the most complete and dynamic learning experience possible. When you add online content to one of your courses, you're adding a lot: automated tests, topic reviews, quick quizzes, and additional case projects with solutions. For more information on how to bring distance learning to your course, contact your local Course Technology sales representative.

Acknowledgments

Writing a book is a team effort rather than an individual one. I would like to take this opportunity to thank my team, especially Jill Braiewa (Senior Content Project Manager), Tricia Coia (Freelance Product Manager), Suzanne Huizenga (Proofreader), Nicole Ashton (Quality Assurance), and the compositors at Integra. Thank you for your support, enthusiasm, patience, and hard work. Last, but certainly not least, I want to thank the following reviewers for their invaluable ideas and comments: Tatyana Feofilaktova, ASA College; Gary Marrer, Maricopa Community College; and David Brett, North Shore Community College. And a special thank you to Sally Douglas (College of Central Florida) for suggesting the YOU DO IT! boxes.

Diane Zak

Read This Before You Begin

Technical Information

Data Files

You will need data files to complete the computer activities in this book. Your instructor may provide the data files to you. You may obtain the files electronically at *www.cengagebrain.com*, and then navigating to the page for this book.

Each chapter in this book has its own set of data files, which are stored in a separate folder within the VB2010 folder. The files for Chapter 1 are stored in the VB2010\Chap01 folder. Similarly, the files for Chapter 2 are stored in the VB2010\Chap02 folder. Throughout this book, you will be instructed to open files from or save files to these folders.

You can use a computer in your school lab or your own computer to complete the steps and Exercises in this book.

Using Your Own Computer

To use your own computer to complete the computer activities in this book, you will need the following:

- A Pentium® 4 processor, 1.6 GHz or higher, personal computer running Microsoft Windows. This book was written and Quality Assurance tested using Microsoft Windows 7.

- Either Microsoft Visual Studio 2010 or the Express Editions of Microsoft Visual Basic 2010 and Microsoft Visual Web Developer 2010 installed on your computer. This book was written using Microsoft Visual Studio 2010 Professional Edition, and Quality Assurance tested using the Express Editions of Microsoft Visual Basic 2010 and Microsoft Visual Web Developer 2010. At the time of this writing, you can download a free copy of the Express Editions at *www.microsoft.com/express/downloads* (Visual Basic 2010 Express) and *www.microsoft.com/express/Downloads/#2010-Visual-Web-Developer* (Visual Web Developer 2010 Express). If necessary, use the following information when installing the Professional or Express Editions of the software:

To configure Visual Studio 2010 or Visual Basic 2010 Express:

1. Start either Visual Studio 2010 or Visual Basic 2010 Express. If the Choose Default Environment Settings dialog box appears when you start Visual Studio, select the Visual Basic Development Settings option.

2. If you are using Visual Basic 2010 Express, click Tools on the menu bar, point to Settings, and then click Expert Settings.

3. Click Tools on the menu bar and then click Options to open the Options dialog box. If necessary, deselect the Show all settings check box. Click the Projects and Solutions node. Use the information shown in Figure 1-4 in Chapter 1 to select and deselect the appropriate check boxes. (Your dialog box will look slightly different if you are using Visual Basic 2010 Express.). When you are finished, click the OK button to close the Options dialog box.

To configure Visual Web Developer 2010 Express:

1. Start Visual Web Developer 2010 Express. Click Tools on the menu bar, point to Settings, and then click Expert Settings.

2. Click Tools on the menu bar and then click Options to open the Options dialog box. If necessary, select the Show all settings check box. Click the Projects and Solutions node. Use the information shown in Figure 12-6 in Chapter 12 to select and deselect the appropriate check boxes. When you are finished, click the OK button to close the Options dialog box.

Figures

The figures in this book reflect how your screen will look if you are using Microsoft Visual Studio 2010 Professional Edition and a Microsoft Windows 7 system. Your screen may appear slightly different in some instances if you are using another version of Microsoft Visual Studio, Microsoft Visual Basic, or Microsoft Windows.

Visit Our Web Site

Additional materials designed for this textbook might be available at *www.cengagebrain.com*. Search this site for more details.

To the Instructor

To complete the computer activities in this book, your students must use a set of data files. The files are included on the Instructor's Resource CD. They also may be obtained electronically at *www.cengagebrain.com*.

The material in this book was written using Microsoft Visual Studio 2010 Professional Edition on a Microsoft Windows 7 system. It was Quality Assurance tested using the Express Editions of Microsoft Visual Basic 2010 and Microsoft Visual Web Developer 2010 on a Microsoft Windows 7 system.

Course Technology Data Files

You are granted a license to copy the data files to any computer or computer network used by individuals who have purchased this book.

An Introduction to Programming

After studying the Overview, you should be able to:

- ◎ Define the terminology used in programming

- ◎ Explain the tasks performed by a programmer

- ◎ Describe the qualities of a good programmer

- ◎ Understand the employment opportunities for programmers and software engineers

- ◎ Run a Visual Basic 2010 application

- ◎ Understand how to use the chapters effectively

2

Programming a Computer

In essence, the word **programming** means *giving a mechanism the directions to accomplish a task*. If you are like most people, you've already programmed several mechanisms. For example, at one time or another, you probably programmed your digital video recorder (DVR) in order to schedule a timed recording of a movie. You also may have programmed the speed dial feature on your cell phone. Or you may have programmed your coffee maker to begin the brewing process before you wake up in the morning. Like your DVR, cell phone, and coffee maker, a computer also is a mechanism that can be programmed. The directions given to a computer are called **computer programs** or, more simply, **programs**. The people who write programs are called **programmers**. Programmers use a variety of special languages, called **programming languages**, to communicate with the computer. Some popular programming languages are Visual Basic, C#, C++, and Java. In this book, you will use the Visual Basic programming language.

The Programmer's Job

When a company has a problem that requires a computer solution, typically it is a programmer who comes to the rescue. The programmer might be an employee of the company; or he or she might be a freelance programmer, which is a programmer who works on temporary contracts rather than for a long-term employer. First the programmer meets with the user, which is the person (or persons) responsible for describing the problem. In many cases, this person also will eventually use the solution. Depending on the complexity of the problem, multiple programmers may be involved. Programming teams often contain subject matter experts, who may or may not be programmers. For example, an accountant might be part of a team working on a program that requires accounting expertise.

The programmer, or team of programmers, may need to meet with the user several times to determine the exact problem and to agree on the desired solution. After the programmer and user agree on the solution, the programmer begins converting the solution into a computer program. During the conversion phase, the programmer meets periodically with the user to determine whether the program fulfills the user's needs and to refine any details of the solution. When the user is satisfied that the program does what he or she wants it to do, the programmer rigorously tests the program with sample data before releasing it to the user. In many cases, the programmer also provides the user with a manual that explains how to use the program. As this process indicates, the creation of a good computer solution to a problem—in other words, the creation of a good program—requires a great deal of interaction between the programmer and the user.

Do You Have What It Takes to Be a Programmer?

According to the 2008–09 Edition of the Occupational Outlook Handbook (OOH), published by the U.S. Department of Labor's Bureau of Labor Statistics, "When hiring programmers, employers look for people with the necessary programming skills who can think logically and pay close attention to detail. Programming calls for patience, persistence, and the ability to work on exacting analytical work, especially under pressure. Ingenuity and creativity also are particularly important when programmers design solutions and test their work for potential failures.... Because programmers are expected to work in teams and interact directly with users, employers want programmers who are able to communicate with nontechnical personnel. Business skills are also important, especially for those wishing to advance to managerial positions." If this description sounds like you, then you probably have what it takes to be a programmer. But if it doesn't sound like you, it's still worth your time to understand the programming process, especially if you are planning a career in business. Knowing even a little bit about the programming process will allow you, the manager of a department, to better communicate your department's needs to a programmer. It also will give you the confidence to question the programmer when he or she claims that the program modification you requested can't be made. In addition, it will help you determine whether the $9,000 quote you received from a freelance programmer seems reasonable. Lastly, understanding the process a computer programmer follows when solving a problem can help you solve problems that don't require a computer solution.

Employment Opportunities

But if, after reading this book, you are excited about the idea of working as a computer programmer, here is some information on employment opportunities. When searching for a job in computer programming, you will encounter ads for "computer programmers" as well as for "computer software engineers." Although job titles and descriptions vary, computer software engineers typically are responsible for designing an appropriate solution to a user's problem, while computer programmers are responsible for translating the solution into a language that the computer can understand. The process of translating the solution is called **coding**. Keep in mind that, depending on the employer and the size and complexity of the user's problem, the design and coding tasks may be performed by the same employee, no matter what his or her job title is. In other words, it's not unusual for a software engineer to code her solution, just as it's not unusual for a programmer to have designed the solution he is coding. Typically, computer software engineers are expected to have at least a bachelor's degree in computer engineering or computer science, along with practical work experience. Computer programmers usually need at least an associate's degree in computer science, mathematics, or information systems, as well as proficiency in one or more programming languages.

Computer programmers and software engineers are employed in almost every industry, such as telecommunications companies, software publishers, financial institutions, insurance carriers, educational institutions, and government agencies. According to the May 2008 Occupational Employment Statistics, programmers held about 394,230 jobs and had a mean annual wage of $73,470. Software engineers, on the other hand, held about 494,160 jobs with a mean annual wage of $87,900. The Bureau of Labor Statistics predicts that employment of programmers will decline slowly, decreasing by 4% from 2006 to 2016. However, the employment of computer software engineers is projected to increase by 38% over the same period. There is a great deal of competition for programming and software engineering jobs, so jobseekers will need to keep up to date with the latest programming languages and technologies. More information about computer programmers and computer

4

software engineers can be found on the Bureau of Labor Statistics Web site at *www.bls.gov.*

Visual Basic 2010

In this book, you will learn how to create programs using the Visual Basic 2010 programming language. Visual Basic 2010 is an **object-oriented programming language**, which is a language that allows the programmer to use objects to accomplish a program's goal. An **object** is anything that can be seen, touched, or used. In other words, an object is nearly any *thing*. The objects used in an object-oriented program can take on many different forms. Programs written for the Windows environment typically use objects such as check boxes, list boxes, and buttons. A payroll program, on the other hand, might utilize objects found in the real world, such as a time card object, an employee object, and a check object. Every object used in an object-oriented program is created from a **class**, which is a pattern that the computer uses to create the object. The class contains the instructions that tell the computer how the object should look and behave. An object created from a class is called an **instance** of the class and is said to be **instantiated** from the class. An analogy involving a cookie cutter and cookies is often used to describe a class and its objects: the class is the cookie cutter, and the objects instantiated from the class are the cookies. You will learn more about classes and objects throughout this book.

You can download a free copy of Visual Basic 2010 Express at *www.microsoft.com/ express/downloads.*

Visual Basic 2010 is available either as a stand-alone product, called Visual Basic 2010 Express, or as part of Visual Studio 2010. Both products include an **integrated development environment (IDE)**, which is an environment that contains all of the tools and features you need to create, run, and test your programs. However, unlike Visual Basic 2010 Express, which contains only the Visual Basic language, Visual Studio 2010 contains four different languages: Visual Basic, Visual C++, Visual C#, and Visual F#.

You can use Visual Basic to create programs, called **applications**, for the Windows environment or for the Web. A Windows application has a Windows user interface and runs on a personal computer. A **user interface** is what the user sees and interacts with while an application is running. Examples of Windows applications include graphics programs, data-entry systems, and games. A Web application, on the other hand, has a Web user interface and runs on a server. You access a Web application using your computer's browser. Examples of Web applications include e-commerce applications available on the Internet, and employee handbook applications accessible on a company's intranet. You also can use Visual Basic to create applications for mobile devices, such as pocket PCs, cell phones, and PDAs (personal digital assistants).

A Visual Basic 2010 Demonstration

In the following set of steps, you will run a Visual Basic 2010 application that shows you some of the objects you will learn about in the chapters. For now, it is not important for you to understand how these objects were created or why the objects perform the way they do. Those questions will be answered in the chapters.

To run the Visual Basic 2010 application:

START HERE

1. Press and hold down the **Windows logo** key on your keyboard as you tap the letter **r**. The Run dialog box opens. Release the logo key.

The Windows logo key looks like this: .

2. Click the **Browse** button to open the Browse dialog box. Locate and then open the VB2010\Overview folder on your computer's hard disk or on the device designated by your instructor.

5

3. Click **Monthly Payment Calculator (Monthly Payment Calculator.exe)** in the list of filenames. (Depending on how Windows is set up on your computer, you may see the .exe extension on the filename.) Click the **Open** button. The Browse dialog box closes and the Run dialog box appears again.

4. Click the **OK** button in the Run dialog box. After a few moments, the Monthly Payment Calculator application shown in Figure 1 appears on the screen. The interface contains a text box, list box, buttons, radio buttons, and labels. You can use the application to calculate the monthly payment for a car loan.

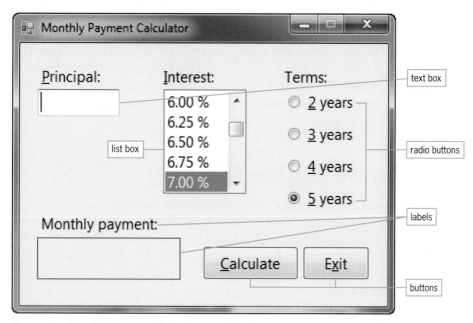

Figure 1   Monthly Payment Calculator application

5. Use the application to calculate the monthly payment for a $20,000 loan at 6.75% interest for five years. Type **20000** in the Principal text box, and then click **6.75 %** in the Interest list box. The radio button corresponding to the five-year term is already selected, so you just need to click the **Calculate** button to compute the monthly payment. The application indicates that your monthly payment would be $393.67. See Figure 2.

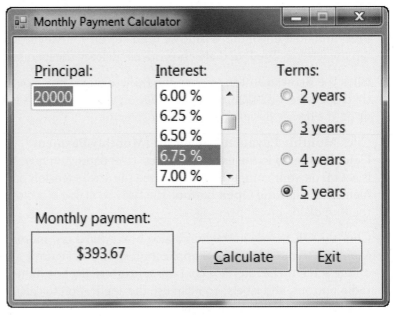

Figure 2 Computed monthly payment

6. Now determine what your monthly payment would be if you borrowed $10,000 at 8% interest for four years. Type **10000** in the Principal text box. Scroll down the Interest list box and then click **8.00 %**. Click the **4 years** radio button and then click the **Calculate** button. The Monthly payment box shows $244.13.

7. Click the **Exit** button to close the application.

Using the Chapters Effectively

This book is designed for a beginning programming course; however, it assumes students are familiar with basic Windows skills and file management. The chapters in this book will help you learn how to write programs using Microsoft Visual Basic 2010. The chapters are designed to be used at your computer. Begin by reading the text that explains the concepts. When you come to the numbered steps, follow the steps on your computer. Read each step carefully and completely before you try it. As you work, compare your screen with the figures to verify your results. The figures in this book reflect how your screen will look if you are using the Professional Edition of Visual Studio 2010 and a Microsoft Windows 7 system. Your screen may appear slightly different in some instances if you are using a different edition of Visual Studio, if you are using Visual Basic Express, or if you are using another version of Microsoft Windows. Don't worry if your screen display differs slightly from the figures. The important parts of the screen display are labeled in each figure. Just be sure you have these parts on your screen.

Do not worry about making mistakes; that's part of the learning process. Tip notes identify common problems and explain how to get back on track. They also provide additional information about a procedure—for example, an alternative method of performing the procedure.

Tip notes are designated by the icon.

Each chapter is divided into three lessons. You might want to take a break between lessons. Following each lesson is a Summary section that lists the important elements of the lesson. After the Summary section is a listing of the key terms (including definitions) covered in the lesson. Following the Key Terms section are questions and exercises designed to review and reinforce the lesson's concepts. You should complete all of the end-of-lesson questions and several exercises before continuing to the next lesson. It takes a great deal of practice to acquire the skills needed to create good programs, and future chapters assume that you have mastered the information found in the previous chapters. Some of the end-of-lesson exercises are Discovery exercises, which allow you to both "discover" the solutions to problems on your own and experiment with material that is not covered in the chapter. Some lessons also contain one or more Debugging exercises. In programming, the term **debugging** refers to the process of finding and fixing any errors, called bugs, in a program. Debugging exercises provide opportunities for you to find and correct the errors in existing applications. Appendix A, which can be covered along with Chapter 3, guides you through the process of locating and correcting two types of errors (bugs): syntax errors and logic errors.

Throughout the book you will find GUI (graphical user interface) design tips. These tips contain guidelines and recommendations for designing applications. You should follow these guidelines and recommendations so that your applications follow the Windows standards.

Summary

- Programs are the step-by-step instructions that tell a computer how to perform a task.

- Programmers use various programming languages to communicate with the computer.

- The creation of a good program requires a great deal of interaction between the programmer and the user.

- Programmers rigorously test a program with sample data before releasing the program to the user.

- All businesspeople should know at least a little about the programming process.

- It's not unusual for the same person to perform the duties of both a software engineer and a programmer.

- An object-oriented programming language, such as Visual Basic 2010, allows programmers to use objects to accomplish a program's goal. An object is anything that can be seen, touched, or used.

- Every object in an object-oriented program is instantiated (created) from a class, which is a pattern that tells the computer how the object should look and behave. An object is referred to as an instance of the class.

- The process of locating and correcting the errors (bugs) in a program is called debugging.

Key Terms

Applications—programs created for the Windows environment, the Web, or mobile devices

Class—a pattern that the computer uses to create (instantiate) an object

Coding—the process of translating a solution into a language that the computer can understand

Computer programs—the directions given to computers; also called programs

Debugging—the process of locating and correcting the errors (bugs) in a program

IDE—integrated development environment

Instance—an object created (instantiated) from a class

Instantiated—the process of creating an object from a class

Integrated development environment—an environment that contains all of the tools and features you need to create, run, and test your programs; also called an IDE

Object—anything that can be seen, touched, or used

Object-oriented programming language—a programming language that allows the programmer to use objects to accomplish a program's goal

Programmers—the people who write computer programs

Programming—the process of giving a mechanism the directions to accomplish a task

Programming languages—languages used to communicate with a computer

Programs—the directions given to computers; also called computer programs

User interface—what the user sees and interacts with while an application is running

CHAPTER 1

An Introduction to Visual Basic 2010

Creating a Splash Screen

In this chapter, you will create a splash screen for the Country Charm Inn, a small bed and breakfast located in rural Kentucky. You will create the splash screen using Visual Basic 2010, Microsoft's newest version of the Visual Basic programming language. A splash screen is the first image that appears when an application is started. It is used to introduce the application and to hold the user's attention while the application is being read into the computer's internal memory.

Previewing the Splash Screen

Before you start the first lesson in this chapter, you will preview a completed splash screen. The splash screen is contained in the VB2010\Chap01 folder.

START HERE

10

The Windows logo key looks like this:  .

To preview a completed splash screen:

1. Press and hold down the **Windows logo** key on your keyboard as you tap the letter **r**. The Run dialog box opens. Release the logo key.

2. Click the **Browse** button to open the Browse dialog box. Locate and then open the VB2010\Chap01 folder on your computer's hard disk or on the device designated by your instructor.

3. Click **Splash** (**Splash.exe**) in the list of filenames. (Depending on how Windows is set up on your computer, you may see the .exe extension on the filename.) Click the **Open** button. The Browse dialog box closes and the Run dialog box appears again.

4. Click the **OK** button in the Run dialog box. After a few moments, the splash screen shown in Figure 1-1 appears on the screen. The splash screen closes when six seconds have elapsed.

Country Charm Inn
Welcome to peace and quiet!

Figure 1-1   Splash screen for the Country Charm Inn

Chapter 1 is designed to help you get comfortable with the Visual Studio 2010 integrated development environment. As you learned in the Overview, an integrated development environment (IDE) is an environment that contains all of the tools and features you need to create, run, and test your programs. As do all the chapters in this book, Chapter 1 contains three lessons. You should complete a lesson in full and do all of the end-of-lesson questions and several exercises before continuing to the next lesson.

LESSON A

After studying Lesson A, you should be able to:

- Start and customize Visual Studio 2010 or Visual Basic 2010 Express

- Create a Visual Basic 2010 Windows application

- Manage the windows in the IDE

- Set the properties of an object

- Restore a property to its default setting

- Save a solution

- Close and open an existing solution

The Splash Screen Application

In this chapter, you will create a splash screen using Visual Basic 2010. As mentioned in the Overview, Visual Basic 2010 is available as a stand-alone product (called Visual Basic 2010 Express) or as part of Visual Studio 2010. Before you can use Visual Basic 2010 to create an application, you first must start either Visual Studio 2010 or Visual Basic 2010 Express.

To start Visual Studio 2010 or Visual Basic 2010 Express:

1. Click the **Start** button on the Windows 7 taskbar and then point to **All Programs**.

2. *If you are using Visual Studio 2010*, click **Microsoft Visual Studio 2010** on the All Programs menu and then click **Microsoft Visual Studio 2010**. If the Choose Default Environment Settings dialog box appears, click **Visual Basic Development Settings** and then click **Start Visual Studio**.

   If you are using Visual Basic 2010 Express, click **Microsoft Visual Studio 2010 Express** on the All Programs menu and then click **Microsoft Visual Basic 2010 Express**.

3. Click **Window** on the menu bar, click **Reset Window Layout**, and then click the **Yes** button. When you start Visual Studio 2010 Professional, your screen will appear similar to Figure 1-2. When you start Visual Basic 2010 Express, your screen will appear similar to Figure 1-3.

   Important note: To select a different window layout, click Tools on the menu bar. If you are using the Express edition, point to Settings. Click Import and Export Settings, select the Reset all settings radio button, click the Next button, select the appropriate radio button, click the Next button, click the preferred settings collection, and then click the Finish button.

The Ch01AVideo file demonstrates all of the steps contained in Lesson A. You can view the video either before or after completing the lesson.

START HERE

11

Start Page window

Solution Explorer window

Toolbox window's tab

Team Explorer window's tab

be sure these check boxes are selected

Figure 1-2 Microsoft Visual Studio 2010 Professional startup screen

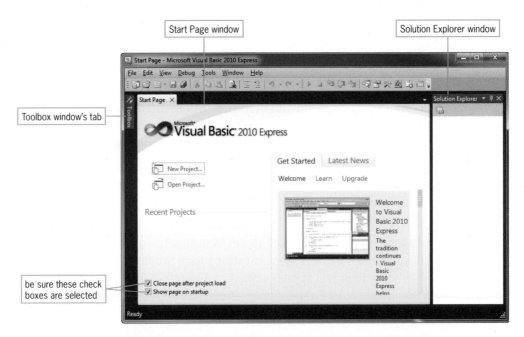

Start Page window

Solution Explorer window

Toolbox window's tab

be sure these check boxes are selected

Figure 1-3 Microsoft Visual Basic 2010 Express startup screen

Next, you will configure Visual Studio or Visual Basic Express so that your screen agrees with the figures and tutorial steps in this book.

START HERE

To configure Visual Studio or Visual Basic Express:

1. *If you are using Visual Basic 2010 Express*, click **Tools** on the menu bar, point to **Settings**, and then click **Expert Settings**.

2. Click **Tools** on the menu bar and then click **Options** to open the Options dialog box. If necessary, deselect the **Show all settings** check box. Click the **Projects and Solutions** node. Use the information

shown in Figure 1-4 to select and deselect the appropriate check boxes. (Your dialog box will look slightly different if you are using Visual Basic 2010 Express.) When you are finished, click the **OK** button to close the Options dialog box.

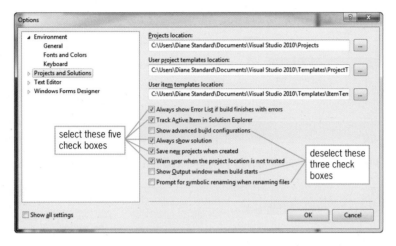

Figure 1-4   Options dialog box

The splash screen will be a Windows application, which means it will have a Windows user interface and run on a desktop computer. Recall that a user interface is what the user sees and interacts with while an application is running. Windows applications in Visual Basic are composed of solutions, projects, and files. A solution is a container that stores the projects and files for an entire application. Although the solutions in this book contain only one project, a solution can contain several projects. A project also is a container, but it stores only the files associated with that particular project.

To create a Visual Basic 2010 Windows application: START HERE

1.   Click **File** on the menu bar and then click **New Project** to open the New Project dialog box.

2.   If necessary, click **Visual Basic** in the Installed Templates list. *If you are using Visual Studio*, expand the Visual Basic node (if necessary) and then (if necessary) click **Windows**.

3.   If necessary, click **Windows Forms Application** in the middle column of the dialog box.

4.   Change the name entered in the Name box to **Splash Project**.

5.   Click the **Browse** button to open the Project Location dialog box. Locate and then click the **VB2010\Chap01** folder. Click the **Select Folder** button to close the Project Location dialog box.

6.   If necessary, select the **Create directory for solution** check box in the New Project dialog box. Change the name entered in the Solution name box to **Splash Solution**. Figures 1-5 and 1-6 show the completed New Project dialog box in Visual Studio 2010 Professional and Visual Basic 2010 Express, respectively. The drive letter will be different if you are saving to a device other than your computer's hard drive—for example, if you are saving to a flash drive.

your drive letter might be different

Figure 1-5 Completed New Project dialog box in Visual Studio 2010 Professional

your drive letter might be different

Figure 1-6 Completed New Project dialog box in Visual Basic 2010 Express

7. Click the **OK** button to close the New Project dialog box. The computer creates a solution and adds a Visual Basic project to the solution. The names of the solution and project, as well as other information pertaining to the project, are recorded in the Solution Explorer window. See Figure 1-7. Notice that, in addition to the windows shown earlier in Figures 1-2 and 1-3, three other windows appear in the IDE: Windows Form Designer, Properties, and Data Sources. (If you are using Visual Basic 2010 Express, your title bar will say "Splash Solution – Microsoft Visual Basic 2010 Express. In addition, your screen will not have the Team Explorer window.)

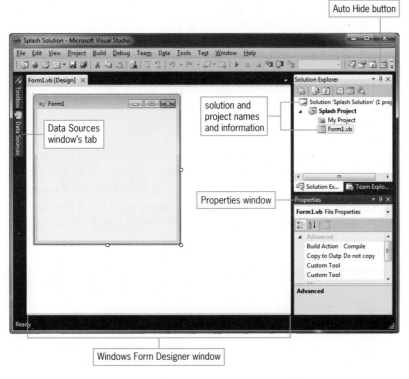

Auto Hide button

solution and
project names
and information

Data Sources
window's tab

Properties window

Windows Form Designer window

Figure 1-7   Solution and Visual Basic project

If you want to widen the Solution Explorer window to match Figure 1-7, position your mouse pointer on the window's left border until the mouse pointer becomes a sizing pointer (a horizontal line with an arrowhead at each end), and then drag the border to the left.

Managing the Windows in the IDE

In most cases, you will find it easier to work in the IDE if you either close or auto-hide the windows you are not currently using. The easiest way to close an open window is to click the Close button on the window's title bar. In most cases, the View menu provides an appropriate option for opening a closed window. Rather than closing a window, you also can auto-hide it. You auto-hide a window using the Auto Hide button (refer to Figure 1-7) on the window's title bar. The Auto Hide button is a toggle button: clicking it once activates it, and clicking it again deactivates it. The Toolbox and Data Sources windows in Figure 1-7 are auto-hidden windows.

To close, open, auto-hide, and display windows in the IDE:

START HERE

1. Click the **Close** button on the Properties window's title bar to close the window. Now, click **View** on the menu bar and then click **Properties Window** to open the window.

2. If your IDE contains the Team Explorer window, click the **window's tab** and then click the **Close** button on its title bar.

3. Click the **Auto Hide** (vertical pushpin) button on the Solution Explorer window. The Solution Explorer window is minimized and appears as a tab on the edge of the IDE.

4. To temporarily display the Solution Explorer window, place your mouse pointer on the Solution Explorer tab. The Solution Explorer window slides into view. Notice that the Auto Hide button is now a horizontal pushpin rather than a vertical pushpin.

5. Move your mouse pointer away from the Solution Explorer window. The window is minimized and appears as a tab again.

6. To permanently display the Solution Explorer window, place your mouse pointer on the Solution Explorer tab and then click the **Auto Hide** (horizontal pushpin) button on the window's title bar. The vertical pushpin replaces the horizontal pushpin on the button.

7. On your own, close the Data Sources window.

8. Figure 1-8 shows the current status of the windows in the IDE. Only the Windows Form Designer, Solution Explorer, and Properties windows are open; the Toolbox window is auto-hidden. If necessary, click **Form1.vb** in the Solution Explorer window. If the items in the Properties window do not appear in alphabetical order, click the **Alphabetical** button.

To reset the window layout in the IDE, click Window on the menu bar, click Reset Window Layout, and then click the Yes button.

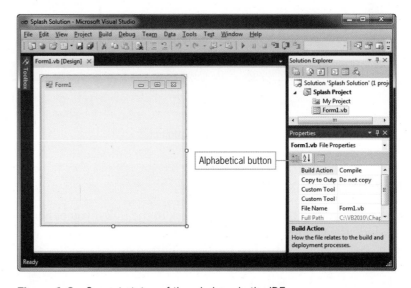

Figure 1-8   Current status of the windows in the IDE

In the next several sections, you will take a closer look at the Windows Form Designer, Solution Explorer, and Properties windows. (The Toolbox window is covered in Lesson B.)

The Windows Form Designer Window

Figure 1-9 shows the **Windows Form Designer window**, where you create (or design) the graphical user interface, referred to as a **GUI**, for your project. Only a Windows Form object appears in the designer window shown in the figure. A **Windows Form object**, or **form**, is the foundation for the user interface in a Windows application. You create the user interface by adding other objects, such as buttons and text boxes, to the form. Notice that a title bar appears at the top of the form. The title bar contains a default caption—in this case, Form1—as well as Minimize, Maximize, and Close buttons. At the top of the designer window is a tab labeled Form1.vb [Design]. [Design] identifies the window as the designer window. Form1.vb is the name of the file (on your computer's hard disk or on another device) that contains the Visual Basic instructions associated with the form.

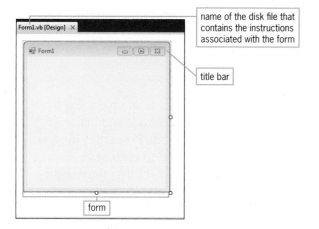

name of the disk file that contains the instructions associated with the form

title bar

form

Figure 1-9 Windows Form Designer window

As you learned in the Overview, all objects in an object-oriented program are instantiated (created) from a class. A form, for example, is an instance of the Windows Form class. The form is automatically instantiated for you when you create a Windows application.

 Recall that a class is a pattern that the computer uses to create an object.

The Solution Explorer Window

The **Solution Explorer window** displays a list of the projects contained in the current solution and the items contained in each project. Figure 1-10 shows the Solution Explorer window for the Splash Solution, which contains one project named Splash Project. Within the Splash Project are the My Project folder and a file named Form1.vb. The project also contains other items, which typically are kept hidden. However, you can display the additional items by clicking the Show All Files button. You would click the button again to hide the items. The .vb on the Form1.vb filename indicates that the file is a Visual Basic source file. A **source file** is a file that contains program instructions, called **code**. The Form1.vb file contains the code associated with the form displayed in the designer window. You can view the code using the Code Editor window, which you will learn about in Lesson C.

Show All Files button

Figure 1-10 Solution Explorer window

The Form1.vb source file is referred to as a **form file**, because it contains the code associated with a form. The code associated with the first form included in a project is automatically stored in a form file named Form1.vb. The code associated with the second form in the same project is stored in a form file named Form2.vb, and so on. Because a project can contain many forms and, therefore, many form files, it is a good practice to give each form file a more meaningful name. Doing this will help you keep track of the various form files in the project. You can use the Properties window to change the filename.

The Properties Window

As is everything in an object-oriented language, a file is an object. Each object has a set of attributes that determine its appearance and behavior. The attributes are called **properties** and are listed in the **Properties window**. When an object is created, a default value is assigned to each of its properties. The Properties window shown in Figure 1-11 lists the default values assigned to the properties of the Form1.vb file. (You do not need to widen your Properties window to match Figure 1-11.) As indicated in the figure, the Properties window includes an Object box and a Properties list. The **Object box** contains the name of the selected object. In this case, it contains Form1.vb, which is the name of the form file. The **Properties list** has two columns. The left column displays the names of the selected object's properties. You can use the Alphabetical and Categorized buttons to display the names either alphabetically or by category, respectively. However, it's usually easier to work with the Properties window when the properties are listed in alphabetical order, as they are in Figure 1-11. The right column in the Properties list is called the **Settings box** and displays the current value (or setting) of each of the properties. A brief description of the selected property appears in the Description pane.

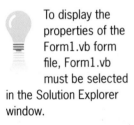 To display the properties of the Form1.vb form file, Form1.vb must be selected in the Solution Explorer window.

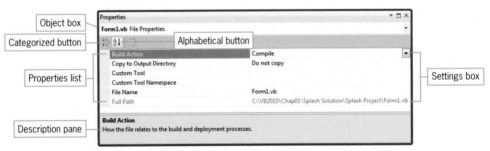

Figure 1-11 Properties window

START HERE **To use the Properties window to change the form file's name:**

1. Form1.vb should be selected in the Solution Explorer window. Click **File Name** in the Properties list and then type **Splash Form.vb**. Be sure to include the .vb extension on the filename; otherwise, the computer will not recognize the file as a source file.

2. Press **Enter**. Splash Form.vb appears in the Solution Explorer and Properties windows and on the designer window's tab, as shown in Figure 1-12.

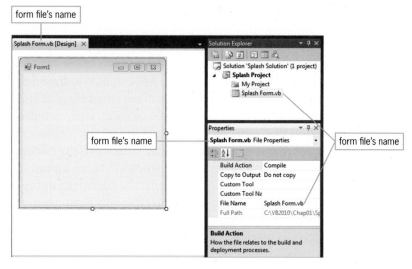

Figure 1-12 Form file's name shown in various locations

You also can change the File Name property by right-clicking Form1.vb in the Solution Explorer window and then clicking Rename on the context menu.

Properties of a Windows Form

Like a file, a Windows form also has a set of properties. The form's properties will appear in the Properties window when you select the form in the designer window.

To view the properties of the form:

START HERE

1. Click the **form** in the designer window. The form's properties appear in the Properties window.

2. If the properties are not listed alphabetically, click the **Alphabetical** button. The Properties window in Figure 1-13 shows a partial listing of the properties of a Windows form.

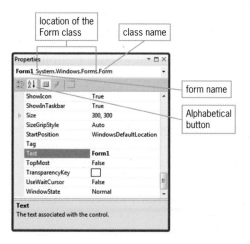

Figure 1-13 Properties window showing a partial listing of the form's properties

Notice that Form1 System.Windows.Forms.Form appears in the Object box in Figure 1-13. Form1 is the name of the form. The name is automatically assigned to the form when the form is instantiated (created). In System.Windows.Forms.Form, Form is the name of the class used to instantiate the form. System.Windows.Forms is the namespace that contains the Form class definition. A **class definition** is a block of code that specifies (or defines) an object's appearance and behavior. All class definitions in Visual Basic 2010 are contained in namespaces, which you can picture as blocks of memory cells inside the computer. Each **namespace** contains the code that defines a group of related classes. The System.Windows.Forms namespace contains the definition of the Windows Form class. It also contains the class definitions for objects you add to a form, such as buttons and text boxes. The period that separates each word in System.Windows.Forms. Form is called the **dot member access operator**. Similar to the backslash (\) in a folder path, the dot member access operator indicates a hierarchy, but of namespaces rather than folders. In other words, the backslash in the path C:\ VB2010\Chap01\Splash Solution\Splash Project\Splash Form.vb indicates that the Splash Form.vb file is contained in (or is a member of) the Splash Project folder, which is a member of the Splash Solution folder, which is a member of the Chap01 folder, which is a member of the VB2010 folder, which is a member of the C: drive. Likewise, the name System.Windows. Forms.Form indicates that the Form class is a member of the Forms namespace, which is a member of the Windows namespace, which is a member of the System namespace. The dot member access operator allows the computer to locate the Form class in the computer's internal memory, similar to the way the backslash (\) allows the computer to locate the Splash Form.vb file on your computer's disk.

The Name Property

As you do to a form file, you should assign a more meaningful name to a Windows form because doing so will help you keep track of the various forms in a project. Unlike a file, a Windows form has a Name property rather than a File Name property. You use the name entered in an object's Name property to refer to the object in code, so each object must have a unique name. The name you assign to an object must begin with a letter and contain only letters, numbers, and the underscore character. The name cannot include punctuation characters or spaces. There are several conventions for naming objects in Visual Basic. In this book, you will use a naming convention called Hungarian notation. Names in Hungarian notation begin with a three (or more) character ID that represents the object's type, with the remaining characters in the name representing the object's purpose. For example, using Hungarian notation, you might assign the name frmSplash to the current form. The "frm" identifies the object as a form, and "Splash" reminds you of the form's purpose. Hungarian notation names are entered using **camel case**, which means you enter the ID characters in lowercase and then capitalize the first letter of each subsequent word in the name. Camel case refers to the fact that the uppercase letters appear as "humps" in the name because they are taller than the lowercase letters.

START HERE **To change the name of the form:**

1. Drag the scroll box in the Properties window to the top of the vertical scroll bar. As you scroll, notice the various properties associated with a form. Also notice that the items within parentheses appear at the top of the Properties list.

2. Click **(Name)** in the Properties list. Type **frmSplash** and press **Enter**. An asterisk (*) appears on the designer window's tab. The asterisk indicates that the form has been changed since the last time it was saved.

The Text Property

In addition to changing the form's Name property, you also should change its Text property, which controls the text displayed in the form's title bar. The text also appears when you hover your mouse pointer over the application's button on the Windows 7 taskbar while the application is running. Form1 is the default value assigned to the Text property of the first form in a project. In this case, "Country Charm Inn" would be a more descriptive value.

To set the Text property of the form: START HERE

1. Scroll down the Properties window until you see the Text property in the Properties list and then click **Text**.

2. Type **Country Charm Inn** and press **Enter**. The new text appears in the property's Settings box and also in the form's title bar.

The Name and Text properties of a Windows form should always be changed to more meaningful values. The Name property is used by the programmer when coding the application. The Text property, on the other hand, is read by the user while the application is running.

The StartPosition Property

When an application is started, the computer uses the form's StartPosition property to determine the form's initial position on the screen. The frmSplash form represents a splash screen, which typically appears in the middle of the screen.

To center a form on the screen when the application is started: START HERE

1. Click **StartPosition** in the Properties list and then click the **list arrow** in the Settings box.

2. Click **CenterScreen** in the list.

The Font Property

A form's Font property determines the type, style, and size of the font used to display the text on the form. A font is the general shape of the characters in the text. Segoe UI, Tahoma, and Microsoft Sans Serif are examples of font types. Font styles include regular, bold, and italic. The numbers 9, 12, and 18 are examples of font sizes, which typically are measured in points, with one **point** equaling 1/72 of an inch. The recommended font for applications created for systems running Windows 7 (or Windows Vista) is Segoe UI, because it offers improved readability. Segoe is pronounced SEE-go, and UI stands for user interface. For most of the elements in the interface, you will use a font size of 9-point. However, to make the figures in the book more readable, some of the interfaces created in this book will use the 11-point Segoe UI font.

START HERE **To set the form's Font property:**

1. Click **Font** in the Properties list and then click the ... (ellipsis) button in the Settings box to open the Font dialog box.

2. Locate and then click the **Segoe UI** font in the Font box. Click **9** in the Size box and then click the **OK** button. (Don't be concerned that the size of the form changed.)

The Size Property

As you can with any Windows object, you can size a form by selecting it and then dragging the sizing handles that appear around it. You also can size an object by selecting it and then pressing and holding down the Shift key as you press the up, down, right, or left arrow key on your keyboard. In addition, you can set the object's Size property.

START HERE **To set the form's Size property:**

1. Click **Size** in the Properties list. Notice that the Size property contains two numbers separated by a comma and a space. The first number represents the width of the form, measured in pixels. The second number represents the height, also measured in pixels. A pixel, which is short for "picture element," is one spot in a grid of thousands of such spots that form an image either produced on the screen by a computer or printed on a page by a printer.

2. Type **685, 460** in the Size property's Settings box and press **Enter**. Expand the Size property by clicking the **arrow** that appears next to the property. Notice that the first number listed in the property represents the width, and the second number represents the height. Click the **arrow** again to collapse the property.

Setting and Restoring a Property's Value

In the next set of steps, you will practice setting and then restoring a property's value. More specifically, you will set and then restore the value of the form's BackColor property, which determines the background color of the form.

START HERE **To set and then restore the form's BackColor property value:**

1. Click **BackColor** in the Properties list and then click the **list arrow** in the Settings box. Click the **Custom** tab and then click a **red square** to change the background color of the form to red.

2. Now, right-click **BackColor** in the Properties list and then click **Reset** on the context menu. The background color of the form returns to its default setting. Figure 1-14 shows the status of the form in the IDE.

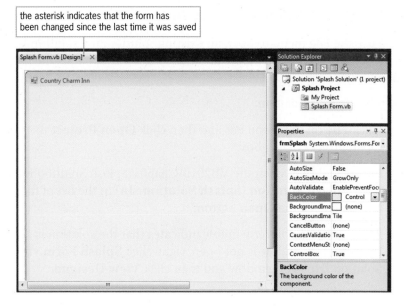

the asterisk indicates that the form has been changed since the last time it was saved

Figure 1-14   Status of the form in the IDE

Saving a Solution

Notice the asterisk (*) that appears on the designer window's tab in Figure 1-14. The asterisk indicates that a change was made to the form since the last time it was saved. It is a good practice to save the current solution every 10 or 15 minutes so that you will not lose a lot of your work if the computer loses power. You can save the solution by clicking File on the menu bar and then clicking Save All. You also can click the Save All button on the Standard toolbar. When you save the solution, the computer saves any changes made to the files included in the solution. Saving the solution also removes the asterisk that appears on the designer window's tab.

To save the current solution: START HERE

1. Click **File** on the menu bar and then click **Save All**. No asterisk appears on the designer window's tab, indicating that all changes made to the form have been saved.

Closing the Current Solution

When you are finished working on a solution, you should close it. Closing a solution closes all projects and files contained in the solution.

To close the Splash Solution: START HERE

1. Click **File** on the menu bar. Notice that the menu contains a Close option and a Close Solution option. The Close option does not close the solution; instead, it merely closes the designer window in the IDE. Only the Close Solution option closes the solution.

2. Click **Close Solution**. The Solution Explorer window indicates that no solution is currently open in the IDE.

23

Opening an Existing Solution

You can use the File menu to open an existing solution. If a solution is already open in the IDE, it is closed before another solution is opened. The names of solution files end with .sln.

START HERE

To open the Splash Solution:

1. Click **File** on the menu bar and then click **Open Project** to open the Open Project dialog box.

2. Locate and then open the VB2010\Chap01\Splash Solution folder. Click **Splash Solution** (**Splash Solution.sln**) in the list of filenames and then click the **Open** button.

3. The Solution Explorer window indicates that the solution is open. If the designer window is not open, right-click **Splash Form.vb** in the Solution Explorer window and then click **View Designer**.

Exiting Visual Studio 2010 or Visual Basic 2010 Express

Finally, you learn how to exit Visual Studio 2010 or Visual Basic 2010 Express. You will complete the splash screen in the remaining two lessons. You can exit Visual Studio or Visual Basic Express using either the Close button on the title bar or the Exit option on the File menu.

START HERE

To exit Visual Studio 2010 or Visual Basic 2010 Express:

1. Click **File** on the menu bar and then click **Exit**.

Lesson A Summary

● To start Visual Studio 2010 or Visual Basic 2010 Express:

If you are using Visual Studio 2010, click the Start button, point to All Programs, click Microsoft Visual Studio 2010, and then click Microsoft Visual Studio 2010. If you are using Visual Basic 2010 Express, click the Start button, point to All Programs, click Microsoft Visual Studio 2010 Express, and then click Microsoft Visual Basic 2010 Express.

● To configure Visual Studio or Visual Basic Express:

If you are using Visual Basic 2010 Express, click Tools, point to Settings, and then click Expert Settings. Click Tools, click Options, deselect the Show all settings check box, click the Projects and Solutions node, and then use the information shown earlier in Figure 1-4 to select and deselect the appropriate check boxes. Click the OK button.

● To create a Visual Basic 2010 Windows application:

Start either Visual Studio 2010 or Visual Basic 2010 Express. Click File and then click New Project. If necessary, click Visual Basic in the Installed Templates list. If you are using Visual Studio, expand the Visual Basic node

24

(if necessary) and then (if necessary) click Windows. If necessary, click Windows Forms Application. Enter an appropriate name and location in the Name and Location boxes, respectively. Select the Create directory for solution check box. Enter an appropriate name in the Solution name box and then click the OK button.

- To reset the window layout in the IDE:

  Click Window, click Reset Window Layout, and then click the Yes button.

- To close and open a window in the IDE:

  Close the window by clicking the Close button on its title bar. Use the appropriate option on the View menu to open the window.

- To auto-hide a window in the IDE:

  Click the Auto Hide (vertical pushpin) button on the window's title bar.

- To temporarily display an auto-hidden window in the IDE:

  Place your mouse pointer on the window's tab.

- To permanently display an auto-hidden window in the IDE:

  Click the Auto Hide (horizontal pushpin) button on the window's title bar.

- To set the value of a property:

  Select the object whose property you want to set and then select the appropriate property in the Properties list. Type the new property value in the selected property's Settings box, or choose the value from the list, color palette, or dialog box.

- To give a more meaningful name to an object:

  Set the object's Name property.

- To control the text appearing in the form's title bar, as well as the text that appears when you hover your mouse pointer over the application's button on the Windows 7 taskbar while the application is running:

  Set the form's Text property.

- To specify the starting location of the form:

  Set the form's StartPosition property.

- To specify the type, style, and size of the font used to display text on the form:

  Set the form's Font property.

- To size a form:

  Drag the form's sizing handles. You also can set the form's Size, Height, and Width values in the Properties window. In addition, you can select the form and then press and hold down the Shift key as you press the up, down, left, or right arrow key on your keyboard.

- To change the background color of a form:

  Set the form's BackColor property.

- To restore a property to its default setting:

  Right-click the property in the Properties list and then click Reset.

- To save a solution:

  Click File on the menu bar and then click Save All. You also can click the Save All button on the Standard toolbar.

- To close a solution:

  Click File on the menu bar and then click Close Solution.

- To open an existing solution:

  Click File on the menu bar and then click Open Project. Locate and then open the application's solution folder. Click the solution filename, which ends with .sln. Click the Open button. If the designer window is not open, right-click the form file's name in the Solution Explorer window and then click View Designer.

- To exit Visual Studio 2010 or Visual Basic 2010 Express:

  Click the Close button on the Visual Studio 2010 or Visual Basic 2010 Express title bar. You also can click File on the menu bar and then click Exit.

Lesson A Key Terms

Camel case—used when entering object names in Hungarian notation; the practice of entering the object's ID characters in lowercase and then capitalizing the first letter of each subsequent word in the name

Class definition—a block of code that specifies (or defines) an object's appearance and behavior

Code—program instructions

Dot member access operator—a period; used to indicate a hierarchy

Form—the foundation for the user interface in a Windows application; also called a Windows Form object

Form file—a file that contains the code associated with a Windows form

GUI—graphical user interface

Namespace—a block of memory cells inside the computer; contains the code that defines a group of related classes

Object box—the section of the Properties window that contains the name of the selected object

Point—used to measure font size; 1/72 of an inch

Properties—the attributes that control an object's appearance and behavior

Properties list—the section of the Properties window that lists the names of the properties associated with the selected object, as well as each property's value

Properties window—the window that lists an object's attributes (properties)

Settings box—the right column of the Properties list; displays each property's current value (setting)

Solution Explorer window—the window that displays a list of the projects contained in the current solution and the items contained in each project

Source file—a file that contains code

Windows Form Designer window—the window in which you create an application's GUI

Windows Form object—the foundation for the user interface in a Windows application; referred to more simply as a form

Lesson A Review Questions

1. When a form has been modified since the last time it was saved, what appears on its tab in the designer window?

    a. an ampersand (&)

    b. an asterisk (*)

    c. a percent sign (%)

    d. a plus sign (+)

2. You use the _____ window to set the characteristics that control an object's appearance and behavior.

    a. Characteristics

    b. Object

    c. Properties

    d. Toolbox

3. The _____ window lists the projects and files included in a solution.

    a. Object

    b. Project

    c. Properties

    d. Solution Explorer

4. The names of solution files in Visual Basic 2010 end with _____.

    a. .prg

    b. .sln

    c. .src

    d. .vb

5. Which of the following statements is true?

   a. You can auto-hide a window by clicking the Auto Hide (vertical pushpin) button on its title bar.

   b. An auto-hidden window appears as a tab on the edge of the IDE.

   c. You temporarily display an auto-hidden window by placing your mouse pointer on its tab.

   d. all of the above

6. The _____ property controls the text displayed in a form's title bar.

   a. Caption

   b. Text

   c. Title

   d. TitleBar

7. You give an object a more meaningful name by setting the object's _____ property.

   a. Application

   b. Caption

   c. Name

   d. Text

8. The _____ property determines the initial position of a form when the application is started.

   a. InitialLocation

   b. Location

   c. StartLocation

   d. StartPosition

9. Explain the difference between a form's Text property and its Name property.

10. Explain the difference between a form file and a form.

11. What does the dot member access operator indicate in the text System.Windows.Forms.Label?

Lesson A Exercises

INTRODUCTORY

1. If necessary, start Visual Studio 2010 or Visual Basic 2010 Express and permanently display the Solution Explorer window. Use the File menu to open the Charities Solution (Charities Solution.sln) file, which is contained in the VB2010\Chap01\Charities Solution folder.

If necessary, right-click the form file's name in the Solution Explorer window and then click View Designer. Change the form's Name property to frmMain. Change the form's BackColor property to light blue. Change the form's Font property to Segoe UI, 9pt. Change the form's StartPosition property to CenterScreen. Change the form's Text property to Charities Unlimited. Click File on the menu bar and then click Save All to save the solution. Click File on the menu bar and then click Close Solution to close the solution.

2. If necessary, start Visual Studio 2010 or Visual Basic 2010 Express and permanently display the Solution Explorer window. Create a Visual Basic Windows application. Use the following names for the solution, project, and form file, respectively: Photo Solution, Photo Project, and Main Form.vb. Save the application in the VB2010\Chap01 folder. Change the form's name to frmMain. The form's title bar should say Photos Incorporated; set the appropriate property. The form should be centered on the screen when it first appears; set the appropriate property. Change the background color of the form to light blue. Any text on the form should appear in the Segoe UI, 9pt font; set the appropriate property. Save and then close the solution.

INTERMEDIATE

3. If necessary, start Visual Studio 2010 or Visual Basic 2010 Express and permanently display the Solution Explorer window. Create a Visual Basic Windows application. Use the following names for the solution, project, and form file, respectively: Yorktown Solution, Yorktown Project, and Main Form.vb. Save the solution in the VB2010\Chap01 folder. Change the form's name to frmMain. The form's title bar should say Yorktown Shopping Center; set the appropriate property and then widen the form. The form should be centered on the screen when it first appears; set the appropriate property. Any text on the form should appear in the Segoe UI, 9pt font; set the appropriate property. Save and then close the solution.

INTERMEDIATE

 Discovery

4. In this exercise, you learn about a form's ControlBox, MaximizeBox, and MinimizeBox properties. If necessary, start Visual Studio 2010 or Visual Basic 2010 Express and permanently display the Solution Explorer window. Open the Greenwood Solution (Greenwood Solution.sln) file contained in the VB2010\Chap01\Greenwood Solution folder. If necessary, open the designer window.

   a. Use the Properties window to view the properties of the form. Click the ControlBox property. What is the purpose of this property? (Hint: Refer to the Description pane in the Properties window.) Set the ControlBox property to False. How does this setting affect the form? Set the ControlBox property to True.

   b. Click the MaximizeBox property. What is the purpose of this property? Set the MaximizeBox property to False. How does this setting affect the form? Set the MaximizeBox property to True.

c. Click the MinimizeBox property. What is the purpose of this property? Set the MinimizeBox property to False. How does this setting affect the form? Set the MinimizeBox property to True. Close the solution without saving it.

5. In this exercise, you research two properties of a form. If necessary, start Visual Studio 2010 or Visual Basic 2010 Express and permanently display the Solution Explorer window. Open the Greenwood Solution (Greenwood Solution.sln) file contained in the VB2010\Chap01\Greenwood Solution folder. If necessary, open the designer window. Use the Properties window to view the properties of the form. What property determines whether an icon is displayed in the form's title bar? What property determines whether the form appears on the Windows taskbar when the application is running? Close the solution without saving it.

LESSON B

After studying Lesson B, you should be able to:

- Add a control to a form

- Set the properties of a label, picture box, and button control

- Select multiple controls

- Center controls on the form

- Open the Project Designer window

- Start and end an application

- Enter code in the Code Editor window

- Terminate an application using the `Me.Close()` instruction

- Run the project's executable file

The Toolbox Window

In Lesson A, you learned about the Windows Form Designer, Solution Explorer, and Properties windows. In this lesson, you will learn about the **Toolbox window**, referred to more simply as the toolbox. The **toolbox** contains the tools you use when creating your application's user interface. Each tool represents a class from which an object, such as a button or text box, can be instantiated. The instantiated objects, called **controls**, will appear on the form.

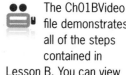

The Ch01BVideo file demonstrates all of the steps contained in Lesson B. You can view the video either before or after completing the lesson.

To open the Splash Solution from Lesson A and then display the Toolbox window:

START HERE

1. If necessary, start Visual Studio 2010 or Visual Basic 2010 Express and open the Solution Explorer window.

2. Open the Splash Solution (Splash Solution.sln) file contained in the VB2010\Chap01\Splash Solution folder. If necessary, open the designer window.

3. Permanently display the Properties and Toolbox windows and then auto-hide the Solution Explorer window.

4. Rest your mouse pointer on the word **Label** in the toolbox. The tool's purpose appears in a box. See Figure 1-15.

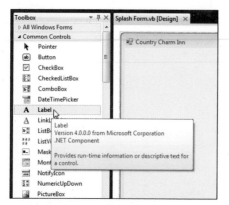

Figure 1-15 Toolbox window showing the purpose of the Label tool

The Label Tool

You use the Label tool to add a label control to a form. The purpose of a **label control** is to display text that the user is not allowed to edit while the application is running. In this case, for example, you do not want the user to change the name of the inn or the welcome message. Therefore, you will display the information using two label controls.

START HERE

To use the Label tool to instantiate a label control:

1. Click the **Label** tool in the toolbox, but do not release the mouse button. Hold down the mouse button as you drag the mouse pointer to the lower-left corner of the form. As you drag the mouse pointer, you will see a solid box, as well as an outline of a rectangle and a plus box, following the mouse pointer. The blue lines that appear between the form's left and bottom borders and the label's left and bottom borders are called margin lines, because their size is determined by the contents of the label's Margin property. The purpose of the margin lines is to assist you in spacing the controls properly on the form. See Figure 1-16.

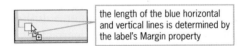

the length of the blue horizontal and vertical lines is determined by the label's Margin property

Figure 1-16 Label tool being dragged to the form

2. Release the mouse button. A label control appears on the form. See Figure 1-17. (If the wrong control appears on the form, right-click the control, click Delete, and then repeat Steps 1 and 2.) Notice that Label1 System.Windows.Forms.Label appears in the Object box in the Properties window. (You may need to widen the Properties window to view the entire contents of the Object box.) Label1 is the default name assigned to the label control. System.Windows.Forms.Label indicates that the control is an instance of the Label class, which is defined in the System.Windows.Forms namespace.

    Important note: You also can add a control to the form by clicking a tool in the toolbox and then clicking the form. In addition, you can click a tool in the toolbox, place the mouse pointer on the form, and then press the left mouse button and drag the mouse pointer until the control is the desired size. You also can double-click a tool in the toolbox.

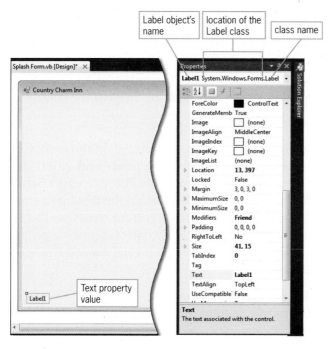

Label object's name | location of the Label class | class name

Figure 1-17 Label control added to the form

Recall from Lesson A that a default value is assigned to each of an object's properties when the object is created. Label1 is the default value assigned to the Text and Name properties of the first label control added to a form. The value of the Text property appears inside the label control, as indicated in Figure 1-17.

To add another label control to the form: ◀ START HERE

1. Click the **Label** tool in the toolbox and then drag the mouse pointer to the form, positioning it above the existing label control. (Do not worry about the exact location.)

2. Release the mouse button. Label2 is assigned to the control's Text and Name properties.

Some programmers assign meaningful names to all of the controls in an interface, while others do so only for controls that are either coded or referred to in code; in subsequent chapters in this book, you will follow the latter convention. In this chapter, however, you will assign a meaningful name to each control in the interface. The three-character ID used for naming labels is lbl.

To assign meaningful names to the label controls: ◀ START HERE

1. Click the **Label1** control on the form. This selects the control and displays its properties in the Properties window. Click **(Name)** in the Properties list. Type **lblName** in the Settings box and then press **Enter**.

2. Click the **Label2** control on the form. Change the control's name to **lblWelcome** and then press **Enter**.

Setting the Text Property

As you learned earlier, a label control's Text property determines the value that appears inside the control. In this application, you want the words "Country Charm Inn" to appear in the lblName control, and the words "Welcome to peace and quiet!" to appear in the lblWelcome control.

START HERE **To set each label control's Text property:**

1. Currently, the lblWelcome control is selected on the form. Click **Text** in the Properties list. Type **Welcome to peace and quiet!** and then press **Enter**. The new text appears in the Text property's Settings box and in the lblWelcome control. Notice that the designer automatically sizes the lblWelcome control to fit its current contents. This is because the default setting of a Label control's AutoSize property is True. (You can verify that fact by viewing the AutoSize property in the Properties window.)

2. Click the **lblName** control on the form. Change its Text property to **Country Charm Inn** and then press **Enter**. The lblName control stretches automatically to fit the contents of its Text property.

Setting the Location Property

The move pointer looks like this: ⬦.

You can move a control to a different location on the form by placing your mouse pointer on the control until it becomes a move pointer, and then dragging the control to the desired location. You also can select the control and then press and hold down the Control (Ctrl) key as you press the up, down, left, or right arrow key on your keyboard. In addition, you can set the control's Location property, which specifies the position of the upper-left corner of the control.

START HERE **To set each label control's Location property:**

1. Click the **lblWelcome** control to select it. Click **Location** in the Properties list. Expand the Location property by clicking the **arrow** that appears next to the property's name. The X value specifies the number of pixels from the left border of the form to the left border of the control. The Y property specifies the number of pixels between the top border of the form and the top border of the control. In other words, the X value refers to the control's horizontal location on the form, whereas the Y value refers to its vertical location.

2. Type **190, 380** in the Location property and then press **Enter**. The lblWelcome control moves to its new location. Click the **arrow** again to collapse the property.

3. In addition to selecting a control by clicking it on the form, you also can select a control by clicking its entry (name and class) in the Object box in the Properties window. Click the **list arrow** in the Properties window's Object box, and then click **lblName System. Windows.Forms.Label** in the list. Set the control's Location property to **220, 350**.

Changing a Property for Multiple Controls

In Lesson A, you changed the form's Font property to Segoe UI, 9pt. When you add a control to the form, the control's Font property is set to the same value as the form's Font property. Using object-oriented programming terminology, the control "inherits" the Font attribute of the form. In this case, for example, the lblName and lblWelcome controls inherit the form's Font property setting: Segoe UI, 9pt. At times, you may want to use a different font type, style, or size for a control's text. One reason for doing this is to bring attention to a specific part of the screen. In the splash screen, for example, you can make the text in the two label controls more noticeable by increasing the size of the font used to display the text. You can change the font size for both controls at the same time by clicking one control and then pressing and holding down the Ctrl (Control) key as you click the other control on the form. You can use the Ctrl+click method to select as many controls as you want. To cancel the selection of one of the selected controls, press and hold down the Ctrl key as you click the control. To cancel the selection of all of the selected controls, release the Ctrl key, then click the form or an unselected control on the form. You also can select a group of controls on the form by placing the mouse pointer slightly above and to the left of the first control you want to select, and then pressing the left mouse button and dragging. A dotted rectangle appears as you drag. When all of the controls you want to select are within (or at least touched by) the dotted rectangle, release the mouse button. All of the controls surrounded or touched by the dotted rectangle will be selected.

To select both label controls, and then set their Font property: START HERE

1. Verify that the lblName control is selected. Press and hold down the **Ctrl** (Control) key as you click the **lblWelcome** control, and then release the Ctrl key. Both controls are selected, as shown in Figure 1-18.

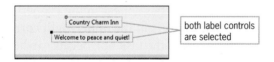

Figure 1-18 Label controls selected on the form

2. Open the Font dialog box by clicking **Font** in the Properties list and then clicking the... (ellipsis) button in the Settings box. Click **16** in the Size box, and then click the **OK** button to close the Font dialog box. The text in the two label controls appears in the new font size.

Using the Format Menu

The Format menu provides options for manipulating the controls on the form. The Align option, for example, allows you to align two or more controls by their left, right, top, or bottom borders. You can use the Make Same Size option to make two or more controls the same width and/or height. Before you can use the Format menu to change the alignment or size of two or more controls, you first must select the controls. The first control you select should always be the one whose size and/or location you want to match. For example, to align the left border of the Label2 control with the left border

To experiment with the Align and Make Same Size options, complete Discovery Exercise 4 at the end of this lesson.

35

of the Label1 control, you first select the Label1 control and then select the Label2 control. However, to make the Label1 control the same size as the Label2 control, you must select the Label2 control before selecting the Label1 control. The first control you select is referred to as the **reference control**. The reference control will have white sizing handles, whereas the other selected controls will have black sizing handles. The Format menu also has a Center in Form option that centers one or more controls either horizontally or vertically on the form. In the next set of steps, you will use the Center in Form option to center the two label controls on the form.

START HERE ▶ **To center the label controls horizontally on the form:**

1. Click the **form** to deselect the two label controls, and then click the **lblName** control. Click **Format** on the menu bar, point to **Center in Form**, and then click **Horizontally**.

2. Use the Format menu to center the lblWelcome control horizontally on the form.

3. Click **File** on the menu bar and then click **Save All** to save the solution.

The PictureBox Tool

The splash screen you previewed at the beginning of the chapter showed an image of a rural countryside. You can include an image on a form using a **picture box control**, which you instantiate using the PictureBox tool.

START HERE ▶ **To add a picture box control to the form:**

1. Click the **PictureBox** tool in the toolbox and then drag the mouse pointer to the upper-left corner of the form. Release the mouse button. The picture box control's properties appear in the Properties list, and a box containing a triangle appears in the upper-right corner of the control. The box is referred to as the task box because, when you click it, it displays a list of the tasks associated with the control. Each task in the list is associated with one or more properties. You can set the properties using the task list or the Properties window.

2. Click the **task box** on the PictureBox1 control. See Figure 1-19.

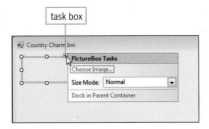

Figure 1-19   Open task list for a picture box

3. Click **Choose Image** to open the Select Resource dialog box. The Choose Image task is associated with the Image property in the Properties window.

4. To include the image file within the project itself, the Project resource file radio button must be selected in the Select Resource dialog box. Verify that the radio button is selected, and then click the **Import** button to open the Open dialog box.

5. Open the VB2010\Chap01 folder. Click **Country Charm** (**Country Charm.jpg**) in the list of filenames and then click the **Open** button. See Figure 1-20.

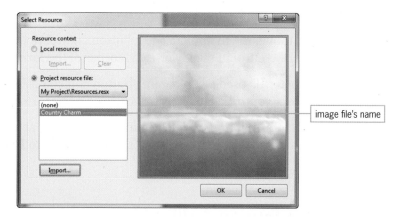

Figure 1-20 Completed Select Resource dialog box

6. Click the **OK** button to close the Select Resource dialog box. A small portion of the image appears in the picture box control on the form, and Splash_Project.My.Resources.Resources.Country_Charm appears in the control's Image property in the Properties window.

7. Click the **list arrow** in the Size Mode box in the task list and then click **StretchImage** in the list. Click the **picture box** control to close the task list.

8. The three-character ID used when naming picture box controls is pic. Use the Properties window to change the picture box's name to **picCountry**.

9. Place your mouse pointer on the sizing handle located in the lower-right corner of the picture box. Drag the control to the size shown in Figure 1-21 and then release the mouse button.

place your mouse pointer on this sizing handle and drag

Figure 1-21 Image shown in the picture box

The Button Tool

Every application should give the user a way to exit the program. Most Windows applications accomplish this task using either an Exit option on a File menu or an Exit button. In this lesson, the splash screen will provide a button for ending the application. In Windows applications, a **button control** is commonly used to perform an immediate action when clicked. The OK and Cancel buttons are examples of button controls found in many Windows applications.

START HERE **To add a button control to the form:**

1. Use the Button tool in the toolbox to add a button control to the form. Position the control in the lower-right corner of the form.

2. The three-character ID used when naming button controls is btn. Change the button control's name to **btnExit**.

3. The button control's Text property determines the text that appears on the button's face. Set the button control's Text property to **Exit**.

4. Save the solution.

Starting and Ending an Application

Now that the user interface is complete, you can start the splash screen application to see how it will appear to the user. Before you start an application for the first time, you should open the Project Designer window and verify the name of the **startup form**, which is the form that the computer automatically displays each time the application is started. You can open the Project Designer window by right-clicking My Project in the Solution Explorer window and then clicking Open on the context menu. Or, you can click Project on the menu bar and then click *<project name>* Properties on the menu.

START HERE **To verify the name of the startup form:**

1. Auto-hide the Toolbox and Properties windows. Temporarily display the Solution Explorer window. Right-click **My Project** in the Solution Explorer window and then click **Open** to open the Project Designer window.

2. If necessary, click the **Application** tab to display the Application pane, which is shown in Figure 1-22. If frmSplash does not appear in the Startup form list box, click the **Startup form** list arrow and then click **frmSplash** in the list.

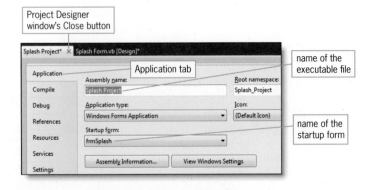

Figure 1-22   Application pane in the Project Designer window

You can start an application by clicking Debug on the menu bar and then clicking Start Debugging. You also can press the F5 key on your keyboard or click the Start Debugging button on the Standard toolbar. When you start a Visual Basic application, the computer automatically creates a file that can be run outside of the IDE (such as from the Run dialog box in Windows). The file is referred to as an **executable file**. The executable file's name is the same as the project's name, except it ends with .exe. The name of the executable file for the Splash Project, for example, is Splash Project.exe. However, you can use the Project Designer window to change the executable file's name. The computer stores the executable file in the project's bin\Debug folder. In this case, the Splash Project.exe file is stored in the VB2010\Chap01\Splash Solution\Splash Project\bin\Debug folder. When you are finished with an application, you typically give the user only the executable file, because it does not allow the user to modify the application's code. To allow someone to modify the code, you need to provide the entire solution.

The Start Debugging button looks like this:

To change the name of the executable file, and then start and end the application:

START HERE

1. The Project Designer window should still be open. Change the file-name in the Assembly name box to **Splash**. Save the solution and then close the Project Designer window by clicking its **Close** button. (Refer to Figure 1-22 for the location of the Close button.)

2. Click **Debug** on the menu bar and then click **Start Debugging** to start the application. See Figure 1-23. (Do not be concerned about any windows that appear at the bottom of the screen.)

form's Close button

startup form

Figure 1-23   Result of starting the splash screen application

3. Recall that the purpose of the Exit button is to allow the user to end the application. Click the **Exit** button on the splash screen. Currently, the button will not work as intended, because you have not yet entered the instructions that tell the button how to respond when clicked.

39

4. Click the **Close** button on the form's title bar to stop the application. (You also can click the designer window to make it the active window, then click Debug on the menu bar, and then click Stop Debugging.)

The Code Editor Window

After creating your application's interface, you can begin entering the Visual Basic instructions (code) that tell the controls how to respond to the user's actions. Those actions—such as clicking, double-clicking, or scrolling—are called **events**. You tell an object how to respond to an event by writing an **event procedure**, which is a set of Visual Basic instructions that are processed only when the event occurs. You enter the procedure's code in the Code Editor window. In this lesson, you will write a Click event procedure for the Exit button, which should end the application when it is clicked.

START HERE   **To open the Code Editor window:**

1. Right-click the **form** and then click **View Code** on the context menu. The Code Editor window opens in the IDE, as shown in Figure 1-24. The Code Editor window contains the Class statement, which is used to define a class in Visual Basic. In this case, the Class statement begins with the `Public Class frmSplash` clause and ends with the `End Class` clause. Within the Class statement you enter the code to tell the form and its objects how to react to the user's actions.

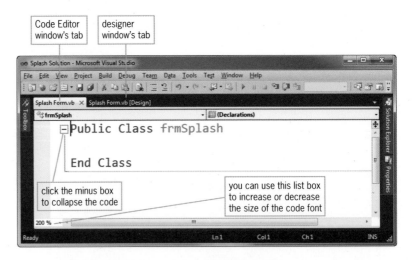

The `Public` keyword in the Class statement indicates that the class can be used by code defined outside of the class.

Figure 1-24   Code Editor window opened in the IDE

If the Code Editor window contains many lines of code, you might want to hide the sections of code that you are not presently working with or that you do not want to print. You hide a section (or region) of code by clicking the minus box that appears next to it. To unhide a region of code, you click the plus box that appears next to the code. Hiding and unhiding code is also referred to as collapsing and expanding the code, respectively.

START HERE   **To collapse and expand a region of code in the Code Editor window:**

1. Click the **minus box** that appears next to the `Public Class frmSplash` clause in the Code Editor window. Doing this collapses the Class statement, as shown in Figure 1-25.

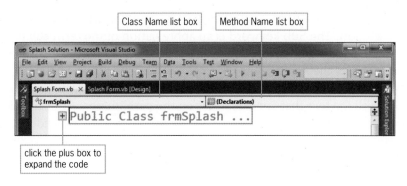

Figure 1-25   Code collapsed in the Code Editor window

2. Now click the **plus box** to expand the code.

As Figure 1-25 indicates, the Code Editor window contains a Class Name list box and a Method Name list box. The **Class Name list box** lists the names of the objects included in the user interface. The **Method Name list box** lists the events to which the selected object is capable of responding. In object-oriented programming (**OOP**), an event is considered a behavior of an object because it represents an action to which the object can respond. In the context of OOP, the Code Editor window "exposes" an object's behaviors to the programmer. You use the Class Name and Method Name list boxes to select the object and event, respectively, that you want to code. In this case, you will select btnExit in the Class Name list box and Click in the Method Name list box. This is because you want the application to end when the Exit button is clicked.

To select the btnExit control's Click event:

START HERE

1. Click the **Class Name** list arrow and then click **btnExit** in the list.

2. Click the **Method Name** list arrow and then click **Click** in the list. A code template for the btnExit control's Click event procedure appears in the Code Editor window. See Figure 1-26.

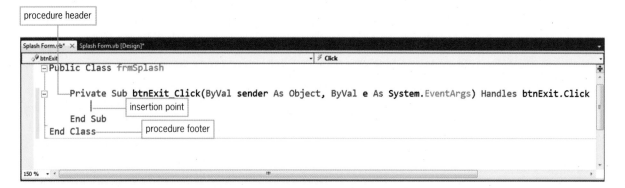

Figure 1-26   btnExit control's Click event procedure

The Code Editor provides the code template to help you follow the rules of the Visual Basic language. The rules of a programming language are called its **syntax**. The first line in the code template is called the **procedure header**, and the last line is called the **procedure footer**. The procedure header begins with the two keywords `Private Sub`. A **keyword** is a word that has a special meaning in a programming language. Keywords appear in a different color from the rest of the code. The `Private` keyword in Figure 1-26 indicates that the button's Click event procedure can be used only within the current Code Editor window. The Sub keyword is an abbreviation of the term **sub procedure**, which is a block of code that performs a specific task. Following the Sub keyword is the name of the object, an underscore, the name of the event, and parentheses containing some text. For now, you do not have to be concerned with the text that appears between the parentheses. After the closing parenthesis is `Handles btnExit.Click`. This part of the procedure header indicates that the procedure handles (or is associated with) the btnExit control's Click event. It tells the computer to process the procedure only when the btnExit control is clicked.

The code template ends with the procedure footer, which contains the keywords `End Sub`. You enter your Visual Basic instructions at the location of the insertion point, which appears between the Private Sub and End Sub clauses in Figure 1-26. The Code Editor automatically indents the line between the procedure header and footer. Indenting the lines within a procedure makes the instructions easier to read and is a common programming practice. In this case, the instruction you enter will tell the btnExit control to end the application when it is clicked.

The Me.Close() Instruction

The `Me.Close()` instruction tells the computer to close the current form. If the current form is the only form in the application, closing it terminates the entire application. In the instruction, `Me` is a keyword that refers to the current form, and Close is one of the methods available in Visual Basic. A **method** is a predefined procedure that you can call (or invoke) when needed. For example, if you want the computer to close the current form when the user clicks the Exit button, you enter the `Me.Close()` instruction in the button's Click event procedure. Notice the empty set of parentheses after the method's name in the instruction. The parentheses are required when calling some Visual Basic methods. However, depending on the method, the parentheses may or may not be empty. If you forget to enter the empty set of parentheses, the Code Editor will enter them for you when you move the insertion point to another line in the Code Editor window.

START HERE **To code the btnExit control's Click event procedure:**

1. You can type the `Me.Close()` instruction on your own or use the Code Editor window's IntelliSense feature. In this set of steps, you will use the IntelliSense feature. Type **me.** (but don't press Enter). When you type the period, the IntelliSense feature displays a list of properties, methods, and so on from which you can select.

   Important note: If the list of choices does not appear, the IntelliSense feature may have been turned off on your computer system. To turn it on, click Tools on the menu bar and then click Options. If necessary, select the Show all settings check box. Expand the Text Editor node and then click Basic. Select the Auto list members check box and then click the OK button.

2. If necessary, click the **Common** tab. The Common tab displays the
    most commonly used items, whereas the All tab displays all of the
    items. Type **cl** (but don't press Enter). The IntelliSense feature high-
    lights the Close method in the list. See Figure 1-27.

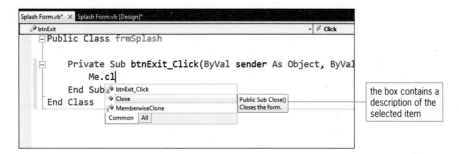

Figure 1-27   List displayed by the IntelliSense feature

3. Press **Tab** to include the Close method in the instruction and then
    press **Enter**. See Figure 1-28.

Figure 1-28   Completed Click event procedure for the btnExit control

It's a good programming practice to test a procedure after you have coded it.
By doing this, you'll know where to look if an error occurs. You can test the
Exit button's Click event procedure by starting the application and then clicking the button. When the button is clicked, the computer will process the
`Me.Close()` instruction contained in the procedure.

To test the Exit button's Click event procedure and the executable file: ◀ START HERE

1. Save the solution and then press the **F5** key to start the application.
    The splash screen appears.

2. Click the **Exit** button to end the application. Close the Code Editor
    window and then close the solution.

3. Press and hold down the **Windows logo** key on your keyboard as you
    tap the letter **r**. The Run dialog box opens. Release the logo key.

4. Click the **Browse** button. Locate and then open the VB2010\Chap01\
    Splash Solution\Splash Project\bin\Debug folder. Click **Splash
    (Splash.exe)** and then click the **Open** button.

5. Click the **OK** button in the Run dialog box. When the splash screen
    appears, click the **Exit** button.

Lesson B Summary

- To add a control to a form:

  Click a tool in the toolbox, but do not release the mouse button. Hold down the mouse button as you drag the mouse pointer to the form, and then release the mouse button. You also can click a tool in the toolbox and then click the form. In addition, you can click a tool in the toolbox, place the mouse pointer on the form, and then press the left mouse button and drag the mouse pointer until the control is the desired size. You also can double-click a tool in the toolbox.

- To display text that the user cannot edit while the application is running:

  Use the Label tool to instantiate a label control. Set the label control's Text property.

- To move a control to a different location on the form:

  Drag the control to the desired location. You also can set the control's Location property. In addition, you can select the control and then press and hold down the Ctrl (Control) key as you press the up, down, right, or left arrow key on your keyboard.

- To specify the type, style, and size of the font used to display text in a control:

  Set the control's Font property.

- To select multiple controls on a form:

  Click the first control you want to select, then Ctrl+click each of the other controls you want to select. You also can select a group of controls on the form by placing the mouse pointer slightly above and to the left of the first control you want to select, then pressing the left mouse button and dragging. A dotted rectangle appears as you drag. When all of the controls you want to select are within (or at least touched by) the dotted rectangle, release the mouse button. All of the controls surrounded or touched by the dotted rectangle will be selected.

- To cancel the selection of one or more controls:

  You cancel the selection of one control by pressing and holding down the Ctrl key as you click the control. You cancel the selection of all of the selected controls by releasing the Ctrl key and then clicking the form or an unselected control on the form.

- To center one or more controls on the form:

  Select the controls you want to center. Click Format on the menu bar, point to Center in Form, and then click either Horizontally or Vertically.

- To align the borders of two or more controls on the form:

  Select the reference control, and then select the other controls you want to align. Click Format on the menu bar, point to Align, and then click the appropriate option.

- To make two or more controls on the form the same size:

  Select the reference control, and then select the other controls you want to size. Click Format on the menu bar, point to Make Same Size, and then click the appropriate option.

- To display a graphic in a control in the user interface:

  Use the PictureBox tool to instantiate a picture box control. Use the task box or Properties window to set the control's Image and SizeMode properties.

- To display a standard button that performs an action when clicked:

  Use the Button tool to instantiate a button control.

- To verify or change the names of the startup form and/or executable file:

  Use the Application pane in the Project Designer window. You can open the Project Designer window by right-clicking My Project in the Solution Explorer window, and then clicking Open on the context menu. Or, you can click Project on the menu bar and then click *<project name>* Properties on the menu.

- To start and stop an application:

  You can start an application by clicking Debug on the menu bar and then clicking Start Debugging. You also can press the F5 key on your keyboard or click the Start Debugging button on the Standard toolbar. You can stop an application by clicking the form's Close button. You also can first make the designer window the active window, and then click Debug on the menu bar and then click Stop Debugging.

- To open the Code Editor window:

  Right-click the form and then click View Code on the context menu.

- To display an object's event procedure in the Code Editor window:

  Open the Code Editor window. Use the Class Name list box to select the object's name, and then use the Method Name list box to select the event.

- To allow the user to close the current form while an application is running:

  Enter the `Me.Close()` instruction in an event procedure.

- To run a project's executable file:

  Open the Run dialog box in Windows. Click the Browse button. Locate and then open the project's bin\Debug folder. Click the executable file's name. Click the Open button to close the Browse dialog box, and then click the OK button.

Lesson B Key Terms

Button control—the control commonly used to perform an immediate action when clicked

Class Name list box—appears in the Code Editor window; lists the names of the objects included in the user interface

Controls—objects (such as a label, picture box, or button) added to a form

Event procedure—a set of Visual Basic instructions that tell an object how to respond to an event

Events—actions to which an object can respond; examples include clicking and double-clicking

Executable file—a file that can be run outside of the Visual Studio IDE, such as from the Run dialog box in Windows; the file has an .exe extension on its filename

Keyword—a word that has a special meaning in a programming language

Label control—the control used to display text that the user is not allowed to edit while an application is running

Method—a predefined Visual Basic procedure that you can call (invoke) when needed

Method Name list box—appears in the Code Editor window; lists the events to which the selected object is capable of responding

OOP—acronym for object-oriented programming

Picture box control—the control used to display an image on a form

Procedure footer—the last line in a procedure

Procedure header—the first line in a procedure

Reference control—the first control selected in a group of controls; this is the control whose size and/or location you want the other selected controls to match

Startup form—the form that appears automatically when an application is started

Sub procedure—a block of code that performs a specific task

Syntax—the rules of a programming language

Toolbox—refers to the Toolbox window

Toolbox window—the window that contains the tools used when creating an interface; each tool represents a class; referred to more simply as the toolbox

Lesson B Review Questions

1. The purpose of the _____ control is to display text that the user is not allowed to edit while the application is running.

   a. Button

   b. DisplayBox

   c. Label

   d. PictureBox

2. The text displayed on a button's face is stored in the button's
   _____ property.

   a. Caption

   b. Label

   c. Name

   d. Text

3. The Format menu contains options that allow you to _____.

   a. align two or more controls

   b. center one or more controls horizontally on the form

   c. make two or more controls the same size

   d. all of the above

4. You can use the _____ instruction to terminate a running
   application.

   a. `Me.Close()`

   b. `Me.Done()`

   c. `Me.Finish()`

   d. `Me.Stop()`

5. Define the term "syntax."

Lesson B Exercises

1. Open the Mechanics Solution (Mechanics Solution.sln) file contained   INTRODUCTORY
   in the VB2010\Chap01\Mechanics Solution folder. If necessary, open
   the designer window.

   a. Change the form file's name to Main Form.vb.

   b. Change the form's name to frmMain. Change its Font property to
      Segoe UI, 9pt. The form's title bar should say IMA; set the appro-
      priate property. The form should be centered on the screen when
      it first appears; set the appropriate property.

   c. Add a label control to the form. The label should contain the text
      "International Mechanics Association" (without the quotation
      marks); set the appropriate property. Display the label's text in
      italics using the Segoe UI, 12pt font. The label should be located
      16 pixels from the top of the form, and it should be centered
      horizontally on the form.

d. Add a button control to the form. Change the button's name to btnExit. The button should display the text "Exit" (without the quotation marks); set the appropriate property. The button should be located 200 pixels from the left border of the form, and 180 pixels from the top of the form.

e. Open the Code Editor window. Enter the `Me.Close()` instruction in the btnExit control's Click event procedure.

f. Display the Project Designer window. Verify that the name of the startup form is frmMain. Also, use the Assembly name box to change the executable file's name to IMA. Close the Project Designer window.

g. Save the solution and then start the application. Use the Exit button to stop the application. Close the Code Editor window and then close the solution.

h. Use the Run dialog box to run the project's executable file.

INTERMEDIATE

2. Create a Visual Basic Windows application. Use the following names for the solution, project, and form file, respectively: Costello Solution, Costello Project, and Main Form.vb. Save the application in the VB2010\Chap01 folder. Create the user interface shown in Figure 1-29. Change the form's Font property to Segoe UI, 9pt. You can use any font style and size for the label controls. The form should be centered on the screen when the application is started. Code the Exit button so that it closes the application when it is clicked. Use the Project Designer window to verify that the name of the startup form is correct, and to change the executable file's name to Costello Motors. Save the solution and then start the application. Use the Exit button to stop the application. Close the Code Editor window and then close the solution. Use the Run dialog box to run the project's executable file.

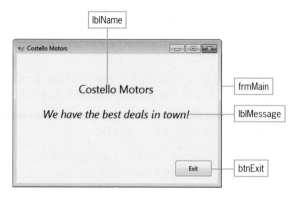

Figure 1-29   User interface for the Costello Motors application

INTERMEDIATE

3. Create a Visual Basic Windows application. Use the following names for the solution, project, and form file, respectively: Tabatha Solution, Tabatha Project, and Main Form.vb. Save the application in the VB2010\Chap01 folder. Create the user interface shown in Figure 1-30. Change the form's Font property to Segoe UI, 9pt. You can use any font style and size for the label control. The form should

be centered on the screen when the application is started. Assign appropriate names to the form, label, button, and picture box. The image is stored in the 00223754.gif file, which is contained in the VB2010\Chap01 folder. Code the Exit button so that it closes the application when it is clicked. Use the Project Designer window to verify that the name of the startup form is correct, and to change the executable file's name to Tabatha. Save the solution and then start the application. Use the Exit button to stop the application. Close the Code Editor window and then close the solution. Use the Run dialog box to run the project's executable file.

Figure 1-30   User interface for the Tabatha's Bed and Breakfast application

Discovery

4. In this exercise, you learn about the Format menu's Align and Make Same Size options.

   a. Open the Jerrods Solution (Jerrods Solution.sln) file contained in the VB2010\Chap01\Jerrods Solution folder. If necessary, open the designer window.

   b. Click one of the button controls on the form, and then press and hold down the Ctrl (Control) key as you click the remaining two button controls. Release the Ctrl key. Notice that the sizing handles on the first button you selected are white, while the sizing handles on the other two buttons are black. The Align and Make Same Size options on the Format menu use the control with the white sizing handles as the reference control when aligning and sizing the selected controls. First, you will practice with the Align option by aligning the three buttons by their left borders. Click Format, point to Align, and then click Lefts. The left borders of the last two buttons you selected are aligned with the left border of the reference control.

   c. The Make Same Size option makes the selected objects the same height, width, or both. Here again, the first object you select determines the size. Click the form to deselect the three buttons. Click Button2, Ctrl+click Button3, and then Ctrl+click Button1. Click Format, point to Make Same Size, and then click Both. The height and width of the last two controls you selected now match the height and width of the reference control.

   d. Click the form to deselect the buttons. Save and then close the solution.

LESSON C

After studying Lesson C, you should be able to:

- Set the properties of a timer control

- Delete a control from the form

- Delete code from the Code Editor window

- Code a timer control's Tick event procedure

- Prevent the user from sizing a form

- Remove and/or disable a form's Minimize, Maximize, and Close buttons

- Print an application's code and interface

 The Ch01CVideo file demonstrates all of the steps contained in Lesson C. You can view the video either before or after completing the lesson.

Using the Timer Tool

In Lesson B, you added an Exit button to the splash screen created for the Country Charm Inn. Splash screens usually do not contain an Exit button. Instead, they use a timer control to automatically remove themselves from the screen after a set period of time. In this lesson, you will remove the Exit button from the splash screen and replace it with a timer control.

To open the Splash Solution from Lesson B:

START HERE

1. If necessary, start Visual Studio 2010 or Visual Basic 2010 Express and open the Solution Explorer window.

2. Open the Splash Solution (Splash Solution.sln) file contained in the VB2010\Chap01\Splash Solution folder. If necessary, open the designer window.

3. Permanently display the Properties and Toolbox windows, and then auto-hide the Solution Explorer window.

You instantiate a timer control using the Timer tool, which is located in the Components section of the toolbox. When you drag the Timer tool to the form and then release the mouse button, the timer control will be placed in the component tray rather than on the form. The **component tray** is a special area of the IDE. Its purpose is to store controls that do not appear in the user interface during **run time**, which occurs while an application is running. In other words, the timer will not be visible to the user when the interface appears on the screen.

 The Boolean values (True and False) are named after the English mathematician George Boole.

The purpose of a **timer control** is to process code at one or more regular intervals. The length of each interval is specified in milliseconds and entered in the timer's Interval property. A millisecond is 1/1000 of a second; in other words, there are 1000 milliseconds in a second. The timer's state—either running or stopped—is determined by its Enabled property, which can be set to either the Boolean value True or the Boolean value False. When its Enabled property is set to True, the timer is running; when it is set to False, the timer is stopped. If the timer is running, its Tick event occurs each time an interval has elapsed. Each time the Tick event occurs, the computer processes the code contained in the Tick event procedure. If the timer is stopped, the Tick event does not occur and, therefore, the code entered in the Tick event procedure is not processed.

To add a timer control to the splash screen:

START HERE

1. If necessary, expand the Components node in the toolbox. Click the **Timer** tool and then drag the mouse pointer to the form. (Do not worry about the exact location.) When you release the mouse button, a timer control appears in the component tray at the bottom of the IDE.

2. The three-character ID used when naming timer controls is tmr. Change the timer's name to **tmrExit**, and then set its Enabled property to **True**.

3. You will have the timer end the application after six seconds, which are 6000 milliseconds. Set the timer's Interval property to **6000** and press **Enter**. See Figure 1-31.

51

Figure 1-31 Timer control placed in the component tray

You no longer need the Exit button, so you can delete it and its associated code. You then will enter the `Me.Close()` instruction in the timer's Tick event procedure.

To delete the Exit button and its code, and then code and test the timer:

START HERE

1. Auto-hide the Toolbox and Properties windows. Click the **Exit** button to select it and then press **Delete** to delete the control from the form.

2. Deleting a control from the form does not delete the control's code, which remains in the Code Editor window. Open the Code Editor window by right-clicking the **form** and then clicking **View Code**. Select (highlight) the entire Click event procedure for the btnExit control, including the blank line above the procedure, as shown in Figure 1-32.

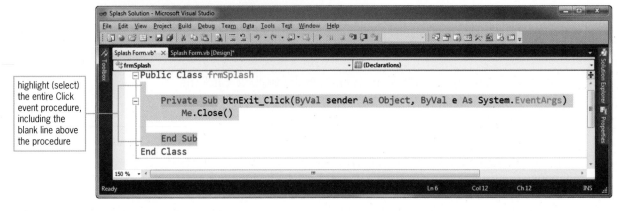

highlight (select)
the entire Click
event procedure,
including the
blank line above
the procedure

Figure 1-32   Exit button's Click event procedure selected in the Code Editor window

3. Press **Delete** to delete the selected code from the Code Editor window.

4. Use the Class Name and Method Name list boxes to open the code template for the tmrExit control's Tick event procedure. Type **Me.Close()** and press **Enter**.

5. Save the solution and then start the application. The splash form appears on the screen.

6. Place your mouse pointer on the form's right border until it becomes a horizontal sizing pointer, and then drag the form's border to the left. Notice that you can change the form's size during run time. Typically, a user is not allowed to change the size of a splash screen. You can prevent the user from sizing the form by changing the form's FormBorderStyle property, which you will do in the next section.

The horizontal
sizing pointer
looks like
this: ⟺.

7. When six seconds have elapsed, the application ends and the splash form disappears. Click the **Splash Form.vb [Design]** tab to make the designer window the active window.

Setting the FormBorderStyle Property

A form's FormBorderStyle property determines the border style of the form. For most applications, you will leave the property at its default setting, Sizable. Doing this allows the user to change the form's size by dragging its borders while the application is running. When a form represents a splash screen, however, you typically set the FormBorderStyle property to either None or FixedSingle. The None setting removes the form's border, whereas the FixedSingle setting draws a fixed, thin line around the form.

START HERE ▶ **To change the FormBorderStyle property:**

1. Click the **form's title bar** to select the form. Temporarily display the Properties window, and then set the FormBorderStyle property to **FixedSingle**.

2. Save the solution and then start the application. Try to size the form by dragging one of its borders. You will notice that you cannot size the form using its border.

3. When six seconds have elapsed, the application ends. Start the application again. Notice that the splash screen's title bar contains a Minimize button, a Maximize button, and a Close button. As a general rule, most splash screens do not contain these elements. You will learn how to remove the elements, as well as the title bar itself, in the next section. Here again, the application ends after six seconds have elapsed.

The MinimizeBox, MaximizeBox, and ControlBox Properties

You can use a form's MinimizeBox property to disable the Minimize button that appears on the form's title bar. Similarly, you can use the MaximizeBox property to disable the Maximize button. You will experiment with both properties in the next set of steps.

To experiment with the MinimizeBox and MaximizeBox properties:

START HERE

1. If necessary, click the **form's title bar** to select the form. First, you will disable the Minimize button. Set the form's MinimizeBox property to **False**. Notice that the Minimize button appears dimmed (grayed out) on the title bar. This indicates that the button is not available for use.

2. Now you will enable the Minimize button and disable the Maximize button. Set the MinimizeBox property to **True**, and then set the MaximizeBox property to **False**. Now only the Maximize button appears dimmed (grayed out) on the title bar.

3. Now observe what happens if both the MinimizeBox and MaximizeBox properties are set to False. Set the MinimizeBox property to **False**. (The MaximizeBox property is already set to False.) Notice that when both properties are set to False, the buttons are not disabled; instead, they are removed from the title bar.

4. Now return the buttons to their original state. Set the MinimizeBox and MaximizeBox properties to **True**.

Unlike most applications, splash screens typically do not contain a title bar. You can remove the title bar by setting the form's ControlBox property to False, and then removing the text from its Text property. You will try this next.

To remove the title bar from the splash screen:

START HERE

1. Set the form's ControlBox property to **False**. Doing this removes the title bar elements (icon and buttons) from the form; however, it does not remove the title bar itself. To remove the title bar, you must delete the contents of the form's Text property. Select the text in the Text property. Press **Delete** and then press **Enter**.

2. Save the solution and then start the application. The splash screen appears without a title bar. See Figure 1-33. The application ends after six seconds have elapsed.

Country Charm Inn
Welcome to peace and quiet!

Figure 1-33   Completed splash screen

Printing the Application's Code and Interface

You should always print a copy of your application's code, because the printout will help you understand and maintain the application in the future. To print the code, the Code Editor window must be the active (current) window. You also should print a copy of the application's user interface. You can print the interface during either design time or run time. In this chapter, you will learn how to print the interface during design time. Printing the interface during run time is covered in Appendix D (which is available at *www.cengagebrain.com*).

START HERE ▶   **To print the splash screen's interface and code:**

1. The designer window should be the active window. Press and hold down the **Alt** key on your keyboard as you tap the **Print Screen** (Prnt Scrn or PrtSc) key and then release the Alt key. Doing this places a picture of the interface on the Clipboard. Start Microsoft Word (or any application that can display a picture) and open a new document (if necessary). Press **Ctrl+v** to paste the contents of the Clipboard in the document. Press **Ctrl+p** to open the Print dialog box. If your computer is connected to a printer, click the **OK** button; otherwise, click the **Cancel** button. Close Microsoft Word (or the application you used to display the picture) without saving the document.

2. Click the **Splash Form.vb** tab to make the Code Editor window the active window. Click **File** on the menu bar, and then click **Print** to open the Print dialog box. See Figure 1-34. Notice that you can include line numbers in the printout. You also can choose to hide the collapsed regions of code. Currently, the Hide collapsed regions check box is grayed out because no code is collapsed in the Code Editor window.

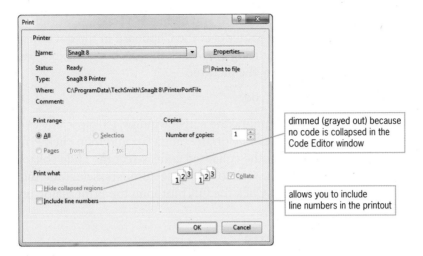

Figure 1-34   Print dialog box

3. If your computer is connected to a printer, click the **OK** button to begin printing; otherwise, click the **Cancel** button. If you clicked the OK button, your printer prints the code.

4. Close the Code Editor window and then close the solution.

Lesson C Summary

- To process code at specified intervals of time:

  Use the Timer tool to instantiate a timer control. Set the timer's Interval property to the number of milliseconds for each interval. Turn on the timer by setting its Enabled property to True. Enter the timer's code in its Tick event procedure.

- To delete a control:

  Select the control you want to delete and then press Delete. If the control contains code, open the Code Editor window and delete the code contained in the control's event procedures.

- To control the border style of the form:

  Set the form's FormBorderStyle property.

- To enable/disable the Minimize button on the form's title bar:

  Set the form's MinimizeBox property.

- To enable/disable the Maximize button on the form's title bar:

  Set the form's MaximizeBox property.

- To control whether the icon and buttons appear in the form's title bar:

  Set the form's ControlBox property.

- To print the user interface:

  Make the designer window the active window. Press and hold down the Alt key on your keyboard as you tap the Print Screen (Prnt Scrn or PrtSc) key and then release the Alt key. Start an application that can display a picture (such as Microsoft Word) and open a new document (if necessary). Press Ctrl+v to paste the contents of the Clipboard in the document. Press Ctrl+p to open the Print dialog box. Click the OK button. Close the application you used to display the picture.

- To print the Visual Basic code:

  Make the Code Editor window the active window. Collapse any code you do not want to print. Click File on the menu bar and then click Print. If you don't want to print the collapsed code, select the Hide collapsed regions check box. If you want to print line numbers, select the Include line numbers check box. Click the OK button in the Print dialog box.

Lesson C Key Terms

Component tray—a special area in the IDE; stores controls that do not appear in the interface during run time

Run time—the state of an application while it is running

Timer control—the control used to process code at one or more regular intervals

Lesson C Review Questions

1. If a timer is running, the code in its _____ event procedure is processed each time an interval has elapsed.

   a. Interval

   b. Tick

   c. Timed

   d. Timer

2. Which of the following is false?

   a. When you add a timer control to a form, the control appears in the component tray.

   b. The user can see a timer control during run time.

   c. You stop a timer by setting its Enabled property to False.

   d. The number entered in a timer's Interval property represents the number of milliseconds for each interval.

3. To disable the Minimize button on a form's title bar, set the form's _____ property to False.

   a. ButtonMinimize

   b. Minimize

   c. MinimizeBox

   d. MinimizeButton

4. You can remove the Minimize, Maximize, and Close buttons from a form's title bar by setting the form's _____ property to False.

   a. ControlBox

   b. ControlButton

   c. TitleBar

   d. TitleBarElements

5. Explain how you delete a control that contains code.

Lesson C Exercises

1. In this exercise, you modify an existing form by replacing its Exit button with a timer.

   a. Open the Jefferson Solution (Jefferson Solution.sln) file contained in the VB2010\Chap01\Jefferson Solution folder. If necessary, open the designer window.

   b. Delete the Exit button from the form and then delete the button's code from the Code Editor window.

   c. Return to the designer window. Add a timer control to the form. Change the timer's name to tmrExit. Set the timer's Enabled property to True. The timer should end the application after eight seconds have elapsed; set the appropriate property. Enter the `Me.Close()` instruction in the appropriate event procedure in the Code Editor window.

   d. Save the solution and then start the application. When eight seconds have elapsed, the application ends.

   e. Set the form's FormBorderStyle property to FixedSingle. Also, remove the elements (icon and buttons) and text from the form's title bar.

   f. Save the solution and then start the application. Close the Code Editor window and then close the solution.

2. Create a Visual Basic Windows application. Use the following names for the solution, project, and form file, respectively: Horse Solution, Horse Project, and Main Form.vb. Save the application in the VB2010\Chap01 folder. Create the interface shown in Figure 1-35. The images are stored in the abby.jpg and rascal.jpg files, which are contained in the VB2010\Chap01 folder. The timer should end the application after five seconds have elapsed. Save the solution and then start the application. Now, remove the icon and buttons from the form's title bar. Also, use the Project Designer window to change the executable file's name to Horse. Save the solution and then start the application. Close the Code Editor window and then close the solution. Use the Run dialog box in Windows to run the Horse.exe file, which is contained in the project's bin\Debug folder.

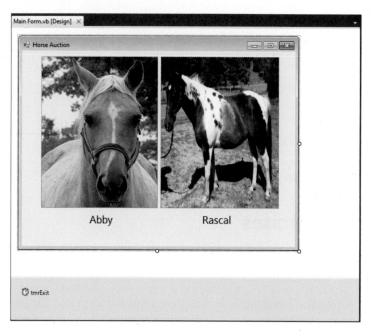

Figure 1-35   Interface for the Horse Auction application

INTERMEDIATE

3. In this exercise, you design your own user interface. Create a Visual Basic Windows application. Use the following names for the solution, project, and form file, respectively: My Splash Solution, My Splash Project, and My Splash Form.vb. Save the application in the VB2010\ Chap01 folder. Create your own splash screen. Save the solution and then start the application. Close the Code Editor window and then close the solution.

Discovery

4. In this exercise, you learn how to enter an assignment statement in an event procedure. You also learn how to display a graphic on the face of a button control.

a. Create a Visual Basic Windows application. Use the following names for the solution, project, and form file, respectively: OnOff Solution, OnOff Project, and Main Form.vb. Save the application in the VB2010\Chap01 folder. Change the form's name to frmMain.

b. Add a picture box control and three buttons to the form. The location and size of the controls are not important. Name the controls picIcon, btnOn, btnOff, and btnExit. Include any graphic in the picture box control. (You can use the Logo.bmp file contained in the VB2010\Chap01 folder.)

c. The captions for the three buttons should be On, Off, and Exit. Change the appropriate property for each button.

d. The Exit button should end the application when clicked. Enter the appropriate code in the Code Editor window.

e. Open the code template for the btnOff control's Click event procedure. In the procedure, enter the instruction `picIcon.Visible = False`. This instruction is called an assignment statement, because it assigns a value to a container. In this case, the container is the Visible property of the picIcon control. When you click the btnOff control, the assignment statement will hide the picture box from view.

f. Open the code template for the btnOn control's Click event procedure. In the procedure, enter an instruction that will display the picture box.

g. Save the solution and then start the application. Use the Off button to hide the picture box, and then use the On button to display the picture box. Finally, use the Exit button to end the application. Close the Code Editor window.

h. You use a button's Image property to specify the graphic you want displayed on the face of the button. You use a button's ImageAlign property to specify the graphic's alignment on the button. Set the On button's Image property to any small graphic file. (You can use the Blue Lace 16.bmp file contained in the VB2010\Chap01 folder.) Set the On button's ImageAlign property to TopLeft. (Hint: When you click the ImageAlign property's list arrow, nine buttons will appear in the list. Select the button in the upper-left corner.) Set the Image and ImageAlign properties of the Off and Exit buttons. (Use any small graphics for the Image properties.) Set each button's TextAlign property to MiddleRight. If necessary, resize the buttons and form.

i. Save the solution and then start and test the application. Close the solution.

5. In this exercise, you learn how to display a tooltip. Open the ToolTip Solution (ToolTip Solution.sln) file contained in the VB2010\Chap01\ ToolTip Solution folder. If necessary, open the designer window. Click the ToolTip tool in the toolbox and then drag the mouse pointer to the form. Notice that a tooltip control appears in the component tray rather than on the form. Set the btnExit control's ToolTip on ToolTip1 property to "Ends the application." (without the quotation marks). Save the solution and then start the application. Hover your mouse pointer over the Exit button. The tooltip "Ends the application." appears in a tooltip box. Click the Exit button and then close the solution.

 ## Swat The Bugs

6. Open the Debug Solution (Debug Solution.sln) file contained in the VB2010\Chap01\Debug Solution folder. If necessary, open the designer window. Start the application. Click the Exit button. Notice that the Exit button does not end the application. Click the Close button on the form's title bar. Locate and then correct the error. Save the solution and then start the application. Click the Exit button, which should end the application. Close the Code Editor window and then close the solution.

CHAPTER 2

Designing Applications

Creating the Playtime Cellular Application

In this chapter, you create an application for Playtime Cellular, a small company that sells toy cell phones. The phones are priced at $25 each and are available in two colors: blue and pink. The application will allow the salespeople to enter the customer's name and address, as well as the number of blue and pink phones ordered. It then will calculate and display the total number of phones ordered and the total price of the order.

Previewing the Playtime Cellular Application

Before you start the first lesson in this chapter, you will preview the completed application. The application is contained in the VB2010\Chap02 folder.

To preview the completed application:

 To open the Run dialog box, press and hold down the Windows logo key as you tap the letter r, and then release the logo key.

1. Use the Run dialog box to run the Playtime (Playtime.exe) file contained in the VB2010\Chap02 folder. The interface shown in Figure 2-1 appears on the screen. In addition to the picture box, label, and button controls that you learned about in Chapter 1, the interface contains seven text boxes. A text box gives a user an area in which to enter data.

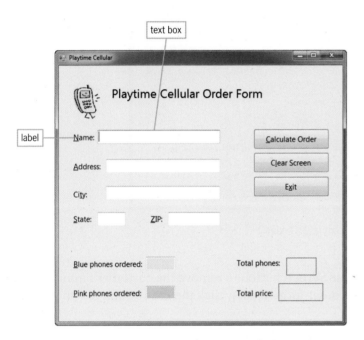

Figure 2-1 Order screen for Playtime Cellular

2. The insertion point is located in the first text box. The label control to the left of the text box identifies the information the user should enter. In this case, the user should enter the customer's name. Type **Ray's Toys** as the customer's name, and then press **Tab** twice to move the insertion point to the City text box.

3. Type **Chicago** as the city name and then press **Shift+Tab** (press and hold down the Shift key as you tap the Tab key) to move the insertion point to the Address text box.

4. Type **2467 Grove Avenue** as the address, press **Tab** twice, type **IL** as the state, and then press **Tab**.

5. Type **60634** as the ZIP code and then press **Tab** to move the insertion point to the Blue phones ordered text box.

6. Type **10** as the number of blue phones ordered and then click the **Calculate Order** button. The button's Click event procedure calculates and displays both the total phones ordered (10) and the total price ($250.00).

7. Click the **Pink phones ordered** text box, type **20**, and then click the **Calculate Order** button. The button's Click event procedure recalculates both the total phones ordered (30) and the total price ($750.00).

8. Change the number of blue phones ordered from 10 to **35** and then click the **Calculate Order** button. The total phones ordered and total price are now 55 and $1,375.00, respectively. See Figure 2-2.

Figure 2-2   Completed order

9. Click the **Clear Screen** button to remove the customer's information from the order form. Finally, click the **Exit** button to end the application.

The Playtime Cellular application is an object-oriented program, because it uses objects (such as buttons and text boxes) to accomplish its goal. In Lesson A, you will learn how a programmer plans an object-oriented program. You will create the Playtime Cellular application in Lessons B and C. Be sure to complete each lesson in full and do all of the end-of-lesson questions and several exercises before continuing to the next lesson.

▌LESSON A

After studying Lesson A, you should be able to:

- Plan an object-oriented Windows application in Visual Basic 2010

- Complete a TOE (Task, Object, Event) chart

- Follow the Windows standards regarding the layout and labeling of controls

Creating an Object-Oriented Application

As Figure 2-3 indicates, the process a programmer follows when creating an object-oriented (OO) application is similar to the process a builder follows when building a home. Like a builder, a programmer first meets with the client to discuss the client's wants and needs. Both then create a plan for the project. After the client approves the plan, the builder builds the home's frame, whereas the programmer builds the user interface, which is the application's frame. Once the frame is built, the builder completes the home by adding the electrical wiring, walls, and so on. The programmer, on the other hand, completes the application by adding the necessary code to the user interface. When the home is complete, the builder makes a final inspection and corrects any problems before the customer moves in. Similarly, the programmer tests the completed application and fixes any problems, called bugs, before releasing the application to the user. The final step in both processes is to assemble the project's documentation (paperwork), which then is given to the customer/user.

A builder's process	A programmer's process
1. Meet with the client	1. Meet with the client
2. Plan the home (blueprint)	2. Plan the application (TOE chart)
3. Build the frame	3. Build the user interface
4. Complete the home	4. Code the application
5. Inspect the home and fix any problems	5. Test and debug the application
6. Assemble the documentation	6. Assemble the documentation

Figure 2-3 Processes used by a builder and a programmer

You will learn how to plan an OO application in this lesson. Steps three through six of the process are covered in Lessons B and C.

Planning an Object-Oriented Application

As any builder will tell you, the most important aspect of a home is not its beauty. Rather, it is how closely the home matches the buyer's wants and needs. The same is true of an OO application. For an application to fulfill the wants and needs of the user, it is essential for the programmer to plan the application jointly with the user. It cannot be stressed enough that the only way to guarantee the success of an application is to actively involve the user in the planning phase. The steps for planning an OO application are listed in Figure 2-4.

---

1. Identify the tasks the application needs to perform.
2. Identify the objects to which you will assign the tasks.
3. Identify the events required to trigger an object into performing its assigned tasks.
4. Draw a sketch of the user interface.

Figure 2-4   Steps for planning an OO application

You can use a TOE (Task, Object, Event) chart to record the application's tasks, objects, and events, which are identified in the first three steps of the planning phase. In the next section, you begin completing a TOE chart for the Playtime Cellular application. The first step is to identify the application's tasks.

Identifying the Application's Tasks

Realizing that it is essential to involve the user when planning the application, you meet with the sales manager of Playtime Cellular, Ms. Garrison, to determine her requirements. You ask Ms. Garrison to bring the form the salespeople currently use to record the orders. Viewing the current forms and procedures will help you gain a better understanding of the application. You also can use the current form as a guide when designing the user interface. Figure 2-5 shows the current order form used by the company.

Playtime Cellular Order Form

Customer name: _____

Address: _____

City: _____   State: _____   ZIP: _____

Number of blue phones ordered	Number of pink phones ordered	Total number of phones ordered	Total price

---

Figure 2-5   Current order form used by Playtime Cellular

When identifying the major tasks an application needs to perform, it is helpful to ask the questions italicized in the following bulleted items. The answers pertaining to the Playtime Cellular application follow each question.

- *What information will the application need to display on the screen and/ or print on the printer?* The Playtime Cellular application should display the customer's name, street address, city, state, ZIP code, number of blue phones ordered, number of pink phones ordered, total number of phones ordered, and total price of the order. In this case, the application does not need to print anything on the printer.

- *What information will the user need to enter into the user interface to display and/or print the desired information?* In the Playtime Cellular application, the salesperson (the user) must enter the customer's name, street address, city, state, ZIP code, and number of blue and pink phones ordered.

- *What information will the application need to calculate to display and/or print the desired information?* The Playtime Cellular application needs to calculate the total number of phones ordered and the total price of the order.

- *How will the user end the application?* All applications should provide a way for the user to end the application. The Playtime Cellular application will use an Exit button for this task.

- *Will previous information need to be cleared from the screen before new information is entered?* After the salesperson enters and calculates an order, he or she will need to clear the customer's information from the screen before entering the next order.

Figure 2-6 shows the Playtime Cellular application's tasks listed in a TOE chart. The tasks do not need to be listed in any particular order. In this case, the data entry tasks are listed first, followed by the calculation tasks, display tasks, application ending task, and screen clearing task.

Task	Object	Event
Get the following order information from the user:		
Customer's name		
Street address		
City		
State		
ZIP code		
Number of blue phones ordered		
Number of pink phones ordered		
Calculate total phones ordered and total price		
Display the following information:		
Customer's name		
Street address		
City		
State		
ZIP code		
Number of blue phones ordered		
Number of pink phones ordered		
Total phones ordered		
Total price		
End the application		
Clear screen for the next order		

Figure 2-6   Tasks entered in a TOE chart

You can draw a TOE chart by hand or use the table feature in a word processor (such as Microsoft Word).

65

Identifying the Objects

After completing the Task column of the TOE chart, you then assign each task to an object in the user interface. For this application, the only objects you will use besides the Windows form itself are the button, label, and text box controls. As you already know, you use a label to display information that you do not want the user to change while the application is running, and you use a button to perform an action immediately after the user clicks it. You use a **text box** to give the user an area in which to enter data.

The first task listed in Figure 2-6 is to get the order information from the user. For each order, the salesperson will need to enter the customer's name, address, city, state, and ZIP code, as well as the number of blue phones ordered and the number of pink phones ordered. Because you need to provide the salesperson with areas in which to enter the information, you will assign the first task to seven text boxes—one for each item of information. The three-character ID used when naming text boxes is txt, so you will name the text boxes txtName, txtAddress, txtCity, txtState, txtZip, txtBlue, and txtPink.

The second task listed in the TOE chart is to calculate both the total number of phones ordered and the total price. So that the salesperson can calculate these amounts at any time, you will assign the task to a button named btnCalc.

The third task listed in the TOE chart is to display the order information, the total number of phones ordered, and the total price. The order information is displayed automatically when the user enters that information in the seven text boxes. The total phones ordered and total price, however, are not entered by the user. Instead, those amounts are calculated by the btnCalc control. Because the user should not be allowed to change the calculated results, you will have the btnCalc control display the total phones ordered and total price in two label controls named lblTotalPhones and lblTotalPrice. Notice that the task of displaying the total phones ordered involves two objects: btnCalc and lblTotalPhones. The task of displaying the total price also involves two objects: btnCalc and lblTotalPrice.

The last two tasks listed in the TOE chart are "End the application" and "Clear screen for the next order." You will assign the tasks to buttons named btnExit and btnClear, respectively; doing this gives the user control over when the tasks are performed. Figure 2-7 shows the TOE chart with the Task and Object columns completed.

Task	Object	Event
Get the following order information from the user:		
Customer's name	txtName	
Street address	txtAddress	
City	txtCity	
State	txtState	
ZIP code	txtZip	
Number of blue phones ordered	txtBlue	
Number of pink phones ordered	txtPink	
Calculate total phones ordered and total price	btnCalc	

Figure 2-7　Tasks and objects entered in a TOE chart *(continues)*

(continued)

Task	Object	Event
Display the following information:		
Customer's name	txtName	
Street address	txtStreet	
City	txtCity	
State	txtState	
ZIP code	txtZip	
Number of blue phones ordered	txtBlue	
Number of pink phones ordered	txtPink	
Total phones ordered	btnCalc, lblTotalPhones	
Total price	btnCalc, lblTotalPrice	
End the application	btnExit	
Clear screen for the next order	btnClear	

Figure 2-7   Tasks and objects entered in a TOE chart

Identifying the Events

After defining the application's tasks and assigning the tasks to objects in the interface, you then determine which event (if any) must occur for an object to carry out its assigned task. The seven text boxes listed in the TOE chart in Figure 2-7 are assigned the task of getting and displaying the order information. Text boxes accept and display information automatically, so no special event is necessary for them to do their assigned task. The two label controls listed in the TOE chart are assigned the task of displaying the total number of phones ordered and the total price of the order. Label controls automatically display their contents; so, here again, no special event needs to occur. (Recall that the two label controls will get their values from the btnCalc control.) The remaining objects listed in the TOE chart are the three buttons. You will have the buttons perform their assigned tasks when the user clicks them. Figure 2-8 shows the completed TOE chart for the Playtime Cellular application.

Task	Object	Event
Get the following order information from the user:		
Customer's name	txtName	None
Street address	txtAddress	None
City	txtCity	None
State	txtState	None
ZIP code	txtZip	None
Number of blue phones ordered	txtBlue	None
Number of pink phones ordered	txtPink	None
Calculate total phones ordered and total price	btnCalc	Click

Figure 2-8   Completed TOE chart ordered by task *(continues)*

(continued)

Task	Object	Event
Display the following information:		
Customer's name	txtName	None
Street address	txtStreet	None
City	txtCity	None
State	txtState	None
ZIP code	txtZip	None
Number of blue phones ordered	txtBlue	None
Number of pink phones ordered	txtPink	None
Total phones ordered	btnCalc, lblTotalPhones	Click, None
Total price	btnCalc, lblTotalPrice	Click, None
End the application	btnExit	Click
Clear screen for the next order	btnClear	Click

Figure 2-8 Completed TOE chart ordered by task

If the application you are creating is small, as is the Playtime Cellular application, you can use the TOE chart in its current form to help you write the Visual Basic code. When the application is large, however, it is often helpful to rearrange the TOE chart so that it is ordered by object rather than by task. To do so, you list all of the objects in the Object column of a new TOE chart, being sure to list each object only once. Then list each object's tasks and events in the Task and Event columns, respectively. Figure 2-9 shows the rearranged TOE chart ordered by object rather than by task.

Task	Object	Event
1. Calculate total phones ordered and total price 2. Display total phones ordered and total price in lblTotalPhones and lblTotalPrice	btnCalc	Click
Clear screen for the next order	btnClear	Click
End the application	btnExit	Click
Display total phones ordered (from btnCalc)	lblTotalPhones	None
Display total price (from btnCalc)	lblTotalPrice	None
Get and display the order information	txtName, txtAddress, txtCity, txtState, txtZip, txtBlue, txtPink	None

Figure 2-9 Completed TOE chart ordered by object

After completing the TOE chart, the next step is to draw a rough sketch of the user interface.

Drawing a Sketch of the User Interface

Although the TOE chart lists the objects to include in the interface, it does not tell you where to place those objects on the form. While the design of an interface is open to creativity, there are some guidelines to which you should adhere so that your application is consistent with the Windows standards. This consistency will make your application easier to both learn and use, because the user interface will have a familiar look to it. The guidelines are referred to as GUI (graphical user interface) guidelines.

The first GUI guideline covered in this book pertains to the organization of the controls in the interface. In Western countries, the user interface should be organized so that the information flows either vertically or horizontally, with the most important information always located in the upper-left corner of the interface. In a vertical arrangement, the information flows from top to bottom: the essential information is located in the first column of the interface, while secondary information is placed in subsequent columns. In a horizontal arrangement, on the other hand, the information flows from left to right: the essential information is placed in the first row of the interface, with secondary information placed in subsequent rows. Related controls should be grouped together using either white (empty) space or one of the tools located in the Containers section of the toolbox. Examples of tools found in the Containers section include the GroupBox, Panel, and TableLayoutPanel tools. The difference between a panel and a group box is that, unlike a group box, a panel can have scroll bars. However, unlike a panel, a group box has a Text property that you can use to indicate the contents of the control. Unlike the panel and group box controls, the table layout panel control provides a table structure in which you place other controls.

Figures 2-10 and 2-11 show two different sketches of the Playtime Cellular interface. In Figure 2-10 the information is arranged vertically, and white space is used to group related controls together. In Figure 2-11 the information is arranged horizontally, with related controls grouped together using tools from the Containers section of the toolbox. Each text box and button in both figures is labeled so the user knows the control's purpose. The "Name:" label that identifies the txtName control tells the user the type of information to enter in the text box. Similarly, the "Calculate Order" caption on the btnCalc control indicates the action the button will perform when it is clicked.

Some companies have their own standards for interfaces used within the company. A company's standards supersede the Windows standards.

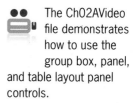

The Ch02AVideo file demonstrates how to use the group box, panel, and table layout panel controls.

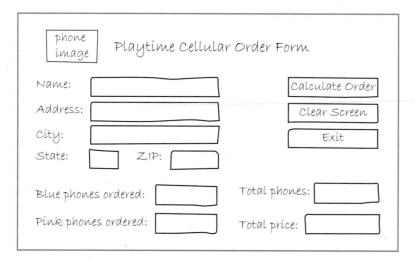

Figure 2-10   Vertical arrangement of the Playtime Cellular application

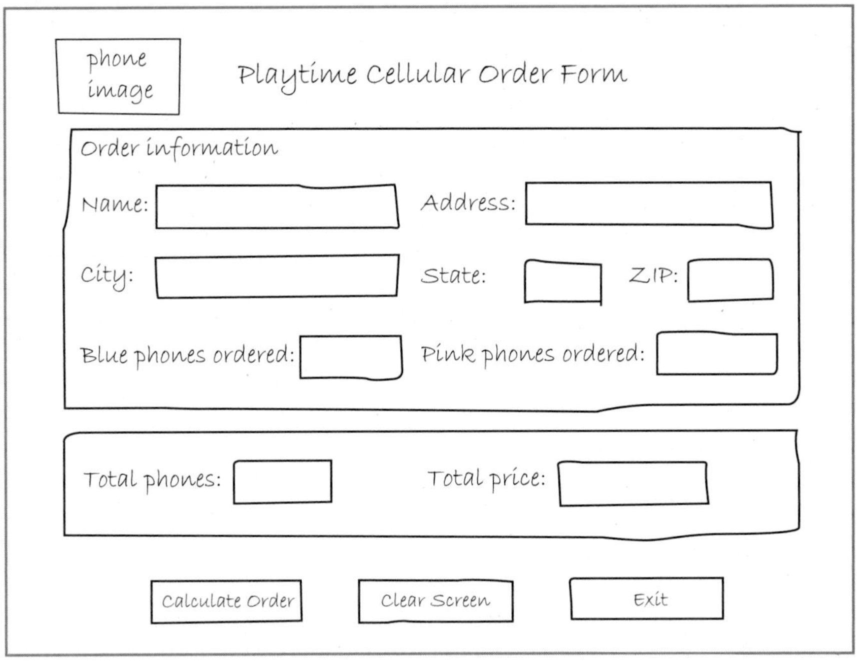

Figure 2-11 Horizontal arrangement of the Playtime Cellular application

Most times, program output (such as the result of calculations) is displayed in a label control in the interface. Label controls that display program output should be labeled to make their contents obvious to the user. In the interfaces shown in Figures 2-10 and 2-11, the "Total phones:" and "Total price:" labels identify the contents of the lblTotalPhones and lblTotalPrice controls, respectively. The text contained in an identifying label should be meaningful and left-aligned within the label. In most cases, an identifying label should be from one to three words only and appear on one line. In addition, the identifying label should be positioned either above or to the left of the control it identifies. An identifying label should end with a colon (:). The colon distinguishes an identifying label from other text in the user interface, such as the heading text "Playtime Cellular Order Form". Some assistive technologies, which are technologies that provide assistance to individuals with disabilities, rely on the colons to make this distinction. The Windows standard is to use sentence capitalization for identifying labels. **Sentence capitalization** means you capitalize only the first letter in the first word and in any words that are customarily capitalized.

As you learned in Chapter 1, buttons are identified by the text that appears on the button's face. The text is often referred to as the button's caption. The caption should be meaningful. In addition, it should be from one to three words only and appear on one line. A button's caption should be entered using **book title capitalization**, which means you capitalize the first letter in each word, except for articles, conjunctions, and prepositions that do not occur at either the beginning or end of the text. When the buttons are positioned horizontally, as they are in Figure 2-11, all the buttons should be the same height; their widths, however, may vary if necessary. If the buttons are stacked vertically, as they are in Figure 2-10, all the buttons should be the same height and width. In a group of buttons, the most commonly used button typically appears first—either on the left (in a horizontal arrangement) or on the top (in a vertical arrangement).

When positioning the controls in the interface, place related controls close to each other and be sure to maintain a consistent margin from the edges of the form. Also, it's helpful to align the borders of the controls wherever possible to minimize the number of different margins appearing in the interface. Doing this allows the user to more easily scan the information. You can align the borders using the snap lines that appear as you are building the interface. Or, you can use the Format menu to align (and also size) the controls.

In this lesson, you learned some basic guidelines to follow when sketching a graphical user interface (GUI). You will learn more GUI guidelines in the remaining lessons and in subsequent chapters. You can find a complete list of the GUI guidelines in Appendix B of this book.

71

GUI DESIGN TIP Layout and Organization of the User Interface

- Organize the user interface so that the information flows either vertically or horizontally, with the most important information always located in the upper-left corner of the screen.

- Group related controls together using either white (empty) space or one of the tools contained in the Containers section of the toolbox.

- Use a label to identify each text box in the user interface. Also use a label to identify other label controls that display program output. The label text should be meaningful. It also should be from one to three words only and appear on one line. Left-align the text within the label, and position the label either above or to the left of the control it identifies. Enter the label text using sentence capitalization, and follow the label text with a colon (:).

- Display a meaningful caption on the face of each button. The caption should indicate the action the button will perform when clicked. Enter the caption using book title capitalization. Place the caption on one line and use from one to three words only.

- When a group of buttons are positioned horizontally, each button in the group should be the same height. When a group of buttons are positioned vertically, each button in the group should be the same height and width. In a group of buttons, the most commonly used button is typically the first button in the group.

- Align the borders of the controls wherever possible to minimize the number of different margins appearing in the interface.

Lesson A Summary

- To create an OO application:

   1. Meet with the client

   2. Plan the application

3.   Build the user interface

4.   Code the application

5.   Test and debug the application

6.   Assemble the documentation

- To plan an OO application in Visual Basic 2010:

  1.   Identify the tasks the application needs to perform.

  2.   Identify the objects to which you will assign the tasks.

  3.   Identify the events required to trigger an object into performing its assigned tasks.

  4.   Draw a sketch of the user interface.

- To assist you in identifying the major tasks an application needs to perform, ask the following questions:

  1.   What information will the application need to display on the screen and/or print on the printer?

  2.   What information will the user need to enter into the user interface to display and/or print the desired information?

  3.   What information will the application need to calculate to display and/or print the desired information?

  4.   How will the user end the application?

  5.   Will previous information need to be cleared from the screen before new information is entered?

Lesson A Key Terms

Book title capitalization—the capitalization used for a button's caption; refers to capitalizing the first letter in each word, except for articles, conjunctions, and prepositions that do not occur at either the beginning or end of the caption

Sentence capitalization—the capitalization used for identifying labels; refers to capitalizing only the first letter in the first word and in any words that are customarily capitalized

Text box—a control that provides an area in the form for the user to enter data

Lesson A Review Questions

1.   When designing a user interface, the most important information should be placed in the _____ corner of the interface.

   a.   lower-left

   b.   lower-right

   c.   upper-left

   d.   upper-right

2. A button's caption should be entered using _____.

   a. book title capitalization

   b. sentence capitalization

   c. either book title capitalization or sentence capitalization

3. Which of the following statements is false?

   a. The text contained in identifying labels should be left-aligned within the label.

   b. An identifying label should be positioned either above or to the left of the control it identifies.

   c. Identifying labels should be entered using book title capitalization.

   d. Identifying labels should end with a colon (:).

4. Listed below are the four steps you should follow when planning an OO application. Put the steps in the proper order by placing a number (1 through 4) on the line to the left of the step.

   _____ Identify the objects to which you will assign the tasks.

   _____ Draw a sketch of the user interface.

   _____ Identify the tasks the application needs to perform.

   _____ Identify the events required to trigger an object into performing its assigned tasks.

5. Listed below are the six steps you should follow when creating an OO application. Put the steps in the proper order by placing a number (1 through 6) on the line to the left of the step.

   _____ Test and debug the application

   _____ Build the user interface

   _____ Code the application

   _____ Assemble the documentation

   _____ Plan the application

   _____ Meet with the client

Lesson A Exercises

1. Sarah Brimley is the accountant at Paper Products. The salespeople at Paper Products are paid a commission, which is a percentage of the sales they make. Sarah wants you to create an application that will compute the commission after she enters the salesperson's name, sales, and commission rate (expressed as a decimal number). For example, if Sarah enters 2000 as the sales and .1 (the decimal equivalent of 10%) as the commission rate, the commission amount should

INTRODUCTORY

be 200. Prepare a TOE chart ordered by task, and then rearrange the TOE chart so that it is ordered by object. Draw a sketch of the user interface.

INTERMEDIATE

2. RM Sales divides its sales territory into four regions: North, South, East, and West. Robert Gonzales, the sales manager, wants an application that allows him to enter the current year's sales for each region and the projected increase (expressed as a decimal number) for each region. He wants the application to compute the following year's projected sales for each region. As an example, if Robert enters 10000 as the current sales for the South region, and then enters .05 (the decimal equivalent of 5%) as the projected increase, the application should display 10500 as the next year's projected sales. Prepare a TOE chart ordered by task, and then rearrange the TOE chart so that it is ordered by object. Draw a sketch of the user interface.

INTERMEDIATE

3. Open the Time Solution (Time Solution.sln) file contained in the VB2010\Chap02\Time Solution folder. If necessary, open the designer window. Lay out and organize the interface so it follows all of the GUI design guidelines you have learned so far. (Refer to Appendix B for a listing of the guidelines.) Code the Exit button's Click event procedure so it ends the application. Save the solution and then start the application. Click the Exit button to end the application and then close the solution.

LESSON B

After studying Lesson B, you should be able to:

- Build the user interface using your TOE chart and sketch

- Follow the Windows standards regarding the use of graphics, fonts, and color

- Set a control's BorderStyle property

- Add a text box to a form

- Lock the controls on the form

- Assign access keys to controls

- Set the TabIndex property

Building the User Interface

In Lesson A, you planned the Playtime Cellular application. Planning the application is the second of the six steps involved in creating an OO application. You now are ready to tackle the third step, which is to build the user interface. You use the TOE chart and sketch you created in the planning step as guides when building the interface, which involves placing the appropriate controls on the form and setting the applicable properties of the controls. To save you time, the VB2010\Chap02\Playtime Solution folder contains a partially completed application for Playtime Cellular. When you open the solution, you will find that most of the user interface has been created and most of the properties have been set. You will complete the interface in this lesson.

 The Ch02BVideo file demonstrates all of the steps contained in Lesson B. You can view the video either before or after completing the lesson.

To open the partially completed application:

START HERE

1. If necessary, start Visual Studio 2010 or Visual Basic 2010 Express and open the Solution Explorer window.

2. Open the Playtime Solution (Playtime Solution.sln) file contained in the VB2010\Chap02\Playtime Solution folder. If necessary, open the designer window.

3. Permanently display the Properties and Toolbox windows and then auto-hide the Solution Explorer window. Figure 2-12 shows the partially completed interface, which resembles the sketch shown in Figure 2-10 in Lesson A.

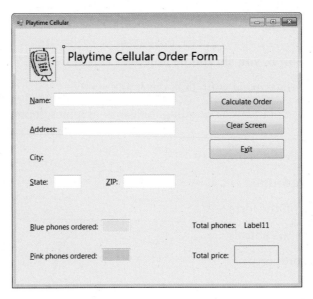

Figure 2-12   Partially completed interface for the Playtime Cellular application

The application's user interface follows the GUI guidelines covered in Lesson A. The information is arranged vertically, and the controls are aligned wherever possible. Each text box and button, as well as each label control that displays program output, is labeled so the user knows the control's purpose. The text contained in the identifying labels is entered using sentence capitalization. In addition, the text ends with a colon and is left-aligned within the label. The identifying labels are positioned to the left of the controls they identify. Each button's caption is entered using book title capitalization. The button captions and identifying labels appear on one line and do not exceed the three-word limit. Because the buttons are stacked in the interface, each button has the same height and width, and the most commonly used button (Calculate Order) is placed at the top of the button group.

When building the user interface, keep in mind that you want to create a screen that no one notices. Interfaces that contain a lot of different colors, fonts, and graphics may get "oohs" and "aahs" during their initial use, but they become tiresome after a while. The most important point to remember is that the interface should not distract the user from doing his or her work. The next three sections provide some guidelines to follow regarding the use of these elements in an interface.

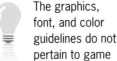

The graphics, font, and color guidelines do not pertain to game applications.

Including Graphics in the User Interface

The human eye is attracted to pictures before text, so use graphics sparingly. Designers typically include graphics to either emphasize or clarify a portion of the screen. However, a graphic also can be used merely for aesthetic purposes, as long as it is small and placed in a location that does not distract the user. The small graphic in the Playtime Cellular interface is included for aesthetics only. The graphic is purposely located in the upper-left corner of the interface, which is where you want the user's eye to be drawn first anyway. The graphic adds a personal touch to the order form without being distracting to the user.

> **GUI DESIGN TIP** Adding Graphics
>
> Use graphics sparingly. If the graphic is used solely for aesthetics, use a small graphic and place it in a location that will not distract the user.

Selecting Fonts for the Interface

As you learned in Chapter 1, an object's Font property determines the type, style, and size of the font used to display the object's text. Recall that Segoe UI, Tahoma, and Microsoft Sans Serif are examples of font types. Font styles include regular, bold, and italic. The numbers 9, 12, and 18 are examples of font sizes. Some font types are serif, while others are sans serif. A serif is a light cross stroke that appears at the top or bottom of a character. The characters in a serif font have the light strokes, whereas the characters in a sans serif font do not. ("Sans" is a French word meaning "without.") Books use serif fonts, because serif fonts are easier to read on the printed page. User interfaces, on the other hand, use sans serif fonts, which are easier to read on the screen. You should use only one font type for all of the text in the interface, and use no more than two different font sizes. In addition, avoid using italics and underlining in an interface, because both font styles make text difficult to read. The use of bold text should be limited to titles, headings, and key items that you want to emphasize.

> **GUI DESIGN TIP** Selecting Font Types, Styles, and Sizes
>
> - Use only one font type for all of the text in the interface. Use a sans serif font, preferably the Segoe UI font.
>
> - Use no more than two different font sizes in the interface.
>
> - Avoid using italics and underlining, because these font styles make text difficult to read.
>
> - Limit the use of bold text to titles, headings, and key items that you want to emphasize.

Adding Color to the Interface

The human eye is attracted to color before black and white; therefore, use color sparingly in an interface. It is a good practice to build the interface using black, white, and gray first, and then add color only if you have a good reason to do so. Keep the following three points in mind when deciding whether to include color in an interface:

1. Many people have some form of either color blindness or color confusion, so they will have trouble distinguishing colors.

2. Color is very subjective: a color that looks pretty to you may be hideous to someone else.

3. A color may have a different meaning in a different culture.

78

You can change the background color of a text box by setting its BackColor property.

Usually, it is best to use black text on a white, off-white, or light gray background, because dark text on a light background is the easiest to read. You should never use a dark color for the background or a light color for the text, because a dark background is hard on the eyes, and light-colored text can appear blurry. If you are going to include color in an interface, limit the number of colors to three, not including white, black, and gray. Be sure that the colors you choose complement each other. Although color can be used to identify an important element in the interface, you should never use it as the only means of identification. In the Playtime Cellular interface, for example, the two colored text boxes help the salesperson quickly identify where to enter the order for blue and pink phones. However, color is not the only means of identifying the purpose of those text boxes; each also has an identifying label.

GUI DESIGN TIP Selecting Colors

- Build the interface using black, white, and gray. Only add color if you have a good reason to do so.

- Use white, off-white, or light gray for the background. Use black for the text.

- Never use a dark color for the background or a light color for the text. A dark background is hard on the eyes, and light-colored text can appear blurry.

- Limit the number of colors in an interface to three, not including white, black, and gray. The colors you choose should complement each other.

- Never use color as the only means of identification for an element in the user interface.

The BorderStyle and AutoSize Properties

A control's border is determined by its BorderStyle property, which can be set to None, FixedSingle, or Fixed3D. Controls with a BorderStyle property set to None have no border. Setting the BorderStyle property to FixedSingle surrounds the control with a thin line, and setting it to Fixed3D gives the control a three-dimensional appearance. In most cases, a text box's BorderStyle property should be left at its default setting: Fixed3D. The BorderStyle property for each text box in the Playtime Cellular interface follows this convention. The appropriate BorderStyle property setting for a label control depends on the control's purpose. Label controls that identify other controls (such as those that identify text boxes) should have a BorderStyle property setting of None, which is the default setting. This is the setting for each identifying label in the Playtime Cellular interface. Label controls that display program output, such as those that display the result of a calculation, typically have a BorderStyle property setting of FixedSingle. The BorderStyle property of the lblTotalPrice control in the Playtime Cellular interface is set to FixedSingle.

A label control's AutoSize property determines whether the control automatically sizes to fit its current contents. The appropriate setting depends on the label's purpose. Label controls that identify other controls use the default setting, which is True. However, you typically set to False the AutoSize property of label controls that display program output. In the next set of steps, you will change the AutoSize and BorderStyle properties of the lblTotalPhones control.

To change the properties of the lblTotalPhones control and then size the control:

START HERE

1. Click the **lblTotalPhones** control, which contains the text Label11.

2. Set the control's AutoSize property to **False**, and then set its BorderStyle property to **FixedSingle**.

3. Next, you will remove Label11 from the Text property. Click **Text** in the Properties list and then select (highlight) Label11. Press **Delete** and then press **Enter**.

4. Now you will tell the computer to center any text appearing in the control. Click **TextAlign** in the Properties list and then click the **list arrow** in the Settings box. Click the **center** button to change the property's setting to MiddleCenter.

5. Finally, you will make the lblTotalPhones control the same height as the lblTotalPrice control. Click the **lblTotalPrice** control, and then press and hold down the Ctrl key as you click the **lblTotalPhones** control. Click **Format** on the menu bar, point to **Make Same Size**, and then click **Height**.

6. Click the **form** to deselect the two labels.

GUI DESIGN TIP Setting the BorderStyle Property of a Text Box or Label

- Keep the BorderStyle property of text boxes at the default value, Fixed3D.

- Keep the BorderStyle property of labels that identify other controls at the default value, None.

- Set to FixedSingle the BorderStyle property of labels that display program output, such as those that display the result of a calculation.

- In Windows applications, a control that contains data that the user is not allowed to edit does not usually appear three-dimensional. Therefore, avoid setting a label control's BorderStyle property to Fixed3D.

GUI DESIGN TIP Setting the AutoSize Property of a Label

- Keep the AutoSize property of identifying labels at the default value, True.

- In most cases, set to False the AutoSize property of label controls that display program output.

A text box is an instance of the TextBox class.

Adding a Text Box Control to the Form

As mentioned earlier, a text box provides an area in the form for the user to enter data. Missing from the Playtime Cellular interface is the text box for entering the city name. You will add the missing text box in the next set of steps.

START HERE

To add the missing text box to the form:

1. Use the TextBox tool in the toolbox to add a text box to the form. Position the text box immediately below the Address text box.

2. Change the text box's name to **txtCity** and press **Enter**.

3. Next, you will make the City text box the same size as the Address text box. Click the **txtAddress** control and then Ctrl+click the **txtCity** control. Click **Format** on the menu bar, point to **Make Same Size**, and then click **Both**.

4. You can align the City text box using either the Format menu or the snap lines. You will use the snap lines. Click the **form** to deselect the City and Address text boxes. Place your mouse pointer on the txtCity control, and then press and hold down the left mouse button as you drag the control to the location shown in Figure 2-13. The blue snap lines help you align the City text box with the Address text box. The pink snap line allows you to align the text in the City text box with the text in its identifying label.

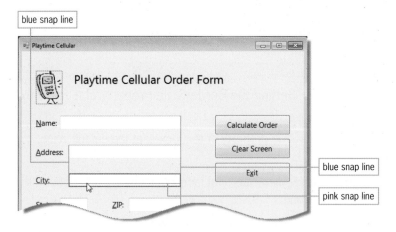

Figure 2-13   Snap lines shown in the interface

5. When the City text box is in the correct location, release the mouse button.

Locking the Controls on a Form

Once you have placed all of the controls in the desired locations on the form, it is a good idea to lock the controls on the form. Locking the controls prevents them from being moved inadvertently as you work in the IDE. You can lock the controls by clicking the form (or any control on the form) and then clicking the Lock Controls option on the Format menu; you can follow the same procedure to unlock the controls. You also can lock and unlock the controls by right-clicking the form (or any control on the form) and then

A locked control can be deleted. It also can be moved by setting its Location property.

clicking Lock Controls on the context menu. When a control is locked, a small lock appears in the upper-left corner of the control.

To lock the controls on the form and then save the solution:

START HERE

1. Right-click the **form** and then click **Lock Controls**. A small lock appears in the upper-left corner of the form.

2. Save the solution. Try dragging one of the controls to a different location on the form. You will not be able to do so.

Assigning Access Keys

The text in many of the controls shown earlier in Figure 2-12 contains an underlined letter. The underlined letter is called an **access key**, and it allows the user to select an object using the Alt key in combination with a letter or number. In Visual Studio, for example, you can select the File menu by pressing Alt+F, because the letter F is the File menu's access key. Access keys are not case sensitive; therefore, you can select the File menu by pressing either Alt+F or Alt+f. Similarly, you can select the Exit button in the Playtime Cellular interface by pressing either Alt+X or Alt+x. Depending on your system's settings, the access keys may or may not appear underlined while an application is running. If you do not see the underlined access keys, you can show them temporarily by pressing the Alt key. You can subsequently hide them by pressing the Alt key again. (To always display access keys, see the Summary section at the end of this lesson.)

You should assign access keys to each of the controls (in the interface) that can accept user input. Examples of such controls include text boxes and buttons, because the user can enter information in a text box and click a button. The only exceptions to this rule are the OK and Cancel buttons, which typically do not have access keys in Windows applications. It is important to assign access keys for the following reasons:

1. Access keys allow a user to work with the application even when the mouse becomes inoperative.

2. Access keys allow users who are fast typists to keep their hands on the keyboard.

3. Access keys allow people with disabilities, which may prevent them from working with a mouse, to use the application.

You assign an access key by including an ampersand (&) in the control's caption or identifying label. If the control is a button, you include the ampersand in the button's Text property, which is where a button's caption is stored. If the control is a text box, you include the ampersand in the Text property of its identifying label. (As you will learn later in this lesson, you also must set the TabIndex properties of the text box and its identifying label appropriately.) You enter the ampersand to the immediate left of the character you want to designate as the access key. For example, to assign the letter C as the access key for the Calculate Order button, you enter &Calculate Order in the button's Text property. To assign the letter N as the access key for the txtName control, you enter &Name: in the Text property of its identifying label. Notice that the Total phones: and Total price: labels in Figure 2-12 do not have access keys. This is because the labels do not identify controls that accept user input; rather, they identify other label controls. Recall that users

82

cannot access label controls while an application is running, so it is inappropriate to assign an access key to the controls.

Each access key in an interface should be unique. The first choice for an access key is the first letter of the caption or identifying label, unless another letter provides a more meaningful association. For example, the letter x is the access key for an Exit button, because it provides a more meaningful association than does the letter E. If you can't use the first letter (perhaps because it already is used as the access key for another control) and no other letter provides a more meaningful association, then use a distinctive consonant in the caption or label. The last choices for an access key are a vowel or a number.

START HERE ▶

To assign access keys to the btnCalc and txtCity controls:

1. Click the **Calculate Order** button. Change the button's Text property to **&Calculate Order** and then press **Enter**. The letter C in the button's caption is now underlined.

2. Click the **City:** label, which identifies the txtCity control. The letter C would be a good choice for an access key; however, the letter is already assigned to the Calculate Order button. (Recall that each access key in an interface must be unique.) Therefore, you will use the letter t instead. Change the label's Text property to **Ci&ty:** and then press **Enter**. The letter t is now underlined.

GUI DESIGN TIP Assigning Access Keys

- Assign a unique access key to each control that can accept user input.

- When assigning an access key to a control, use the first letter of the caption or identifying label, unless another letter provides a more meaningful association. If you can't use the first letter and no other letter provides a more meaningful association, then use a distinctive consonant. Lastly, use a vowel or a number.

Controlling the Tab Order

Most controls have a TabIndex property, which contains a number that represents the order in which the control was added to the form. The first control added to a form has a TabIndex value of 0. The second control has a TabIndex of 1, and so on. The TabIndex values determine the tab order, which is the order in which each control receives the **focus** when the user either presses the Tab key or employs an access key while an application is running. A control whose TabIndex is 2 will receive the focus immediately after the control whose TabIndex is 1. Likewise, a control with a TabIndex of 18 will receive the focus immediately after the control whose TabIndex is 17. When a control has the focus, it can accept user input.

When a text box has the focus, an insertion point appears inside it. When a button has the focus, it has a darkened border.

Most times, you will need to reset the TabIndex values for an interface, because controls rarely are added to a form in the desired tab order. To determine the appropriate TabIndex values, you first make a list of the controls that can accept user input. The list should reflect the order in which the user will want to access the controls. In the Playtime Cellular interface, the user typically will want to access the txtName control first, followed by the txtAddress control, txtCity control, and so on. If a control that accepts user input is identified by a label control, you also include the label control in the list. (A text box is an example of a control that accepts user input and is identified by a label control.) You place the name of the label control immediately above the name of the control it identifies in the list. In the Playtime Cellular interface, the Label2 control (which contains Name:) identifies the txtName control. Therefore, Label2 should appear immediately above txtName in the list. The names of controls that do not accept user input and are not used to identify controls that do should be listed at the bottom of the list; these names do not need to appear in any specific order. After listing the control names, you then assign each control in the list a TabIndex value, beginning with the number 0. If a control does not have a TabIndex property, you do not assign it a TabIndex value in the list. You can tell whether a control has a TabIndex property by viewing its Properties list.

Figure 2-14 shows the list of controls and TabIndex values for the Playtime Cellular interface. Notice that the TabIndex value assigned to each text box's identifying label is one number less than the value assigned to the text box itself. For example, the Label2 control has a TabIndex value of 0 and its corresponding text box (txtName) has a TabIndex value of 1. For a text box's access key (which is defined in the identifying label) to work appropriately, you must be sure to set the identifying label's TabIndex property to a value that is one number less than the value stored in the text box's TabIndex property.

Controls that accept user input, along with their identifying labels	TabIndex value
Label2 (Name:)	0
txtName	1
Label3 (Address:)	2
txtAddress	3
Label4 (City:)	4
txtCity	5
Label5 (State:)	6
txtState	7
Label6 (ZIP:)	8
txtZip	9
Label7 (Blue phones ordered:)	10
txtBlue	11
Label8 (Pink phones ordered:)	12
txtPink	13
btnCalc	14
btnClear	15
btnExit	16
Other controls	
Label1 (Playtime Cellular Order Form)	17
Label9 (Total phones:)	18
Label10 (Total price:)	19
lblTotalPhones	20
lblTotalPrice	21
PictureBox1	N/A

Figure 2-14 List of controls and TabIndex values

83

You can set each control's TabIndex property using either the Properties window or the Tab Order option on the View menu. The Tab Order option is available only when the designer window is the active window.

START HERE

To set the TabIndex values and then verify the tab order:

1. Click the **form** to make the designer window the active window. Click **View** on the menu bar and then click **Tab Order**. The current TabIndex values appear in blue boxes on the form. (The picture box control does not have a TabIndex property.)

   Important note: If the View menu does not contain the Tab Order option, click Tools on the menu bar, point to Settings, and then click Expert Settings.

2. You begin specifying the desired tab order by clicking the first control you want in the tab order. According to Figure 2-14, the first control in the tab order should be the Label2 control, which displays the <u>N</u>ame: text. Click the **blue box that contains the number 1**. (You also can click the Label2 control directly.) The number 0 replaces the number 1 in the box, and the color of the box changes from blue to white to indicate that you have set the TabIndex value for that control.

3. The second control in the tab order should be the txtName control, which currently has a TabIndex value of 6. Click the **blue box that contains the number 6**. The number 1 replaces the number 6 in the box, and the color of the box changes from blue to white.

4. Use the information shown in Figure 2-15 to set the TabIndex properties for the remaining controls, which have TabIndex values of 2 through 21. Be sure to set the values in numerical order. If you make a mistake, press the Esc key to remove the TabIndex boxes from the form, and then repeat Steps 1 through 4. When you have finished setting all of the TabIndex values, the color of the boxes will automatically change from white to blue, as shown in Figure 2-15.

You also can remove the TabIndex boxes using the Tab Order option on the View menu.

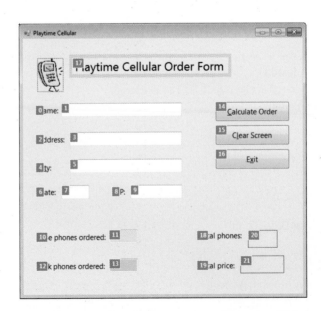

Figure 2-15   TabIndex boxes showing the correct TabIndex values

5. Press **Esc** to remove the TabIndex boxes from the form.

6. Save the solution and then start the application. When you start an application, the computer sends the focus to the control whose TabIndex is 0. In the Playtime Cellular interface, that control is the Label2 (<u>N</u>ame:) control. However, because label controls cannot receive the focus, the computer sends the focus to the next control in the tab order sequence. In this case, it sends the focus to the txtName control. The blinking insertion point indicates that the text box has the focus and is ready to receive input from you.

7. Type **Toys For All** in the txtName control. The information you entered is recorded in the text box's Text property.

8. In Windows applications, the Tab key moves the focus forward, and the Shift+Tab key combination moves the focus backward. Press **Tab** to move the focus to the txtAddress control, and then press **Shift+Tab** to move the focus back to the txtName control.

9. Now use the Tab key to verify the tab order of the controls in the interface. Press **Tab**, slowly, seven times. The focus moves to the following controls: txtAddress, txtCity, txtState, txtZip, txtBlue, txtPink, btnCalc. Notice that when a button has the focus, its border is darkened. Press **Tab** two more times to move the focus first to the btnClear control and then to the btnExit control.

10. Pressing the Enter key when a button has the focus invokes the button's Click event, causing the computer to process any code contained in the Click event procedure. Press **Enter** to have the computer process the btnExit control's Click event procedure, which contains the `Me.Close()` instruction. The application ends.

11. You also can move the focus using a text box's access key. Start the application. Press **Alt+b** to move the focus to the txtBlue control. Now press **Alt+n** to move the focus to the txtName control. On your own, try the access keys for the remaining text boxes in the interface.

12. Unlike pressing a text box's access key, which moves the focus, pressing a button's access key invokes the button's Click event. Press **Alt+x** to invoke the Exit button's Click event, which ends the application.

13. Close the solution.

GUI DESIGN TIP Using the TabIndex Property to Control the Focus

- Assign a TabIndex value (starting with 0) to each control in the interface, except for controls that do not have a TabIndex property. The TabIndex values should reflect the order in which the user will want to access the controls.

- To give users keyboard access to a text box, assign an access key to the text box's identifying label. Set the identifying label's TabIndex property to a value that is one number less than the value stored in the text box's TabIndex property.

Lesson B Summary

- To specify a control's border:

  Set the control's BorderStyle property.

- To specify whether a label control should automatically size to fit its current contents:

  Set the label control's AutoSize property.

- To lock/unlock the controls on the form:

  Right-click the form or any control on the form and then select Lock Controls on the context menu. You also can click the Lock Controls option on the Format menu.

- To assign an access key to a control:

  Type an ampersand (&) in the Text property of the control or identifying label. The ampersand should appear to the immediate left of the character that you want to designate as the access key.

- To provide keyboard access to a text box:

  Assign an access key to the text box's identifying label. Set the identifying label's TabIndex property to a value that is one number less than the text box's TabIndex value.

- To employ an access key:

  Press and hold down the Alt key as you tap the access key.

- To set the tab order:

  Set each control's TabIndex property to a number (starting with 0) that represents the order in which the control should receive the focus. You can set the TabIndex property using either the Properties window or the Tab Order option on the View menu.

- To always display access keys:

  To always display access keys in Windows 7, click the Start button on the Windows 7 taskbar. Click Control Panel and then click Appearance and Personalization. In the Ease of Access Center section, click Turn on easy access keys. Select the Underline keyboard shortcuts and access keys check box, and then click the OK button. Close the Control Panel window.

  To always display access keys in Windows Vista, click Start on the Windows Vista taskbar. Click Control Panel and then click Appearance and Personalization. In the Ease of Access Center section, click Underline keyboard shortcuts and access keys, and then select the Underline keyboard shortcuts and access keys check box. (You may need to scroll down to view the check box.) Click the Save button and then close the Ease of Access Center dialog box.

To always display access keys when using the Classic View in Windows Vista, click the Start button on the Windows Vista taskbar. Click Control Panel, double-click Ease of Access Center, click Make the keyboard easier to use, and then select the Underline keyboard shortcuts and access keys check box. Click the Save button and then close the Ease of Access Center dialog box.

Lesson B Key Terms

Access key—the underlined character in an object's identifying label or caption; allows the user to select the object using the Alt key in combination with the underlined character

Focus—indicates that a control is ready to accept user input

Lesson B Review Questions

1. Which property determines the tab order for the controls in an interface?

    a. SetOrder

    b. TabIndex

    c. TabNumber

    d. TabOrder

2. An Exit button's access key is always the letter _____.

    a. E

    b. i

    c. t

    d. x

3. You assign an access key using a control's _____ property.

    a. Access

    b. Caption

    c. Key

    d. Text

4. Which of the following specifies the letter D as the access key?

    a. &Display

    b. #Display

    c. ^Display

    d. D&isplay

5. Explain the method for providing keyboard access to a text box.

Lesson B Exercises

INTRODUCTORY

1. Open the Paper Solution (Paper Solution.sln) file contained in the VB2010\Chap02\Paper Solution folder. If necessary, open the designer window. Figure 2-16 shows the completed interface. Finish building the interface by adding a text box named txtName to the form. Lock the controls on the form. Assign the access keys (shown in the figure) to the text boxes and buttons. Set the TabIndex values appropriately. Save the solution and then start the application. Verify that the tab order is correct. Also verify that the access keys work appropriately. Use the Exit button to end the application. Close the solution. (You will code the Calculate Commission and Clear Screen buttons in Lesson C's Exercise 1.)

Figure 2-16   User interface for the Paper Products application

INTERMEDIATE

2. Open the RM Sales Solution (RM Sales Solution.sln) file contained in the VB2010\Chap02\RM Sales Solution folder. If necessary, open the designer window. Figure 2-17 shows the completed interface. Finish building the interface by adding a label control named lblNorth to the form. Lock the controls on the form. Change the label's BorderStyle property to the appropriate setting. Set the tab order to allow the user to enter the North region's sales and increase percentage before entering the South region's sales and increase percentage, and so on. Save the solution and then start the application. Verify that the tab order is correct. Also verify that the access keys work appropriately. Use the Exit button to end the application. Close the solution. (You will code the Calculate Projected Sales and Clear Screen buttons in Lesson C's Exercise 2.)

Figure 2-17   User interface for the RM Sales application

3.   In this exercise, you modify the application from Lesson A's Exercise 3.   INTERMEDIATE
     Open the Time Solution (Time Solution.sln) file contained in the
     VB2010\Chap02\Time Solution folder. If necessary, open the designer
     window. Lock the controls on the form. Assign access keys to the con-
     trols that can accept user input. Set each control's TabIndex property.
     Save the solution and then start the application. Verify that the tab
     order is correct. Also verify that the access keys work appropriately.
     Use the Exit button to end the application. Close the solution. (You
     will code the Calculate Hours button in Lesson C's Exercise 3.)

LESSON C

After studying Lesson C, you should be able to:

- Code an application using its TOE chart
- Plan an object's code using pseudocode or a flowchart
- Write an assignment statement
- Send the focus to a control during run time
- Include internal documentation in the code
- Write arithmetic expressions
- Use the Val and Format functions
- Locate and correct syntax errors

Coding the Application

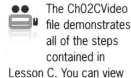

The Ch02CVideo file demonstrates all of the steps contained in Lesson C. You can view the video either before or after completing the lesson.

In Lessons A and B, you created a TOE chart and user interface for the Playtime Cellular application. The user interface and TOE chart are shown in Figures 2-18 and 2-19, respectively. After planning an application and building its user interface, you then can begin coding the application. You code an application so that the objects in the interface perform their assigned tasks when the appropriate event occurs. The objects and events that need to be coded, as well as the tasks assigned to each object and event, are listed in the application's TOE chart. The TOE chart in Figure 2-19 indicates that only the three buttons require coding, as they are the only objects with an event listed in the third column of the chart.

Figure 2-18 Playtime Cellular application's interface

Task	Object	Event
1. Calculate total phones ordered and total price	btnCalc	Click
2. Display total phones ordered and total price in lblTotalPhones and lblTotalPrice		
Clear screen for the next order	btnClear	Click
End the application	btnExit	Click
Display total phones ordered (from btnCalc)	lblTotalPhones	None
Display total price (from btnCalc)	lblTotalPrice	None
Get and display the order information	txtName, txtAddress, txtCity, txtState, txtZip, txtBlue, txtPink	None

Figure 2-19   Playtime Cellular application's TOE chart (ordered by object)

Before you begin coding an object's event procedure, you should plan it. Many programmers use planning tools such as pseudocode or flowcharts. You do not need to create both a flowchart and pseudocode for a procedure; you need to use only one of these planning tools. The tool you use is really a matter of personal preference. For simple procedures, pseudocode works just fine. When a procedure becomes more complex, however, the procedure's steps may be easier to understand in a flowchart. The programmer uses either the procedure's pseudocode or its flowchart as a guide when coding the procedure.

Using Pseudocode to Plan a Procedure

Pseudocode uses short phrases to describe the steps a procedure must take to accomplish its goal. Even though the word "pseudocode" might be unfamiliar to you, you already have written pseudocode without even realizing it. Consider the last time you gave directions to someone. You wrote each direction down on paper, in your own words; your directions were a form of pseudocode.

Figure 2-20 shows the pseudocode for the procedures that need to be coded in the Playtime Cellular application. As the pseudocode indicates, the btnCalc control's Click event procedure will calculate the total phones ordered and the total price, and then display the calculated results in the appropriate label controls in the interface. The btnClear control's Click event procedure will prepare the screen for the next order by removing the previous order's information from the text boxes and two label controls. It then will send the focus to the txtName control so the user can begin entering the next order. The btnExit control's Click event procedure will simply end the application.

---

btnCalc Click event procedure
1. calculate total phones ordered = blue phones ordered + pink phones ordered
2. calculate total price = total phones ordered ∗ phone price
3. display total phones ordered and total price in lblTotalPhones and lblTotalPrice

btnClear Click event procedure
1. clear the Text property of the 7 text boxes
2. clear the Text property of the lblTotalPhones and lblTotalPrice controls
3. send the focus to the txtName control so the user can begin entering the next order

btnExit Click event procedure
end the application

Figure 2-20 Pseudocode for the Playtime Cellular application

Using a Flowchart to Plan a Procedure

Unlike pseudocode, which consists of short phrases, a **flowchart** uses standardized symbols to show the steps a procedure must follow to reach its goal. Figure 2-21 shows the flowcharts for the procedures that need to be coded in the Playtime Cellular application. The logic illustrated in the flowcharts is the same as the logic shown in the pseudocode in Figure 2-20. The flowcharts contain three different symbols: an oval, a rectangle, and a parallelogram. The oval symbol is called the **start/stop symbol**. The start and stop ovals indicate the beginning and end, respectively, of the flowchart. The rectangles are called **process symbols**. You use the process symbol to represent tasks such as making assignments and calculations. The parallelogram in a flowchart is called the **input/output symbol** and is used to represent input tasks (such as getting information from the user) and output tasks (such as displaying information). The parallelogram in Figure 2-21 represents an output task. The lines connecting the symbols in a flowchart are called **flowlines**.

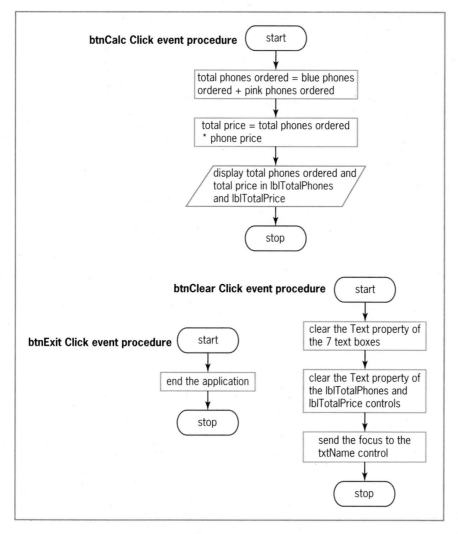

btnCalc Click event procedure — start
→ total phones ordered = blue phones ordered + pink phones ordered
→ total price = total phones ordered * phone price
→ display total phones ordered and total price in lblTotalPhones and lblTotalPrice
→ stop

btnClear Click event procedure — start
→ clear the Text property of the 7 text boxes
→ clear the Text property of the lblTotalPhones and lblTotalPrice controls
→ send the focus to the txtName control
→ stop

btnExit Click event procedure — start
→ end the application
→ stop

Figure 2-21 Flowcharts for the Playtime Cellular application

Coding the btnClear Control's Click Event Procedure

According to its pseudocode and flowchart, the btnClear control's Click event procedure should clear the Text property of the seven text boxes and two of the labels in the interface. It then should send the focus to the txtName control. You can clear the Text property of an object by assigning a zero-length string to it. A **string** is defined as zero or more characters enclosed in quotation marks. The word "Jones" is a string. Likewise, "45" is a string, but 45 (without the quotes) is a number. "Jones" is a string with a length of five, because there are five characters between the quotation marks. "45" is a string with a length of two, because there are two characters between the quotation marks. Following this logic, a **zero-length string**, also called an **empty string**, is a set of quotation marks with nothing between them, like this: "". Assigning a zero-length string to the Text property of an object during run time removes the contents of the object. You also can clear an object's Text property by assigning the value **String.Empty** to it while an application is running. When you do this, the computer assigns an empty string to the Text property, thereby removing its contents.

 You also can use the Clear method to clear the contents of a text box. The Clear method is covered in Discovery Exercise 12 at the end of this lesson.

Assigning a Value to a Property During Run Time

In Chapter 1, you learned how to use the Properties window to set an object's properties during design time, which is when you are building the interface. You also can set an object's properties during run time; you do this using an assignment statement. An **assignment statement** is one of many different types of Visual Basic instructions. Its purpose is to assign a value to something (such as to the property of an object) while an application is running. The syntax of an assignment statement that assigns a value to an object's property is *object.property = expression*. In the syntax, *object* and *property* are the names of the object and property, respectively, to which you want the value of the *expression* assigned. The expression can be a number, a string, a calculation, or a keyword. You use a period to separate the object name from the property name. Recall that the period is the dot member access operator. In this case, the operator indicates that the *property* is a member of the *object*. You use an equal sign between the *object.property* information and the *expression*. The equal sign in an assignment statement is called the **assignment operator**.

When the computer processes an assignment statement, it assigns the value of the expression that appears on the right side of the assignment operator to the object and property that appear on the left side of the assignment operator. The assignment statement `txtName.Text = String.Empty`, for example, assigns the empty string to the txtName control's Text property. Similarly, the assignment statement `txtState.Text = "IL"` assigns the string "IL" to the Text property of the txtState control. You will use assignment statements to code the btnClear control's pseudocode.

START HERE ▶ **To open the btnClear control's Click event procedure:**

1. If necessary, start Visual Studio 2010 or Visual Basic 2010 Express and open the Solution Explorer window.

2. Open the Playtime Solution (Playtime Solution.sln) file from Lesson B. The file is contained in the VB2010\Chap02\Playtime Solution folder. If necessary, open the designer window.

3. Auto-hide the Solution Explorer window. If necessary, auto-hide the Properties and Toolbox windows.

4. Open the Code Editor window. Notice that the btnExit control's Click event procedure has already been coded for you.

5. Use the Class Name and Method Name list boxes to open the code template for the btnClear control's Click event procedure.

6. Press **Enter** to insert a blank line below the procedure header.

Step 1 in the procedure's pseudocode (shown earlier in Figure 2-20) is to clear the Text property of the seven text boxes in the interface. You can do this using either the *textbox*`.Text = String.Empty` instruction or the *textbox*`.Text = ""` instruction, where *textbox* is the name of the appropriate text box. As you learned in Chapter 1, you can either type the Visual Basic instructions on your own or use the IntelliSense feature that is built into the Code Editor. In the next set of steps, you will use the IntelliSense feature.

To begin coding the btnClear control's Click event procedure: START HERE

1. First, you will enter the `txtName.Text = String.Empty`
   assignment statement in the procedure. Type the two letters **tx**. The
   IntelliSense feature lists the names of the seven text boxes.
   See Figure 2-22.

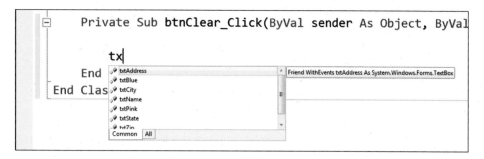

Figure 2-22 Listing of text box names

2. Type **tn** to highlight txtName in the list and then press **Tab** to enter
   txtName in the assignment statement.

3. Now type **.** (a period) to display a listing of the properties and methods of the txtName control. If Text is not highlighted in the list, type
   te. At this point, you can either press the Tab key to enter the Text
   choice in the assignment statement, or you can type the character
   that follows Text in the statement. In this case, the next character
   is the assignment operator. Type **=** to enter the Text choice in the
   statement.

4. Next, type **st** to highlight String in the list, and then type **.e** to highlight Empty. Press **Enter**. The `txtName.Text = String.Empty`
   statement appears in the Code Editor window.

When entering code, you can type the names of commands, objects, and
properties in lowercase letters. When you move to the next line, the Code
Editor automatically changes your code to reflect the proper capitalization
of those elements. This provides a quick way of verifying that you entered an
object's name and property correctly, and that you entered the code using the
correct syntax. If the capitalization does not change, it means that the Code
Editor does not recognize the object, command, or property. In this book you
always will be given the complete instruction to enter, including the appropriate capitalization. Keep in mind that you can type the instruction on your
own, or you can use the IntelliSense feature to enter the instruction.

To continue coding the btnClear control's Click event procedure: START HERE

1. Enter the following six assignment statements:

   txtAddress.Text = String.Empty
   txtCity.Text = String.Empty
   txtState.Text = String.Empty
   txtZip.Text = String.Empty
   txtBlue.Text = String.Empty
   txtPink.Text = String.Empty

2. The second step in the procedure's pseudocode is to clear the Text property of the lblTotalPhones and lblTotalPrice controls. Enter the following two assignment statements. Press **Enter** twice after typing the last statement.

lblTotalPhones.Text = String.Empty
lblTotalPrice.Text = String.Empty

The last step in the procedure's pseudocode is to send the focus to the txtName control. You can accomplish this task using the Focus method. Recall that a method is a predefined Visual Basic procedure that you can call (or invoke) when needed.

Using the Focus Method

You can use the **Focus method** to move the focus to a specified control while an application is running. As you learned in Lesson B, a control that has the focus can accept user input. The Focus method's syntax is *object*.**Focus()**, in which *object* is the name of the object to which you want the focus sent.

START HERE **To enter the Focus method in the btnClear control's Click event procedure:**

1. Type **txtName.Focus()** and press **Enter**.

2. Save the solution.

Internally Documenting the Program Code

It is a good practice to include comments, called internal documentation, as reminders in the Code Editor window. Programmers use comments to indicate a procedure's purpose and also to explain various sections of a procedure's code. Including comments in your code will make the code more readable and easier to understand by anyone viewing it. You create a comment in Visual Basic by placing an apostrophe (') before the text that represents the comment. The computer ignores everything that appears after the apostrophe on that line. Although it is not required, some programmers use a space to separate the apostrophe from the comment text.

START HERE **To add comments to the btnClear control's Click event procedure:**

1. Click the **blank line** above the txtName.Text = String.Empty statement. Type **' prepare the screen for the next order** (be sure to type the apostrophe followed by a space) and press **Enter**. Notice that comments appear in a different color from the rest of the code.

2. Click the **blank line** above the txtName.Focus() statement. Type **' send the focus to the Name text box**. See Figure 2-23.

```
  Private Sub btnClear_Click(ByVal sender As Obj
        ' prepare the screen for the next order

        txtName.Text = String.Empty
        txtAddress.Text = String.Empty
        txtCity.Text = String.Empty
        txtState.Text = String.Empty
        txtZip.Text = String.Empty
        txtBlue.Text = String.Empty
        txtPink.Text = String.Empty
        lblTotalPhones.Text = String.Empty
        lblTotalPrice.Text = String.Empty
        ' send the focus to the Name text box
        txtName.Focus()

    End Sub
```

Figure 2-23   btnClear control's Click event procedure

It is a good programming practice to test an object's code before coding the next object. This way, if something is wrong with the program, you know exactly where to look for the error.

To test the btnClear control's Click event procedure: START HERE

1. Save the solution and then start the application. Type your name and address information (including the city, state, and ZIP) in the appropriate text boxes. Also type any numbers in the Blue phones ordered and Pink phones ordered boxes.

2. Click the **Clear Screen** button. The computer processes the instructions contained in the button's Click event procedure. The instructions remove the contents of nine of the controls and then send the focus to the Name text box. Click the **Exit** button to end the application.

Many programmers also use comments to document the project's name and purpose, the programmer's name, and the date the code was either created or modified. Such comments are placed above the Public Class clause in the Code Editor window. The area above the Public Class clause is called the **General Declarations section**.

To include comments in the General Declarations section: START HERE

1. Click **before the letter P** in the `Public Class frmMain` line and then press **Enter** to insert a blank line. Now, click the **blank line**.

2. Type the comments shown in Figure 2-24 and then save the solution. In the comments, replace <your name> and <current date> with your name and the current date, respectively.

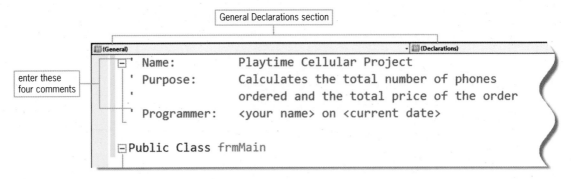

Figure 2-24   Comments entered in the General Declarations section

Before you can code the btnCalc control's Click event procedure, you need to learn how to write arithmetic expressions in Visual Basic.

Writing Arithmetic Expressions

Most applications require the computer to perform at least one calculation. You instruct the computer to perform a calculation by writing an arithmetic expression, which is an expression that contains one or more arithmetic operators. Figure 2-25 lists the most commonly used arithmetic operators available in Visual Basic, along with their precedence numbers. The precedence numbers indicate the order in which the computer performs the operation in an expression. Operations with a precedence number of 1 are performed before operations with a precedence number of 2, which are performed before operations with a precedence number of 3, and so on. However, you can use parentheses to override the order of precedence, because operations within parentheses are always performed before operations outside parentheses.

Operator	Operation	Precedence number
^	exponentiation (raises a number to a power)	1
–	negation	2
*, /	multiplication and division	3
\	integer division	4
Mod	modulus	5
+, –	addition and subtraction	6

Figure 2-25   Most commonly used arithmetic operators

Although the negation and subtraction operators listed in Figure 2-25 use the same symbol (a hyphen), there is a difference between both operators: the negation operator is unary, whereas the subtraction operator is binary. Unary and binary refer to the number of operands required by the operator. Unary operators require one operand; binary operators require two operands. For example, the expression –10 uses the negation operator to turn its one operand (the positive number 10) into a negative number. The expression 8 – 2, on the other hand, uses the subtraction operator to subtract its second operand (the number 2) from its first operand (the number 8).

Two of the arithmetic operators listed in Figure 2-25 might be less familiar to you: the integer division operator (\) and the modulus operator (Mod). You use the **integer division operator** to divide two integers (whole numbers) and then return the result as an integer. For instance, the expression 211 \ 4 results in 52, which is the integer result of dividing 211 by 4. (If you use the standard division operator [/] to divide 211 by 4, the result is 52.75 rather than 52.) You might use the integer division operator in a program that determines the number of quarters, dimes, and nickels to return as change to a customer. For example, if a customer should receive 53 cents in change, you could use the expression 53 \ 25 to determine the number of quarters to return; the expression evaluates to 2. The **modulus operator** also is used to divide two numbers, but the numbers do not have to be integers. After dividing the numbers, the modulus operator returns the remainder of the division. For instance, 211 Mod 4 equals 3, which is the remainder of 211 divided by 4. A common use for the modulus operator is to determine whether a number is even or odd. If you divide the number by 2 and the remainder is 0, the number is even; if the remainder is 1, however, the number is odd. Figure 2-26 shows several examples of using the integer division and Mod operators.

Examples	Results
211 \ 4	52
211 Mod 4	3
53 \ 25	2
53 Mod 25	3
75 \ 2	37
75 Mod 2	1
100 \ 2	50
100 Mod 2	0

Figure 2-26   Examples of the integer division and Mod operators

You may have noticed that some of the operators listed in Figure 2-25 have the same precedence number. For example, both the addition and subtraction operators have a precedence number of 6. When an expression contains more than one operator having the same priority, those operators are evaluated from left to right. In the expression 7 – 8 / 2 + 5, for instance, the division (/) is performed first, then the subtraction (–), and then the addition (+). The result of the expression is the number 8, as shown in Figure 2-27. You can use parentheses to change the order in which the operators in an expression are evaluated. For example, as Figure 2-27 shows, the expression 7 – (8 / 2 + 5) evaluates to –2 rather than to 8. This is because the parentheses tell the computer to perform the division first, then the addition, and then the subtraction.

Original expression	$7 - 8 / 2 + 5$
The division is performed first	$7 - 4 + 5$
The subtraction is performed next	$3 + 5$
The addition is performed last	8
Original expression	$7 - (8 / 2 + 5)$
The division is performed first	$7 - (4 + 5)$
The addition is performed next	$7 - 9$
The subtraction is performed last	-2

Figure 2-27   Expressions containing more than one operator having the same precedence

When entering an arithmetic expression in code, you do not enter a comma or special characters, such as the dollar sign or percent sign. If you want to include a percentage in an arithmetic expression, you do so using its decimal equivalent; for example, you enter .05 rather than 5%.

Coding the Calculate Order Button

According to the Playtime Cellular application's TOE chart (shown earlier in Figure 2-19), the btnCalc control is responsible for calculating both the total number of phones ordered and the total price of the order, and then displaying the calculated amounts in the lblTotalPhones and lblTotalPrice controls. The instructions to accomplish the button's tasks should be placed in the button's Click event procedure, because you want the instructions processed when the user clicks the button. The pseudocode shown in Figure 2-28 lists the steps the procedure must take to accomplish its tasks.

btnCalc Click event procedure
1.   calculate total phones ordered = blue phones ordered + pink phones ordered
2.   calculate total price = total phones ordered * phone price
3.   display total phones ordered and total price in lblTotalPhones and lblTotalPrice

Figure 2-28   Pseudocode for the btnCalc control's Click event procedure

Step 1 in the pseudocode is to calculate the total number of phones ordered by adding together the number of blue phones ordered and the number of pink phones ordered. The number of blue phones ordered is recorded in the txtBlue control's Text property as the user enters that information in the interface. Likewise, the number of pink phones ordered is recorded in the txtPink control's Text property. You can use an assignment statement to add together the Text property of the two text boxes, and then assign the sum to the Text property of the lblTotalPhones control. The total phones ordered calculation is illustrated in Figure 2-29.

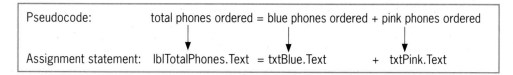

Figure 2-29   Illustration of the total phones ordered calculation

The next step in the procedure's pseudocode is to calculate the total price of the order by multiplying the total number of phones ordered (which is recorded in the lblTotalPhones control) by the phone price ($25). The total price should be displayed in the lblTotalPrice control. The total price calculation is illustrated in Figure 2-30.

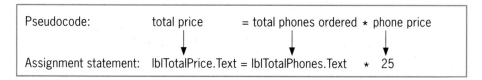

Figure 2-30   Illustration of the total price calculation

The last step in the procedure's pseudocode is to display the total phones ordered and total price in the appropriate label controls. The assignment statements shown in Figures 2-29 and 2-30 accomplish this task.

To code the btnCalc control's Click event procedure and then test it: START HERE

1. Open the code template for the btnCalc control's Click event procedure. Type **' calculates number of phones ordered and total price** and press **Enter** twice.

2. Next, enter the following two assignment statements:

   lblTotalPhones.Text = txtBlue.Text + txtPink.Text
   lblTotalPrice.Text = lblTotalPhones.Text * 25

3. Save the solution and then start the application. Click the **Blue phones ordered** text box. Type **5** and then press **Tab**. Type **10** as the number of pink phones ordered and then click the **Calculate Order** button. The button's Click event procedure calculates the total number of phones ordered and total price, displaying the results in the two label controls. As Figure 2-31 indicates, the displayed results are incorrect. Instead of mathematically adding the two order quantities together, giving 15, the second order quantity was appended to the first order quantity, giving 510. When the total phones ordered amount is incorrect, the total price also will be incorrect, because the total phones ordered amount is used in the total price calculation.

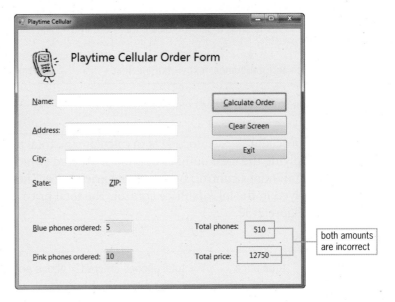

Figure 2-31 Interface showing the incorrect results of the calculations

4. Click the **Exit** button to end the application.

Even though you do not see quotation marks around the value, a value stored in the Text property of an object is treated as a string rather than as a number. Adding strings together does not give you the same result as adding numbers together. For example, adding the string "5" to the string "10" results in the string "510", whereas adding the number 5 to the number 10 results in the number 15. To add together the contents of two text boxes, you need to tell the computer to treat the contents as numbers rather than as strings. You can do this using either the Val function or the TryParse method. In this chapter (and only in this chapter), you will use the Val function, because it is the easiest to learn. However, keep in mind that most programmers now use the TryParse method, which you will learn about in Chapter 3.

The Val Function

A **function** is a predefined procedure that performs a specific task and then returns a value after completing the task. The **Val function**, for instance, temporarily converts a string to a number and then returns the number. The number is stored in the computer's internal memory only while the function is processing. The syntax of the Val function is **Val(*string*)**. The item within the parentheses is called an argument and represents information that the function needs to perform its task. In this case, the *string* argument represents the string you want treated as a number. Because the computer must be able to interpret the string as a numeric value, the string cannot include a letter, comma, or special character (such as the dollar sign or percent sign); it can, however, include a period or a space. When the computer encounters an invalid character in the Val function's string, it stops converting the string to a number at that point. Figure 2-32 shows some examples of how the Val function converts various strings.

Val function	Numeric result
Val("456")	456
Val("24,500")	24
Val("123X")	123
Val("25%")	25
Val(" 12 34 ")	1234
Val("$56.88")	0
Val("Abc")	0
Val("")	0

Figure 2-32 Examples of the Val function

To include the Val function in the btnCalc control's code: ◄ START HERE

1. Change the two assignment statements as follows:

   lblTotalPhones.Text = Val(txtBlue.Text) + Val(txtPink.Text)
   lblTotalPrice.Text = Val(lblTotalPhones.Text) * 25

2. Save the solution. The changes made to the procedure are highlighted in Figure 2-33.

```
Private Sub btnCalc_Click(ByVal sender As Object, ByVal e As System
        ' calculates number of phones ordered and total price

    lblTotalPhones.Text = Val(txtBlue.Text) + Val(txtPink.Text)
    lblTotalPrice.Text = Val(lblTotalPhones.Text) * 25

End Sub
```

Figure 2-33 Val function entered in the assignment statements

3. Start the application. Enter **5** as the number of blue phones ordered, and then enter **10** as the number of pink phones ordered. Click the **Calculate Order** button. The application correctly calculates and displays the total number of phones ordered (15) and total price of the order (375). In the next section, you will improve the appearance of the total price amount by including a dollar sign, a thousands separator, and two decimal places.

4. Click the **Exit** button.

The Format Function

You can use the **Format function** to improve the appearance of numbers in an interface. The function's syntax is **Format(*expression*, *style*)**. The *expression* argument specifies the number, date, time, or string whose appearance you want to format. The *style* argument can be a predefined Visual Basic format style. It also can be a string containing special symbols that indicate how you want the expression displayed. (You can display the Help screen for the Format function to learn more about these special symbols.) In this case, you will use one of the predefined Visual Basic format styles, some of which are explained in Figure 2-34.

Format style	Description
Currency	Formats the number with a dollar sign, two decimal places, and (if appropriate) a thousands separator; negative numbers are enclosed in parentheses
Fixed	Formats the number with at least one digit to the left and two digits to the right of the decimal point
Standard	Formats the number with at least one digit to the left of the decimal point, two digits to the right of the decimal point, and (if appropriate) a thousands separator
Percent	Multiplies the number by 100 and then formats the result with a percent sign and two digits to the right of the decimal point

Figure 2-34   Some of the predefined format styles in Visual Basic

START HERE ▶   **To format the total price amount:**

1. Click the **blank line** below the total price assignment statement, and then enter the following statement:

    lblTotalPrice.Text = Format(lblTotalPrice.Text, "Currency")

2. Save the solution. The change made to the procedure is highlighted in Figure 2-35.

```
Private Sub btnCalc_Click(ByVal sender As Object, ByVal e As System
    ' calculates number of phones ordered and total price

    lblTotalPhones.Text = Val(txtBlue.Text) + Val(txtPink.Text)
    lblTotalPrice.Text = Val(lblTotalPhones.Text) * 25
    lblTotalPrice.Text = Format(lblTotalPrice.Text, "Currency")

End Sub
```

Figure 2-35   Format function entered in the procedure

You also can include the Format function in the statement that calculates the total price, like this:
lblTotalPrice.Text = Format(Val(lblTotal-Phones.Text) * 25, "Currency").

3. Start the application. Enter **5** as the number of blue phones ordered, and then enter **10** as the number of pink phones ordered. Click the **Calculate Order** button. See Figure 2-36.

Blue phones ordered: 5   Total phones: 15

Pink phones ordered: 10   Total price: $375.00   ⟶ result of formatting the total price to Currency

Figure 2-36   Formatted total price shown in the interface

4. Click the **Exit** button.

You have completed the first four of the six steps involved in creating an OO application: meeting with the client, planning the application, building the user interface, and coding the application. The fifth step is to test and debug the application.

Testing and Debugging the Application

You test an application by starting it and entering some sample data. The sample data should include both valid and invalid data. **Valid data** is data that the application is expecting the user to enter, whereas **invalid data** is data that the application is not expecting the user to enter. The Playtime Cellular application, for instance, expects the user to enter a numeric value in the txtBlue control; it does not expect the user to enter a letter. In most cases, invalid data is a result of a typing error made by the user. You should test an application as thoroughly as possible. Doing this helps to ensure that the application displays the correct output when valid data is entered, and does not end abruptly when invalid data is entered.

Debugging refers to the process of locating and correcting the errors, called **bugs**, in a program. Program bugs typically are caused by either syntax errors or logic errors. As you learned in Chapter 1, the term "syntax" refers to the set of rules you must follow when using a programming language. A **syntax error** occurs when you break one of the language's rules. Most syntax errors are a result of typing errors that occur when entering instructions, such as typing `Me.Clse()` instead of `Me.Close()`. The Code Editor detects most syntax errors as you enter the instructions. Logic errors, on the other hand, are much more difficult to find because the Code Editor cannot detect them for you. A **logic error** can occur for a variety of reasons, such as forgetting to enter an instruction or entering the instructions in the wrong order. Some logic errors occur as a result of calculation statements that are correct syntactically but incorrect mathematically. For example, consider the statement `lblSquared.Text = Val(txtNum.Text) + Val(txtNum.Text)`, which is supposed to square the number entered in the txtNum control. The statement's syntax is correct; however, the statement is incorrect mathematically, because you square a value by multiplying it by itself, not by adding it to itself.

To test and debug the Playtime Cellular application: ◄ START HERE

1. Start the application. First, test the application by clicking the **Calculate Order** button without entering any data. The application displays 0 and $0.00 as the total number of phones ordered and total price, respectively. (Recall that the Val function converts the empty string to the number 0.)

2. Click the **Clear Screen** button to clear the calculated results from the label controls. Enter the letter **r** as the number of blue phones ordered and the letter **p** as the number of pink phones ordered. Click the **Calculate Order** button. The application displays 0 and $0.00 as the total number of phones ordered and total price, respectively. (Recall that the Val function converts a letter to the number 0.)

3. Click the **Clear Screen** button. Now enter the following correct order:

Toys For All
123 Main Street
Chicago, IL, 60631
25 blue phones ordered
20 pink phones ordered

4. Click the **Calculate Order** button. See Figure 2-37.

Figure 2-37   Result of calculating the Toys For All order

5. Click the **Clear Screen** button and then practice with other entries to see how the application responds. When you are finished testing the application, click the **Exit** button to end the application.

In the following set of steps, you will introduce syntax errors in the application's code. You also will learn how to locate and correct the errors.

START HERE **To introduce syntax errors in the code and also debug the code:**

1. Change the statement in the btnExit control's Click event procedure to **Me.Clse()** and then click the **blank line** above the procedure header. The jagged blue line indicates that the statement contains a syntax error. Change the statement to **Me.Close()** and then click the **blank line** above the procedure header. The jagged blue line disappears.

2. In the btnCalc control's Click event procedure, delete the ending parenthesis in the last assignment statement and then click the **blank line** below the statement. The jagged blue line indicates that the statement contains a syntax error. The red rectangle indicates that the Code Editor has some suggestions for fixing the error.

3. Hover your mouse pointer over the red rectangle until you see the Error Correction Options box, and then click the **list arrow** in the box. A suggestion for fixing the error appears in the Error Correction window. See Figure 2-38.

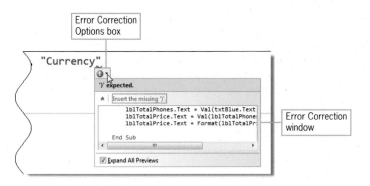

Figure 2-38   Suggestion for fixing the error

4. Move the scroll bar in the Error Correction window all the way to the right. The window indicates that the missing parenthesis will be inserted at the end of the assignment statement that contains the syntax error. You can type the missing parenthesis yourself. Or, you can simply click the suggestion in the Error Correction window. Click the **Insert the missing ')'.** suggestion to insert the missing parenthesis.

5. If you are not paying close attention to the Code Editor window, you may not notice that a statement contains a syntax error. In this step, you will observe what happens when you start an application whose code contains a syntax error. First, delete the ending parenthesis in the last assignment statement in the btnCalc control's Click event procedure, and then click the **blank line** below the statement. Save the solution and then start the application. The message dialog box shown in Figure 2-39 appears.

Figure 2-39   Message dialog box

6. Click the **No** button. The Error List window shown in Figure 2-40 opens at the bottom of the IDE. The window indicates that the code contains one error. The window provides a description of the error and the location of the error in the Code Editor window.

Figure 2-40   Error List window in the IDE

7. Double-click the **error message** in the Error List window. The Code Editor opens the Error Correction window shown earlier in Figure 2-38. Click the **Insert the missing ')'** suggestion to insert the missing parenthesis. The Code Editor inserts the missing parenthesis and then removes the error message from the Error List window.

8. Close the Error List window. Save the solution and then start the application. Test the application to verify that it works correctly, and then click the **Exit** button to end the application.

Assembling the Documentation

After you have tested an application thoroughly, you can move to the last step involved in creating an OO application: assemble the documentation. Assembling the documentation refers to putting your planning tools and a printout of the application's interface and code in a safe place, so you can refer to them if you need to change the application in the future. Your planning tools include the TOE chart, a sketch of the user interface, and either the flowcharts or pseudocode.

START HERE ▶   **To print the application's interface and code:**

1. Click the **designer window's tab**. Press **Alt+Print Screen** (Prnt Scrn or PrtSc) to place a picture of the interface on the Clipboard. Start Microsoft Word (or any application that can display a picture) and open a new document (if necessary). Press **Ctrl+v** to paste the contents of the Clipboard in the document. Press **Ctrl+p** to open the Print dialog box. If your computer is connected to a printer, click the **OK** button; otherwise, click the **Cancel** button. Close Microsoft Word (or the application you used to display the picture) without saving the document.

2. Click the **Code Editor window's tab**. Click **File** on the menu bar and then click **Print**. If necessary, select the **Include line numbers** check box. If your computer is connected to a printer, click the **OK** button; otherwise, click the **Cancel** button.

3. Close the Code Editor window and then close the solution.

The code for the Playtime Cellular application is shown in Figure 2-41.

```
 1 ' Name:        Playtime Cellular Project
 2 ' Purpose:     Calculates the total number of phones
 3 '              ordered and the total price of the order
 4 ' Programmer:  <your name> on <current date>
 5
 6 Public Class frmMain
 7
 8    Private Sub btnExit_Click(ByVal sender As Object,
      ByVal e As System.EventArgs) Handles btnExit.Click
 9       Me.Close()
10    End Sub
11
12    Private Sub btnClear_Click(ByVal sender As Object,
      ByVal e As System.EventArgs) Handles btnClear.Click
```

Figure 2-41 Playtime Cellular application's code *(continues)*

(continued)

```
13        ' prepare the screen for the next order
14
15        txtName.Text = String.Empty
16        txtAddress.Text = String.Empty
17        txtCity.Text = String.Empty
18        txtState.Text = String.Empty
19        txtZip.Text = String.Empty
20        txtBlue.Text = String.Empty
21        txtPink.Text = String.Empty
22        lblTotalPhones.Text = String.Empty
23        lblTotalPrice.Text = String.Empty
24        ' send the focus to the Name text box
25        txtName.Focus()
26
27    End Sub
28
29    Private Sub btnCalc_Click(ByVal sender As Object,
      ByVal e As System.EventArgs) Handles btnCalc.Click
30        ' calculates number of phones ordered and total price
31
32        lblTotalPhones.Text = Val(txtBlue.Text) +
          Val(txtPink.Text)
33        lblTotalPrice.Text = Val(lblTotalPhones.Text) * 25
34        lblTotalPrice.Text = Format(lblTotalPrice.Text,
          "Currency")
35
36    End Sub
37 End Class
```

Figure 2-41   Playtime Cellular application's code

Lesson C Summary

- To plan an object's code:

  Use pseudocode or a flowchart.

- To clear the text property of an object while an application is running:

  Assign either the **String.Empty** value or the empty string ("") to the object's Text property.

- To assign a value to an object's property while an application is running:

  Use an assignment statement that follows the syntax *object.property = expression*.

- To move the focus to an object while an application is running:

  Use the Focus method. The method's syntax is *object*.**Focus()**.

- To create a comment in Visual Basic:

  Begin the comment text with an apostrophe (').

- To divide two integers and then return the result as an integer:

  Use the integer division operator (\).

109

- To divide two numbers and then return the remainder as an integer:
  Use the modulus operator (Mod).
- To temporarily convert a string to a number:
  Use the Val function. The function's syntax is **Val**(*string*).
- To improve the appearance of numbers in the user interface:
  Use the Format function. The function's syntax is **Format**(*expression*, *style*).

Lesson C Key Terms

Assignment operator—the equal sign in an assignment statement

Assignment statement—an instruction that assigns a value to something, such as to the property of an object

Bugs—the errors in a program

Debugging—the process of locating and correcting the bugs (errors) in a program

Empty string—a set of quotation marks with nothing between them (""); also called a zero-length string

Flowchart—a planning tool that uses standardized symbols to show the steps a procedure must take to accomplish its goal

Flowlines—the lines connecting the symbols in a flowchart

Focus method—moves the focus to a specified control during run time

Format function—used to improve the appearance of numbers in an interface

Function—a procedure that processes a specific task and returns a value

General Declarations section—the area above the Public Class clause in the Code Editor window

Input/output symbol—the parallelogram in a flowchart; used to represent input and output tasks

Integer division operator—represented by a backslash (\); divides two integers and then returns the quotient as an integer

Invalid data—data that an application is not expecting the user to enter

Logic error—occurs when you neglect to enter an instruction or enter the instructions in the wrong order; also occurs as a result of calculation statements that are correct syntactically but incorrect mathematically

Modulus operator—represented by the keyword Mod; divides two numbers and returns the remainder of the division

Process symbols—the rectangle symbols in a flowchart; used to represent assignment and calculation tasks

Pseudocode—a planning tool that uses phrases to describe the steps a procedure must take to accomplish its goal

Start/stop symbol—the oval symbol in a flowchart; used to indicate the beginning and end of the flowchart

String—zero or more characters enclosed in quotation marks

String.Empty—the value that represents the empty string in Visual Basic

Syntax error—occurs when an instruction in an application's code breaks one of a programming language's rules

Val function—temporarily converts a string to a number and then returns the number

Valid data—data that an application is expecting the user to enter

Zero-length string—a set of quotation marks with nothing between them (""); also called an empty string

Lesson C Review Questions

1. Which of the following assignment statements will not calculate correctly?

   a. `lblTotal.Text = Val(txtSales1.Text) + Val(txtSales2.Text)`

   b. `lblTotal.Text = Val(txtSales1.Text + txtSales2.Text)`

   c. `lblTotal.Text = Val(txtQuantity.Text) * 2`

   d. `lblTotal.Text = Val(lblTotal.Text) * 1.1`

2. The _____ function temporarily converts a string to a number, and then returns the number.

   a. Format

   b. StringToNumber

   c. Val

   d. Value

3. Which symbol is used in a flowchart to represent a calculation task?

   a. circle

   b. oval

   c. parallelogram

   d. rectangle

4. What value is assigned to the lblNum control when the `lblNum.Text = 73 \ 25` instruction is processed by the computer?

5. What value is assigned to the lblNum control when the `lblNum.Text = 73 Mod 25` instruction is processed by the computer?

Lesson C Exercises

Important note: In several of the exercises in this lesson, you perform the second through sixth steps involved in creating an OO application. Recall that the six steps are:

1. Meet with the client.

2. Plan the application. (Prepare a TOE chart that is ordered by object, and then draw a sketch of the user interface.)

3. Build the user interface. (Refer to Appendix B for a listing of the GUI guidelines you have learned so far. To help you remember the names of the controls as you are coding, print the application's interface and then write the names next to each object.)

4. Code the application. (Either write pseudocode or draw a flowchart for each of the objects that will be coded. Include appropriate comments in the code.)

5. Test and debug the application.

6. Assemble the documentation (your planning tools and a printout of the interface and code).

INTRODUCTORY

1. In this exercise, you complete the application saved in Lesson B's Exercise 1. Open the Paper Solution (Paper Solution.sln) file contained in the VB2010\Chap02\Paper Solution folder. If necessary, open the designer window.

   a. Code the Calculate Commission button; be sure to use the Val function. Use the Format function to display the commission with a dollar sign, a thousands separator, and two decimal places. Use the Focus method to send the focus to the Clear Screen button.

   b. Code the Clear Screen button. Send the focus to the Name text box.

   c. Save the solution and then start the application. Test the application using the following valid data: Pat Brown, 2000, and .1. Also test the application using invalid data. Close the Code Editor window and then close the solution.

INTRODUCTORY

2. In this exercise, you complete the application saved in Lesson B's Exercise 2. Open the RM Sales Solution (RM Sales Solution.sln) file contained in the VB2010\Chap02\RM Sales Solution folder. If necessary, open the designer window.

   a. Code the Calculate Projected Sales button; be sure to use the Val function. Use the Format function to display the projected sales using the Standard format style.

   b. Code the Clear Screen button. Send the focus to the txtNorthSales control.

c. Save the solution and then start the application. Test the application using valid and invalid data. Use the following information for the valid data:

North sales and percentage: 25000, .1

South sales and percentage: 10000, .05

East sales and percentage: 10000, .04

West sales and percentage: 15000, .11

d. Close the Code Editor window and then close the solution.

3. In this exercise, you complete the application saved in Lesson B's Exercise 3. Open the Time Solution (Time Solution.sln) file contained in the VB2010\Chap02\Time Solution folder. If necessary, open the designer window. Code the Calculate Hours button; be sure to use the Val function. Send the focus to the Monday text box. Save the solution and then start the application. Test the application using valid and invalid data. Close the Code Editor window and then close the solution.

> INTRODUCTORY

4. John Lee wants an application that displays his ending balance after he enters the following three pieces of information: his cash balance at the beginning of the month, the amount of money he earned during the month, and the amount of money he spent during the month.

> INTRODUCTORY

a. Create a Visual Basic Windows application. Use the following names for the solution, project, and form file, respectively: JohnLee Solution, JohnLee Project, and Main Form.vb. Save the application in the VB2010\Chap02 folder.

b. Assign the name frmMain to the form. Perform the steps involved in creating an OO application. (See the Important note at the beginning of the Exercises section.) Use the following valid and invalid data when testing the application:

Beginning cash balance: 5000   Earnings: 2500   Expenses: 3000
Beginning cash balance: xyz   Earnings: xyz   Expenses: xyz

c. Close the Code Editor window and then close the solution.

5. In this exercise, you modify the Playtime Cellular application from the chapter. Use Windows to make a copy of the Playtime Solution folder contained in the VB2010\Chap02 folder. Rename the copy Modified Playtime Solution. Open the Playtime Solution (Playtime Solution.sln) file contained in the Modified Playtime Solution folder. Open the designer window. Modify the interface so that it allows the user to enter the phone price. Also modify the application's code. Save the solution and then start and test the application. Close the Code Editor window and then close the solution.

> INTERMEDIATE

6. Lana Jones wants an application that will display the average of any three numbers she enters. Create a Visual Basic Windows application. Use the following names for the solution, project, and form file,

> INTERMEDIATE

respectively: LanaJones Solution, LanaJones Project, and Main Form.vb. Save the application in the VB2010\Chap02 folder. Assign the name frmMain to the form. Perform the steps involved in creating an OO application. (See the Important note at the beginning of the Exercises section.) Use the valid and invalid data shown here when testing the application. Close the Code Editor window and then close the solution.

First Number: 27	Second Number: 9	Third Number: 18
First Number: A	Second Number: B	Third Number: C

INTERMEDIATE

7. Martha Arenso, the manager of Bookworms Inc., needs an inventory application. Martha will enter the title of a book, the number of paperback versions of the book currently in inventory, the number of hardcover versions of the book currently in inventory, the cost of the paperback version, and the cost of the hardcover version. Martha wants the application to display the value of the paperback versions of the book, the value of the hardcover versions of the book, the total number of paperback and hardcover versions, and the total value of the paperback and hardcover versions combined. Create a Visual Basic Windows application. Use the following names for the solution, project, and form file, respectively: Bookworms Solution, Bookworms Project, and Main Form.vb. Save the application in the VB2010\Chap02 folder. Assign the name frmMain to the form. Perform the steps involved in creating an OO application. (See the Important note at the beginning of the Exercises section.) Format the calculated dollar amounts to show a dollar sign, thousands separator, and two decimal places. Use the valid and invalid data shown here when testing the application. Close the Code Editor window and then close the solution.

Book Title: An Introduction to Visual Basic 2010

Paperback versions: 100	Paperback cost: 40
Hardcover versions: 50	Hardcover cost: 75

Book Title: Advanced Visual Basic 2010

Paperback versions: A	Paperback cost: B
Hardcover versions: C	Hardcover cost: D

INTERMEDIATE

8. Jackets Unlimited is having a 25% off sale. The store manager wants an application that allows the clerk to enter the original price of a jacket. The application should display the discount and new price. Create a Visual Basic Windows application. Use the following names for the solution, project, and form file, respectively: Jackets Solution, Jackets Project, and Main Form.vb. Save the application in the VB2010\Chap02 folder. Assign the name frmMain to the form. Perform the steps involved in creating an OO application. (See the Important note at the beginning of the Exercises section.) Format the discount and new price using the Standard format style. Test the application using valid and invalid data. Close the Code Editor window and then close the solution.

9. Typing Salon charges $.10 per typed envelope and $.25 per typed page. The company accountant wants an application to help her prepare bills. She will enter the customer's name, the number of typed envelopes, and the number of typed pages. The application should calculate and display the customer's total bill. Create a Visual Basic Windows application. Use the following names for the solution, project, and form file, respectively: TypingSalon Solution, TypingSalon Project, and Main Form.vb. Save the application in the VB2010\Chap02 folder. Assign the name frmMain to the form. Perform the steps involved in creating an OO application. (See the Important note at the beginning of the Exercises section.) Format the total bill using the Currency format style. Use the valid and invalid data shown here when testing the application. Close the Code Editor window and then close the solution.

Customer's name: Alice Wong
Number of typed envelopes: 250   Number of typed pages: 200

Customer's name: Alice Wong
Number of typed envelopes: $4   Number of typed pages: AB

10. Suman Gadhari, the payroll clerk at Sun Projects, wants an application that displays the net pay for each of the company's employees. Suman will enter the employee's name, hours worked, and rate of pay. For this application, you do not have to worry about overtime, because this company does not allow anyone to work more than 40 hours. Suman wants the application to calculate and display the gross pay, the federal withholding tax (FWT), the Social Security tax (FICA), the state income tax, and the net pay. The FWT is 20% of the gross pay. The FICA tax is 8% of the gross pay. The state income tax is 2.5% of the gross pay. Create a Visual Basic Windows application. Use the following names for the solution, project, and form file, respectively: Sun Solution, Sun Project, and Main Form.vb. Save the application in the VB2010\Chap02 folder. Assign the name frmMain to the form. Perform the steps involved in creating an OO application. (See the Important note at the beginning of the Exercises section.) Format the calculated amounts using the Standard format style. Test the application using valid and invalid data. Close the Code Editor window and then close the solution.

11. Colfax Industries needs an application that allows the shipping clerk to enter the quantity of an item in inventory and the number of the items that can be packed in a box for shipping. When the shipping clerk clicks a button, the application should compute and display the number of full boxes that can be packed and the number of items left over. Create a Visual Basic Windows application. Use the following names for the solution, project, and form file, respectively: Colfax Solution, Colfax Project, and Main Form.vb. Save the application in the VB2010\Chap02 folder. Assign the name frmMain to the form. Perform the steps involved in creating an OO application. (See the Important note at the beginning of the Exercises section.) Save the

solution and then start the application. Colfax has 45 skateboards in inventory. If six skateboards can fit into a box for shipping, how many full boxes can the company ship and how many skateboards will remain in inventory? Close the Code Editor window and then close the solution.

Discovery

12. In this exercise, you learn about the TabStop property and the Clear method.

   a. Use Windows to make a copy of the Playtime Solution folder from the chapter. Rename the copy Discovery Playtime Solution.

   b. Open the Playtime Solution (Playtime Solution.sln) file contained in the Discovery Playtime Solution folder. Open the designer window.

   c. Most of Playtime Cellular's customers reside in Illinois. Use the Properties window to set the txtState control's Text property to IL.

   d. Because the txtState control already contains IL, there is no need for the user to tab into the control when entering data. You can use the control's TabStop property to bypass (or skip over) the control. If the user wants to change the State value, he or she can click the control or use the control's access key. Change the txtState control's TabStop property to False. Save the solution and then start the application. Verify that the txtState control is bypassed when you tab through the controls in the interface.

   e. Click the Clear Screen button. Notice that the button removes the IL from the txtState control. Stop the application. Modify the btnClear control's Click event procedure to assign the string "IL" (rather than the **String.Empty** value) to the txtState control.

   f. Save the solution and then start the application. Click the txtState control. Replace the IL in the control with TX and then click the Clear Screen button. The button should assign the value IL to the txtState control. Stop the application.

   g. You can use a text box control's Clear method to remove the contents of the control while an application is running. The method's syntax is *textbox*.**Clear()**. Use the Clear method in the btnClear control's Click event procedure to remove the contents of the text boxes (except the txtState text box). (You cannot use the Clear method to remove the contents of label controls.)

   h. Save the solution and then start the application. Enter an order and then click the Calculate Order button. Click the Clear Screen button. Close the Code Editor window and then close the solution.

Swat The Bugs

13. Open the Debug Solution (Debug Solution.sln) file contained in the VB2010\Chap02\Debug Solution folder. If necessary, open the designer window. Open the Code Editor window. Locate and then correct the syntax errors in the code. Save the solution and then start and test the application. Close the Code Editor window and then close the solution.

CHAPTER 3

Using Variables and Constants

Revising the Playtime Cellular Application

In this chapter, you modify the Playtime Cellular application from Chapter 2. The modified application will calculate a 3% sales tax and then display the result in the interface. It also will display the name of the salesperson who recorded the order.

Previewing the Modified Playtime Cellular Application

Before you start the first lesson in this chapter, you will preview the completed application. The application is contained in the VB2010\Chap03 folder.

To preview the completed application:

START HERE

119

 To open the Run dialog box, press and hold down the Windows logo key as you tap the letter r, and then release the logo key.

1. Use the Run dialog box to run the Playtime (Playtime.exe) file contained in the VB2010\Chap03 folder. An order form similar to the one created in Chapter 2 appears on the screen.

2. Enter the following customer information on the order form:

   Johansen's
   3400 Esquire Drive
   Chicago, IL, 60654

3. Type **25** in the Blue phones ordered box and then type **5** in the Pink phones ordered box.

4. Although the Calculate Order button does not have the focus, you can select it by pressing the Enter key. This is because the Calculate Order button is the default button in the user interface. You will learn how to designate a default button in Lesson B. Press **Enter** to calculate the order. A Name Entry dialog box appears and requests the salesperson's name, as shown in Figure 3-1.

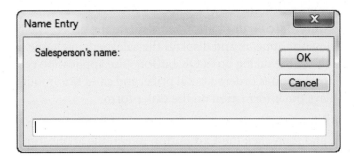

Figure 3-1   Name Entry dialog box

5. Type **Harriet Nozinski** as the salesperson's name and then press **Enter** to select the dialog box's OK button. The application calculates the order. The completed order form is shown in Figure 3-2. Notice that the sales tax amount and the salesperson's name appear on the order form. The application uses string concatenation, which is covered in Lesson B, to display the information.

Figure 3-2 Completed order form

6. Change the number of pink phones ordered to **10**. The application clears the contents of the label controls that display the total phones ordered, total price, and message. In Lesson C, you will learn how to clear the contents of a control when a change is made to the value stored in a different control.

7. Click the **Calculate Order** button to calculate the order. The Name Entry dialog box appears and displays the salesperson's name. Press **Enter** to select the dialog box's OK button. The application recalculates the total phones ordered, total price, and sales tax amount, and then displays the information on the order form.

8. Click the **Clear Screen** button to clear the order information from the form, and then click the **Exit** button to end the application.

In Lesson A, you will learn how to store information, temporarily, in memory locations inside the computer. You will modify the Playtime Cellular application in Lessons B and C. Be sure to complete each lesson in full and do all of the end-of-lesson questions and several exercises before continuing to the next lesson.

LESSON A

After studying Lesson A, you should be able to:

- Declare variables and named constants

- Assign data to an existing variable

- Convert string data to a numeric data type using the TryParse method

- Convert numeric data to a different data type using the Convert class methods

- Explain the scope and lifetime of variables and named constants

- Explain the purpose of Option Explicit, Option Infer, and Option Strict

Using Variables to Store Information

All of the order information in the Playtime Cellular application from Chapter 2 is temporarily stored in the properties of various controls on the order form. For example, the numbers of blue and pink phones ordered are stored in the Text properties of the txtBlue and txtPink controls, respectively. The application uses the Text properties of those controls in the statement that calculates the total phones ordered, like this: `lblTotalPhones.Text = Val(txtBlue.Text) + Val(txtPink.Text)`. The statement assigns the calculated result to the Text property of the lblTotalPhones control. The application then uses the lblTotalPhones control's Text property in the statement that calculates the total price of the order, like this: `lblTotalPrice.Text = Val(lblTotalPhones.Text) * 25`.

Besides storing data in the properties of controls, a programmer also can store data, temporarily, in memory locations inside the computer. The memory locations are called **variables**, because the contents of the locations can change as the application is running. It may be helpful to picture a variable as a small box inside the computer. You can enter and store data in the box, but you cannot actually see the box. One use for a variable is to hold information that is not stored in a control on the form. For example, if you didn't need to display the total number of phones ordered on the Playtime Cellular order form, you could eliminate the lblTotalPhones control from the form and store the total number of phones ordered in a variable instead. You then would use the value stored in the variable, rather than the value stored in the Text property of the lblTotalPhones control, in the total price calculation.

You also can use a variable to store the data contained in a control's property, such as the data contained in a control's Text property. Programmers typically do this when the data is a numeric amount that will be used in a calculation. As you will learn in the next section, assigning numeric data to a variable allows you to control the preciseness of the data. It also makes your code run more efficiently, because the computer can process data stored in a variable much faster than it can process data stored in the property of a control.

Every variable has a data type, name, scope, and lifetime. First, you will learn how to select an appropriate data type for a variable.

Selecting a Data Type for a Variable

Each variable used in an application should be assigned a data type by the programmer. The **data type** determines the type of data the variable can store. Figure 3-3 describes most of the basic data types available in Visual Basic 2010. Each data type is a class, which means that each data type is a pattern from which one or more objects—in this case, variables—are instantiated (created). As the figure indicates, variables assigned the Integer, Long, or Short data type can store integers, which are whole numbers—positive or negative numbers without any decimal places. The differences among these three data types are in the range of integers each type can store and the amount of memory each type needs to store the integer. Decimal, Double, and Single variables, on the other hand, can store numbers containing a decimal place. Here again, the differences among these three data types are in the range of numbers each type can store and the amount of memory each type needs to store the numbers. However, calculations involving Decimal variables are not subject to the small rounding errors that may occur when using Double or Single variables. In most cases, the small rounding errors do not create any problems in an application. One exception to this is when the application contains complex equations dealing with money, where you need accuracy to the penny. In those cases, the Decimal data type is the best type to use.

Also listed in Figure 3-3 are the Char, String, Boolean, Date, and Object data types. The Char data type can store one Unicode character, while the String data type can store from zero to approximately two billion Unicode characters. **Unicode** is the universal coding scheme for characters. It assigns a unique numeric value to each character used in the written languages of the world. (For more information, see The Unicode Standard at *www.unicode.org*.) You use a Boolean variable to store a Boolean value (either True or False), and a Date variable to store date and time information. The Object data type can store any type of data. However, your application will pay a price for this flexibility: it will run more slowly, because the computer has to determine the type of data currently stored in an Object variable. It is best to avoid using the Object data type.

Data type	Stores	Memory required
Boolean	a logical value (True, False)	2 bytes
Char	one Unicode character	2 bytes
Date	date and time information Date range: January 1, 0001 to December 31, 9999 Time range: 0:00:00 (midnight) to 23:59:59	8 bytes
Decimal	a number with a decimal place Range with no decimal place: +/–79,228,162,514,264,337,593,543,950,335 Range with a decimal place: +/–7.9228162514264337593543950335	16 bytes
Double	a number with a decimal place Range: +/–4.94065645841247 X 10^{-324} to +/–1.79769313486231 X 10^{308}	8 bytes
Integer	integer Range: –2,147,483,648 to 2,147,483,647	4 bytes
Long	integer Range: –9,223,372,036,854,775,808 to 9,223,372,036,854,775,807	8 bytes
Object	data of any type	4 bytes
Short	integer Range: –32,768 to 32,767	2 bytes
Single	a number with a decimal place Range: +/–1.401298 X 10^{-45} to +/–3.402823 X 10^{38}	4 bytes
String	text; 0 to approximately 2 billion characters	

Figure 3-3 Basic data types in Visual Basic

The applications in this book will use the Integer data type for variables that will store integers used in calculations, even when the integers are small enough to fit into a Short variable. This is because a calculation containing Integer variables takes less time to process than the equivalent calculation containing Short variables. Either the Decimal data type or the Double data type will be used for numbers that contain decimal places and are used in calculations. The applications will use the String data type for variables that contain either text or numbers not used in calculations, and the Boolean data type to store Boolean values.

Selecting a Name for a Variable

In addition to assigning a data type to an application's variables, the programmer also must assign a name to each variable. The name, also called the identifier, should describe the contents of the variable. A good variable name is one that is meaningful right after you finish a program and also years later when you (or perhaps a co-worker) need to modify the program. There are several conventions for naming variables in Visual Basic. In this book, you will use Hungarian notation, which is the same naming convention used for controls. Variable names in Hungarian notation begin with a three-character ID that represents the variable's data type. The names of Integer variables begin with int, while the names of Decimal and Double variables begin with dec and dbl, respectively. String variable names begin with str, and Boolean variable names begin with bln. The remaining characters in a variable's name represent the variable's purpose. Using Hungarian notation, you might assign the name `intAge` to an Integer variable that stores a person's age, and the name `decGrossPay` to a Decimal variable that stores the amount of an employee's gross pay. Like control names, variable names are entered using camel case, which means you lowercase the ID and then uppercase the first letter of each word in the name. Figure 3-4 lists the rules for naming variables and includes examples of valid and invalid variable names.

Rules for naming variables

1. The name must begin with a letter or an underscore.
2. The name can contain only letters, numbers, and the underscore character. No punctuation characters, special characters, or spaces are allowed in the name.
3. Although the name can contain thousands of characters, 32 characters is the recommended maximum number of characters to use.
4. The name cannot be a reserved word, such as `Sub` or `Double`.

Valid names
`intJan_Sales, decSales2013, dblWestRegion, strFirstName, blnIsValid`

Invalid names	Problem
`2ndQuarterSales`	the name must begin with a letter or an underscore
`dblWest Region`	the name cannot contain a space
`strFirst.Name`	the name cannot contain punctuation
`decSales$North`	the name cannot contain a special character

Figure 3-4 Variable naming rules and examples

"Dim" comes from the word "dimension," which is how programmers in the 1960s referred to the process of allocating the computer's memory. "Dimension" refers to the "size" of something.

Declaring a Variable

Now that you know how to select an appropriate data type and name for a variable, you can learn how to declare a variable in code. Declaring a variable tells the computer to set aside a small section of its internal memory, and it allows you to refer to the section by the variable's name. The size of the section is determined by the variable's data type. You declare a variable using a declaration statement. Figure 3-5 shows the syntax of a declaration statement and includes examples of declaring variables. The {Dim | `Private` | `Static`} portion of the syntax indicates that you can select only one of the keywords appearing within the braces. In most instances, you declare a variable using the `Dim` keyword. (You will learn about the `Private` and `Static` keywords later in this lesson.)

VariableName and *dataType* in the syntax are the variable's name and data type, respectively. As mentioned earlier, a variable is considered an object in Visual Basic and is an instance of the class specified in the *dataType* information. The `Dim dblHoursWorked As Double` statement, for example, creates an object named `dblHoursWorked`; the object is an instance of the Double class. *InitialValue* in the syntax is the value you want stored in the variable when it is created in the computer's internal memory. The square brackets in the syntax indicate that the "*= initialValue*" part of a variable declaration statement is optional. If you do not assign an initial value to a variable when it is declared, the computer stores a default value in the variable; the default value depends on the variable's data type. A variable declared using one of the numeric data types is automatically initialized to—in other words, given a beginning value of—the number 0. The computer automatically initializes a Boolean variable using the keyword `False`, and a Date variable to 1/1/0001 12:00:00 AM. Object and String variables are automatically initialized using the keyword `Nothing`. Variables initialized to `Nothing` do not actually contain the word "Nothing"; rather, they contain no data at all.

125

Variable declaration statement

Syntax
{**Dim** | **Private** | **Static**} *variableName* **As** *dataType* [= *initialValue*]

Example 1
```
Dim intHours As Integer
Dim dblPayRate As Double
```
declares an Integer variable named `intHours` and a Double variable named `dblPayRate`; the variables are automatically initialized to 0

Example 2
```
Dim decDiscount As Decimal
```
declares a Decimal variable named `decDiscount`; the variable is automatically initialized to 0

Example 3
```
Dim blnIsValid As Boolean = True
```
declares a Boolean variable named `blnIsValid` and initializes it using the keyword `True`

Example 4
```
Dim strMessage As String = "Good Morning"
```
declares a String variable named `strMessage` and initializes it using the string "Good Morning"

Figure 3-5   Syntax and examples of a variable declaration statement

Assigning Data to an Existing Variable

In Chapter 2, you learned how to use an assignment statement to assign a value to a control's property during run time. An assignment statement also is used to assign a value to a variable during run time. The syntax for doing this is *variableName = expression*, where *expression* can contain items such as literal constants, object properties, variables, keywords, or arithmetic

Recall that the equal sign in an assignment statement is called the assignment operator.

126

operators. A **literal constant** is an item of data whose value does not change while the application is running; examples include the string literal constant "Mary" and the numeric literal constant 500. When the computer processes an assignment statement, it assigns the value of the expression that appears on the right side of the assignment operator to the variable (memory location) whose name appears on the left side of the assignment operator. In other words, the computer evaluates the expression and then stores the result in the variable.

The data type of the value assigned to a variable should be the same data type as the variable itself. Figure 3-6 shows examples of assigning values to variables having the same data type. The `intQuantity = 500` assignment statement in Example 1 stores the numeric literal constant 500 (an integer) in an Integer variable named `intQuantity`. Similarly, the `strFirstName = "Mary"` assignment statement in Example 2 stores the string literal constant "Mary" in a String variable named `strFirstName`. Notice that string literal constants are enclosed in quotation marks, but numeric literal constants and variable names are not. The quotation marks differentiate a string from both a number and a variable name. In other words, "500" is a string, but 500 is a number. Similarly, "Mary" is a string, but Mary (without the quotation marks) would be interpreted by the computer as the name of a variable. When the computer processes an assignment statement that assigns a string to a String variable, it assigns only the characters that appear between the quotation marks; the computer does not assign the quotation marks themselves.

The `strZipCode = txtZip.Text` statement in Example 3 in Figure 3-6 assigns the string contained in the txtZip control's Text property to a String variable named `strZipCode`. The `dblDiscountRate = .03` statement in Example 4 assigns the Double number .03 to a Double variable named `dblDiscountRate`. This is because a numeric literal constant that has a decimal place is automatically treated as a Double number in Visual Basic. When entering a numeric literal constant, you do not enter a comma or special characters, such as the dollar sign or percent sign. If you want to include a percentage in an assignment statement, you do so using its decimal equivalent; for example, you enter .03 rather than 3%.

The `decTaxRate = .05D` statement in Example 5 in Figure 3-6 shows how you convert a numeric literal constant of the Double data type to the Decimal data type, and then assign the result to a Decimal variable. The D that follows the number .05 in the statement is one of the literal type characters in Visual Basic. A **literal type character** forces a literal constant to assume a data type other than the one its form indicates. In this case, the D forces the Double number .05 to assume the Decimal data type. The `dblCommission = dblSales * .1` statement in Example 6 multiplies the contents of the `dblSales` variable by the Double number .1 and then assigns the result to the `dblCommission` variable. When an assignment statement's expression contains the name of a variable, the computer uses the value stored inside the variable to evaluate the expression.

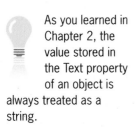

As you learned in Chapter 2, the value stored in the Text property of an object is always treated as a string.

You will learn about another literal type character, the letter C, in Chapter 8.

Assigning values to variables having the same data type

Example 1
```
intQuantity = 500
```
assigns the integer 500 to the `intQuantity` variable

Example 2
```
strFirstName = "Mary"
```
assigns the string "Mary" to the `strFirstName` variable

Example 3
```
strZipCode = txtZip.Text
```
assigns the string contained in the txtZip control's Text property to the `strZipCode` variable

Example 4
```
dblDiscountRate = .03
```
assigns the Double number .03 to the `dblDiscountRate` variable

Example 5
```
decTaxRate = .05D
```
converts the Double number .05 to Decimal and then assigns the result to the `decTaxRate` variable

Example 6
```
dblCommission = dblSales * .1
```
multiplies the contents of the `dblSales` variable by .1 and then assigns the result to the `dblCommission` variable

---

Figure 3-6 Assignment statements in which the value's data type matches the variable's data type

A variable can store only one value at any one time. When you use an assignment statement to assign another value to the variable, the new value replaces the existing value. To illustrate this point, assume that a button's Click event procedure contains the following two lines of code: `Dim intNumber As Integer = 500` and `intNumber = intNumber * 2`. When you start the application and click the button, the two lines of code are processed as follows:

1. The declaration statement creates the `intNumber` variable in memory and initializes it to the number 500.

2. The assignment statement first multiplies the contents of the `intNumber` variable by the number 2, giving 1000. The assignment statement then replaces the current contents of the `intNumber` variable (500) with 1000. Notice that the calculation appearing on the right side of the assignment operator is performed first, and then the result is assigned to the variable whose name appears on the left side of the assignment operator.

In all of the assignment statements in Figure 3-6, the data type of the value matches the data type of the variable to which the value is assigned. At times, however, the value's data type might be different from the variable's data type. You can change the value's data type to match the variable's data type using either the TryParse method or one of the methods in the Convert class.

128

The TryParse Method

You will learn more about the TryParse method in Chapter 4.

Like the Val function, which you learned about in Chapter 2, the **TryParse method** converts a string to a number. However, unlike the Val function, which always returns a Double number, the TryParse method allows the programmer to specify the number's data type; for this reason, most programmers prefer to use the TryParse method. Every numeric data type in Visual Basic has a TryParse method that converts a string to that particular data type.

Figure 3-7 shows the basic syntax of the TryParse method along with examples of using the method. In the syntax, *dataType* is one of the numeric data types available in Visual Basic. The dot member access operator in the TryParse method's syntax indicates that the method is a member of the *dataType* class. The method's arguments (*string* and *numericVariableName*) represent information that the method needs to perform its task. The *string* argument is the string you want converted to a number of the *dataType* type and typically is either the Text property of a control or the name of a String variable. The *numericVariableName* argument is the name of a numeric variable in which the TryParse method can store the number. The numeric variable must have the same data type as specified in the *dataType* portion of the syntax. In other words, when using the TryParse method to convert a string to a Double number, you need to provide the method with the name of a Double variable in which to store the number. The TryParse method parses its *string* argument, which means it looks at each character in the string, to determine whether the string can be converted to a number of the specified data type. If the string can be converted, the TryParse method converts the string to a number and stores the number in the variable specified in the *numericVariableName* argument. If the TryParse method determines that the string cannot be converted to the appropriate data type, it assigns the number 0 to the variable.

Using the TryParse method

<u>Basic syntax</u>
dataType.**TryParse(***string*, *numericVariableName***)**

<u>Example 1</u>
```
Double.TryParse(txtSales.Text, dblSales)
```
If the string contained in the txtSales control's Text property can be converted to a Double number, the TryParse method converts the string and then stores the result in the `dblSales` variable; otherwise, it stores the number 0 in the `dblSales` variable.

Figure 3-7   Basic syntax and examples of the TryParse method *(continues)*

(continued)

Example 2
```
Decimal.TryParse(txtGross.Text, decGross)
```
If the string contained in the txtGross control's Text property can be converted to a Decimal number, the TryParse method converts the string and then stores the result in the decGross variable; otherwise, it stores the number 0 in the decGross variable.

Example 3
```
Integer.TryParse(strNumber, intNumber)
```
If the string contained in the strNumber variable can be converted to an Integer number, the TryParse method converts the string and then stores the result in the intNumber variable; otherwise, it stores the number 0 in the intNumber variable.

Figure 3-7 Basic syntax and examples of the TryParse method

Figure 3-8 shows how the TryParse method of the Double, Decimal, and Integer data types would convert various strings. As the figure indicates, the three methods can convert a string that contains only numbers. They also can convert a string that contains a leading sign, as well as one that contains leading or trailing spaces. In addition, the Double.TryParse and Decimal. TryParse methods can convert a string that contains a decimal point or a comma. However, none of the three methods can convert a string that contains a dollar sign, a percent sign, a letter, or a space within the string.

string	Double.TryParse	Decimal.TryParse	Integer.TryParse
"62"	62	62	62
"–9"	–9	–9	–9
"12.55"	12.55	12.55	0
"–4.23"	–4.23	–4.23	0
"1,457"	1457	1457	0
" 33 "	33	33	33
"$5"	0	0	0
"7%"	0	0	0
"122a"	0	0	0
"1 345"	0	0	0
empty string	0	0	0

Figure 3-8 Results of the TryParse method for the Double, Decimal, and Integer data types

You can experiment with the Visual Basic conversion functions by completing Discovery Exercise 5 at the end of Lesson C.

The Convert Class

At times, you may need to convert a number (rather than a string) from one data type to another. Visual Basic provides several ways of accomplishing this task. One way is to use the Visual Basic conversion functions, which are listed in Appendix C in this book. You also can use one of the methods defined in the **Convert class**. In this book you will use the Convert class methods, because they have an advantage over the conversion functions: the methods can be used in any of the languages built into Visual Studio, whereas the conversion functions can be used only in the Visual Basic language. The more commonly used methods in the Convert class are the ToDecimal, ToDouble, ToInt32, and ToString methods. The methods convert a value to the Decimal, Double, Integer, and String data types, respectively.

The syntax for using the Convert class methods is shown in Figure 3-9. The dot member access operator in the syntax indicates that the *method* is a member of the Convert class. In most cases, the *value* argument is a numeric value that you want converted either to the String data type or to a different numeric data type (for example, from Double to Decimal). Although you can use the Convert methods to convert a string to a numeric data type, the TryParse method is the recommended method to use for that task. This is because, unlike the Convert methods, the TryParse method does not produce an error when it tries to convert the empty string; instead, the TryParse method assigns the number 0 to its *numericVariableName* argument.

Also included in Figure 3-9 are examples of using the Convert class methods. In the statement shown in Example 1, the Convert.ToDecimal method converts the Double number .05 to Decimal. (Recall that a number with a decimal place is automatically treated as a Double number in Visual Basic.) The statement then assigns the result to the `decTaxRate` variable. You also could write the statement in Example 1 as `decTaxRate = .05D`; however, many programmers would argue that using the Convert.ToDecimal method, rather than the literal type character (D), makes the code clearer. In Example 2's statement, the Convert.ToString method converts the integer stored in the `intTotalScore` variable to String before the statement assigns the result to the lblTotal control's Text property. The statement in Example 3 uses the Convert.ToDecimal method to convert the Double number .1 to Decimal. The statement multiplies the result by the contents of the `decSales` variable and then assigns the product to the `decCommission` variable. You also could write this statement as `decCommission = decSales * .1D`.

Using the Convert class methods

Syntax
Convert.*method*(*value*)

Example 1
```
decTaxRate = Convert.ToDecimal(.05)
```
converts the Double number .05 to Decimal and then assigns the result to the
`decTaxRate` variable

Figure 3-9   Syntax and examples of the Convert class methods *(continues)*

(continued)

Example 2
```
lblTotal.Text = Convert.ToString(intTotalScore)
```
converts the integer stored in the `intTotalScore` variable to String and then assigns the result to the lblTotal control's Text property

Example 3
```
decCommission = decSales * Convert.ToDecimal(.1)
```
converts the Double number .1 to Decimal, then multiplies the result by the contents of the `decSales` variable, and then assigns that result to the `decCommission` variable

Figure 3-9 Syntax and examples of the Convert class methods

YOU DO IT 1!

Create a Visual Basic Windows application named YouDoIt 1. Save the application in the VB2010\Chap03 folder. Add a text box, a label, and a button to the form. The button's Click event procedure should store the contents of the text box in a Double variable named `dblCost`. It then should display the variable's contents in the label. Code the procedure. Save the solution and then start and test the application. Close the solution.

The Scope and Lifetime of a Variable

Besides a name, data type, and initial value, every variable also has a scope and a lifetime. A variable's **scope** indicates where the variable can be used in an application's code, and its **lifetime** indicates how long the variable remains in the computer's internal memory. Variables can have class scope, procedure scope, or block scope. However, most of the variables used in an application will have procedure scope. This is because fewer unintentional errors occur in applications when the variables are declared using the minimum scope needed, which usually is procedure scope.

A variable's scope and lifetime are determined by where you declare the variable—in other words, where you enter the variable's declaration statement. Typically, you enter the declaration statement either in a procedure (such as an event procedure) or in the Declarations section of a form. A form's Declarations section is not the same as the General Declarations section, which you learned about in Chapter 2. The General Declarations section is located above the Public Class clause in the Code Editor window, whereas the form's Declarations section is located between the Public Class and End Class clauses. Variables declared in a form's Declarations section have class scope. Variables declared in a procedure, on the other hand, have either procedure scope or block scope, depending on where in the procedure they are declared. In the next two sections, you will learn about procedure scope variables and class scope variables. Variables having block scope are covered in Chapter 4.

 Variables also can have namespace scope and are referred to as namespace variables, global variables, or public variables. Such variables can lead to unintentional errors in a program and should be avoided, if possible. For this reason, they are not covered in this book.

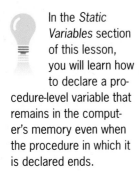

Procedure-level variables are also called local variables and their scope is often referred to as local scope.

In the *Static Variables* section of this lesson, you will learn how to declare a procedure-level variable that remains in the computer's memory even when the procedure in which it is declared ends.

Variables with Procedure Scope

When you declare a variable in a procedure, the variable is called a **procedure-level variable** and it has **procedure scope**, because only that procedure can use the variable. Procedure-level variables typically are declared at the beginning of a procedure, and they remain in the computer's internal memory only while that procedure is running. Procedure-level variables are removed from memory when the procedure in which they are declared ends. In other words, a procedure-level variable has the same lifetime as the procedure that declares it. As mentioned earlier, most of the variables in your applications will be procedure-level variables.

The Sales Tax Calculator application that you view next illustrates the use of procedure-level variables. As the interface shown in Figure 3-10 indicates, the application allows the user to enter a sales amount. It then calculates and displays either a 2% sales tax or a 5% sales tax, depending on the button selected by the user.

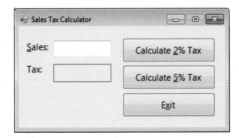

Figure 3-10 User interface for the Sales Tax Calculator application

Figure 3-11 shows the Click event procedures for the Calculate 2% Tax and Calculate 5% Tax buttons. When the user clicks the Calculate 2% Tax button in the interface, the Dim statements in the button's Click event procedure create and initialize two procedure-level Double variables named `dblSales` and `dblTax2`; both variables can be used only by that procedure. Next, the TryParse method converts the sales amount entered in the txtSales control to Double and then stores the result in the `dblSales` variable. The first assignment statement in the procedure multiplies the contents of the `dblSales` variable by the Double number .02 and then stores the result in the `dblTax2` variable. The last assignment statement in the procedure converts the contents of the `dblTax2` variable to String, assigning the result to the lblTax control's Text property. When the procedure ends, the computer removes the `dblSales` and `dblTax2` variables from memory. The variables will be created again the next time the user clicks the Calculate 2% Tax button. A similar process is followed when the user clicks the Calculate 5% Tax button, except the variable that stores the tax amount is named `dblTax5` and the tax is calculated using a rate of .05 rather than .02.

```
Private Sub btnCalcTax2_Click(ByVal sender As Object,
ByVal e As System.EventArgs) Handles btnCalcTax2.Click
    ' calculates a 2% sales tax

    ' declare variables
    Dim dblSales As Double
    Dim dblTax2 As Double

    ' calculate and display the sales tax
    Double.TryParse(txtSales.Text, dblSales)
    dblTax2 = dblSales * 0.02
    lblTax.Text = Convert.ToString(dblTax2)
End Sub

Private Sub btnCalcTax5_Click(ByVal sender As Object,
ByVal e As System.EventArgs) Handles btnCalcTax5.Click
    ' calculates a 5% sales tax

    ' declare variables
    Dim dblSales As Double
    Dim dblTax5 As Double

    ' calculate and display the sales tax
    Double.TryParse(txtSales.Text, dblSales)
    dblTax5 = dblSales * 0.05
    lblTax.Text = Convert.ToString(dblTax5)
End Sub
```

procedure-level variables in the btnCalcTax2 Click event procedure

procedure-level variables in the btnCalcTax5 Click event procedure

Figure 3-11 Click event procedures using procedure-level variables

Notice that both procedures in Figure 3-11 declare a variable named
dblSales. When you use the same name to declare a variable in more than
one procedure, each procedure creates its own variable when the procedure
is invoked. Each procedure also destroys its own variable when the procedure
ends. In other words, although the **dblSales** variables in both procedures
have the same name, they are not the same variable. Rather, each refers to a
different section in the computer's internal memory, and each is created and
destroyed independently from the other.

To code and then test the Sales Tax Calculator application:

START HERE

1. If necessary, start Visual Studio 2010 or Visual Basic 2010 Express.
   Open the Sales Tax Solution (Sales Tax Solution.sln) file contained in
   the VB2010\Chap03\Sales Tax Solution-Procedure-level folder. If necessary, open the designer window. The user interface shown earlier in
   Figure 3-10 appears on the screen.

2. Open the Code Editor window. For now, do not be concerned about
   the three Option statements that appear in the window. You will
   learn about the Option statements later in this lesson. Replace <your
   name> and <current date> in the comments with your name and the
   current date, respectively.

3. Open the code template for the btnCalcTax2 control's Click event
   procedure. Also open the code template for the btnCalcTax5 control's
   Click event procedure. In the procedures, enter the comments and
   code shown in Figure 3-11.

4. Save the solution and then start the application. Type **1000** in the Sales box and then click the **Calculate 2% Tax** button. The button's Click event procedure calculates and displays a tax of 20. Click the **Calculate 5% Tax** button. The button's Click event procedure calculates and displays a tax of 50.

5. Change the sales amount from 1000 to the letter **a** and then click the **Calculate 2% Tax** button. The button's Click event procedure calculates and displays a tax of 0. Click the **Calculate 5% Tax** button. The button's Click event procedure calculates and displays a tax of 0.

6. Click the **Exit** button. Close the Code Editor window and then close the solution.

Variables with Class Scope

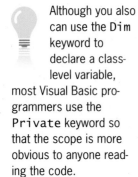

Although you also can use the Dim keyword to declare a class-level variable, most Visual Basic programmers use the Private keyword so that the scope is more obvious to anyone reading the code.

In addition to declaring a variable in a procedure, you also can declare a variable in the form's Declarations section, which begins with the Public Class clause and ends with the End Class clause. When you declare a variable in the form's Declarations section, the variable is called a **class-level variable** and it has **class scope**. Class-level variables can be used by all of the procedures in the form, including the procedures associated with the controls contained on the form, and they retain their values and remain in the computer's internal memory until the application ends. In other words, a class-level variable has the same lifetime as the application itself. Unlike a procedure-level variable, which is declared using the Dim keyword, you declare a class-level variable using the Private keyword. You typically use a class-level variable when you need more than one procedure in the same form to use the same variable. However, a class-level variable also can be used when a procedure needs to retain a variable's value after the procedure ends. The Total Sales application, which you view next, illustrates this use of a class-level variable. The application's interface is shown in Figure 3-12. As the interface indicates, the application displays the total of the sales amounts entered by the user.

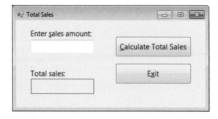

Figure 3-12   User interface for the Total Sales application

Figure 3-13 shows the Total Sales application's code. The code uses a class-level variable named `decTotal` to accumulate (add together) the sales amounts entered by the user. Class-level variables should be entered after the Public Class clause, but before the first Private Sub clause, in the form's Declarations section. When the user starts the Total Sales application, the computer processes the `Private decTotal As Decimal` statement in the form's Declarations section. The statement creates and initializes a

Decimal variable named `decTotal`. The variable is created and initialized only once, when the application starts. It remains in the computer's internal memory until the application ends. Each time the user clicks the Calculate Total Sales button in the interface, the button's Click event procedure creates and initializes a procedure-level variable named `decSales`. Next, the TryParse method in the procedure converts the sales amount entered in the txtSales control to Decimal, storing the result in the `decSales` variable. The first assignment statement in the procedure adds the contents of the procedure-level `decSales` variable to the contents of the class-level `decTotal` variable. At this point, the `decTotal` variable contains the sum of all of the sales amounts entered so far. The last assignment statement in the procedure converts the contents of the `decTotal` variable to String and then assigns the result to the lblTotalSales control. The procedure then sends the focus to the txtSales control. When the procedure ends, the computer removes the procedure-level `decSales` variable from its memory; however, it does not remove the class-level `decTotal` variable. The `decTotal` variable is removed from the computer's memory only when the application ends.

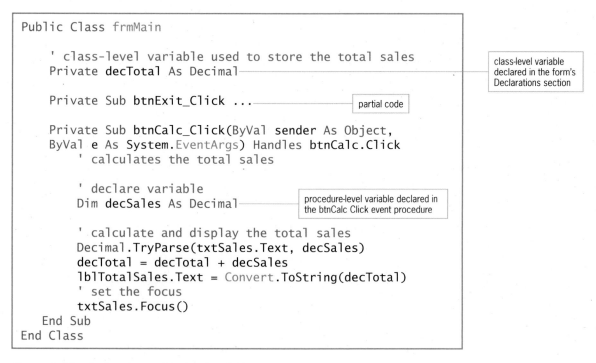

```
Public Class frmMain

    ' class-level variable used to store the total sales
    Private decTotal As Decimal ──────────────────────────  class-level variable
                                                            declared in the form's
                                                            Declarations section

    Private Sub btnExit_Click ... ──────────  partial code

    Private Sub btnCalc_Click(ByVal sender As Object,
    ByVal e As System.EventArgs) Handles btnCalc.Click
        ' calculates the total sales

        ' declare variable                procedure-level variable declared in
        Dim decSales As Decimal ────────  the btnCalc Click event procedure

        ' calculate and display the total sales
        Decimal.TryParse(txtSales.Text, decSales)
        decTotal = decTotal + decSales
        lblTotalSales.Text = Convert.ToString(decTotal)
        ' set the focus
        txtSales.Focus()
    End Sub
End Class
```

Figure 3-13   Code using a class-level variable

To code and then test the Total Sales application: **START HERE**

1. Open the Total Sales Solution (Total Sales Solution.sln) file contained in the VB2010\Chap03\Total Sales Solution-Class-level folder. If necessary, open the designer window. The user interface shown earlier in Figure 3-12 appears on the screen.

2. Open the Code Editor window. Here again, do not be concerned about the three Option statements that appear in the window. You will learn about the Option statements later in this lesson. Replace <your name> and <current date> in the comments with your name and the current date, respectively.

3. First, declare the class-level `decTotal` variable in the form's Declarations section. Click the **blank line** below the `' class-level variable used to store the total sales` comment and then enter the following declaration statement:

Private decTotal As Decimal

4. Open the code template for the btnCalc control's Click event procedure. In the procedure, enter the comments and code shown in Figure 3-13.

5. Save the solution and then start the application.

6. Type **2000** as the sales amount and then click the **Calculate Total Sales** button. The button's Click event procedure calculates and displays the total sales: 2000.

7. Change the sales amount from 2000 to **4000** and then click the **Calculate Total Sales** button. The number 6000 appears in the Total sales box.

8. Change the sales amount from 4000 to **500** and then click the **Calculate Total Sales** button. The number 6500 appears in the Total sales box.

9. Click the **Exit** button. Close the Code Editor window and then close the solution.

Static Variables

Recall that you can declare a variable using the `Dim`, `Private`, or `Static` keywords. You already know how to use the `Dim` and `Private` keywords to declare procedure-level and class-level variables, respectively. In this section, you will learn how to use the `Static` keyword to declare a special type of procedure-level variable, called a static variable. A **static variable** is a procedure-level variable that remains in memory, and also retains its value, even when the procedure in which it is declared ends. Like a class-level variable, a static variable is not removed from the computer's internal memory until the application ends. However, unlike a class-level variable, which can be used by all of the procedures in a form, a static variable can be used only by the procedure in which it is declared. In other words, a static variable has a narrower scope than does a class-level variable. As mentioned earlier, you can prevent many unintentional errors from occurring in an application by declaring the variables using the minimum scope needed.

The `Static` keyword can be used only in a procedure.

In the previous section, you viewed the interface (Figure 3-12) and code (Figure 3-13) for the Total Sales application. Recall that the application uses a class-level variable to accumulate the sales amounts entered by the user. Rather than using a class-level variable for that purpose, you also can use a static variable. Figure 3-14 shows the Total Sales application's code using a static variable. The first time the user clicks the Calculate Total

Sales button in the interface, the button's Click event procedure creates and initializes (to 0) a procedure-level variable named `decSales` and a static variable named `decTotal`. Next, the TryParse method converts the sales amount in the txtSales control to Decimal, storing the result in the `decSales` variable. The first assignment statement in the procedure adds the contents of the `decSales` variable to the contents of the `decTotal` variable. The last assignment statement in the procedure converts the contents of the `decTotal` variable to String and assigns the result to the lblTotalSales control. The procedure then sends the focus to the txtSales control. When the procedure ends, the computer removes from its internal memory the variable declared using the `Dim` keyword (`decSales`). But it does not remove the variable declared using the `Static` keyword (`decTotal`). Each subsequent time the user clicks the Calculate Total Sales button, the computer re-creates and re-initializes the `decSales` variable declared in the button's Click event procedure. However, it does not re-create or re-initialize the `decTotal` variable because that variable, as well as its current value, is still in the computer's memory. After re-creating and re-initializing the `decSales` variable, the computer processes the remaining instructions contained in the button's Click event procedure. Here again, each time the procedure ends, the `decSales` variable is removed from the computer's internal memory. The `decTotal` variable is removed only when the application ends.

137

```
Public Class frmMain

    Private Sub btnExit_Click(ByVal sender As Object,
    ByVal e As System.EventArgs) Handles btnExit.Click
        Me.Close()
    End Sub

    Private Sub btnCalc_Click(ByVal sender As Object,
    ByVal e As System.EventArgs) Handles btnCalc.Click
        ' calculates the total sales

        ' declare variables ──────────────        [modified comment]
        Dim decSales As Decimal
        Static decTotal As Decimal ──────    [static variable declared in the btnCalc
                                              Click event procedure]

        ' calculate and display the total sales
        Decimal.TryParse(txtSales.Text, decSales)
        decTotal = decTotal + decSales
        lblTotalSales.Text = Convert.ToString(decTotal)
        ' set the focus
        txtSales.Focus()
    End Sub
End Class
```

Figure 3-14 Code using a static variable

To use a static variable in the Total Sales application:

1. Use Windows to make a copy of the Total Sales Solution-Class-level folder contained in the VB2010\Chap03 folder. Rename the copy **Total Sales Solution-Static**.

2. Open the Total Sales Solution (Total Sales Solution.sln) file contained in the Total Sales Solution-Static folder. Open the designer window. The user interface shown earlier in Figure 3-12 appears on the screen.

3. Open the Code Editor window. Delete the comment and Private declaration statement entered in the form's Declarations section.

4. Modify the btnCalc control's Click event procedure so that it uses a static variable rather than a class-level variable. Use the code shown in Figure 3-14 as a guide.

5. Save the solution and then start the application.

6. Type the following three sales amounts, one at a time. Click the **Calculate Total Sales** button after typing each sales amount: **2000**, **4000**, and **500**. The number 6500 appears in the Total sales box.

7. Click the **Exit** button. Close the Code Editor window and then close the solution.

YOU DO IT 2!

Create a Visual Basic Windows application named YouDoIt 2. Save the application in the VB2010\Chap03 folder. Add a label and a button to the form. The button's Click event procedure should add the number 1 to the contents of a class-level Integer variable named `intNumber`. It then should display the variable's contents in the label. Code the application. Save the solution and then start and test the application. Now change the class-level variable to a static variable. Save the solution and then start and test the application. Close the solution.

Named Constants

In addition to using literal constants and variables in your code, you also can use named constants. Like a variable, a **named constant** is a memory location inside the computer. However, unlike a variable's value, a named constant's value cannot be changed while the application is running. You create a named constant using the **Const statement**. Figure 3-15 shows the statement's syntax and includes examples of declaring named constants. To differentiate the name of a constant from the name of a variable, many programmers lowercase the three-character ID that represents the constant's data type and then uppercase the remaining characters in the name, as shown in the examples in the figure. The Const statement stores the value of the *expression* in the named constant. The expression's value must have the same data type as the named constant. The expression can contain a literal constant, another named constant, or an arithmetic operator; however, it cannot contain a variable or a method.

When entered in a procedure, the Const statements shown in the first three examples in Figure 3-15 create procedure-level named constants. To create a class-level named constant, you precede the **Const** keyword with the **Private** keyword, as shown in Example 4. In addition, you enter the Const statement in the form's Declarations section. At this point, you may be wondering why the Convert.ToDecimal method was not used to convert the Double number in Example 3 to the Decimal data type. This is because, as mentioned earlier, the expression assigned to a named constant cannot contain a method.

Declaring a named constant

<u>Syntax</u>
[Private] Const *constantName* **As** *dataType* = *expression*

<u>Example 1</u>
`Const dblPI As Double = 3.141593`
declares `dblPI` as a Double named constant and initializes it to the Double number 3.141593

<u>Example 2</u>
`Const intMAX_HOURS As Integer = 40`
declares `intMAX_HOURS` as an Integer named constant and initializes it to the integer 40

<u>Example 3</u>
`Const decTAX_RATE As Decimal = .05D` ———————— the D literal type character changes the number to the Decimal data type
declares `decTAX_RATE` as a Decimal named constant and initializes it to the Decimal number .05

<u>Example 4</u>
`Private Const strHEADING As String = "ABC Company"`
declares `strHEADING` as a String named constant and initializes it to the string "ABC Company"

Figure 3-15 Syntax and examples of the Const statement

Named constants make code more self-documenting and easier to modify, because they allow you to use meaningful words in place of values that are less clear. The named constant **dblPI**, for example, is much more meaningful than the number 3.141593, which is the value of pi rounded to six decimal places. Once you create a named constant, you then can use the constant's name, rather than its value, in the application's code. Unlike the value stored in a variable, the value stored in a named constant cannot be inadvertently changed while the application is running. Using a named constant to represent a value has another advantage: if the value changes in the future, you will need to modify only the Const statement in the program, rather than all of the program statements that use the value. The Area Calculator application that you view next illustrates the use of a named constant. The application's interface is shown in Figure 3-16. As the interface indicates, the application allows the user to enter the radius of a circle. It then calculates and displays the area of the circle. The formula for calculating the area of a circle is πr^2, where π stands for pi (3.141593).

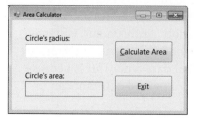

Figure 3-16   User interface for the Area Calculator application

Figure 3-17 shows the code for the Calculate Area button's Click event procedure. The declaration statements in the procedure declare and initialize a named constant and two variables. Next, the TryParse method converts (to Double) the radius value entered in the txtRadius control, and it stores the result in the **dblRadius** variable. The first assignment statement in the procedure calculates the circle's area using the values stored in the **dblPI** named constant and **dblRadius** variable; it then assigns the result to the **dblArea** variable. The second assignment statement displays the contents of the **dblArea** variable (converted to String) in the lblArea control. When the procedure ends, the computer removes the named constant and two variables from its internal memory.

You also can calculate the area using the expression **dblPI * dblRadius ^ 2**.

```vb
Private Sub btnCalc_Click(ByVal sender As Object,
ByVal e As System.EventArgs) Handles btnCalc.Click
    ' calculates the area of a circle

    ' declare named constant and variables
    Const dblPI As Double = 3.141593
    Dim dblRadius As Double
    Dim dblArea As Double

    ' calculate and display the area
    Double.TryParse(txtRadius.Text, dblRadius)
    dblArea = dblPI * dblRadius * dblRadius
    lblArea.Text = Convert.ToString(dblArea)
End Sub
```

named constant declaration statement

assignment statement containing the named constant

Figure 3-17   Calculate Area button's Click event procedure

START HERE

To code and then test the Area Calculator application:

1. Open the Area Calculator Solution (Area Calculator Solution.sln) file contained in the VB2010\Chap03\Area Calculator Solution folder. If necessary, open the designer window. The user interface shown earlier in Figure 3-16 appears on the screen.

2. Open the Code Editor window. Replace <your name> and <current date> in the comments with your name and the current date, respectively.

3. Open the code template for the btnCalc control's Click event procedure, and then enter the comments and code shown in Figure 3-17.

4. Save the solution and then start the application.

5. Type **10** in the Circle's radius box and then click the **Calculate Area** button. The button's Click event procedure calculates and displays the area: 314.1593.

6. Click the **Exit** button. Close the Code Editor window and then close the solution.

Option Explicit, Option Infer, and Option Strict

It is important to declare the variables used in an application, because doing so allows you to control their data type. It also makes the application more self-documenting, which means it will be clearer and easier to understand by anyone reading your code. A word of caution is in order at this point: in Visual Basic you can create variables "on the fly." This means that if your code contains the name of an undeclared variable, Visual Basic creates the variable for you and assigns the Object data type to it. (An undeclared variable is a variable that does not appear in a declaration statement, such as a Dim statement.) Recall that the Object type is not a very efficient data type, and its use should be limited. Because it is so easy to forget to declare a variable—and so easy to misspell a variable's name while coding, thereby inadvertently creating an undeclared variable—Visual Basic provides a way that prevents you from using undeclared variables in your code. You simply enter the statement Option Explicit On in the General Declarations section of the Code Editor window. The statement tells the Code Editor to alert you if your code contains the name of an undeclared variable. When you also enter the Option Infer Off statement in the General Declarations section, the Code Editor ensures that every variable and named constant is declared with a data type. In other words, the statement tells the computer not to infer (or assume) a memory location's data type based on the data assigned to the memory location.

Recall that the General Declarations section is located above the Public Class clause in the Code Editor window.

As you learned earlier, the data type of the value assigned to a memory location (variable or named constant) should be the same as the data type of the memory location itself. If the value's data type does not match the memory location's data type, the computer uses a process called **implicit type conversion** to convert the value to fit the memory location. For example, when processing the statement Dim dblSales As Double = 9, the computer converts the integer 9 to a Double number before storing the value in the variable. It does this by appending a decimal point and the number 0 to the end of the integer. In this case, the integer 9 will be converted to the Double number 9.0 before the number is assigned to the dblSales variable. When a value is converted from one data type to another data type that can store either larger numbers or numbers with greater precision, the value is said to be **promoted**. In this case, if the dblSales variable is used subsequently in a calculation, the results of the calculation will not be adversely affected by the implicit promotion of the number 9 to the number 9.0.

On the other hand, if you inadvertently assign a Double number to a memory location that can store only integers—as does the statement Dim intScore As Integer = 78.4—the computer converts the Double number to an integer before storing the value in the memory location. It does this by rounding the number to the nearest whole number and then truncating (dropping off) the decimal portion of the number. In this case, the computer converts the Double number 78.4 to the integer 78, which then is assigned to the `intScore` variable. When a value is converted from one data type to another data type that can store only smaller numbers or numbers with less precision, the value is said to be **demoted**. If the `intScore` variable is used subsequently in a calculation, the results of the calculation probably will be adversely affected by the implicit demotion of the number 78.4 to the number 78. More than likely, the demotion will cause the calculated results to be incorrect.

With implicit type conversions, data loss can occur when a value is converted from one data type to a narrower data type, which is a data type with less precision or smaller capacity. You can eliminate the problems that occur as a result of implicit type conversions by entering the `Option Strict On` statement in the General Declarations section of the Code Editor window. When the `Option Strict On` statement appears in an application's code, the computer uses the type conversion rules listed in Figure 3-18. The figure also includes examples of these rules.

According to the first rule listed in Figure 3-18, the computer will not implicitly convert a string to a number. As a result, the Code Editor will issue the warning "Option Strict On disallows implicit conversions from 'String' to 'Double'" when your code contains the statement `dblHours = txtHours.Text`, because the statement tells the computer to store a string in a Double variable. As you learned earlier, you should use the TryParse method to explicitly convert a string to the Double data type before assigning it to a Double variable. In this case, the appropriate statement to use is `Double.TryParse(txtHours.Text, dblHours)`.

According to the second rule listed in Figure 3-18, the computer will not implicitly convert a number to a string. Therefore, the Code Editor will issue the warning "Option Strict On disallows implicit conversions from 'Decimal' to 'String'" when your code contains the statement `lblGross.Text = decGrossPay`, because the statement assigns a number to a string. Recall that you can use the Convert class methods to explicitly convert a number to the String data type. The appropriate statement to use here is `lblGross.Text = Convert.ToString(decGrossPay)`.

The third rule listed in Figure 3-18 states that wider data types will not be implicitly demoted to narrower data types. A data type is wider than another data type if it can store either larger numbers or numbers with greater precision. Because of this rule, a Double number will not be implicitly demoted to the Decimal or Integer data types. If your code contains the statement `Dim decRate As Decimal = .05`, the Code Editor will issue the "Option Strict On disallows implicit conversions from 'Double' to 'Decimal'" warning, because the statement assigns a Double number to a Decimal variable. The correct statement to use in this case is either `Dim decRate As Decimal = .05D` or `Dim decRate As Decimal = Convert.ToDecimal(.05)`. According to the last type conversion rule listed in Figure 3-18, the computer will implicitly convert narrower data types to wider data types. For example, when processing the statement `dblAverage = dblTotal / intNum`, the computer will implicitly promote the integer stored in the `intNum` variable to Double before dividing it into the contents of the `dblTotal` variable. The result, a Double number, will be assigned to the `dblAverage` variable.

Type conversion rules

1. Strings will not be implicitly converted to numbers. The Code Editor will display a warning message when a statement attempts to use a string where a number is expected.

Incorrect:	`dblHours = txtHours.Text`
Correct:	`Double.TryParse(txtHours.Text, dblHours)`

2. Numbers will not be implicitly converted to strings. The Code Editor will display a warning message when a statement attempts to use a number where a string is expected.

Incorrect:	`lblGross.Text = decGrossPay`
Correct:	`lblGross.Text = Convert.ToString(decGrossPay)`

3. Wider data types will not be implicitly demoted to narrower data types. The Code Editor will display a warning message when a statement attempts to use a wider data type where a narrower data type is expected.

Incorrect:	`Dim decRate As Decimal = .05`
Correct:	`Dim decRate As Decimal =.05D`
Correct:	`Dim decRate As Decimal = Convert.ToDecimal(.05)`

4. Narrower data types will be implicitly promoted to wider data types.

Correct:	`dblAverage = dblTotal / intNum`

Figure 3-18   Rules and examples of type conversions

Figure 3-19 shows the three Option statements entered in the General Declarations section of the Code Editor window. If a project contains more than one form, the statements must be entered in each form's Code Editor window.

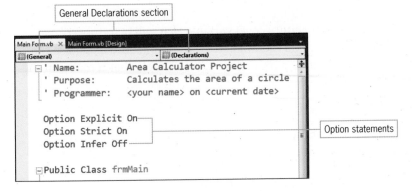

Figure 3-19   Option statements entered in the General Declarations section

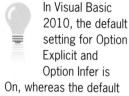

In Visual Basic 2010, the default setting for Option Explicit and Option Infer is On, whereas the default setting for Option Strict is Off.

Rather than entering the Option statements in the Code Editor window, you also can set the options using either the Project Designer window or the Options dialog box. However, it is strongly recommended that you enter the Option statements in the Code Editor window, because doing so ensures that the options are set appropriately; it also makes your code more self-documenting. The steps for setting the options in the Project Designer window and Options dialog box are listed in the Lesson A Summary section.

YOU DO IT 3!

Create a Visual Basic Windows application named YouDoIt 3. Save the application in the VB2010\Chap03 folder. Add a text box, a label, and a button to the form. In the General Declarations section of the Code Editor window, enter the following three Option statements: `Option Explicit On`, `Option Strict Off`, and `Option Infer Off`. In the button's Click event procedure, declare a Double variable named `dblNum`. Use an assignment statement to assign the contents of the text box to the Double variable. Then, use an assignment statement to assign the contents of the Double variable to the label. Save the solution and then start and test the application. Now change the `Option Strict Off` statement to `Option Strict On`, and then make the necessary modifications to the code. Save the solution and then start and test the application. Close the solution.

Lesson A Summary

- To declare a variable:

  The syntax of a variable declaration statement is {**Dim** | **Private** | **Static**} *variableName* **As** *dataType* [= *initialValue*]. Use camel case for a variable's name.

- To declare a procedure-level variable:

  Enter the variable declaration statement in a procedure; use the `Dim` keyword to declare a procedure-level variable that will be removed from the computer's internal memory when the procedure ends; use the `Static` keyword to declare a procedure-level variable that remains in the computer's internal memory until the application ends.

- To declare a class-level variable:

  Enter the variable declaration statement in a form's Declarations section; use the `Private` keyword.

- To use an assignment statement to assign data to a variable:

  Use the syntax *variableName* = *expression*.

145

- To force a Double literal constant to assume the Decimal data type:

  Append the letter D to the end of the Double literal constant.

- To convert a string to a numeric data type:

  Use the TryParse method. The method's syntax is *dataType.*
  TryParse(*string*, *numericVariableName***)**.

- To convert a numeric value to a different data type:

  Use one of the Convert class methods. Each method's syntax is
  Convert.*method***(***value***)**.

- To create a named constant:

  Use the Const statement. The statement's syntax is **Const** *constantName*
  As *dataType* = *expression*. Lowercase the three-character ID and then
  uppercase the remainder of the name.

- To create a procedure-level named constant:

  Enter the Const statement in a procedure.

- To create a class-level named constant:

  Enter the Const statement, preceded by the keyword `Private`, in a form's
  Declarations section.

- To prevent the computer from creating an undeclared variable:

  Enter the `Option Explicit On` statement in the General Declarations
  section of the Code Editor window.

- To prevent the computer from inferring a variable's data type:

  Enter the `Option Infer Off` statement in the General Declarations section of the Code Editor window.

- To prevent the computer from making implicit type conversions that may
  result in a loss of data:

  Enter the `Option Strict On` statement in the General Declarations
  section of the Code Editor window.

- To use the Project Designer window to set Option Explicit, Option Strict,
  and Option Infer for an entire project:

  Open the solution that contains the project. Right-click My Project in
  the Solution Explorer window and then click Open to open the Project
  Designer window. Click the Compile tab. Use the Option explicit, Option
  strict, and Option infer boxes to set the options. Save the solution and
  then close the Project Designer window.

- To use the Options dialog box to set Option Explicit, Option Strict, and
  Option Infer for all of the projects you create:

  Click Tools on the Visual Studio menu bar and then click Options. When
  the Options dialog box opens, expand the Projects and Solutions node and
  then click VB Defaults. Use the Option Explicit, Option Strict, and Option
  Infer boxes to set the options. Click the OK button to close the Options
  dialog box.

Lesson A Key Terms

Class scope—the scope of a class-level variable; refers to the fact that the variable can be used by any procedure in the form

Class-level variable—a variable declared in a form's Declarations section; the variable has class scope

Const statement—the statement used to create a named constant

Convert class—contains methods that return the result of converting a value to a specified data type

Data type—indicates the type of data a memory location (variable or named constant) can store

Demoted—the process of converting a value from one data type to another data type that can store only smaller numbers or numbers with less precision

Implicit type conversion—the process by which a value is automatically converted to fit the memory location to which it is assigned

Lifetime—indicates how long a variable or named constant remains in the computer's internal memory

Literal constant—an item of data whose value does not change during run time

Literal type character—a character (such as the letter D) appended to a literal constant for the purpose of forcing the literal constant to assume a different data type (such as Decimal)

Named constant—a computer memory location whose contents cannot be changed during run time; created using the Const statement

Procedure scope—the scope of a procedure-level variable; refers to the fact that the variable can be used only by the procedure in which it is declared

Procedure-level variable—a variable declared in a procedure; the variable has procedure scope

Promoted—the process of converting a value from one data type to another data type that can store either larger numbers or numbers with greater precision

Scope—indicates where a memory location (variable or named constant) can be used in an application's code

Static variable—a procedure-level variable that remains in memory, and also retains its value, until the application (rather than the procedure) ends

TryParse method—used to convert a string to a number of a specified data type

Unicode—the universal coding scheme that assigns a unique numeric value to each character used in the written languages of the world

Variables—computer memory locations where programmers can temporarily store data, as well as change the data, while an application is running

Lesson A Review Questions

1. Which of the following are computer memory locations that can temporarily store information?

    a. literal constants

    b. named constants

    c. variables

    d. both b and c

2. Which of the following is a data item whose value does not change while the application is running?

    a. literal constant

    b. literal variable

    c. named constant

    d. variable

3. If both Option Explicit and Option Strict are off, which data type will the computer assign to the `intAge` variable when processing the statement `Dim intAge`?

    a. Decimal

    b. Integer

    c. Object

    d. String

4. You use the _____ keyword to declare a class-level variable.

    a. `Class`

    b. `Dimension`

    c. `Global`

    d. `Private`

5. Which of the following statements declares a procedure-level variable that retains its value until the application ends?

    a. `Dim Static intScore As Integer`

    b. `Private Static intScore As Integer`

    c. `Static intScore As Integer`

    d. both b and c

6. Which of the following declares a procedure-level String variable?

    a. `Dim String strCity`

    b. `Dim strCity As String`

c. `Private strCity As String`

d. `String strCity`

7. If Option Strict is on, you would use the _____ statement to assign the contents of the txtSales control to a Double variable named `dblSales`.

a. `dblSales = txtSales.Text`

b. `dblSales = txtSales.Text.Convert.ToDouble`

c. `Double.TryParse(txtSales.Text, dblSales)`

d. `TryParse.Double(txtSales.Text, dblSales)`

8. Which of the following declares a named constant having the Double data type?

a. `Const dblRATE As Double = .09`

b. `Const dblRATE As Double`

c. `Constant dblRATE = .09`

d. both a and b

9. If Option Strict is on, you would use the _____ statement to assign the sum of two Integer variables to the Text property of the lblTotal control.

a. `lblTotal.Text = Convert.ToInteger(intN1 + intN2)`

b. `lblTotal.Text = Convert.ToInt32(intN1 + intN2)`

c. `lblTotal.Text = Convert.ToString(intN1) + Convert.ToString(intN2)`

d. none of the above

10. Which of the following statements prevents data loss due to implicit type conversions?

a. `Option Explicit On`

b. `Option Strict On`

c. `Option Implicit Off`

d. `Option Convert Off`

Lesson A Exercises

INTRODUCTORY

1. A procedure needs to store an item's name and price (which may have decimal places). Write the appropriate Dim statements to declare the necessary procedure-level variables.

INTRODUCTORY

2. A procedure needs to store the name of an item in inventory and the item's height and weight. The height may have a decimal place; the

weight will always be a whole number. Write the appropriate Dim statements to declare the necessary procedure-level variables.

3. A procedure needs to store the name of an inventory item, the number of units in stock at the beginning of the current month, the number of units purchased during the current month, the number of units sold during the current month, and the number of units in stock at the end of the current month. The number of units is always a whole number. Write the appropriate Dim statements to declare the necessary procedure-level variables.

INTRODUCTORY

4. Write an assignment statement that assigns Miami to a String variable named `strCity`.

INTRODUCTORY

5. Write an assignment statement that assigns Desk to a String variable named `strItemName`. Also write assignment statements that assign the numbers 40 and 20 to Integer variables named `intQuantityInStock` and `intQuantityOnOrder`, respectively.

INTRODUCTORY

6. Write the statement to declare a procedure-level named constant named decTAX_RATE whose value is .05.

INTRODUCTORY

7. Write the statement to store the contents of the txtUnits control in an Integer variable named `intNumberOfUnits`.

INTRODUCTORY

8. Write the statement to assign the contents of an Integer variable named `intNumberOfUnits` to the lblUnits control.

INTRODUCTORY

9. An application needs to store the part number of an item and its cost (which may contain a decimal place). An example of a part number for this application is A103. Write the appropriate Private statements to declare the necessary class-level variables.

INTRODUCTORY

10. Write an assignment statement that adds together the contents of the `dblNorthSales` and `dblSouthSales` variables and then assigns the sum to the `dblTotalSales` variable.

INTRODUCTORY

11. Write an assignment statement that multiplies the contents of the `decSalary` variable by the number 1.5 and then assigns the result to the `decSalary` variable.

INTERMEDIATE

12. Write the statement to assign the sum of the values stored in the `decWestSales` and `decEastSales` variables to a String variable named `strTotalSales`.

INTERMEDIATE

13. Write the statement to declare a String variable that can be used by two procedures in the same form. Name the variable `strEmployeeName`. Also specify where you will need to enter the statement in the Code Editor window and whether the variable is a procedure-level or class-level variable.

INTERMEDIATE

Discovery

14. In this exercise, you experiment with procedure-level and class-level variables. Open the Scope Solution (Scope Solution.sln) file contained in the VB2010\Chap03\Scope Solution folder. The Scope application allows the user to calculate either a 5% or 10% commission on a sales amount. It displays the sales and commission amounts in the lblSales and lblCommission controls, respectively.

a. Open the Code Editor window and then open the code template for the btnSales control's Click event procedure. Code the procedure so that it declares a variable named dblSales. The procedure also should use an assignment statement to assign the number 500 to the variable. In addition, the procedure should display the contents of the variable in the lblSales control on the form.

b. Save the solution and then start the application. Click the Display Sales button. What does the button's Click event procedure display in the lblSales control? When the Click event procedure ends, what happens to the dblSales variable? Click the Exit button.

c. Open the code template for the btnComm5 control's Click event procedure. In the procedure, enter an assignment statement that multiplies a variable named dblSales by .05, assigning the result to the lblCommission control. When you press the Enter key after typing the assignment statement, a jagged line appears below dblSales in the instruction. The jagged line indicates that there is something wrong with the code. To determine the problem, rest your mouse pointer on the variable name, dblSales. The message in the box indicates that the variable is not declared. In other words, the btnComm5 control's Click event procedure cannot locate the variable's declaration statement, which you previously entered in the btnSales control's Click event procedure. As you learned in Lesson A, only the procedure in which a variable is declared can use the variable. No other procedure is even aware that the variable exists.

d. Now observe what happens when you use the same name to declare a variable in more than one procedure. Insert a blank line above the assignment statement in the btnComm5 control's Click event procedure. In the blank line, type a statement that declares the dblSales variable, and then click the assignment statement to move the insertion point away from the current line. Notice that the jagged line disappears from the assignment statement. Save the solution and then start the application. Click the Display Sales button. The value stored in the dblSales variable declared in the btnSales control's Click event procedure (500) appears in the lblSales control. Click the 5% Commission button. Why does the number 0 appear in the lblCommission control? What happens to the dblSales variable declared in the btnComm5 control's Click event procedure when the procedure ends? Click the Exit button. As this example shows, when you use the same name to declare a variable in more than one procedure, each procedure creates its own procedure-level variable. Although the variables have the same name, each refers to a different location in memory.

e. Next, you use a class-level variable in the application. Click the blank line above the btnExit control's Click event procedure. The Class Name and Method Name boxes show frmMain and (Declarations), respectively. Press Enter to insert a blank line. In the blank line, type a statement that declares a class-level variable named db1Sales.

f. Delete the Dim statement from the btnSales control's Click event procedure. Also delete the Dim statement from the btnComm5 control's Click event procedure.

g. Open the code template for the btnComm10 control's Click event procedure. In the procedure, enter an assignment statement that multiplies the db1Sales variable by .1, assigning the result to the lblCommission control.

h. Save the solution and then start the application. The variable declaration statement in the form's Declarations section creates the db1Sales variable and initializes it to 0. Click the Display Sales button. The button's Click event procedure stores the number 500 in the db1Sales variable and then displays the contents of the variable (500) in the lblSales control. Click the 5% Commission button. The button's Click event procedure multiplies the contents of the db1Sales variable (500) by .05 and then displays the result (25) in the lblCommission control. Click the 10% Commission button. The button's Click event procedure multiplies the contents of the db1Sales variable (500) by .1 and then displays the result (50) in the lblCommission control. As this example shows, any procedure in the form can use a class-level variable. Click the Exit button. What happens to the db1Sales variable when the application ends? Close the Code Editor window and then close the solution.

 ## Swat The Bugs

15. Open the Debug Solution (Debug Solution.sln) file contained in the VB2010\Chap03\Debug Solution-Lesson A folder. The application is supposed to display the number of times the Count button is pressed, but it is not working correctly.

a. Start the application. Click the Count button. The message indicates that you have pressed the Count button once, which is correct. Click the Count button several more times. The message still displays the number 1. Click the Exit button.

b. Open the Code Editor window and study the code. What are two ways that you can use to correct the code? Which way is the preferred way? Modify the code using the preferred way. Save the solution and then start the application. Click the Count button several times. Each time you click the Count button, the message should change to indicate the number of times the button was pressed. Click the Exit button. Close the Code Editor window and then close the solution.

LESSON B

After studying Lesson B, you should be able to:

- Include procedure-level and class-level variables in an application
- Concatenate strings
- Get user input using the InputBox function
- Include the `ControlChars.NewLine` constant in code
- Designate the default button for a form
- Format numbers using the ToString method

Modifying the Playtime Cellular Application

Recall that your task in this chapter is to modify the Playtime Cellular application created in Chapter 2. The modified application will calculate and display a 3% sales tax. It also will display the name of the salesperson who recorded the order. Before making modifications to an application's existing code, you should review the application's documentation and revise the necessary documents. In this case, you need to revise the Playtime Cellular application's TOE chart and also the pseudocode for the Calculate Order button, which is responsible for making the application's calculations. The revised TOE chart is shown in Figure 3-20. Changes made to the original TOE chart, which is shown in Chapter 2's Figure 2-19, are shaded in the figure. (You will view the revised pseudocode for the Calculate Order button later in this lesson.)

Task	Object	Event
1. Calculate total phones ordered and total price	btnCalc	Click
2. Display total phones ordered and total price in lblTotalPhones and lblTotalPrice		
3. Calculate the sales tax		
4. Display the sales tax and salesperson's name in lblMessage		
Clear screen for the next order	btnClear	Click
End the application	btnExit	Click
Display total phones ordered (from btnCalc)	lblTotalPhones	None
Display total price (from btnCalc)	lblTotalPrice	None
Get and display the order information	txtName, txtAddress, txtCity, txtState, txtZip, txtBlue, txtPink	None
Get the salesperson's name	frmMain	Load
Show the sales tax and salesperson's name (from btnCalc)	lblMessage	None

Figure 3-20 Revised TOE chart for the Playtime Cellular application

Notice that the btnCalc control's Click event procedure has two additional tasks to perform: it must calculate the sales tax and also display the sales tax and salesperson's name in the lblMessage control. Two additional objects (frmMain and lblMessage) also are included in the revised TOE chart. The frmMain Load event procedure, which occurs before the form is displayed the first time, is responsible for getting the salesperson's name when the application starts. The lblMessage control will show the sales tax and salesperson's name. As the revised TOE chart indicates, you need to change the code in the btnCalc control's Click event procedure, and you also need to code the form's Load event procedure. The lblMessage control, however, does not need to be coded.

> ●● The Ch03BVideo file demonstrates all of the steps contained in Lesson B. You can view the video either before or after completing the lesson.

153

To open the Playtime Cellular application:

◄ START HERE

1. If necessary, start Visual Studio 2010 or Visual Basic 2010 Express.

2. Open the Playtime Solution (Playtime Solution.sln) file contained in the VB2010\Chap03\Playtime Solution folder. If necessary, open the designer window. Figure 3-21 shows the application's user interface.

Figure 3-21 Playtime Cellular application's user interface

Two modifications were made to the application created in Chapter 2: the lblMessage control was added to the interface and the statement `lblMessage.Text = String.Empty` was added to the btnClear control's Click event procedure. The statement will remove the contents of the lblMessage control when the user clicks the Clear Screen button.

Modifying the Calculate Order Button's Code

Currently, the Calculate Order button uses the Val function and the Text properties of controls to calculate the total phones ordered and total price. In this lesson, you will modify the button's code to use the TryParse method and variables. Because you will be using variables, you will enter the three Option statements in the Code Editor window.

START HERE

To begin modifying the application's code:

1. Open the Code Editor window. Replace <your name> and <current date> with your name and the current date, respectively.

2. Click the **blank line** above the Public Class clause and then press **Enter** to insert another blank line. Enter the following three statements:

   Option Explicit On
   Option Strict On
   Option Infer Off

3. Scroll down the Code Editor window until the entire btnCalc_Click procedure is visible. Notice that jagged blue lines appear below the expressions in the two calculations. The jagged lines indicate that the expressions contain an error.

4. Position your mouse pointer on the first jagged blue line, as shown in Figure 3-22. An explanation of the error appears in a box. The error message says "Option Strict On disallows implicit conversions from 'Double' to 'String'." You received this error message because the assignment statement tells the computer to assign a Double number to the Text property of a control. (As you learned in Lesson A, the Val function returns a Double number.)

```
                                              mouse pointer

Private Sub btnCalc_Click(ByVal sender As Object, ByVal e As Syst
        ' calculates number of phones ordered and total price

    lblTotalPhones.Text = Val(txtBlue.Text) + Val(txtPink.Text)
    lblTotalPrice.Text = V| Option Strict On disallows implicit conversions from 'Double' to 'String'. |
    lblTotalPrice.Text = Format(lblTotalPrice.Text, "Currency")

End Sub
```

Figure 3-22   Jagged blue lines indicate errors in the statements

5. Select the three lines of code and the blank line that appears below them, as shown in Figure 3-23. Press **Delete** to remove the selected lines from the procedure.

```
            Private Sub btnCalc_Click(ByVal sender As Object, ByVal e As Syst
                    ' calculates number of phones ordered and total price

                lblTotalPhones.Text = Val(txtBlue.Text) + Val(txtPink.Text)
                lblTotalPrice.Text = Val(lblTotalPhones.Text) * 25
                lblTotalPrice.Text = Format(lblTotalPrice.Text, "Currency")

            End Sub
```

highlight these lines

Figure 3-23   Lines to delete from the procedure

Figure 3-24 shows the revised pseudocode for the btnCalc control's Click event procedure. Changes made to the original pseudocode, which is shown in Figure 2-28 in Chapter 2, are shaded in the figure. The Click event procedure includes two additional calculations: one for a subtotal and other for the sales tax. The subtotal is computed by multiplying the total number of phones ordered by the phone price. The sales tax is computed by multiplying the subtotal by the sales tax rate. Notice that the total price equation has changed: it now adds the subtotal to the sales tax. Lastly, the Click event procedure displays the sales tax and the salesperson's name in the lblMessage control.

btnCalc Click event procedure
1. calculate total phones ordered = blue phones ordered + pink phones ordered
2. calculate subtotal = total phones ordered * phone price
3. calculate sales tax = subtotal * sales tax rate
4. calculate total price = subtotal + sales tax
5. display total phones ordered and total price in lblTotalPhones and lblTotalPrice
6. display the sales tax and salesperson's name in lblMessage

Figure 3-24   Revised pseudocode for the btnCalc control's Click event procedure

Before you begin coding a procedure, you first study the procedure's pseudocode to determine the variables and named constants (if any) the procedure will use. When determining the named constants, look for items whose value will be the same each time the procedure is invoked. In the btnCalc control's Click event procedure, the phone price and sales tax rate will always be $25 and .03 (the decimal equivalent of 3%), respectively; therefore, you will assign both values to Decimal named constants. At this point, you may be wondering why the phone price is assigned to a Decimal constant rather than to an Integer constant. Although the phone price does not currently contain any decimal places, it is possible that the price may include a decimal place in the future. By using the Decimal data type now, you can change the constant's value to include a decimal place without having to remember to also change its data type.

When determining a procedure's variables, look in the pseudocode for items whose value probably will change each time the procedure is processed. In the btnCalc control's Click event procedure, the numbers of blue and pink phones ordered probably will be different each time the procedure is processed, and so will the total number of phones ordered, subtotal, sales tax, and total price. Therefore, you will assign those values to variables. Integer variables are a good choice for storing the numbers of blue and pink phones and the total phones, because a customer can order only a whole number of phones. You will use Decimal variables to store the subtotal, sales tax, and total price, because these amounts may contain a decimal place. Figure 3-25 lists the names and data types of the two named constants and six variables you will use in the btnCalc control's Click event procedure.

Named constant/Variable	Data type
decPHONE_PRICE	Decimal
decTAX_RATE	Decimal
intBluePhones	Integer
intPinkPhones	Integer
intTotalPhones	Integer
decSubtotal	Decimal
decSalesTax	Decimal
decTotalPrice	Decimal

Figure 3-25 List of named constants and variables

START HERE
To declare the named constants and variables:

1. The insertion point should be located in the blank line above the End Sub clause. If necessary, press **Tab** twice to align the blinking insertion point with the apostrophe in the comment.

2. First, you will declare the named constants. When declaring named constants and variables, be sure to enter the name using the exact capitalization you want. Then, any time you want to refer to the named constant or variable in the code, you can enter its name using any case. The Code Editor will automatically adjust the name to match the case used in the declaration statement. Enter the following declaration statements. (For now, don't be concerned about the green jagged line that appears below each statement after you press Enter.)

   Const decPHONE_PRICE As Decimal = 25D
   Const decTAX_RATE As Decimal = .03D

3. Next, enter the following six variable declaration statements. Press **Enter** twice after typing the last statement.

   Dim intBluePhones As Integer
   Dim intPinkPhones As Integer
   Dim intTotalPhones As Integer
   Dim decSubtotal As Decimal
   Dim decSalesTax As Decimal
   Dim decTotalPrice As Decimal

4. Place your mouse pointer on the green jagged line that appears below the last Dim statement. A box containing a message appears, as shown in Figure 3-26. The message indicates that, although the decTotalPrice variable has been declared, it has not been used yet. In other words, the variable name does not appear in any other statement in the code. The green jagged line will disappear when you include the variable name in another statement in the procedure.

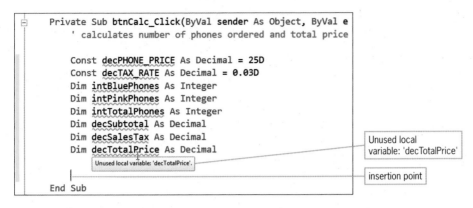

```
Private Sub btnCalc_Click(ByVal sender As Object, ByVal e
    ' calculates number of phones ordered and total price

    Const decPHONE_PRICE As Decimal = 25D
    Const decTAX_RATE As Decimal = 0.03D
    Dim intBluePhones As Integer
    Dim intPinkPhones As Integer
    Dim intTotalPhones As Integer
    Dim decSubtotal As Decimal
    Dim decSalesTax As Decimal
    Dim decTotalPrice As Decimal
        Unused local variable: 'decTotalPrice'.

    |

    End Sub
```

Unused local variable: 'decTotalPrice'

insertion point

Figure 3-26   Const and Dim statements entered in the procedure

After declaring the named constants and variables, you can begin coding each step in the procedure's pseudocode (shown earlier in Figure 3-24). Keep in mind that some steps may require more than one line of code. The first step in the pseudocode is to calculate the total number of phones ordered. The calculation is made by adding the number of blue phones ordered (which is stored in the Text property of the txtBlue control) to the number of pink phones ordered (which is stored in the Text property of the txtPink control). You will use the TryParse method to convert the Text properties of both text boxes to integers, which you will store in the `intBluePhones` and `intPinkPhones` variables. You then will use an assignment statement to add together the contents of both variables, assigning the sum to the `intTotalPhones` variable.

To continue coding the btnCalc control's Click event procedure:

START HERE

1. The insertion point should be positioned as shown earlier in Figure 3-26. Enter the following comment and TryParse methods. When you press Enter after typing each TryParse method, the Code Editor removes the green jagged line that appears below the respective variable's Dim statement.

   ' calculate the total number of phones ordered
   Integer.TryParse(txtBlue.Text, intBluePhones)
   Integer.TryParse(txtPink.Text, intPinkPhones)

2. Next, enter the following assignment statement, which calculates the total number of phones ordered. Press **Enter** twice after typing the assignment statement. (Notice that all of the variables in the assignment statement have the same data type: Integer.)

   intTotalPhones = intBluePhones + intPinkPhones

3. The second step in the pseudocode is to calculate the subtotal by multiplying the total number of phones ordered by the phone price. You will assign the subtotal to the **decSubtotal** variable. Enter the following comment and assignment statement. Press **Enter** twice after typing the assignment statement. When processing the assignment statement, the computer will implicitly convert the integer stored in the `intTotalPhones` variable to Decimal before multiplying it by

157

the decimal number stored in the `decPHONE_PRICE` constant. It then will assign the result to the `decSubtotal` variable.

' calculate the subtotal
decSubtotal = intTotalPhones * decPHONE_PRICE

4. The third step in the pseudocode is to calculate the sales tax by multiplying the subtotal by the sales tax rate. You will assign the sales tax to the `decSalesTax` variable. Enter the following comment and assignment statement. Press **Enter** twice after typing the assignment statement. Notice that the variables and named constant in the assignment statement have the same data type: Decimal.

' calculate the sales tax
decSalesTax = decSubtotal * decTAX_RATE

5. The fourth step in the pseudocode is to calculate the total price by adding together the subtotal and the sales tax. You will assign the result to the `decTotalPrice` variable. Enter the following comment and assignment statement. Press **Enter** twice after typing the assignment statement. Notice that all of the variables in the assignment statement have the same data type: Decimal.

' calculate the total price
decTotalPrice = decSubtotal + decSalesTax

6. Step 5 in the pseudocode is to display the total phones ordered and the total price in the lblTotalPhones and lblTotalPrice controls, respectively. The total number of phones ordered is stored in the `intTotalPhones` variable, and the total price is stored in the `decTotalPrice` variable. Because both variables have a numeric data type, you will need to convert their contents to the String data type before assigning the contents to the label controls. You can use the ToString method of the Convert class to make the conversions. Enter the following comment and assignment statements. Press **Enter** twice after typing the last assignment statement.

' display total amounts
lblTotalPhones.Text = Convert.ToString(intTotalPhones)
lblTotalPrice.Text = Convert.ToString(decTotalPrice)

7. The last step in the pseudocode is to display the sales tax and the salesperson's name in the lblMessage control. For now, you will display only the sales tax. Enter the following comment and assignment statement:

' display tax and salesperson's name
lblMessage.Text = Convert.ToString (decSalesTax)

8. Save the solution. Figure 3-27 shows the code entered in the btnCalc control's Click event procedure.

```
Private Sub btnCalc_Click(ByVal sender As Object,
ByVal e As System.EventArgs) Handles btnCalc.Click
    ' calculates number of phones ordered and total price

    Const decPHONE_PRICE As Decimal = 25D
    Const decTAX_RATE As Decimal = 0.03D
    Dim intBluePhones As Integer
    Dim intPinkPhones As Integer
    Dim intTotalPhones As Integer
    Dim decSubtotal As Decimal
    Dim decSalesTax As Decimal
    Dim decTotalPrice As Decimal

    ' calculate the total number of phones ordered
    Integer.TryParse(txtBlue.Text, intBluePhones)
    Integer.TryParse(txtPink.Text, intPinkPhones)
    intTotalPhones = intBluePhones + intPinkPhones

    ' calculate the subtotal
    decSubtotal = intTotalPhones * decPHONE_PRICE

    ' calculate the sales tax
    decSalesTax = decSubtotal * decTAX_RATE

    ' calculate the total price
    decTotalPrice = decSubtotal + decSalesTax

    ' display total amounts
    lblTotalPhones.Text = Convert.ToString(intTotalPhones)
    lblTotalPrice.Text = Convert.ToString(decTotalPrice)

    ' display tax and salesperson's name
    lblMessage.Text = Convert.ToString(decSalesTax)

End Sub
```

Figure 3-27 Code entered in the btnCalc control's Click event procedure

To start and then test the application:

START HERE

1. Start the application. Enter **10** and **5** as the number of blue and pink phones ordered, respectively. Click the **Calculate Order** button. The total number of phones ordered, total price, and sales tax appear in the interface, as shown in Figure 3-28. However, it's not obvious to the user that the 11.25 is the sales tax. You can fix this problem by displaying the message "The sales tax was" before the sales tax amount. Before you can accomplish this task, you need to learn how to concatenate (link together) strings. String concatenation is covered in the next section.

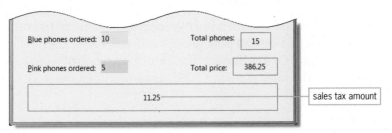

Figure 3-28 Calculated amounts shown in the interface

160

2. Click the **Clear Screen** button to clear the order form, and then click the **Exit** button.

Concatenating Strings

> You also can use the plus sign (+) to concatenate strings. To avoid confusion, however, you should use the plus sign for addition and the ampersand for concatenation.

You use the **concatenation operator**, which is the ampersand (**&**), to concatenate (connect or link together) strings. When concatenating strings, you must be sure to include a space before and after the ampersand; otherwise, the Code Editor will not recognize the ampersand as the concatenation operator. Figure 3-29 shows some examples of string concatenation.

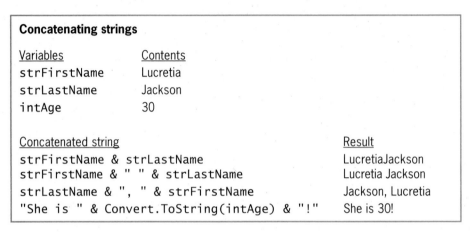

Concatenating strings

Variables	Contents
strFirstName	Lucretia
strLastName	Jackson
intAge	30

Concatenated string	Result
strFirstName & strLastName	LucretiaJackson
strFirstName & " " & strLastName	Lucretia Jackson
strLastName & ", " & strFirstName	Jackson, Lucretia
"She is " & Convert.ToString(intAge) & "!"	She is 30!

Figure 3-29   Examples of string concatenation

You will use the concatenation operator to concatenate the following three strings: "The sales tax was ", the contents of the decSalesTax variable after it has been converted to a string, and "." (a period). Using the examples shown in Figure 3-29 as a guide, the correct assignment statement is lblMessage.Text = "The sales tax was " & Convert.ToString(decSalesTax) & ".".

START HERE **To concatenate the strings and then test the code:**

1. Change the last assignment statement in the procedure as shown in Figure 3-30.

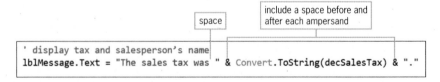

```
                                                        include a space before and
                                          space          after each ampersand
' display tax and salesperson's name
lblMessage.Text = "The sales tax was " & Convert.ToString(decSalesTax) & "."
```

Figure 3-30   String concatenation included in the assignment statement

2. Save the solution and then start the application. Enter **10** and **5** as the number of blue and pink phones ordered, respectively. Click the **Calculate Order** button. The lblMessage control contains the sentence "The sales tax was 11.25.", as shown in Figure 3-31.

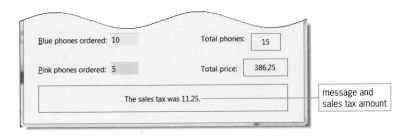

Figure 3-31 Concatenated strings displayed in the lblMessage control

3. Click the **Exit** button.

Recall that you also need to display the salesperson's name in the lblMessage control. You can use the InputBox function to obtain the name from the user.

The InputBox Function

The **InputBox function** displays an input dialog box, which is one of the standard dialog boxes available in Visual Basic. An example of an input dialog box is shown in Figure 3-32. The input dialog box contains a message, an OK button, a Cancel button, and an input area where the user can enter information. The message in the dialog box should prompt the user to enter the appropriate information in the input area. The user closes the dialog box by clicking the OK button, Cancel button, or Close button. The value returned by the InputBox function depends on the button the user chooses. If the user clicks the OK button, the InputBox function returns the value contained in the input area of the dialog box; the return value is always treated as a string. If the user clicks either the Cancel button in the dialog box or the Close button on the dialog box's title bar, the InputBox function returns an empty (or zero-length) string.

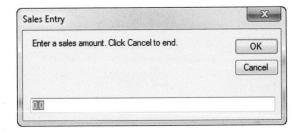

Figure 3-32 Example of an input dialog box

Figure 3-33 shows the basic syntax of the InputBox function. The *prompt* argument contains the message to display inside the dialog box. The optional *title* and *defaultResponse* arguments control the text that appears in the dialog box's title bar and input area, respectively. If you omit the title argument, the project name appears in the title bar. If you omit the defaultResponse argument, a blank input area appears when the dialog box opens. In the input dialog box shown in Figure 3-32, "Enter a sales amount. Click Cancel to end." is the prompt, "Sales Entry" is the title, and "0.0" is the defaultResponse. When entering the InputBox function in the Code Editor window, the prompt, title, and defaultResponse arguments must be enclosed in quotation marks, unless that information is stored in a String named constant or a String variable. The Windows standard is to use sentence capitalization for the prompt, but book title capitalization for the title. The capitalization (if any) you use for the defaultResponse depends on the text itself. In most cases, you assign the value returned by the InputBox function to a String variable, as shown in the first three examples in Figure 3-33.

Using the InputBox function

<u>Syntax</u>
InputBox(prompt[, title][, defaultResponse]**)**

<u>Example 1</u>
```
strSales =
    InputBox("Enter a sales amount. Click Cancel to end.",
    "Sales Entry", "0.0")
```
Displays the input dialog box shown earlier in Figure 3-32. When the user closes the dialog box, the assignment statement assigns the user's response to the strSales variable.

<u>Example 2</u>
```
strState = InputBox("State name:", "State")
```
Displays an input dialog box that shows State name: as the prompt, State in the title bar, and an empty input area. When the user closes the dialog box, the assignment statement assigns the user's response to the strState variable.

<u>Example 3</u>
```
Const strPROMPT As String = "Enter the interest rate:"
Const strTITLE As String = "Interest Rate"
strRate = InputBox(strPROMPT, strTITLE, ".00")
```
Displays an input dialog box that shows the contents of the strPROMPT constant as the prompt, the contents of the strTITLE constant in the title bar, and .00 in the input area. When the user closes the dialog box, the assignment statement assigns the user's response to the strRate variable.

<u>Example 4</u>
```
Integer.TryParse(InputBox("How old are you?",
    "Discount Verification"), intAge)
```
Displays an input dialog box that shows How old are you? as the prompt, Discount Verification in the title bar, and an empty input area. When the user closes the dialog box, the TryParse method converts the user's response from String to Integer and then stores the result in the intAge variable.

The InputBox function's syntax also includes optional *XPos* and *YPos* arguments for specifying the dialog box's horizontal and vertical positions, respectively. If both arguments are omitted, the dialog box appears centered on the screen.

Figure 3-33   Basic syntax and examples of the InputBox function

GUI DESIGN TIP   InputBox Function's Prompt and Title Capitalization

Use sentence capitalization for the prompt, but book title capitalization for the title.

You will use the InputBox function in the Playtime Cellular application to prompt the salesperson to enter his or her name. The InputBox function should be entered in the frmMain Load event procedure because that is the procedure responsible for getting the salesperson's name. Recall that a form's Load event occurs before the form appears on the screen. After the Load event procedure obtains the salesperson's name, you then will have the btnCalc control's Click event procedure concatenate the name to the message displayed in the lblMessage control.

Before entering the InputBox function in the Load event procedure, you must decide where to declare the String variable that will store the function's return value. In other words, should the variable have procedure scope or class scope? When deciding, consider the fact that the form's Load event procedure needs to assign the InputBox function's return value to the variable. The Calculate Order button's Click event procedure also needs to use the variable, because the procedure must concatenate the variable to the message displayed in the lblMessage control. Recall from Lesson A that when two procedures in the same form need to use the same variable, you declare the variable as a class-level variable. You do this by entering the variable declaration statement in the form's Declarations section.

To continue coding the Playtime Cellular application:

◀ START HERE

1. Scroll to the top of the Code Editor window. Click the **blank line** immediately below the `Public Class frmMain` clause. When you do so, frmMain and (Declarations) appear in the Class Name and Method Name boxes, respectively. Press **Enter** to insert a blank line.

2. First, you will declare a class-level String variable named `strSalesPerson`. Enter the comment and declaration statement shown in Figure 3-34.

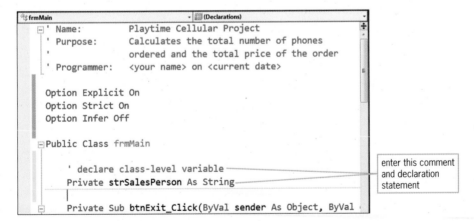

Figure 3-34 Class-level variable declared in the form's Declarations section

3. Now you will enter the InputBox function in the form's Load event procedure, so the function will be processed as soon as the salesperson starts the application. You access the form's procedures by selecting (frmMain Events) in the Class Name list box. Click the **Class Name** list arrow and then click (**frmMain Events**) in the list. Click the

Method Name list arrow to view a list of the form's procedures. Scroll down the list until you see Load, and then click **Load** in the list. The frmMain Load event procedure appears in the Code Editor window.

4. To make the assignment statement that contains the InputBox function shorter and easier to understand, you will create named constants for the function's prompt and title arguments, and then use the named constants (rather than the longer strings) in the function. You are using named constants rather than variables because the prompt and title arguments will not change as the application is running. Enter the comments and code shown in Figure 3-35.

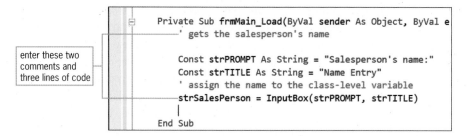

enter these two comments and three lines of code

```
Private Sub frmMain_Load(ByVal sender As Object, ByVal e
    ' gets the salesperson's name

    Const strPROMPT As String = "Salesperson's name:"
    Const strTITLE As String = "Name Entry"
    ' assign the name to the class-level variable
    strSalesPerson = InputBox(strPROMPT, strTITLE)

End Sub
```

Figure 3-35 frmMain Load event procedure

5. Next, you will concatenate the **strSalesPerson** variable to the message assigned to the lblMessage control. Locate the btnCalc control's Click event procedure. Click at the **end of the last assignment statement** in the procedure. Press the **Spacebar** and then type **& strSalesPerson**. This changes the assignment statement to **lblMessage.Text = "The sales tax was " & Convert. ToString(decSalesTax) & "." & strSalesPerson**.

6. Save the solution and then start the application. The Name Entry dialog box created by the InputBox function appears first. See Figure 3-36.

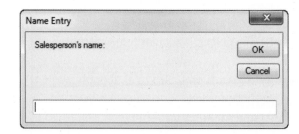

Figure 3-36 Dialog box created by the InputBox function

7. Type your name in the input area of the dialog box and then click the **OK** button. The order form appears. Type **10** in the Blue phones ordered box and then click the **Calculate Order** button. Notice that your name appears much too close to the period in the lblMessage control. You can correct the spacing problem in the lblMessage control by replacing the period (".") in the assignment statement with a period and two spaces (". "). Or, you can use the ControlChars.New-Line constant to display the salesperson's name on the next line in the lblMessage control. Click the **Exit** button.

The ControlChars.NewLine Constant

The **ControlChars.NewLine constant** instructs the computer to advance the insertion point to the next line in a control. (You also can use it to advance the insertion point in a file or on the printer.) Whenever you want to start a new line, you simply type the ControlChars.NewLine constant at the appropriate location in your code. In this case, you want to advance to a new line after displaying the period—in other words, before displaying the salesperson's name. The appropriate assignment statement is `lblMessage.Text = "The sales tax was " & Convert.ToString(decSalesTax) & "." & ControlChars.NewLine & strSalesPerson`. The assignment statement is rather long and, depending on the size of the font used in the Code Editor window, you may not be able to view the entire statement without scrolling the window. You can break a line of code into two or more physical lines in the Code Editor window, as long as you break the line either before a closing parenthesis or after one of the following: a comma, an opening parenthesis, or an operator (arithmetic, assignment, comparison, logical, or concatenation). If you want to break a line of code anywhere else, you will need to use the **line continuation character**, which is an underscore (_) that is immediately preceded by a space. If you use the line continuation character, it must appear at the end of a physical line of code.

 The `Control Chars. NewLine` constant is an intrinsic constant, which is a named constant built into Visual Basic.

To display the salesperson's name on a separate line in the lblMessage control:

◄ START HERE

1. In the btnCalc control's Click event procedure, modify the last assignment statement as indicated in Figure 3-37.

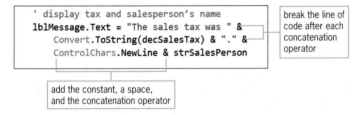

Figure 3-37   Modified assignment statement

2. Save the solution and then start the application. The Name Entry dialog box created by the InputBox function appears first. See Figure 3-38. Notice that the OK button in the dialog box has a darkened border, even though it does not have the focus. The input area in the dialog box has the focus, as indicated by the position of the insertion point. In Windows terminology, a button that has a highlighted border when it does not have the focus is called the default button. You can select a default button by pressing Enter at any time.

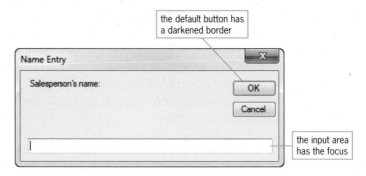

the default button has
a darkened border

the input area
has the focus

Figure 3-38   Name Entry input dialog box

3. Type **Mary Jones** in the input area of the dialog box. Then, instead of clicking the OK button, simply press **Enter**. The order form appears.

4. Type **5** in the Blue phones ordered box and then click the **Calculate Order** button. The salesperson's name now appears on a separate line in the lblMessage control, as shown in Figure 3-39. Click the **Exit** button.

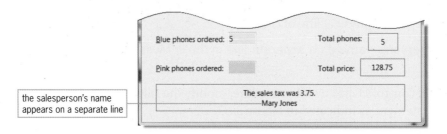

the salesperson's name
appears on a separate line

Figure 3-39   Salesperson's name shown on the order form

Designating a Default Button

A form's CancelButton property specifies the button whose Click event procedure is processed when the user presses the Esc key. A form can have only one cancel button. You can experiment with the Cancel property by completing Discovery Exercise 10 at the end of this lesson.

As you already know from using Windows applications, you can select a button by clicking it or by pressing the Enter key when the button has the focus. If you make a button the **default button**, you also can select it by pressing the Enter key even when the button does not have the focus. When a button is selected, the computer processes the code contained in the button's Click event procedure. An interface does not have to have a default button. However, if one is used, it should be the button that is most often selected by the user, except in cases where the tasks performed by the button are both destructive and irreversible. For example, a button that deletes information should not be designated as the default button. If you assign a default button in an interface, it typically is the first button, which means that it is on the left when the buttons are positioned horizontally on the form, but on the top when the buttons are stacked vertically. A form can have only one default button. You specify the default button (if any) by setting the form's AcceptButton property to the name of the button.

GUI DESIGN TIP Assigning a Default Button

The default button should be the button that is most often selected by the user, except in cases where the tasks performed by the button are both destructive and irreversible. In most interfaces, the default button is the first button.

To make the Calculate Order button the default button:

START HERE

1. Click the **Main Form.vb [Design]** tab to return to the designer window. Set the form's AcceptButton property to **btnCalc**. A darkened border appears around the Calculate Order button.

2. Save the solution and then start the application. Type your name in the Name Entry dialog box and then press **Enter**. The order form appears.

3. Type **5** in the Blue phones ordered box and then press **Enter** to select the Calculate Order button. The numbers 5 and 128.75 appear in the Total phones and Total price boxes, respectively. In addition, the message "The sales tax was 3.75." and your name appear in the lblMessage control. Click the **Exit** button.

Finally, you will modify the btnCalc control's Click event procedure so that it displays a dollar sign and comma (if appropriate) in the total price amount.

Using the ToString Method to Format Numbers

Numbers representing monetary amounts are usually displayed with either zero or two decimal places and may include a dollar sign and a thousands separator. Similarly, numbers representing percentage amounts are usually displayed with zero or more decimal places and a percent sign. Specifying the number of decimal places and the special characters to display in a number is called **formatting**. In Chapter 2, you learned how to use the Format function to format a number for output as a string. Although you can still use the Format function in Visual Basic 2010, many programmers now use the ToString method because the method can be used in any of the languages built into Visual Studio. The ToString method's syntax is *numericVariableName.* **ToString(***formatString***)**. In the syntax, *numericVariableName* is the name of a numeric variable. The **ToString method** formats the number stored in the numeric variable and then returns the result as a string. The *formatString* argument in the syntax specifies the format you want to use. The *formatString* argument must take the form "*Axx*", where *A* is an alphabetic character called the format specifier, and *xx* is a sequence of digits called the precision specifier. The format specifier must be one of the built-in format characters. The most commonly used format characters are listed in Figure 3-40. Notice that you can use either an uppercase letter or a lowercase letter as the format specifier. When used with one of the format characters listed in Figure 3-40, the precision specifier controls the number of digits that will appear after the decimal point in the formatted number. Also included in Figure 3-40 are examples of using the ToString method.

Using the ToString method to format a number

Syntax
numericVariableName.**ToString**(*formatString*)

Format specifier (Name)	Description
C or c (Currency)	displays the string with a dollar sign; includes a thousands separator (if appropriate); negative values are enclosed in parentheses
N or n (Number)	similar to the Currency format, but does not include a dollar sign and negative values are preceded by a minus sign
F or f (Fixed-point)	same as the Number format, but does not include a thousands separator
P or p (Percent)	multiplies the value by 100 and displays the result with a percent sign; negative values are preceded by a minus sign

Example 1
```
Dim intCommission As Integer = 1250
lblCommission.Text = intCommission.ToString("C2")
```
assigns the string "$1,250.00" to the lblCommission control's Text property

Example 2
```
Dim decTotal As Decimal = 123.675D
lblTotal.Text = decTotal.ToString("N2")
```
assigns the string "123.68" to the lblTotal control's Text property

Example 3
```
Dim dblRate As Double = .06
lblRate.Text = dblRate.ToString("P0")
```
assigns the string "6 %" to the lblRate control's Text property

Figure 3-40   Syntax and examples of the ToString method

In the Playtime Cellular application, you will format the total price to include a dollar sign, a thousands separator, and two decimal places.

START HERE

To format the total price:

1. Click the **Main Form.vb** tab to return to the Code Editor window. In the btnCalc control's Click event procedure, change the `lblTotalPrice.Text = Convert.ToString(decTotalPrice)` statement as follows:

   lblTotalPrice.Text = decTotalPrice.ToString("C2")

2. Save the solution and then start the application. Type **Perry Hormel** in the input area of the dialog box and then press **Enter**. The order form appears.

3. Type **15** in the Blue phones ordered box, type **25** in the Pink phones ordered box, and then press **Enter** to calculate the order. The total price appears with a dollar sign, a thousands separator, and two decimal places. See Figure 3-41.

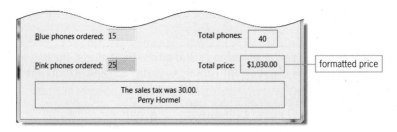

Figure 3-41   Formatted price shown on the order form

4. Click the **Exit** button. Close the Code Editor window and then close the solution.

Figure 3-42 shows the application's code at the end of Lesson B.

```
1  ' Name:          Playtime Cellular Project
2  ' Purpose:       Calculates the total number of phones
3  '                ordered and the total price of the order
4  ' Programmer:    <your name> on <current date>
5
6  Option Explicit On
7  Option Strict On
8  Option Infer Off
9
10 Public Class frmMain
11
12    ' declare class-level variable
13    Private strSalesPerson As String
14
15    Private Sub btnExit_Click(ByVal sender As Object,
      ByVal e As System.EventArgs) Handles btnExit.Click
16       Me.Close()
17    End Sub
18
19    Private Sub btnClear_Click(ByVal sender As Object,
      ByVal e As System.EventArgs) Handles btnClear.Click
20       ' prepare the screen for the next order
21
22    txtName.Text = String.Empty
23    txtAddress.Text = String.Empty
24    txtCity.Text = String.Empty
25    txtState.Text = String.Empty
26    txtZip.Text = String.Empty
27    txtBlue.Text = String.Empty
28    txtPink.Text = String.Empty
29    lblTotalPhones.Text = String.Empty
30    lblTotalPrice.Text = String.Empty
```

Figure 3-42   Playtime Cellular application's code at the end of Lesson B (*continues*)

170

(continued)

```
31          lblMessage.Text = String.Empty
32          ' send the focus to the Name text box
33          txtName.Focus()
34
35      End Sub
36
37      Private Sub btnCalc_Click(ByVal sender As Object,
        ByVal e As System.EventArgs) Handles btnCalc.Click
38          ' calculates number of phones ordered and total price
39
40          Const decPHONE_PRICE As Decimal = 25D
41          Const decTAX_RATE As Decimal = 0.03D
42          Dim intBluePhones As Integer
43          Dim intPinkPhones As Integer
44          Dim intTotalPhones As Integer
45          Dim decSubtotal As Decimal
46          Dim decSalesTax As Decimal
47          Dim decTotalPrice As Decimal
48
49          ' calculate the total number of phones ordered
50          Integer.TryParse(txtBlue.Text, intBluePhones)
51          Integer.TryParse(txtPink.Text, intPinkPhones)
52          intTotalPhones = intBluePhones + intPinkPhones
53
54          ' calculate the subtotal
55          decSubtotal = intTotalPhones * decPHONE_PRICE
56
57          ' calculate the sales tax
58          decSalesTax = decSubtotal * decTAX_RATE
59
60          ' calculate the total price
61          decTotalPrice = decSubtotal + decSalesTax
62
63          ' display total amounts
64          lblTotalPhones.Text = Convert.ToString(intTotalPhones)
65          lblTotalPrice.Text = decTotalPrice.ToString("C2")
66
67          ' display tax and salesperson's name
68          lblMessage.Text = "The sales tax was " &
69              Convert.ToString(decSalesTax) & "." &
70              ControlChars.NewLine & strSalesPerson
71
72      End Sub
73
74      Private Sub frmMain_Load(ByVal sender As Object,
        ByVal e As System.EventArgs) Handles Me.Load
75          ' gets the salesperson's name
76
77          Const strPROMPT As String = "Salesperson's name:"
78          Const strTITLE As String = "Name Entry"
79          ' assign the name to the class-level variable
80          strSalesPerson = InputBox(strPROMPT, strTITLE)
81
82      End Sub
83 End Class
```

Figure 3-42   Playtime Cellular application's code at the end of Lesson B

Lesson B Summary

- To concatenate strings:

    Use the concatenation operator (&). Be sure to include a space before and after the ampersand.

- To display an input dialog box:

    Use the InputBox function. The function's syntax is **InputBox(**_prompt_ **[,** _title_**][,** _defaultResponse_**])**. The _prompt_, _title_, and _defaultResponse_ arguments must be enclosed in quotation marks, unless the information is stored in a String named constant or a String variable. Use sentence capitalization for the prompt, but book title capitalization for the title.

    If the user clicks the OK button, the InputBox function returns the value contained in the input area of the dialog box. The return value is always treated as a string. If the user clicks either the Cancel button in the dialog box or the Close button on the dialog box's title bar, the InputBox function returns an empty string.

- To advance the insertion point to the next line:

    Use the `ControlChars.NewLine` constant in code.

- To break up a long instruction into two or more physical lines in the Code Editor window:

    Break the line after a comma, after an opening parenthesis, before a closing parenthesis, or after an operator (arithmetic, assignment, comparison, logical, or concatenation). You also can use the line continuation character, which is an underscore (_). The line continuation character must be immediately preceded by a space and appear at the end of a physical line of code.

- To make a button the default button:

    Set the form's AcceptButton property to the name of the button.

- To format a number for output as a string:

    Use the ToString method. The method's syntax is _numericVariableName_.**ToString(**_formatString_**)**.

Lesson B Key Terms

&—the concatenation operator

Concatenation operator—the ampersand (&); used to concatenate strings; must be both preceded and followed by a space character

ControlChars.NewLine constant—used to advance the insertion point to the next line

Default button—a button that can be selected by pressing the Enter key even when the button does not have the focus

Formatting—specifying the number of decimal places and the special characters to display in a number

InputBox function—a Visual Basic function that displays an input dialog box containing a message, OK and Cancel buttons, and an input area

Line continuation character—an underscore that is immediately preceded by a space and located at the end of a physical line of code; used to split a long instruction into two or more physical lines in the Code Editor window

ToString method—formats a number stored in a numeric variable and then returns the result as a string

Lesson B Review Questions

1. The InputBox function displays a dialog box containing which of the following?

   a. input area

   b. OK and Cancel buttons

   c. prompt

   d. all of the above

2. Which of the following is the concatenation operator?

   a. @

   b. &

   c. $

   d. #

3. The `strRegion1` and `strRegion2` variables contain the strings "North" and "West", respectively. Which of the following will display the string "NorthWest" (one word) in the lblRegion control?

   a. `lblRegion.Text = strRegion1 & strRegion2`

   b. `lblRegion.Text = "strRegion1" & "strRegion2"`

   c. `lblRegion.Text = strRegion1 @ strRegion2`

   d. `lblRegion.Text = strRegion1 # strRegion2`

4. The `strCity` and `strState` variables contain the strings "Boston" and "MA", respectively. Which of the following will display the string "Boston, MA" (the city, a comma, a space, and the state) in the lblAddress control?

   a. `lblAddress.Text = strCity , & strState`

   b. `lblAddress.Text = "strCity" & "," & "strState"`

   c. `lblAddress.Text = strCity & ", " & strState`

   d. none of the above

5. Which of the following Visual Basic constants advances the insertion point to the next line?

   a. `Advance`

   b. `ControlChars.Advance`

   c. `ControlChars.NewLine`

   d. `ControlChars.NextLine`

6. Which property of a form designates the form's default button?

   a. AcceptButton

   b. DefaultButton

   c. EnterButton

   d. FocusButton

7. Which of the following statements correctly assigns the InputBox function's return value to a Double variable named `dblNum`?

   a. `Double.TryParse(InputBox(strMSG,`
      `      "Number"), dblNum)`

   b. `dblNum = Double.TryParse(`
      `      InputBox(strMSG, "Number"))`

   c. `dblNum = InputBox(strMSG, "Number")`

   d. `TryParse.Double(InputBox(strMSG,`
      `      "Number"), dblNum)`

8. Which of the following statements correctly assigns the InputBox function's return value to a String variable named `strCity`?

   a. `String.TryParse(InputBox(strMSG,`
      `      "City"), strCity)`

   b. `strCity = String.TryParse(`
      `      InputBox(strMSG, "City"))`

   c. `strCity = InputBox(strMSG, "City")`

   d. none of the above

9. The InputBox function's prompt argument should be entered using _____.

   a. book title capitalization

   b. sentence capitalization

10. If the **decSales** variable contains the number 12345.89, which of the following statements displays the number as 12,345.89?

    a. `lblSales.Text = decSales.ToString("C2")`

    b. `lblSales.Text = decSales.ToString("N2")`

    c. `lblSales.Text = decSales.ToString("D2")`

    d. `lblSales.Text = decSales.ToString("F2")`

Lesson B Exercises

INTRODUCTORY

1. The **strCity** and **strState** variables contain the strings "Madison" and "WI", respectively. Write an assignment statement to display the string "Madison, WI" in the lblAddress control.

INTRODUCTORY

2. The **strZip** variable contains the string "53711". Write an assignment statement to display the string "My ZIP code is 53711." in the lblMsg control.

INTRODUCTORY

3. In this exercise, you modify the Playtime Cellular application from this lesson. Use Windows to make a copy of the Playtime Solution folder. Rename the copy Modified Playtime Solution. Open the Playtime Solution (Playtime Solution.sln) file contained in the Modified Playtime Solution folder. Open the designer window. Modify the btnCalc control's Click event procedure so that it displays the sales tax amount with a dollar sign, two decimal places, and a thousands separator (if necessary). Save the solution and then start and test the application. Close the Code Editor window and then close the solution.

INTRODUCTORY

4. Open the Commission Solution (Commission Solution.sln) file contained in the VB2010\Chap03\Commission Solution folder. If necessary, open the designer window. The application calculates and displays a salesperson's commission, using a commission rate of 10%. Make the Calculate Commission button the default button. Open the Code Editor window and review the code in the Calculate Commission button's Click event procedure. Modify the procedure's code to use variables. (Do not use the Val function.) Use a named constant for the commission rate. Be sure to enter the **Option Explicit On**, **Option Strict On**, and **Option Infer Off** statements in the General Declarations section. Use the ToString method to display the commission amount with a dollar sign, two decimal places, and a thousands separator (if necessary). Save the solution and then start the application. Test the application by calculating the commission for sales of 7500. The commission should be $750.00. Close the Code Editor window and then close the solution.

INTERMEDIATE

5. The **strCity** and **strState** variables contain the strings "Madison" and "WI", respectively. Write an assignment statement to display the string "The capital of WI is Madison." in the lblMsg control.

6. Open the Mingo Solution (Mingo Solution.sln) file contained in the VB2010\Chap03\Mingo Solution folder. If necessary, open the designer window. The application allows the sales manager to enter the sales made in three states. It then calculates and displays both the total sales made and the total commission earned in the three states.

   a. Make the Calculate button the default button.

   b. Enter the appropriate Option statements in the Code Editor window.

   c. Code the Exit button so that it ends the application when it is clicked.

   d. Use the pseudocode shown in Figure 3-43 to code the Calculate button's Click event procedure. Be sure to use variables. (Do not use the Val function.) The commission rate is 5%. Use the ToString method to display a thousands separator (if necessary) and two decimal places in the total sales and commission amounts.

   e. Save the solution and then start the application. Test the application by calculating the total sales and commission for the following amounts: New York sales of 15000, Maine sales of 25000, and Florida sales of 10500.

   f. Close the Code Editor window and then close the solution.

   ---
   btnCalc Click event procedure
   1. calculate total sales = New York sales + Maine sales + Florida sales
   2. calculate commission = total sales * commission rate
   3. display total sales and commission in lblTotalSales and lblCommission
   4. send the focus to the txtNewYork control

Figure 3-43   Pseudocode for Exercise 6

7. In this exercise, you modify the Mingo Sales application from Exercise 6. Use Windows to make a copy of the Mingo Solution folder. Rename the copy Modified Mingo Solution. Open the Mingo Solution (Mingo Solution.sln) file contained in the Modified Mingo Solution folder. Open the designer window. Code the form's Load event procedure so that it uses the InputBox function to ask the user for the commission rate before the form appears. Modify the code in the btnCalc control's Click event procedure so that it uses the commission rate entered by the user. Save the solution and then start the application. When you are prompted to enter the commission rate, type .1 (the decimal equivalent of 10%) and then click the OK button. Test the application using 26000 as the New York sales, 34000 as the Maine sales, and 17000 as the Florida sales. Close the Code Editor window and then close the solution.

8. Open the IMY Solution (IMY Solution.sln) file contained in the VB2010\Chap03\IMY Solution folder. If necessary, open the designer window. The application calculates the new hourly pay for each of

three job codes, given the current hourly pay for each job code and the raise percentage (entered as a decimal number). The application should display the message "Raise percentage: *XX* %" in a label control on the form. The *XX* in the message should be replaced by the actual raise percentage.

a. Code the Exit button so that it ends the application when it is clicked.

b. Before the form appears, use the InputBox function to prompt the personnel clerk to enter the raise percentage. You will use the raise percentage to calculate the new hourly pay for each job code.

c. Use the pseudocode shown in Figure 3-44 to code the Calculate button's Click event procedure. Create a named constant for the "Raise percentage:" message. Format the new hourly pays using the "N2" *formatString*. Format the raise rate (in the message) using the "P0" *formatString*.

d. Save the solution and then start the application. When you are prompted to enter the raise percentage, type .05 (the decimal equivalent of 5%) and then click the OK button. Use the following information to calculate the new hourly pay for each job code:

Current hourly pay for job code 1:   5
Current hourly pay for job code 2:   6.5
Current hourly pay for job code 3:   8.75

e. Close the Code Editor window and then close the solution.

---

btnCalc Click event procedure
1. calculate each new hourly pay = current hourly pay * raise rate + current hourly pay
2. display the new hourly pays in the appropriate label controls
3. display the message and raise rate in the lblMessage control
4. send the focus to the txtCode1 control

Figure 3-44 Pseudocode for Exercise 8

ADVANCED

9. In this exercise, you modify the IMY Industries application from Exercise 8. The modified application will allow the user to enter a separate raise percentage for each job code. Use Windows to make a copy of the IMY Solution folder. Rename the copy Modified IMY Solution. Open the IMY Solution (IMY Solution.sln) file contained in the Modified IMY Solution folder. Open the designer window.

a. Modify the application's code so that it asks the personnel clerk to enter the raise for each job code separately. Display the following information on separate lines in the lblMessage control. Be sure to replace the *XX* in each line with the appropriate raise percentage. (You will need to change the size of the form and lblMessage control.)

Job Code 1:   XX %
Job Code 2:   XX %
Job Code 3:   XX %

b. Save the solution and then start the application. When you are prompted to enter the raise percentages for the job codes, use .03 for job code 1, .05 for job code 2, and .04 for job code 3. Use the following information to calculate the new hourly pay for each job code:

Current hourly pay for job code 1:   5
Current hourly pay for job code 2:   6.5
Current hourly pay for job code 3:   8.75

c. Close the Code Editor window and then close the solution.

Discovery

10. In this exercise, you learn about the CancelButton property of a Windows form. Open the Cancel Solution (Cancel Solution.sln) file contained in the VB2010\Chap03\Cancel Solution folder. If necessary, open the designer window.

a. Open the Code Editor window and review the existing code. Start the application. Type your first name in the text box and then press Enter to select the Clear button, which is the form's default button. The Clear button removes your name from the text box. Click the Undo button. Your name reappears in the text box. Click the Exit button.

b. Return to the designer window. Set the form's CancelButton property to btnUndo. Doing this tells the computer to process the code in the Undo button's Click event procedure when the user presses the Esc key. Save the solution and then start the application. Type your first name in the text box and then press Enter to select the Clear button. Press Esc to select the Undo button. Your name reappears in the text box. Close the Code Editor window and then close the solution.

LESSON C

After studying Lesson C, you should be able to:

- Include a static variable in code
- Code the TextChanged event procedure
- Create a procedure that handles more than one event

Modifying the Load and Click Event Procedures

Currently, the Playtime Cellular application allows the user to enter the salesperson's name only when the application first starts. In this lesson you will modify the application's code so that it asks for the salesperson's name before each order is calculated. By doing this, another salesperson will be able to use the same computer to take an order without having to start the application again. As you learned in Lesson B, you should review an application's documentation and revise the necessary documents before making modifications to the code. Figure 3-45 shows the revised TOE chart. Changes made to the TOE chart from Lesson B are shaded in the figure. (Lesson B's TOE chart is shown in Figure 3-20.) Notice that the Calculate Order button's Click event procedure, rather than the frmMain Load event procedure, is responsible for getting the salesperson's name.

Task	Object	Event
1. Get the salesperson's name 2. Calculate total phones ordered and total price 3. Display total phones ordered and total price in lblTotalPhones and lblTotalPrice 4. Calculate the sales tax 5. Display the sales tax and salesperson's name in lblMessage	btnCalc	Click
Clear screen for the next order	btnClear	Click
End the application	btnExit	Click
Display total phones ordered (from btnCalc)	lblTotalPhones	None
Display total price (from btnCalc)	lblTotalPrice	None
Get and display the order information	txtName, txtAddress, txtCity, txtState, txtZip, txtBlue, txtPink	None
Get the salesperson's name	frmMain	Load
Show the sales tax and salesperson's name (from btnCalc)	lblMessage	None

Figure 3-45 Revised TOE chart

Figure 3-46 shows the revised pseudocode for the Calculate Order button's Click event procedure. Changes made to the pseudocode from Lesson B are shaded in the figure. (Lesson B's pseudocode is shown in Figure 3-24.)

```
btnCalc Click event procedure
1.  get the salesperson's name
2.  calculate total phones ordered = blue phones ordered + pink phones ordered
3.  calculate subtotal = total phones ordered * phone price
4.  calculate sales tax = subtotal * sales tax rate
5.  calculate total price = subtotal + sales tax
6.  display total phones ordered and total price in lblTotalPhones and lblTotalPrice
7.  display the sales tax and salesperson's name in lblMessage
```

Figure 3-46   Revised pseudocode for the Calculate Order button

The Ch03CVideo file demonstrates all of the steps contained in Lesson C. You can view the video either before or after completing the lesson.

First, you will open the Playtime Cellular application from Lesson B. You then will move the code contained in the frmMain Load event procedure to the btnCalc control's Click event procedure.

To open the Playtime Cellular application and then move some of the code:

START HERE

1. If necessary, start Visual Studio 2010 or Visual Basic 2010 Express.

2. Open the Playtime Solution (Playtime Solution.sln) file from Lesson B. The file is contained in the VB2010\Chap03\Playtime Solution folder. If necessary, open the designer window.

3. Open the Code Editor window. Locate the frmMain Load event procedure, and then highlight the two Const statements in the procedure. Press **Ctrl+x** to cut the two Const statements from the procedure.

4. Locate the btnCalc control's Click event procedure. Click the **blank line** above the first Const statement in the procedure, and then press **Enter** to insert a new blank line. With the insertion point in the new blank line, press **Ctrl+v**. The two Const statements that you cut from the Load event procedure now appear in the Click event procedure.

5. Return to the frmMain Load event procedure. Highlight the second comment and the assignment statement. Press **Ctrl+x** to remove the comment and the assignment statement from the procedure.

6. Return to the btnCalc control's Click event procedure. Click the **blank line** below the last Dim statement, and then press **Enter** to insert a new blank line. With the insertion point in the new blank line, press **Ctrl+v**. The comment and assignment statement that you cut from the Load event procedure now appear in the Click event procedure. Press **Enter** to insert a new blank line below the assignment statement, and then delete the `class-level` text from the comment.

7. Return to the frmMain Load event procedure and then delete the entire procedure from the Code Editor window.

Now that you have moved the InputBox function from the frmMain Load event procedure to the btnCalc control's Click event procedure, only one procedure—the btnCalc control's Click event procedure—needs to use the `strSalesPerson` variable. Therefore, you can move the statement that declares the variable from the form's Declarations section to the btnCalc control's Click event procedure. In addition, you will need to change the keyword in the declaration statement from `Private` to `Dim`. Recall that you use the `Private` keyword to declare class-level variables, but you use the `Dim` keyword to declare procedure-level variables.

START HERE

To move the declaration statement and then modify it:

1. Delete the `' declare class-level variable` comment from the form's Declarations section. Highlight the `Private strSalesPerson As String` statement, and then press **Ctrl+x** to cut the statement from the Declarations section.

2. Click the **blank line** below the last Dim statement in the btnCalc control's Click event procedure. Press **Ctrl+v** to paste the Private statement in the procedure, and then press **Enter** to insert a blank line below the statement.

3. The blue jagged line that appears below the `Private` keyword indicates that there is something wrong with the statement. You can determine the problem by resting your mouse pointer somewhere on the word (or words) immediately above the jagged line. Rest your mouse pointer on the `Private` keyword. The error message indicates that the `Private` keyword is not valid on a local variable declaration. Change `Private` in the variable declaration statement to **Dim**.

4. Save the solution and then start the application. Click the **Calculate Order** button on the order form. Type your name in the Name Entry dialog box and then press **Enter**. The message "The sales tax was 0.00." and your name appear in the lblMessage control.

5. Click the **Calculate Order** button again. Notice that the Name Entry dialog box requires the user to enter the salesperson's name again. It would be more efficient for the user if the salesperson's name appeared as the default response the second and subsequent times the Calculate Order button is clicked.

6. Click the **Cancel** button in the dialog box. No name appears in the lblMessage control; this is because the InputBox function returns an empty string when you click the Cancel button in the dialog box. Click the **Exit** button.

To display the salesperson's name in the dialog box when the Calculate Order button is clicked the second and subsequent times, you can declare the `strSalesPerson` variable as either a class-level variable or a static variable, and then use the variable as the *defaultResponse* argument in the InputBox function. In this case, a static variable is a better choice, because static variables have a lesser scope than class-level variables. Recall that a static variable is really just a special type of procedure-level variable. As you learned in Lesson A, fewer unintentional errors occur in applications when variables are declared using the minimum scope needed. In this case, for example, only the btnCalc control's Click event procedure needs to use the `strSalesPerson` variable, so a variable with procedure scope is a much better choice than one with class scope.

To declare the strSalesPerson variable as a static variable and then modify the InputBox function:

START HERE

1. Change the `Dim` in the `Dim strSalesPerson As String` statement in the btnCalc control's Click event procedure to **Static**.

2. Now change the statement that contains the InputBox function as follows, and then click the **blank line** below the statement:

    strSalesPerson = InputBox(strPROMPT, strTITLE, strSalesPerson)

3. Save the solution and then start the application. Type **5** in the Blue phones ordered box, type **10** in the Pink phones ordered box, and then press **Enter**. Type your name in the Name Entry dialog box and then press **Enter**. The application calculates and displays the total phones ordered (15) and total price ($386.25). In addition, the message "The sales tax was 11.25." and your name appear in the lblMessage control.

4. Change the number of blue phones ordered to **20**. At this point, the calculated amounts on the order form are incorrect, because they do not reflect the change in the order of blue phones. To display the correct amounts, you will need to recalculate the order by selecting the Calculate Order button. Press **Enter** to select the Calculate Order button. Your name appears highlighted in the input area of the Name Entry dialog box.

5. Press **Enter** to select the OK button in the dialog box. The application calculates and displays the total phones ordered (30) and total price ($772.50). The message "The sales tax was 22.50." and your name appear in the lblMessage control. Click the **Exit** button.

Having the previously calculated amounts remain on the screen when a change is made to the interface could be misleading. A better approach is to clear the amounts when a change is made to either the number of blue phones ordered or the number of pink phones ordered.

Coding the TextChanged Event Procedure

A control's **TextChanged event** occurs when a change is made to the contents of the control's Text property. This can happen as a result of either the user entering data into the control or the application's code assigning data to the control's Text property. In the next set of steps, you will code the txtBlue control's TextChanged event procedure so that it clears the contents of the lblTotalPhones, lblTotalPrice, and lblMessage controls when the user changes the number of blue phones ordered.

To code the txtBlue control's TextChanged event procedure:

START HERE

1. Open the code template for the txtBlue control's TextChanged event procedure. Type the following comment and then press **Enter** twice:

    ' clears the total phones, total price, and message

2. Enter the following three assignment statements:

    lblTotalPhones.Text = String.Empty
    lblTotalPrice.Text = String.Empty
    lblMessage.Text = String.Empty

3. Save the solution and then start the application. Type **5** in the Blue phones ordered box and then press **Enter**.

4. Type your name in the Name Entry dialog box and then press **Enter**. The application calculates and displays the total phones ordered (5), total price ($128.75), and sales tax (3.75).

5. Change the number of blue phones ordered to **3**. When you make a change to the number of blue phones ordered, the txtBlue control's TextChanged event procedure clears the total phones ordered, total price, and message information from the form. Click the **Exit** button.

Recall that you also want to clear the calculated amounts when a change is made to the number of pink phones ordered. You could code the TextChanged event procedure for the txtPink control separately, as you did with the txtBlue control. However, an easier way is simply to create one procedure for the computer to process when the TextChanged event of either of the two controls occurs.

Associating a Procedure with Different Objects and Events

The Handles clause in an event procedure's header indicates the object and event associated with the procedure. The `Handles txtBlue.TextChanged` clause in Figure 3-47, for example, indicates that the txtBlue_TextChanged procedure is associated with the TextChanged event of the txtBlue control. As a result, the procedure will be processed when the txtBlue control's TextChanged event occurs.

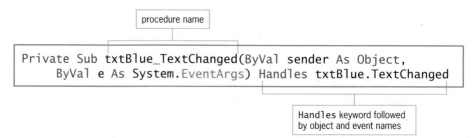

```
procedure name

Private Sub txtBlue_TextChanged(ByVal sender As Object,
    ByVal e As System.EventArgs) Handles txtBlue.TextChanged

                                        Handles keyword followed
                                        by object and event names
```

Figure 3-47   txtBlue control's TextChanged event procedure

Although an event procedure's name contains the names of its associated object and event, that is not a requirement. You can change the name of an event procedure to almost anything you like, as long as the name follows the same rules for naming variables. Unlike variable names, however, procedure names are entered using **Pascal case**, which means you capitalize the first letter in the name and the first letter of each subsequent word in the name. For example, you can change the name of the procedure in Figure 3-47 from txtBlue_TextChanged to ClearLabels and the procedure will still work correctly. This is because the Handles clause, rather than the event procedure's name, determines when the procedure is invoked.

You can associate a procedure with more than one object and event, as long as each event contains the same parameters in its procedure header. To do so, you list each object and event in the procedure's Handles clause. You separate the object and event with a period, like this: *object.event*. You use a comma to separate each *object.event* from the next *object.event*. In the Playtime Cellular application, you will change the name of the txtBlue_TextChanged procedure to ClearLabels. You then will associate the ClearLabels procedure with the txtBlue.TextChanged and txtPink.TextChanged events.

To change the procedure's name and then associate the procedure with different objects and events:

START HERE

1. Change `txtBlue_TextChanged`, which appears after Private Sub in the procedure header, to **ClearLabels**.

2. In the ClearLabels procedure header, click **immediately before the letter H** in the keyword `Handles`. Type _ (an underscore, which is the line continuation character). Be sure there is a space between the ending parenthesis and the underscore.

3. Press **Enter** to move the Handles clause to the next line in the procedure.

4. Click **immediately after TextChanged** in the Handles clause. The Clear-Labels procedure is already associated with the txtBlue.TextChanged event. You just need to associate it with the txtPink.TextChanged event. Type **,** (a comma). Scroll the list of object names until you see txtPink. Click **txtPink** in the list, and then press **Tab** to enter the object name in the procedure.

5. Type **.** (a period). Scroll the list of event names (if necessary) until you see TextChanged. Click **TextChanged** and then press **Tab**. Figure 3-48 shows the completed ClearLabels procedure.

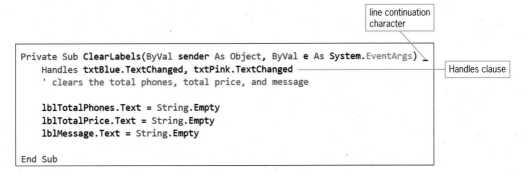

line continuation character

Handles clause

```
Private Sub ClearLabels(ByVal sender As Object, ByVal e As System.EventArgs) _
    Handles txtBlue.TextChanged, txtPink.TextChanged
    ' clears the total phones, total price, and message

    lblTotalPhones.Text = String.Empty
    lblTotalPrice.Text = String.Empty
    lblMessage.Text = String.Empty

End Sub
```

Figure 3-48   Completed ClearLabels procedure

6. Save the solution and then start the application. Type **15** in the Pink phones ordered box and then press **Enter**.

7. Type your name in the Name Entry dialog box and then press **Enter**. The application calculates the total phones ordered (15), total price ($386.25), and sales tax (11.25).

8. Change the number of pink phones ordered to **4**. The ClearLabels procedure clears the total phones ordered, total price, and message information from the form.

9. Press **Enter** to select the Calculate Order button, and then press **Enter** to select the OK button in the Name Entry dialog box. The application calculates the total phones ordered (4), total price ($103.00), and sales tax (3.00).

10. Type **2** in the Blue phones ordered box. The ClearLabels procedure clears the total phones ordered, total price, and message information from the form.

11. Click the **Exit** button. Close the Code Editor window and then close the solution.

Figure 3-49 shows the application's code at the end of Lesson C.

```
 1 ' Name:          Playtime Cellular Project
 2 ' Purpose:       Calculates the total number of phones
 3 '                ordered and the total price of the order
 4 ' Programmer:    <your name> on <current date>
 5
 6 Option Explicit On
 7 Option Strict On
 8 Option Infer Off
 9
10 Public Class frmMain
11
12    Private Sub btnExit_Click(ByVal sender As Object,
      ByVal e As System.EventArgs) Handles btnExit.Click
13       Me.Close()
14    End Sub
15
16    Private Sub btnClear_Click(ByVal sender As Object,
      ByVal e As System.EventArgs) Handles btnClear.Click
17       ' prepare the screen for the next order
18
19       txtName.Text = String.Empty
20       txtAddress.Text = String.Empty
21       txtCity.Text = String.Empty
22       txtState.Text = String.Empty
23       txtZip.Text = String.Empty
24       txtBlue.Text = String.Empty
25       txtPink.Text = String.Empty
26       lblTotalPhones.Text = String.Empty
27       lblTotalPrice.Text = String.Empty
28       lblMessage.Text = String.Empty
29       ' send the focus to the Name text box
30       txtName.Focus()
31
32    End Sub
33
34    Private Sub btnCalc_Click(ByVal sender As Object,
      ByVal e As System.EventArgs) Handles btnCalc.Click
35       ' calculates number of phones ordered and total price
36
37       Const strPROMPT As String = "Salesperson's name:"
38       Const strTITLE As String = "Name Entry"
39       Const decPHONE_PRICE As Decimal = 25D
40       Const decTAX_RATE As Decimal = 0.03D
41       Dim intBluePhones As Integer
42       Dim intPinkPhones As Integer
43       Dim intTotalPhones As Integer
44       Dim decSubtotal As Decimal
45       Dim decSalesTax As Decimal
46       Dim decTotalPrice As Decimal
47       Static strSalesPerson As String
```

Figure 3-49 Playtime Cellular application's code at the end of Lesson C *(continues)*

(continued)

```
48
49          ' assign the name to the variable
50          strSalesPerson = InputBox(strPROMPT,
            strTITLE, strSalesPerson)
51
52          ' calculate the total number of phones ordered
53          Integer.TryParse(txtBlue.Text, intBluePhones)
54          Integer.TryParse(txtPink.Text, intPinkPhones)
55          intTotalPhones = intBluePhones + intPinkPhones
56
57          ' calculate the subtotal
58          decSubtotal = intTotalPhones * decPHONE_PRICE
59
60          ' calculate the sales tax
61          decSalesTax = decSubtotal * decTAX_RATE
62
63          ' calculate the total price
64          decTotalPrice = decSubtotal + decSalesTax
65
66          ' display total amounts
67          lblTotalPhones.Text = Convert.ToString(intTotalPhones)
68          lblTotalPrice.Text = decTotalPrice.ToString("C2")
69
70          ' display tax and salesperson's name
71          lblMessage.Text = "The sales tax was " &
72              Convert.ToString(decSalesTax) & "." &
73              ControlChars.NewLine & strSalesPerson
74
75      End Sub
76
77      Private Sub ClearLabels(ByVal sender As Object,
        ByVal e As System.EventArgs) _
78          Handles txtBlue.TextChanged, txtPink.TextChanged
79          ' clears the total phones, total price, and message
80
81          lblTotalPhones.Text = String.Empty
82          lblTotalPrice.Text = String.Empty
83          lblMessage.Text = String.Empty
84
85      End Sub
86 End Class
```

Figure 3-49 Playtime Cellular application's code at the end of Lesson C

Lesson C Summary

- To process code when a change is made to the contents of a control's Text property:

  Enter the code in the control's TextChanged event procedure.

- To associate a procedure with more than one object or event:

  List each object and event (using the syntax *object.event*) after the **Handles** keyword in the procedure header. Use a comma to separate an object and event from the previous object and event.

Lesson C Key Terms

Pascal case—used when entering procedure names; the process of capitalizing the first letter in the name and the first letter of each subsequent word in the name

TextChanged event—occurs when a change is made to the contents of a control's Text property

Lesson C Review Questions

1. A _____ variable is a procedure-level variable that retains its value after the procedure in which it is declared ends.

   a. constant

   b. static

   c. stationary

   d. term

2. The _____ event occurs when the contents of a text box have changed.

   a. Change

   b. Changed

   c. TextChanged

   d. TextChange

3. Which of the following Handles clauses indicates that a procedure should be processed when the user clicks either the txtNum1 control or the txtNum2 control?

   a. `Handles txtNum1.Click, txtNum2.Click`

   b. `Handles txtNum1, txtNum2`

   c. `Handles txtNum1.Click Or txtNum2.Click`

   d. `Handles txtNum1_Click, txtNum2_Click`

4. Which of the following statements declares a procedure-level variable that retains its value after the procedure in which it is declared ends?

   a. `Const intCounter As Integer`

   b. `Dim intCounter As Constant`

   c. `Dim intCounter As Integer`

   d. `Static intCounter As Integer`

Lesson C Exercises

INTRODUCTORY

1. Open the Name Solution (Name Solution.sln) file contained in the VB2010\Chap03\Name Solution folder. Code the form's Load event procedure so that it uses two InputBox functions to prompt the user to enter his or her first name and last name. Assign the results of both functions to variables. Code the Display button's Click event procedure so that it displays the user's last name, a comma, a space, and the user's first name in the lblName control. Save the solution and then start the application. Test the application by entering your first and last names. Click the Display button. Close the Code Editor window and then close the solution.

INTRODUCTORY

2. In this exercise, you create an application that converts American dollars to British pounds and Mexican pesos. Create a Visual Basic Windows application. Use the following names for the solution, project, and form file, respectively: Currency Calculator Solution, Currency Calculator Project, and Main Form.vb. Save the application in the VB2010\Chap03 folder. Create the interface shown in Figure 3-50. Make the Calculate button the default button. Code the application appropriately. Calculate the number of pounds by multiplying the number of dollars by .56773. Calculate the number of pesos by multiplying the number of dollars by 10.4682. The number of pounds and pesos should be displayed with three decimal places. Clear the number of pounds and pesos when a change is made to the number of dollars. Save the solution and then start and test the application. Close the Code Editor window and then close the solution.

Figure 3-50   Interface for Exercise 2

INTERMEDIATE

3. In this exercise, you create an application that allows your friend Martin to enter the number of pennies he has in a jar. The application should calculate the number of dollars, quarters, dimes, nickels, and pennies he will receive when he cashes in the pennies at a bank. Create a Visual Basic Windows application. Use the following names for the solution, project, and form file, respectively: Pennies Solution, Pennies Project, and Main Form.vb. Save the application in the VB2010\Chap03 folder. Create the interface shown in Figure 3-51. Make the Calculate button the default button. Code the application

appropriately. (It might be helpful to review the information in Figures 2-25 and 2-26 in Chapter 2.) Clear the calculated amounts when a change is made to the number of pennies entered by the user. Save the solution and then start the application. Test the application twice, using the following data: 2311 pennies and 7333 pennies. Close the Code Editor window and then close the solution.

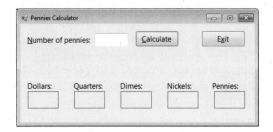

Figure 3-51   Interface for Exercise 3

ADVANCED

4. In this exercise, you create an application that can help students in grades 1 through 6 learn how to make change. The application should allow the student to enter the amount of money a customer owes and the amount of money the customer paid. It then should calculate the amount of change, as well as the number of dollars, quarters, dimes, nickels, and pennies to return to the customer. For now, you do not have to worry about the situation where the amount owed is greater than the amount paid. You can assume that the customer pays either the exact amount or more than the exact amount. Create a Visual Basic Windows application. Use the following names for the solution, project, and form file, respectively: Change Solution, Change Project, and Main Form.vb. Save the application in the VB2010\Chap03 folder. Create the interface shown in Figure 3-52. Make the Calculate Change button the default button. Code the application appropriately. (It might be helpful to review the information in Figures 2-25 and 2-26 in Chapter 2.) Clear the calculated amounts when a change is made to either the amount owed or amount paid. Save the solution and then start the application. Test the application three times, using the following data: 75.33 as the amount owed and 80.00 as the amount paid, 39.67 as the amount owed and 50.00 as the amount paid, and 45.55 as the amount owed and 45.55 as the amount paid. Close the Code Editor window and then close the solution.

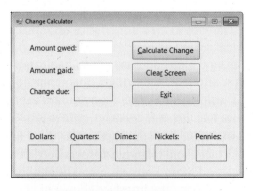

Figure 3-52   Interface for Exercise 4

Discovery

5. In this exercise, you experiment with the Visual Basic conversion functions listed in Appendix C. Open the Conversion Functions Solution (Conversion Functions Solution.sln) file contained in the VB2010\Chap03\Conversion Functions Solution folder. Modify the code so that it uses the Visual Basic conversion functions listed in Appendix C. For example, to convert the item price to Decimal, use `decPrice = CDec(txtPrice.Text)`. Save the solution and then start and test the application. Close the Code Editor window and then close the solution.

Swat The Bugs

6. Open the Debug Solution (Debug Solution.sln) file contained in the VB2010\Chap03\Debug Solution-Lesson C folder. If necessary, open the designer window. Start and then test the application. Locate and correct any errors. When the application is working correctly, close the Code Editor window and then close the solution.

CHAPTER 4

The Selection Structure

Creating the Monthly Payment Calculator Application

While shopping for her dream car, Jennifer Johnston has noticed that many auto dealers are offering buyers a choice of either a large cash rebate or an extremely low financing rate, much lower than the rate Jennifer would pay by financing the car through her local credit union. Jennifer is not sure whether to take the lower financing rate from the dealer, or take the rebate and then finance the car through the credit union. In this chapter, you will create an application that Jennifer can use to calculate and display her monthly car payment using both scenarios.

Previewing the Monthly Payment Calculator Application

Before you start the first lesson in this chapter, you will preview the completed application. The application is contained in the VB2010\Chap04 folder.

To preview the completed application:

START HERE

191

1. Use the Run dialog box to run the Monthly Payment (Monthly Payment.exe) file contained in the VB2010\Chap04 folder. The application's user interface appears on the screen.

2. First, you will calculate the monthly payment on a $9000 loan at 5% interest for 3 years. Type **9000** in the Principal box and type **5** in the Rate box. Click the **Calculate Monthly Payment** button. The message box shown in Figure 4-1 appears on the screen. You will learn how to create a message box in Lesson B.

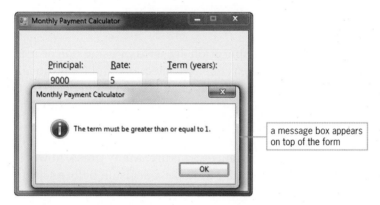

a message box appears on top of the form

Figure 4-1 Message box

3. Click the **OK** button to close the message box. Type **3** in the Term (years) box and then click the **Calculate Monthly Payment** button. The application calculates and displays the monthly payment amount. See Figure 4-2.

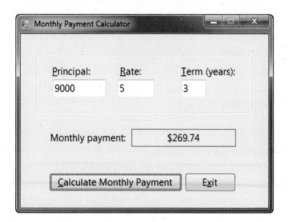

Figure 4-2 Monthly payment amount shown in the interface

4. Click the **Exit** button to end the application.

The Monthly Payment Calculator application uses the selection structure, which you will learn about in Lesson A. In Lesson B, you will complete the application's interface and also begin coding the application. You will finish coding the application in Lesson C. Be sure to complete each lesson in full and do all of the end-of-lesson questions and several exercises before continuing to the next lesson.

LESSON A

After studying Lesson A, you should be able to:

- Write pseudocode for the selection structure
- Create a flowchart to help you plan an application's code
- Write an If…Then…Else statement
- Include comparison operators and logical operators in a selection structure's condition
- Change the case of a string
- Determine the success of the TryParse method

Making Decisions in a Program

All of the procedures in an application are written using one or more of three basic control structures: sequence, selection, and repetition. The procedures in the previous three chapters used the sequence structure only. When one of the procedures was invoked during run time, the computer processed its instructions sequentially—in other words, in the order the instructions appeared in the procedure. Every procedure you write will contain the sequence structure. Many times, however, a procedure will need the computer to make a decision before selecting the next instruction to process. A procedure that calculates an employee's gross pay, for example, typically has the computer determine whether the number of hours the employee worked is greater than 40. The computer then would select either an instruction that computes regular pay only or an instruction that computes regular pay plus overtime pay. Procedures that need the computer to make a decision require the use of the selection structure (also called the decision structure). The **selection structure** indicates that a decision (based on some condition) needs to be made, followed by an appropriate action derived from that decision. There are three types of selection structures: single-alternative, dual-alternative, and multiple-alternative. You will learn about single-alternative and dual-alternative selection structures in this chapter. Multiple-alternative selection structures are covered in Chapter 5.

Although the idea of using the selection structure in a procedure is new to you, you already are familiar with the concept of the selection structure because you use it each day to make hundreds of decisions. Figure 4-3 shows examples of selection structures you might use today. The examples are written in pseudocode. Each example contains a **condition** that specifies the decision you are making. The condition must be phrased so that it results in either a true or false answer only. The selection structure in Example 1 is a **single-alternative selection structure**, because it requires a specific set of tasks to be performed only when the condition is true. The set of tasks to perform when the condition is true is called the **true path**. Example 2 contains a **dual-alternative selection structure**, because it contains one set of tasks to perform when the condition is true, but a different set of tasks to perform when the condition is false. The set of tasks to perform when the condition is false is called the **false path**. When writing pseudocode, most programmers use the words "if" and "end if" to denote the beginning and end, respectively, of a selection structure, and the word "else" to denote the beginning of the false path. They also indent the instructions within the selection structure, as shown in Figure 4-3.

Example 1 – single-alternative selection structure

```
        ┌───────────┐
        │ condition │
        └───────────┘

if it is raining
    wear a raincoat ──────────┐
    bring an umbrella ──── │ true path │
end if
```

Example 2 – dual-alternative selection structure

```
          ┌───────────┐
          │ condition │
          └───────────┘

if you have a test tomorrow
        study tonight ──── │ true path │
else
        watch a movie ──── │ false path │
end if
```

Figure 4-3   Selection structures you might use today

But how does a programmer determine whether a procedure in an application requires a selection structure? The answer to this question is by studying the problem specification. The first problem specification you will examine in this chapter is for Kanton Boutique. The problem specification is shown in Figure 4-4.

Kanton Boutique wants an application that allows the store clerk to enter an item's price and the quantity purchased by a customer. The application should calculate the total amount the customer owes by multiplying the price by the quantity purchased. It then should display the total amount owed.

Figure 4-4   Problem specification for Kanton Boutique

Figure 4-5 shows an appropriate interface for the Kanton Boutique application, and Figure 4-6 shows the pseudocode for the Calculate button's Click event procedure. The procedure requires only the sequence structure. It does not need a selection structure, because no decisions are necessary to calculate and display the total amount owed.

Figure 4-5   Interface for the Kanton Boutique application

btnCalc Click event procedure
1.   store user input (price and quantity purchased) in variables
2.   total owed = price * quantity purchased
3.   display total owed in lblTotal

Figure 4-6   Pseudocode containing only the sequence structure

Now we'll make a slight change to the problem specification from Figure 4-4. This time, Kanton Boutique offers a 10% discount when the quantity purchased is over five. Consider the changes you will need to make to the Calculate button's original pseudocode, which is shown in Figure 4-6. The first two steps in the original pseudocode are to store the user input in variables and then calculate the total owed by multiplying the price by the quantity purchased. The modified pseudocode will still need both of these steps. Step 3 in the original pseudocode is to display the total owed in the lblTotal control. Before the modified procedure can display the total owed, it will need to make a decision regarding the number of items purchased. More specifically, the modified procedure will need to determine whether the quantity purchased is over five; if it is, the modified procedure will need to calculate the discount and then subtract the discount from the total owed. The modified problem specification and pseudocode are shown in Figure 4-7. The pseudocode contains a single-alternative selection structure. In this case, a single-alternative selection structure is appropriate because the procedure needs to perform a special set of actions only when the condition is true, which occurs when the customer purchases more than five of the item.

Kanton Boutique wants an application that allows the store clerk to enter an item's price and the quantity purchased by a customer. The application should calculate the total amount the customer owes by multiplying the price by the quantity purchased and then subtracting any discount. It then should display the total amount owed. Kanton Boutique gives customers a 10% discount when the quantity purchased is over five.

btnCalc Click event procedure
1. store user input (price and quantity purchased) in variables
2. total owed = price * quantity purchased

          [condition]

3. if the quantity purchased is over 5
        discount = total owed * .1
        total owed = total owed – discount   [true path]
    end if
4. display total owed in lblTotal

Figure 4-7   Modified problem specification and pseudocode containing a single-alternative selection structure

Figure 4-8 shows the Calculate button's Click event procedure in flowchart form. Recall that the oval in a flowchart is the start/stop symbol, the rectangle is the process symbol, and the parallelogram is the input/output symbol. The diamond in a flowchart is called the **decision symbol**, because it is used to represent the condition (decision) in both the selection and repetition structures. The diamond in Figure 4-8 represents the condition in a selection structure. (You will learn how to use the diamond to represent a repetition structure's condition in Chapter 6.) The condition in Figure 4-8's diamond checks whether the customer purchased more than five items. Notice that the condition results in an answer of either true or false only. Also notice that the diamond has one flowline entering it and two flowlines leaving it. One of the flowlines leading out of the diamond in a flowchart should be marked with a T (for true) and the other should be marked with an F (for false). The T flowline points to the next instruction to be processed when the condition is true. In Figure 4-8, the next instruction calculates the 10% discount. The F flowline points to the next instruction to be processed when the condition is false; in Figure 4-8, that instruction displays the total owed. The flowchart in Figure 4-8 illustrates a single-alternative selection structure, because only the true path contains a special set of actions.

You also can mark the flow-lines leading out of a diamond with a Y and an N (for yes and no).

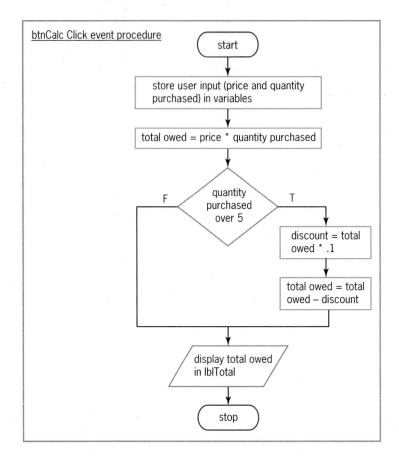

Figure 4-8 Single-alternative selection structure shown in a flowchart

Next, we'll modify the Kanton Boutique problem specification one more time. In addition to the 10% discount for purchasing more than five of an item, Kanton Boutique is now offering a 5% discount when the quantity purchased is five or less. The modified problem specification and pseudocode are shown in Figure 4-9, and the corresponding flowchart is shown in Figure 4-10. The pseudocode and flowchart contain a dual-alternative selection structure. In this case, a dual-alternative selection structure is appropriate because the procedure needs to perform one action when the condition is true, but a different action when the condition is false. The condition will be true when the customer purchases more than five of the item, and false when the customer purchases five or less of the item.

Kanton Boutique wants an application that allows the store clerk to enter an item's price and the quantity purchased by a customer. The application should calculate the total amount the customer owes by multiplying the price by the quantity purchased and then subtracting any discount. It then should display the total amount owed. Kanton Boutique gives customers a 10% discount when the quantity purchased is over five; otherwise, it gives a 5% discount.

btnCalc Click event procedure
1.   store user input (price and quantity purchased) in variables
2.   total owed = price * quantity purchased

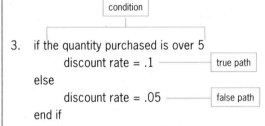

3.   if the quantity purchased is over 5
            discount rate = .1 ——————— true path
      else
            discount rate = .05 ——————— false path
      end if
4.   discount = total owed * discount rate
5.   total owed = total owed – discount
6.   display total owed in lblTotal

Figure 4-9   Modified problem specification and pseudocode containing a dual-alternative selection structure

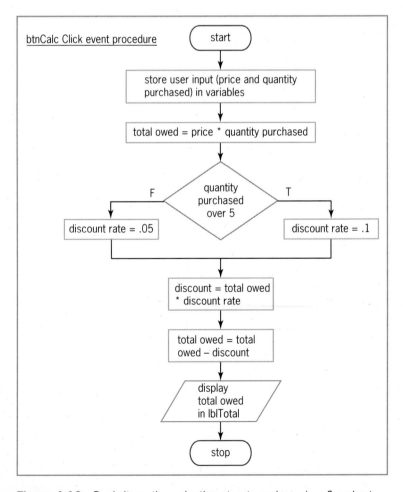

Figure 4-10   Dual-alternative selection structure shown in a flowchart

Coding Single-Alternative and Dual-Alternative Selection Structures

Visual Basic provides the **If...Then...Else statement** for coding single-alternative and dual-alternative selection structures. The statement's syntax is shown in Figure 4-11. The square brackets in the syntax indicate that the Else portion, referred to as the Else clause, is optional. Boldfaced items in a statement's syntax are required. In this case, the keywords If, Then, and End If are required. The Else keyword is necessary only in a dual-alternative selection structure. Italicized items in a statement's syntax indicate where the programmer must supply information. In the If...Then...Else statement, the programmer must supply the *condition* that the computer needs to evaluate before further processing can occur. The condition must be a Boolean expression, which is an expression that results in a Boolean value (either True or False). The condition can contain variables, constants, properties, methods, keywords, arithmetic operators, comparison operators, and logical operators. (You will learn about comparison operators and logical operators in this lesson.) Besides providing the condition, the programmer must provide the statements to be processed in the true path and (optionally) in the false path. The set of statements contained in each path is referred to as a **statement block**. Also included in Figure 4-11 are two examples of using the If...Then...Else statement to code selection structures. Example 1 shows how you use the statement to code the single-alternative selection structure shown earlier in Figures 4-7 and 4-8. Example 2 shows how you use the statement to code the dual-alternative selection structure shown earlier in Figures 4-9 and 4-10.

> In Visual Basic, a statement block is a set of statements terminated by an Else, End If, Loop, or Next clause. You will learn about the Loop and Next clauses in Chapters 6 and 7.

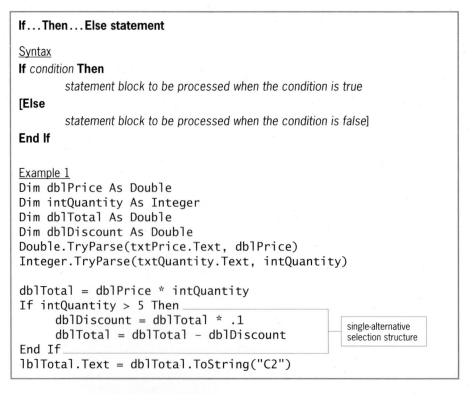

If...Then...Else statement

Syntax
If *condition* **Then**
       statement block to be processed when the condition is true
[Else
       statement block to be processed when the condition is false]
End If

Example 1
```
Dim dblPrice As Double
Dim intQuantity As Integer
Dim dblTotal As Double
Dim dblDiscount As Double
Double.TryParse(txtPrice.Text, dblPrice)
Integer.TryParse(txtQuantity.Text, intQuantity)

dblTotal = dblPrice * intQuantity
If intQuantity > 5 Then
    dblDiscount = dblTotal * .1
    dblTotal = dblTotal - dblDiscount
End If
lblTotal.Text = dblTotal.ToString("C2")
```
single-alternative selection structure

Figure 4-11   Syntax and examples of the If...Then...Else statement *(continues)*

198

(continued)

```
Example 2
Dim dblPrice As Double
Dim intQuantity As Integer
Dim dblTotal As Double
Dim dblDiscount As Double
Dim dblDiscountRate As Double
Double.TryParse(txtPrice.Text, dblPrice)
Integer.TryParse(txtQuantity.Text, intQuantity)

dblTotal = dblPrice * intQuantity
If intQuantity > 5 Then
        dblDiscountRate = .1
Else
        dblDiscountRate = .05
End If
dblDiscount = dblTotal * dblDiscountRate
dblTotal = dblTotal - dblDiscount
lblTotal.Text = dblTotal.ToString("C2")
```

dual-alternative selection structure

Figure 4-11   Syntax and examples of the If...Then...Else statement

YOU DO IT 1!

Create a Visual Basic Windows application named YouDoIt 1. Save the application in the VB2010\Chap04 folder. Add a text box, a label, and a button to the form. The button's Click event procedure should display the string "Over 1" in the label when the value in the text box is greater than the number 1; otherwise, it should display the string "Not Over 1". Code the procedure. Save the solution and then start and test the application. Close the solution.

Comparison Operators

As mentioned earlier, the condition in an If...Then...Else statement can contain comparison operators. The operators are called **comparison operators** because they are used to compare two values. The comparison always results in a Boolean value. Figure 4-12 lists the most commonly used comparison operators in Visual Basic and includes examples of using the operators in an If...Then...Else statement's condition.

Comparison operators are also referred to as relational operators.

199

Keep in mind that = is the opposite of <>, > is the opposite of <=, and < is the opposite of >=.

Comparison operator	Operation
=	equal to
>	greater than
>=	greater than or equal to
<	less than
<=	less than or equal to
<>	not equal to

Example 1
```
If decNorthSales = decSouthSales Then
```
The condition evaluates to True when both variables contain the same value; otherwise, it evaluates to False.

Example 2
```
If intAge >= 21 Then
```
The condition evaluates to True when the value stored in the `intAge` variable is greater than or equal to 21; otherwise, it evaluates to False.

Example 3
```
If decPrice < 67.89D Then
```
The condition evaluates to True when the value stored in the `decPrice` variable is less than 67.89; otherwise, it evaluates to False. You also can write the condition as `decPrice < Convert.ToDecimal(67.89)`.

Example 4
```
If strState <> "KY" Then
```
The condition evaluates to True when the `strState` variable does not contain the string "KY"; otherwise, it evaluates to False.

Figure 4-12   Listing and examples of commonly used comparison operators

Unlike arithmetic operators, comparison operators do not have an order of precedence. When an expression contains more than one comparison operator, the computer evaluates the comparison operators from left to right in the expression, similar to what is done with arithmetic operators. Comparison operators are evaluated after any arithmetic operators in an expression. For example, when processing the expression $10 - 2 > 3 * 2$, the computer will evaluate the two arithmetic operators before it evaluates the comparison operator. The result of the expression is the Boolean value True, as shown in Figure 4-13.

Evaluation steps	Result
Original expression	$10 - 2 > 3 * 2$
The multiplication is performed first	$10 - 2 > 6$
The subtraction is performed next	$8 > 6$
The > comparison is performed last	True

Figure 4-13   Evaluation steps for an expression containing arithmetic and comparison operators

YOU DO IT 2!

Create a Visual Basic Windows application named YouDoIt 2. Save the application in the VB2010\Chap04 folder. Add a label and a button to the form. The button's Click event procedure should display the result of the following expression: 8 + 3 – 6 + 85 < 5 * 26. Code the procedure. Save the solution and then start and test the application. Close the solution.

In the next two sections, you will view two examples of procedures that contain a comparison operator in an If...Then...Else statement's condition. The first procedure uses a single-alternative selection structure, and the second procedure uses a dual-alternative selection structure.

Using Comparison Operators: Swapping Numeric Values

Figure 4-14 shows a sample run of an application that displays the lowest and highest of two numbers entered by the user. Figures 4-15 and 4-16 show the pseudocode and flowchart, respectively, for the Display button's Click event procedure. The procedure contains a single-alternative selection structure that determines whether the first number entered by the user is greater than the second number, and then takes the appropriate action if it is.

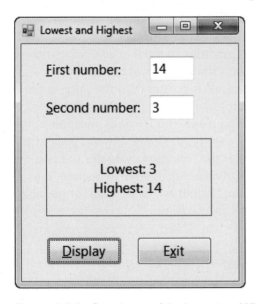

Figure 4-14 Sample run of the Lowest and Highest application

btnDisplay Click event procedure
1. store the text box values in two variables
2. if the number in the first variable is greater than the number in the second variable
      swap both numbers so that the first variable contains the lowest of the two numbers
   end if
3. display the lowest number and the highest number in lblMessage

Figure 4-15 Pseudocode containing a single-alternative selection structure

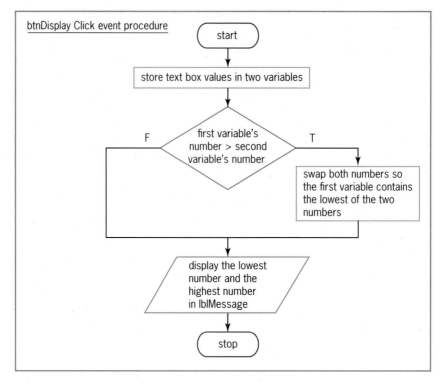

Figure 4-16   Flowchart containing a single-alternative selection structure

Figure 4-17 shows the code entered in the Display button's Click event procedure. The `intNum1 > intNum2` condition in the If clause compares the contents of the `intNum1` variable with the contents of the `intNum2` variable. If the value in the `intNum1` variable is greater than the value in the `intNum2` variable, the condition evaluates to True and the four instructions in the If…Then…Else statement's true path swap both values. Swapping the values places the smaller number in the `intNum1` variable and places the larger number in the `intNum2` variable. If the condition evaluates to False, on the other hand, the true path instructions are skipped over because the `intNum1` variable already contains a number that is smaller than (or possibly equal to) the number stored in the `intNum2` variable.

```
Private Sub btnDisplay_Click(ByVal sender As Object,
ByVal e As System.EventArgs) Handles btnDisplay.Click
    ' displays the lowest and highest of two numbers

    Dim intNum1 As Integer
    Dim intNum2 As Integer

    ' store input in variables
    Integer.TryParse(txtFirst.Text, intNum1)
    Integer.TryParse(txtSecond.Text, intNum2)
```

Figure 4-17   Display button's Click event procedure *(continues)*

(continued)

```
    ' swap numbers, if necessary
    If intNum1 > intNum2 Then
        Dim intTemp As Integer
        intTemp = intNum1
        intNum1 = intNum2
        intNum2 = intTemp
    End If

    ' display lowest and highest numbers
    lblMessage.Text = "Lowest: " &
        Convert.ToString(intNum1) &
        ControlChars.NewLine & "Highest: " &
        Convert.ToString(intNum2)
End Sub
```

comparison operator

single-alternative selection structure

Figure 4-17   Display button's Click event procedure

203

Study closely the instructions used to swap the values stored in the intNum1 and intNum2 variables. The first instruction is a Dim statement that declares a variable named intTemp. Like the variables declared at the beginning of a procedure, variables declared within a statement block—referred to as **block-level variables**—remain in memory until the procedure ends. However, unlike variables declared at the beginning of a procedure, block-level variables have block scope rather than procedure scope. As you know, a variable that has procedure scope can be used anywhere within the procedure. A variable that has **block scope**, however, can be used only within the statement block in which it is declared. More specifically, it can be used only below its declaration statement within the statement block. In this case, the intNum1 and intNum2 variables can be used anywhere within the Display button's Click event procedure, but the intTemp variable can be used only after its Dim statement within the If…Then…Else statement's true path. You may be wondering why the intTemp variable is not declared at the beginning of the procedure, along with the other variables. Although there is nothing wrong with declaring all variables at the beginning of a procedure, the intTemp variable is not needed unless a swap is necessary, so there is no reason to create the variable ahead of time.

The second instruction in the If…Then…Else statement's true path assigns the value in the intNum1 variable to the intTemp variable. If you do not store the intNum1 variable's value in the intTemp variable, the value will be lost when the computer processes the next statement, intNum1 = intNum2, which replaces the contents of the intNum1 variable with the contents of the intNum2 variable. Finally, the intNum2 = intTemp instruction assigns the intTemp variable's value to the intNum2 variable; this completes the swap. Figure 4-18 illustrates the concept of swapping, assuming the user enters the numbers 14 and 3 in the txtFirst and txtSecond controls, respectively.

	intNum1	intNum2	intTemp
values stored in the variables immediately before the intTemp = intNum1 statement is processed	14	3	0
result of the intTemp = intNum1 statement	14	3	14
result of the intNum1 = intNum2 statement	3	3	14
result of the intNum2 = intTemp statement	3	14	14

the values were swapped

Figure 4-18 Illustration of the swapping concept

START HERE **To code and then test the Lowest and Highest application:**

1. If necessary, start Visual Studio 2010 or Visual Basic 2010 Express. Open the Lowest and Highest Solution (Lowest and Highest Solution.sln) file contained in the VB2010\Chap04\Lowest and Highest Solution folder. If necessary, open the designer window.

2. Open the Code Editor window. Replace <your name> and <current date> in the comments with your name and the current date, respectively.

3. Open the code template for the btnDisplay control's Click event procedure. Enter the comments and code shown earlier in Figure 4-17.

4. Save the solution and then start the application. Type **14** in the First number box and then type **3** in the Second number box. Click the **Display** button. The button's Click event procedure displays the lowest and highest numbers, as shown earlier in Figure 4-14.

5. Click the **Exit** button. Close the Code Editor window and then close the solution.

Using Comparison Operators: Displaying the Sum or Difference

Figure 4-19 shows a sample run of an application that displays either the sum of two numbers entered by the user or the difference between both numbers. Figures 4-20 and 4-21 show the pseudocode and flowchart, respectively, for the Calculate button's Click event procedure. The procedure uses a dual-alternative selection structure to determine the appropriate operation to perform.

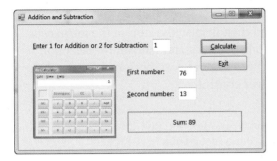

Figure 4-19   Sample run of the Addition and Subtraction application

btnCalc Click event procedure
1.   store operation, first number, and second number in variables
2.   if the user wants to perform addition
              calculate the sum by adding together the first number and the second number
              display the message "Sum:" along with the sum in lblAnswer
     else
              calculate the difference by subtracting the second number from the first number
              display the message "Difference:" along with the difference in lblAnswer
     end if

Figure 4-20   Pseudocode containing a dual-alternative selection structure

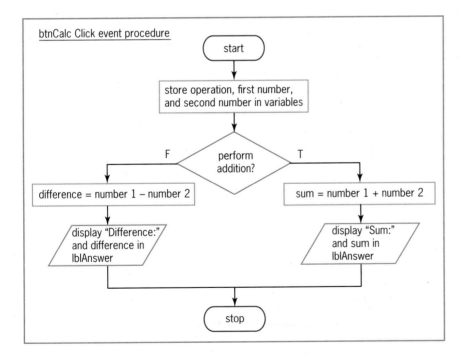

Figure 4-21   Flowchart containing a dual-alternative selection structure

Figure 4-22 shows the code entered in the Calculate button's Click event procedure. The Dim statements in the procedure declare four procedure-level variables. The next three statements store the contents of the text boxes in the appropriate variables. The condition in the If clause compares the contents of the `strOperation` variable with the string "1". If the condition evaluates to

True, the statements in the selection structure's true path calculate the sum of the numbers entered by the user and then display the sum in the lblAnswer control. If the condition evaluates to False, the statements in the selection structure's false path calculate the difference between both numbers and then display the difference in the lblAnswer control.

```
Private Sub btnCalc_Click(ByVal sender As Object,
ByVal e As System.EventArgs) Handles btnCalc.Click
    ' calculates either a sum or a difference

    Dim strOperation As String
    Dim intNum1 As Integer
    Dim intNum2 As Integer
    Dim intAnswer As Integer

    ' store input in variables
    strOperation = txtOperation.Text
    Integer.TryParse(txtNum1.Text, intNum1)
    Integer.TryParse(txtNum2.Text, intNum2)

    ' calculate and display the sum or difference
    If strOperation = "1" Then
        intAnswer = intNum1 + intNum2
        lblAnswer.Text =
            "Sum: " & Convert.ToString(intAnswer)
    Else
        intAnswer = intNum1 - intNum2
        lblAnswer.Text =
            "Difference: " & Convert.ToString(intAnswer)
    End If
End Sub
```

comparison operator

dual-alternative
selection structure

Figure 4-22   Calculate button's Click event procedure

START HERE

To code and then test the Addition and Subtraction application:

1. Open the Addition and Subtraction Solution (Addition and Subtraction Solution.sln) file contained in the VB2010\Chap04\ Addition and Subtraction Solution folder. If necessary, open the designer window.

2. Open the Code Editor window. Replace <your name> and <current date> in the comments with your name and the current date, respectively.

3. Open the code template for the btnCalc control's Click event procedure. Enter the comments and code shown earlier in Figure 4-22.

4. Save the solution and then start the application. Type **1** in the Enter 1 for Addition or 2 for Subtraction box, **76** in the First number box, and **13** in the Second number box. Click the **Calculate** button. The button's Click event procedure displays the sum of both numbers, as shown earlier in Figure 4-19.

5. Change the 1 in the Enter 1 for Addition or 2 for Subtraction box to **2** and then click the **Calculate** button. The button's Click event procedure displays the difference between both numbers.

6. Click the **Exit** button. Close the Code Editor window and then close the solution.

YOU DO IT 3!

Create a Visual Basic Windows application named YouDoIt 3. Save the application in the VB2010\Chap04 folder. Add a text box, a label, and a button to the form. If the user enters the number 1 in the text box, the button's Click event procedure should display the result of multiplying the number 20 by the number 5; otherwise, it should display the result of dividing the number 20 by the number 5. Code the procedure. Save the solution and then start and test the application. Close the solution.

Logical Operators

An If...Then...Else statement's condition also can contain logical operators, often referred to as Boolean operators. Visual Basic provides six logical operators, which are listed along with their order of precedence in Figure 4-23. Keep in mind, however, that logical operators are evaluated after any arithmetic or comparison operators in an expression. All of the **logical operators**, with the exception of the Not operator, allow you to combine two or more conditions, called sub-conditions, into one compound condition. The compound condition will always evaluate to either True or False. Also included in Figure 4-23 are examples of using logical operators in the If...Then...Else statement's condition.

Logical operator	Operation	Precedence number
Not	reverses the truth-value of the condition; True becomes False, and False becomes True	1
And	all sub-conditions must be true for the compound condition to evaluate to True	2
AndAlso	same as the And operator, except performs short-circuit evaluation	2
Or	only one of the sub-conditions needs to be true for the compound condition to evaluate to True	3
OrElse	same as the Or operator, except performs short-circuit evaluation	3
Xor	one and only one of the sub-conditions can be true for the compound condition to evaluate to True	4

Figure 4-23 Listing and examples of logical operators (continues)

(continued)

Example 1
```
If Not blnIsInsured Then
```
The condition evaluates to True when the `blnIsInsured` variable contains the Boolean value False; otherwise, it evaluates to False. The clause also could be written as `If Not blnIsInsured = True` Then; or, more clearly as `If blnIsInsured = False Then`.

Example 2
```
If dblHours > 0 AndAlso dblHours <= 40 Then
```
The compound condition evaluates to True when the value in the `dblHours` variable is greater than 0 and, at the same time, less than or equal to 40; otherwise, it evaluates to False.

Example 3
```
If strState = "TN" AndAlso decSales > 50000D Then
```
The compound condition evaluates to True when the `strState` variable contains the string "TN" and, at the same time, the value in the `decSales` variable is greater than 50000; otherwise, it evaluates to False.

Example 4
```
If strState = "TN" OrElse decSales > 50000D Then
```
The compound condition evaluates to True when the `strState` variable contains the string "TN" or when the value in the `decSales` variable is greater than 50000; otherwise, it evaluates to False.

Example 5
```
If strCoupon1 = "USE" Xor strCoupon2 = "USE" Then
```
The compound condition evaluates to True when only one of the variables contains the string "USE"; otherwise, it evaluates to False.

Figure 4-23   Listing and examples of logical operators

As already mentioned, all expressions containing a logical operator evaluate to a Boolean value: either True or False. The tables shown in Figure 4-24, called **truth tables**, summarize how the computer evaluates the logical operators in an expression. As the figure indicates, the **Not operator** reverses the truth-value of the *condition*. If the value of the *condition* is True, then the value of Not *condition* is False. Likewise, if the value of the *condition* is False, then the value of Not *condition* is True. When you use either the **And operator** or the **AndAlso operator** to combine two sub-conditions, the resulting compound condition evaluates to True only when both sub-conditions are True. If either sub-condition is False or if both sub-conditions are False, then the compound condition evaluates to False. The difference between the And and AndAlso operators is that the And operator always evaluates both sub-conditions, while the AndAlso operator performs a **short-circuit evaluation**, which means it does not always evaluate sub-condition2. Because both sub-conditions combined with the AndAlso operator need to be True for the compound condition to evaluate to True, the AndAlso operator does not evaluate sub-condition2 when sub-condition1 is False; this makes the AndAlso operator more efficient than the And operator.

As indicated in Figure 4-24, when you combine conditions using either the **Or operator** or the **OrElse operator**, the compound condition evaluates to False only when both sub-conditions are False. If either sub-condition is True or if both sub-conditions are True, then the compound condition evaluates to True. The difference between the Or and OrElse operators is that the Or operator always evaluates both sub-conditions, while the OrElse operator performs a short-circuit evaluation. In this case, because only one of the sub-conditions combined with the OrElse operator needs to be True for the compound condition to evaluate to True, the OrElse operator does not evaluate sub-condition2 when sub-condition1 is True. As a result, the OrElse operator is more efficient than the Or operator. Finally, when you combine conditions using the Xor operator, the compound condition evaluates to True only when one and only one sub-condition is True. If both sub-conditions are True or both sub-conditions are False, then the compound condition evaluates to False.

Truth table for the Not operator

value of condition	value of Not condition
True	False
False	True

Truth table for the And operator

sub-condition1	sub-condition2	sub-condition1 And sub-condition2
True	True	True
True	False	False
False	True	False
False	False	False

Truth table for the AndAlso operator

sub-condition1	sub-condition2	sub-condition1 AndAlso sub-condition2
True	True	True
True	False	False
False	(not evaluated)	False

Truth table for the Or operator

sub-condition1	sub-condition2	sub-condition1 Or sub-condition2
True	True	True
True	False	True
False	True	True
False	False	False

Truth table for the OrElse operator

sub-condition1	sub-condition2	sub-condition1 OrElse sub-condition2
True	(not evaluated)	True
False	True	True
False	False	False

Truth table for the Xor operator

sub-condition1	sub-condition2	sub-condition1 Xor sub-condition2
True	True	False
True	False	True
False	True	True
False	False	False

Figure 4-24   Truth tables for the logical operators

Using the Truth Tables

A procedure needs to calculate a commission for each A-rated salesperson whose monthly sales are more than $9000. The procedure uses the `strRating` and `dblSales` variables to store the salesperson's rating and sales amount, respectively. Therefore, you can phrase sub-condition1 as `strRating = "A"` and phrase sub-condition2 as `dblSales > 9000`. Which logical operator should you use to combine both sub-conditions into one compound condition? You can use the truth tables from Figure 4-24 to help you answer this question. For a salesperson to receive a commission, both sub-condition1 and sub-condition2 must be True at the same time. If either sub-condition is False or if both sub-conditions are False, then the compound condition should be False and the salesperson should not receive a commission. According to the truth tables, the And, AndAlso, Or, and OrElse operators evaluate a compound condition as True when both sub-conditions are True. However, only the And and AndAlso operators evaluate the compound condition as False when either one or both of the sub-conditions are False. The Or and OrElse operators evaluate the compound condition as False only when both sub-conditions are False. Therefore, the correct compound condition to use here is either `strRating = "A" And dblSales > 9000` or `strRating = "A" AndAlso dblSales > 9000`. However, remember that the AndAlso operator is more efficient than the And operator.

Now assume you want to send a letter to all A-rated salespeople and all B-rated salespeople. If the rating is stored in the `strRating` variable, you can phrase sub-condition1 as `strRating = "A"` and phrase sub-condition2 as `strRating = "B"`. Now which logical operator should you use to combine both sub-conditions? At first it might appear that either the And or the AndAlso operator is the correct one to use, because the example says to send the letter to "all A-rated salespeople and all B-rated salespeople." In everyday conversations, people sometimes use the word "and" when what they really mean is "or." Although both words do not mean the same thing, using "and" instead of "or" generally does not cause a problem, because we are able to infer what another person means. Computers, however, cannot infer anything; they simply process the directions you give them, word for word. In this case, you actually want to send a letter to all salespeople with either an A rating or a B rating (a salesperson can have only one rating), so you will need to use either the Or or the OrElse operator. As the truth tables indicate, the Or and OrElse operators are the only operators that evaluate the compound condition as True when at least one of the sub-conditions is True. Therefore, the correct compound condition to use in this case is either `strRating = "A" Or strRating = "B"` or `strRating = "A" OrElse strRating = "B"`. However, the OrElse operator is more efficient than the Or operator.

Finally, assume that when placing an order, a customer is allowed to use only one of two coupons. If a procedure uses the variables `strCoupon1` and `strCoupon2` to keep track of the coupons, you can phrase sub-condition1 as `strCoupon1 = "USE"` and phrase sub-condition2 as `strCoupon2 = "USE"`. Now which operator should you use to combine both sub-conditions? According to the truth tables, the Xor operator is the only operator that evaluates the compound condition as True when one and only one sub-condition is True. Therefore, the correct compound condition to use here is `strCoupon1 = "USE" Xor strCoupon2 = "USE"`.

Using Logical Operators: Calculating Gross Pay

A procedure needs to calculate and display an employee's gross pay. To keep this example simple, no one at the company works more than 40 hours per week and everyone earns the same hourly rate, $11.55. Before making the gross pay calculation, the procedure should verify that the number of hours entered by the user is greater than or equal to zero, but less than or equal to 40. Programmers refer to the process of verifying that the input data is within the expected range as **data validation**. In this case, if the number of hours is valid, the procedure should calculate and display the gross pay; , it should display an error message alerting the user that the input data is incorrect.

Figure 4-25 shows two ways of writing the procedure's code; both contain a dual-alternative selection structure whose compound condition includes a logical operator. The compound condition in Example 1 uses the AndAlso operator to determine whether the value stored in the dblHours variable is greater than or equal to zero and, at the same time, less than or equal to 40. If the compound condition evaluates to True, the selection structure's true path calculates and displays the gross pay; otherwise, its false path displays the "Error" message. The compound condition in Example 2 uses the OrElse operator to determine whether the value stored in the dblHours variable is either less than zero or greater than 40. If the compound condition evaluates to True, the selection structure's true path displays the "Error" message; otherwise, its false path calculates and displays the gross pay. Both examples in Figure 4-25 produce the same result and simply represent two different ways of performing the same task.

Procedures containing logical operators

Example 1 – using the AndAlso operator
```
Const dblRATE As Double = 11.55
Dim dblHours As Double
Dim dblGross As Double

Double.TryParse(txtHours.Text, dblHours)

If dblHours >= 0 AndAlso dblHours <= 40 Then
     ' calculate and display the gross pay
     dblGross = dblHours * dblRATE
     lblGross.Text = dblGross.ToString("C2")
Else
     ' display an error message
     lblGross.Text = "Error"
End If


Example 2 – using the OrElse operator
Const dblRATE As Double = 11.55
Dim dblHours As Double
Dim dblGross As Double
```

Figure 4-25   Examples of using the AndAlso and OrElse logical operators in a procedure
(continues)

(continued)

```
Double.TryParse(txtHours.Text, dblHours)

If dblHours < 0 OrElse dblHours > 40 Then
    ' display an error message
    lblGross.Text = "Error"
Else
    ' calculate and display the gross pay
    dblGross = dblHours * dblRATE
    lblGross.Text = dblGross.ToString("C2")
End If
```

Figure 4-25   Examples of using the AndAlso and OrElse logical operators in a procedure

START HERE

To code and then test the Gross Pay Calculator application:

1. Open the Gross Pay Solution (Gross Pay Solution.sln) file contained in the VB2010\Chap04\Gross Pay Solution folder. If necessary, open the designer window.

2. Open the Code Editor window. Replace <your name> and <current date> in the comments with your name and the current date, respectively.

3. Locate the code template for the btnCalc control's Click event procedure. Enter the comments and code from either of the two examples shown earlier in Figure 4-25.

4. Save the solution and then start the application. Type **20** in the Hours worked box and then press **Enter** to select the Calculate button. The button's Click event procedure displays the gross pay amount in the lblGross control. See Figure 4-26.

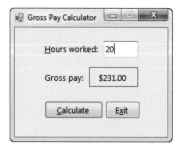

Figure 4-26   Sample run of the application using valid data

5. Change the number of hours worked to **52** and then press **Enter**. The Calculate button's Click event procedure displays the "Error" message in the lblGross control. See Figure 4-27.

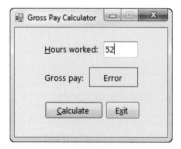

Figure 4-27   Sample run of the application using invalid data

6. Click the **Exit** button. Close the Code Editor window and then close the solution.

YOU DO IT 4!

Create a Visual Basic Windows application named YouDoIt 4. Save the application in the VB2010\Chap04 folder. Add a text box, a label, and a button to the form. If the user enters a number that is either less than 0 or greater than 100, the button's Click event procedure should display the string "Invalid number" in the label; otherwise, it should display the string "Valid number". Code the procedure. Save the solution and then start and test the application. Close the solution.

In addition to comparing numeric values and numbers treated as strings, an If...Then...Else statement's condition also can compare letters or Boolean values. First, you will learn how to compare strings containing letters.

Comparing Strings Containing Letters

A procedure needs to display the word "Pass" when the user enters the letter P (in either uppercase or lowercase) in the txtLetter control, and the word "Fail" when the user enters anything else. Figure 4-28 shows four ways of writing the procedure's code. The `strLetter = "P" OrElse strLetter = "p"` compound condition in Example 1 determines whether the value stored in the `strLetter` variable is either the uppercase letter P or the lowercase letter p. When the variable contains one of those two letters, the compound condition evaluates to True and the selection structure displays the word "Pass" on the screen; otherwise, it displays the word "Fail". You may be wondering why you need to compare the contents of the `strLetter` variable with both the uppercase and lowercase forms of the letter P. As is true in many programming languages, string comparisons in Visual Basic are case sensitive, which means that the uppercase version of a letter is not the same as its lowercase counterpart. So, although a human being recognizes P and p as being the same letter, a computer does not; to a computer, a P is different from a p. The reason for this differentiation is that each character on the computer keyboard is stored using a different Unicode character in the computer's internal memory.

In Example 2 in Figure 4-28, the compound condition `strLetter <> "P" AndAlso strLetter <> "p"` determines whether the value stored in the `strLetter` variable is not equal to either the uppercase letter P or the lowercase letter p. When the variable does not contain either of those two letters, the compound condition evaluates to True and the selection structure displays the word "Fail" on the screen; otherwise, it displays the word "Pass".

Rather than using a dual-alternative selection structure, as in Examples 1 and 2, Example 3 uses two single-alternative selection structures. Although the selection structures in Example 3 produce the same results as the ones in Examples 1 and 2, they do so less efficiently. To illustrate this point, assume that the user enters the letter P in the txtLetter control. The compound condition in the first selection structure in Example 3 determines whether the value stored in the `strLetter` variable is equal to either P or p. In this case, the compound condition evaluates to True, because the variable contains the letter P. As a result, the first selection structure's true path displays the word "Pass". Although the appropriate word ("Pass") already appears in the interface, the procedure still evaluates the second selection structure's compound condition to determine whether to display the "Fail" message. The second evaluation is unnecessary and makes Example 3's code less efficient than the code shown in Examples 1 and 2.

Finally, the selection structure in Example 4 in Figure 4-28 also contains a string comparison in its condition. However, notice that the condition does not use a logical operator; rather, it uses the ToUpper method. You will learn about the ToUpper method in the next section.

Procedures containing string comparisons

Example 1 – using the OrElse operator
```
Dim strLetter As String
strLetter = txtLetter.Text
If strLetter = "P" OrElse strLetter = "p" Then
      lblMessage.Text = "Pass"
Else
      lblMessage.Text = "Fail"
End If
```

Example 2 – using the AndAlso operator
```
Dim strLetter As String
strLetter = txtLetter.Text
If strLetter <> "P" AndAlso strLetter <> "p" Then
      lblMessage.Text = "Fail"
Else
      lblMessage.Text = "Pass"
End If
```

Example 3 – correct, but less efficient, solution
```
Dim strLetter As String
strLetter = txtLetter.Text
If strLetter = "P" OrElse strLetter = "p" Then
      lblMessage.Text = "Pass"
End If
If strLetter <> "P" AndAlso strLetter <> "p" Then
      lblMessage.Text = "Fail"
End If
```

Example 4 – using the ToUpper method
```
Dim strLetter As String
strLetter = txtLetter.Text
If strLetter.ToUpper = "P" Then
      lblMessage.Text = "Pass"
Else
      lblMessage.Text = "Fail"
End If
```

Figure 4-28   Examples of using string comparisons in a procedure

Converting a String to Uppercase or Lowercase

As already mentioned, string comparisons in Visual Basic are case-sensitive, which means that the string "Yes" is not the same as either the string "YES" or the string "yes". A problem occurs when a comparison needs to include a string that is either entered by the user or read from a file, because you cannot always control the case of the string. Although you can change a text box's CharacterCasing property from its default value of Normal to either Upper (which converts the user's entry to uppercase) or Lower (which converts the user's entry to lowercase), you may not want to change the case of the user's entry as he or she is typing it. And it's entirely possible that you may not be aware of the case of strings that are read from a file. Before using a string in a comparison, you can convert it to either uppercase or lowercase and then use the converted string in the comparison. Visual Basic provides the **ToUpper method** for converting a string to uppercase, and the **ToLower method** for converting a string to lowercase. The ToUpper and ToLower methods affect only characters that represent letters of the alphabet, as these are the only characters that have uppercase and lowercase forms.

> You will use the CharacterCasing property in Discovery Exercise 18 at the end of this lesson.

215

Figure 4-29 shows the syntax of the ToUpper and ToLower methods and includes examples of using the methods. In each syntax, *string* typically is either the name of a String variable or the Text property of an object. Both methods temporarily convert the *string* to the specified case. When using the ToUpper method in a comparison, be sure that everything you are comparing is uppercase; otherwise, the comparison will not evaluate correctly. For example, the condition `strLetter.ToUpper = "p"` is not correct: the condition will always evaluate to False, because the uppercase letter P will never be equal to a lowercase letter p. Likewise, when using the ToLower method in a comparison, be sure that everything you are comparing is lowercase. You also can use the ToUpper and ToLower methods to permanently convert the contents of either a String variable or a control's Text property to uppercase or lowercase, respectively. You do this using an assignment statement, as shown in Example 6 in Figure 4-29.

ToUpper and ToLower methods

Syntax
string.**ToUpper**
string.**ToLower**

Example 1
```
If strLetter.ToUpper = "P" Then
```
compares the uppercase version of the string stored in the `strLetter` variable with the uppercase letter P

Example 2
```
If strItem1.ToUpper = strItem2.ToUpper Then
```
compares the uppercase version of the string stored in the `strItem1` variable with the uppercase version of the string stored in the `strItem2` variable

---

Figure 4-29 Syntax and examples of the ToUpper and ToLower methods *(continues)*

(continued)

Example 3
```
If strLetter.ToLower > "f" Then
```
compares the lowercase version of the string stored in the `strLetter` variable with the lowercase letter f

Example 4
```
If "paris" = txtCity.Text.ToLower Then
```
compares the lowercase string "paris" with the lowercase version of the string stored in the txtCity control's Text property

Example 5
```
lblName.Text = strCustomer.ToUpper
```
assigns the uppercase version of the string stored in the `strCustomer` variable to the lblName control's Text property

Example 6
```
strName = strName.ToUpper
txtState.Text = txtState.Text.ToLower
```
changes the contents of the `strName` variable to uppercase, and changes the contents of the txtState control's Text property to lowercase

---

Figure 4-29 Syntax and examples of the ToUpper and ToLower methods

Using the ToUpper and ToLower Methods: Displaying a Message

A procedure needs to display the message "We have a store in this state." when the user enters any of the following three state IDs: Il, In, Ky. When the user enters an ID other than these, the procedure should display the message "We don't have a store in this state." Figure 4-30 shows three ways of writing the procedure's code. When the computer processes the compound condition in Example 1, it temporarily converts the contents of the `strState` variable to uppercase and then compares the result to the string "IL". If the comparison evaluates to False, the computer again temporarily converts the contents of the variable to uppercase, this time comparing the result to the string "IN". If the comparison evaluates to False, the computer again converts the contents of the variable to uppercase; this time, it compares the result to the string "KY". Notice that, depending on the result of each condition, the computer might need to convert the contents of the `strState` variable to uppercase three times.

Example 2 in Figure 4-30 provides a more efficient way of writing Example 1's code. The `strState = txtState.Text.ToUpper` statement in Example 2 temporarily converts the contents of the txtState control's Text property to uppercase and then assigns the result to the `strState` variable. The compound condition then compares the contents of the `strState` variable (which now contains uppercase letters) to the string "IL". If the comparison evaluates to False, the computer compares the variable's contents to the string "IN". If this comparison evaluates to False, the computer compares the variable's contents to the string "KY". Notice that the value in the txtState control's Text property is converted to uppercase only once, rather than three times. However, although the code shown in Example 2 is more efficient than the code shown in Example 1, there may be times when you will not want to change the case of the string stored in a variable. For example, you may need to display (on the screen or in a printed report) the variable's contents using the exact case entered by the user.

The `strState = txtState.Text.ToLower` statement in Example 3 in Figure 4-30 assigns the contents of the txtState control's Text property, in lowercase, to the `strState` variable. The compound condition in Example 3 is processed similarly to the compound condition in Example 2. However, the comparisons are made using lowercase letters rather than uppercase letters, and the comparisons test for inequality rather than equality. The three examples in Figure 4-30 produce the same result and simply represent different ways of performing the same task.

Procedures containing the ToUpper and ToLower methods

Example 1 – using the ToUpper method in a condition
```
Dim strState As String
strState = txtState.Text
If strState.ToUpper = "IL" OrElse
    strState.ToUpper = "IN" OrElse
    strState.ToUpper = "KY" Then
    lblMsg.Text = "We have a store in this state."
Else
    lblMsg.Text = "We don't have a store in this state."
End If
```

Example 2 – using the ToUpper method in an assignment statement
```
Dim strState As String
strState = txtState.Text.ToUpper
If strState = "IL" OrElse
    strState = "IN" OrElse strState = "KY" Then
    lblMsg.Text = "We have a store in this state."
Else
    lblMsg.Text = "We don't have a store in this state."
End If
```

Example 3 – using the ToLower method in an assignment statement
```
Dim strState As String
strState = txtState.Text.ToLower
If strState <> "il" AndAlso
    strState <> "in" AndAlso strState <> "ky" Then
    lblMsg.Text = "We don't have a store in this state."
Else
    lblMsg.Text = "We have a store in this state."
End If
```

Figure 4-30 Examples of using the ToUpper and ToLower methods in a procedure

START HERE **To code and then test the Store Locator application:**

1. Open the State Solution (State Solution.sln) file contained in the VB2010\Chap04\State Solution folder. If necessary, open the designer window.

2. Open the Code Editor window. Replace <your name> and <current date> in the comments with your name and the current date, respectively.

3. Open the code template for the btnToUpper1 control's Click event procedure. Enter the code shown in Example 1 in Figure 4-30.

4. Open the code template for the btnToUpper2 control's Click event procedure. Enter the code shown in Example 2 in Figure 4-30.

5. Open the code template for the btnToLower control's Click event procedure. Enter the code shown in Example 3 in Figure 4-30.

6. Save the solution and then start the application. Type **ky** in the State ID box and then click the **ToUpper Example 1** button. The button's Click event procedure displays the appropriate message in the lblMsg control. See Figure 4-31.

Figure 4-31   Message shown in the interface

7. Change the state ID to **tn** and then click the **ToUpper Example 1** button. The button's Click event procedure displays the "We don't have a store in this state." message.

8. On your own, test the code for the ToUpper Example 2 and ToLower Example 3 buttons.

9. When you are finished testing the code, click the **Exit** button. Close the Code Editor window and then close the solution.

YOU DO IT 5!

Create a Visual Basic Windows application named YouDoIt 5. Save the application in the VB2010\Chap04 folder. Add a text box, a label, and a button to the form. If the user enters the letter A (in either uppercase or lowercase), the button's Click event procedure should display the string "Addition" in the label; otherwise, it should display the string "Subtraction". Code the procedure. Save the solution and then start and test the application. Close the solution.

Comparing Boolean Values

You also can compare Boolean values in an If...Then...Else statement's condition, as shown in the examples in Figure 4-32. Each example uses a Boolean variable named `blnIsInsured`. As you learned in Chapter 3, a Boolean variable can store either the Boolean value True or the Boolean value False. The `blnIsInsured = True` condition in Example 1 and the `blnIsInsured` condition in Example 2 produce the same result: both conditions evaluate to True when the `blnIsInsured` variable contains the Boolean value True. In the last two examples, the `blnIsInsured = False` condition and the `Not blnIsInsured` condition also produce the same result. In this case, both conditions evaluate to True when the `blnIsInsured` variable contains the Boolean value False.

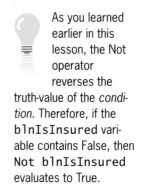

As you learned earlier in this lesson, the Not operator reverses the truth-value of the *condition*. Therefore, if the `blnIsInsured` variable contains False, then `Not blnIsInsured` evaluates to True.

219

Boolean values used in a condition

Example 1
```
If blnIsInsured = True Then
```
The condition evaluates to True when the `blnIsInsured` variable contains the Boolean value True; otherwise, it evaluates to False.

Example 2
```
If blnIsInsured Then
```
Same as Example 1.

Example 3
```
If blnIsInsured = False Then
```
The condition evaluates to True when the `blnIsInsured` variable contains the Boolean value False; otherwise, it evaluates to True.

Example 4
```
If Not blnIsInsured Then
```
Same as Example 3.

Figure 4-32 Examples of using Boolean values in a condition

Comparing Boolean Values: Determining Whether a String Can Be Converted to a Number

In Chapter 3, you learned how to use the TryParse method to convert a string to a number of a specific data type. Recall that if the conversion is successful, the TryParse method stores the number in the variable specified in the method's *numericVariableName* argument; otherwise, it stores the number 0 in the variable. In addition to storing a value in the variable, the TryParse method also returns a Boolean value that indicates whether the conversion was successful. It returns the Boolean value True when the string can be converted to the specified numeric data type, and returns the Boolean value False when the string cannot be converted. You can assign the value returned by the TryParse method to a Boolean variable, as shown in the syntax and example in Figure 4-33. You then can use an If...Then...Else statement to take the appropriate action based on the result of the conversion.

Using the Boolean value returned by the TryParse method

<u>Syntax</u>
booleanVariable = *dataType*.**TryParse**(*string*, *numericVariableName*)

<u>Example</u>
`blnIsSalesOk = Double.TryParse(txtSales.Text, dblSales)`
If the string contained in the txtSales control can be converted to a Double number, the TryParse method converts the string and stores the result in the `dblSales` variable. It also assigns the Boolean value True to the `blnIsSalesOk` variable. If the string cannot be converted to a Double number, the TryParse method stores the number 0 in the `dblSales` variable and also assigns the Boolean value False to the `blnIsSalesOk` variable.

Figure 4-33   Syntax and an example of using the Boolean value returned by the TryParse method

START HERE

To use the TryParse method's Boolean value in a procedure:

1. Open the New Pay Solution (New Pay Solution.sln) file contained in the VB2010\Chap04\New Pay Solution folder. If necessary, open the designer window.

2. Open the Code Editor window. Replace <your name> and <current date> in the comments with your name and the current date, respectively.

3. Locate the btnCalc control's Click event procedure. Notice that the code does not use the Boolean value returned by the TryParse method. Before modifying the code, you will observe how the procedure currently works. Start the application. Type **10** in the Old pay box and then click the **Calculate** button. Even though no raise rate was entered, the btnCalc control's Click event procedure displays a new pay amount in the lblNew control. In this case, it displays the old pay amount ($10.00) as the new pay amount.

4. Type **a** in the Raise rate box and then click the **Calculate** button. Here again, the procedure displays $10.00 as the new pay amount, even though the raise rate is invalid. See Figure 4-34.

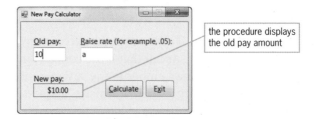

Figure 4-34   New pay displayed by the current Click event procedure

5. Change the raise rate to **.05** and then click the **Calculate** button. The procedure displays $10.50 as the new pay amount, which is correct. Click the **Exit** button.

6. Use the code shown in Figure 4-35 to modify the btnCalc control's Click event procedure. The modifications are shaded in the figure.

```
Private Sub btnCalc_Click(ByVal sender As Object,
ByVal e As System.EventArgs) Handles btnCalc.Click
    ' calculates and displays the new pay

    Dim dblOld As Double
    Dim dblRate As Double
    Dim dblNew As Double
    Dim blnIsOldOk As Boolean
    Dim blnIsRateOk As Boolean

    ' convert the input to numbers
    blnIsOldOk = Double.TryParse(txtOld.Text, dblOld)
    blnIsRateOk = Double.TryParse(txtRate.Text, dblRate)

    ' determine whether the conversions were successful
    If blnIsOldOk AndAlso blnIsRateOk Then
        ' calculate and display the new pay
        dblNew = dblOld + dblOld * dblRate
        lblNew.Text = dblNew.ToString("C2")
    Else
        lblNew.Text = "Invalid data"
    End If

    ' set the focus
    txtOld.Focus()
End Sub
```

Figure 4-35   Modified btnCalc control's Click event procedure

7. Save the solution and then start the application. Type **10** in the Old pay box and then click the **Calculate** button. Because no raise rate was entered, the procedure displays the "Invalid data" message in the lblNew control.

8. Type **.05** in the Raise rate box and then click the **Calculate** button. The procedure calculates and displays $10.50 as the new pay amount, which is correct.

9. Change the old pay to the letter **a** and then click the **Calculate** button. The procedure displays the "Invalid data" message, which is correct.

10. Click the **Exit** button. Close the Code Editor window and then close the solution.

YOU DO IT 6!

Create a Visual Basic Windows application named YouDoIt 6. Save the application in the VB2010\Chap04 folder. Add a text box, a label, and a button to the form. If the user enters a value that can be converted to an Integer, the button's Click event procedure should display the integer in the label; otherwise, it should display the string "Can't be converted". Code the procedure. Save the solution and then start and test the application. Close the solution.

Summary of Operators

Figure 4-36 shows the order of precedence for the arithmetic, concatenation, comparison, and logical operators you have learned so far. Notice that logical operators are evaluated after any arithmetic operators or comparison operators in an expression. As a result, when the computer processes the expression 30 > 75 / 3 AndAlso 5 < 10 * 2, it evaluates the arithmetic operators first, followed by the comparison operators and then the logical operator. The expression evaluates to True, as shown in the example included in Figure 4-36.

Operator	Operation	Precedence number
^	exponentiation (raises a number to a power)	1
–	negation	2
*, /	multiplication and division	3
\	integer division	4
Mod	modulus	5
+, –	addition and subtraction	6
&	concatenation	7
=, >, >=, <, <=, <>	equal to, greater than, greater than or equal to, less than, less than or equal to, not equal to	8
Not	reverses the truth-value of the condition; True becomes False, and False becomes True	9
AndAlso, And	all sub-conditions must be True for the compound condition to evaluate to True	10
OrElse, Or	only one of the sub-conditions needs to be True for the compound condition to evaluate to True	11
Xor	one and only one of the sub-conditions can be True for the compound condition to evaluate to True	12

Example

Evaluation steps	Result
Original expression	30 > 75 / 3 AndAlso 5 < 10 * 2
75 / 3 is evaluated first	30 > 25 AndAlso 5 < 10 * 2
10 * 2 is evaluated second	30 > 25 AndAlso 5 < 20
30 > 25 is evaluated third	True AndAlso 5 < 20
5 < 20 is evaluated fourth	True AndAlso True
True AndAlso True is evaluated last	True

Figure 4-36   Listing of arithmetic, concatenation, comparison, and logical operators

Lesson A Summary

- To code single-alternative and dual-alternative selection structures:

  Use the If...Then...Else statement. The statement's syntax is shown in Figure 4-11.

- To compare two values:

  Use the comparison operators listed in Figure 4-12.

- To swap the values contained in two variables:

  Assign the first variable's value to a temporary variable. Assign the second variable's value to the first variable, and then assign the temporary variable's value to the second variable.

- To create a compound condition:

  Use the logical operators listed in Figure 4-23. The truth tables for the logical operators are shown in Figure 4-24.

- To convert the user's text box entry to either uppercase or lowercase as the user is typing the text:

  Change the text box's CharacterCasing property from Normal to either Upper or Lower.

- To temporarily convert a string to uppercase:

  Use the ToUpper method. The method's syntax is *string*.**ToUpper**.

- To temporarily convert a string to lowercase:

  Use the ToLower method. The method's syntax is *string*.**ToLower**.

- To determine whether the TryParse method converted a string to a number of the specified data type:

  Use the syntax *booleanVariable* = *dataType*.**TryParse**(*string*, *numericVariableName*). The TryParse method returns the Boolean value True when the string can be converted to the numeric *dataType*; otherwise, it returns the Boolean value False.

- To evaluate an expression containing arithmetic, comparison, and logical operators:

  Evaluate the arithmetic operators first, followed by the comparison operators and then the logical operators. Figure 4-36 shows the order of precedence for the arithmetic, concatenation, comparison, and logical operators you have learned so far.

Lesson A Key Terms

And operator—one of the logical operators; when used to combine two sub-conditions, the resulting compound condition evaluates to True only when both sub-conditions are True

AndAlso operator—one of the logical operators; same as the And operator, but more efficient because it performs a short-circuit evaluation

Block scope—the scope of a variable declared within a statement block; a variable with block scope can be used only within the statement block in which it is declared, and only after its declaration statement

Block-level variables—variables declared within a statement block; the variables have block scope

Comparison operators—operators used to compare values in an expression; also called relational operators

Condition—specifies the decision you are making and must be phrased so that it evaluates to a Boolean value: either True or False

Data validation—the process of verifying that a program's input data is within the expected range

Decision symbol—the diamond in a flowchart; used to represent the condition in selection and repetition structures

Dual-alternative selection structure—a selection structure that requires one set of actions to be performed when the structure's condition evaluates to True, but a different set of actions to be performed when the structure's condition evaluates to False

False path—contains the instructions to be processed when a selection structure's condition evaluates to False

If...Then...Else statement—used to code single-alternative and dual-alternative selection structures in Visual Basic

Logical operators—operators used to combine two or more sub-conditions into one compound condition; also called Boolean operators

Not operator—one of the logical operators; reverses the truth-value of a condition

Or operator—one of the logical operators; when used to combine two sub-conditions, the resulting compound condition evaluates to False only when both sub-conditions are False

OrElse operator—one of the logical operators; same as the Or operator, but more efficient because it performs a short-circuit evaluation

Selection structure—one of the three basic control structures; tells the computer to make a decision based on some condition and then select the appropriate action; also called the decision structure

Short-circuit evaluation—refers to the way the computer evaluates two sub-conditions connected by either the AndAlso or OrElse operators; when the AndAlso operator is used, the computer does not evaluate sub-condition2 when sub-condition1 is False; when the OrElse operator is used, the computer does not evaluate sub-condition2 when sub-condition1 is True

Single-alternative selection structure—a selection structure that requires a special set of actions to be performed only when the structure's condition evaluates to True

Statement block—in a selection structure, the set of statements terminated by an Else or End If clause

ToLower method—temporarily converts a string to lowercase

ToUpper method—temporarily converts a string to uppercase

True path—contains the instructions to be processed when a selection structure's condition evaluates to True

Truth tables—tables that summarize how the computer evaluates the logical operators in an expression

225

Lesson A Review Questions

1. What is the scope of variables declared in an If...Then...Else statement's false path?

   a. the entire application

   b. the procedure in which the If...Then...Else statement appears

   c. the entire If...Then...Else statement

   d. only the false path in the If...Then...Else statement

2. Which of the following is a valid condition for an If...Then...Else statement?

   a. `dblSales > 500 AndAlso < 800`

   b. `dblCost > 100 AndAlso dblCost <= 1000`

   c. `strState.ToUpper = "Alaska" OrElse`
      `strState.ToUpper = "Hawaii"`

   d. none of the above

3. Which of the following conditions should you use in an If...Then...Else statement to compare the string contained in the txtName control with the name Bob? (Be sure the condition will handle Bob, BOB, bob, and so on.)

   a. `txtName.Text = ToUpper("BOB")`

   b. `txtName.Text = ToUpper("Bob")`

   c. `ToUpper(txtName.Text) = "BOB"`

   d. `txtName.Text.ToUpper = "BOB"`

4. The six logical operators are listed below. Indicate their order of precedence by placing a number (1, 2, and so on) on the line to the left of the operator. (If two or more operators have the same precedence, assign the same number to each.)

   _____ Xor

   _____ And

   _____ Not

   _____ Or

   _____ AndAlso

   _____ OrElse

5. An expression can contain arithmetic, comparison, and logical operators. Indicate the order of precedence for the three types of operators by placing a number (1, 2, or 3) on the line to the left of the operator type.

_____ Arithmetic

_____ Logical

_____ Comparison

6. The expression `3 > 6 AndAlso 7 > 4` evaluates to _____.

   a. True

   b. False

7. The expression `4 > 6 OrElse 10 < 2 * 6` evaluates to _____.

   a. True

   b. False

8. The expression `7 >= 3 + 5 OrElse 6 < 4 AndAlso 2 < 5` evaluates to _____.

   a. True

   b. False

9. The expression `5 * 2 > 5 * 3 AndAlso True` evaluates to _____.

   a. True

   b. False

10. The expression `5 * 3 > 3 ^ 2` evaluates to _____.

    a. True

    b. False

11. The expression `5 * 3 > 3 ^ 2 AndAlso True OrElse False` evaluates to _____.

    a. True

    b. False

Use the selection structure shown in Figure 4-37 to answer Questions 12 and 13.

```
If intNumber <= 100 Then
     intNumber = intNumber * 2
Else
     intNumber = intNumber * 3
End If
```

Figure 4-37 Code for Review Questions 12 and 13

12. If the `intNumber` variable contains the number 90, what value will be in the variable after the selection structure in Figure 4-37 is processed?

    a. 0

    b. 90

    c. 180

    d. 270

13. If the `intNumber` variable contains the number 1000, what value will be in the variable after the selection structure in Figure 4-37 is processed?

    a. 0

    b. 1000

    c. 2000

    d. 3000

14. If the txtPrice control contains the value 75, what value will the `Decimal.TryParse(txtPrice.Text, decPrice)` method return?

    a. False

    b. True

    c. 75

    d. 75.00

Lesson A Exercises

1. Draw the flowchart corresponding to the pseudocode shown in Figure 4-38.

    INTRODUCTORY

    ```
    if the hours are greater than 40
            display "Overtime pay"
    else
            display "Regular pay"
    end if
    ```

    Figure 4-38 Pseudocode for Exercise 1

INTRODUCTORY

2. Write an If…Then…Else statement that displays the string "Pontiac" in the lblCarMake control when the txtCar control contains the string "Grand Am" (in any case).

INTRODUCTORY

3. Write an If…Then…Else statement that displays the string "Please enter your ZIP code" in the lblMsg control when the txtZip control does not contain any data.

INTRODUCTORY

4. Write an If…Then…Else statement that displays the string "Entry error" in the lblMsg control when the intUnits variable contains a number that is less than 0; otherwise, display the string "Valid number".

INTRODUCTORY

5. Write an If…Then…Else statement that displays the string "Reorder" in the lblMsg control when the intQuantity variable contains a number that is less than 10; otherwise, display the string "OK".

INTRODUCTORY

6. Write an If…Then…Else statement that assigns the number 10 to the intBonus variable when the dblSales variable contains a number that is less than or equal to $250; otherwise, assign the number 15.

INTRODUCTORY

7. Write an If…Then…Else statement that displays the value 25 in the lblShipping control when the strState variable contains the string "Hawaii" (in any case); otherwise, display the value 50.

INTRODUCTORY

8. A procedure contains the blnIsSalesOk = Double.TryParse(txtSales.Text, dblSales) statement. Write an If…Then…Else statement that displays the string "Please enter a number" in the lblMsg control when the contents of the txtSales control cannot be converted to a Double number; otherwise, multiply the contents of the dblSales variable by 10% and display the result in the lblMsg control.

INTRODUCTORY

9. Write an If…Then…Else statement that displays the string "Dog" in the lblAnimal control when the strAnimal variable contains the letter "D" (in any case); otherwise, display the string "Cat". Also draw the flowchart.

INTRODUCTORY

10. A procedure should calculate a 3% sales tax when the strState variable contains the string "Colorado" (in any case); otherwise, it should calculate a 4% sales tax. The sales tax is calculated by multiplying the tax rate by the contents of the dblSales variable. Store the sales tax in the dblTax variable. Display the sales tax amount in the lblTax control. Draw the flowchart and then write the Visual Basic code.

INTERMEDIATE

11. A procedure should calculate an employee's gross pay. Employees working more than 40 hours receive time and one-half for the hours over 40. Use the variables decHours, decHourRate, and decGross. Display the contents of the decGross variable in the lblGross control. Write the pseudocode and then write the Visual Basic code.

12. A procedure should calculate a 10% discount on desks sold to customers in Colorado. Use the variables `strItem`, `strState`, `dblSales`, and `dblDiscount`. Format the discount using the "C2" format and display it in the lblDiscount control. Write the Visual Basic code.

INTERMEDIATE

13. A procedure should calculate a 2% price increase on all red shirts, but a 1% price increase on all other items. In addition to calculating the price increase, the procedure also should calculate the new price. You can use the variables `strItemColor`, `strItem`, `decOrigPrice`, `decIncrease`, and `decNewPrice`. Format the original price, price increase, and new price using the "N2" format. Display the original price, price increase, and new price in the lblOriginal, lblIncrease, and lblNewPrice controls, respectively. Write the Visual Basic code.

INTERMEDIATE

229

14. Write the Visual Basic code that swaps the values stored in the `decLowSales` and `decHighSales` variables, but only if the value stored in the `decHighSales` variable is less than the value stored in the `decLowSales` variable.

INTERMEDIATE

15. In this exercise, you modify the Addition and Subtraction application from this lesson. Use Windows to make a copy of the Addition and Subtraction Solution folder. Rename the copy Modified Addition and Subtraction Solution. Open the Addition and Subtraction Solution (Addition and Subtraction Solution.sln) file contained in the Modified Addition and Subtraction Solution folder. Open the designer window. Change Label1's text from "Enter 1 for Addition or 2 for Subtraction" to "Enter A for Addition or S for Subtraction". Open the Code Editor window. Make the appropriate modifications to the btnCalc control's Click event procedure. (The user should be able to enter the operation letter in either uppercase or lowercase.) Save the solution and then start and test the application. Close the Code Editor window and then close the solution.

INTERMEDIATE

16. Open the Bonus Solution (Bonus Solution.sln) file contained in the VB2010\Chap04\Bonus Solution folder. If necessary, open the designer window. The btnCalc control's Click event procedure should calculate a 5% bonus and then display the result (formatted using the "C2" format) in the lblBonus control. Calculate and display the bonus only when the TryParse method is successful; otherwise, display the message "Invalid sales" in the lblBonus control. Code the procedure. Save the solution and then start and test the application. Close the Code Editor window and then close the solution.

INTERMEDIATE

17. Open the Sum Solution (Sum Solution.sln) file contained in the VB2010\Chap04\Sum Solution folder. If necessary, open the designer window. The btnCalc control's Click event procedure should calculate the sum of the two values entered by the user, and then display the result in the lblSum control. Calculate and display the sum only when both values can be converted to the Integer data type; otherwise, display the message "Please enter two integers" in the lblSum control. Code the procedure. Save the solution and then start and test the application. Close the Code Editor window and then close the solution.

INTERMEDIATE

Discovery

18. In this exercise, you learn how to use a text box's CharacterCasing property. Open the CharCase Solution (CharCase Solution.sln) file contained in the VB2010\Chap04\CharCase Solution folder. If necessary, open the designer window.

   a. Open the Code Editor window and study the code contained in the btnDisplay control's Click event procedure. The code compares the text entered by the user with the strings "IL", "IN", and "KY". However, it does not convert the contents of the text box to uppercase. Start the application. Enter ky as the state ID and then click the Display button. The button's Click event procedure displays the "We don't have a store in this state." message, which is incorrect. Click the Exit button.

   b. Use the Properties window to change the txtState control's CharacterCasing property to Upper. Save the solution and then start the application. Enter ky as the state ID. Notice that the letters appear in uppercase in the text box. Click the Display button. The button's Click event procedure displays the "We have a store in this state." message, which is correct. Close the Code Editor window and then close the solution.

LESSON B

After studying Lesson B, you should be able to:

- Group objects using a GroupBox control
- Calculate a periodic payment using the Financial.Pmt method
- Create a message box using the MessageBox.Show method
- Determine the value returned by a message box

231

Creating the Monthly Payment Calculator Application

Recall that your task in this chapter is to create an application that calculates and displays the monthly payment on a car loan. To make the calculation, the application must know the loan amount (principal), the annual percentage rate (APR) of interest, and the life of the loan (term) in years.

The Ch04BVideo file demonstrates all of the steps contained in Lesson B. You can view the video either before or after completing the lesson.

To open the partially completed Monthly Payment Calculator application:

> START HERE

1. If necessary, start Visual Studio 2010 or Visual Basic 2010 Express.

2. Open the Payment Solution (Payment Solution.sln) file contained in the VB2010\Chap04\Payment Solution folder. If necessary, open the designer window. Missing from the interface is a group box control.

Adding a Group Box to the Form

You use the GroupBox tool to add a group box to the interface. The GroupBox tool is located in the Containers section of the toolbox, because a group box serves as a container for other controls. You can use a **group box** to visually separate related controls from other controls on the form. The group box in the Monthly Payment Calculator interface will visually separate the controls relating to the principal, rate, and term information from the rest of the controls. The group box and the controls contained in the group box are treated as one unit. When you move the group box, the controls inside the group box also move. Likewise, when you delete the group box, the controls inside the group box also are deleted. You can include an identifying label on a group box by setting the group box's Text property. Labeling a group box is optional; but if you do label it, the label should be entered using sentence capitalization.

GUI DESIGN TIP Labeling a Group Box

Use sentence capitalization for the optional identifying label, which is entered in the group box's Text property.

To utilize a group box in the interface:

> START HERE

1. If necessary, expand the Containers node in the toolbox. Click the **GroupBox** tool and then drag the mouse pointer to the form. You do not need to worry about the exact location. Release the mouse button. The GroupBox1 control appears on the form.

2. Position and size the group box as shown in Figure 4-39.

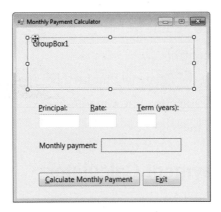

Figure 4-39   Interface showing the location and size of the group box

3. Delete the contents of the group box's Text property, because the group box will not need an identifying label in this interface.

To select more than one control, click the first control and then press and hold down the Ctrl (Control) key as you click the other controls you want to select. The move pointer mentioned in Step 4 looks like this:

4. Next, you will drag the controls related to the principal, rate, and term into the group box. You then will center the controls within the group box. Select the following six controls: Label1 (Principal:), txtPrincipal, Label2 (Rate:), txtRate, Label3 (Term (years):), and txtTerm. Place your mouse pointer on one of the selected controls. The mouse pointer turns into the move pointer. Press and hold down the left mouse button as you drag the selected controls into the group box, and then release the mouse button.

5. Use the Format menu to center the selected controls both horizontally and vertically in the group box, and then click the **form** to deselect the controls.

6. Select the remaining two labels and buttons, and then move the selected controls up so they are closer to the group box. In addition, shorten the form. See Figure 4-40.

Figure 4-40   Completed interface

7. Now you will lock the controls in place and then set the tab order. Right-click the **form** and then click **Lock Controls**. Click **View** on the menu bar and then click **Tab Order**. The current TabIndex values appear in blue boxes on the form. Notice that the TabIndex values of the controls contained within the group box begin with the number 10, which is the TabIndex value of the group box itself. The number 10 indicates that the controls belong to the group box rather than to the

form. As mentioned earlier, if you move or delete the group box, the controls that belong to the group box also will be moved or deleted. The numbers that appear after the period in the TabIndex values indicate the order in which each control was added to the group box.

8. Use the information shown in Figure 4-41 to set each control's TabIndex value. When you are finished, press **Esc** to remove the TabIndex boxes, and then save the solution.

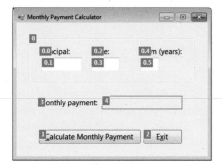

Figure 4-41   Correct TabIndex values for the interface

Coding the Monthly Payment Calculator Application

According to the application's TOE chart, which is shown in Figure 4-42, the Click event procedures for the two buttons need to be coded. The TextChanged, KeyPress, and Enter events for the three text boxes also need to be coded. When you open the Code Editor window, you will notice that the btnExit control's Click event procedure and the TextChanged event procedures for the three text boxes have been coded for you. In this lesson, you will code the btnCalc control's Click event procedure. You will code the KeyPress and Enter event procedures in Lesson C.

Task	Object	Event
1. Calculate the monthly payment 2. Display the monthly payment in lblPayment	btnCalc	Click
End the application	btnExit	Click
Display the monthly payment (from btnCalc)	lblPayment	None
Get and display the principal, rate, and term	txtPrincipal, txtRate, txtTerm	None
Clear the contents of lblPayment		TextChanged
Allow the text box to accept only numbers, the period, and the Backspace key		KeyPress
Select the contents of the text box		Enter

Figure 4-42   TOE chart for the Monthly Payment Calculator application

Coding the btnCalc Control's Click Event Procedure

The btnCalc control's Click event procedure is responsible for calculating the monthly payment and then displaying the result in the lblPayment control. The procedure's pseudocode is shown in Figure 4-43. Notice that the user input (principal, rate, and term) will be assigned to variables. This is because those values probably will change each time the Click event procedure is invoked.

---

btnCalc Click event procedure
1. store user input (principal, rate, and term) in variables
2. if the rate >= 1
        divide the rate by 100 to get its decimal equivalent
    end if
3. if the term >= 1
        calculate the monthly payment using the principal, rate, and term information
        display the monthly payment
    else
        display the message "The term must be greater than or equal to 1."
    end if

Figure 4-43   Pseudocode for the btnCalc control's Click event procedure

START HERE ▶   **To begin coding the btnCalc control's Click event procedure:**

1. Open the Code Editor window. Replace <your name> and <current date> in the comments with your name and the current date, respectively.

2. Open the code template for the btnCalc control's Click event procedure. Type the following comment and then press **Enter** twice:

    ' calculates and displays a monthly payment

First, study the procedure's pseudocode to determine any other variables or named constants the procedure will use. When determining the named constants, look for items whose value will be the same each time the procedure is invoked. In the btnCalc control's Click event procedure, the number 1 that appears in Steps 2 and 3, as well as the number 100 in Step 2 and the message in Step 3, will be the same each time the procedure is invoked. Although you could create named constants for the numbers 1 and 100, doing so is unnecessary because those values are already self-documenting and are unlikely to change. You will, however, create a named constant for the message. The named constant will make the code easier to understand. In addition, it will allow you (or another programmer) to quickly locate the message should it need to be changed in the future. When determining the procedure's variables, look in the pseudocode for items, other than the input items, whose value probably will change each time the procedure is processed. In this case, in addition to the input items (principal, rate, and term), the monthly payment amount probably will be different each time the Calculate Monthly Payment button is clicked; therefore, you will assign that value to a variable.

To continue coding the btnCalc control's Click event procedure: START HERE

1. Enter the following Const and Dim statements. Press **Enter** twice after typing the last Dim statement.

   Const strMSG As String =
       "The term must be greater than or equal to 1."
   Dim dblPrincipal As Double
   Dim dblRate As Double
   Dim dblTerm As Double
   Dim dblMonthlyPayment As Double

2. Step 1 in the pseudocode is to store the input items in variables. Enter the following TryParse methods. Press **Enter** twice after typing the last TryParse method.

   Double.TryParse(txtPrincipal.Text, dblPrincipal)
   Double.TryParse(txtRate.Text, dblRate)
   Double.TryParse(txtTerm.Text, dblTerm)

3. Next, you will use a selection structure to handle Step 2 in the pseudocode. Step 2 determines whether the interest rate needs to be converted to its decimal equivalent. This is necessary because the user might enter the rate as either a whole number or a decimal number. For example, an interest rate of 5% might be entered as either 5 or .05. Enter the following comment and If clause. When you press Enter after typing the If clause, the Code Editor will automatically enter the End If clause for you.

   ' convert the rate to decimal form, if necessary
   If dblRate >= 1 Then

4. Type **dblRate = dblRate / 100** and then click **at the end of the End If clause**. Press **Enter** twice to insert two blank lines after the clause.

5. The last step in the pseudocode is to determine whether the term entered by the user is valid. To be valid, the term must be greater than or equal to one year. Enter the following comment and If clause. When you press Enter after typing the If clause, the Code Editor will automatically enter the End If clause for you.

   ' verify that the term is valid
   If dblTerm >= 1 Then

6. Save the solution. Figure 4-44 shows the code currently entered in the procedure.

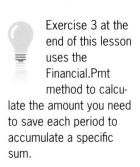

Using a blank line to separate related blocks of code in the Code Editor window makes the code easier to read and understand.

```
btnCalc                                          Click
    Private Sub btnCalc_Click(ByVal sender As Object, ByVal
        ' calculates and displays a monthly payment

        Const strMSG As String =
            "The term must be greater than or equal to 1. "
        Dim dblPrincipal As Double
        Dim dblRate As Double
        Dim dblTerm As Double
        Dim dblMonthlyPayment As Double

        Double.TryParse(txtPrincipal.Text, dblPrincipal)
        Double.TryParse(txtRate.Text, dblRate)
        Double.TryParse(txtTerm.Text, dblTerm)

        ' convert the rate to decimal form, if necessary
        If dblRate >= 1 Then
            dblRate = dblRate / 100
        End If

        ' verify that the term is valid
        If dblTerm >= 1 Then
                                                        ─── insertion point

        End If
    End Sub
```

Figure 4-44　Partially completed Click event procedure

If the term is valid, the procedure should calculate the monthly payment and then display the result. You can calculate the monthly payment using the Financial.Pmt method.

Using the Financial.Pmt Method

The **Financial.Pmt method** calculates a periodic payment on either a loan or an investment, and it returns the calculated value as a Double number. Figure 4-45 shows the method's basic syntax and lists the meaning of each argument. The *Rate* and *NPer* (number of periods) arguments must be expressed using the same units. If Rate is a monthly interest rate, then NPer must specify the number of monthly payments. Similarly, if Rate is an annual interest rate, then NPer must specify the number of annual payments. Figure 4-45 also includes examples of using the Financial.Pmt method. Example 1 calculates the annual payment for a loan of $9000 for 3 years at 5% interest. As the example indicates, the annual payment rounded to the nearest cent is −3304.88. This means that if you borrow $9000 for 3 years at 5% interest, you will need to make three annual payments of $3304.88 to pay off the loan. Notice that the Financial.Pmt method returns a negative number. You can change the negative number to a positive number by preceding the method with the negation operator, like this: −Financial.Pmt(.05, 3, 9000). As you learned in Chapter 2, the purpose of the negation operator is to reverse the sign of a number. A negative number preceded by the negation operator becomes a positive number, and vice versa. The Financial.Pmt method shown in Example 2 calculates the monthly payment for a loan of $12000 for 5 years at 6% interest. In this example, the Rate and NPer arguments are expressed in monthly terms rather than in annual terms. You change an annual rate to a monthly rate by dividing the annual rate by 12. You change the term from years to months by multiplying the number of years by 12. The monthly payment for the loan in Example 2, rounded to the nearest cent and expressed as a positive number, is 231.99.

Exercise 3 at the end of this lesson uses the Financial.Pmt method to calculate the amount you need to save each period to accumulate a specific sum.

Financial.Pmt method

Syntax
Financial.Pmt(*Rate***, *NPer***, *PV***)**

Argument	Meaning
Rate	interest rate per period
NPer	total number of payment periods (the term)
PV	present value of the loan (the loan amount)

Example 1
`Financial.Pmt(.05, 3, 9000)`
Calculates the annual payment for a loan of $9000 for 3 years at 5% interest. *Rate* is .05, *NPer* is 3, and *PV* is 9000. The annual payment (rounded to the nearest cent) is –3304.88.

Example 2
`-Financial.Pmt(.06 / 12, 5 * 12, 12000)`
Calculates the monthly payment for a loan of $12000 for 5 years at 6% interest. *Rate* is .06 / 12, *NPer* is 5 * 12, and *PV* is 12000. The monthly payment (rounded to the nearest cent and expressed as a positive number) is 231.99.

You can use the PMT function in Microsoft Excel to verify that the payments shown in Figure 4-45 are correct.

Figure 4-45 Basic syntax and examples of the Financial.Pmt method

To continue coding the btnCalc control's Click event procedure: START HERE

1. The insertion point should be positioned as shown earlier in Figure 4-44. Enter the following comment and assignment statement. Be sure to enter the negation operator before the Financial.Pmt method so that a positive number is assigned to the dblMonthlyPayment variable.

   ' calculate and display the monthly payment
   dblMonthlyPayment =
      –Financial.Pmt(dblRate/12, dblTerm * 12, dblPrincipal)

2. Next, you will format the monthly payment to show a dollar sign and two decimal places, and then display the formatted amount in the lblPayment control. Enter the following assignment statement:

   lblPayment.Text = dblMonthlyPayment.ToString("C2")

3. Save the solution. Figure 4-46 shows the selection structure's true path coded in the procedure.

```
negation operator

        ' verify that the term is valid
        If dblTerm >= 1 Then
            ' calculate and display the monthly payment
            dblMonthlyPayment =
                -Financial.Pmt(dblRate / 12, dblTerm * 12, dblPrincipal)
            lblPayment.Text = dblMonthlyPayment.ToString("C2")
                                                                        insertion point

        End If
    End Sub
```

Figure 4-46 Selection structure's true path coded in the procedure

When the term entered by the user is not greater than or equal to 1, the procedure should display an appropriate message. In the next section, you will learn how to display the message in a message box.

The MessageBox.Show Method

At times, an application may need to communicate with the user during run time; one means of doing this is through a message box. You display a message box using the **MessageBox.Show method**. The message box contains text, one or more buttons, and an icon. Figure 4-47 shows the method's syntax and lists the meaning of each argument. The figure also includes examples of using the method. Figures 4-48 and 4-49 show the message boxes created by the two examples.

MessageBox.Show method

<u>Syntax</u>
MessageBox.Show(_text, caption, buttons, icon_[, _defaultButton_]**)**

<u>Argument</u>	<u>Meaning</u>
text	text to display in the message box; use sentence capitalization
caption	text to display in the message box's title bar; use book title capitalization

buttons	buttons to display in the message box; can be one of the following constants:
	`MessageBoxButtons.AbortRetryIgnore`
	`MessageBoxButtons.OK` (default setting)
	`MessageBoxButtons.OKCancel`
	`MessageBoxButtons.RetryCancel`
	`MessageBoxButtons.YesNo`
	`MessageBoxButtons.YesNoCancel`

icon	icon to display in the message box; typically, one of the following constants: `MessageBoxIcon.Exclamation` ⚠ `MessageBoxIcon.Information` ⓘ `MessageBoxIcon.Question` ❓ `MessageBoxIcon.Stop` ✖

defaultButton	button automatically selected when the user presses Enter; can be one of the following constants:
	`MessageBoxDefaultButton.Button1` (default setting)
	`MessageBoxDefaultButton.Button2`
	`MessageBoxDefaultButton.Button3`

<u>Example 1</u>
```
MessageBox.Show("Record deleted.", "Payroll",
     MessageBoxButtons.OK, MessageBoxIcon.Information)
```
displays an information message box that contains the message "Record deleted."

Figure 4-47 Syntax and examples of the MessageBox.Show method (_continues_)

(continued)

Example 2
```
MessageBox.Show("Delete this record?", "Payroll",
      MessageBoxButtons.YesNo, MessageBoxIcon.Exclamation,
      MessageBoxDefaultButton.Button2)
```
displays a warning message box that contains the message "Delete this record?"

Figure 4-47 Syntax and examples of the MessageBox.Show method

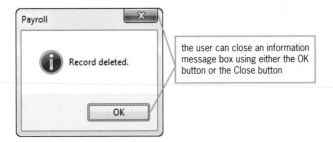

Figure 4-48 Message displayed by the code in Example 1 in Figure 4-47

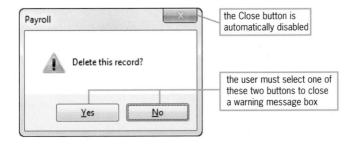

Figure 4-49 Message displayed by the code in Example 2 in Figure 4-47

GUI DESIGN TIP MessageBox.Show Method

- Use sentence capitalization for the *text* argument, but book title capitalization for the *caption* argument.

- Display either the Exclamation icon or the Question icon to alert the user that he or she must make a decision before the application can continue. You can phrase the message as a question.

- Display the Information icon along with an OK button in a message box that displays an informational message.

- Display the Stop icon to alert the user of a serious problem that must be corrected before the application can continue.

- The default button in the dialog box should be the one that represents the user's most likely action, as long as that action is not destructive.

After displaying the message box, the MessageBox.Show method waits for the user to choose one of the buttons. It then closes the message box and returns an integer indicating the button chosen by the user. Sometimes you are not interested in the value returned by the MessageBox.Show method. This is the case when the message box is for informational purposes only, like the message box shown in Figure 4-48. Many times, however, the button selected by the user determines the next task performed by the computer. Selecting the Yes button in the message box shown in Figure 4-49 tells the application to delete the record; selecting the No button tells it *not* to delete the record.

Figure 4-50 lists the integer values returned by the MessageBox.Show method. Each value is associated with a button that can appear in a message box. The figure also lists the DialogResult values assigned to each integer, and the meaning of the integers and DialogResult values. As the figure indicates, the MessageBox.Show method returns the integer 6 when the user selects the Yes button. The integer 6 is represented by the DialogResult value, `DialogResult.Yes`. When referring to the method's return value in code, you should use the DialogResult values rather than the integers, because the values make the code more self-documenting and easier to understand. Also included in Figure 4-50 are two examples of using the MessageBox.Show method's return value. In the first example, the value is assigned to a DialogResult variable named `dlgButton`. The selection structure in the example compares the contents of the `dlgButton` variable with the `DialogResult.Yes` value. In the second example, the method's return value is not stored in a variable. Instead, the method appears in the selection structure's condition, where its return value is compared with the `DialogResult.Yes` value. The selection structure in Example 2 performs one set of tasks when the user selects the Yes button in the message box, but a different set of tasks when the user selects the No button. It is a good programming practice to document the Else portion of the selection structure as shown in Figure 4-50, because it makes it clear that the Else portion is processed only when the user selects the No button.

MessageBox.Show method's return values

Integer	DialogResult value	Meaning
1	`DialogResult.OK`	user chose the OK button
2	`DialogResult.Cancel`	user chose the Cancel button
3	`DialogResult.Abort`	user chose the Abort button
4	`DialogResult.Retry`	user chose the Retry button
5	`DialogResult.Ignore`	user chose the Ignore button
6	`DialogResult.Yes`	user chose the Yes button
7	`DialogResult.No`	user chose the No button

Example 1
```
Dim dlgButton As DialogResult
dlgButton =
     MessageBox.Show("Delete this record?", "Payroll",
     MessageBoxButtons.YesNo, MessageBoxIcon.Exclamation,
     MessageBoxDefaultButton.Button2)
If dlgButton = DialogResult.Yes Then
     instructions to delete the record
End If
```

Figure 4-50   Values returned by the MessageBox.Show method *(continues)*

(continued)

Example 2
```
If MessageBox.Show("Play another game?", "Math Monster",
    MessageBoxButtons.YesNo,
    MessageBoxIcon.Exclamation) = DialogResult.Yes Then
    instructions to start another game
Else    ' No button
    instructions to close the game application
End If
```

Figure 4-50   Values returned by the MessageBox.Show method

In the current application, the btnCalc control's Click event procedure should display a message box when the term entered by the user is not greater than or equal to 1. The message box is for informational purposes only. Therefore, it should contain the Information icon and the OK button, and you do not need to be concerned with its return value. The message to display in the message box is stored in the **strMSG** constant.

To complete the btnCalc control's Click event procedure and then test the code:

START HERE

1. The insertion point should be positioned in the blank line above the End If clause, as shown earlier in Figure 4-46. Enter the following lines of code:

    Else
    >   **MessageBox.Show(strMSG, "Monthly Payment Calculator",**
    >   **MessageBoxButtons.OK,**
    >   **MessageBoxIcon.Information)**

2. If necessary, delete the blank line above the End If clause.

3. Save the solution and then start the application. First, calculate the monthly payment for a loan of $12000 for 5 years at 6% interest. Type **12000** as the principal, **6** as the rate, and **5** as the term. Click the **Calculate Monthly Payment** button. The button's Click event procedure calculates and displays the monthly payment. See Figure 4-51.

Figure 4-51   Monthly payment shown in the interface

4. Next, verify that the application works correctly when the user enters an incorrect term. Change the term from 5 to **0** and then click the **Calculate Monthly Payment** button. The message box shown in Figure 4-52 appears.

Figure 4-52   Message box created by the MessageBox.Show method

5. Click the **OK** button to close the message box.

6. Now verify that the application works correctly when the user enters the interest rate as a decimal number. Change the rate from 6 to **.06**, and change the term from 0 to **5**. Click the **Calculate Monthly Payment** button. The button's Click event procedure calculates and displays a monthly payment of $231.99, which is the same monthly payment shown in Figure 4-51.

7. Click the **Exit** button. Close the Code Editor window and then close the solution.

Figure 4-53 shows the application's code at the end of Lesson B.

```
1 ' Name:          Payment Project
2 ' Purpose:       Calculates the monthly payment on a loan
3 ' Programmer:    <your name> on <current date>
4
5 Option Explicit On
6 Option Strict On
7 Option Infer Off
8
9 Public Class frmMain
10
11    Private Sub btnExit_Click(ByVal sender As Object,
      ByVal e As System.EventArgs) Handles btnExit.Click
12        Me.Close()
13    End Sub
14
15    Private Sub ClearPayment(ByVal sender As Object,
      ByVal e As System.EventArgs
      ) Handles txtPrincipal.TextChanged,
      txtRate.TextChanged, txtTerm.TextChanged
16        lblPayment.Text = String.Empty
17    End Sub
18
19    Private Sub btnCalc_Click(ByVal sender As Object,
      ByVal e As System.EventArgs) Handles btnCalc.Click
```

Figure 4-53   Monthly Payment Calculator application's code at the end of Lesson B
(continued)

(continued)

```
20       ' calculates and displays a monthly payment
21
22       Const strMSG As String =
23           "The term must be greater than or equal to 1. "
24       Dim dblPrincipal As Double
25       Dim dblRate As Double
26       Dim dblTerm As Double
27       Dim dblMonthlyPayment As Double
28
29       Double.TryParse(txtPrincipal.Text, dblPrincipal)
30       Double.TryParse(txtRate.Text, dblRate)
31       Double.TryParse(txtTerm.Text, dblTerm)
32
33       ' convert the rate to decimal form, if necessary
34       If dblRate >= 1 Then
35           dblRate = dblRate / 100
36       End If
37
38       ' verify that the term is valid
39       If dblTerm >= 1 Then
40           ' calculate and display the monthly payment
41           dblMonthlyPayment =
42               -Financial.Pmt(dblRate / 12,
                 dblTerm * 12, dblPrincipal)
43           lblPayment.Text = dblMonthlyPayment.ToString("C2")
44       Else
45           MessageBox.Show(strMSG, "Monthly Payment Calculator",
46                        MessageBoxButtons.OK,
47                        MessageBoxIcon.Information)
48       End If
49   End Sub
50 End Class
```

Figure 4-53   Monthly Payment Calculator application's code at the end of Lesson B

Lesson B Summary

- To group controls together using a group box:

  Use the GroupBox tool to add a group box to the form. Drag controls from either the form or the toolbox into the group box. To include an optional identifying label on a group box, set the group box's Text property. The TabIndex value of a control contained within a group box is composed of two numbers separated by a period. The number to the left of the period is the TabIndex value of the group box itself. The number to the right of the period indicates the order in which the control was added to the group box.

- To calculate a periodic payment on either a loan or an investment:

  Use the Financial.Pmt method. The method's basic syntax is **Financial. Pmt(***Rate***,** *NPer***,** *PV***)**. Refer to Figure 4-45 for a description of each argument, as well as examples of using the method to calculate a periodic payment.

243

- To display a message box that contains text, one or more buttons, and an icon:

  Use the MessageBox.Show method. The method's syntax is **MessageBox. Show**(*text*, *caption*, *buttons*, *icon*[, *defaultButton*]). Refer to Figure 4-47 for a description of each argument, as well as examples of using the method to display a message box. Refer to Figure 4-50 for a listing and description of the method's return values.

Lesson B Key Terms

Financial.Pmt method—used to calculate a periodic payment on either a loan or an investment

Group box—a control that is used to contain other controls; instantiated using the GroupBox tool, which is located in the Containers section of the toolbox

MessageBox.Show method—displays a message box that contains text, one or more buttons, and an icon; allows an application to communicate with the user while the application is running

Lesson B Review Questions

1. Which of the following statements is false?

   a. When you delete a group box, the controls contained within the group box remain on the form.

   b. A group box's identifying label should be entered using sentence capitalization.

   c. You can include an identifying label on a group box by setting the group box's Text property.

   d. You can drag a control from the form into a group box.

2. The TabIndex value of a group box is 5. If the txtName control was the first control added to the group box, its TabIndex value will be _____.

   a. 1

   b. 1.5

   c. 5.0

   d. 5.1

3. Which of the following calculates the monthly payment on a loan of $5000 for 2 years at 4% interest? Payments should be expressed as a positive number.

   a. -Financial.Pmt(.04 / 12, 2 * 12, 5000)

   b. -Financial.Pmt(24, .04 / 12, 5000)

   c. -Financial.Pmt(5000, .04 / 12, 2 * 12)

   d. none of the above

4. Which of the following calculates the quarterly payment on a loan of $6000 for 3 years at 9% interest? Payments should be expressed as a negative number.

    a. `Financial.Pmt(.09 / 4, 3 * 12, 6000)`

    b. `Financial.Pmt(.09 / 4, 3 * 4, 6000)`

    c. `Financial.Pmt(.09 / 12, 3 * 12, 6000)`

    d. none of the above

5. You use the _____ constant to include the Exclamation icon in a message box.

    a. `MessageBox.Exclamation`

    b. `MessageBox.IconExclamation`

    c. `MessageBoxIcon.Exclamation`

    d. `MessageBox.WarningIcon`

6. If a message is for informational purposes only and does not require the user to make a decision, the message box should display which of the following?

    a. an OK button and the Information icon

    b. an OK button and the Exclamation icon

    c. a Yes button and the Information icon

    d. any button and the Information icon

7. If the user clicks the OK button in a message box, the message box returns the number 1, which is equivalent to which value?

    a. `DialogResult.OK`

    b. `DialogResult.OKButton`

    c. `MessageBox.OK`

    d. `MessageResult.OK`

Lesson B Exercises

1. In this exercise, you create an application that calculates and displays the quarterly payment on a loan. Create a Visual Basic Windows application. Use the following names for the solution, project, and form file, respectively: Quarterly Payment Solution, Quarterly Payment Project, and Main Form.vb. Save the application in the VB2010\Chap04 folder. Create the interface shown in Figure 4-54. Code the application. Clear the quarterly payment when a change is made to any of the text boxes. Convert the interest rate to its decimal form, if necessary. Use the MessageBox.Show method to display an appropriate message when the term is less than one year. Save the solution and then start the application. Test the application

    INTRODUCTORY

using 10000 as the loan amount, 4 as the interest rate, and 3 as the term. The quarterly payment should be $888.49. Close the Code Editor window and then close the solution.

Figure 4-54   Interface for Exercise 1

INTRODUCTORY

2. In this exercise, you code an application that calculates and displays a customer's discount and the total amount the customer owes. Create a Visual Basic Windows application. Use the following names for the solution, project, and form file, respectively: Mingo Solution, Mingo Project, and Main Form.vb. Save the application in the VB2010\ Chap04 folder. Create the interface shown in Figure 4-55. The user will enter the quantity ordered and price (per unit) in the text boxes. Code the Calculate button's Click event procedure. The procedure should verify that the text boxes contain valid data. (Hint: Use the Boolean value returned by the TryParse method.) If both text boxes contain valid data, the procedure should calculate and display both a 10% discount and the total amount the customer owes; otherwise, it should display an appropriate message in a message box. Display the discount with two decimal places. Display the total due with a dollar sign and two decimal places. The discount and total due should be removed from the interface when a change is made to the contents of a text box. Save the solution and then start and test the application. Close the Code Editor window and then close the solution.

Figure 4-55   Interface for Exercise 2

3. Open the Investment Solution (Investment Solution.sln) file contained in the VB2010\Chap04\Investment Solution folder. If necessary, open the designer window. The application should calculate the amount you need to save each month to accumulate a specific amount, given the term and interest rate. You can calculate this amount using the Financial.Pmt method. However, you need to use the following syntax: **Financial.Pmt(*Rate*, *NPer*, *PV*, *FV*)**. As you learned in this lesson, the Rate argument is the interest rate per period, and the NPer argument is the total number of payment periods. The PV argument is the present value of the investment, which is 0 (zero). The FV argument is the future value of the investment and represents the amount you want to accumulate. Code the Calculate button's Click event procedure. Calculate the monthly amount only when the three input items can be converted to numbers; otherwise, display an appropriate message. Display the monthly amount as a positive number. Save the solution and then start the application. Test the application by calculating the amount you need to save to accumulate $40000 at the end of 20 years, assuming a 6% interest rate. The application should show that you need to save $86.57 per month. Close the Code Editor window and then close the solution.

4. In this exercise, you modify the Mingo Sales application from Exercise 2. Use Windows to make a copy of the Mingo Solution folder. Rename the copy Modified Mingo Solution. Open the Mingo Solution (Mingo Solution.sln) file contained in the Modified Mingo Solution folder. Open the designer and Code Editor windows. Before calculating the discount and total due, the btnCalc control's Click event procedure should display the message "Are you a wholesaler?" in a message box. Only wholesalers receive the 10% discount. Make the appropriate modifications to the btnCalc control's Click event procedure. Save the solution and then start the application. Test the application by calculating the total due for a wholesaler ordering 4 units of product at $10 per unit. Then, test the application by calculating the total due for a non-wholesaler ordering 2 units of product at $5 per unit. Close the Code Editor window and then close the solution.

LESSON C

After studying Lesson C, you should be able to:

- Prevent the entry of unwanted characters in a text box

- Select the existing text in a text box

The Ch04CVideo file demonstrates all of the steps contained in Lesson C. You can view the video either before or after completing the lesson.

Coding the KeyPress Event Procedures

To complete the Monthly Payment Calculator application from Lesson B, you need to code the KeyPress and Enter event procedures for the three text boxes. You will code the KeyPress event procedures first.

START HERE

To open the Monthly Payment Calculator application:

1. If necessary, start Visual Studio 2010 or Visual Basic 2010 Express.

2. Open the Payment Solution (Payment Solution.sln) file from Lesson B. The file is contained in the VB2010\Chap04\Payment Solution folder. If necessary, open the designer window.

The Monthly Payment Calculator application provides text boxes for the user to enter the principal, rate, and term. The user should enter those items using only numbers and the period. The items should not contain any letters, spaces, punctuation marks (except for the period), or special characters. Unfortunately, you can't stop the user from trying to enter an inappropriate character into a text box. However, you can prevent the text box from accepting the character; you do this by coding the text box's KeyPress event procedure.

START HERE

To view the code template for the txtPrincipal control's KeyPress event procedure:

1. Open the Code Editor window and then open the code template for the txtPrincipal control's KeyPress event procedure. See Figure 4-56.

```
                                        sender parameter          e parameter

    Private Sub txtPrincipal_KeyPress(ByVal sender As Object, ByVal e As S

    End Sub
```

Figure 4-56   Code template for the txtPrincipal control's KeyPress event procedure

A control's **KeyPress event** occurs each time the user presses a key while the control has the focus. The procedure associated with the KeyPress event has two parameters, which appear within the parentheses in the procedure header: sender and e. A **parameter** represents information that is passed to the procedure when the event occurs. When the KeyPress event occurs, a character corresponding to the pressed key is sent to the KeyPress event's e parameter. For example, when the user presses the period (.) while entering data into a text box, the text box's KeyPress event occurs and a period is sent to the event's e parameter. Similarly, when the Shift key along with a letter is pressed, the uppercase version of the letter is sent to the e parameter. To prevent a text box from accepting an inappropriate character, you first use the e parameter's **KeyChar property** to determine the pressed key. (KeyChar stands for "key character.") You then use the e parameter's **Handled property** to cancel the key if it is an inappropriate one. You cancel the key by setting the Handled property to True, like this: e.Handled = True.

Figure 4-57 shows examples of using the KeyChar and Handled properties in the KeyPress event procedure. The selection structure in Example 1 prevents the txtSales control from accepting the dollar sign. It does this by first comparing the contents of the KeyChar property with a dollar sign. If the condition evaluates to True, the e.Handled = True instruction cancels the $ key before it is entered in the txtSales control. You can use the selection structure in Example 2 to allow the text box to accept only numbers and the Backspace key (which is used for editing). You refer to the Backspace key on your keyboard using Visual Basic's **ControlChars.Back constant**.

The KeyPress event automatically allows the use of the Delete key for editing.

Controlling the characters accepted by a text box

Example 1
```
Private Sub txtSales_KeyPress(ByVal sender As Object,
ByVal e As System.Windows.Forms.KeyPressEventArgs
) Handles txtSales.KeyPress
    ' prevents the text box from accepting the dollar sign

    If e.KeyChar = "$" Then
        e.Handled = True
    End If
End Sub
```

Example 2
```
Private Sub txtAge_KeyPress(ByVal sender As Object,
ByVal e As System.Windows.Forms.KeyPressEventArgs
) Handles txtAge.KeyPress
    ' allows the text box to accept only numbers
    ' and the Backspace key

    If (e.KeyChar < "0" OrElse e.KeyChar > "9") AndAlso
        e.KeyChar <> ControlChars.Back Then
        e.Handled = True
    End If
End Sub
```

Figure 4-57   Examples of using the KeyChar and Handled properties in the KeyPress event procedure

According to the application's TOE chart, each text box's KeyPress event procedure should allow the text box to accept only numbers, the period, and the Backspace key. All other keys should be canceled. (The TOE chart is shown in Figure 4-42 in Lesson B.)

250

START HERE **To allow the three text boxes to accept only numbers, the period, and the Backspace key:**

1. Change txtPrincipal_KeyPress in the procedure header to **CancelKeys**.

2. Click **immediately before the)** (closing parenthesis) in the procedure header and then press **Enter** to move the parenthesis and Handles clause to the next line in the procedure. Press the **Backspace** key until the closing parenthesis is aligned with the letter a in `Private`. (You can look ahead to Figure 4-58.)

3. Click **at the end of the Handles clause**. Type the following text and press **Enter**. (Be sure to type the comma after `txtPrincipal.KeyPress`.)

   , txtRate.KeyPress, txtTerm.KeyPress

4. Enter the following comments. Press **Enter** twice after typing the second comment.

   ' allows the text box to accept only numbers, the
   ' period, and the Backspace key

5. Enter the following If clause. When you press Enter after typing Then, the Code Editor will automatically enter the End If clause for you.

   If (e.KeyChar < "0" OrElse e.KeyChar > "9") AndAlso
   **   e.KeyChar <> "." AndAlso**
   **   e.KeyChar <> ControlChars.Back Then**

6. Enter the following comment and assignment statement:

   ' cancel the key
   e.Handled = True

7. If necessary, delete the blank lines above the End If and End Sub clauses. Figure 4-58 shows the completed CancelKeys procedure, which is associated with each text box's KeyPress event.

```
Private Sub CancelKeys(ByVal sender As Object, ByVal e As System.Windows
        ) Handles txtPrincipal.KeyPress, txtRate.KeyPress, txtTerm.KeyPress
        ' allows the text box to accept only numbers, the
        ' period, and the Backspace key

        If (e.KeyChar < "0" OrElse e.KeyChar > "9") AndAlso
            e.KeyChar <> "." AndAlso
            e.KeyChar <> ControlChars.Back Then
            ' cancel the key
            e.Handled = True
        End If
    End Sub
```

the procedure is associated with each text box's KeyPress event

Figure 4-58   CancelKeys procedure

In the next set of steps, you will test the CancelKeys procedure to verify that it allows the text boxes to accept only numbers, the period, and the Backspace key.

START HERE **To test the CancelKeys procedure:**

1. Save the solution and then start the application.

2. Try entering a letter in the Principal box, and then try entering a dollar sign. Type **30000** in the Principal box and then press **Backspace** to delete the last zero. The text box now contains 3000.

3. Try entering a letter in the Rate box, and then try entering a percent sign. Type **.045** in the Rate box and then press **Backspace** to delete the number 5. The text box now contains .04.

4. Try entering a letter in the Term box, and then try entering an ampersand. Type **20** in the Term box and then press **Backspace** to delete the zero. The text box now contains 2.

5. Click the **Calculate Monthly Payment** button. The monthly payment is $130.27.

6. Press **Tab** twice to move the focus to the txtPrincipal control. Notice that the insertion point appears at the end of the number 3000. It is customary in Windows applications to have a text box's existing text selected (highlighted) when the text box receives the focus. You will learn how to select the existing text in the next section. Click the **Exit** button to end the application.

Coding the Enter Event Procedures

To complete the Monthly Payment Calculator application, you just need to code the Enter event procedures for the three text boxes. A text box's **Enter event** occurs when the text box receives the focus, which can happen as a result of the user tabbing to the control or using the control's access key. It also occurs when the Focus method is used to send the focus to the control. In the current application, the Enter event procedure for each text box is responsible for selecting (highlighting) the contents of the text box. When the text is selected in a text box, the user can remove the text simply by pressing a key on the keyboard, such as the letter n; the pressed key—in this case, the letter n—replaces the selected text. Visual Basic provides the **SelectAll method** for selecting a text box's existing text. The method's syntax is shown in Figure 4-59 along with an example of using the method. In the syntax, *textbox* is the name of the text box whose contents you want to select.

SelectAll method

Syntax
textbox.**SelectAll()**

Example
`txtName.SelectAll()`
selects the contents of the txtName control

Figure 4-59   Syntax and an example of the SelectAll method

You will use the SelectAll method to select the contents of the text boxes in the Monthly Payment Calculator application. You will enter the method in each text box's Enter event procedure so that the method is processed when the text box receives the focus.

To code each text box's Enter event procedure and then test the procedures: ◄ START HERE

1. Open the code template for the txtPrincipal control's Enter event procedure. Type the following comment and then press **Enter** twice:

   ' selects the contents when the text box receives the focus

2. Type **txtPrincipal.SelectAll()**.

3. Open the code template for the txtRate control's Enter event procedure. Copy the comment and SelectAll method from the txtPrincipal control's Enter event procedure to the txtRate control's Enter event procedure. Change txtPrincipal in the SelectAll method to **txtRate**.

4. Open the code template for the txtTerm control's Enter event procedure. Copy the comment and SelectAll method from the txtPrincipal control's Enter event procedure to the txtTerm control's Enter event procedure. Change txtPrincipal in the SelectAll method to **txtTerm**.

5. Save the solution and then start the application. Type **10000** in the Principal box, **8** in the Rate box, and **5** in the Term box. Click the **Calculate Monthly Payment** button. A monthly payment amount of $202.76 appears in the Monthly payment box.

6. Press **Tab** twice to move the focus to the txtPrincipal control. The control's Enter event procedure selects the contents of the text box, as shown in Figure 4-60.

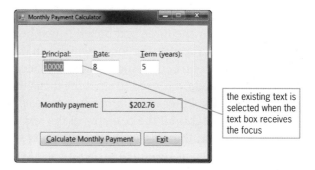

Figure 4-60   Existing text selected in the txtPrincipal control

7. Press **Tab** twice to move the focus to the txtRate and txtTerm controls. Each control's Enter event procedure selects the contents of its associated text box.

8. Click the **Exit** button. Close the Code Editor window and then close the solution.

Figure 4-61 shows the application's code at the end of Lesson C.

```
1 ' Name:         Payment Project
2 ' Purpose:      Calculates the monthly payment on a loan
3 ' Programmer:   <your name> on <current date>
4
5 Option Explicit On
6 Option Strict On
7 Option Infer Off
8
9 Public Class frmMain
10
11    Private Sub btnExit_Click(ByVal sender As Object,
         ByVal e As System.EventArgs) Handles btnExit.Click
```

Figure 4-61   Monthly Payment Calculator application's code at the end of Lesson C
(continues)

(continued)

```
12      Me.Close()
13   End Sub
14
15   Private Sub txtPrincipal_Enter(ByVal sender As Object,
     ByVal e As System.EventArgs) Handles txtPrincipal.Enter
16      ' selects the contents when the text box receives
        the focus
17
18      txtPrincipal.SelectAll()
19   End Sub
20
21   Private Sub txtRate_Enter(ByVal sender As Object,
     ByVal e As System.EventArgs) Handles txtRate.Enter
22      ' selects the contents when the text box receives
        the focus
23
24      txtRate.SelectAll()
25   End Sub
26
27   Private Sub txtTerm_Enter(ByVal sender As Object,
     ByVal e As System.EventArgs) Handles txtTerm.Enter
28      ' selects the contents when the text box receives
        the focus
29
30      txtTerm.SelectAll()
31   End Sub
32
33   Private Sub CancelKeys(ByVal sender As Object,
     ByVal e As System.Windows.Forms.KeyPressEventArgs
34      ) Handles txtPrincipal.KeyPress, txtRate.KeyPress,
        txtTerm.KeyPress
35      ' allows the text box to accept only numbers, the
36      ' period, and the Backspace key
37
38      If (e.KeyChar < "0" OrElse e.KeyChar > "9") AndAlso
39          e.KeyChar <> "." AndAlso
40          e.KeyChar <> ControlChars.Back Then
41          ' cancel the key
42          e.Handled = True
43      End If
44   End Sub
45
46   Private Sub ClearPayment(ByVal sender As Object,
     ByVal e As System.EventArgs
        ) Handles txtPrincipal.TextChanged,
        txtRate.TextChanged, txtTerm.TextChanged
47      lblPayment.Text = String.Empty
48   End Sub
49
50   Private Sub btnCalc_Click(ByVal sender As Object,
     ByVal e As System.EventArgs) Handles btnCalc.Click
51      ' calculates and displays a monthly payment
52
53      Const strMSG As String =
54          "The term must be greater than or equal to 1. "
55      Dim dblPrincipal As Double
```

Figure 4-61 Monthly Payment Calculator application's code at the end of Lesson C

(continues)

(continued)

```
56      Dim dblRate As Double
57      Dim dblTerm As Double
58      Dim dblMonthlyPayment As Double
59
60      Double.TryParse(txtPrincipal.Text, dblPrincipal)
61      Double.TryParse(txtRate.Text, dblRate)
62      Double.TryParse(txtTerm.Text, dblTerm)
63
64      ' convert the rate to decimal form, if necessary
65      If dblRate >= 1 Then
66          dblRate = dblRate / 100
67      End If
68
69      ' verify that the term is valid
70      If dblTerm >= 1 Then
71          ' calculate and display the monthly payment
72          dblMonthlyPayment =
73              -Financial.Pmt(dblRate / 12,
                    dblTerm * 12, dblPrincipal)
74          lblPayment.Text = dblMonthlyPayment.ToString("C2")
75      Else
76          MessageBox.Show(strMSG, "Monthly Payment Calculator",
77                      MessageBoxButtons.OK,
78                      MessageBoxIcon.Information)
79      End If
80   End Sub
81 End Class
```

Figure 4-61 Monthly Payment Calculator application's code at the end of Lesson C

Lesson C Summary

- To allow a text box to accept only certain keys:

  Code the text box's KeyPress event procedure. The key the user pressed is stored in the e.KeyChar property. You use the **e.Handled = True** instruction to cancel the key pressed by the user.

- To select the existing text in a text box:

  Use the SelectAll method. The method's syntax is *textbox*.**SelectAll()**.

- To process code when a control receives the focus:

  Enter the code in the control's Enter event procedure.

Lesson C Key Terms

ControlChars.Back constant—the Visual Basic constant that represents the Backspace key on your keyboard

Enter event—occurs when a control receives the focus, which can happen as a result of the user either tabbing to the control or using the control's access key; also occurs when the Focus method is used to send the focus to the control

Handled property—a property of the KeyPress event procedure's **e** parameter; when assigned the value True, it cancels the key pressed by the user

KeyChar property—a property of the KeyPress event procedure's **e** parameter; stores the character associated with the key pressed by the user

KeyPress event—occurs each time the user presses a key while a control has the focus

Parameter—an item contained within parentheses in a procedure header; represents information passed to the procedure when the procedure is invoked

SelectAll method—used to select all of the text contained in a text box

Lesson C Review Questions

1. A control's _____ event occurs each time a user presses a key while the control has the focus.

   a. Key

   b. KeyPress

   c. Press

   d. PressKey

2. When entered in the appropriate event, which of the following statements cancels the key pressed by the user?

   a. `Cancel = True`

   b. `e.Cancel = True`

   c. `e.Handled = True`

   d. `Key = Null`

3. Which of the following If clauses determines whether the user pressed the Backspace key?

   a. `If ControlChars.Back = True Then`

   b. `If e.KeyChar = Backspace Then`

   c. `If e.KeyChar = ControlChars.Backspace Then`

   d. `If e.KeyChar = ControlChars.Back Then`

4. Which of the following If clauses determines whether the user pressed the $ key?

   a. `If ControlChars.DollarSign = True Then`

   b. `If e.KeyChar = "$" Then`

   c. `If e.KeyChar = Chars.DollarSign Then`

   d. `If KeyChar.ControlChars = "$" Then`

5. When a user tabs to a text box, the text box's _____ event occurs.

    a. Access

    b. Enter

    c. TabOrder

    d. TabbedTo

6. Which of the following tells the computer to highlight all of the text contained in the txtCity control?

    a. `txtCity.SelectAll()`

    b. `txtCity.HighlightAll()`

    c. `Highlight(txtCity)`

    d. `SelectAll(txtCity.Text)`

Lesson C Exercises

INTRODUCTORY

1. Open the State ID Solution (State ID Solution.sln) file contained in the VB2010\Chap04\State ID Solution folder. If necessary, open the designer window. The txtState control should accept only letters and the Backspace key; code the appropriate procedure. When the txtState control receives the focus, its existing text should be selected; code the appropriate procedure. Save the solution and then start the application. Test the application with both valid data (uppercase and lowercase letters and the Backspace key) and invalid data (numbers and special characters). Close the Code Editor window and then close the solution.

INTRODUCTORY

2. Use Windows to make a copy of the Playtime Solution folder contained in the VB2010\Chap04 folder. Rename the copy Modified Playtime Solution. Open the Playtime Solution (Playtime Solution.sln) file contained in the Modified Playtime Solution folder. Open the designer window. When a text box receives the focus, its existing text should be selected; code the appropriate procedures. The txtBlue and txtPink controls should accept only numbers and the Backspace key; code the appropriate procedures. Save the solution and then start and test the application. Close the Code Editor window and then close the solution.

INTRODUCTORY

3. Open the MessageBox Value Solution (MessageBox Value Solution.sln) file contained in the VB2010\Chap04\MessageBox Value Solution folder. If necessary, open the designer window. Open the Code Editor window. The btnCalc control's Click event procedure should use the MessageBox.Show method to ask whether the user wants to include a dollar sign in the gross pay amount. Include Yes and No buttons in the message box. If the user clicks the Yes button, the procedure should display the gross pay amount using the "C2" format. If the user clicks the No button, the procedure should display the gross pay amount using the "N2" format. Modify the btnCalc control's code. In addition, when

the text box receives the focus, its existing text should be selected; code the appropriate procedure. Save the solution and then start and test the application. Close the Code Editor window and then close the solution.

4. In this exercise, you create an application for Micro Seminars. The application displays the total amount a company owes for a seminar. The seminar charge is $80 per person. Create a Visual Basic Windows application. Use the following names for the solution, project, and form file, respectively: Micro Solution, Micro Project, and Main Form.vb. Save the application in the VB2010\Chap04 folder. Create the interface shown in Figure 4-62. Code the application. Allow the text box to accept only numbers and the Backspace key. When a change is made to the number of registrants, clear the contents of the label control that displays the total owed. When the text box receives the focus, select its existing text. The Calculate button's Click event procedure should display an appropriate message when the number of registrants is either less than 1 or greater than 50. It should display the total owed with a dollar sign and two decimal places. Save the solution and then start and test the application. Close the Code Editor window and then close the solution.

INTRODUCTORY

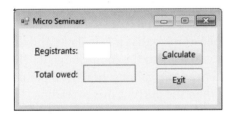

Figure 4-62   Interface for Exercise 4

5. Open the Shipping Solution (Shipping Solution.sln) file contained in the VB2010\Chap04\Shipping Solution folder. If necessary, open the designer window. Code the Display Shipping Charge button's Click event procedure. The procedure should display $32.00 as the shipping charge for the following ZIP codes: 60618, 60320, and 60544. All other ZIP codes are charged $37.75 for shipping. Save the solution and then start and test the application. Close the Code Editor window and then close the solution.

INTRODUCTORY

6. In this exercise, you create an application designed to teach the Spanish words for red, blue, and green. The Spanish words are rojo, azul, and verde. Create a Visual Basic Windows application. Use the following names for the solution, project, and form file, respectively: Spanish Colors Solution, Spanish Colors Project, and Main Form.vb. Save the application in the VB2010\Chap04 folder. Create the interface shown in Figure 4-63. The interface contains three text boxes, five buttons, and one label. After entering the Spanish word corresponding to a button's color, the user should click the button to verify the entry. If the Spanish word is correct, the button's Click event procedure should change the color of the text box to match the button's color. (Hint: Assign the button's BackColor property to the text box's BackColor property.) Otherwise, the Click event procedure should

INTERMEDIATE

display the appropriate Spanish word in a message box. The Clear button should change each text box's background color to white, using the Visual Basic constant `Color.White`; it also should clear the contents of each text box. Save the solution and then start and test the application. Close the Code Editor window and then close the solution.

Figure 4-63   Interface for Exercise 6

INTERMEDIATE

7. In this exercise, you code an application that calculates a customer's water bill. Create a Visual Basic Windows application. Use the following names for the solution, project, and form file, respectively: Allenton Solution, Allenton Project, and Main Form.vb. Save the application in the VB2010\Chap04 folder. Create the interface shown in Figure 4-64. Code the application so that it calculates and displays the number of gallons of water used and the total charge for the water. The charge for water is $1.75 per 1000 gallons, or .00175 per gallon. Make the calculations only when the current meter reading is greater than or equal to the previous meter reading; otherwise, display an appropriate message in a message box. Display the total charge with a dollar sign and two decimal places. The text boxes should accept only numbers and the Backspace key. Clear the number of gallons used and the total charge when a change is made to the contents of a text box on the form. When a text box receives the focus, select its existing text. Save the solution and then start and test the application. Close the Code Editor window and then close the solution.

Figure 4-64   Interface for Exercise 7

INTERMEDIATE

8. Create a Visual Basic Windows application. Use the following names for the solution, project, and form file, respectively: Marcy Solution, Marcy Project, and Main Form.vb. Save the application in

the VB2010\Chap04 folder. Marcy's Department Store is having a BoGoHo (Buy One, Get One Half Off) sale. The application should allow the user to enter the prices of two items. It then should calculate and display the total owed. The half-off should always be taken on the item having the lowest price. For example, if one item costs $24.99 and the second item costs $12.50, the $12.50 item would be half-off. (In other words, the second item would cost $6.25.) The total owed would be $31.24 ($24.99 + $6.25). Create a suitable interface and then code the application. Save the solution and then start and test the application. Close the Code Editor window and then close the solution.

ADVANCED

9. Create a Visual Basic Windows application. Use the following names for the solution, project, and form file, respectively: Novelty Solution, Novelty Project, and Main Form.vb. Save the application in the VB2010\Chap04 folder. Create the interface shown in Figure 4-65. When the user clicks the Calculate Total button, the button's Click event procedure should add the item price to the total of the prices already entered; this amount represents the subtotal owed by the customer. The procedure should display the subtotal on the form. It also should display a 3% sales tax, the shipping charge, and the grand total owed by the customer. The grand total is calculated by adding together the subtotal, the 3% sales tax, and a $15 shipping charge. For example, if the user enters 26.75 as the price and then clicks the Calculate Total button, the button's Click event procedure should display 26.75 as the subtotal, 0.80 as the sales tax, 15.00 as the shipping charge, and 42.55 as the grand total. If the user subsequently enters 30 as the price and then clicks the Calculate Total button, the button's Click event procedure should display 56.75 as the subtotal, 1.70 as the sales tax, 15.00 as the shipping charge, and 73.45 as the grand total. However, when the subtotal is at least $100, the shipping charge is 0.00. Code the application. Save the solution and then start and test the application. Close the Code Editor window and then close the solution.

Figure 4-65   Interface for Exercise 9

Discovery

10. In this exercise, you learn how to specify the maximum number of characters that can be entered in a text box. Open the Zip Solution (Zip Solution.sln) file contained in the VB2010\Chap04\Zip Solution folder. If necessary, open the designer window. Click the txtZip control. Look in the Properties list for a property that allows you to specify the maximum number of characters that can be entered in the text box. When you locate the property, set its value to 10. Save the solution and then start the application. Test the application by trying to enter more than 10 characters in the text box. Close the Code Editor window and then close the solution.

Swat The Bugs

11. Open the Debug Solution (Debug Solution.sln) file contained in the VB2010\Chap04\Debug Solution-Lesson C folder. Open the Code Editor window and review the existing code. The btnCalc control's Click event procedure should calculate a 10% bonus when the code entered by the user is either 1 or 2 and, at the same time, the sales amount is greater than $10000; otherwise, the bonus rate is 5%. Also, the CancelKeys procedure should allow the two text boxes to accept only numbers and the Backspace key.

   a. Start the application. Type the number 1 in the Code box and then press the Backspace key. Notice that the Backspace key is not working correctly. Stop the application and then make the appropriate change to the CancelKeys procedure.

   b. Save the solution and then start the application. Type the number 12 in the Code box and then press the Backspace key to delete the 2. The Code box now contains the number 1.

   c. Type 200 in the Sales amount box and then click the Calculate Bonus button. A message box appears and indicates that the bonus amount is $20.00 (10% of $200), which is incorrect; it should be $10.00 (5% of $200). Close the message box. Stop the application and then make the appropriate change to the btnCalc control's Click event procedure.

   d. Save the solution and then start the application. Type the number 1 in the Code box. Type 200 in the Sales amount box and then click the Calculate Bonus button. The message box should indicate that the bonus amount is $10.00. Close the message box. Close the Code Editor window and then close the solution.

CHAPTER 5

More on the Selection Structure

Creating the Math Practice Application

In this chapter, you create an application for Susan Chen, the principal of a local primary school. The application will be used by the first and second grade students to practice both adding and subtracting numbers. The application should display a math problem on the screen, and then allow the student to both enter the answer and verify that the answer is correct. The application should give the student as many chances as necessary to answer the problem correctly. The math problems for first grade students should use numbers from 1 through 10 only, whereas the ones for second grade students should use numbers from 10 through 99. Because the first and second grade students have not learned about negative numbers yet, the subtraction problems should never ask them to subtract a larger number from a smaller one. Ms. Chen also wants the application to keep track of the number of correct and incorrect responses made by the student; this information will help her assess the student's math ability. Finally, she wants to be able to control the display of the assessment information to keep students from being distracted or pressured by the number of right and wrong answers.

Previewing the Math Practice Application

Before you start the first lesson in this chapter, you will preview the completed application. The application is contained in the VB2010\Chap05 folder.

START HERE

To preview the completed application:

1. Use the Run dialog box to run the Math (Math.exe) file contained in the VB2010\Chap05 folder. The application's user interface appears on the screen. See Figure 5-1. Because the application displays random numbers, the numbers on your screen may not match the ones shown in the figure. Random numbers are covered in Lesson B along with radio button and check box controls.

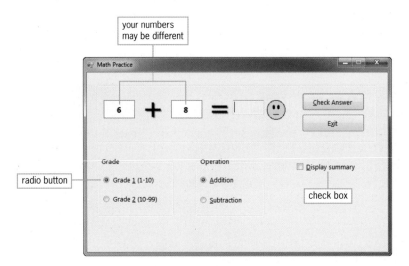

Figure 5-1   Math Practice application's interface

2. Type the correct answer to the addition problem appearing in the interface, and then press **Enter** to select the Check Answer button, which is the default button on the form. When you answer the math problem correctly, a happy face icon appears in the picture box located to the left of the Check Answer button, and a new problem appears in the interface.

3. Click the **Display summary** check box to select it. A check mark appears inside the check box, and a group box appears below the check box. The label controls contained in the group box display the number of correct and incorrect responses. In this case, you have made 1 correct response and 0 incorrect responses. See Figure 5-2.

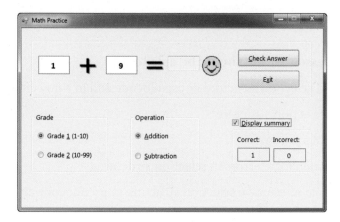

Figure 5-2 Number of correct and incorrect responses shown in the interface

4. Click the **Subtraction** radio button. A colored dot appears in the center of the Subtraction radio button to indicate that the radio button is selected, and the math problem changes to one involving subtraction.

5. Click the **text box** in which you enter the answer. Type an incorrect answer to the subtraction problem appearing on the screen and then press **Enter**. The application replaces the happy face icon in the picture box with an icon whose facial expression is neutral. It also displays the "Try again!" message in a message box.

6. Press **Enter** to close the message box. The application highlights the incorrect answer in the text box and gives you another chance to enter a correct response. The interface shows that you have made 1 correct response and 1 incorrect response.

7. Type the correct answer to the subtraction problem and then press **Enter**. The happy face icon reappears in the picture box, and the number of correct responses now says 2. In addition, a new math problem appears in the interface.

8. Click the **Display summary** check box to deselect it. The application removes the check mark from the check box and hides the group box that contains the summary information. Click the **Exit** button to end the application.

The Math Practice application uses a multiple-alternative selection structure, which you will learn about in Lesson A. You also will learn about nested selection structures. As mentioned earlier, random numbers and radio button and check box controls are covered in Lesson B. You will code the Math Practice application in Lessons B and C. Be sure to complete each lesson in full and do all of the end-of-lesson questions and several exercises before continuing to the next lesson.

264

LESSON A

After studying Lesson A, you should be able to:

- Include a nested selection structure in pseudocode and in a flowchart
- Code a nested selection structure
- Desk-check an algorithm
- Recognize common logic errors in selection structures
- Include a multiple-alternative selection structure in pseudocode and in a flowchart
- Code a multiple-alternative selection structure

Nested Selection Structures

In Chapter 4, you learned that you use the selection structure when you want the computer to make a decision and then select the appropriate path—either the true path or the false path—based on the result. Both paths in a selection structure can include instructions that declare variables, perform calculations, and so on. In this chapter, you will learn that both paths also can include other selection structures. When either a selection structure's true path or its false path contains another selection structure, the inner selection structure is referred to as a **nested selection structure**, because it is contained (nested) within the outer selection structure.

You already are familiar with the concept of nested selection structures, examples of which are shown in Figure 5-3. The examples are written in pseudocode. Example 1 contains an outer single-alternative selection structure and a nested dual-alternative selection structure. The outer selection structure begins with "if the customer orders a cup of coffee", and it ends with the last "end if". The nested selection structure begins with "if the customer wants regular coffee" and ends with the first "end if". The "else" in Example 1 separates the nested selection structure's true path from its false path. Notice that the instructions in both paths are indented within the nested selection structure. Indenting in this manner clearly indicates the instructions to be followed when the condition is true, as well as the ones to be followed when the condition is false.

Example 2 in Figure 5-3 contains an outer dual-alternative selection structure and a nested dual-alternative selection structure. The outer selection structure begins with "if the video store has *Inception* in stock", and it ends with the last "end if". The first "else" belongs to the outer selection structure. The nested selection structure begins with "if the video store has *Salt* in stock" and ends with the first "end if". The second "else" belongs to the nested selection structure. Keep in mind that for a nested selection structure to work correctly, it must be contained entirely within one of the paths in the outer selection structure. The nested selection structure in Example 1, for instance, appears entirely within the outer selection structure's true path. The nested selection structure in Example 2, on the other hand, appears entirely within the outer selection structure's false path.

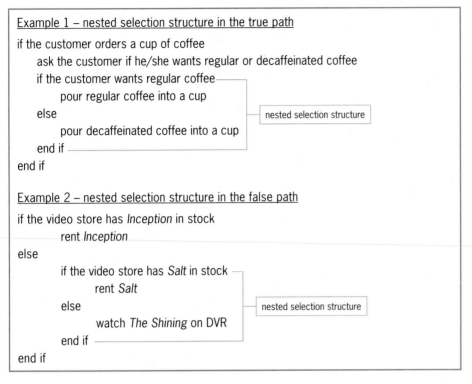

Example 1 – nested selection structure in the true path

if the customer orders a cup of coffee
    ask the customer if he/she wants regular or decaffeinated coffee
    if the customer wants regular coffee
        pour regular coffee into a cup
    else
        pour decaffeinated coffee into a cup
    end if
end if

nested selection structure

Example 2 – nested selection structure in the false path

if the video store has *Inception* in stock
    rent *Inception*
else
    if the video store has *Salt* in stock
        rent *Salt*
    else
        watch *The Shining* on DVR
    end if
end if

nested selection structure

Figure 5-3   Selection structures you might use today

The Voter Eligibility Application

Figure 5-4 shows the problem specification for the Voter Eligibility application. The application determines whether a person can vote and then displays one of three different messages. The appropriate message depends on the person's age and voter registration status. For example, if the person is younger than 18 years old, the application should display the message "You are too young to vote." However, if the person is at least 18 years old, the application should display one of two messages; the correct message is determined by the person's voter registration status. If the person is registered, then the appropriate message is "You can vote."; otherwise, it is "You must register before you can vote." Notice that determining the person's voter registration status is important only *after* his or her age is determined. Because of this, the decision regarding the age is considered the primary decision, while the decision regarding the registration status is considered the secondary decision, because whether it needs to be made depends on the result of the primary decision. A primary decision is always made by an outer selection structure, while a secondary decision is always made by a nested selection structure.

The Scottsville city manager wants an application that determines voter eligibility and displays one of three messages. The messages and criteria for displaying each message are as follows:

Message	Criteria
You are too young to vote.	person is younger than 18 years old
You can vote.	person is at least 18 years old and is registered to vote
You must register before you can vote.	person is at least 18 years old but is not registered to vote

Figure 5-4   Problem specification for the Voter Eligibility application

Figure 5-5 shows a sample run of the Voter Eligibility application, and Figure 5-6 shows the flowchart for the Display Message button's Click event procedure. The first diamond in the flowchart represents the outer selection structure's condition, which checks whether the age entered by the user is greater than or equal to 18. If the condition evaluates to False, it means that the person is not old enough to vote. In that case, the outer selection structure's false path displays the "You are too young to vote." message before the outer selection structure ends. However, if the outer selection structure's condition evaluates to True, it means that the person *is* old enough to vote. In that case, the outer selection structure's true path first asks whether the person is registered to vote. The nested selection structure then determines the appropriate action to take based on the person's registration status. The nested selection structure's condition is represented by the second diamond in Figure 5-6. If the person is registered, the nested selection structure's true path displays the "You can vote." message; otherwise, its false path displays the "You must register before you can vote." message. After the appropriate message is displayed, the outer and nested selection structures end. Notice that the nested selection structure is processed only when the outer selection structure's condition evaluates to True.

Figure 5-5   Sample run of the Voter Eligibility application

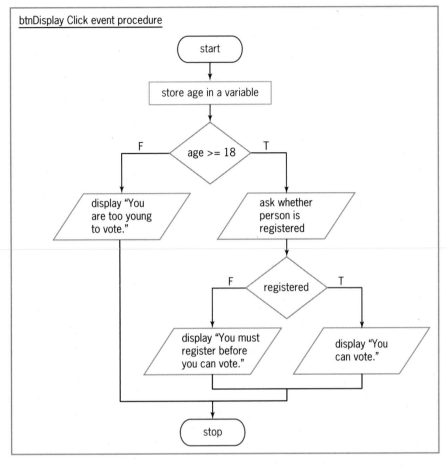

btnDisplay Click event procedure

Figure 5-6 Flowchart showing the nested selection structure in the true path

Even small procedures can have more than one solution. Figure 5-7 shows another version of the Display Message button's Click event procedure, also in flowchart form. As in the previous solution, the outer selection structure in this solution determines the age (the primary decision), and the nested selection structure determines the voter registration status (the secondary decision). In this solution, however, the outer selection structure's condition checks whether the age is less than 18. In addition, the nested selection structure appears in the outer selection structure's false path in this solution, which means it will be processed only when the outer selection structure's condition evaluates to False. The solutions in Figures 5-6 and 5-7 produce the same result. Neither solution is better than the other. Each simply represents a different way of solving the same problem.

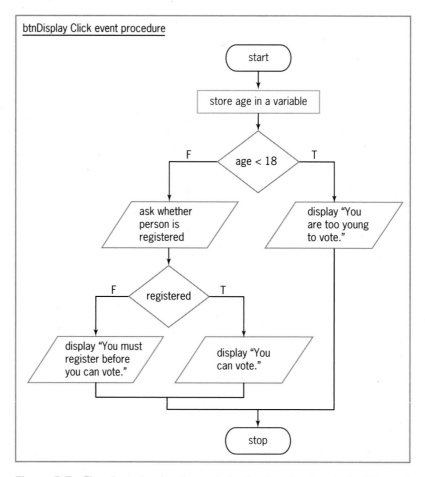

Figure 5-7 Flowchart showing the nested selection structure in the false path

Figure 5-8 shows the code corresponding to the flowcharts in Figures 5-6 and 5-7.

Code for the flowchart in Figure 5-6

```
Private Sub btnDisplay_Click(ByVal sender As Object,
ByVal e As System.EventArgs) Handles btnDisplay.Click
    ' displays a message

    Const strMSG1 As String = "You are too young to vote."
    Const strMSG2 As String =
        "You must register before you can vote."
    Const strMSG3 As String = "You can vote."
    Const strPROMPT As String =
        "Are you registered to vote?"
    Dim intAge As Integer
    Dim dlgButton As DialogResult

    Integer.TryParse(txtAge.Text, intAge)

    If intAge >= 18 Then
        dlgButton = MessageBox.Show(strPROMPT,
            "Voter Eligibility",
```

Figure 5-8 Code for the flowcharts in Figures 5-6 and 5-7 *(continues)*

(continued)

```
                MessageBoxButtons.YesNo,
                MessageBoxIcon.Exclamation)
        If dlgButton = DialogResult.Yes Then
                lblMsg.Text = strMSG3
        Else
                lblMsg.Text = strMSG2
        End If
    Else
            lblMsg.Text = strMSG1
    End If
End Sub


Code for the flowchart in Figure 5-7

Private Sub btnDisplay_Click(ByVal sender As Object,
ByVal e As System.EventArgs) Handles btnDisplay.Click
    ' displays a message

    Const strMSG1 As String = "You are too young to vote."
    Const strMSG2 As String =
        "You must register before you can vote."
    Const strMSG3 As String = "You can vote."
    Const strPROMPT As String =
        "Are you registered to vote?"
    Dim intAge As Integer
    Dim dlgButton As DialogResult

    Integer.TryParse(txtAge.Text, intAge)

    If intAge < 18 Then
            lblMsg.Text = strMSG1
    Else
            dlgButton = MessageBox.Show(strPROMPT,
                "Voter Eligibility",
                MessageBoxButtons.YesNo,
                MessageBoxIcon.Exclamation)
        If dlgButton = DialogResult.Yes Then
                lblMsg.Text = strMSG3
        Else
                lblMsg.Text = strMSG2
        End If
    End If
End Sub
```

Figure 5-8   Code for the flowcharts in Figures 5-6 and 5-7

To code and then test the Voter Eligibility application:

1. If necessary, start Visual Studio 2010 or Visual Basic 2010 Express. Open the Voter Solution (Voter Solution.sln) file contained in the VB2010\Chap05\Voter Solution folder. If necessary, open the designer window.

2. Open the Code Editor window. Replace <your name> and <current date> in the comments with your name and the current date, respectively.

3. Open the code template for the btnDisplay control's Click event procedure. Enter the comments and code shown in either of the procedures in Figure 5-8.

269

START HERE

4. Save the solution and then start the application. Type **16** in the Age box and then press **Enter**. The Display Message button's Click event procedure displays the "You are too young to vote." message, as shown earlier in Figure 5-5.

5. Change the age to **25** and then press **Enter**. A message box opens and displays the "Are you registered to vote?" message. Press **Enter** to select the Yes button. The "You can vote." message appears in the interface.

6. Click the **Display Message** button and then click the **No** button in the message box. The "You must register before you can vote." message appears in the interface.

7. Click the **Exit** button. Close the Code Editor window and then close the solution.

YOU DO IT 1!

Create a Visual Basic Windows application named YouDoIt 1. Save the application in the VB2010\Chap05 folder. Add a label and two buttons to the form. The application should display the price of a CD (compact disc) in the label. The prices are shown here. Code the first button's Click event procedure using a nested selection structure in the outer selection structure's true path. Code the second button's Click event procedure using a nested selection structure in the outer selection structure's false path. Use message boxes to get the coupon information from the user. Save the solution and then start and test the application. Close the solution.

Price	Criteria
$12	customer does not have a coupon
$10	customer has a $2 coupon
$8	customer has a $4 coupon

Logic Errors in Selection Structures

In the next few sections, you will observe some of the common logic errors made when writing selection structures. Being aware of these errors will help prevent you from making them. In most cases, logic errors in selection structures are a result of one of the following three mistakes: using a compound condition rather than a nested selection structure; reversing the primary and secondary decisions; or using an unnecessary nested selection structure. The XYZ Company's bonus procedure will be used to demonstrate each of these logic errors. The company pays its salespeople an 8% bonus on their sales. However, salespeople having a sales code of X receive an additional $150 bonus when their sales are greater than or equal to $10000; otherwise, they receive an additional $125 bonus. Notice that the salesperson's code is a factor in determining whether the salesperson is eligible for the additional bonus amount. If the salesperson is entitled to the additional bonus, then the amount of his or her sales determines the appropriate additional amount. In this case, the decision regarding the salesperson's code is the primary decision, and the decision regarding the sales amount is the secondary decision, because whether the sales amount decision needs to be made depends on the result of the code decision. The pseudocode shown in Figure 5-9 represents a correct algorithm for the bonus procedure. An **algorithm** is the set of step-by-step instructions for accomplishing a task.

Correct algorithm for the bonus procedure
1. store user input (code and sales) in variables
2. calculate the bonus by multiplying the sales by .08
3. if the code is X
    if the sales are greater than or equal to 10000
        add 150 to the bonus
    else
        add 125 to the bonus
    end if
  end if
4. display the bonus

Figure 5-9 A correct algorithm for the bonus procedure

271

> You also can write the nested selection structure's condition in Figure 5-9 as follows: if the sales are less than 10000. You then would reverse the instructions in the true and false paths.

You can verify that the algorithm in Figure 5-9 works correctly by desk-checking it. **Desk-checking** refers to the process of reviewing the algorithm while seated at your desk rather than in front of the computer. Desk-checking is also called **hand-tracing**, because you use a pencil and paper to follow each of the algorithm's instructions by hand. You desk-check an algorithm to verify that it is not missing any steps, and that the existing steps are correct and in the proper order. Any errors you find will need to be corrected before you begin coding the algorithm.

Before you begin desk-checking an algorithm, you first choose a set of sample data for the input values, which you then use to manually compute the expected output values. You will desk-check the algorithm in Figure 5-9 three times. For the first desk-check, you will use X as the code and $15000 as the sales amount. Using this test data, the algorithm should display a bonus amount of $1350. For the second desk-check, you will use X as the code and $9000 as the sales amount; in this case, the algorithm should display a bonus amount of $845. For the third desk-check, you will use A as the code and $13000 as the sales amount. With this set of test data, the algorithm should display a bonus amount of $1040.

Using the first set of test data (X and 15000), the algorithm multiplies the sales amount by .08, giving 1200. The outer selection structure's condition then determines whether the salesperson's code is X; it is, so the nested selection structure's condition checks whether the sales amount is greater than or equal to 10000. The sales amount is greater than 10000, so the nested selection structure's true path adds 150 to the bonus amount, giving 1350, which is correct. After doing this, both selection structures end. The last step in the algorithm displays the bonus amount of 1350.

Using the second set of test data (X and 9000), the algorithm multiplies the sales amount by .08, giving 720. The outer selection structure's condition then determines whether the salesperson's code is X; it is, so the nested selection structure's condition checks whether the sales amount is greater than or equal to 10000. The sales amount is not greater than or equal to 10000, so the nested selection structure's false path adds 125 to the bonus amount, giving 845, which is correct. After doing this, both selection structures end. The last step in the algorithm displays the bonus amount of 845.

Using the third set of test data (A and 13000), the algorithm multiplies the sales amount by .08, giving 1040. The outer selection structure's condition then determines whether the salesperson's code is X. The code is not X, so the outer selection structure ends. Notice that the nested selection structure is not processed when the outer selection structure's condition is false. The last step in the algorithm displays the bonus amount of 1040. Figure 5-10 shows the results of desk-checking the correct algorithm.

Desk-check		Result
First:	using X as the code and 15000 as the sales	1350
Second:	using X as the code and 9000 as the sales	845
Third:	using A as the code and 13000 as the sales	1040

Figure 5-10   Results of desk-checking the correct algorithm

Using a Compound Condition Rather than a Nested Selection Structure

A common error made when writing selection structures is to use a compound condition in the outer selection structure's condition when a nested selection structure is needed. Figure 5-11 shows an example of this error in the bonus algorithm. The correct algorithm is included in the figure for comparison. Notice that the incorrect algorithm uses one selection structure rather than two selection structures, and the selection structure contains a compound condition. Consider why the selection structure in the incorrect algorithm cannot be used in place of the selection structures in the correct algorithm. In the correct algorithm, the outer and nested selection structures indicate that a hierarchy exists between the code and sales decisions: the code decision is always made first, followed by the sales decision (if necessary). In the incorrect algorithm, the compound condition indicates that no hierarchy exists between both decisions; each has equal weight and neither is dependent on the other, which is incorrect.

a logical operator used rather than a nested selection structure

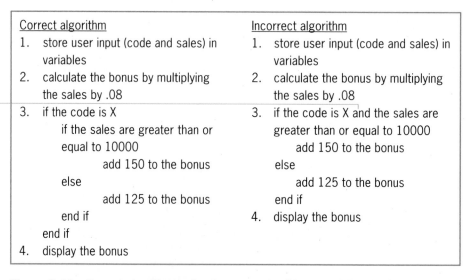

Figure 5-11   Correct algorithm and an incorrect algorithm containing the first logic error

To better understand why the incorrect algorithm in Figure 5-11 will not work correctly, you will desk-check it using the same test data used to desk-check the correct algorithm. Using the first set of test data (X and 15000), the incorrect algorithm multiplies the sales amount by .08, giving 1200. The selection structure's compound condition is evaluated next. The compound condition evaluates to True, because both sub-conditions are True. Therefore, the selection structure's true path adds 150 to the bonus amount, giving 1350. The incorrect algorithm then displays the bonus amount of 1350. Even though the algorithm's selection structure is phrased incorrectly, notice that the incorrect algorithm produces the same result as the correct algorithm using the first set of test data.

Using the second set of test data (X and 9000), the incorrect algorithm multiplies the sales amount by .08, giving 720. The selection structure's compound condition is evaluated next. The compound condition evaluates to False, because the sales amount is not greater than or equal to 10000. Therefore, the selection structure's false path adds 125 to the bonus amount, giving 845. The incorrect algorithm then displays the bonus amount of 845. Here again, using the second set of test data, the incorrect algorithm produces the same result as the correct algorithm.

Using the third set of test data (A and 13000), the incorrect algorithm multiplies the sales amount by .08, giving 1040. The selection structure's compound condition is evaluated next. The compound condition evaluates to False, because the salesperson's code is not X. As a result, the selection structure's false path adds 125 to the bonus amount, giving 1165. The incorrect algorithm then displays the bonus amount of 1165. Notice that the incorrect algorithm produces erroneous results for the third set of test data; it should have displayed 1040 as the bonus amount. It is important to desk-check an algorithm several times using different test data. In this case, if you had used only the first two sets of data to desk-check the incorrect algorithm, you would not have discovered the error. Figure 5-12 shows the results of desk-checking the incorrect algorithm shown in Figure 5-11. As indicated in the figure, the results of the first and second desk-checks are correct, but the result of the third desk-check is not correct.

Desk-check		Result
First:	using X as the code and 15000 as the sales	1350 (correct)
Second:	using X as the code and 9000 as the sales	845 (correct)
Third:	using A as the code and 13000 as the sales	1165 (incorrect)

Figure 5-12   Results of desk-checking the incorrect algorithm shown in Figure 5-11

Reversing the Primary and Secondary Decisions

Another common error made when writing a selection structure that contains a nested selection structure is to reverse the primary and secondary decisions—in other words, put the secondary decision in the outer selection structure, and put the primary decision in the nested selection structure. Figure 5-13 shows an example of this error in the bonus algorithm. The correct algorithm is included in the figure for comparison. Unlike the selection structures in the correct algorithm, which determine the code before determining the sales amount, the selection structures in the incorrect algorithm determine the sales amount before determining the code. Consider how this difference changes the algorithm. In the correct algorithm, the selection structures indicate that only salespeople who have a code of X receive an additional bonus, which is correct. The selection structures in the incorrect algorithm, on the other hand, indicate that the additional bonus is given to all salespeople whose sales are greater than or equal to 10000, which is not correct. Figure 5-14 shows the results of desk-checking the incorrect algorithm. As indicated in the figure, only the result of the first desk-check is correct.

Correct algorithm	Incorrect algorithm
1. store user input (code and sales) in variables	1. store user input (code and sales) in variables
2. calculate the bonus by multiplying the sales by .08	2. calculate the bonus by multiplying the sales by .08
3. if the code is X	3. if the sales are greater than or equal to 10000
if the sales are greater than or equal to 10000	if the code is X *primary and secondary decisions reversed*
add 150 to the bonus	add 150 to the bonus
else	else
add 125 to the bonus	add 125 to the bonus
end if	end if
end if	end if
4. display the bonus	4. display the bonus

Figure 5-13   Correct algorithm and an incorrect algorithm containing the second logic error

Desk-check		Result
First:	using X as the code and 15000 as the sales	1350 (correct)
Second:	using X as the code and 9000 as the sales	720 (incorrect)
Third:	using A as the code and 13000 as the sales	1165 (incorrect)

Figure 5-14   Results of desk-checking the incorrect algorithm shown in Figure 5-13

Using an Unnecessary Nested Selection Structure

Another common error made when writing selection structures is to include an unnecessary nested selection structure. In most cases, a selection structure containing this error still will produce the correct results; however, it will do so less efficiently than selection structures that are properly structured. Figure 5-15 shows an example of this error in the bonus algorithm. The correct algorithm is included in the figure for comparison. Unlike the correct algorithm, which contains two selection structures, the inefficient algorithm contains three selection structures. Notice that the condition in the third selection structure determines whether the sales are less than 10000 and is processed only when the condition in the second selection structure is false. In other words, it is processed only when the sales are not greater than or equal to 10000. However, if the sales are not greater than or equal to 10000, then they would have to be less than 10000, so the third selection structure is unnecessary. Figure 5-16 shows the results of desk-checking the inefficient algorithm. As indicated in the figure, although the results of the three desk-checks are correct, the result of the second desk-check is obtained in a less efficient manner.

Correct algorithm
1. store user input (code and sales) in variables
2. calculate the bonus by multiplying the sales by .08
3. if the code is X
        if the sales are greater than or equal to 10000
                add 150 to the bonus
        else
                add 125 to the bonus
        end if
    end if
4. display the bonus

Incorrect algorithm
1. store user input (code and sales) in variables
2. calculate the bonus by multiplying the sales by .08
3. if the code is X
        if the sales are greater than or equal to 10000
                add 150 to the bonus
        else
                if the sales are less ──────┐ unnecessary nested
                than 10000   selection structure
                        add 125 to the bonus
                end if ──────────────────────┘
        end if
    end if
4. display the bonus

Figure 5-15   Correct algorithm and an incorrect algorithm containing the third logic error

Desk-check		Result
First:	using X as the code and 15000 as the sales	1350 (correct)
Second:	using X as the code and 9000 as the sales	845 (correct) — result obtained in a less efficient manner
Third:	using A as the code and 13000 as the sales	1040 (correct)

Figure 5-16   Results of desk-checking the incorrect algorithm shown in Figure 5-15

Multiple-Alternative Selection Structures

At times, you may need to create a selection structure that can choose from several alternatives. Such selection structures are referred to as **multiple-alternative selection structures**. An example of this is a selection structure that displays a message based on a letter grade entered by the user. The valid letter grades and their corresponding messages are shown in Figure 5-17. As the figure indicates, when the letter grade is an A, the selection structure should display the message "Excellent." When the letter grade is a B, the selection structure should display the message "Above Average," and so on.

Multiple-alternative selection structures are also called extended selection structures.

Letter grade	Message
A	Excellent
B	Above Average
C	Average
D	Below Average
F	Below Average

Figure 5-17   Letter grades and messages

Figures 5-18 and 5-19 show the pseudocode and flowchart, respectively, for the btnDisplay control's Click event procedure, which uses a multiple-alternative selection structure to display the appropriate letter grade. The diamond in the flowchart represents the multiple-alternative selection structure's condition. As you already know, the diamond is also used to represent the condition in both the single-alternative and dual-alternative selection structures. However, unlike the diamond in both of those selection structures, the diamond in a multiple-alternative selection structure has several flowlines (rather than only two flowlines) leading out of the symbol. Each flowline represents a possible path and must be marked appropriately, indicating the value or values necessary for the path to be chosen.

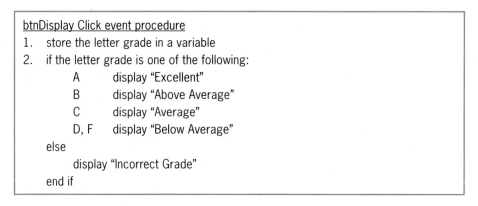

Figure 5-18   Pseudocode containing a multiple-alternative selection structure

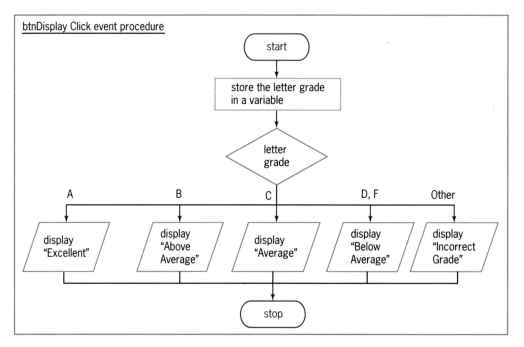

Figure 5-19   Flowchart containing a multiple-alternative selection structure

Figure 5-20 shows two versions of the code for the btnDisplay control's Click event procedure. Both versions use If...Then...Else statements to code the multiple-alternative selection structure. Both versions of the code produce the same result. However, the second version contains a more convenient way of writing a multiple-alternative selection structure.

```
Version 1—multiple-alternative selection structure
Private Sub btnDisplay_Click(ByVal sender As Object,
ByVal e As System.EventArgs) Handles btnDisplay.Click
    ' displays a message corresponding to a grade

    Dim strGrade As String

    ' display appropriate message
    strGrade = txtGrade.Text.ToUpper
    If strGrade = "A" Then
            lblMsg.Text = "Excellent"
    Else
        If strGrade = "B" Then
                lblMsg.Text = "Above Average"
        Else
            If strGrade = "C" Then
                lblMsg.Text = "Average"
            Else
                If strGrade = "D" OrElse strGrade = "F" Then
                    lblMsg.Text = "Below Average"
                Else
                    lblMsg.Text = "Incorrect Grade"
                End If
            End If
        End If
    End If
End Sub
```

you get here when the grade is not A

you get here when the grade is not A and not B

you get here when the grade is not A, B, or C

you get here when the grade is not A, B, C, D, or F

four End If clauses are required

```
Version 2—multiple-alternative selection structure
Private Sub btnDisplay_Click(ByVal sender As Object,
ByVal e As System.EventArgs) Handles btnDisplay.Click
    ' displays a message corresponding to a grade

    Dim strGrade As String

    ' display appropriate message
    strGrade = txtGrade.Text.ToUpper
    If strGrade = "A" Then
        lblMsg.Text = "Excellent"
    ElseIf strGrade = "B" Then
        lblMsg.Text = "Above Average"
    ElseIf strGrade = "C" Then
        lblMsg.Text = "Average"
    ElseIf strGrade = "D" OrElse strGrade = "F" Then
        lblMsg.Text = "Below Average"
    Else
        lblMsg.Text = "Incorrect Grade"
    End If
End Sub
```

only one End If clause is required

Figure 5-20 Two versions of the code containing a multiple-alternative selection structure

To code and then test the Grade application:

START HERE

1. Open the Grade Solution (Grade Solution.sln) file contained in the VB2010\Chap05\Grade Solution-If folder. If necessary, open the designer window.

2. Open the Code Editor window. Replace <your name> and <current date> in the comments with your name and the current date, respectively.

3. Open the code template for the btnDisplay control's Click event procedure. Enter the code shown in Version 2 in Figure 5-20.

4. Save the solution and then start the application. Type the letter **a** and then press **Enter**. The "Excellent" message appears in the interface. See Figure 5-21.

Figure 5-21   Excellent message shown in the interface

5. On your own, test the application using the following grades: **b**, **c**, **d**, **x**, and **f**. When you are finished testing, click the **Exit** button. Close the Code Editor window and then close the solution.

YOU DO IT 2!

Create a Visual Basic Windows application named YouDoIt 2. Save the application in the VB2010\Chap05 folder. Add a text box, a label, and a button to the form. The button's Click event procedure should display (in the label) either the price of a concert ticket or an error message. The ticket price is based on the code entered in the text box, as shown here. Code the procedure. Save the solution and then start and test the application. Close the solution.

Code	Ticket price
1	$15
2	$15
3	$25
4	$35
5	$37
Other	Invalid code

The Select Case Statement

When a multiple-alternative selection structure has many paths from which to choose, it is often simpler and clearer to code the selection structure using the **Select Case statement** rather than several If...Then...Else statements. The Select Case statement's syntax is shown in Figure 5-22. The figure also shows how you can use the Select Case statement to code the multiple-alternative selection structure from Figure 5-20. The statement begins with the keywords `Select Case`, followed by a *selectorExpression*. The selectorExpression can contain any combination of variables, constants, keywords, functions, methods, operators, and properties. In the example in Figure 5-22, the selectorExpression is a String variable named `strGrade`. The Select Case statement ends with the End Select clause. Between the Select Case and End Select clauses are the individual Case clauses. Each Case clause represents a different path that the computer can follow. It is customary to indent each Case clause and the instructions within each Case clause, as shown in the figure. You can have as many Case clauses as necessary in a Select Case statement. However, if the Select Case statement includes a Case Else clause, the Case Else clause must be the last clause in the statement.

Each of the individual Case clauses, except the Case Else clause, must contain an *expressionList*, which can include one or more expressions. To include more than one expression in an expressionList, you separate each expression with a comma, as in the expressionList `Case "D", "F"`. The selectorExpression needs to match only one of the expressions listed in an expressionList. The data type of the expressions must be compatible with the data type of the selectorExpression. If the selectorExpression is numeric, the expressions in the Case clauses should be numeric. Likewise, if the selectorExpression is a string, the expressions should be strings. In the example in Figure 5-22, the selectorExpression (`strGrade`) is a string, and so are the expressions: "A", "B", "C", "D", and "F".

Select Case statement

<u>Syntax</u>
Select Case *selectorExpression*
    Case *expressionList1*
      instructions for the first Case
    [**Case** *expressionList2*
      instructions for the second Case]
    [**Case** *expressionListN*
      instructions for the Nth Case]
    [**Case Else**
      instructions for when the selectorExpression does not match any of the
      expressionLists]
End Select

<u>Example</u>
```
Private Sub btnDisplay_Click(ByVal sender As Object,
ByVal e As System.EventArgs) Handles btnDisplay.Click
    ' displays a message corresponding to a grade

    Dim strGrade As String

    ' display appropriate message
    strGrade = txtGrade.Text.ToUpper
    Select Case strGrade
        Case "A"
            lblMsg.Text = "Excellent"
        Case "B"
            lblMsg.Text = "Above Average"
        Case "C"
            lblMsg.Text = "Average"
        Case "D", "F"
            lblMsg.Text = "Below Average"
        Case Else
            lblMsg.Text = "Incorrect Grade"
    End Select
End Sub
```

Figure 5-22 Syntax and an example of the Select Case statement

When processing the Select Case statement, the computer first compares the value of the selectorExpression with the values listed in expressionList1. If a match is found, the computer processes the instructions for the first Case, stopping when it reaches either another Case clause or the End Select clause; it then skips to the instruction following the End Select clause. For example, if the `strGrade` variable contains the string "A", the Select Case statement in Figure 5-22 will assign the string "Excellent" to the lblMsg control before the statement ends. If a match is not found in expressionList1, the computer skips to the second Case clause, where it compares the selectorExpression with the values listed in expressionList2. If a match is found, the computer processes the instructions for the second Case clause and then skips to the instruction following the End Select clause. If a match is not found, the computer skips to the third Case clause, and so on.

If a Case clause contains more than one value, as does the `Case "D", "F"` clause, the selectorExpression needs to match only one of the values. As a result, the Select Case statement in Figure 5-22 will assign the string "Below Average" when the `strGrade` variable contains either the string "D" or the string "F". If the selectorExpression does not match any of the values listed in any of the expressionLists, the computer processes the instructions listed in the Case Else clause (if there is one) and then skips to the instruction following the End Select clause. Keep in mind that if the selectorExpression matches a value in more than one Case clause, only the instructions in the first match are processed.

START HERE

To use the Select Case statement to code the Grade application:

1. Open the Grade Solution (Grade Solution.sln) file contained in the VB2010\Chap05\Grade Solution-Select Case folder. If necessary, open the designer window.

2. Open the Code Editor window. Replace <your name> and <current date> in the comments with your name and the current date, respectively.

3. Open the code template for the btnDisplay control's Click event procedure. Enter the code shown in Figure 5-22.

4. Save the solution and then start the application. Type the letter **a** and then press **Enter**. The "Excellent" message appears in the interface.

5. On your own, test the application using the following grades: **b, c, d, x**, and **f**. When you are finished testing, click the **Exit** button. Close the Code Editor window and then close the solution.

Specifying a Range of Values in a Case Clause

In addition to specifying one or more discrete values in a Case clause, you also can specify a range of values, such as the values 1 through 4 or values greater than 10. You do this using either the keyword `To` or the keyword `Is`. You use the `To` keyword when you know both the upper and lower values in the range. The `Is` keyword is appropriate when you know only one end of the range (either the upper or lower end). Figure 5-23 shows the syntax for using both keywords. It also contains an example of a Select Case statement that assigns a price based on the number of items ordered. According to the price chart in Figure 5-23, the price for 1 to 5 items is $25 each. Using discrete values, the first Case clause would look like this: `Case 1, 2, 3, 4, 5`. However, a more convenient way of writing that range of numbers is to use the **To** keyword, like this: `Case 1 To 5`. The expression `1 To 5` specifies the range of numbers from 1 to 5, inclusive. The expression `6 To 10` in the second Case clause specifies the range of numbers from 6 through 10. Notice that both Case clauses state both the lower (1 and 6) and upper (5 and 10) values in each range.

The third Case clause, `Case Is > 10`, contains the **Is** keyword rather than the **To** keyword. Recall that you use the **Is** keyword when you know only one end of the range of values. In this case, you know only the lower end of the range, 10. The **Is** keyword is always used in combination with one of the following comparison operators: =, <, <=, >, >=, <>. The `Case Is > 10` clause specifies all numbers greater than the number 10. Because `intOrdered` is an Integer variable, you also can write this Case clause as `Case Is >= 11`. The Case Else clause in the example in Figure 5-23 is processed only when the `intOrdered` variable contains a value that is not included in any of the previous Case clauses.

If you neglect to type the **Is** keyword in an expression—for example, if you enter `Case > 10`—the Code Editor will change the clause to `Case Is > 10`.

Be sure to test your code thoroughly, because the computer will not display an error message when the value preceding **To** in a Case clause is greater than the value following **To**. Instead, the Select Case statement will not give the correct results.

Specifying a range of values in a Case clause

<u>Syntax</u>
Case *smallest value in the range* **To** *largest value in the range*
Case Is *comparisonOperator value*

<u>Example</u>
ABC Corporation Price Chart

Numbered ordered	Price per item
1 – 5	$25
6 – 10	$23
More than 10	$20
Less than 1	$0

```
Select Case intOrdered
    Case 1 To 5
        intPrice = 25
    Case 6 To 10
        intPrice = 23
    Case Is > 10
        intPrice = 20
    Case Else
        intPrice = 0
End Select
```

Figure 5-23 Syntax and an example of specifying a range of values

To code and then test the ABC Corporation application:

START HERE

1. Open the ABC Solution (ABC Solution.sln) file contained in the VB2010\Chap05\ABC Solution folder. If necessary, open the designer window.

2. Open the Code Editor window. Replace <your name> and <current date> in the comments with your name and the current date, respectively.

3. Locate the btnDisplay control's Click event procedure. Click the **blank line** below the `' determine the price per item` comment and then enter the Select Case statement shown in Figure 5-23.

4. Save the solution and then start the application. Type **3** in the Number ordered box and then press **Enter**. $25.00 appears in the Price per item box, as shown in Figure 5-24.

Figure 5-24 Price per item shown in the interface

5. On your own, test the application using **6**, **11**, and **0** as the number ordered. When you are finished testing, click the **Exit** button. Close the Code Editor window and then close the solution.

YOU DO IT 3!

Create a Visual Basic Windows application named YouDoIt 3. Save the application in the VB2010\Chap05 folder. Add a text box, a label, and a button to the form. The button's Click event procedure should display (in the label) either the price of a concert ticket or an error message. The ticket price is based on the code entered in the text box, as shown here. Code the procedure using the Select Case statement. Save the solution and then start and test the application. Close the solution.

Code	Ticket price
1	$15
2	$15
3	$25
4	$35
5	$37
Other	Invalid code

Lesson A Summary

- To create a selection structure that evaluates both a primary and a secondary decision:

  Place (nest) the secondary decision's selection structure within either the true or false path of the primary decision's selection structure.

- To verify that an algorithm works correctly:

  Desk-check (hand-trace) the algorithm.

- To code a multiple-alternative selection structure:

  Use either If...Then...Else statements or the Select Case statement.

- To specify a range of values in a Select Case statement's Case clause:

  Use the To keyword when you know both the upper and lower values in the range. Use the Is keyword when you know only one end of the range. The Is keyword is used in combination with one of the following comparison operators: =, <, <=, >, >=, <>.

Lesson A Key Terms

Algorithm—a set of step-by-step instructions for accomplishing a task

Desk-checking—the process of manually walking through the steps in an algorithm, using sample data; also called hand-tracing

Hand-tracing—another term for desk-checking

Multiple-alternative selection structures—selection structures that contain several alternatives; also called extended selection structures; can be coded using either If...Then...Else statements or the Select Case statement

Nested selection structure—a selection structure that is wholly contained (nested) within either the true or false path of another selection structure

Select Case statement—used to code a multiple-alternative selection structure in Visual Basic

Lesson A Review Questions

Use the code shown in Figure 5-25 to answer Review Questions 1 through 3.

```
If intNum <= 100 Then
      intNum = intNum * 2
ElseIf intNum > 500 Then
      intNum = intNum * 3
End If
```

Figure 5-25 Code for Review Questions 1 through 3

1. If the intNum variable contains the number 90, what value will be in the variable after the code in Figure 5-25 is processed?

    a. 0

    b. 90

    c. 180

    d. 270

2. If the `intNum` variable contains the number 1000, what value will be in the variable after the code in Figure 5-25 is processed?

   a. 0

   b. 1000

   c. 2000

   d. 3000

3. If the `intNum` variable contains the number 200, what value will be in the variable after the code in Figure 5-25 is processed?

   a. 0

   b. 200

   c. 400

   d. 600

Use the code shown in Figure 5-26 to answer Review Questions 4 through 7.

```
If intId = 1 Then
      lblName.Text = "Janet"
ElseIf intId = 2 OrElse intId = 3 Then
      lblName.Text = "Mark"
ElseIf intId = 4 Then
      lblName.Text = "Jerry"
Else
      lblName.Text = "Sue"
End If
```

Figure 5-26   Code for Review Questions 4 through 7

4. What will the code in Figure 5-26 display when the `intId` variable contains the number 2?

   a. Janet

   b. Jerry

   c. Mark

   d. Sue

5. What will the code in Figure 5-26 display when the `intId` variable contains the number 4?

   a. Janet

   b. Jerry

   c. Mark

   d. Sue

6. What will the code in Figure 5-26 display when the `intId` variable contains the number 3?

   a. Janet

   b. Jerry

   c. Mark

   d. Sue

7. What will the code in Figure 5-26 display when the `intId` variable contains the number 8?

   a. Janet

   b. Jerry

   c. Mark

   d. Sue

8. A nested selection structure can appear in _____ of another selection structure.

   a. only the true path

   b. only the false path

   c. either the true or false path

9. Which of the following Case clauses is valid in a Select Case statement whose selectorExpression is an Integer variable named `intCode`?

   a. `Case Is > 7`

   b. `Case 3, 5`

   c. `Case 1 To 4`

   d. all of the above

Use the code shown in Figure 5-27 to answer Review Questions 10 through 12.

```
Select Case intId
    Case 1
        lblName.Text = "Janet"
    Case 2 To 4
        lblName.Text = "Mark"
    Case 5, 7
        lblName.Text = "Jerry"
    Case Else
        lblName.Text = "Sue"
End Select
```

Figure 5-27   Code for Review Questions 10 through 12

10. What will the code in Figure 5-27 display when the `intId` variable contains the number 2?

    a. Janet

    b. Mark

    c. Jerry

    d. Sue

11. What will the code in Figure 5-27 display when the `intId` variable contains the number 3?

    a. Janet

    b. Mark

    c. Jerry

    d. Sue

12. What will the code in Figure 5-27 display when the `intId` variable contains the number 6?

    a. Janet

    b. Mark

    c. Jerry

    d. Sue

13. A procedure needs to display the appropriate fee to charge a golfer. Club members are free. Non-members golfing on Monday through Thursday are charged $15. Non-members golfing on Friday through Sunday are charged $25. In this procedure, which is the primary decision and which is the secondary decision? Why?

14. List the three errors commonly made when writing selection structures. Which error produces the correct results, but in a less efficient way?

15. Explain the meaning of the term "desk-checking."

Lesson A Exercises

INTRODUCTORY

1. Write the Visual Basic code for the algorithm shown in Figure 5-9 in this lesson. The salesperson's code and sales amount are entered in the txtCode and txtSales controls, respectively. Store the text box values and bonus amount in variables. Display the appropriate bonus amount in the lblMsg control. Format the bonus amount using the "C2" format.

INTRODUCTORY

2. Write the Visual Basic code that displays the message "Highest honors" when a student's test score is 90 or above. When the test score is 70

through 89, display the message "Good job". For all other test scores, display the message "Retake the test". The test score is stored in the `intScore` variable. Display the appropriate message in the lblMsg control. Code the multiple-alternative selection structure using the If...Then...Else statement.

3. Rewrite the code from Exercise 2 using the Select Case statement.

INTRODUCTORY

287

4. Write the Visual Basic code that compares the contents of the `intQuantity` variable with the number 10. When the variable contains a number that is equal to 10, display the string "Equal" in the lblMsg control. When the variable contains a number that is greater than 10, display the string "Over 10". When the variable contains a number that is less than 10, display the string "Not over 10". Code the multiple-alternative selection structure using the If...Then...Else statement.

INTRODUCTORY

5. Rewrite the code from Exercise 4 using the Select Case statement.

INTRODUCTORY

6. Open the Animal Solution (Animal Solution.sln) file contained in the VB2010\Chap05\Animal Solution folder. If necessary, open the designer window.

INTRODUCTORY

   a. Open the Code Editor window. The If...Then...Else button's Click event procedure should display the string "Dog" when the `intAnimal` variable contains the number 1, the string "Cat" when the variable contains the number 2, and the string "Bird" when the variable contains anything other than the numbers 1 or 2. Display the appropriate string in the lblMsg control. Use the If...Then...Else statement to code the multiple-alternative selection structure. Save the solution and then start the application. Test the If...Then...Else button's code three times, using the numbers 1, 2, and 5.

   b. The Select Case button's Click event procedure should display the string "Dog" when the `strAnimal` variable contains either the letter "D" or the letter "d", the string "Cat" when the variable contains either the letter "C" or the letter "c", and the string "Bird" when the variable contains anything other than the letters "D", "d", "C", or "c". Display the appropriate string in the lblMsg control. Use the Select Case statement to code the multiple-alternative selection structure. Save the solution and then start the application. Test the Select Case button's code three times, using the letters D, c, and x.

   c. Close the Code Editor window and then close the solution.

7. Code the partial flowchart shown in Figure 5-28. Use an Integer variable named `intCode` and a Double variable named `dblRate`. Display the rate formatted with a percent sign and no decimal places. Use the Select Case statement to code the multiple-alternative selection structure in the figure.

INTERMEDIATE

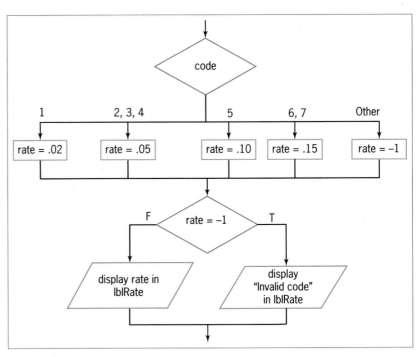

Figure 5-28   Flowchart for Exercise 7

INTERMEDIATE

8. A procedure needs to display a shipping charge based on the state name stored in the **strState** variable. The state name is stored using uppercase letters. Write a Select Case statement that assigns the shipping charge to the **dblShipping** variable. The shipping charge for Hawaii is $25. The shipping charge for Oregon is $30. The shipping charge for California is $32.50. Display an appropriate message in the lblMsg control when the **strState** variable contains a value that is not one of these three states; also assign the number 0 to the **dblShipping** variable. Display the shipping charge in the lblShipping control. Format the shipping charge using the "N2" format.

INTERMEDIATE

9. Rewrite the code from Exercise 8 using the If...Then...Else statement.

INTERMEDIATE

10. The price of a concert ticket depends on the seat location stored in the **strSeat** variable. The seat location is stored using uppercase letters. Write a Select Case statement that displays the ticket price in the lblPrice control. Box seats are $75. Pavilion seats are $30. Lawn seats are $21. Display an appropriate message in the lblPrice control when the **strSeat** variable contains a value that is not one of these three seat locations.

INTERMEDIATE

11. Rewrite the code from Exercise 10 using the If...Then...Else statement.

INTERMEDIATE

12. Open the Month Solution (Month Solution.sln) file contained in the VB2010\Chap05\Month Solution folder. If necessary, open the designer window.

   a. Open the Code Editor window. The If...Then...Else button's Click event procedure should display the name of the month corresponding to the number entered by the user. For example, if the user enters the number 1, the procedure should display the string

"January". If the user enters an invalid number, which is one that is not in the range 1 through 12, the procedure should display an appropriate message. Display the month name or message in the lblMsg control. Use the If...Then...Else statement to code the multiple-alternative selection structure. Save the solution and then start the application. Test the If...Then...Else button's code three times, using the numbers 3, 7, and 20.

b. Now assume that the user will enter the first three characters of the month's name (rather than the month number) in the text box. Complete the Select Case button's Click event procedure by writing a Select Case statement that displays the name of the month corresponding to the characters entered by the user. For example, if the user enters the three characters "Jan" (in any case), the procedure should display the string "January". If the user enters "Jun", the procedure should display "June". If the three characters entered by the user do not match any of the expressions in the Case clauses, the procedure should display an appropriate message. Display the appropriate month name or message in the lblMsg control. Save the solution and then start the application. Test the Select Case button's code three times, using the following data: jun, dec, xyz.

c. Close the Code Editor window and then close the solution.

13. Open the Bonus Solution (Bonus Solution.sln) file contained in the VB2010\Chap05\Bonus Solution folder. If necessary, open the designer window. Open the Code Editor window. The Calculate button's Click event procedure should assign the number 25 to the intBonus variable when the user enters a sales amount that is greater than or equal to $100, but less than or equal to $250. When the user enters a sales amount that is greater than $250, the procedure should assign the number 50 to the variable. When the user enters a sales amount that is less than $100, the procedure should assign the number 0 as the bonus. Use the If...Then...Else statement to code the multiple-alternative selection structure. Save the solution and then start the application. Test the Calculate button's code three times, using sales amounts of 100, 300, and 40. Close the Code Editor window and then close the solution.

> INTERMEDIATE

14. Open the Seminar Solution (Seminar Solution.sln) file contained in the VB2010\Chap05\Seminar Solution folder. If necessary, open the designer window. Computer Workshop offers programming seminars to companies. The price per person depends on the number of people the company registers. The first 4 people registered are charged $100 per person. Registrants 5 through 10 are charged $80 per person. Registrants 11 and over are charged $60 per person. For example, if the company registers 7 people, then the total amount owed is $640. The $640 is calculated by first multiplying 4 by 100, giving 400. You then multiply 3 by 80, giving 240. You then add the 400 to the 240, giving 640. Display the total amount owed in the lblTotal control. Use the Select Case statement to complete the Calculate button's Click event procedure. Save the solution and then start and test the application. Close the Code Editor window and then close the solution.

> ADVANCED

LESSON B

After studying Lesson B, you should be able to:

- Include a group of radio buttons in an interface

- Designate a default radio button

- Include a check box in an interface

- Create and call an independent Sub procedure

- Generate random numbers

Creating the Math Practice Application

Recall that Susan Chen, the principal of a local primary school, wants an application that the first and second grade students can use to practice both adding and subtracting numbers. The application should display the math problem on the screen and then allow the student to both enter the answer and verify that the answer is correct. The application should give the student as many chances as necessary to answer the problem correctly. The math problems for the first grade students should use numbers from 1 through 10 only. The math problems for the second grade students should use numbers from 10 through 99. Because the students have not learned about negative numbers yet, the subtraction problems should never ask them to subtract a larger number from a smaller one. Recall that Ms. Chen wants the application to keep track of the number of correct and incorrect responses made by the student, and she wants the ability to control the display of that information.

 The Ch05BVideo file demonstrates all of the steps contained in Lesson B. You can view the video either before or after completing the lesson.

START HERE

To open the partially completed Math Practice application:

1. If necessary, start Visual Studio 2010 or Visual Basic 2010 Express.

2. Open the Math Solution (Math Solution.sln) file contained in the VB2010\Chap05\Math Solution folder. If necessary, open the designer window. The interface contains one text box, two buttons, three radio buttons, seven picture boxes, four group boxes, and various labels. Missing from the interface are the Subtraction radio button and the Display summary check box.

Adding a Radio Button to the Form

You use the RadioButton tool to add a radio button to a form. **Radio buttons** allow you to limit the user to only one choice in a group of two or more related but mutually exclusive choices. The radio buttons in the Math Practice application will limit the user to one grade level selection and one mathematical operation selection. During run time, you can determine whether a radio button is selected or unselected by looking at the value in its Checked property. If the property contains the Boolean value True, the radio button is selected. If it contains the Boolean value False, the radio button is not selected.

Each radio button in an interface should be labeled so that the user knows its purpose. You enter the label using sentence capitalization in the radio button's Text property. Each radio button also should have a unique access key, which allows the user to select the button using the keyboard. In the next set of steps, you will add the missing Subtraction radio button to the form.

To add a radio button to the form:

START HERE

1. Click the **RadioButton** tool in the toolbox and then drag the mouse pointer into the Operation group box, placing it below the Addition radio button. Release the mouse button. The RadioButton1 control appears in the group box.

2. The three-character ID for a radio button's name is rad. Change the RadioButton1 control's name to **radSubtraction**, and then change its Text property to **&Subtraction**. Also change its AutoSize property to **False**. Position and size the radio button as shown in Figure 5-29.

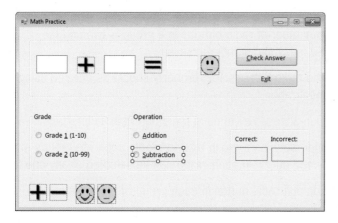

Figure 5-29　Subtraction radio button added to the Operation group box

Two groups of radio buttons appear in the Math Practice interface: one group contains the two Grade radio buttons and the other contains the two Operation radio buttons. To include two groups of radio buttons in an interface, at least one of the groups must be placed within a container, such as a group box. Otherwise, the radio buttons are considered to be in the same group and only one can be selected at any one time. In this case, the radio buttons pertaining to the grade choice are contained in the Grade group box, and the radio buttons pertaining to the operation choice are contained in the Operation group box. Placing each group of radio buttons in a separate group box allows the user to select one button from each group.

Keep in mind that the minimum number of radio buttons in a group is two, because the only way to deselect a radio button is to select another radio button. The recommended maximum number of radio buttons in a group is seven. It is customary in Windows applications to have one of the radio buttons in each group already selected when the user interface first appears. The automatically selected radio button is called the **default radio button** and is either the radio button that represents the user's most likely choice or the first radio button in the group. You designate the default radio button by setting the button's Checked property to the Boolean value True. In the Math Practice application, you will make the first radio button in each group the default radio button.

START HERE ▶ **To designate a default radio button in each group:**

1. Click the **Grade 1 (1-10)** radio button and then set its Checked property to **True**. When you set the Checked property to True in the Properties window, a colored dot appears inside the button's circle to indicate that the button is selected.

2. Click the **Addition** radio button and then set its Checked property to **True**. A colored dot appears inside the circle in the Addition radio button.

GUI DESIGN TIP   Radio Button Standards

- Use radio buttons to limit the user to one choice in a group of related but mutually exclusive choices.

- The minimum number of radio buttons in a group is two and the recommended maximum number is seven.

- The label in the radio button's Text property should be entered using sentence capitalization.

- Assign a unique access key to each radio button in an interface.

- Use a container (such as a group box) to create separate groups of radio buttons. Only one button in each group can be selected at any one time.

- Designate a default radio button in each group of radio buttons.

Adding a Check Box to the Interface

You use the CheckBox tool in the toolbox to add a check box to a form. Like radio buttons, check boxes can be either selected or deselected. Also like radio buttons, you can determine whether a check box is selected by looking at the value in its Checked property during run time: a True value indicates that the check box is selected, whereas a False value indicates that it is not selected. However, unlike radio buttons, **check boxes** provide one or more independent and nonexclusive items from which the user can choose. Whereas only one button in a group of radio buttons can be selected at any one time, any number of check boxes on a form can be selected at the same time. Each check box on a form should be labeled to make its purpose obvious. You enter the label using sentence capitalization in the check box's Text property. Each check box also should have a unique access key.

START HERE ▶ **To add a check box to the interface:**

1. Click the **CheckBox** tool in the toolbox and then drag the mouse pointer onto the form, positioning it immediately above the grpSummary control. (See Figure 5-30 for the location of the grpSummary control.) Release the mouse button. The CheckBox1 control appears on the form.

2. The three-character ID for a check box's name is chk. Change the CheckBox1 control's name to **chkSummary**, and then change its Text property to **&Display summary**. Position the check box as shown in Figure 5-30.

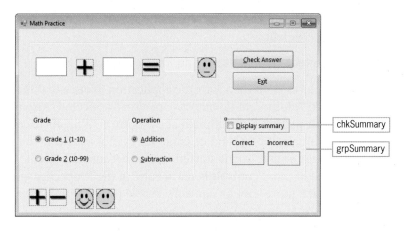

Figure 5-30 Display summary check box added to the form

GUI DESIGN TIP Check Box Standards

- Use check boxes to allow the user to select any number of choices from a group of one or more independent and nonexclusive choices.

- The label in the check box's Text property should be entered using sentence capitalization.

- Assign a unique access key to each check box in an interface.

Now that you have completed the user interface, you can lock the controls in place and then set each control's TabIndex property.

To lock the controls and then set each control's TabIndex property:

START HERE

1. Right-click the **form** and then click **Lock Controls** on the context menu.

2. Click **View** on the menu bar and then click **Tab Order**. Use the information shown in Figure 5-31 to set the TabIndex values for the controls. (As you learned in Chapter 2, picture boxes do not have a TabIndex property.) When you are finished, press **Esc** to remove the TabIndex boxes from the form.

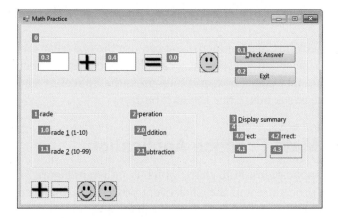

Figure 5-31 Correct TabIndex values

Next, you will start the application to observe how you select and deselect radio buttons and check boxes.

START HERE

To select and deselect radio buttons and check boxes:

1. Save the solution and then start the application. Notice that the Grade 1 (1-10) and Addition radio buttons are already selected. Also notice that the four picture boxes located at the bottom of the form, as well as the grpSummary control and its contents, do not appear in the interface when the application is started. This is because the Visible property of each of those controls is set to False in the Properties window. You will learn more about a control's Visible property in Lesson C.

2. You can select a different radio button by clicking it. You can click either the circle or the text that appears inside the radio button. Click the **Subtraction** radio button. The computer selects the Subtraction radio button as it deselects the Addition radio button. This is because both radio buttons belong to the same group and only one radio button in a group can be selected at any one time.

3. Click the **Grade 2 (10-99)** radio button. The computer selects the Grade 2 (10-99) radio button as it deselects the Grade 1 (1-10) radio button. Here again, the Grade radio buttons belong to the same group, so selecting one deselects the other.

4. After selecting a radio button in a group, you can use the up and down arrow keys on your keyboard to select another radio button in the group. Press the **up arrow** key to select the Grade 1 (1-10) radio button, and then press the **down arrow** key to select the Grade 2 (10-99) radio button.

5. Press **Tab**. Notice that the focus moves to the Subtraction radio button rather than to the Addition radio button. In a group of radio buttons, only the selected radio button receives the focus when the user tabs to the group.

6. You can select a check box by clicking either the square or the text that appears inside the control. Click the **Display summary** check box to select it. A check mark appears inside the check box to indicate that the check box is selected.

7. Click the **Display summary** check box to deselect it. The computer removes the check mark from the check box.

8. When a check box has the focus, you can use the Spacebar on your keyboard to select and deselect it. Press the **Spacebar** to select the Display summary check box, and then press the **Spacebar** again to deselect the check box. Click the **Exit** button.

Coding the Math Practice Application

According to the application's TOE chart, which is shown in Figure 5-32, the form's Load event procedure and the Click event procedures for seven of the controls need to be coded. In this lesson, you will code all but the Click event procedures for the btnExit control (which has already been coded for you) and the btnCheckAnswer and chkSummary controls (which you will code in Lesson C).

Task	Object	Event
End the application	btnExit	Click
Display an addition problem	frmMain	Load
1. Display the plus sign in picOperator 2. Generate and display two random integers in lblNum1 and lblNum2	radAddition	Click
1. Display the minus sign in picOperator 2. Generate and display two random integers in lblNum1 and lblNum2	radSubtraction	Click
Generate and display two random integers in lblNum1 and lblNum2	radGrade1, radGrade2	Click
Show or hide the grpSummary control	chkSummary	Click
1. Calculate the correct answer to the math problem 2. Compare the correct answer to the user's answer 3. Display either the happy face or neutral face in picFace 4. If the user's answer is correct, generate and display two random integers in lblNum1 and lblNum2 5. If the user's answer is incorrect, display the "Try again!" message 6. Add 1 to the number of either correct or incorrect responses 7. Display the number of correct and incorrect responses in lblCorrect and lblIncorrect, respectively 8. Send the focus to txtAnswer	btnCheckAnswer	Click
Display the number of correct responses (from btnCheckAnswer)	lblCorrect	None
Display the number of incorrect responses (from btnCheckAnswer)	lblIncorrect	None
Display two random integers (from radGrade1, radGrade2, radAddition, radSubtraction, btnCheckAnswer)	lblNum1, lblNum2	None
Display either the plus sign or the minus sign (from radAddition and radSubtraction)	picOperator	None
Display either the happy face or neutral face (from btnCheckAnswer)	picFace	None
Get and display the user's answer	txtAnswer	None

Figure 5-32   TOE chart for the Math Practice application

Notice that the task of generating and displaying two random integers in the lblNum1 and lblNum2 controls appears in the Task column for five of the controls. The task is listed as Step 2 for the radAddition and radSubtraction controls. It is listed as the only task for the radGrade1 and radGrade2 controls, and it also appears in Step 4 for the btnCheckAnswer control. Rather than entering the appropriate code in the Click event procedures for each of the five controls, you will enter the code in an independent Sub procedure. You then will have the five Click event procedures call (invoke) the Sub procedure.

Creating an Independent Sub Procedure

There are two types of Sub procedures in Visual Basic: event procedures and independent Sub procedures. The procedures coded in the previous chapters were event procedures. An event procedure is a Sub procedure that is associated with a specific object and event, such as a button's Click event or a text box's TextChanged event. The computer automatically processes an event procedure when the event occurs. An **independent Sub procedure**, on the other hand, is a procedure that is independent of any object and event. An independent Sub procedure is processed only when called (invoked) from code.

Programmers use independent Sub procedures for several reasons. First, they allow the programmer to avoid duplicating code when different sections of a program need to perform the same task. Rather than enter the code in each of those sections, the programmer can enter the code in a procedure and then have each section call the procedure to perform its task when needed. Second, consider an event procedure that must perform many tasks. To keep the event procedure's code from getting unwieldy and difficult to understand, the programmer can assign some of the tasks to one or more independent Sub procedures. Doing this makes the event procedure easier to code, because it allows the programmer to concentrate on one small piece of the code at a time. And finally, independent Sub procedures are used extensively in large and complex programs, which typically are written by a team of programmers. The programming team will break up the program into small and manageable tasks, and then assign some of the tasks to different team members to be coded as independent Sub procedures. Doing this allows more than one programmer to work on the program at the same time, decreasing the time it takes to write the program.

Figure 5-33 shows the syntax for creating an independent Sub procedure in Visual Basic. It also includes an example of an independent Sub procedure, as well as the steps for entering an independent Sub procedure in the Code Editor window. Some programmers enter independent Sub procedures above the first event procedure, while others enter them below the last event procedure. Still others enter them either immediately above or immediately below the procedure from which they are invoked. In this book, the independent Sub procedures will usually be entered above the first event procedure in the Code Editor window.

As the syntax in Figure 5-33 shows, independent Sub procedures have both a procedure header and a procedure footer. In most cases, the procedure header begins with the `Private` keyword, which indicates that the procedure can be used only within the current Code Editor window. Following the `Private` keyword is the `Sub` keyword, which identifies the procedure as a Sub procedure. After the `Sub` keyword is the procedure name. The rules for naming an independent Sub procedure are the same as those for naming variables; however, procedure names are usually entered using Pascal case. The Sub procedure's name should indicate the task the procedure performs. It is a common practice to begin the name with a verb. For example, a good name for a Sub procedure that clears the contents of three label controls is ClearLabels.

When you enter a procedure below the last event procedure in the Code Editor window, be sure to enter it above the End Class clause.

Using Pascal case, you capitalize the first letter in the procedure name and the first letter of each subsequent word in the name.

Following the procedure name in the procedure header is a set of parentheses that contains an optional *parameterList*. The parameterList lists the data type and name of one or more parameters. As you learned in Chapter 4, the parameters store the information passed to the procedure when it is invoked. If the procedure does not require any information to be passed to it, an empty set of parentheses follows the procedure name in the procedure header. You will learn more about parameters in Chapter 7. A Sub procedure ends with its procedure footer, which is always **End Sub**. Between the procedure header and procedure footer, you enter the instructions to be processed when the procedure is invoked.

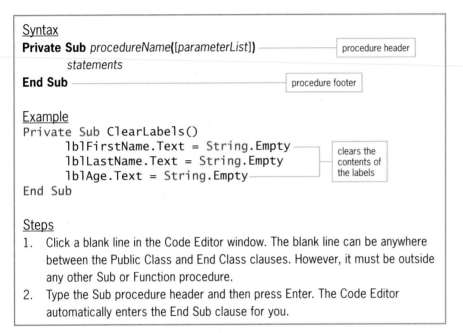

Syntax
Private Sub *procedureName([parameterList])* ——— | procedure header |
    statements
End Sub ——————————— | procedure footer |

Example
```
Private Sub ClearLabels()
    lblFirstName.Text = String.Empty
    lblLastName.Text = String.Empty
    lblAge.Text = String.Empty
End Sub
```
| clears the contents of the labels |

Steps
1. Click a blank line in the Code Editor window. The blank line can be anywhere between the Public Class and End Class clauses. However, it must be outside any other Sub or Function procedure.
2. Type the Sub procedure header and then press Enter. The Code Editor automatically enters the End Sub clause for you.

Figure 5-33 Independent Sub procedure syntax, example, and steps

The Math Practice application will use an independent Sub procedure named GenerateAndDisplayIntegers. The procedure's pseudocode is shown in Figure 5-34.

GenerateAndDisplayIntegers procedure
1. declare variables to store the two random integers
2. if the Grade 1 radio button is selected
       generate two random integers from 1 through 10
       and store them in variables
   else
       generate two random integers from 10 through 99
       and store them in variables
   end if
3. if the Subtraction radio button is selected and the first random integer is less than the second random integer
       swap the two random integers stored in the variables
   end if
4. display the random integers in the lblNum1 and lblNum2 controls

Figure 5-34 Pseudocode for the GenerateAndDisplayIntegers procedure

START HERE ▶

To begin coding the GenerateAndDisplayIntegers procedure:

1. Open the Code Editor window. Replace <your name> and <current date> in the comments with your name and the current date, respectively.

2. Click the **blank line** below the `Public Class frmMain` clause, and then press **Enter** to insert another blank line. In the new blank line, type the following procedure header and then press **Enter**. When you press Enter, the Code Editor will automatically enter the End Sub clause for you.

   Private Sub GenerateAndDisplayIntegers()

3. Type the following comment and then press **Enter** twice:

   ' generates and displays two random integers

4. The procedure will use two Integer variables to store the two random integers it generates. Enter the following two Dim statements. Press **Enter** twice after typing the second Dim statement.

   Dim intRandom1 As Integer
   Dim intRandom2 As Integer

5. Step 2 in the pseudocode is a selection structure whose condition determines whether the Grade 1 radio button is selected. Enter the following comment and If clause:

   ' generate random integers
   If radGrade1.Checked Then

You also can write the If clause in Step 5 as `If radGrade1.Checked = True Then`.

If the Grade 1 radio button is selected, then the GenerateAndDisplayIntegers procedure should generate two random integers from 1 through 10.

Generating Random Integers

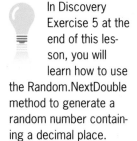

In Discovery Exercise 5 at the end of this lesson, you will learn how to use the Random.NextDouble method to generate a random number containing a decimal place.

Most programming languages provide a **pseudo-random number generator**, which is a device that produces a sequence of numbers that meet certain statistical requirements for randomness. Pseudo-random numbers are chosen with equal probability from a finite set of numbers. The chosen numbers are not completely random, because a definite mathematical algorithm is used to select them. However, they are sufficiently random for practical purposes. The pseudo-random number generator in Visual Basic is an object whose data type is Random.

Figure 5-35 shows the syntax for generating random integers in Visual Basic, and it includes examples of using the syntax. As the figure indicates, you first create a **Random object** to represent the pseudo-random number generator. You create the Random object by declaring it in a Dim statement. You enter the Dim statement in the procedure that will use the number generator. After the Random object is created, you can use the object's Random.Next method to generate random integers. In the method's syntax, *randomObjectName* is the name of the Random object. The *minValue* and *maxValue* arguments in the syntax must be integers, and minValue must be less than maxValue. The **Random.Next method** returns an integer that is greater than or equal to min-Value, but less than maxValue.

Generating random integers

<u>Syntax</u>
Dim *randomObjectName* **As New Random**
randomObjectName.**Next(***minValue*, *maxValue***)**

<u>Example 1</u>
```
Dim randomGenerator As New Random
intNumber = randomGenerator.Next(1, 51)
```
The Dim statement creates a Random object named `randomGenerator`. The assignment statement generates a random integer that is greater than or equal to 1, but less than 51, and then assigns the random integer to the `intNumber` variable.

<u>Example 2</u>
```
Dim randomGen As New Random
intNum = randomGen.Next(-10, 0)
```
The Dim statement creates a Random object named `randomGen`. The assignment statement generates a random integer that is greater than or equal to –10, but less than 0, and then assigns the random integer to the `intNum` variable.

Figure 5-35 Syntax and examples of generating random integers

To continue coding the GenerateAndDisplayIntegers procedure: START HERE

1. Click the **blank line** below the second Dim statement and then enter the following Dim statement:

   Dim randomGenerator As New Random

2. If the Grade 1 radio button is selected, the procedure should generate two random integers from 1 through 10. To generate integers within that range, you use the number 1 as the Random.Next method's minValue and the number 11 as its maxValue. Click the **blank line** above the End If clause and then enter the following two assignment statements:

   intRandom1 = randomGenerator.Next(1, 11)
   intRandom2 = randomGenerator.Next(1, 11)

3. If the Grade 1 radio button is not selected, then the Grade 2 radio button must be selected. In that case, the procedure should generate two integers from 10 through 99. Enter the additional code shown in Figure 5-36 and then position the insertion point as shown in the figure.

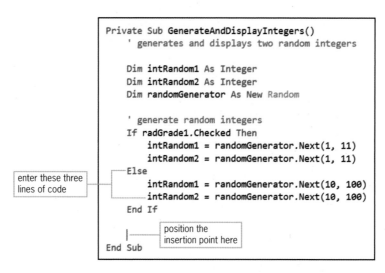

```
Private Sub GenerateAndDisplayIntegers()
    ' generates and displays two random integers

    Dim intRandom1 As Integer
    Dim intRandom2 As Integer
    Dim randomGenerator As New Random

    ' generate random integers
    If radGrade1.Checked Then
        intRandom1 = randomGenerator.Next(1, 11)
        intRandom2 = randomGenerator.Next(1, 11)
    Else
        intRandom1 = randomGenerator.Next(10, 100)
        intRandom2 = randomGenerator.Next(10, 100)
    End If

    |

End Sub
```

enter these three
lines of code

position the
insertion point here

Figure 5-36   Random number generation code entered
in the procedure

4. Step 3 in the procedure's pseudocode is another selection struc-
    ture. This selection structure's condition determines whether the
    Subtraction radio button is selected and also whether the first ran-
    dom integer is less than the second random integer. If both sub-
    conditions are true, then the procedure should swap (interchange)
    the two random integers, because no subtraction problem should
    result in a negative number. Enter the additional comments and code
    shown in Figure 5-37 and then position the insertion point as shown
    in the figure.

```
    ' swap integers if the subtraction problem
    ' would result in a negative answer
    If radSubtraction.Checked AndAlso intRandom1 < intRandom2 Then
        Dim intTemp As Integer
        intTemp = intRandom1
        intRandom1 = intRandom2
        intRandom2 = intTemp
    End If

    |

End Sub
```

enter these comments
and six lines of code

position the insertion
point here

Figure 5-37   Additional comments and code entered in the procedure

5. The last step in the pseudocode is to display the random integers in
    the lblNum1 and lblNum2 controls. Enter the following comment and
    assignment statements and then save the solution:

    ' display integers
    lblNum1.Text = Convert.ToString(intRandom1)
    lblNum2.Text = Convert.ToString(intRandom2)

Coding the Grade Radio Buttons' Click Event Procedures

According to the application's TOE chart (shown earlier in Figure 5-32), the radGrade1 and radGrade2 controls should generate and display two random integers when clicked. The code to generate and display the random integers is entered in the GenerateAndDisplayIntegers procedure. The radio buttons can use the procedure's code by invoking the procedure. You can invoke an independent Sub procedure using the **Call statement**. The statement's syntax is shown in Figure 5-38. In the syntax, *procedureName* is the name of the procedure you are calling (invoking), and *argumentList* (which is optional) is a comma-separated list of arguments you want passed to the procedure. If you have no information to pass to the procedure that you are calling, as is the case in the GenerateAndDisplayIntegers procedure, you include an empty set of parentheses after the procedureName in the Call statement. (You will learn how to pass information to a procedure in Chapter 7.)

Figure 5-38 also shows two examples of calling the GenerateAndDisplayIntegers procedure from the Click event procedures for the radGrade1 and radGrade2 controls. In Example 1, the Call statement is entered in both Click event procedures. In Example 2, the Call statement is entered in a procedure named ProcessGradeRadioButtons. According to its Handles clause, the ProcessGradeRadioButtons procedure is invoked when the Click event occurs for either the radGrade1 or radGrade2 control. In this case, neither example is better than the other; both simply represent different ways of performing the same task.

Call Statement

Syntax
Call *procedureName*(**[**argumentList**]**)

Example 1
```
Private Sub radGrade1_Click(ByVal sender As Object,
    ByVal e As System.EventArgs) Handles radGrade1.Click
    Call GenerateAndDisplayIntegers()
End Sub

Private Sub radGrade2_Click(ByVal sender As Object,
    ByVal e As System.EventArgs) Handles radGrade2.Click
    Call GenerateAndDisplayIntegers()
End Sub
```

Example 2
```
Private Sub ProcessGradeRadioButtons(ByVal sender As Object,
            ByVal e As System.EventArgs
            ) Handles radGrade1.Click, radGrade2.Click
    Call GenerateAndDisplayIntegers()
End Sub
```

Figure 5-38   Syntax and examples of the Call statement

The Call keyword is optional when invoking a Sub procedure. Therefore, you also can call the procedure in Figure 5-38 using the statement GenerateAndDisplay Integers().

301

START HERE **To call the GenerateAndDisplayIntegers procedure when either Grade radio button is clicked:**

1. Open the code template for the radGrade1 control's Click event procedure. Change `radGrade1_Click` in the procedure header to **ProcessGradeRadioButtons**.

2. Modify the procedure header as shown in Figure 5-39. Be sure to add the radGrade2 control's Click event to the Handles clause. Also type the Call statement shown in the figure.

```
Private Sub ProcessGradeRadioButtons(ByVal sender As Object,
                                     ByVal e As System.EventArgs
                                     ) Handles radGrade1.Click, radGrade2.Click
    Call GenerateAndDisplayIntegers()
End Sub
```

Figure 5-39 Completed ProcessGradeRadioButtons procedure

When the user clicks either of the two Grade radio buttons, the computer will process the Call statement contained in the ProcessGradeRadioButtons procedure. When processing the Call statement, the computer leaves the ProcessGradeRadioButtons procedure, temporarily, to process the instructions contained in the GenerateAndDisplayIntegers procedure. When the GenerateAndDisplayIntegers procedure ends, the computer returns to the line below the Call statement in the ProcessGradeRadioButtons procedure. The line below the Call statement is the End Sub clause, which ends the ProcessGradeRadioButtons procedure. In the next set of steps, you will test the code you have entered so far to verify that it is working correctly.

START HERE **To test the code you have entered so far:**

1. Save the solution and then start the application. Click the **Grade 2 (10-99)** radio button. Two random integers from 10 through 99 appear in the interface, as shown in Figure 5-40. Your random integers might be different from the ones shown in the figure.

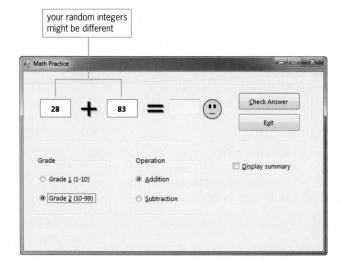

Figure 5-40 Random integers shown in the interface

2. Click the **Grade 1 (1-10)** radio button. Two random integers from 1 through 10 appear in the interface. Click the **Exit** button.

Coding the Operation Radio Buttons' Click Event Procedures

According to the application's TOE chart, the Click event procedures for both Operation radio buttons should display the appropriate mathematical operator (either a plus sign or a minus sign) in the picOperator control. The plus and minus signs are stored in the picPlus and picMinus controls, respectively, which are located at the bottom of the form. Both procedures also should generate two random integers and then display the integers in the lblNum1 and lblNum2 controls.

To code the Click event procedures for the Operation radio buttons: ◁ START HERE

1. Open the code template for the radAddition control's Click event procedure. Type the following comment and then press **Enter** twice:

   ' display the plus sign and random numbers

2. You can display the plus sign in the picOperator control by assigning the value stored in the picPlus control's Image property to the picOperator control's Image property. Enter the following assignment statement:

   picOperator.Image = picPlus.Image

3. Now, enter the following Call statement:

   Call GenerateAndDisplayIntegers()

4. Open the code template for the radSubtraction control's Click event procedure. Type the following comment and then press **Enter** twice:

   ' display the minus sign and random numbers

5. Next, enter the following assignment and Call statements:

   picOperator.Image = picMinus.Image
   Call GenerateAndDisplayIntegers()

6. Save the solution and then start the application. Notice that an addition problem does not automatically appear in the interface, even though the Grade 1 and Addition radio buttons are selected. You will fix that problem in the next section.

7. Click the **Subtraction** radio button. A minus sign appears in the picOperator control, and two random integers from 1 through 10 appear in the interface.

8. Click the **Addition** radio button. A plus sign appears in the picOperator control, and two random integers from 1 through 10 appear in the interface.

9. Click the **Grade 2 (10-99)** radio button. Two random integers from 10 through 99 appear in the interface. Click the **Exit** button.

During run time, you can remove a graphic from a picture box by assigning the keyword Nothing to the picture box's Image property.

The application should automatically display an addition problem when the Math Practice form first appears on the screen. You can accomplish this task in two ways: you can either use the Call statement to call the GenerateAndDisplayIntegers procedure, or use the PerformClick method to invoke the radAddition control's Click event procedure. Whichever way you choose, the appropriate code must be entered in the form's Load event procedure, which is the last procedure you code in this lesson.

Coding the Form's Load Event Procedure

As you learned in Chapter 3, a form's Load event occurs when the application is started and the form is displayed the first time. The form does not appear on the screen until all of the instructions in its Load event procedure are processed. To automatically display an addition problem when the Math Practice form appears, you can enter either one of the following statements in the Load event procedure: `Call GenerateAndDisplayIntegers()` or `radAddition.PerformClick()`. The latter statement uses the **PerformClick method** to invoke the Addition radio button's Click event, which causes the computer to process the code contained in the Click event procedure. The PerformClick method's syntax is *object*.**PerformClick()**, where *object* is the name of the object whose Click event you want invoked.

START HERE

To automatically display an addition problem when the form first appears:

1. Click the **Class Name** list arrow in the Code Editor window and then click **(frmMain Events)** in the list. Click the **Method Name** list arrow and then click **Load** in the list. The template for the frmMain Load event procedure appears in the Code Editor window.

2. Type the following comment and then press **Enter** twice:

   ' display an addition problem

3. Next, enter the following PerformClick method:

   radAddition.PerformClick()

4. Save the solution and then start the application. An addition problem appears in the interface.

5. Click the **Exit** button. Close the Code Editor window and then close the solution.

Figure 5-41 shows the application's code at the end of Lesson B.

```
 1 ' Name:              Math Project
 2 ' Purpose:           Displays math problems
 3 ' Programmer:        <your name> on <current date>
 4
 5 Option Explicit On
 6 Option Strict On
 7 Option Infer Off
 8
 9 Public Class frmMain
10
11    Private Sub GenerateAndDisplayIntegers()
12        ' generates and displays two random integers
13
14        Dim intRandom1 As Integer
15        Dim intRandom2 As Integer
16        Dim randomGenerator As New Random
17
18        ' generate random integers
19        If radGrade1.Checked Then
20            intRandom1 = randomGenerator.Next(1, 11)
21            intRandom2 = randomGenerator.Next(1, 11)
```

Figure 5-41   Math Practice application's code at the end of Lesson B *(continues)*

(continued)

```
22      Else
23          intRandom1 = randomGenerator.Next(10, 100)
24          intRandom2 = randomGenerator.Next(10, 100)
25      End If
26
27      ' swap integers if the subtraction problem
28      ' would result in a negative answer
29      If radSubtraction.Checked AndAlso
        intRandom1 < intRandom2 Then
30          Dim intTemp As Integer
31          intTemp = intRandom1
32          intRandom1 = intRandom2
33          intRandom2 = intTemp
34      End If
35
36      ' display integers
37      lblNum1.Text = Convert.ToString(intRandom1)
38      lblNum2.Text = Convert.ToString(intRandom2)
39
40  End Sub
41  Private Sub btnExit_Click(ByVal sender As Object,
    ByVal e As System.EventArgs) Handles btnExit.Click
42      Me.Close()
43  End Sub
44
45  Private Sub ProcessGradeRadioButtons(
    ByVal sender As Object,
46  ByVal e As System.EventArgs
47  ) Handles radGrade1.Click, radGrade2.Click
48      Call GenerateAndDisplayIntegers()
49  End Sub
50
51  Private Sub radAddition_Click(ByVal sender As Object,
    ByVal e As System.EventArgs) Handles radAddition.Click
52      ' display the plus sign and random numbers
53
54      picOperator.Image = picPlus.Image
55      Call GenerateAndDisplayIntegers()
56
57  End Sub
58
59  Private Sub radSubtraction_Click(ByVal sender As Object,
    ByVal e As System.EventArgs) Handles radSubtraction.Click
60      ' display the minus sign and random numbers
61
62      picOperator.Image = picMinus.Image
63      Call GenerateAndDisplayIntegers()
64
65  End Sub
66
67  Private Sub frmMain_Load(ByVal sender As Object,
    ByVal e As System.EventArgs) Handles Me.Load
68      ' display an addition problem
69
70      radAddition.PerformClick()
71
72  End Sub
73 End Class
```

Figure 5-41 Math Practice application's code at the end of Lesson B

Lesson B Summary

- To limit the user to only one choice in a group of two or more related but mutually exclusive choices:

  Use the RadioButton tool to add a radio button control to the form. To include two groups of radio buttons on a form, at least one of the groups must be placed within a container, such as a group box.

- To allow the user to select any number of choices from a group of one or more independent and nonexclusive choices:

  Use the CheckBox tool to add a check box control to the form.

- To create a collection of code that can be invoked from one or more places in a program:

  Create an independent Sub procedure. The Sub procedure's name should indicate the task performed by the procedure. The name typically begins with a verb and is entered using Pascal case.

- To generate random integers:

  Create a Random object to represent the pseudo-random number generator. Typically, the syntax for creating a Random object is **Dim** *randomObjectName* **As New Random**. You then use the Random.Next method to generate a random integer. The method's syntax is *randomObjectName*.**Next(***minValue*, *maxValue***)**. The Random.Next method returns an integer that is greater than or equal to minValue, but less than maxValue.

- To call (invoke) an independent Sub procedure:

  Use the Call statement. The statement's syntax is **Call** *procedureName* (*[argumentList]*). In the syntax, *procedureName* is the name of the procedure you want to call, and *argumentList* (which is optional) contains the information you want to send to the Sub procedure.

- To invoke an object's Click event from code:

  Use the PerformClick method. The method's syntax is *object*.**PerformClick()**, in which *object* is the name of the object whose Click event you want invoked.

Lesson B Key Terms

Call statement—the Visual Basic statement used to invoke an independent Sub procedure

Check boxes—controls used to offer the user one or more independent and nonexclusive choices

Default radio button—the radio button that is automatically selected when an interface first appears

Independent Sub procedure—a procedure that is not associated with any specific object or event and is processed only when invoked (called) from code

PerformClick method—the method used to invoke a control's Click event

Pseudo-random number generator—a device that produces a sequence of numbers that meet certain statistical requirements for randomness; the pseudo-random number generator in Visual Basic is an object whose data type is Random

Radio buttons—controls used to limit the user to only one choice from a group of two or more related but mutually exclusive choices

Random object—represents the pseudo-random number generator in Visual Basic

Random.Next method—used to generate a random integer that is greater than or equal to a minimum value, but less than a maximum value

Lesson B Review Questions

1. What is the minimum number of radio buttons in a group?

    a. one

    b. two

    c. three

    d. There is no minimum number of radio buttons.

2. The text appearing in check boxes and radio buttons should be entered using _____.

    a. sentence capitalization

    b. book title capitalization

    c. either book title capitalization or sentence capitalization

3. It is customary in Windows applications to designate a default check box.

    a. True

    b. False

4. A form contains six radio buttons. Three of the radio buttons are contained in a group box. How many of the radio buttons in the interface can be selected at the same time?

    a. one

    b. two

    c. three

    d. six

5. A form contains six check boxes. Three of the check boxes are contained in a group box. How many of the check boxes can be selected at the same time?

   a. one

   b. two

   c. three

   d. six

6. If a radio button is selected, its _____ property contains the Boolean value True.

   a. Checked

   b. On

   c. Selected

   d. Selection

7. Which of the following statements declares an object to represent the pseudo-random number generator in a procedure?

   a. `Dim randGen As New RandomNumber`

   b. `Dim randGen As New Generator`

   c. `Dim randGen As New Random`

   d. `Dim randGen As New RandomObject`

8. Which of the following statements generates a random integer from 1 to 25, inclusive?

   a. `intNum = randGen.Next(1, 25)`

   b. `intNum = randGen.Next(1, 26)`

   c. `intNum = randGen(1, 25)`

   d. `intNum = randGen.NextNumber(1, 26)`

9. You can use the _____ statement to invoke an independent Sub procedure.

   a. Call

   b. Get

   c. Invoke

   d. ProcedureCall

10. Which of the following statements invokes the radAlaska control's Click event?

   a. `radAlaska.Click()`

   b. `radAlaska.ClickIt()`

   c. `radAlaska.PerformClick()`

   d. `PerformClick.radAlaska()`

Lesson B Exercises

1. In this exercise, you modify the Math Practice application from this lesson. Use Windows to make a copy of the Math Solution folder. Rename the copy Math Solution-Call. Open the Math Solution (Math Solution.sln) file contained in the Math Solution-Call folder. Open the designer and Code Editor windows. Replace the `radAddition.PerformClick()` statement in the form's Load event procedure with a Call statement that invokes the GenerateAndDisplayIntegers procedure. Save the solution and then start the application. An addition problem automatically appears in the interface. Close the Code Editor window and then close the solution.

   INTRODUCTORY

2. In this exercise, you code an application that allows the user to select the name of a state and the name of a city. After making both selections, the user can click the Verify Answer button to verify that the selected city is the capital of the selected state. Open the Capitals Solution (Capitals Solution.sln) file contained in the VB2010\Chap05\ Capitals Solution folder. If necessary, open the designer window.

   INTRODUCTORY

   a. Designate the first radio button in each group as the default radio button for the group.

   b. Enter the code to invoke the Click event for the two default radio buttons when the form first appears on the screen.

   c. Declare two class-level String variables named `strCapital` and `strChoice`.

   d. The Click event procedure for each State radio button should assign the appropriate capital to the `strCapital` variable and then remove the contents of the lblMsg control. Code each State radio button's Click event procedure.

   e. The Click event procedure for each Capital radio button should assign the selected capital to the `strChoice` variable and then remove the contents of the lblMsg control. Code each Capital radio button's Click event procedure.

   f. The Verify Answer button's Click event procedure should compare the correct capital with the capital chosen by the user. If the user selected the correct capital, the procedure should display the word "Correct" in the lblMsg control; otherwise, it should display the word "Incorrect" in the lblMsg control. Code the button's Click event procedure.

    g. Save the solution and then start the application. Test the application by selecting Illinois from the State group and Salem from the Capital group. Click the Verify Answer button. The word "Incorrect" should appear in the lblMsg control. Now select Wisconsin from the State group and Madison from the Capital group. Click the Verify Answer button. The word "Correct" should appear in the lblMsg control. Close the Code Editor window and then close the solution.

INTERMEDIATE

3. Open the Juarez Solution (Juarez Solution.sln) file contained in the VB2010\Chap05\Juarez Solution folder. If necessary, open the designer window.

    a. The Display Grade button's Click event procedure should display a letter grade. The appropriate letter grade is based on the average of three test scores, as indicated in Figure 5-42. Each test is worth 100 points. The procedure should display an appropriate message if any of the test scores cannot be converted to the Double data type. Code the Click event procedure.

    b. When the user makes a change to the contents of a text box, the application should remove the contents of the lblGrade control. Code the appropriate event procedures.

    c. The application should select a text box's existing text when the text box receives the focus. Code the appropriate event procedures.

    d. Save the solution and then start and test the application. Use the following scores for the first test: 90, 95, and 100. Use the following scores for the second test: 83, 72, and 65. Use the following scores for the third test: 40, 30, and 20. Next, test the application using letters, and then test it using an empty text box. Close the Code Editor window and then close the solution.

Average	Grade
90 – 100	A
80 – 89	B
70 – 79	C
60 – 69	D
Below 60	F

Figure 5-42　Grade information for Exercise 3

INTERMEDIATE

4. In this exercise, you create an application that allows the user to enter both the number of calories and the number of grams of fat contained in a specific food. The application should calculate and display two values: the food's fat calories (the number of calories attributed to fat) and its fat percentage (the ratio of the food's fat calories to its total calories). You calculate the number of fat calories in a food by multiplying the number of fat grams contained in the food by the number 9, because each gram of fat contains 9 calories. To calculate the fat percentage, you divide the food's fat calories by its total calories and then multiply the result by 100. The application should display the message "This food is

high in fat." when the fat percentage is over 30%; otherwise, it should display the message "This food is not high in fat." Create a Visual Basic Windows application. Use the following names for the solution, project, and form file, respectively: Fat Calculator Solution, Fat Calculator Project, and Main Form.vb. Save the application in the VB2010\Chap05 folder. Create the interface shown in Figure 5-43, and then code the application. Display an appropriate message if the user's entries cannot be converted to numbers. Save the solution and then start and test the application. Close the Code Editor window and then close the solution.

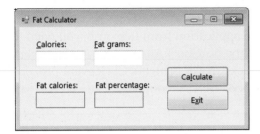

Figure 5-43   Interface for Exercise 4

Discovery

5. In this exercise, you learn how to generate and display random numbers containing decimal places. Open the Random Double Solution (Random Double Solution.sln) file contained in the VB2010\Chap05\Random Double Solution folder. If necessary, open the designer window.

 a. You can use the Random.NextDouble method to return a random number that is greater than or equal to 0.0, but less than 1.0. The syntax of the Random.NextDouble method is *randomObjectName.***NextDouble**. Code the Display Random Number button's Click event procedure so that it displays a random number in the lblNumber control. Save the solution and then start the application. Click the Display Random Number button several times. Each time you click the button, a random number that is greater than or equal to 0.0, but less than 1.0, appears in the lblNumber control.

 b. You can use the following formula to generate random numbers within a specified range: (*maxValue* − *minValue* + **1**) * *randomObjectName*.**NextDouble** + *minValue*. For example, assuming the Random object's name is `randGen`, the formula `(10 - 1 + 1) * randGen.NextDouble + 1` generates random numbers that are greater than or equal to 1.0, but less than 11.0. Modify the Display Random Number button's Click event procedure so that it displays a random number that is greater than or equal to 25.0, but less than 51.0. Display two decimal places in the number.

 c. Save the solution and then start the application. Click the Display Random Number button several times. Each time you click the button, a random number that is greater than or equal to 25.0, but less than 51.0, appears in the lblNumber control. Close the Code Editor window and then close the solution.

LESSON C

After studying Lesson C, you should be able to:

- Code a check box's Click event procedure

- Show and hide a control

Coding the Check Answer Button's Click Event Procedure

To complete the Math Practice application from Lesson B, you need to code the Click event procedures for the btnCheckAnswer and chkSummary controls. You will code the btnCheckAnswer control's Click event procedure first. Figure 5-44 shows the procedure's pseudocode.

---

btnCheckAnswer Click event procedure

1. declare the necessary memory locations (variables and any named constants)
2. store the two random numbers and the user's answer in variables
3. if the Addition radio button is selected
         calculate the correct answer by adding together the values in the
         lblNum1 and lblNum2 controls
     else
         calculate the correct answer by subtracting the value in the lblNum2
         control from the value in the lblNum1 control
     end if
4. if the user's answer equals the correct answer
         display the happy face icon in the picFace control
         add 1 to the number of correct responses
         clear the contents of the txtAnswer control
         call the GenerateAndDisplayIntegers procedure to generate
         and display two random integers
     else
         display the neutral face icon in the picFace control
         add 1 to the number of incorrect responses
         display the "Try again!" message in a message box
         select the existing text in the txtAnswer control
     end if
5. send the focus to the txtAnswer control
6. display the number of correct and incorrect responses in lblCorrect and lblIncorrect

---

Figure 5-44 Pseudocode for the btnCheckAnswer control's Click event procedure

Figure 5-45 lists the memory locations the procedure will use. Notice that two of the variables will be declared as static variables. As you learned in Chapter 3, a static variable is a procedure-level variable that retains its value even when the procedure in which it is declared ends. In this case, the two variables need to be static variables because they must keep a running tally of the number of correct and incorrect responses.

The Ch05CVideo file demonstrates all of the steps contained in Lesson C. You can view the video either before or after completing the lesson.

Named constant	Purpose
strMSG	store the "Try again!" message

Variables	Purpose
intNum1	store the random number contained in the lblNum1 control
intNum2	store the random number contained in the lblNum2 control
intUserAnswer	store the user's answer (from the txtAnswer control)
intCorrectAnswer	store the correct answer
intCorrectResponses	store the number of correct responses made by the user; declare as a static variable
intIncorrectResponses	store the number of incorrect responses made by the user; declare as a static variable

Figure 5-45 Memory locations used by the btnCheckAnswer control's Click event procedure

To begin coding the btnCheckAnswer control's Click event procedure: START HERE

1. If necessary, start Visual Studio 2010 or Visual Basic 2010 Express.

2. Open the Math Solution (Math Solution.sln) file from Lesson B. The file is contained in the VB2010\Chap05\Math Solution folder. If necessary, open the designer window.

3. Open the Code Editor window and then open the code template for the btnCheckAnswer control's Click event procedure. Enter the following comments. Press **Enter** twice after typing the last comment.

   ' calculates the correct answer and then compares
   ' the correct answer to the user's answer
   ' keeps track of the number of correct
   ' and incorrect responses

4. Next, enter the following Const, Dim, and Static statements. Press **Enter** twice after typing the last Static statement.

   Const strMSG As String = "Try again!"
   Dim intNum1 As Integer
   Dim intNum2 As Integer
   Dim intUserAnswer As Integer
   Dim intCorrectAnswer As Integer
   Static intCorrectResponses As Integer
   Static intIncorrectResponses As Integer

5. Step 2 in the procedure's pseudocode is to store the random numbers and the user's answer in variables. Enter the following comment and three assignment statements. Press **Enter** twice after typing the last assignment statement.

   ' store random numbers and user's answer in variables
   Integer.TryParse(lblNum1.Text, intNum1)
   Integer.TryParse(lblNum2.Text, intNum2)
   Integer.TryParse(txtAnswer.Text, intUserAnswer)

6. Step 3 in the pseudocode is a selection structure whose condition determines whether the Addition radio button is selected. If it is, the procedure should add the two random numbers together. Otherwise, it should subtract the second random number from the first random number.

314

Enter the comments and selection structure shown in Figure 5-46 and then position the insertion point as shown in the figure.

enter these comments and six lines of code

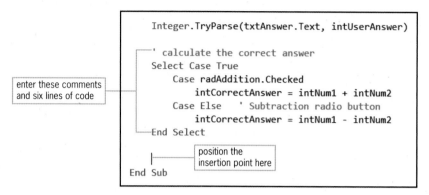

```
Integer.TryParse(txtAnswer.Text, intUserAnswer)

' calculate the correct answer
Select Case True
    Case radAddition.Checked
        intCorrectAnswer = intNum1 + intNum2
    Case Else    ' Subtraction radio button
        intCorrectAnswer = intNum1 - intNum2
End Select
```

position the insertion point here

```
End Sub
```

Figure 5-46   Comments and selection structure entered in the procedure

7. Step 4 in the pseudocode is a selection structure whose condition determines whether the user's answer is correct. You can make this determination by comparing the contents of the `intUserAnswer` variable with the contents of the `intCorrectAnswer` variable. Enter the following comment and If clause:

' determine whether the user's answer is correct
If intUserAnswer = intCorrectAnswer Then

8. If the user's answer is correct, the procedure should perform the following four tasks: display the happy face icon in the picFace control, add 1 to the number of correct responses, clear the contents of the txtAnswer control, and call the GenerateAndDisplayIntegers procedure to generate and display two random integers. Enter the following four statements:

picFace.Image = picHappy.Image
intCorrectResponses = intCorrectResponses + 1
txtAnswer.Text = String.Empty
Call GenerateAndDisplayIntegers()

9. If the user's answer is not correct, the procedure should perform the following four tasks: display the neutral face icon in the picFace control, add 1 to the number of incorrect responses, display the "Try again!" message in a message box, and select the existing text in the txtAnswer control. Enter the additional code shown in Figure 5-47 and then position the insertion point as shown in the figure.

enter these seven lines of code

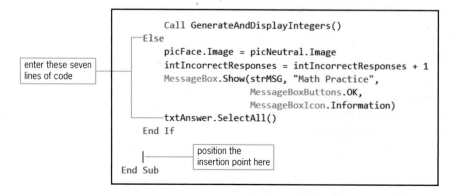

```
        Call GenerateAndDisplayIntegers()
Else
        picFace.Image = picNeutral.Image
        intIncorrectResponses = intIncorrectResponses + 1
        MessageBox.Show(strMSG, "Math Practice",
                        MessageBoxButtons.OK,
                        MessageBoxIcon.Information)
        txtAnswer.SelectAll()
    End If
```

position the insertion point here

```
End Sub
```

Figure 5-47   Code entered in the selection structure's false path

10. The last two steps in the procedure's pseudocode are to send the focus to the txtAnswer control and then display the number of correct and incorrect responses in the appropriate label controls. Enter the following three lines of code and then save the solution:

    txtAnswer.Focus()
    lblCorrect.Text = intCorrectResponses.ToString
    lblIncorrect.Text = intIncorrectResponses.ToString

Coding the Display Summary Check Box's Click Event Procedure

Recall that the four picture boxes located at the bottom of the form do not appear in the interface during run time. This is because their **Visible property** is set to False in the Properties window. The Visible property of the grpSummary control also is set to False, which explains why you do not see the control and its contents when the form appears on the screen. According to the application's TOE chart (shown earlier in Figure 5-32), the chkSummary control's Click event procedure is responsible for both showing and hiding the grpSummary control. The procedure should show the group box when the user selects the check box, and it should hide the group box when the user deselects the check box. Recall that you can determine whether a check box was either selected or deselected during run time by looking at the Boolean value in its Checked property. When it is coded, the Click event procedure for a check box always will contain a selection structure that determines whether the check box was selected or deselected by the user. A selection structure is not necessary in a radio button's Click event procedure, because clicking a radio button always selects the button; the user cannot deselect a radio button by clicking it.

To code the chkSummary control's Click event procedure: ◄ START HERE

1. Open the code template for the chkSummary control's Click event procedure. Type the following comment and then press **Enter** twice:

    ' shows/hides the grpSummary control

2. If the user selects the check box, the procedure should display the grpSummary control. This is accomplished by setting the control's Visible property to the Boolean value True. Enter the following If clause and assignment statement:

    If chkSummary.Checked Then
    **   grpSummary.Visible = True**

 You also can write the If clause in Step 2 as `If chkSummary. Checked = True Then`.

3. If the user deselects the check box, the procedure should hide the grpSummary control. This is accomplished by setting the control's Visible property to the Boolean value False. Enter the following Else clause and assignment statement:

    Else
    **   grpSummary.Visible = False**

4. If necessary, delete the blank line above the End If clause in the procedure.

5. Save the solution and then start the application. Type the correct answer to the addition problem and then press **Enter** to select the Check Answer button, which is the default button on the form. The happy face icon and a new addition problem appear in the interface.

6. Click the **Display summary** check box to select it. A check mark appears in the check box, and the grpSummary control and its contents appear in the interface. Notice that the label controls within the group box indicate that you have made 1 correct response and 0 incorrect responses.

7. Click the **text box** in which you enter the answer. Type an incorrect answer to the current addition problem and then press **Enter**. A neutral face icon appears in the interface, and a message box appears on the screen, as shown in Figure 5-48.

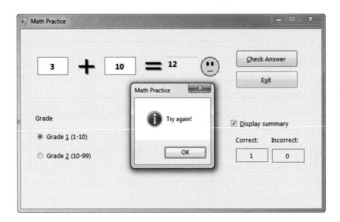

Figure 5-48   Result of entering an incorrect response to the addition problem

8. Press **Enter** to close the message box. The number of incorrect responses changes from 0 to 1, and the incorrect answer is selected in the txtAnswer control. Type the correct answer to the current addition problem and then press **Enter**. The number of correct responses changes from 1 to 2, and the happy face icon appears in the interface.

9. Click the **Display summary** check box to deselect it. The check mark is removed from the check box, and the grpSummary control and its contents are hidden.

10. Click the **Exit** button. Close the Code Editor window and then close the solution.

Figure 5-49 shows the application's code at the end of Lesson C.

```
 1 ' Name:            Math Project
 2 ' Purpose:         Displays math problems
 3 ' Programmer:      <your name> on <current date>
 4
 5 Option Explicit On
 6 Option Strict On
 7 Option Infer Off
 8
 9 Public Class frmMain
10
11    Private Sub GenerateAndDisplayIntegers()
12        ' generates and displays two random integers
13
14        Dim intRandom1 As Integer
15        Dim intRandom2 As Integer
16        Dim randomGenerator As New Random
17
18        ' generate random integers
19        If radGrade1.Checked Then
20            intRandom1 = randomGenerator.Next(1, 11)
21            intRandom2 = randomGenerator.Next(1, 11)
22        Else
23            intRandom1 = randomGenerator.Next(10, 100)
24            intRandom2 = randomGenerator.Next(10, 100)
25        End If
26
27        ' swap integers if the subtraction problem
28        ' would result in a negative answer
29        If radSubtraction.Checked AndAlso
           intRandom1 < intRandom2 Then
30            Dim intTemp As Integer
31            intTemp = intRandom1
32            intRandom1 = intRandom2
33            intRandom2 = intTemp
34        End If
35
36        ' display integers
37        lblNum1.Text = Convert.ToString(intRandom1)
38        lblNum2.Text = Convert.ToString(intRandom2)
39
40    End Sub
41    Private Sub btnExit_Click(ByVal sender As Object,
       ByVal e As System.EventArgs) Handles btnExit.Click
42        Me.Close()
43    End Sub
44
45    Private Sub ProcessGradeRadioButtons(
       ByVal sender As Object,
46       ByVal e As System.EventArgs
47    ) Handles radGrade1.Click, radGrade2.Click
48        Call GenerateAndDisplayIntegers()
49    End Sub
50
51    Private Sub radAddition_Click(ByVal sender As Object,
       ByVal e As System.EventArgs) Handles radAddition.Click
52        ' display the plus sign and random numbers
53
54        picOperator.Image = picPlus.Image
```

Figure 5-49   Math Practice application's code at the end of Lesson C *(continues)*

318

(continued)

```
55        Call GenerateAndDisplayIntegers()
56
57   End Sub
58
59   Private Sub radSubtraction_Click(ByVal sender As Object,
     ByVal e As System.EventArgs) Handles radSubtraction.Click
60        ' display the minus sign and random numbers
61
62        picOperator.Image = picMinus.Image
63        Call GenerateAndDisplayIntegers()
64
65   End Sub
66
67   Private Sub frmMain_Load(ByVal sender As Object,
     ByVal e As System.EventArgs) Handles Me.Load
68        ' display an addition problem
69
70        radAddition.PerformClick()
71
72   End Sub
73
74   Private Sub btnCheckAnswer_Click(ByVal sender As Object,
     ByVal e As System.EventArgs) Handles btnCheckAnswer.Click
75        ' calculates the correct answer and then compares
76        ' the correct answer to the user's answer
77        ' keeps track of the number of correct
78        ' and incorrect responses
79
80        Const strMSG As String = "Try again!"
81        Dim intNum1 As Integer
82        Dim intNum2 As Integer
83        Dim intUserAnswer As Integer
84        Dim intCorrectAnswer As Integer
85        Static intCorrectResponses As Integer
86        Static intIncorrectResponses As Integer
87
88        ' store random numbers and user's answer in variables
89        Integer.TryParse(lblNum1.Text, intNum1)
90        Integer.TryParse(lblNum2.Text, intNum2)
91        Integer.TryParse(txtAnswer.Text, intUserAnswer)
92
93        ' calculate the correct answer
94        Select Case True
95           Case radAddition.Checked
96                intCorrectAnswer = intNum1 + intNum2
97           Case Else ' Subtraction radio button
98                intCorrectAnswer = intNum1 - intNum2
99        End Select
100
101       ' determine whether the user's answer is correct
102       If intUserAnswer = intCorrectAnswer Then
103           picFace.Image = picHappy.Image
104           intCorrectResponses = intCorrectResponses + 1
105           txtAnswer.Text = String.Empty
106           Call GenerateAndDisplayIntegers()
107       Else
108           picFace.Image = picNeutral.Image
```

Figure 5-49   Math Practice application's code at the end of Lesson C *(continues)*

(continued)

```
109             intIncorrectResponses = intIncorrectResponses + 1
110             MessageBox.Show(strMSG, "Math Practice",
111                     MessageBoxButtons.OK,
112                     MessageBoxIcon.Information)
113             txtAnswer.SelectAll()
114         End If
115
116         txtAnswer.Focus()
117         lblCorrect.Text = intCorrectResponses.ToString
118         lblIncorrect.Text = intIncorrectResponses.ToString
119
120     End Sub
121
122     Private Sub chkSummary_Click(ByVal sender As Object,
        ByVal e As System.EventArgs) Handles chkSummary.Click
123         ' shows/hides the grpSummary control
124
125         If chkSummary.Checked Then
126             grpSummary.Visible = True
127         Else
128             grpSummary.Visible = False
129         End If
130     End Sub
131 End Class
```

Figure 5-49   Math Practice application's code at the end of Lesson C

Lesson C Summary

- To show or hide a control:

  Set the control's Visible property to the Boolean value True to show the control. Set the control's Visible property to the Boolean value False to hide the control.

- To code a check box's Click event procedure:

  Use a selection structure to determine whether the check box was either selected or deselected by the user.

Lesson C Key Term

Visible property—determines whether a control is visible in the interface while an application is running

Lesson C Review Questions

1. Which of the following statements will hide the picDivision control?

    a. `picDivision.Hide`

    b. `picDivision.Hide = True`

    c. `Hide.picDivision = True`

    d. none of the above

2. If a check box is deselected, its _____ property contains the Boolean value False.

    a. Checked

    b. Deselected

    c. On

    d. none of the above

3. When it is coded, a radio button's Click event procedure always will contain a selection structure that determines whether the radio button was selected or deselected by the user.

    a. True

    b. False

4. Like a check box, a radio button can be deselected by clicking it.

    a. True

    b. False

Lesson C Exercises

INTRODUCTORY

1. In this exercise, you modify the Math Practice application from this lesson. Use Windows to make a copy of the Math Solution folder. Rename the copy Modified Math Solution. Open the Math Solution (Math Solution.sln) file contained in the Modified Math Solution folder. Open the designer and Code Editor windows.

    a. Change the If...Then...Else statement in the chkSummary control's Click event procedure to a Select Case statement.

    b. Change the first selection structure in the btnCheckAnswer control's Click event procedure to an If...Then...Else statement.

    c. Change the second selection structure in the btnCheckAnswer control's Click event procedure to a Select Case statement.

    d. Save the solution and then start and test the application. Close the Code Editor window and then close the solution.

320

2. Open the Washington Solution (Washington Solution.sln) file contained in the VB2010\Chap05\Washington Solution folder. If necessary, open the designer window. Center the rank in the label control. Set the text box's MaxLength property so that the user can enter only one character in the text box. Code the Display button's Click event procedure so that it displays the rank associated with the code entered by the user. The codes and ranks are shown in Figure 5-50. Allow the text box to accept only the numeric keys 1, 2, 3, and 4 and the Backspace key. When a change is made to the code entered in the text box, clear the contents of the label control that displays the rank. Save the solution and then start and test the application. Close the Code Editor window and then close the solution.

Code	Rank
1	Freshman
2	Sophomore
3	Junior
4	Senior

Figure 5-50   Information for Exercise 2

3. Create a Visual Basic Windows application. Use the following names for the solution, project, and form file, respectively: Lottery Solution, Lottery Project, and Main Form.vb. Save the application in the VB2010\Chap05 folder. Create the interface shown in Figure 5-51. The Select Numbers button should display six lottery numbers. Each lottery number can range from 1 to 54 only. (An example of six lottery numbers would be: 4 8 35 15 20 3.) Code the application. For now, do not worry if the lottery numbers are not unique. You will learn how to display unique numbers in Chapter 9. Save the solution and then start and test the application. Close the Code Editor window and then close the solution.

Figure 5-51   Interface for Exercise 3

4. Open the Ferris Solution (Ferris Solution.sln) file contained in the VB2010\Chap05\Ferris Solution folder. If necessary, open the designer window. Ferris Seminars offers computer seminars to various companies. The owner of Ferris Seminars wants an application that the registration clerks can use to calculate the registration fee for a company. The clerk will enter the number registered for the seminar and then select one of the Seminar radio buttons. If a company is entitled to a 10% discount, the clerk will need to select the 10%

discount check box. The Calculate Total Due button should calculate the total registration fee. Seminar 1 is $100 per person, and Seminar 2 is $120 per person. Code the application. Remove the total fee when a change is made to the number registered, the seminar, or the discount. The text box should accept only numbers and the Backspace key. Save the solution and then start and test the application. Close the Code Editor window and then close the solution.

5. In this exercise, you modify the Monthly Payment Calculator application from Chapter 4. Use Windows to copy the Payment Solution folder from the VB2010\Chap04 folder to the VB2010\Chap05 folder. Open the Payment Solution (Payment Solution.sln) file contained in the VB2010\Chap05\Payment Solution folder. Open the designer and Code Editor windows. Delete the ClearPayment procedure and then create an independent Sub procedure named ClearPayment. The independent Sub procedure should clear the contents of the lblPayment control. Call the independent Sub procedure when a change is made to any of the three text boxes. Save the solution and then start and test the application. Close the Code Editor window and then close the solution.

6. Create a Visual Basic Windows application. Use the following names for the solution, project, and form file, respectively: Health Solution, Health Project, and Main Form.vb. Save the application in the VB2010\Chap05 folder. Create the interface shown in Figure 5-52. The application should calculate and display a health club member's monthly dues.

   a. Declare a class-level variable to keep track of the additional charges.

   b. Each check box's Click event procedure should add the appropriate additional charge to the class-level variable when the check box is selected, and subtract the additional charge from the class-level variable when the check box is deselected. The additional charges are $30 per month for tennis, $25 per month for golf, and $20 per month for racquetball. Each check box's Click event procedure also should display the contents of the class-level variable in the Additional box, as well as clear the contents of the Monthly dues box. Code the Click event procedures.

   c. Code the Calculate button's Click event procedure so that it calculates the monthly dues. The dues are calculated by adding the basic fee to the total additional charge. Display the total due with a dollar sign and two decimal places.

   d. When the user makes a change to the Basic fee box, the application should clear the contents of the Monthly dues box. Code the appropriate event procedure.

   e. The Basic fee box should accept only numbers and the Backspace key. Code the appropriate event procedure.

   f. Save the solution and then start the application. Test the application by entering 80 as the basic fee and then selecting the Golf check box. The number 25 appears as the additional charge. Click the Calculate button. The monthly dues are $105.00.

g. Next, select the Tennis and Racquetball check boxes and deselect the Golf check box. The number 50 appears as the additional charge. Click the Calculate button. The monthly dues are $130.00. Close the Code Editor window and then close the solution.

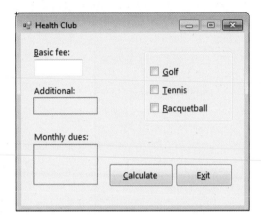

Figure 5-52   Interface for Exercise 6

7. Create a Visual Basic Windows application. Use the following names for the solution, project, and form file, respectively: Barren Solution, Barren Project, and Main Form.vb. Save the application in the VB2010\Chap05 folder. Create the interface shown in Figure 5-53. The application should display a seminar fee. The fee is based on the membership status and age entered by the user. The fee for club members younger than 65 years old is $10. The fee for club members at least 65 years old is $5. The fee for non-members is $20. When the user clicks a radio button, clear the contents of the label control that displays the fee. Code the application. Save the solution and then start and test the application. Close the Code Editor window and then close the solution.

INTERMEDIATE

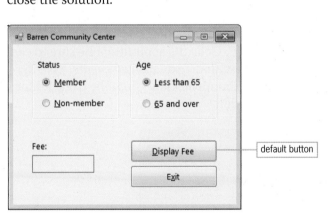

Figure 5-53   Interface for Exercise 7

8. Create a Visual Basic Windows application. Use the following names for the solution, project, and form file, respectively: Golf Pro Solution, Golf Pro Project, and Main Form.vb. Save the application in the VB2010\Chap05 folder. Create the interface shown in Figure 5-54. Each salesperson at Golf Pro receives a commission based on the total of

INTERMEDIATE

his or her domestic and international sales. The commission rates are shown in Figure 5-55. The text boxes should accept only numbers and the Backspace key. Select the existing text when a text box receives the focus. Clear the Commission box when the value in a text box changes. Code the application. Save the solution and then start and test the application. Close the Code Editor window and then close the solution.

Figure 5-54   Interface for Exercise 8

Sales ($)	Commission
1 – 100,000.99	2% of sales
100,001 – 400,000.99	$2000 plus 5% of the sales over $100,000
400,001 and over	$17000 plus 10% of the sales over $400,000

Figure 5-55   Commission rates for Exercise 8

INTERMEDIATE

9. Create a Visual Basic Windows application. Use the following names for the solution, project, and form file, respectively: Marshall Solution, Marshall Project, and Main Form.vb. Save the application in the VB2010\Chap05 folder. Create the interface shown in Figure 5-56. Each salesperson at Marshall Sales Corporation receives a commission based on the amount of his or her sales. The commission rates are shown in Figure 5-57. Code the application. Be sure to code the text box's Enter, KeyPress, and TextChanged events. Save the solution and then start and test the application. Close the Code Editor window and then close the solution.

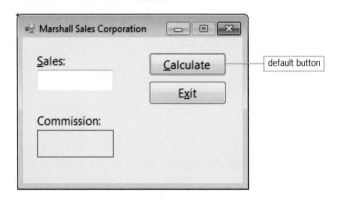

Figure 5-56   Interface for Exercise 9

Sales ($)	Commission
1 – 100,000.99	2% of sales
100,001 – 200,000.99	4% of sales
200,001 – 300,000.99	6% of sales
300,001 – 400,000.99	8% of sales
400,001 and over	10% of sales

Figure 5-57 Commission rates for Exercise 9

10. Create a Visual Basic Windows application. Name the solution, project, and form file Willow Solution, Willow Project, and Main Form.vb, respectively. Save the application in the VB2010\Chap05 folder. Create the interface shown in Figure 5-58. The application should calculate and display the number of daily calories needed to maintain your current weight. Use the information shown in Figure 5-59 when coding the application. Be sure to code the text box's Enter and KeyPress events. Clear the daily calories when the weight, gender, or activity changes. Save the solution and then start and test the application. Close the Code Editor window and then close the solution.

INTERMEDIATE

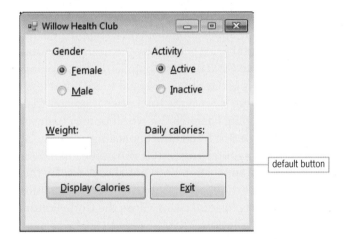

Figure 5-58 Interface for Exercise 10

Moderately active female	daily calories = weight * 12 calories per pound
Relatively inactive female	daily calories = weight * 10 calories per pound
Moderately active male	daily calories = weight * 15 calories per pound
Relatively inactive male	daily calories = weight * 13 calories per pound

Figure 5-59 Daily calories information for Exercise 10

11. In this exercise, you create an application for Johnson Products. The application calculates and displays the price of an order, based on the number of units ordered and the customer's status (either wholesaler or retailer). The price per unit is shown in Figure 5-60. Create a Visual Basic Windows application. Use the following names for the solution, project, and form file, respectively: Johnson Solution, Johnson

ADVANCED

Project, and Main Form.vb. Save the application in the VB2010\
Chap05 folder. Design an appropriate interface. Use radio buttons to
determine the customer's status. Code the application. Save the solution and then start and test the application. Close the Code Editor
window and then close the solution.

Wholesaler		Retailer	
Number of units	Price per unit ($)	Number of units	Price per unit ($)
1–4	10	1–3	15
5 and over	9	4–8	14
		9 and over	12

Figure 5-60   Pricing chart for Exercise 11

 Swat The Bugs

12. The purpose of this exercise is to demonstrate the importance of
testing an application thoroughly. Open the Debug Solution (Debug
Solution.sln) file contained in the VB2010\Chap05\Debug Solution-
Lesson C folder. If necessary, open the designer window. Open the
Code Editor window. The application displays a shipping charge,
which is based on the total price entered by the user. If the total price
is greater than or equal to $100 but less than $501, the shipping charge
is $10. If the total price is greater than or equal to $501 but less than
$1001, the shipping charge is $7. If the total price is greater than or
equal to $1001, the shipping charge is $5. No shipping charge is due if
the total price is less than $100. Start the application. Test the appli-
cation using the following total prices: 100, 501, 1500, 500.75, 30,
1000.33. Notice that the application does not always display the correct
shipping charge. Correct the application's code. Save the solution and
then start and test the application again. Close the Code Editor window and then close the solution.

The Repetition Structure

Creating the Shoppers Haven Application

In this chapter, you create an application that allows the user to enter an item's original price and its discount rate. The discount rates range from 10% through 30% in increments of 5%. The application will calculate and display the amount of the discount and also the discounted.price.

Previewing the Shoppers Haven Application

Before you start the first lesson in this chapter, you will preview the completed application. The application is contained in the VB2010\Chap06 folder.

START HERE

To preview the completed application:

1. Use the Run dialog box to run the Shoppers (Shoppers.exe) file contained in the VB2010\Chap06 folder. The application's user interface appears on the screen. The interface contains a list box. List box controls are covered in Lesson C.

2. Type **56.99** in the Original price box. Click **15** in the list of discount rates and then click the **Calculate** button. The item's discount and discounted price appear in the interface. See Figure 6-1.

Figure 6-1 Discount and discounted price shown in the interface

3. Click the **Exit** button to end the application.

The Shoppers Haven application uses the repetition structure, which is covered in Lessons A and B. You will code the Shoppers Haven application in Lesson C. Be sure to complete each lesson in full and do all of the end-of-lesson questions and several exercises before continuing to the next lesson.

LESSON A

After studying Lesson A, you should be able to:

- Differentiate between a looping condition and a loop exit condition
- Explain the difference between a pretest loop and a posttest loop

- Include pretest and posttest loops in pseudocode and a flowchart
- Write a Do...Loop statement
- Stop an infinite loop
- Utilize counters and accumulators
- Explain the purpose of the priming and update reads
- Abbreviate assignment statements using the arithmetic assignment operators
- Code a counter-controlled loop using the For...Next statement

Repeating Program Instructions

Recall that all of the procedures in an application are written using one or more of three basic control structures: sequence, selection, and repetition. You learned about the sequence and selection structures in previous chapters. This chapter covers the repetition structure. Programmers use the **repetition structure**, referred to more simply as a **loop**, when they need the computer to repeatedly process one or more program instructions. If and for how long the instructions are repeated is determined by the loop's condition.

Like the condition in a selection structure, the condition in a loop must evaluate to either True or False. The condition is evaluated with each repetition (or iteration) of the loop and can be phrased in one of two ways: it can specify either the requirement for repeating the instructions or the requirement for *not* repeating them. The requirement for repeating the instructions is referred to as the **looping condition**, because it indicates when the computer should continue "looping" through the instructions. The requirement for *not* repeating the instructions is referred to as the **loop exit condition**, because it tells the computer when to exit (or stop) the loop. An example may help illustrate the difference between the looping condition and the loop exit condition. You've probably heard the old adage "Make hay while the sun shines." The "while the sun shines" is the looping condition, because it tells you when to continue making hay. The adage also could be phrased as "Make hay until the sun stops shining." In this case, the "until the sun stops shining" is the loop exit condition, because it indicates when you should stop making hay. Every looping condition has an opposing loop exit condition; in other words, one is the opposite of the other. See Figure 6-2.

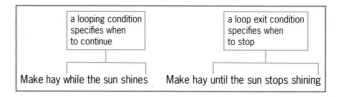

Figure 6-2   Example of a looping condition and a loop exit condition

The programmer determines whether a problem's solution requires a loop by studying the problem specification. The first problem specification you will examine in this chapter is for the Quarter of a Million Club. The problem specification is shown in Figure 6-3.

> The Quarter of a Million Club wants an application that allows a club member to enter two items: the amount of money deposited into a savings account at the beginning of the year and the annual interest rate. The application should display the balance in the savings account at the end of the year, assuming the interest is compounded annually and no withdrawals or additional deposits are made.

Figure 6-3   Problem specification for the Quarter of a Million Club application

Figure 6-4 shows a sample run of the Quarter of a Million Club application. The .00 in the Annual interest rate (.00): label indicates that the user should enter the interest rate in decimal form.

Figure 6-4   Sample run of the Quarter of a Million Club application

Figure 6-5 shows the pseudocode and Visual Basic code for the Calculate button's Click event procedure. The procedure requires only the sequence structure. It does not need a selection structure or a loop, because no decisions need to be made and no instructions need to be repeated to calculate and display the account balance at the end of one year.

```
btnCalc Click event procedure
1. store deposit in balance variable
2. store rate in rate variable
3. interest = balance * rate
4. add interest to balance
5. display balance

Private Sub btnCalc_Click(ByVal sender As Object,
ByVal e As System.EventArgs) Handles btnCalc.Click
    ' display account balance

    Dim dblBalance As Double
    Dim dblRate As Double
    Dim dblInterest As Double

    Double.TryParse(txtDeposit.Text, dblBalance)
    Double.TryParse(txtRate.Text, dblRate)

    dblInterest = dblBalance * dblRate
    dblBalance = dblBalance + dblInterest

    lblBalance.Text = dblBalance.ToString("C2")
End Sub
```

Figure 6-5 Pseudocode and code containing only the sequence structure

Next, we'll make a slight change to the problem specification from Figure 6-3. The Quarter of a Million Club application will now need to display the number of years required for the savings account to reach one-quarter of a million dollars, and the balance in the account at that time. Consider the changes you will need to make to the Calculate button's original pseudocode. The first two steps in the original pseudocode are to store the input items (deposit and interest rate) in variables; the modified pseudocode will still need both of these steps. Steps 3 and 4 are to calculate the interest and then add the interest to the savings account balance. The modified pseudocode will need to repeat both of those steps either while the balance is less than one-quarter of a million dollars (looping condition) or until the balance is greater than or equal to one-quarter of a million dollars (loop exit condition). Notice that the loop exit condition is the opposite of the looping condition. The loop in the modified pseudocode also will need to keep track of the number of times the instructions in Steps 3 and 4 are processed, because each time represents a year. The last step in the original pseudocode is to display the account balance. The modified pseudocode will need to display the account balance and the number of years.

The modified problem specification is shown in Figure 6-6 along with four versions of the modified pseudocode. (As mentioned in Chapter 5, even small procedures can have more than one solution.) Only the loop is different in each version. In Versions 1 and 2, the loop is a pretest loop. In a **pretest loop**, the condition is evaluated *before* the instructions within the loop are processed. The condition in Version 1 is a looping condition, because it tells the computer when to continue repeating the loop instructions. Version 2's condition, on the other hand, is a loop exit condition, because it tells the computer when to *stop* repeating the instructions. Depending on the result of

The condition appears at the beginning of a pretest loop, but at the end of a posttest loop. For that reason, pretest and post-test loops are also called top-driven and bottom-driven loops, respectively.

You can nest loops, which means you can place one loop within another loop.

the evaluation, the instructions in a pretest loop may never be processed. For example, if the user enters a deposit that is greater than or equal to 250,000 (one-quarter of a million), the looping condition in Version 1 will evaluate to False and the loop instructions will be skipped over. Similarly, the loop exit condition in Version 2 will evaluate to True, causing the loop instructions to be bypassed.

The loops in Versions 3 and 4, on the other hand, are posttest loops. In a **posttest loop**, the condition is evaluated *after* the instructions within the loop are processed. The condition in Version 3 is a looping condition, whereas the condition in Version 4 is a loop exit condition. Unlike the instructions in a pretest loop, the instructions in a posttest loop will always be processed at least once. In this case, if the user enters a deposit that is greater than or equal to 250,000, the instructions in the two posttest loops will be processed once before the loop ends. Posttest loops should be used only when you are certain that the loop instructions should be processed at least once.

The Quarter of a Million Club wants an application that allows a club member to enter two items: the amount of money deposited into a savings account at the beginning of the year and the annual interest rate. The application should display the number of years required for the balance in the savings account to reach one-quarter of a million dollars, assuming the interest is compounded annually and no withdrawals or additional deposits are made. It also should display the account balance at that time.

Version 1 – pretest loop
1. store deposit in balance variable
2. store rate in rate variable
3. repeat while balance < 250,000   [looping condition specifies when to continue]
    interest = balance * rate
    add interest to balance
    add 1 to number of years
    end repeat while
4. display number of years and balance

Version 2 – pretest loop
1. store deposit in balance variable
2. store rate in rate variable
3. repeat until balance >= 250,000   [loop exit condition specifies when to stop]
    interest = balance * rate
    add interest to balance
    add 1 to number of years
    end repeat until
4. display number of years and balance

Version 3 – posttest loop
1. store deposit in balance variable
2. store rate in rate variable
3. repeat
    interest = balance * rate   [looping condition specifies when to continue]
    add interest to balance
    add 1 to number of years
    end repeat while balance < 250,000
4. display number of years and balance

Version 4 – posttest loop
1. store deposit in balance variable
2. store rate in rate variable
3. repeat
    interest = balance * rate   [loop exit condition specifies when to stop]
    add interest to balance
    add 1 to number of years
    end repeat until balance >= 250,000
4. display number of years and balance

Figure 6-6 Modified problem specification and pseudocode containing a loop

The Visual Basic language provides three different statements for coding loops: Do…Loop, For…Next, and For Each…Next. The Do…Loop statement can be used to code both pretest and posttest loops, whereas the For…Next and For Each…Next statements are used only for pretest loops. You will learn about the Do…Loop and For…Next statements in this lesson. The For Each…Next statement is covered in Chapter 9.

The Do...Loop Statement

You can use the **Do...Loop statement** to code both pretest and posttest loops. Figure 6-7 shows two versions of the statement's syntax: one for coding a pretest loop and the other for coding a posttest loop. In both versions of the syntax, the statement begins with the Do clause and ends with the Loop clause. Between both clauses, you enter the instructions you want the computer to repeat. The instructions between the Do and Loop clauses are referred to as the **loop body**.

The {While | Until} portion in each syntax indicates that you can select only one of the keywords appearing within the braces. You follow the keyword with a *condition*, which can be phrased as either a looping condition or a loop exit condition. You use the `While` keyword in a looping condition to specify that the loop body should be processed *while* (in other words, as long as) the condition is true. You use the `Until` keyword in a loop exit condition to specify that the loop body should be processed *until* the condition becomes true, at which time the loop should stop. Like the condition in an If...Then...Else statement, the condition in a Do...Loop statement can contain variables, constants, properties, methods, keywords, and operators; it also must evaluate to a Boolean value. The condition is evaluated with each repetition of the loop and determines whether the computer processes the loop body. Notice that the keyword (either `While` or `Until`) and the condition appear in the Do clause in a pretest loop, but they appear in the Loop clause in a posttest loop. Also included in Figure 6-7 are examples of using both syntax versions to display the numbers 1, 2, and 3 in message boxes.

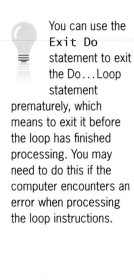

You can use the `Exit Do` statement to exit the Do...Loop statement prematurely, which means to exit it before the loop has finished processing. You may need to do this if the computer encounters an error when processing the loop instructions.

333

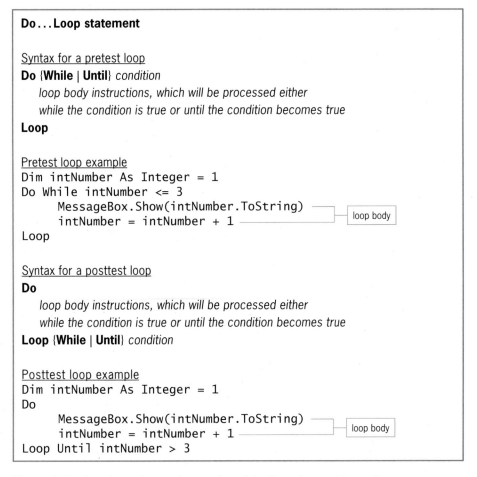

```
Do...Loop statement


Syntax for a pretest loop
Do {While | Until} condition
     loop body instructions, which will be processed either
     while the condition is true or until the condition becomes true
Loop


Pretest loop example
Dim intNumber As Integer = 1
Do While intNumber <= 3
     MessageBox.Show(intNumber.ToString)        ┐
     intNumber = intNumber + 1                  ┘─  loop body
Loop


Syntax for a posttest loop
Do
     loop body instructions, which will be processed either
     while the condition is true or until the condition becomes true
Loop {While | Until} condition


Posttest loop example
Dim intNumber As Integer = 1
Do
     MessageBox.Show(intNumber.ToString)        ┐
     intNumber = intNumber + 1                  ┘─  loop body
Loop Until intNumber > 3
```

Figure 6-7   Syntax versions and examples of the Do...Loop statement

Figure 6-8 describes the way the computer processes the code shown in the examples in Figure 6-7.

Processing steps for the pretest loop example

1. The computer creates the `intNumber` variable and initializes it to 1.
2. The computer processes the Do clause, which checks whether the value in the `intNumber` variable is less than or equal to 3. It is.
3. The MessageBox.Show method displays 1 (the contents of the `intNumber` variable).
4. The `intNumber = intNumber + 1` statement adds 1 to the contents of the `intNumber` variable, giving 2.
5. The computer processes the Loop clause, which returns processing to the Do clause (the beginning of the loop).
6. The computer processes the Do clause, which checks whether the value in the `intNumber` variable is less than or equal to 3. It is.
7. The MessageBox.Show method displays 2 (the contents of the `intNumber` variable).
8. The `intNumber = intNumber + 1` statement adds 1 to the contents of the `intNumber` variable, giving 3.
9. The computer processes the Loop clause, which returns processing to the Do clause.
10. The computer processes the Do clause, which checks whether the value in the `intNumber` variable is less than or equal to 3. It is.
11. The MessageBox.Show method displays 3 (the contents of the `intNumber` variable).
12. The `intNumber = intNumber + 1` statement adds 1 to the contents of the `intNumber` variable, giving 4.
13. The computer processes the Loop clause, which returns processing to the Do clause.
14. The computer processes the Do clause, which checks whether the value in the `intNumber` variable is less than or equal to 3. It isn't, so the computer stops processing the Do...Loop statement. Processing continues with the statement following the Loop clause.

Processing steps for the posttest loop example

1. The computer creates the `intNumber` variable and initializes it to 1.
2. The computer processes the Do clause, which marks the beginning of the loop.
3. The MessageBox.Show method displays 1 (the contents of the `intNumber` variable).
4. The `intNumber = intNumber + 1` statement adds 1 to the contents of the `intNumber` variable, giving 2.
5. The computer processes the Loop clause, which checks whether the value in the `intNumber` variable is greater than 3. It isn't, so processing returns to the Do clause (the beginning of the loop).
6. The MessageBox.Show method displays 2 (the contents of the `intNumber` variable).
7. The `intNumber = intNumber + 1` statement adds 1 to the contents of the `intNumber` variable, giving 3.
8. The computer processes the Loop clause, which checks whether the value in the `intNumber` variable is greater than 3. It isn't, so processing returns to the Do clause.
9. The MessageBox.Show method displays 3 (the contents of the `intNumber` variable).
10. The `intNumber = intNumber + 1` statement adds 1 to the contents of the `intNumber` variable, giving 4.
11. The computer processes the Loop clause, which checks whether the value in the intNumber variable is greater than 3. It is, so the computer stops processing the Do...Loop statement. Processing continues with the statement following the Loop clause.

Figure 6-8   Processing steps for the loop examples from Figure 6-7

Although it appears that the pretest and posttest loops produce the same results—in this case, both examples in Figure 6-7 display the numbers 1 through 3—that will not always be the case. In other words, the two loops are not always interchangeable. For instance, if the `intNumber` variable in the pretest loop in Figure 6-7 is initialized to 10 rather than to 1, the instructions in the pretest loop will not be processed because the `intNumber <= 3` condition (which is evaluated before the instructions are processed) evaluates to False. However, if the `intNumber` variable in the posttest loop in Figure 6-7 is initialized to 10 rather than to 1, the instructions in the posttest loop will be processed one time because the `intNumber > 3` condition is evaluated after (rather than before) the loop instructions are processed.

It's often easier to understand loops when viewed in flowchart form. Figure 6-9 shows the flowcharts associated with the loop examples from Figure 6-7. The loop's condition in a flowchart is represented by the decision symbol, which is a diamond. Inside each diamond is a comparison that evaluates to either True or False only. Recall that the result of the comparison determines whether the instructions within the loop are processed. The diamonds in both figures have one flowline entering the symbol and two flowlines leaving the symbol. The two flowlines leading out of the diamond should be marked so that anyone reading the flowchart can distinguish the true path from the false path. You mark the flowline leading to the true path with a T and the flowline leading to the false path with an F. You also can mark the flowlines leading out of the diamond with a Y and an N (for yes and no). In the pretest loop's flowchart, the flowline entering the diamond, along with the diamond and the symbols and flowlines within the true path, form a circle or loop. In the posttest loop's flowchart, the loop is formed by all of the symbols and flowlines in the false path. It is this loop, or circle, that distinguishes the repetition structure from the selection structure in a flowchart.

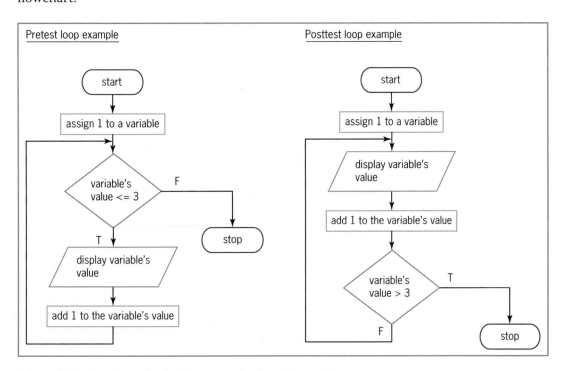

Figure 6-9 Flowcharts for the loop examples from Figure 6-7

YOU DO IT 1!

Create a Visual Basic Windows application named YouDoIt 1. Save the application in the VB2010\Chap06 folder. Add two buttons to the form. Both buttons should display the following numbers in message boxes: 1, 3, 5, and 7. Code the first button's Click event procedure using a pretest loop. Code the second button's Click event procedure using a posttest loop. Save the solution and then start and test the application. Close the solution.

Coding the Modified Quarter of a Million Club Application

Figure 6-10 shows the pseudocode and Visual Basic code for the Calculate button's Click event procedure in the modified Quarter of a Million Club application. (The pseudocode is Version 1 from Figure 6-6.) The looping condition in the Do...Loop statement tells the computer to repeat the loop body as long as (or while) the number in the **dblBalance** variable is less than 250,000, which is one-quarter of a million. Rather than using a looping condition in the Do clause, you also can use a loop exit condition, as follows: Do Until dblBalance >= 250000. (Recall that >= is the opposite of <.) Figure 6-11 shows a sample run of the modified application.

```
btnCalc Click event procedure
1.   store deposit in balance variable
2.   store rate in rate variable
3.   repeat while balance < 250,000
          interest = balance * rate
          add interest to balance
          add 1 to number of years
     end repeat while
4.   display number of years and balance

Private Sub btnCalc_Click(ByVal sender As Object,
ByVal e As System.EventArgs) Handles btnCalc.Click
     ' display account balance and number of years

    Dim dblBalance As Double
    Dim dblRate As Double
    Dim dblInterest As Double
    Dim intYears As Integer

    Double.TryParse(txtDeposit.Text, dblBalance)
    Double.TryParse(txtRate.Text, dblRate)

    Do While dblBalance < 250000
        dblInterest = dblBalance * dblRate
        dblBalance = dblBalance + dblInterest
        intYears = intYears + 1
    Loop

    lblBalance.Text = "You will have " &
        dblBalance.ToString("C2") &
        " in " & intYears.ToString & " years."
End Sub
```

Figure 6-10   Modified pseudocode and code for the Calculate button's Click event procedure

Figure 6-11   Sample run of the modified Quarter of a Million Club application

To code and then test the modified Quarter of a Million Club application: START HERE

1. If necessary, start Visual Studio 2010 or Visual Basic 2010 Express.

2. Open the Million Solution (Million Solution.sln) file contained in the VB2010\Chap06\Million Solution folder. If necessary, open the designer window.

3. Open the Code Editor window. Replace <your name> and <current date> in the comments with your name and the current date, respectively.

4. Open the code template for the btnCalc control's Click event procedure. Enter the comment and code shown earlier in Figure 6-10.

5. Save the solution and then start the application.

6. Enter **50000** as the deposit and **.04** as the annual interest rate. Click the **Calculate** button. The button's Click event procedure displays the message shown in Figure 6-11.

7. Now, delete the **50000** in the Deposit box and then click the **Calculate** button. After a short period of time, the error message box shown in Figure 6-12 appears. (It may take as long as 30 seconds for the error message box to appear.) Place your mouse pointer on `intYears`, as shown in the figure.

337

338

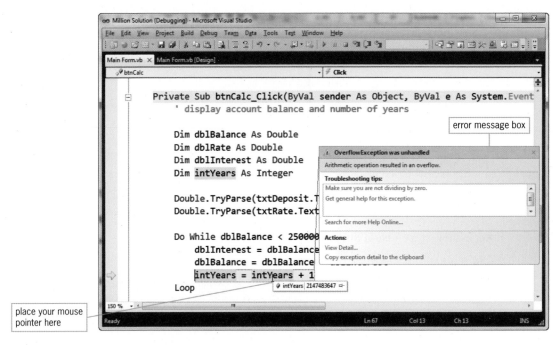

Figure 6-12 Error message box

The ranges of values associated with the different data types are listed in Figure 3-3 in Chapter 3.

An overflow error is similar to trying to fill an 8 ounce glass with 10 ounces of water.

The error message informs you that an arithmetic operation—in this case, adding 1 to the `intYears` variable—resulted in an overflow. An overflow error occurs when the computer tries to store in a memory location a value that is too large for the location's data type. In this case, the `intYears` variable already contains the highest value that can be stored in an Integer variable (2,147,483,647). Therefore, increasing the variable's value by 1 causes the overflow error. But why does the `intYears` variable contain 2,147,483,647? In this case, because you didn't provide the initial deposit amount, the loop's condition (`dblBalance < 250000`) always evaluated to True; it never evaluated to False, which is required for stopping the loop. A loop that has no way to end is called an **infinite loop** or an **endless loop**. An infinite loop also will occur if you enter an initial deposit that is less than 250,000, but you neglect to enter an interest rate. You can stop a program that has an infinite loop by clicking Debug on the menu bar and then clicking Stop Debugging.

START HERE

To continue testing the application:

1. Click **Debug** on the menu bar and then click **Stop Debugging**.

2. Add the shaded selection structure shown in Figure 6-13 to the btnCalc control's Click event procedure.

```
Private Sub btnCalc_Click(ByVal sender As Object,
ByVal e As System.EventArgs) Handles btnCalc.Click
     ' display account balance and number of years

     Dim dblBalance As Double
     Dim dblRate As Double
     Dim dblInterest As Double
     Dim intYears As Integer

     Double.TryParse(txtDeposit.Text, dblBalance)
     Double.TryParse(txtRate.Text, dblRate)

     If dblBalance > 0 AndAlso dblRate > 0 Then
         Do While dblBalance < 250000
             dblInterest = dblBalance * dblRate
             dblBalance = dblBalance + dblInterest
             intYears = intYears + 1
         Loop
     End If

     lblBalance.Text = "You will have " &
         dblBalance.ToString("C2") &
         " in " & intYears.ToString & " years."
End Sub
```

Figure 6-13 Selection structure added to the procedure

3. Save the solution and then start the application. Click the **Calculate** button. The button's Click event procedure displays the message "You will have $0.00 in 0 years."

4. Enter **50000** as the deposit and **.04** as the annual interest rate. Click the **Calculate** button. The button's Click event procedure displays the message shown earlier in Figure 6-11.

5. On your own, test the application using different deposits and annual interest rates. When you are finished, click the **Exit** button. Close the Code Editor window and then close the solution.

The Click event procedure shown in Figure 6-13 used a counter to keep track of the number of years, and an accumulator to keep track of the account balance. You learn about counters and accumulators in the next section.

Counters and Accumulators

Some procedures require you to calculate a subtotal, a total, or an average. You make these calculations using a loop that includes a counter, an accumulator, or both. A **counter** is a numeric variable used for counting something, such as the number of employees paid in a week. An **accumulator** is a numeric variable used for accumulating (adding together) something, such as the total dollar amount of a week's payroll. The intYears variable in the code shown earlier in Figure 6-13 is a counter, because it keeps track of the number of years required for the account balance to reach 250,000. The dblBalance variable in the code is an accumulator, because it adds together the annual interest amounts.

339

Two tasks are associated with counters and accumulators: initializing and updating. **Initializing** means to assign a beginning value to the counter or accumulator. Typically, counters and accumulators are initialized to the number 0. However, they can be initialized to any number, depending on the value required by the procedure. In Figure 6-13, the `intYears` variable is initialized to 0 in the last Dim statement. Although the `dblBalance` variable in the figure is also initialized to 0 in a Dim statement, it technically gets its initial value in the first TryParse method. The initialization task is performed before the loop is processed, because it needs to be performed only once.

Updating, often referred to as **incrementing**, means adding a number to the value stored in the counter or accumulator. The number can be either positive or negative, integer or non-integer. A counter is always updated by a constant value—typically the number 1—whereas an accumulator is updated by a value that varies. The `intYears` variable in Figure 6-13 is updated by 1, while the `dblBalance` variable is updated by the value in the `dblInterest` variable. The assignment statement that updates a counter or an accumulator is placed within the loop body, because the update task must be performed each time the loop instructions are processed. The Sales Express Company application, which you view next, uses both a counter and an accumulator.

The Sales Express Company Application

Figure 6-14 shows the problem specification for the Sales Express Company application, which uses a loop, a counter, and an accumulator to calculate the average sales amount entered by the sales manager. Figure 6-15 shows a sample run of the application, assuming the sales manager entered the following four sales amounts: 7000, 15000, 4575, and 23400. The txtSales control in the interface has its Multiline and ReadOnly properties set to True, and its ScrollBars property set to Vertical. When a text box's **Multiline property** is set to True, the text box can both accept and display multiple lines of text; otherwise, only one line of text can be entered in the text box. Changing a text box's **ReadOnly property** from its default value (False) to True prevents the user from changing the contents of the text box during run time. A text box's **ScrollBars property** specifies whether the text box has no scroll bars (the default), a horizontal scroll bar, a vertical scroll bar, or both horizontal and vertical scroll bars.

The Sales Express Company wants an application that displays the average amount the company sold during the prior year. The sales manager will enter the amount of each salesperson's sales. The application will use a counter to keep track of the number of sales amounts entered and an accumulator to total the sales amounts. When the sales manager has finished entering the sales amounts, the application will calculate the average sales amount by dividing the value stored in the accumulator by the value stored in the counter. It then will display the average sales amount. If the sales manager does not enter any sales amounts, the application will display the message "N/A" (for "not available").

Figure 6-14   Problem specification for the Sales Express Company application

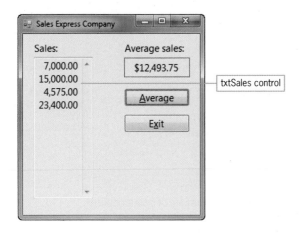

Figure 6-15 Sample run of the Sales Express Company application

Figure 6-16 shows the pseudocode for the Average button's Click event procedure. Step 1 in the pseudocode is to remove the contents of the txtSales control, and Step 2 is to get a sales amount from the user. Step 3 is a pretest loop whose loop body is processed as long as the user enters a sales amount. The first instruction in the loop body adds the number 1 to the counter, which keeps track of the number of sales amounts the user enters. The second instruction adds the sales amount to the accumulator, which keeps track of the total sales. The third instruction in the loop body displays the sales amount in the txtSales control, and the fourth instruction requests another sales amount from the user. The loop's condition then checks whether a sales amount was entered; this is necessary to determine whether the loop body should be processed again.

When the user has finished entering sales amounts, the loop ends and processing continues with Step 4 in the pseudocode. Step 4 is a selection structure whose condition verifies that the value stored in the sales counter is greater than the number 0. This verification is necessary because the first instruction in the selection structure's true path uses the sales counter as the divisor when calculating the average sales amount. Before using a counter variable (or any variable) as the divisor in an expression, you always should verify that the variable does not contain the number 0 because, as in mathematics, division by zero is not possible. Dividing by zero in a procedure will cause the application to end abruptly with an error. As Step 4 indicates, if the sales counter's value is greater than 0, the average sales amount is calculated and then displayed; otherwise, the string "N/A" is displayed.

341

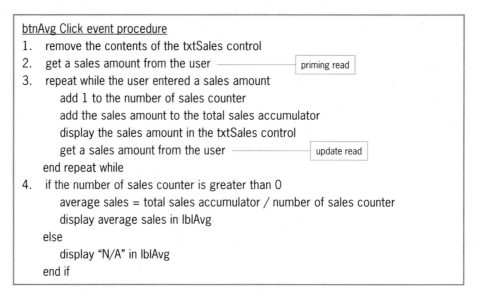

Figure 6-16   Pseudocode for the Average button's Click event procedure

Notice that the pseudocode in Figure 6-16 contains two "get a sales amount from the user" instructions. One of the instructions appears above the loop, and the other appears as the last instruction in the loop body. The "get a sales amount from the user" instruction above the loop is referred to as the **priming read**, because it is used to prime (prepare or set up) the loop. The priming read initializes the loop condition by providing its first value. In this case, the priming read gets only the first sales amount from the user. Because the loop in Figure 6-16 is a pretest loop, the first sales amount determines whether the instructions in the loop body are processed at all.

If the loop body instructions are processed, the "get a sales amount from the user" instruction in the loop body gets the remaining sales amounts (if any) from the user. The "get a sales amount from the user" instruction in the loop body is referred to as the **update read**, because it allows the user to update the value of the input item (in this case, the sales amount) that controls the loop's condition. The update read is often an exact copy of the priming read. Keep in mind that if you don't include the update read in the loop body, there will be no way to enter a value that will stop the loop after it has been processed the first time. This is because the priming read is processed only once and gets only the first sales amount from the user. As you learned earlier, a loop that has no way to end is called an infinite (or endless) loop. Recall that you can stop an infinite loop by clicking Debug on the menu bar and then clicking Stop Debugging.

Figure 6-17 shows the Average button's Click event procedure in flowchart form. Notice that the priming read's parallelogram is located above the loop's condition, while the update read's parallelogram is located at the end of the loop body.

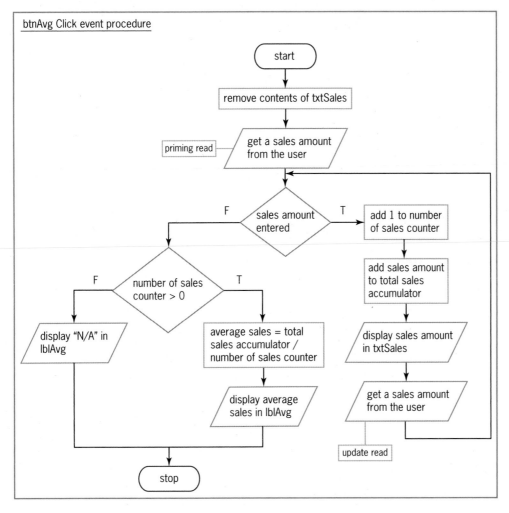

Figure 6-17 Flowchart for the Average button's Click event procedure

To open the Sales Express Company application:

START HERE

1. Open the Sales Express Solution (Sales Express Solution.sln) file contained in the VB2010\Chap06\Sales Express Solution folder. If necessary, open the designer window.

2. Open the Code Editor window. Replace <your name> and <current date> in the comments with your name and the current date, respectively.

3. Locate the btnAvg control's Click event procedure. The procedure declares two named constants and five variables. The named constants and **strInputSales** variable will be used, along with the InputBox function, to get a sales amount from the user. The **decSales** variable will store the sales amount after it has been converted to Decimal. The **intNumSales** variable will keep track of the number of sales amounts entered, and the **decTotalSales** variable will be used to accumulate the sales amounts. The **decAvgSales** variable will store the average sales amount after it has been calculated.

As shown earlier in Figure 6-13, an accumulator also can be initialized in a TryParse method. The same is true for a counter.

Recall that counters and accumulators must be initialized. Because the Dim statement automatically assigns the number 0 to Integer and Decimal variables when the variables are created, you do not need to enter any additional code to initialize the `intNumSales` and `decTotalSales` variables. In cases where you need to initialize a counter or accumulator to a value other than 0, you can do so either in the Dim statement that declares the variable or in an assignment statement. For example, to initialize the `intNumSales` variable to the number 1, you could use either the declaration statement `Dim intNumSales As Integer = 1` or the assignment statement `intNumSales = 1` in your code. However, to use the assignment statement, the `intNumSales` variable must already be declared.

START HERE

To begin coding the Sales Express Company application:

1. Click the **blank line** below the ` ' get first sales amount` comment and then enter the following assignment statement:

    strInputSales = InputBox(strPROMPT, strTITLE, "0")

2. Click the **blank line** below the ` ' repeat as long as the user enters a sales amount` comment and then enter the loop shown in Figure 6-18.

enter these comments and lines of code

```
' repeat as long as the user enters a sales amount
Do While strInputSales <> String.Empty
    ' convert the sales amount to a number
    Decimal.TryParse(strInputSales, decSales)

    ' update the counter and accumulator
    intNumSales = intNumSales + 1
    decTotalSales = decTotalSales + decSales

    ' display the sales amount in the text box
    txtSales.Text = txtSales.Text &
        decSales.ToString("N2") & ControlChars.NewLine

    ' get next sales amount
    strInputSales = InputBox(strPROMPT, strTITLE)
Loop

' verify that the counter is greater than 0
```

Figure 6-18   Loop entered in the btnAvg control's Click event procedure

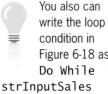

You also can write the loop condition in Figure 6-18 as `Do While strInputSales <> ""`.

The first statement in the loop converts the string returned by the InputBox function to the Decimal data type. The second statement, `intNumSales = intNumSales + 1`, updates the counter variable by adding a constant value of 1 to it. Notice that the counter variable appears on both sides of the assignment operator. The statement tells the computer to add 1 to the contents of the variable and then place the result back in the variable. The counter variable's value will be incremented by 1 each time the loop is processed.

The third statement in the loop, `decTotalSales = decTotalSales + decSales`, updates the accumulator variable by adding the current sales amount to it. Like the counter variable in the previous statement, the accumulator variable appears on both sides of the assignment operator. The statement tells the computer to add the contents of the `decSales` variable to the contents of the accumulator variable and then place the result back in the accumulator variable. The accumulator variable's value will be incremented by a sales amount, which will vary, each time the loop is processed.

The next statement in the loop displays the sales amount in the txtSales control. The last statement in the loop prompts the user for another sales amount and then assigns the user's entry to the `strInputSales` variable. Notice that the statement appears twice in the code: before the Do...Loop statement and within the Do...Loop statement. (You can verify this in Figure 6-19.) As you learned earlier, the input instruction located above the loop is referred to as the priming read, and its task is to get only the first sales amount from the user. The input instruction located within the loop gets each of the remaining sales amounts (if any).

To complete the procedure and then test the code: ◄ START HERE

1. Click the **blank line** below the ` verify that the counter is greater than 0` comment and then enter the following dual-alternative selection structure:

   If intNumSales > 0 Then
       decAvgSales = decTotalSales / intNumSales
       lblAvg.Text = decAvgSales.ToString("C2")
   Else
       lblAvg.Text = "N/A"
   End If

2. Save the solution and then start the application. Click the **Average** button, which opens the Sales Entry dialog box. Click the **Cancel** button in the dialog box. The btnAvg control's Click event procedure displays N/A in the lblAvg control.

3. Click the **Average** button again. Use the Sales Entry dialog box to enter the following four sales amounts, one at a time: **7000**, **15000**, **4575**, and **23400**.

4. Click the **Cancel** button in the dialog box. The btnAvg control's Click event procedure calculates and displays the average sales amount ($12,493.75), as shown earlier in Figure 6-15.

5. Click the **Exit** button. Close the Code Editor window and then close the solution. Figure 6-19 shows the code entered in the btnAvg control's Click event procedure.

```
Private Sub btnAvg_Click(ByVal sender As Object,
ByVal e As System.EventArgs) Handles btnAvg.Click
    ' calculates and displays the average sales amount

    Const strPROMPT As String =
            "Enter a sales amount. " &
            ControlChars.NewLine &
            "Click Cancel or leave blank to end."
    Const strTITLE As String = "Sales Entry"
```

Figure 6-19 btnAvg control's Click event procedure *(continues)*

(continued)

```
        Dim strInputSales As String
        Dim decSales As Decimal
        Dim intNumSales As Integer
        Dim decTotalSales As Decimal
        Dim decAvgSales As Decimal

        ' remove contents of text box
        txtSales.Text = String.Empty

        ' get first sales amount
        strInputSales = InputBox(strPROMPT, strTITLE, "0")

        ' repeat as long as the user enters a sales amount
        Do While strInputSales <> String.Empty
            ' convert the sales amount to a number
            Decimal.TryParse(strInputSales, decSales)

            ' update the counter and accumulator
            intNumSales = intNumSales + 1
            decTotalSales = decTotalSales + decSales

            ' display the sales amount in the text box
            txtSales.Text = txtSales.Text &
                decSales.ToString("N2") & ControlChars.NewLine

            ' get next sales amount
            strInputSales = InputBox(strPROMPT, strTITLE)
        Loop

        ' verify that the counter is greater than 0
        If intNumSales > 0 Then
            decAvgSales = decTotalSales / intNumSales
            lblAvg.Text = decAvgSales.ToString("C2")
        Else
            lblAvg.Text = "N/A"
        End If
    End Sub
```

Figure 6-19   btnAvg control's Click event procedure

YOU DO IT 2!

Create a Visual Basic Windows application named YouDoIt 2. Save the application in the VB2010\Chap06 folder. Add three labels and a button to the form. The button's Click event procedure should allow the user to enter one or more prices. It then should display (in the labels) the number of prices entered, the total of the prices entered, and the average price entered. If the user does not enter any numbers, the procedure should display the string "None" in the three labels. Code the button's Click event procedure using a pretest loop and the InputBox function. Save the solution and then start and test the application. Close the solution.

Arithmetic Assignment Operators

In addition to the standard arithmetic operators listed in Figure 2-25 in Chapter 2, Visual Basic also provides several arithmetic assignment operators. The **arithmetic assignment operators** allow you to abbreviate an assignment statement that contains an arithmetic operator, as long as the assignment statement has the following format, in which *variableName* is the name of the same variable: *variableName = variableName arithmeticOperator value*. For example, you can use the addition assignment operator (+=) to abbreviate the statement `intAge = intAge + 1` as follows: `intAge += 1`. Both statements tell the computer to add the number 1 to the contents of the `intAge` variable and then store the result in the `intAge` variable. Figure 6-20 shows the syntax of a Visual Basic statement that uses an arithmetic assignment operator. The figure also lists the most commonly used arithmetic assignment operators, and it includes examples of using arithmetic assignment operators to abbreviate assignment statements. Notice that each arithmetic assignment operator consists of an arithmetic operator followed immediately by the assignment operator (=). The arithmetic assignment operators do not contain a space. In other words, the multiplication assignment operator is *=, not * =.

347

It's easy to abbreviate an assignment statement. Simply remove the variable name that appears on the left side of the assignment operator (=) in the statement, and then put the assignment operator immediately after the arithmetic operator.

Arithmetic assignment operators

Syntax

variableName arithmeticAssignmentOperator value

Operator	Purpose
+=	addition assignment
-=	subtraction assignment
*=	multiplication assignment
/=	division assignment

Example 1

Original statement: `intAge = intAge + 1`

Abbreviated statement: `intAge += 1`

Both statements add 1 to the number stored in the `intAge` variable and then assign the result to the variable.

Example 2

Original statement: `decPrice = decPrice - decDiscount`

Abbreviated statement: `decPrice -= decDiscount`

Both statements subtract the number stored in the `decDiscount` variable from the number stored in the `decPrice` variable and then assign the result to the `decPrice` variable.

Example 3

Original statement: `dblSales = dblSales * 1.05`

Abbreviated statement: `dblSales *= 1.05`

Both statements multiply the number stored in the `dblSales` variable by 1.05 and then assign the result to the variable.

Figure 6-20 Syntax and examples of the arithmetic assignment operators *(continues)*

(continued)

> Example 4
> Original statement: `dblNum = dblNum / 2`
> Abbreviated statement: `dblNum /= 2`
> Both statements divide the number stored in the `dblNum` variable by 2 and
> then assign the result to the variable.

Figure 6-20   Syntax and examples of the arithmetic assignment operators

START HERE ▶

To use the arithmetic assignment operators in the Sales Express Company application:

1. Use Windows to make a copy of the Sales Express Solution folder. Rename the copy **Sales Express Solution-Arithmetic Assignment**.

2. Open the Sales Express Solution (Sales Express Solution.sln) file contained in the Sales Express Solution-Arithmetic Assignment folder. Open the designer window.

3. Open the Code Editor window. Locate the btnAvg control's Click event procedure. Modify the statements that update the counter and accumulator variables as shown in Figure 6-21.

modify these two
statements as shown →

```
' update the counter and accumulator
intNumSales += 1
decTotalSales += decSales
```

Figure 6-21   Modified update statements using arithmetic assignment operators

4. Save the solution and then start the application. Click the **Average** button. Use the Sales Entry dialog box to enter the following three sales amounts: **10**, **14**, and **22**. Click the **Cancel** button in the dialog box. The btnAvg control's Click event procedure displays $15.33 in the lblAvg control.

5. Click the **Exit** button. Close the Code Editor window and then close the solution.

The For...Next Statement

The For Each...Next statement is covered in Chapter 9.

As already mentioned, Visual Basic provides three different statements for coding repetition structures (loops): Do...Loop, For...Next, and For Each...Next. You learned about the Do...Loop statement earlier in this lesson; recall that the statement can be used to code both pretest and posttest loops. In the remainder of this lesson, you will learn how to use the **For...Next statement** to code a specific type of pretest loop, called a counter-controlled loop. A **counter-controlled loop** is just what its name implies: It's a loop whose processing is controlled by a counter. You use a counter-controlled loop when you want the computer to process the loop instructions a precise number of times. Although you also can use the Do...Loop statement to code a counter-controlled loop, the For...Next statement provides a more compact and convenient way of writing that type of loop.

Figure 6-22 shows the For...Next statement's syntax and includes examples of using the statement. You enter the loop body, which contains the instructions you want the computer to repeat, between the statement's For and Next clauses. Notice that *counterVariableName* appears in both clauses. *CounterVariableName* is the name of a numeric variable that the computer can use to keep track of (in other words, count) the number of times it processes the loop body. Although, technically, you do not need to specify the name of the counter variable in the Next clause, doing so is highly recommended because it makes your code more self-documenting.

You can use the **As** *dataType* portion of the For clause to declare the counter variable, as shown in the first two examples in Figure 6-22. When you declare a variable in the For clause, the variable has block scope and can be used only within the For...Next loop. Alternatively, you can declare the counter variable in a Dim statement, as shown in Example 3. As you know, a variable declared in a Dim statement at the beginning of a procedure has procedure scope and can be used within the entire procedure. When deciding where to declare the counter variable, keep in mind that if the variable is needed only by the For...Next loop, then it is a better programming practice to declare the variable in the For clause. As mentioned in Chapter 3, fewer unintentional errors occur in applications when the variables are declared using the minimum scope needed. Block-level variables have the smallest scope, followed by procedure-level variables, followed by class-level variables. You should declare the counter variable in a Dim statement only when its value is required by statements outside the For...Next loop in the procedure.

The *startValue*, *endValue*, and *stepValue* items in the For clause control the number of times the loop body is processed. The startValue and endValue tell the computer where to begin and end counting, respectively. The stepValue tells the computer how much to count by—in other words, how much to add to the counter variable each time the loop body is processed. If you omit the stepValue, a stepValue of positive 1 is used. In Example 1 in Figure 6-22, the startValue is 10, the endValue is 13, and the stepValue (which is omitted) is 1. Those values tell the computer to start counting at 10 and, counting by 1s, stop at 13—in other words, count 10, 11, 12, and 13. The computer will process the instructions in Example 1's loop body four times.

The startValue, endValue, and stepValue items must be numeric and can be either positive or negative, integer or non-integer. If the stepValue is a positive number, the startValue must be less than or equal to the endValue for the loop instructions to be processed. For instance, the `For intNum As Integer = 10 To 13` clause is correct, but the `For intNum As Integer = 13 To 10` clause is not correct because you cannot count from 13 (the startValue) to 10 (the endValue) by adding increments of 1 (the stepValue). If, on the other hand, the stepValue is a negative number, then the startValue must be greater than or equal to the endValue for the loop instructions to be processed. As a result, the `For intNum As Integer = 5 To 1 Step -1` clause is correct, but the `For intNum As Integer = 1 To 5 Step -1` clause is not correct because you cannot count from 1 to 5 by adding increments of negative 1. Adding increments of a negative number is referred to as **decrementing**. In other words, adding increments of negative 1 is the same as decrementing by 1. In addition to the syntax and examples of the For...Next statement, Figure 6-22 also shows the tasks performed by the computer when processing the statement.

You can use the `Exit For` statement to exit the For...Next statement prematurely, which means to exit it before the loop has finished processing. You may need to do this if the computer encounters an error when processing the loop instructions.

For...Next statement

<u>Syntax</u>

For *counterVariableName* [**As** *dataType*] = *startValue* **To** *endValue* [**Step** *stepValue*]
    loop body instructions

    If the stepValue is a positive number, the computer will process the loop
    body instructions while the counter variable's value is less than or equal to
    the endValue. It will stop processing the instructions when the counter
    variable's value is greater than the endValue.

    If the stepValue is a negative number, the computer will process the loop body
    instructions while the counter variable's value is greater than or equal to
    the endValue. It will stop processing the instructions when the counter
    variable's value is less than the endValue.

Next *counterVariableName*

<u>Example 1</u>
```
For intNum As Integer = 10 To 13
      MessageBox.Show(intNum.ToString)          loop body
Next intNum
```
displays 10, 11, 12, and 13 in message boxes

<u>Example 2</u>
```
Dim strCity As String
For intNum As Integer = 5 To 1 Step -1
      strCity = InputBox("City:", "City Entry")
      txtCities.Text = txtCities.Text &            loop body
          strCity & ControlChars.NewLine
Next intNum
```
displays five city names in the txtCities control

<u>Example 3</u>
```
Dim dblRate As Double
For dblRate = .05 To .1 Step .01
      lblRates.Text = lblRates.Text &
          dblRate.ToString("P0") &            loop body
          ControlChars.NewLine
Next dblRate
```
displays 5 %, 6 %, 7 %, 8 %, 9 %, and 10 % in the lblRates control

<u>Processing tasks</u>
1. If the counter variable is declared in the For clause, the computer creates and then initializes the variable to the startValue; otherwise, it just performs the initialization task. This is done only once, at the beginning of the loop.
2. The computer evaluates the loop condition by comparing the value in the counter variable with the endValue. If the stepValue is a positive number, the comparison determines whether the counter variable's value is greater than the endValue. If the stepValue is a negative number, the comparison determines whether the counter variable's value is less than the endValue. Notice that the computer evaluates the loop condition before processing the instructions within the loop.

Figure 6-22   For...Next statement's syntax, examples, and processing tasks *(continues)*

(continued)

3. If the loop condition evaluates to True, the computer stops processing the loop; processing continues with the statement following the Next clause. If the loop condition evaluates to False, the computer processes the loop body and then task 4 is performed.
4. Task 4 is performed only when the loop condition evaluates to False. In this task, the computer adds the stepValue to the contents of the counter variable. It then repeats tasks 2, 3, and 4 until the loop condition evaluates to True.

Figure 6-22 For...Next statement's syntax, examples, and processing tasks

Figure 6-23 describes the steps the computer follows when processing the loop shown in Example 1 in Figure 6-22. As Step 2 indicates, the loop's condition is evaluated before the loop body is processed. This is because the loop created by the For...Next statement is a pretest loop. Notice that the `intNum` variable contains the number 14 when the For...Next statement ends. The number 14 is the first integer that is greater than the loop's endValue of 13.

Processing steps for Example 1

1. The computer creates the `intNum` variable and initializes it to 10.
2. The computer checks whether the `intNum` variable's value is greater than 13. It's not, so the computer displays the number 10 in a message box and then increments the `intNum` variable's value by 1, giving 11.
3. The computer again checks whether the `intNum` variable's value is greater than 13. It's not, so the computer displays the number 11 in a message box and then increments the `intNum` variable's value by 1, giving 12.
4. The computer again checks whether the `intNum` variable's value is greater than 13. It's not, so the computer displays the number 12 in a message box and then increments the `intNum` variable's value by 1, giving 13.
5. The computer again checks whether the `intNum` variable's value is greater than 13. It's not, so the computer displays the number 13 in a message box and then increments the `intNum` variable's value by 1, giving 14.
6. The computer again checks whether the `intNum` variable's value is greater than 13. It is, so the computer stops processing the loop body. Processing continues with the statement following the Next clause.

Figure 6-23 Processing steps for Example 1 in Figure 6-22

You will use the For...Next statement to code the Monthly Payment Calculator application.

The Monthly Payment Calculator Application

Figure 6-24 shows the problem specification for the Monthly Payment Calculator application, and Figure 6-25 shows a sample run of the application.

Jacobsen Loans wants an application that displays the monthly payments on a car loan, using a term of 5 years and annual interest rates of 5%, 6%, 7%, 8%, 9%, and 10%.

Figure 6-24 Problem specification for the Monthly Payment Calculator application

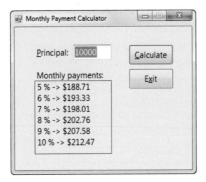

Figure 6-25   Sample run of the Monthly Payment Calculator application

Figure 6-26 shows the pseudocode and flowchart for the Calculate button's Click event procedure. Many programmers use a hexagon, which is a six-sided figure, to represent the For clause in a flowchart. Within the hexagon, you record the four items contained in a For clause: *counterVariableName*, *startValue*, *endValue*, and *stepValue*. The counterVariableName and stepValue are placed at the top and bottom, respectively, of the hexagon. The startValue and endValue are placed on the left and right side, respectively. The hexagon in Figure 6-26 indicates that the counterVariableName is **dblRate**, the startValue is 5%, the endValue is 10%, and the stepValue is 1%. Notice that a greater than sign (>) precedes the endValue in the hexagon. The > sign indicates that the loop will stop when the counter variable's value is greater than 10%.

btnCalc Click event procedure

1. remove contents of lblPayments
2. store the principal in a variable
3. repeat for interest rates from 5% to 10% in increments of 1%
      calculate the monthly payment
      display the monthly payment in lblPayments
   end repeat for
4. send focus to txtPrincipal
5. select existing text in txtPrincipal

Figure 6-26   Pseudocode and flowchart for the Calculate button's Click event procedure
(continues)

(continued)

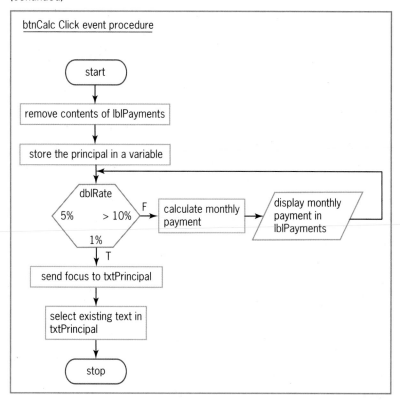

btnCalc Click event procedure

Figure 6-26 Pseudocode and flowchart for the Calculate button's Click event procedure

To code the Monthly Payment Calculator application:

START HERE

1. Open the Payment Calculator Solution (Payment Calculator Solution.sln) file contained in the VB2010\Chap06\Payment Calculator Solution folder. If necessary, open the designer window.

2. Open the Code Editor window, which contains the following procedures: btnExit_Click, txtPrincipal_Enter, txtPrincipal_KeyPress, txtPrincipal_TextChanged, and btnCalc_Click.

3. Replace <your name> and <current date> in the comments with your name and the current date, respectively.

4. Locate the btnCalc control's Click event procedure. The procedure declares an Integer named constant for the term. It also declares two Double variables to store the principal and monthly payment amounts. Next, the procedure clears the contents of the lblPayments control. It then uses the TryParse method to convert the contents of the txtPrincipal control to a Double number.

5. Click the **blank line** below the ' calculate and display payments comment and then enter the following For clause, which tells the computer to repeat the instructions in the loop six times,

using interest rates of .05, .06, .07, .08, .09, and .1. When you press Enter after typing the For clause, the Code Editor automatically enters the Next clause for you.

For dblRate As Double = .05 To .1 Step .01

6. Change the Next clause to **Next dblRate**.

7. Now enter the additional lines of code indicated in Figure 6-27.

```vbnet
Private Sub btnCalc_Click(ByVal sender As Object, ByVal e As System.E
    ' calculates the monthly payments on a loan
    ' using a term of 5 years and interest rates of 5% through 10%

    Const intTERM As Integer = 5
    Dim dblPrincipal As Double
    Dim dblPayment As Double

    lblPayments.Text = String.Empty
    Double.TryParse(txtPrincipal.Text, dblPrincipal)

    ' calculate and display payments
    For dblRate As Double = 0.05 To 0.1 Step 0.01
        dblPayment =
            -Financial.Pmt(dblRate / 12, intTERM * 12, dblPrincipal)
        lblPayments.Text = lblPayments.Text &
            dblRate.ToString("P0") & " -> " &
            dblPayment.ToString("C2") & ControlChars.NewLine
    Next dblRate

    txtPrincipal.Focus()
    txtPrincipal.SelectAll()
End Sub
```

enter these five lines of code →

Figure 6-27   Completed Calculate button's Click event procedure

8. Save the solution and then start the application. Type **10000** in the Principal box and then click the **Calculate** button. The button's Click event procedure displays the monthly payments in the Monthly payments box, as shown earlier in Figure 6-25.

9. Click the **Exit** button. Close the Code Editor window and then close the solution.

Comparing the For...Next and Do...Loop Statements

As mentioned earlier, you can code a counter-controlled loop using either the For...Next statement or the Do...Loop statement; however, the For...Next statement is more convenient to use. Figure 6-28 shows an example of using both loops to display the string "Hi" three times. Notice that, when using the Do...Loop statement to code a counter-controlled loop, you must include a statement to declare and initialize the counter variable, as well as a statement to update the counter variable. In addition, you must include the appropriate comparison in the Do clause. In a For...Next statement, the declaration, initialization, update, and comparison tasks are handled by the For clause.

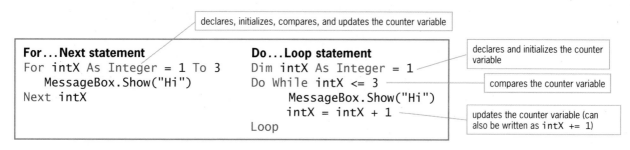

Figure 6-28   Comparison of the For...Next and Do...Loop statements

YOU DO IT 3!

Create a Visual Basic Windows application named YouDoIt 3. Save the application in the VB2010\Chap06 folder. Add two labels and a button to the form. The button's Click event procedure should display (in the labels) the number of integers from 14 through 23 and the sum of those integers. Code the procedure using the For...Next statement. Save the solution and then start and test the application. Close the solution.

Lesson A Summary

- To have the computer repeatedly process one or more program instructions while the looping condition is true (or until the loop exit condition has been met):

  Use a repetition structure (loop). You can code a repetition structure in Visual Basic using one of the following statements: For...Next, Do...Loop, and For Each...Next. (The For Each...Next statement is covered in Chapter 9.)

- To use the Do...Loop statement to code a loop:

  Refer to Figure 6-7 for the two versions of the Do...Loop statement's syntax. The Do...Loop statement can be used to code both pretest and posttest loops. In a pretest loop, the loop condition appears in the Do clause; it appears in the Loop clause in a posttest loop. The loop condition must evaluate to a Boolean value.

- To represent the loop condition in a flowchart:

  Use the decision symbol, which is a diamond.

- To stop an endless (infinite) loop:

  Click Debug on the menu bar and then click Stop Debugging.

- To use a counter:

  Initialize (if necessary) and update the counter. The initialization is done outside of the loop that uses the counter; the update is done within the loop. You update a counter by incrementing (or decrementing) its value by a constant amount, which can be either positive or negative, integer or non-integer.

- To use an accumulator:

  Initialize (if necessary) and update the accumulator. The initialization is done outside of the loop that uses the accumulator; the update is done within the loop. You update an accumulator by incrementing (or decrementing) its value by an amount that varies. The amount can be either positive or negative, integer or non-integer.

- To abbreviate an assignment statement:

  Use the arithmetic assignment operators listed in Figure 6-20. The assignment statement you want to abbreviate must follow this format, in which *variableName* is the name of the same variable: *variableName = variableName arithmeticOperator value*.

- To use the For...Next statement to code a counter-controlled loop:

  Refer to Figure 6-22 for the For...Next statement's syntax. The statement can be used to code pretest loops only. In the syntax, counterVariableName is the name of a numeric variable that the computer uses to keep track of the number of times it processes the loop body. The startValue, endValue, and stepValue items control the number of times the loop body is processed. The startValue, endValue, and stepValue items must be numeric and can be positive or negative, integer or non-integer. If you omit the stepValue, a stepValue of positive 1 is used.

- To flowchart a For...Next loop:

  Many programmers use a hexagon to represent the For clause. Inside the hexagon, you record the counter variable's name and its startValue, stepValue, and endValue.

Lesson A Key Terms

Accumulator—a numeric variable used for accumulating (adding together) something

Arithmetic assignment operators—composed of an arithmetic operator followed by the assignment operator; used to abbreviate an assignment statement that has the following format, in which *variableName* is the name of the same variable: *variableName = variableName arithmeticOperator value*

Counter—a numeric variable used for counting something

Counter-controlled loop—a loop whose processing is controlled by a counter; the loop body will be processed a precise number of times

Decrementing—adding increments of a negative number

Do...Loop statement—a Visual Basic statement that can be used to code both pretest loops and posttest loops

Endless loop—a loop whose instructions are processed indefinitely; also called an infinite loop

For...Next statement—a Visual Basic statement that is used to code a specific type of pretest loop, called a counter-controlled loop

Incrementing—another name for updating

Infinite loop—another name for an endless loop

Initializing—the process of assigning a beginning value to a memory location, such as a counter or an accumulator variable

Loop—another name for the repetition structure

Loop body—the instructions within a loop

Loop exit condition—the requirement that must be met for the computer to stop processing the loop body instructions

Looping condition—the requirement that must be met for the computer to continue processing the loop body instructions

Multiline property—determines whether a text box can accept and display only one line of text or multiple lines of text

Posttest loop—a loop whose condition is evaluated *after* the instructions in its loop body are processed

Pretest loop—a loop whose condition is evaluated *before* the instructions in its loop body are processed

Priming read—the input instruction that appears above the loop that it controls; used to get the first input item from the user

ReadOnly property—controls whether the user is allowed to change the contents of a text box during run time

Repetition structure—the control structure used to repeatedly process one or more program instructions; also called a loop

ScrollBars property—a property of a text box; specifies whether the text box has scroll bars

Update read—the input instruction that appears within a loop and is associated with the priming read

Updating—the process of adding a number to the value stored in a counter or accumulator variable; also called incrementing

Lesson A Review Questions

1. Which of the following statements can be used to code a loop whose instructions you want processed 10 times?

    a. Do...Loop

    b. For...Next

    c. either a or b

2. The instructions in a _____ loop are always processed at least once, whereas the instructions in a _____ loop might not be processed at all.

   a. posttest, pretest

   b. pretest, posttest

3. Which of the following clauses stops the loop when the value in the intAge variable is less than the number 0?

   a. `Do While intAge >= 0`

   b. `Do Until intAge < 0`

   c. `Loop While intAge >= 0`

   d. all of the above

4. How many times will the MessageBox.Show method in the following code be processed?

```
Dim intCount As Integer
Do While intCount > 3
    MessageBox.Show("Hello")
    intCount = intCount + 1
Loop
```

   a. 0

   b. 1

   c. 3

   d. 4

5. How many times will the MessageBox.Show method in the following code be processed?

```
Dim intCount As Integer
Do
    MessageBox.Show("Hello")
    intCount += 1
Loop While intCount > 3
```

   a. 0

   b. 1

   c. 3

   d. 4

6. How many times will the MessageBox.Show method in the following code be processed?

```
For intCount As Integer = 4 To 11 Step 2
    MessageBox.Show("Hello")
Next intCount
```

   a. 3

   b. 4

   c. 5

   d. 8

7. What value is stored in the intCount variable when the loop in Review Question 6 ends?

   a. 10

   b. 11

   c. 12

   d. 13

8. A procedure allows the user to enter one or more values. The first input instruction will get the first value only and is referred to as the _____ read.

   a. entering

   b. initializer

   c. priming

   d. starter

Refer to Figure 6-29 to answer Questions 9 through 12.

9. Which of the following control structures are used in flowchart A in Figure 6-29? (Select all that apply.)

   a. sequence

   b. selection

   c. repetition

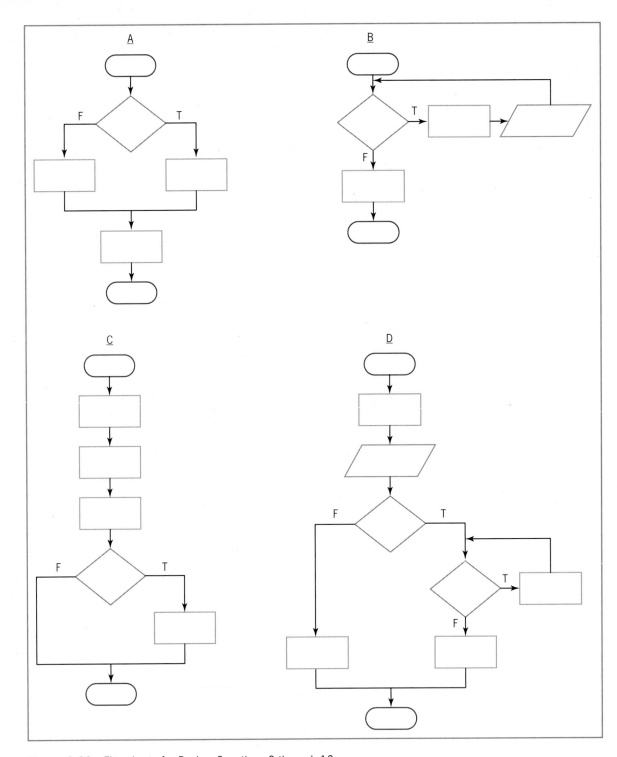

Figure 6-29   Flowcharts for Review Questions 9 through 12

10. Which of the following control structures are used in flowchart B in Figure 6-29? (Select all that apply.)

   a. sequence

   b. selection

   c. repetition

11. Which of the following programming structures are used in flowchart C in Figure 6-29? (Select all that apply.)

   a. sequence

   b. selection

   c. repetition

12. Which of the following programming structures are used in flowchart D in Figure 6-29? (Select all that apply.)

   a. sequence

   b. selection

   c. repetition

Lesson A Exercises

1. Write a Visual Basic Do clause that processes the loop instructions as long as the value in the `intQuantity` variable is greater than the number 0. Use the `While` keyword. Now rewrite the Do clause using the `Until` keyword.   INTRODUCTORY

2. Write a Visual Basic Do clause that stops the loop when the value in the `intInStock` variable is less than or equal to the value in the `intReorder` variable. Use the `Until` keyword. Now rewrite the Do clause using the `While` keyword.   INTRODUCTORY

3. Write a Visual Basic Loop clause that processes the loop instructions as long as the value in the `strLetter` variable is either Y or y. Use the `While` keyword. Now rewrite the Loop clause using the `Until` keyword.   INTRODUCTORY

4. Write a Visual Basic Do clause that processes the loop instructions as long as the value in the `strEmpName` variable is not "Done" (in any case). Use the `While` keyword. Now rewrite the Do clause using the `Until` keyword.   INTRODUCTORY

5. What will the following code display in message boxes?   INTRODUCTORY

```
Dim intX As Integer
Do While intX < 5
    MessageBox.Show(intX.ToString)
    intX = intX + 1
Loop
```

INTRODUCTORY

6. What will the following code display in message boxes?

```
Dim intX As Integer
Do
    MessageBox.Show(intX.ToString)
    intX += 1
Loop Until intX > 5
```

INTRODUCTORY

7. Write a Visual Basic assignment statement that updates the intQuantity counter variable by 2.

INTRODUCTORY

8. Write a Visual Basic assignment statement that updates the decTotal accumulator variable by the value stored in the decPurchase variable.

INTERMEDIATE

9. Write a Visual Basic assignment statement that updates the intTotal counter variable by −3.

INTERMEDIATE

10. Write a Visual Basic assignment statement that subtracts the contents of the decReturns variable from the contents of the decSales accumulator variable.

INTERMEDIATE

11. Write the Visual Basic code for a pretest loop that uses an Integer variable named intEvenNum to display the even integers from 2 through 10 in the lblNumbers control. Use the For...Next statement. Display each number on a separate line in the control.

INTERMEDIATE

12. Rewrite the pretest loop from Exercise 11 using the Do...Loop statement.

INTERMEDIATE

13. Change the pretest loop from Exercise 12 to a posttest loop.

INTERMEDIATE

14. Write the Visual Basic code that corresponds to the flowchart shown in Figure 6-30. Display the calculated results on separate lines in the lblCount control.

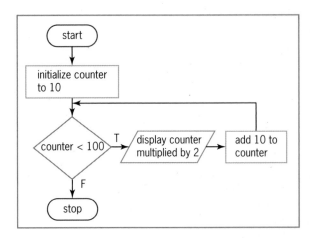

Figure 6-30 Flowchart for Exercise 14

15. Write a For...Next statement that displays the numbers from 0 through 117, in increments of 9, in the lblNumbers control. Display each number on a separate line in the control.

16. Write a For...Next statement that calculates and displays the squares of the even numbers from 2 through 12. Display the results in the lblNumbers control. Display each number on a separate line in the control.

17. What will the following code display?

```
Dim intTotal As Integer
Do While intTotal <= 5
    MessageBox.Show(intTotal.ToString)
    intTotal += 2
Loop
```

18. What will the following code display?

```
Dim intTotal As Integer = 1
Do
    MessageBox.Show(intTotal.ToString)
    intTotal = intTotal + 2
Loop Until intTotal >= 3
```

19. In this exercise, you modify the Monthly Payment Calculator application from this lesson. Use Windows to make a copy of the Payment Calculator Solution folder. Rename the copy Modified Payment Calculator Solution. Open the Payment Calculator Solution (Payment Calculator Solution.sln) file contained in the Modified Payment Calculator Solution folder. Open the designer and Code Editor windows. Change the For...Next statement in the btnCalc control's Click event procedure to a Do...Loop statement. Save the solution and then start and test the application. Close the Code Editor window and then close the solution.

20. In this exercise, you modify the Sales Express Company application from this lesson. Use Windows to make a copy of the Sales Express Solution folder. Rename the copy Modified Sales Express Solution. Open the Sales Express Solution (Sales Express Solution.sln) file contained in the Modified Sales Express Solution folder. Open the designer and Code Editor windows. Each time the application is started, the user will enter five sales amounts. Change the Do...Loop statement in the btnAvg control's Click event procedure to a For...Next statement. If a sales amount cannot be converted to a number, use the Exit For statement to exit the loop. Calculate the average only when the user enters five valid sales amounts; otherwise, display an appropriate message in a message box and the number 0 in the lblAvg control. Save the solution and then start and test the application. Close the Code Editor window and then close the solution.

Swat The Bugs

21. The following code should display a 10% bonus for each sales amount that is entered, but it is not working correctly. Correct the code.

```
Dim strInput As String
Dim dblSales As Double
Dim dblBonus As Double
strInput = InputBox("Sales amount:", "Sales")
Do While strInput <> String.Empty
    Double.TryParse(strInput, dblSales)
    dblBonus = dblSales * .1
    MessageBox.Show(dblBonus.ToString("C2"))
Loop
```

22. The following code should display the numbers 1 through 4, but it is not working correctly. Correct the code.

```
Dim intNumber As Integer = 1
Do While intNumber < 5
    MessageBox.Show(intNumber.ToString)
Loop
```

23. The following code should display the numbers 10 through 1, but it is not working correctly. Correct the code.

```
Dim intNumber As Integer = 10
Do
    MessageBox.Show(intNumber.ToString)
Loop Until intNumber = 0
```

24. The following code should display a 5% commission for each sales amount that is entered, but it is not working correctly. Correct the code.

```
Dim strInput As String
Dim dblSales As Double
Dim dblComm As Double
strInput = InputBox("Sales:", "Sales")
Double.TryParse(strInput, dblSales)
Do
    strInput = InputBox("Sales:", "Sales")
    Double.TryParse(strInput, dblSales)
    dblComm = dblSales * .05
    MessageBox.Show(dblComm.ToString("C2"))
Loop Until dblSales <= 0
```

LESSON B

After studying Lesson B, you should be able to:

- Nest repetition structures

- Refresh the screen

- Delay program execution

Nested Repetition Structures

Like selection structures, repetition structures can be nested. In other words, you can place one loop (called the nested or inner loop) within another loop (called the outer loop). Both loops can be pretest loops, or both can be posttest loops. Or, one can be a pretest loop and the other a posttest loop. You already are familiar with the concept of nested loops, because a clock uses nested loops to keep track of the time. For simplicity, consider a clock's minute and second hands only. The second hand on a clock moves one position, clockwise, for every second that has elapsed. After the second hand moves 60 positions, the minute hand moves one position, also clockwise. The second hand then begins its journey around the clock again. Figure 6-31 shows the logic used by a clock's minute and second hands. The outer loop controls the minute hand, while the inner (nested) loop controls the second hand. Notice that the entire nested loop is contained within the outer loop; this must be true for the loop to be nested and for it to work correctly.

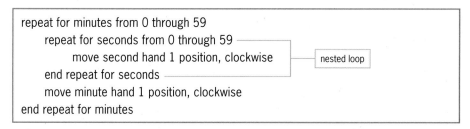

Figure 6-31 Logic used by a clock's minute and second hands

To code and then test the Clock application: START HERE

1. If necessary, start Visual Studio 2010 or Visual Basic 2010 Express. Open the Clock Solution (Clock Solution.sln) file contained in the VB2010\Chap06\Clock Solution folder. If necessary, open the designer window. See Figure 6-32.

Figure 6-32   Clock application's interface

2. Open the Code Editor window. Replace <your name> and <current date> in the comments with your name and the current date, respectively.

3. Open the code template for the btnStart control's Click event procedure. The procedure will use an outer loop to display the number of minutes, and a nested loop to display the number of seconds. For simplicity in watching the minutes and seconds tick away, you will display minute values from 0 through 2, and display second values from 0 through 5. Enter the following comments. Press **Enter** twice after typing the last comment.

    ' displays minutes (from 0 through 2 only)
    ' and seconds (from 0 through 5 only)

4. Now enter the following outer and nested loops:

    For intMinutes As Integer = 0 To 2
    **   lblMinutes.Text = intMinutes.ToString**
    **   For intSeconds As Integer = 0 To 5**
    **   lblSeconds.Text = intSeconds.ToString**
    **   Next intSeconds**
    Next intMinutes

5. Save the solution and then start the application. Click the **Start** button. The computer processes the code entered in the button's Click event procedure. However, it processes the code so quickly that you don't get a chance to see each of the values assigned to the label controls. Rather, only the final values (2 and 5) appear in the label controls. You can fix this problem by refreshing the interface and then delaying program execution each time the value in the lblSeconds control changes.

The Refresh and Sleep Methods

You can refresh (or redraw) the interface using the form's Refresh method. The **Refresh method** ensures that the computer processes any previous lines of code that affect the interface's appearance. The Refresh method's syntax is **Me.Refresh()**, in which Me refers to the current form. To delay program execution, you can use the **Sleep method** in the following syntax: **System. Threading.Thread.Sleep(***milliseconds***)**. The *milliseconds* argument is the number of milliseconds to suspend the program. A millisecond is 1/1000 of a second; in other words, there are 1000 milliseconds in a second. In the Clock application, you will delay program execution for a half of a second, which is 500 milliseconds.

To include the Refresh and Sleep methods in the procedure and then test the code: START HERE

1. Enter the additional comment and two lines of code indicated in Figure 6-33.

```
Private Sub btnStart_Click(ByVal sender As Object, ByVal e
    ' displays minutes (from 0 through 2 only)
    ' and seconds (from 0 through 5 only)

    For intMinutes As Integer = 0 To 2
        lblMinutes.Text = intMinutes.ToString
        For intSeconds As Integer = 0 To 5
            lblSeconds.Text = intSeconds.ToString
            ' refresh interface and then pause execution      enter this comment
            Me.Refresh()                                      and these two lines
            System.Threading.Thread.Sleep(500)                of code
        Next intSeconds
    Next intMinutes
End Sub
```

Figure 6-33 Refresh and Sleep methods added to the procedure

2. Save the solution and then start the application. Click the **Start** button. The number 0 appears in the lblMinutes control, and the numbers 0 through 5 appear (one at a time) in the lblSeconds control. Notice that the number of minutes is increased by 1 when the number of seconds changes from 5 to 0. When the procedure ends, the lblMinutes and lblSeconds controls contain the numbers 2 and 5, respectively. (If you want to end the procedure prematurely, click the form in the designer window, click Debug on the menu bar, and then click Stop Debugging.)

3. Click the **Exit** button. Close the Code Editor window and then close the solution.

Revisiting the Monthly Payment Calculator Application

Figure 6-34 shows the modified problem specification for the Monthly Payment Calculator application from Lesson A. The solution to this problem will require two loops, one nested within the other. The outer loop will control the interest rates, which range from 5% to 10% in increments of 1%. The inner loop will control the terms, which are 3 years, 4 years, and 5 years.

> Jacobsen Loans wants an application that displays the monthly payments on a car loan, using terms of 3, 4, and 5 years and annual interest rates of 5%, 6%, 7%, 8%, 9%, and 10%.

Figure 6-34 Modified problem specification for the Monthly Payment Calculator application

START HERE ▶ **To code and then test the modified application:**

1. Open the Payment Calculator Solution (Payment Calculator Solution.sln) file contained in the VB2010\Chap06\Nested Payment Calculator Solution folder. If necessary, open the designer window.

2. Open the Code Editor window, which contains the following procedures: btnExit_Click, txtPrincipal_Enter, txtPrincipal_KeyPress, txtPrincipal_TextChanged, and btnCalc_Click. Replace <your name> and <current date> in the comments with your name and the current date, respectively.

3. Locate the code template for the btnCalc control's Click event procedure. Click the **blank line** below the `' calculate and display payments` comment. First, you will enter the loop that controls the interest rates. Enter the following For clause:

   For dblRate As Double = .05 To .1 Step .01

4. Change the Next clause to **Next dblRate**.

5. Click the **blank line** below the For clause. You will display the current rate (formatted as a percentage) in the lblPayments control. Enter the following lines of code. Be sure to include four spaces between the last set of quotation marks. Press **Enter** twice after typing the last line.

   lblPayments.Text = lblPayments.Text &
   **   dblRate.ToString("P0") & "   "**

6. Next, you will enter the loop that controls the term. Enter the following For clause:

   For intTerm As Integer = 3 To 5

7. Change the Next clause to **Next intTerm**.

8. Click the **blank line** below the nested For clause. Now you will enter the code to calculate and display the monthly payments. Type the lines of code indicated in Figure 6-35. Be sure to include four spaces between the last set of quotation marks.

```
' calculate and display payments
For dblRate As Double = 0.05 To 0.1 Step 0.01
    lblPayments.Text = lblPayments.Text &
        dblRate.ToString("P0") & "     "

    For intTerm As Integer = 3 To 5
        dblPayment = -Financial.Pmt(dblRate / 12,
                                 intTerm * 12, dblPrincipal)
        lblPayments.Text = lblPayments.Text &
            dblPayment.ToString("N2") & "     "
    Next intTerm
Next dblRate
```

enter these four lines of code

Figure 6-35   Outer and nested loops entered in the procedure

Although both loops in Figure 6-35 are pretest loops, you also can use two posttest loops or a combination of a pretest and a posttest loop.

9. Finally, you will display a blank line after each rate in the lblPayments control. Click **immediately after the letter m** in the `Next intTerm` clause and then press **Enter** twice. Enter the following assignment statement:

   lblPayments.Text =
   **   lblPayments.Text & ControlChars.NewLine**

10. Save the solution and then start the application. Type **10000** in the Principal box and then press **Enter** to select the Calculate button. The button's Click event procedure displays the monthly payments, as shown in Figure 6-36.

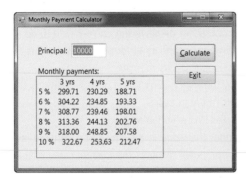

Figure 6-36 Monthly payments shown in the interface

11. Click the **Exit** button. Close the Code Editor window and then close the solution.

Figure 6-37 describes the way the computer processes the loops contained in the Calculate button's Click event procedure. Notice that when the inner loop ends, the value stored in the `intTerm` variable is 6. When the outer loop ends, the value stored in the `dblRate` variable is 0.11.

Processing steps for the loops in the btnCalc_Click procedure

1. The computer creates the `dblRate` variable and initializes it to 0.05.
2. The computer checks whether the value in the `dblRate` variable is greater than 0.1. It's not, so the computer displays the current rate (5 %) in the lblPayments control and then processes the inner loop as follows:
   a. The computer creates the `intTerm` variable and initializes it to 3.
   b. The computer checks whether the value in the `intTerm` variable is greater than 5. It's not, so the computer calculates the monthly payment (using 0.05 as the rate and 3 as the term) and then displays the result in the lblPayments control.
   c. The computer adds 1 to the `intTerm` variable, giving 4.
   d. The computer again checks whether the value in the `intTerm` variable is greater than 5. It's not, so the computer calculates the monthly car payment (using 0.05 as the rate and 4 as the term) and then displays the result in the lblPayments control.
   e. The computer adds 1 to the `intTerm` variable, giving 5.
   f. The computer again checks whether the value in the `intTerm` variable is greater than 5. It's not, so the computer calculates the monthly car payment (using 0.05 as the rate and 5 as the term) and then displays the result in the lblPayments control.
   g. The computer adds 1 to the `intTerm` variable, giving 6.
   h. The computer again checks whether the value in the `intTerm` variable is greater than 5. It is, so the computer removes the `intTerm` variable from memory and then stops processing the inner loop. Processing continues with the statement immediately below the `Next intTerm` clause.

Figure 6-37 Processing steps for the loops *(continues)*

(continued)

3. The statement immediately below the `Next intTerm` clause positions the cursor on the next line in the lblPayments control.
4. The computer adds 0.01 to the `dblRate` variable, giving 0.06.
5. The computer again checks whether the value in the `dblRate` variable is greater than 0.1. It's not, so the computer displays the current rate (6 %) in the lblPayments control. It then processes the inner loop as shown in Steps 2a through 2h; however, this time it uses 0.06 as the rate.
6. The statement immediately below the `Next intTerm` clause positions the cursor on the next line in the lblPayments control.
7. The computer adds 0.01 to the `dblRate` variable, giving 0.07.
8. The computer again checks whether the value in the `dblRate` variable is greater than 0.1. It's not, so the computer displays the current rate (7 %) in the lblPayments control. It then processes the inner loop as shown in Steps 2a through 2h; however, this time it uses 0.07 as the rate.
9. The statement immediately below the `Next intTerm` clause positions the cursor on the next line in the lblPayments control.
10. The computer adds 0.01 to the `dblRate` variable, giving 0.08.
11. The computer again checks whether the value in the `dblRate` variable is greater than 0.1. It's not, so the computer displays the current rate (8 %) in the lblPayments control. It then processes the inner loop as shown in Steps 2a through 2h; however, this time it uses 0.08 as the rate.
12. The statement immediately below the `Next intTerm` clause positions the cursor on the next line in the lblPayments control.
13. The computer adds 0.01 to the `dblRate` variable, giving 0.09.
14. The computer again checks whether the value in the `dblRate` variable is greater than 0.1. It's not, so the computer displays the current rate (9 %) in the lblPayments control. It then processes the inner loop as shown in Steps 2a through 2h; however, this time it uses 0.09 as the rate.
15. The statement immediately below the `Next intTerm` clause positions the cursor on the next line in the lblPayments control.
16. The computer adds 0.01 to the `dblRate` variable, giving 0.1.
17. The computer again checks whether the value in the `dblRate` variable is greater than 0.1. It's not, so the computer displays the current rate (10 %) in the lblPayments control. It then processes the inner loop as shown in Steps 2a through 2h; however, this time it uses 0.1 as the rate.
18. The statement immediately below the `Next intTerm` clause positions the cursor on the next line in the lblPayments control.
19. The computer adds 0.01 to the `dblRate` variable, giving 0.11.
20. The computer again checks whether the value in the `dblRate` variable is greater than 0.1. It is, so the computer removes the `dblRate` variable from memory and then stops the outer loop. Processing continues with the statement immediately below the `Next dblRate` clause.

Figure 6-37   Processing steps for the loops

Lesson B Summary

- To nest a repetition structure:

  Place the entire inner loop within the outer loop.

- To refresh the interface:

  Use the Refresh method. The method's syntax is **Me.Refresh()**.

- To pause program execution:

  Use the Sleep method. The method's syntax is **System.Threading.Thread.Sleep(***milliseconds***)**.

Lesson B Key Terms

Refresh method—can be used to refresh (redraw) a form

Sleep method—can be used to delay program execution

Lesson B Review Questions

1. What will the following code display in the lblAsterisks control?

    ```
    For intX As Integer = 1 To 2
        For intY As Integer = 1 To 3
            lblAsterisks.Text = lblAsterisks.Text & "*"
        Next intY
        lblAsterisks.Text = lblAsterisks.Text &
            ControlChars.NewLine
    Next intX
    ```

    a. ```
        ***
        ***
        ```

    b.  ```
        ***
        ***
        ***
        ```

    c. ```
        **
        **
        **
        ```

    d.  ```
        ***
        ***
        ***
        ***
        ```

372

2. What will the following code display in the lblSum control?

```
Dim intSum As Integer
Dim intY As Integer
Do While intY < 3
    For intX As Integer = 1 To 4
        intSum = intSum + intX
    Next intX
    intY = intY + 1
Loop
lblSum.Text = Convert.ToString(intSum)
```

a. 5

b. 8

c. 15

d. 30

3. Which of the following statements pauses program execution for 1 second?

a. `System.Threading.Thread.Pause(1000)`

b. `System.Threading.Thread.Pause(1)`

c. `System.Threading.Thread.Sleep(1000)`

d. `System.Threading.Thread.Sleep(100)`

Lesson B Exercises

INTRODUCTORY

1. In this exercise, you modify the Clock application from this lesson. Use Windows to make a copy of the Clock Solution folder. Rename the copy Clock Solution-Introductory. Open the Clock Solution (Clock Solution.sln) file contained in the Clock Solution-Introductory folder. Open the designer and Code Editor windows. Change the outer For…Next statement to a Do…Loop statement. Save the solution and then start and test the application. Close the Code Editor window and then close the solution.

INTRODUCTORY

2. In this exercise, you modify the Monthly Payment Calculator application from this lesson. Use Windows to make a copy of the Nested Payment Calculator Solution folder. Rename the copy Nested Payment Calculator Solution-Introductory. Open the Payment Calculator Solution (Payment Calculator Solution.sln) file contained in the Nested Payment Calculator Solution-Introductory folder. Open the designer and Code Editor windows. Change the For…Next statement that controls the term to a Do…Loop statement. Save the solution and then start and test the application. Close the Code Editor window and then close the solution.

3. In this exercise, you modify the Clock application from this lesson. Use Windows to make a copy of the Clock Solution folder. Rename the copy Clock Solution-Intermediate. Open the Clock Solution (Clock Solution.sln) file contained in the Clock Solution-Intermediate folder. Open the designer and Code Editor windows. Change the inner For...Next statement to a Do...Loop statement. Save the solution and then start and test the application. Close the Code Editor window and then close the solution.

INTERMEDIATE

4. In this exercise, you modify the Monthly Payment Calculator application from this lesson. Use Windows to make a copy of the Nested Payment Calculator Solution folder. Rename the copy Nested Payment Calculator Solution-Intermediate. Open the Payment Calculator Solution (Payment Calculator Solution.sln) file contained in the Nested Payment Calculator Solution-Intermediate folder. Open the designer and Code Editor windows. Change both For...Next statements to Do...Loop statements. Save the solution and then start and test the application. Close the Code Editor window and then close the solution.

INTERMEDIATE

5. Professor Arkins wants an application that allows him to assign a grade to any number of students. Each student's grade is based on three test scores, with each test worth 100 points. The application should total the test scores and then assign the appropriate grade using the information shown in Figure 6-38. Open the Grade Calculator Solution (Grade Calculator Solution.sln) file contained in the VB2010\Chap06\Grade Calculator Solution folder. If necessary, open the designer window. Code the application. Save the solution and then start and test the application. Close the Code Editor window and then close the solution.

INTERMEDIATE

Total points earned	Grade
270–300	A
240–269	B
210–239	C
180–209	D
below 180	F

Figure 6-38 Grade information for Exercise 5

6. Open the Car Solution (Car Solution.sln) file contained in the VB2010\Chap06\Car Solution folder. The Click Me button's Click event procedure should make the "I WANT THIS CAR!" message blink 10 times. In other words, the message should disappear and then reappear, disappear and then reappear, and so on. Use the For...Next statement. Save the solution and then start and test the application. Close the Code Editor window and then close the solution.

ADVANCED

LESSON C

After studying Lesson C, you should be able to:

- Include a list box on a form
- Select a list box item from code
- Determine the selected item in a list box

The Ch06CVideo file demonstrates all of the steps contained in Lesson C. You can view the video either before or after completing the lesson.

Creating the Shoppers Haven Application

Recall that your task is to create an application that allows the user to enter an item's original price and its discount rate. The discount rates range from 10% through 30% in increments of 5%. The application will calculate and display the amount of the discount and also the discounted price. Figure 6-39 shows the application's TOE chart.

Task	Object	Event
End the application	btnExit	Click
1. Calculate the discount and discounted price 2. Display the discount and discounted price in lblDiscount and lblDiscountPrice	btnCalc	Click
Get and display the original price Select the existing text Clear lblDiscount and lblDiscountPrice	txtOrigPrice	None Enter TextChanged
1. Fill lstRate with values 2. Select a default value in lstRate	frmMain	Load
Display the discount (from btnCalc)	lblDiscount	None
Display the discounted price (from btnCalc)	lblDiscountPrice	None
Get and display the discount rates Clear lblDiscount and lblDiscountPrice	lstRate	None SelectedValueChanged

Figure 6-39   TOE chart for the Shoppers Haven application

START HERE ▶ **To open the partially-completed Shoppers Haven application:**

1. If necessary, start Visual Studio 2010 or Visual Basic 2010 Express.

2. Open the Shoppers Haven Solution (Shoppers Haven Solution.sln) file contained in the VB2010\Chap06\Shoppers Haven Solution folder. If necessary, open the designer window. Missing from the interface is a list box control.

Including a List Box in an Interface

You add a list box to an interface using the ListBox tool in the toolbox. A **list box** displays a list of choices from which the user can select zero choices, one choice, or multiple choices. The number of choices the user can select is controlled by the list box's **SelectionMode property**. The default value for the property is One, which allows the user to select only one choice at a time. You can make a list box any size you want. However, the Windows standard for list boxes is to display a minimum of three choices and a maximum of eight choices at a time. If you have more items than can fit into the list box, the control automatically displays a scroll bar for viewing the complete list of items. You should use a label control to provide keyboard access to the list box. For the access key to work correctly, you must set the label's TabIndex property to a value that is one less than the list box's TabIndex value.

 You can learn more about the SelectionMode property in Exercise 10 at the end of this lesson.

375

 If you have only two choices to offer the user, you should use two radio buttons rather than a list box.

To complete the user interface:

START HERE

1. Click the **ListBox** tool in the toolbox and then drag the mouse pointer to the form. Position the mouse pointer below the Discount rate label and then release the mouse button.

2. The three-character ID for list box names is lst. Change the list box's name to **lstRate**. Do not be concerned that the list box's name appears inside the control. The name will not appear when the application is started.

3. Set the list box's Size property to **66, 64**.

4. Lock the controls on the form and then use the information in Figure 6-40 to set the TabIndex values. When you are finished, press **Esc** to remove the TabIndex boxes from the form and then save the solution.

Figure 6-40 Correct TabIndex values

Adding Items to a List Box

The items in a list box belong to a collection called the **Items collection**. A **collection** is a group of individual objects treated as one unit. The first item in the Items collection appears as the first item in the list box. The second item in the collection appears as the second item in the list box, and so on. A unique number called an index identifies each item in the Items collection. The first item in the collection (which also is the first item in the list box) has an index of 0. The second item has an index of 1, and so on. You specify each item to display in a list box using the Items collection's **Add method**. Figure 6-41 shows the method's syntax and includes examples of using the method. In the syntax, *object* is the name of the list box control, and the *item* argument is the text you want to add to the control's list. The three Add methods in Example 1 will add the strings "Dog", "Cat", and "Horse" to the lstAnimal control. In Example 2, the Add method appears in the body of a pretest loop that repeats its instructions for `intCode` values of 100 through 105. As a result, the Add method will add the values 100, 101, 102, 103, 104, and 105 (each converted to the String data type) to the lstCode control. You also can write the Add method in Example 2 as follows: `lstCode.Items.Add(Convert.ToString(intCode))`. In most cases, you enter the Add methods in the Load event procedure of a form, because you typically want the list box to display its values when the form first appears on the screen.

To learn about the Items collection's Insert, Remove, RemoveAt, and Clear methods, as well as its Count property, complete Exercise 11 at the end of this lesson.

To learn how to use the String Collection Editor window to add items to a list box, complete Exercise 12 at the end of this lesson.

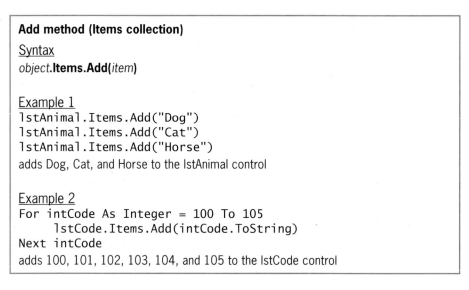

Add method (Items collection)

<u>Syntax</u>
object.**Items.Add**(*item*)

<u>Example 1</u>
```
lstAnimal.Items.Add("Dog")
lstAnimal.Items.Add("Cat")
lstAnimal.Items.Add("Horse")
```
adds Dog, Cat, and Horse to the lstAnimal control

<u>Example 2</u>
```
For intCode As Integer = 100 To 105
     lstCode.Items.Add(intCode.ToString)
Next intCode
```
adds 100, 101, 102, 103, 104, and 105 to the lstCode control

Figure 6-41   Syntax and examples of the Items collection's Add method

Figure 6-42 shows the lstAnimal and lstCode controls after the computer processes the code shown in Figure 6-41.

Figure 6-42   Result of processing the code from Figure 6-41

The Sorted Property

The position of an item in a list box depends on the value stored in the list box's **Sorted property**. When the Sorted property is set to False (the default value), the item is added at the end of the list. The Sorted property of both list boxes in Figure 6-42 is set to False. When the Sorted property is set to

True, the item is sorted along with the existing items and then placed in its proper position in the list. Visual Basic sorts the list box items in dictionary order, which means that numbers are sorted before letters, and a lowercase letter is sorted before its uppercase equivalent. The items in a list box are sorted based on the leftmost characters in each item. As a result, the items "Personnel", "Inventory", and "Payroll" will appear in the following order when the lstDepartment control's Sorted property is set to True: Inventory, Payroll, Personnel. Likewise, the items 1, 2, 3, and 10 will appear in the following order when the lstNumber control's Sorted property is set to True: 1, 10, 2, 3. Both list boxes are shown in Figure 6-43.

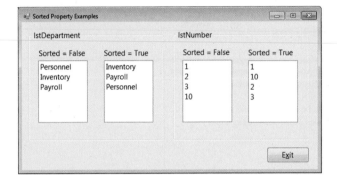

Figure 6-43 Examples of the list box's Sorted property

The requirements of the application you are creating determine whether you display the list box items in either sorted order or the order in which they are added to the list box. If several list items are selected much more frequently than other items, you typically leave the list box's Sorted property set to False and then add the frequently used items first; doing this ensures that the items appear at the beginning of the list. However, if the list box items are selected fairly equally, you typically set the list box's Sorted property to True, because it is easier to locate items when they appear in a sorted order.

GUI DESIGN TIP List Box Standards

- A list box should contain a minimum of three items.

- A list box should display a minimum of three items and a maximum of eight items at a time.

- Use a label control to provide keyboard access to the list box. Set the label's TabIndex property to a value that is one less than the list box's TabIndex value.

- List box items are either arranged by use, with the most used entries appearing first in the list, or sorted in ascending order.

Coding the Shoppers Haven Application

When the Shoppers Haven interface appears on the screen, the appropriate discount rates should be listed in the lstRate control. You can accomplish this by entering the appropriate Add methods in the form's Load event procedure.

START HERE **To specify the discount rates to display in the lstRate control:**

1. Open the Code Editor window. Replace <your name> and <current date> in the comments with your name and the current date, respectively.

2. Click the **Class Name** list arrow and then click **(frmMain Events)**. Click the **Method Name** list arrow and then click **Load**. Type the following comment and then press **Enter** twice:

   ' fill the list box with values

3. Enter the For...Next loop shown in Figure 6-44, and then position the insertion point as shown in the figure. (Be sure to change the Next clause to `Next dblRates`.)

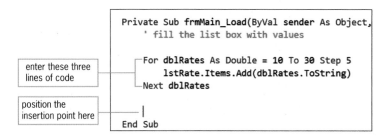

enter these three lines of code

position the insertion point here

```
Private Sub frmMain_Load(ByVal sender As Object,
      ' fill the list box with values

   For dblRates As Double = 10 To 30 Step 5
        lstRate.Items.Add(dblRates.ToString)
   Next dblRates

End Sub
```

Figure 6-44 For...Next loop entered in the Load event procedure

4. Save the solution and then start the application. The numbers 10, 15, and 20 appear in the list box. (Depending on your screen's resolution, the number 25 also may appear in the list box.) Scroll down the list box to verify that it also contains the numbers 25 and 30.

5. Scroll to the top of the list box and then click **15** in the list. See Figure 6-45. When you select an item in a list box, the item appears highlighted in the list. In addition, the item's value (in this case, the string "15") is stored in the list box's SelectedItem property, and the item's index (in this case, the number 1) is stored in the list box's SelectedIndex property. You will learn more about the SelectedItem and SelectedIndex properties in the next section. Click the **Exit** button.

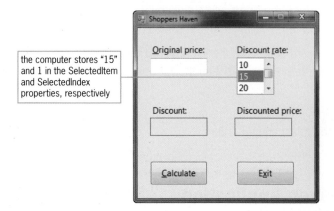

the computer stores "15" and 1 in the SelectedItem and SelectedIndex properties, respectively

Figure 6-45 Second item selected in the list box

The SelectedItem and SelectedIndex Properties

You can use either the **SelectedItem property** or the **SelectedIndex property** to determine whether an item is selected in a list box. When no item is selected, the SelectedItem property contains the empty string, and the SelectedIndex property contains the number −1 (negative 1). Otherwise, the SelectedItem and SelectedIndex properties contain the value of the selected item and the item's index, respectively. Figure 6-46 shows examples of using the SelectedItem and SelectedIndex properties.

SelectedItem and SelectedIndex properties

Example 1 (SelectedItem property)
```
lblAnimal.Text = Convert.ToString(lstAnimal.SelectedItem)
```
The assignment statement converts the item selected in the lstAnimal control to String and then assigns the result to the lblAnimal control's Text property.

Example 2 (SelectedItem property)
```
If Convert.ToInt32(lstCode.SelectedItem) = 103 Then
```
The If clause converts the item selected in the lstCode control to Integer and then compares the result with the integer 103. The condition evaluates to True when item 103 is selected in the lstCode control; otherwise, it evaluates to False. You also can convert the item to String and then compare the result with the string "103" as follows:
```
If Convert.ToString(lstCode.SelectedItem) = "103".
```

Example 3 (SelectedItem property)
```
If Convert.ToString(lstCode.SelectedItem) <> String.Empty Then
```
The If clause converts the item selected in the lstCode control to String and then compares the result to the empty string. The condition evaluates to True when an item is selected in the lstCode control; otherwise, it evaluates to False.

Example 4 (SelectedIndex property)
```
MessageBox.Show(lstAnimal.SelectedIndex.ToString)
```
The MessageBox.Show method displays (in a message box) the index of the item selected in the lstAnimal control. You also can use the
```
MessageBox.Show(Convert.ToString(lstAnimal.SelectedIndex))
```
statement.

Example 5 (SelectedIndex property)
```
If lstCode.SelectedIndex = 0 Then
```
The If clause compares the index of the item selected in the lstCode control with the number 0. The condition evaluates to True when the first item in the list box is selected; otherwise, it evaluates to False.

Figure 6-46 Examples of the list box's SelectedItem and SelectedIndex properties

If a list box allows the user to make only one selection, it is customary in Windows applications to have one of the list box items already selected when the interface appears. The selected item, called the **default list box item**, should be either the item selected most frequently or the first item in the list. You can use either the SelectedItem property or the SelectedIndex property to select the default list box item from code, as shown in the examples in Figure 6-47. (The examples refer to the list boxes shown earlier in

Figure 6-42.) In most cases, you enter the appropriate code in the form's Load event procedure.

Selecting the default list box item

Example 1 (SelectedItem property)
`lstAnimal.SelectedItem = "Cat"`
selects the Cat item in the lstAnimal control

Example 2 (SelectedItem property)
`lstCode.SelectedItem = "101"`
selects the 101 item in the lstCode control

Example 3 (SelectedIndex property)
`lstCode.SelectedIndex = 2`
selects the third item in the lstCode control

Figure 6-47   Examples of selecting the default list box item

START HERE ▶   **To select a default item in the lstRate control:**

1. The insertion point should be positioned two lines below the `Next dblRates` clause in the form's Load event procedure. Enter the following assignment statement:

   lstRate.SelectedIndex = 0

2. Save the solution and then start the application. The form's Load event procedure fills the list box with the discount rates and then selects the first item in the list. See Figure 6-48. Click the **Exit** button.

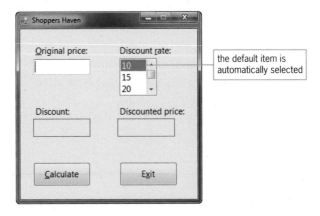

Figure 6-48   Default item selected in the list box

GUI DESIGN TIP   Default List Box Item

If a list box allows the user to make only one selection, a default item should be selected when the interface first appears. The default item should be either the item selected most frequently or the first item in the list. However, if a list box allows more than one selection at a time, you do not select a default item.

The SelectedValueChanged and SelectedIndexChanged Events

Each time either the user or a statement selects an item in a list box, the list box's **SelectedValueChanged event** and its **SelectedIndexChanged event** occur. You can use the procedures associated with these events to perform one or more tasks when the selected item has changed. In the Shoppers Haven application, you will code the lstRate control's SelectedValueChanged procedure so that it clears both the discount and discounted price amounts whenever a change is made to the discount rate.

To code the list box's SelectedValueChanged event procedure:

START HERE

1. Open the code template for the lstRate control's SelectedValueChanged event. Type the following comment and then press **Enter** twice:

   ' clear the calculated results

2. Now enter the following assignment statements:

   lblDiscount.Text = String.Empty
   lblDiscountPrice.Text = String.Empty

3. Save the solution.

Coding the btnCalc Control's Click Event Procedure

To complete the Shoppers Haven application, you need to code the btnCalc control's Click event procedure. The procedure's pseudocode is shown in Figure 6-49.

btnCalc Click event procedure
1. store the user input (original price and discount rate) in variables
2. calculate the discount = original price * discount rate / 100
3. calculate the discounted price = original price – discount
4. display the discount and discounted price in the lblDiscount and lblDiscountPrice controls

Figure 6-49 Pseudocode for the btnCalc control's Click event procedure

To code and then test the btnCalc control's Click event procedure:

1. Open the code template for the btnCalc control's Click event procedure. Type the following comment and then press **Enter** twice:

   ' calculate the discount and discounted price

2. Recall that before you begin coding a procedure, you first study the procedure's pseudocode to determine the variables and named constants (if any) the procedure will use. In this case, the procedure will not use any named constants; however, it will use four variables. The `dblOriginal` variable will store the original price. The `dblRate`

variable will store the discount rate. The **dblDiscount** and **dblDiscountPrice** variables will store the discount and discounted price, respectively. Enter the following four Dim statements. Press **Enter** twice after typing the last Dim statement.

Dim dblOriginal As Double
Dim dblRate As Double
Dim dblDiscount As Double
Dim dblDiscountPrice As Double

3. The first step in the pseudocode is to store the user input (original price and discount rate) in variables. Enter the following TryParse methods. Press **Enter** twice after typing the second TryParse method.

Double.TryParse(txtOrigPrice.Text, dblOriginal)
Double.TryParse(lstRate.SelectedItem.ToString, dblRate)

4. The second step in the pseudocode is to calculate the discount amount. Enter the following assignment statement:

dblDiscount = dblOriginal * dblRate / 100

5. The third step in the pseudocode is to calculate the discounted price. Enter the following assignment statement:

dblDiscountPrice = dblOriginal – dblDiscount

6. The last step in the pseudocode is to display the discount and discounted price in the appropriate label controls. Enter the following assignment statements:

lblDiscount.Text = dblDiscount.ToString("C2")
lblDiscountPrice.Text = dblDiscountPrice.ToString("C2")

7. Save the solution and then start the application. Type **100** in the Original price box and then click **20** in the list of discount rates. Click the **Calculate** button. The button's Click event procedure displays the discount and discounted price. See Figure 6-50.

Figure 6-50 Calculated amounts shown in the interface

8. Click **10** in the Discount rate list box. The list box's SelectedValueChanged procedure removes the discount and discounted price from the label controls.

9. Click the **Calculate** button. The button's Click event procedure displays $10.00 and $90.00 as the discount and discounted price, respectively.

10. Click the **Exit** button. Close the Code Editor window and then close the solution.

Figure 6-51 shows the application's code.

```
1 ' Name:          Shoppers Haven Project
2 ' Purpose:       Displays the discount and discounted price
3 ' Programmer:    <your name> on <current date>
4
5 Option Explicit On
6 Option Strict On
7 Option Infer Off
8
9 Public Class frmMain
10
11    Private Sub btnExit_Click(ByVal sender As Object,
      ByVal e As System.EventArgs) Handles btnExit.Click
12        Me.Close()
13    End Sub
14
15    Private Sub txtOrigPrice_Enter(ByVal sender As Object,
      ByVal e As System.EventArgs) Handles txtOrigPrice.Enter
16        txtOrigPrice.SelectAll()
17    End Sub
18
19    Private Sub txtOrigPrice_KeyPress(ByVal sender As Object,
      ByVal e As System.Windows.Forms.KeyPressEventArgs
      ) Handles txtOrigPrice.KeyPress
20        ' allows only numbers, the period, and the Backspace
21
22        If (e.KeyChar < "0" OrElse e.KeyChar > "9") AndAlso
23            e.KeyChar <> "." AndAlso
24            e.KeyChar <> ControlChars.Back Then
25            e.Handled = True
26        End If
27    End Sub
28
29    Private Sub txtOrigPrice_TextChanged(ByVal sender As Object,
      ByVal e As System.EventArgs
      ) Handles txtOrigPrice.TextChanged
30        ' clear the calculated results
31
32        lblDiscount.Text = String.Empty
33        lblDiscountPrice.Text = String.Empty
34    End Sub
35
36    Private Sub frmMain_Load(ByVal sender As Object,
      ByVal e As System.EventArgs) Handles Me.Load
37        ' fill the list box with values
38
39        For dblRates As Double = 10 To 30 Step 5
40            lstRate.Items.Add(dblRates.ToString)
```

Figure 6-51 Shoppers Haven application's code *(continues)*

(continued)

```
41        Next dblRates
42
43        lstRate.SelectedIndex = 0
44
45    End Sub
46
47    Private Sub lstRate_SelectedValueChanged(
      ByVal sender As Object, ByVal e As System.EventArgs
      ) Handles lstRate.SelectedValueChanged
48        ' clear the calculated results
49
50        lblDiscount.Text = String.Empty
51        lblDiscountPrice.Text = String.Empty
52
53    End Sub
54
55    Private Sub btnCalc_Click(ByVal sender As Object,
      ByVal e As System.EventArgs) Handles btnCalc.Click
56        ' calculate the discount and discounted price
57
58        Dim dblOriginal As Double
59        Dim dblRate As Double
60        Dim dblDiscount As Double
61        Dim dblDiscountPrice As Double
62
63        Double.TryParse(txtOrigPrice.Text, dblOriginal)
64        Double.TryParse(lstRate.SelectedItem.ToString, dblRate)
65
66        dblDiscount = dblOriginal * dblRate / 100
67        dblDiscountPrice = dblOriginal - dblDiscount
68        lblDiscount.Text = dblDiscount.ToString("C2")
69        lblDiscountPrice.Text = dblDiscountPrice.ToString("C2")
70
71    End Sub
72 End Class
```

Figure 6-51   Shoppers Haven application's code

Lesson C Summary

- To add a list box control to a form:

  Use the ListBox tool in the toolbox.

- To specify whether the user can select zero choices, one choice, or multiple choices in a list box:

  Set the list box's SelectionMode property.

- To add items to a list box:

  Use the Items collection's Add method. The method's syntax is *object*.**Items.Add**(*item*). In the syntax, *object* is the name of the list box control, and the *item* argument is the text you want to add to the control's list.

- To automatically sort the items in a list box:

  Set the list box's Sorted property to True.

- To determine the item selected in a list box, or to select a list box item from code:

  Use either the list box's SelectedItem property or its SelectedIndex property.

- To perform tasks when a different item is selected in a list box:

  Enter the code in either the list box's SelectedValueChanged procedure or its SelectedIndexChanged procedure.

Lesson C Key Terms

Add method—the Items collection's method used to add items to a list box

Collection—a group of individual objects treated as one unit

Default list box item—the item automatically selected in a list box when the interface appears on the screen

Items collection—the collection composed of the items in a list box

List box—a control used to display a list of choices from which the user can select zero choices, one choice, or multiple choices

SelectedIndex property—stores the index of the item selected in a list box

SelectedIndexChanged event—occurs when an item is selected in a list box

SelectedItem property—stores the value of the item selected in a list box

SelectedValueChanged event—occurs when an item is selected in a list box

SelectionMode property—determines the number of items that can be selected in a list box

Sorted property—specifies whether the list box items should appear in the order they are entered or in sorted order

Lesson C Review Questions

1. Which of the following methods allows you to add items to a list box?

    a. Add

    b. AddList

    c. Item

    d. ItemAdd

2. The items in a list box belong to the _____ collection.

    a. Items

    b. List

    c. ListItems

    d. Values

3. Which of the following properties stores the index of the item selected in a list box?

    a. Index

    b. SelectedIndex

    c. Selection

    d. SelectionIndex

4. Which of the following statements selects the "Horse" item, which appears third in the lstAnimal control?

    a. `lstAnimal.SelectedIndex = 2`

    b. `lstAnimal.SelectedIndex = 3`

    c. `lstAnimal.SelectedItem = 2`

    d. `lstAnimal.SelectedItem = 3`

5. The _____ event occurs when the user selects a different item in a list box.

    a. SelectionChanged

    b. SelectedItemChanged

    c. SelectedValueChanged

    d. none of the above

Lesson C Exercises

INTRODUCTORY

1. In this exercise, you modify the Shoppers Haven application from this lesson. Use Windows to make a copy of the Shoppers Haven Solution folder. Rename the copy Modified Shoppers Haven Solution. Open the Shoppers Haven Solution (Shoppers Haven Solution.sln) file contained in the Modified Shoppers Haven Solution folder. Open the designer and Code Editor windows. Change the For...Next statement in the form's Load event procedure to a Do...Loop statement. Save the solution and then start and test the application. Close the Code Editor window and then close the solution.

INTRODUCTORY

2. In this exercise, you create an application that displays the telephone extension corresponding to the name selected in a list box. The names and extensions are shown in Figure 6-52. Create a Visual Basic Windows application. Use the following names for the solution, project, and form file, respectively: Phone Solution, Phone Project, and Main Form.vb. Save the application in the VB2010\Chap06 folder. Create the interface shown in Figure 6-53. The items in the list box should be sorted; set the appropriate property. Code the application. The form's Load event procedure should add the names shown in Figure 6-52 to the list box and then select the first name in the

list. The list box's SelectedValueChanged event procedure should assign the item selected in the list box to a variable. It then should use the Select Case statement to display the telephone extension corresponding to the name. Save the solution and then start and test the application. Close the Code Editor window and then close the solution.

Name	Extension
Smith, Joe	3388
Jones, Mary	3356
Adkari, Joel	2487
Lin, Sue	1111
Li, Vicky	2222

Figure 6-52 Information for Exercise 2

Figure 6-53 Interface for Exercise 2

3. In this exercise, you modify the application from Exercise 2. Use Windows to make a copy of the Phone Solution folder. Rename the copy Modified Phone Solution. Open the Phone Solution (Phone Solution.sln) file contained in the Modified Phone Solution folder. Open the designer and Code Editor windows. Modify the list box's SelectedValueChanged event procedure so that it assigns the index of the item selected in the list box to a variable. Modify the Select Case statement so that it displays the telephone extension corresponding to the index stored in the variable. Save the solution and then start and test the application. Close the Code Editor window and then close the solution.

    INTRODUCTORY

4. In this exercise, you create an application that displays a multiplication table similar to the one shown in Figure 6-54. Open the Multiplication Solution (Multiplication Solution.sln) file contained in the VB2010\Chap06\Multiplication Solution folder. Code the application. Save the solution and then start and test the application. Close the Code Editor window and then close the solution.

    INTRODUCTORY

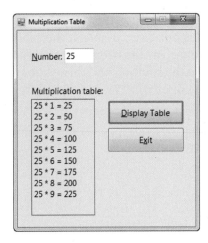

Figure 6-54   Sample run of the Multiplication Table application

INTERMEDIATE

5. Powder Skating Rink holds a weekly ice-skating competition. Competing skaters must perform a two-minute program in front of a panel of judges. The number of judges varies from week to week. At the end of a skater's program, each judge assigns a score of 0 through 10 to the skater. The manager of the ice rink wants an application that calculates and displays a skater's average score. The application also should display the skater's total score and the number of scores entered. Create a Visual Basic Windows application. Use the following names for the solution, project, and form file, respectively: Powder Solution, Powder Project, and Main Form.vb. Save the application in the VB2010\Chap06 folder. Create the interface shown in Figure 6-55. Code the application. Save the solution and then start and test the application. Close the Code Editor window and then close the solution.

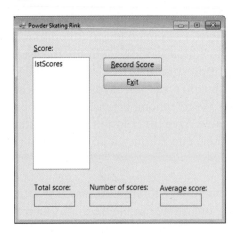

Figure 6-55   Interface for Exercise 5

INTERMEDIATE

6. In this exercise, you create an application that allows the user to enter the gender (either F or M) and GPA for any number of students. The application should calculate the average GPA for all students, the average GPA for male students, and the average GPA for female students. The list box should list GPAs from 1.0 through 4.0 in increments of .1. (For example, 1.0, 1.1, 1.2, 1.3, and so on.) Create a Visual

Basic Windows application. Use the following names for the solution, project, and form file, respectively: GPA Solution, GPA Project, and Main Form.vb. Save the application in the VB2010\Chap06 folder. Create the interface shown in Figure 6-56. Code the application. Save the solution and then start and test the application. Close the Code Editor window and then close the solution.

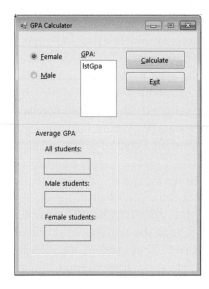

Figure 6-56   Interface for Exercise 6

7. In this exercise, you code an application that allows the user 10 chances to guess a random number generated by the computer. The random number should be an integer from 1 through 50, inclusive. Each time the user makes an incorrect guess, the application should display a message that tells the user either to guess a higher number or to guess a lower number. When the user guesses the random number, the application should display a "Congratulations!" message. However, if the user is not able to guess the random number after 10 tries, the application should display the random number in a message. Open the Random Solution (Random Solution.sln) file contained in the VB2010\Chap06\Random Solution folder. If necessary, open the designer window. Code the application. Save the solution and then start and test the application. Close the Code Editor window and then close the solution.

   ADVANCED

8. In this exercise, you code an application that displays the first 10 Fibonacci numbers: 1, 1, 2, 3, 5, 8, 13, 21, 34, and 55. Notice that, beginning with the third number in the series, each Fibonacci number is the sum of the prior two numbers. In other words, 2 is the sum of 1 plus 1, 3 is the sum of 1 plus 2, 5 is the sum of 2 plus 3, and so on. Open the Fibonacci Solution (Fibonacci Solution.sln) file contained in the VB2010\Chap06\Fibonacci Solution folder. If necessary, open the designer window. Code the application. Display the numbers in the lblNumbers control. Save the solution and then start and test the application. Close the Code Editor window and then close the solution.

   ADVANCED

ADVANCED

9. The accountant at Sonheim Manufacturing Company wants an application that calculates an asset's annual depreciation. The accountant will enter the asset's cost, useful life (in years), and salvage value (which is the value of the asset at the end of its useful life). Use a list box to display the useful life, which should range from 3 through 20 years. The application should use the double-declining balance method to calculate the annual depreciation amounts; it then should display the amounts in the interface. You can use the Financial. DDB method to calculate the depreciation. The method's syntax is **Financial.DDB**(*cost*, *salvage*, *life*, *period*). In the syntax, the *cost*, *salvage*, and *life* arguments are the asset's cost, salvage value, and useful life, respectively. The *period* argument is the period for which you want the depreciation amount calculated. The method returns the depreciation amount as a Double number. Figure 6-57 shows a sample depreciation schedule for an asset with a cost of $1000, a useful life of 4 years, and a salvage value of $100. Create a Visual Basic Windows application. Use the following names for the solution, project, and form file, respectively: Sonheim Solution, Sonheim Project, and Main Form.vb. Save the application in the VB2010\Chap06 folder. Create the interface shown in Figure 6-57. Set the txtSchedule control's Multiline and ReadOnly properties to True, and set its ScrollBars property to Vertical. Code the application. Save the solution and then start and test the application. Close the Code Editor window and then close the solution.

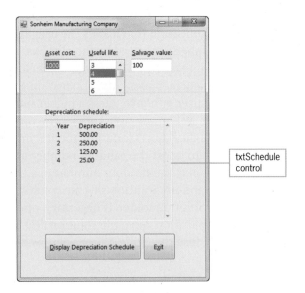

Figure 6-57   Sample run of the Sonheim Manufacturing Company application

Discovery

10. In this exercise, you learn how to create a list box that allows the user to select more than one item at a time. Open the Multi Solution (Multi Solution.sln) file contained in the VB2010\Chap06\Multi Solution folder. If necessary, open the designer window. The interface contains a list box named lstNames. The list box's Sorted and SelectionMode properties are set to True and One, respectively.

   a. Open the Code Editor window. Notice that the form's Load event procedure adds five names to the lstNames control. Code the btnSingle control's Click event procedure so that it displays, in the lblResult control, the item selected in the list box. For example, if the user clicks Debbie in the list box and then clicks the Single Selection button, the name Debbie should appear in the lblResult control. (Hint: Use the Convert.ToString method.)

   b. Save the solution and then start the application. Click Debbie in the list box, then click Ahmad, and then click Bill. Notice that, when the list box's SelectionMode property is set to One, you can select only one item at a time in the list.

   c. Click the Single Selection button. The name Bill appears in the lblResult control. Click the Exit button.

   d. Change the list box's SelectionMode property to MultiSimple. Save the solution and then start the application. Click Debbie in the list box, then click Ahmad, then click Bill, and then click Ahmad. Notice that, when the list box's SelectionMode property is set to MultiSimple, you can select more than one item at a time in the list. Also notice that you click to both select and deselect an item. (You also can use Ctrl+click and Shift+click, as well as press the Spacebar, to select and deselect items when the list box's SelectionMode property is set to MultiSimple.) Click the Exit button.

   e. Change the list box's SelectionMode property to MultiExtended. Save the solution and then start the application. Click Debbie in the list, and then click Jim. Notice that, in this case, clicking Jim deselects Debbie. When a list box's SelectionMode property is set to MultiExtended, you use Ctrl+click to select multiple items in the list. You also use Ctrl+click to deselect items in the list. Click Debbie in the list, Ctrl+click Ahmad, and then Ctrl+click Debbie.

   f. Next, click Bill in the list, and then Shift+click Jim; this selects all of the names from Bill through Jim. Click the Exit button.

g. As you know, when a list box's SelectionMode property is set to One, the item selected in the list box is stored in the SelectedItem property, and the item's index is stored in the SelectedIndex property. However, when a list box's SelectionMode property is set to either MultiSimple or MultiExtended, the items selected in the list box are stored (as strings) in the SelectedItems property, and the indices of the items are stored (as integers) in the SelectedIndices property. Code the btnMulti control's Click event procedure so that it first clears the contents of the lblResult control. The procedure should then display the selected names (which are stored in the SelectedItems property) on separate lines in the lblResult control.

h. Save the solution and then start the application. Click Ahmad in the list box, and then Shift+click Jim. Click the Multi-Selection button. The five names should appear on separate lines in the lblResult control. Close the Code Editor window and then close the solution.

11. In this exercise, you learn how to use the Items collection's Insert, Remove, RemoveAt, and Clear methods. You also learn how to use the Items collection's Count property. Open the Items Solution (Items Solution.sln) file contained in the VB2010\Chap06\Items Solution folder. If necessary, open the designer window.

a. The Items collection's Insert method allows you to add an item at a desired position in a list box during run time. The Insert method's syntax is *object*.**Items.Insert**(*position*, *item*), where *position* is the index of the *item*. Code the Insert button's Click event procedure so it adds your name as the fourth item in the list box.

b. The Items collection's Remove method allows you to remove an item from a list box during run time. The Remove method's syntax is *object*.**Items.Remove**(*item*), where *item* is the item's value. Code the Remove button's Click event procedure so it removes your name from the list box.

c. Like the Remove method, the Items collection's RemoveAt method also allows you to remove an item from a list box while an application is running. However, in the RemoveAt method, you specify the item's index rather than its value. The RemoveAt method's syntax is *object*.**Items.RemoveAt**(*index*), where *index* is the item's index. Code the Remove At button's Click event procedure so it removes the second name from the list box.

d. The Items collection's Clear method allows you to remove all items from a list box during run time. The Clear method's syntax is *object*.**Items.Clear**(). Code the Clear button's Click event procedure so it clears the items from the list box.

e. The Items collection's Count property stores the number of items contained in a list box. Code the Count button's Click event procedure so it displays (in a message box) the number of items listed in the lstNames control.

f. Save the solution and then start and test the application. Close the Code Editor window and then close the solution.

12. In this exercise, you learn how to use the String Collection Editor window to fill a list box with values. Open the ListBox Solution (ListBox Solution.sln) file contained in the VB2010\Chap06\ListBox Solution folder. If necessary, open the designer window. Open the Code Editor window. Remove the Add methods and the For...Next statement from the form's Load event procedure. Close the Code Editor window. Click the lstAnimal control on the form. Click the Items property in the Properties list and then click the ellipsis (...) button in the Settings box. The String Collection Editor window opens. Type Dog and then press Enter. Type Cat and then press Enter. Finally, type Horse and then press Enter. Click the OK button to close the dialog box. Use the String Collection Editor window to enter the following codes in the lstCode control: 100, 101, 102, 103, 104, and 105. Save the solution and then start the application. Close the solution.

 ## Swat The Bugs

13. Open the Debug Solution (Debug Solution.sln) file contained in the VB2010\Chap06\Debug Solution-Lesson C folder. If necessary, open the designer window. Open the Code Editor window and review the existing code. Start and then test the application. Be sure to include non-integers in your test data. (If you need to stop an endless loop, click Debug on the menu bar and then click Stop Debugging.) Correct any errors in the code. Save the solution and then start and test the application again. Close the Code Editor window and then close the solution.

CHAPTER 7

Sub and Function Procedures

Creating the Harvey Industries Application

In this chapter, you create an application for Jefferson Williams, the payroll manager at Harvey Industries. Currently, Mr. Williams manually calculates each employee's weekly gross pay, federal withholding tax (FWT), Social Security and Medicare (FICA) tax, and net pay. Making these calculations manually is both time-consuming and prone to mathematical errors. Mr. Williams has asked you to create an application that he can use to perform the payroll calculations both efficiently and accurately.

Previewing the Harvey Industries Application

Before you start the first lesson in this chapter, you will preview the completed application. The application is contained in the VB2010\Chap07 folder.

To preview the completed application:

START HERE

1. Use the Run dialog box to run the Harvey (Harvey.exe) file contained in the VB2010\Chap07 folder. The application's user interface appears on the screen.

2. Type **Kent Montara** in the Name box and then click the Married radio button.

3. Scroll down the Hours list box and then click **41.0** in the list. Scroll down the Rate list box and then click **13.00** in the list.

4. The interface contains a combo box that allows you to either type the number of withholding allowances or select the number from a list. Click the **list arrow** in the Allowances combo box and then click **3** in the list.

5. Click the **Calculate** button. The gross pay, taxes, and net pay appear in the interface. See Figure 7-1.

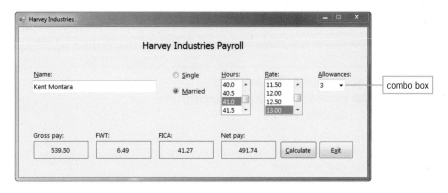

Figure 7-1 Interface showing the payroll calculations

6. Click the **Exit** button. The "Do you want to exit?" message appears in a message box. Click the **No** button. Notice that the form remains on the screen. In Lesson C, you will learn how to prevent the computer from closing a form.

7. Click the **Exit** button and then click the **Yes** button in the message box. The application ends.

The Harvey Industries application uses a combo box and a Function procedure. You will learn about Function procedures in Lesson A. Combo boxes are covered in Lesson B. You will code the Harvey Industries application in Lesson C. Be sure to complete each lesson in full and do all of the end-of-lesson questions and several exercises before continuing to the next lesson.

LESSON A

After studying Lesson A, you should be able to:

- Explain the difference between a Sub procedure and a Function procedure
- Create a procedure that receives information passed to it
- Explain the difference between passing data *by value* and passing data *by reference*
- Create a Function procedure

More About Sub Procedures

As you learned in Chapter 5, there are two types of Sub procedures in Visual Basic: event procedures and independent Sub procedures. An event procedure is a Sub procedure that is associated with a specific object and event, such as a button's Click event or a text box's TextChanged event. The computer automatically processes an event procedure when the event occurs. An independent Sub procedure, on the other hand, is a procedure that is independent of any object and event. An independent Sub procedure is processed only when called (invoked) from code. You learned how to create an independent Sub procedure in Chapter 5. You also learned how to use the Call statement to invoke a procedure. Figure 7-2 shows the syntax of an independent Sub procedure, as well as the syntax of the Call statement.

Syntax of an independent Sub procedure
Private Sub *procedureName*(**[***parameterList***]**)
       statements
End Sub

Syntax of the Call statement
Call *procedureName*(**[***argumentList***]**)

Figure 7-2 Syntax of an independent Sub procedure and the Call statement

An independent Sub procedure can contain one or more parameters in its procedure header. Each parameter has procedure scope and each stores an item of data. The data is passed to the procedure through the *argumentList* in the Call statement. The number of arguments in the Call statement's argumentList should agree with the number of parameters in the procedure's parameterList. If the parameterList contains one parameter, then the argumentList should have one argument. Similarly, a procedure that contains three parameters requires three arguments in the Call statement. (Refer to the Tip on this page for an exception to this general rule.) In addition to having the same number of arguments as parameters, the data type and position of each argument should agree with the data type and position of its corresponding parameter. For example, if the first parameter has a data type of String and the second a data type of Double, then the first argument in the Call statement should have the String data type and the second should have the Double data type. This is because, when the procedure is called,

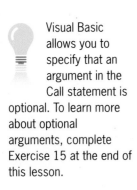

Visual Basic allows you to specify that an argument in the Call statement is optional. To learn more about optional arguments, complete Exercise 15 at the end of this lesson.

the computer stores the value of the first argument in the procedure's first parameter, the value of the second argument in the second parameter, and so on. An argument can be a literal constant, named constant, keyword, or variable; however, in most cases, it will be a variable.

Passing Variables

Every variable has both a value and a unique address that represents its location in the computer's internal memory. Visual Basic allows you to pass either a copy of the variable's value or the variable's address to the receiving procedure. Passing a copy of the variable's value is referred to as **passing by value**. Passing a variable's address is referred to as **passing by reference**. The method you choose—*by value* or *by reference*—depends on whether you want the receiving procedure to have access to the variable in memory. In other words, it depends on whether you want to allow the receiving procedure to change the variable's contents.

The internal memory of a computer is similar to a large post office. Like each post office box, each memory cell has a unique address.

Although the idea of passing information *by value* and *by reference* may sound confusing at first, it is a concept with which you already are familiar. To illustrate, assume you have a savings account at a local bank. During a conversation with your friend Melissa, you mention the amount of money you have in the account. Sharing this information with Melissa is similar to passing a variable *by value*. Knowing your account balance does not give Melissa access to your bank account. It merely provides information that she can use to compare to the balance in her savings account. The savings account example also provides an illustration of passing information *by reference*. To deposit money to or withdraw money from your account, you must provide the bank teller with your account number. The account number represents the location of your account at the bank and allows the teller to change the account balance. Giving the teller your bank account number is similar to passing a variable *by reference*. The account number allows the teller to change the contents of your bank account, similar to the way the variable's address allows the receiving procedure to change the contents of the variable.

Passing Variables by Value

To pass a variable *by value*, you include the keyword `ByVal` before the name of its corresponding parameter in the receiving procedure's parameterList. When you pass a variable *by value*, the computer passes a copy of the variable's contents to the receiving procedure. When only a copy of the contents is passed, the receiving procedure is not given access to the variable in memory. Therefore, it cannot change the value stored inside the variable. It is appropriate to pass a variable *by value* when the receiving procedure needs to *know* the variable's contents, but it does not need to *change* the contents. Unless you specify otherwise, variables in Visual Basic are automatically passed *by value*. In the next set of steps, you will finish coding the Pet Information application, which passes two variables *by value* to an independent Sub procedure.

START HERE ▶ **To code and then test the Pet Information application:**

1. If necessary, start Visual Studio 2010 or Visual Basic 2010 Express. Open the Pet Information Solution (Pet Information Solution.sln) file contained in the VB2010\Chap07\Pet Information Solution folder. If necessary, open the designer window.

2. Open the Code Editor window. Replace <your name> and <current date> in the comments with your name and the current date, respectively.

3. Locate the btnDisplay control's Click event procedure. Before the event procedure ends, it will call an independent Sub procedure named ShowMsg. The ShowMsg procedure will calculate the age of the pet on his or her next birthday and then display the pet's name and updated age in the lblMsg control. The Click event procedure will need to pass the pet's name and current age to the ShowMsg procedure. The pet's name and age are stored in the `strInputName` and `intCurrentAge` variables, respectively. You will pass both variables *by value*, because the ShowMsg procedure will not need to change their values. Click the **blank line** above the End Sub clause in the Click event procedure and then enter the following Call statement:

> Recall that it is a common practice to begin a procedure's name with a verb and to enter the name using Pascal case.

Call ShowMsg(strInputName, intCurrentAge)

4. Now you will create the ShowMsg procedure. The procedure will need to receive the two values passed to it: a string followed by an integer. You will have the computer store the first value in a parameter named `strName`, and store the second value in a parameter named `intAge`. Click the **blank line** below the `Public Class frmMain` clause and then press **Enter** to insert another blank line. Enter the following procedure header and comments. Press **Enter** twice after typing the last comment.

Private Sub ShowMsg(ByVal strName As String,
ByVal intAge As Integer)
' calculates the age on the next birthday and
' then displays the name and updated age

5. Next, you will declare a variable that the procedure can use to update the pet's age. Enter the following Dim statement:

Dim intNextAge As Integer

6. Now you will perform the appropriate calculation. Enter the following assignment statement:

intNextAge = intAge + 1

7. Finally, you will display the name and updated age in the lblMsg control. Enter the additional lines of code indicated in Figure 7-3.

```
Dim intNextAge As Integer
intNextAge = intAge + 1
lblMsg.Text = "On his or her next birthday, your pet " &
    strName & " will be " &
    intNextAge.ToString & " years old."

End Sub
```

enter these three lines of code

Figure 7-3 Additional lines of code entered in the ShowMsg procedure

8. Save the solution and then start the application. Click the **Display Message** button. Type **Chester** in the Name Entry dialog box and then press **Enter**. Type **6** in the Age Entry dialog box and then press **Enter**. The message shown in Figure 7-4 appears in the lblMsg control.

Figure 7-4 Message displayed in the interface

9. Click the **Exit** button. Close the Code Editor window and then close the solution.

Figure 7-5 shows the code entered in both the ShowMsg procedure and btnDisplay control's Click event procedure. Notice that the number, data type, and sequence of the arguments in the Call statement match the number, data type, and sequence of the corresponding parameters in the ShowMsg procedure header. Also notice that the names of the arguments do not need to be identical to the names of the corresponding parameters. In fact, to avoid confusion, it usually is better to use different names for the arguments and parameters.

```
Private Sub ShowMsg(ByVal strName As String,          parameterList
                    ByVal intAge As Integer)
    ' calculates the age on the next birthday and
    ' then displays the name and updated age

    Dim intNextAge As Integer
    intNextAge = intAge + 1
    lblMsg.Text = "On his or her next birthday, your pet " &
        strName & " will be " &
        intNextAge.ToString & " years old."

End Sub

Private Sub btnDisplay_Click(ByVal sender As Object,
ByVal e As System.EventArgs) Handles btnDisplay.Click
    ' gets the pet information and then calls a procedure to
    ' display the information

    Dim strInputName As String
    Dim strInputAge As String
    Dim intCurrentAge As Integer

    strInputName = InputBox("Pet's name:", "Name Entry")
    strInputAge = InputBox("Pet's current age (years):",
        "Age Entry")
    Integer.TryParse(strInputAge, intCurrentAge)

    Call ShowMsg(strInputName, intCurrentAge)

End Sub                       argumentList
```

Figure 7-5 ShowMsg procedure and btnDisplay Click event procedure

 The Call statement does not indicate whether a variable is being passed *by value* or *by reference*. To make that determination, you need to look at the receiving procedure's header.

399

YOU DO IT 1!

Create a Visual Basic Windows application named YouDoIt 1. Save the application in the VB2010\Chap07 folder. Add a text box, a label, and a button to the form. The button's Click event procedure should assign the text box value to a Double variable and then pass a copy of the variable's value to an independent Sub procedure named ShowDouble. The ShowDouble procedure should multiply the variable's value by two and then display the result in the label control. Code the button's Click event procedure and the ShowDouble procedure. Save the solution and then start and test the application. Close the solution.

Passing Variables by Reference

Instead of passing a copy of a variable's value to a procedure, you can pass the variable's address. In other words, you can pass the variable's location in the computer's internal memory. As you learned earlier, passing a variable's address is referred to as passing *by reference*, and it gives the receiving procedure access to the variable being passed. You pass a variable *by reference* when you want the receiving procedure to change the contents of the variable. To pass a variable *by reference* in Visual Basic, you include the keyword **ByRef** before the name of its corresponding parameter in the receiving procedure's header. The **ByRef** keyword tells the computer to pass the variable's address rather than its contents. In the next set of steps, you will finish coding the Gross Pay Calculator application, which passes three variables to an independent Sub procedure: two *by value* and one *by reference*.

START HERE ▶   **To code and then test the Gross Pay Calculator application:**

1. Open the Gross Pay Solution (Gross Pay Solution.sln) file contained in the VB2010\Chap07\Gross Pay Solution-Sub folder. If necessary, open the designer window. The application will calculate and display an employee's gross pay, which is based on the hours worked and pay rate entered by the user.

2. Open the Code Editor window. Replace <your name> and <current date> in the comments with your name and the current date, respectively.

3. Locate the btnCalc control's Click event procedure. Before displaying the gross pay, the procedure will call an independent Sub procedure named CalcGrossPay to calculate the gross pay. For the CalcGrossPay procedure to perform its task, it needs to know the number of hours worked and the pay rate; those values are stored in the `dblHoursWkd` and `dblRateOfPay` variables, respectively. The CalcGrossPay procedure will not need to change the values stored in the variables, so you will pass the variables *by value*. The CalcGrossPay procedure also needs to know where to store the gross pay after it has been calculated. To have the procedure store the gross pay in the `dblGrossPay` variable, you will need to pass it the variable's address. In other words, you will need to pass the variable *by reference*. Click the **blank line** below the `' use a Sub procedure to calculate the gross`

pay comment in the Click event procedure and then enter the following Call statement:

Call CalcGrossPay(dblHoursWkd, dblRateOfPay, dblGrossPay)

4. Now you will create the CalcGrossPay procedure. The procedure will need to receive a copy of the values stored in the **dblHoursWkd** and **dblRateOfPay** variables, as well as the address of the **dblGrossPay** variable. You will use **dblHours**, **dblRate**, and **dblGross** for the names of the parameters. Click the **blank line** below the **Public Class frmMain** clause and then press **Enter** to insert another blank line. Enter the following procedure header and comment. Press **Enter** twice after typing the comment.

> **Private Sub CalcGrossPay(ByVal dblHours As Double,**
> **ByVal dblRate As Double,**
> **ByRef dblGross As Double)**
> **' calculates the gross pay**

5. The gross pay is calculated by multiplying the hours worked by the pay rate. Enter the following assignment statement:

dblGross = dblHours * dblRate

6. However, if the employee worked more than 40 hours, he or she should receive overtime pay. In this application, overtime pay is an additional half-time for the hours worked over 40. Enter the comment and selection structure shown in Figure 7-6.

```
dblGross = dblHours * dblRate
' add overtime, if necessary ──────┐
If dblHours > 40 Then              │ ┌──────────────────────┐
    dblGross = dblGross +          │ │ enter this comment and │
        (dblHours - 40) * dblRate / 2 │ selection structure    │
End If ────────────────────────────┘ └──────────────────────┘
```

Figure 7-6   Comment and selection structure entered in the CalcGrossPay procedure

7. Save the solution and then start the application. Locate and then click **43.0** in the Hours list box and **7.75** in the Rate list box. Click the **Calculate** button. See Figure 7-7.

Figure 7-7   Gross pay shown in the interface

8. Click the **Exit** button. Close the Code Editor window and then close the solution.

401

Figure 7-8 shows the code entered in both the CalcGrossPay procedure and btnCalc control's Click event procedure. Here again, notice that the number, data type, and sequence of the arguments in the Call statement match the number, data type, and sequence of the corresponding parameters in the receiving procedure's header. Also notice that the names of the arguments are not identical to the names of their corresponding parameters. The parameterList indicates that the first two variables in the argumentList are passed *by value*, and the third variable is passed *by reference*.

The Call statement does not indicate whether a variable is being passed *by value* or *by reference*. To make that determination, you need to look at the receiving procedure's header.

```
Private Sub CalcGrossPay(ByVal dblHours As Double,
                         ByVal dblRate As Double,       parameterList
                         ByRef dblGross As Double)
    ' calculates the gross pay

    dblGross = dblHours * dblRate
    ' add overtime, if necessary
    If dblHours > 40 Then
        dblGross = dblGross +
            (dblHours - 40) * dblRate / 2
    End If
End Sub

Private Sub btnCalc_Click(ByVal sender As Object,
ByVal e As System.EventArgs) Handles btnCalc.Click
    ' calculates and displays a gross pay amount

    Dim dblHoursWkd As Double
    Dim dblRateOfPay As Double
    Dim dblGrossPay As Double

    Double.TryParse(lstHours.SelectedItem.ToString,
        dblHoursWkd)
    Double.TryParse(lstRate.SelectedItem.ToString,
        dblRateOfPay)

    ' use a Sub procedure to calculate the gross pay
    Call CalcGrossPay(dblHoursWkd, dblRateOfPay, dblGrossPay)

                        passed by value        passed by reference

    lblGross.Text = dblGrossPay.ToString("C2")
End Sub
```

Figure 7-8   CalcGrossPay procedure and btnCalc control's Click event procedure

Desk-checking the procedures shown in Figure 7-8 will help clarify the difference between passing *by value* and passing *by reference*. When the user clicks the Calculate button after selecting 43.0 and 7.75 as the hours and rate, respectively, the Dim statements in the button's Click event procedure create and initialize three Double variables. Next, the two TryParse methods store the hours and pay rate in the `dblHoursWkd` and `dblRateOfPay` variables. Figure 7-9 shows the contents of the variables before the Call statement is processed.

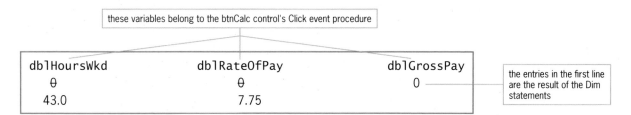

Figure 7-9   Desk-check table before the Call statement is processed

The computer processes the Call statement next. The statement invokes the CalcGrossPay procedure, passing it three arguments. At this point, the computer temporarily leaves the Click event procedure to process the code contained in the CalcGrossPay procedure; the procedure header is processed first. The **ByVal** keyword indicates that the first two parameters are receiving values from the Call statement—in this case, copies of the numbers stored in the **dblHoursWkd** and **dblRateOfPay** variables. As a result, the computer creates the **dblHours** and **dblRate** variables listed in the parameterList, and stores the numbers 43.0 and 7.75, respectively, in the variables. The **ByRef** keyword indicates that the third parameter is receiving the address of a variable. When you pass a variable's address to a procedure, the computer uses the address to locate the variable in its internal memory. It then assigns the parameter name to the memory location. In this case, the computer locates the **dblGrossPay** variable in memory and assigns the name **dblGross** to it. At this point, the memory location has two names: one assigned by the btnCalc control's Click event procedure and the other assigned by the CalcGrossPay procedure, as indicated in Figure 7-10. Notice that two of the variables in the figure belong strictly to the Click event procedure, and two belong strictly to the CalcGrossPay procedure. One memory location, however, belongs to both procedures. Although both procedures can access the memory location, each procedure uses a different name to do so. The Click event procedure uses the name **dblGrossPay**, whereas the CalcGrossPay procedure uses the name **dblGross**.

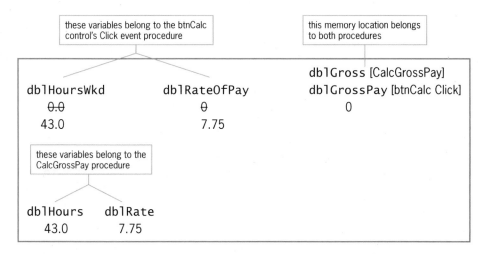

Figure 7-10   Desk-check table after the Call statement and CalcGrossPay procedure header are processed

 Although the **dblGrossPay** and **dblGross** names refer to the same location in memory, the **dblGrossPay** name is recognized only within the btnCalc control's Click event procedure, and the **dblGross** name is recognized only within the CalcGrossPay procedure.

403

After processing the CalcGrossPay procedure header, the computer processes the code contained in the procedure. The first statement calculates the gross pay by multiplying the contents of the **dblHours** variable (43.0) by the contents of the **dblRate** variable (7.75), and then assigns the result (333.25) to the **dblGross** variable. Figure 7-11 shows the desk-check table after the calculation statement is processed. Notice that when the value in the **dblGross** variable changes, the value in the **dblGrossPay** variable also changes. This happens because the names **dblGross** and **dblGrossPay** refer to the same location in the computer's internal memory.

changing the value in the dblGross variable also changes the value in the dblGrossPay variable

dblHoursWkd	dblRateOfPay	dblGross [CalcGrossPay] dblGrossPay [btnCalc Click]
~~0.0~~	~~0~~	~~0~~
43.0	7.75	333.25

dblHours	dblRate
43.0	7.75

Figure 7-11   Desk-check table after the first statement in the CalcGrossPay procedure is processed

The **dblHours** variable contains a value that is greater than 40, so the statement in the selection structure's true path calculates the overtime pay (11.63) and adds it to the regular pay (333.25). The statement assigns the result (344.88) to the **dblGross** variable. Figure 7-12 shows the desk-check table after the statement is processed.

dblHoursWkd	dblRateOfPay	dblGross [CalcGrossPay] dblGrossPay [btnCalc Click]
~~0.0~~	~~0~~	~~0~~
43.0	7.75	~~333.25~~
		344.88

dblHours	dblRate
43.0	7.75

Figure 7-12   Desk-check table after the statement in the selection structure's true path is processed

The CalcGrossPay procedure's End Sub clause is processed next and ends the procedure. At this point, the computer removes the **dblHours** and **dblRate** variables from memory. It also removes the **dblGross** name from the appropriate location in memory, as indicated in Figure 7-13. Notice that the **dblGrossPay** memory location now has only one name: the name assigned to it by the btnCalc control's Click event procedure.

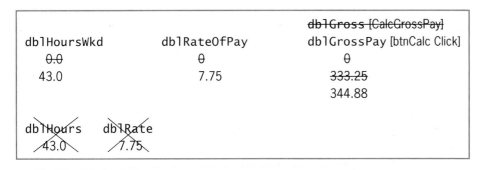

Figure 7-13   Desk-check table after the CalcGrossPay procedure ends

After the CalcGrossPay procedure ends, the computer returns to the line of code below the Call statement in the btnCalc control's Click event procedure. In this case, it returns to the statement that displays the gross pay in the lblGross control. Finally, the computer processes the Click event procedure's End Sub clause. When the Click event procedure ends, the computer removes the procedure's variables (`dblHoursWkd`, `dblRateOfPay`, and `dblGrossPay`) from memory.

YOU DO IT 2!

Create a Visual Basic Windows application named YouDoIt 2. Save the application in the VB2010\Chap07 folder. Add a text box, a label, and a button to the form. The button's Click event procedure should assign the text box value to an Integer variable and then pass a copy of the variable's value, along with the address of a different Integer variable, to an independent Sub procedure named CalcDouble. The CalcDouble procedure should multiply the first Integer variable's value by two and then store the result in the second Integer variable. The button's Click event procedure should display the contents of the second Integer variable in the label control. Code the button's Click event procedure and the CalcDouble procedure. Save the solution and then start and test the application. Close the solution.

Function Procedures

In addition to creating Sub procedures in Visual Basic, you also can create Function procedures. The difference between both types of procedures is that a **Function procedure** returns a value after performing its assigned task, whereas a Sub procedure does not return a value. Function procedures are referred to more simply as **functions**. Figure 7-14 shows the syntax for creating a function in Visual Basic. The header and footer in a function are almost identical to the header and footer in a Sub procedure, except the function's header and footer contain the `Function` keyword rather than the `Sub` keyword. Also different from a Sub procedure header, a function's header includes the `As` *dataType* section, which specifies the data type of the value returned by the function. As is true with a Sub procedure, a function can receive information either *by value* or *by reference*. The information it receives is listed in the parameterList in the header. Between the function's header and footer, you enter the instructions to process when the function is invoked. In most cases, the **Return statement** is the last statement within a function. The statement's syntax is `Return` *expression*, where *expression* represents the one and only value that will be returned to the statement invoking the function. The data type of the *expression* must agree with the data type specified in the `As` *dataType* section of the header.

In addition to the syntax, Figure 7-14 also includes two examples of a function, as well as the steps you follow to enter a function in the Code Editor window. As with Sub procedures, you can enter your functions above the first event procedure, below the last event procedure, or immediately above or below the procedure from which they are invoked. In this book, you usually will enter the functions above the first event procedure. Like Sub procedure names, function names are entered using Pascal case and typically begin with a verb. The name should indicate the task the function performs. For example, a good name for a function that returns a new price is GetNewPrice.

> Using Pascal case, you capitalize the first letter in the function name and the first letter of each subsequent word in the name.

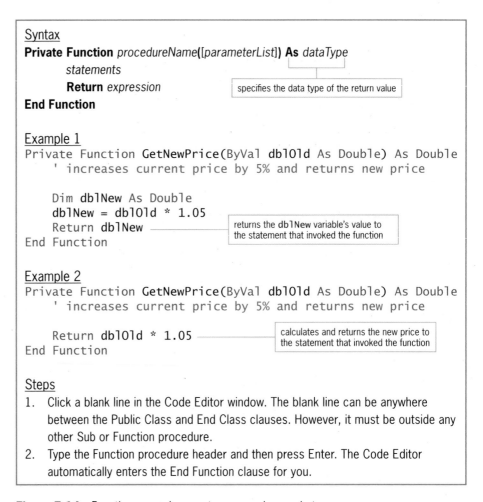

Syntax
Private Function *procedureName*(**[***parameterList***]**) **As** *dataType*
    statements
      Return *expression* ——— specifies the data type of the return value
End Function

Example 1
```
Private Function GetNewPrice(ByVal dblOld As Double) As Double
     ' increases current price by 5% and returns new price

    Dim dblNew As Double
    dblNew = dblOld * 1.05
    Return dblNew
End Function
```
returns the dblNew variable's value to the statement that invoked the function

Example 2
```
Private Function GetNewPrice(ByVal dblOld As Double) As Double
     ' increases current price by 5% and returns new price

    Return dblOld * 1.05
End Function
```
calculates and returns the new price to the statement that invoked the function

Steps
1. Click a blank line in the Code Editor window. The blank line can be anywhere between the Public Class and End Class clauses. However, it must be outside any other Sub or Function procedure.
2. Type the Function procedure header and then press Enter. The Code Editor automatically enters the End Function clause for you.

Figure 7-14   Function procedure syntax, examples, and steps

You can invoke a function from one or more places in an application's code. You invoke a function that you create in exactly the same way as you invoke one of Visual Basic's built-in functions, such as the InputBox function. You do this by including the function's name and arguments (if any) in a statement. The number, data type, and position of the arguments should agree with the number, data type, and position of the function's parameters. In most cases, the statement that invokes a function assigns the function's return value to a variable. However, it also may use the return value in a calculation or simply display the return value. Figure 7-15 shows examples of invoking the GetNewPrice function from Figure 7-14. The `GetNewPrice(dblCurrentPrice)` entry in each example invokes the function, passing it the value stored in the `dblCurrentPrice` variable.

Example 1 – assigning the return value to a variable
`dblNewPrice = GetNewPrice(dblCurrentPrice)`

Example 2 – using the return value in a calculation
`dblTotalDue = intQuantity * GetNewPrice(dblCurrentPrice)`
the assignment statement multiplies the function's return value by the value in the `intQuantity` variable and then assigns the result to the `dblTotalDue` variable

Example 3 – displaying the return value
`lblNewPrice.Text = GetNewPrice(dblCurrentPrice).ToString`

Figure 7-15 Examples of invoking the GetNewPrice function

In the next set of steps, you will modify the Gross Pay Calculator application that you completed in the previous section. The modified application will use a function (rather than a Sub procedure) to calculate and return the gross pay.

To modify the Gross Pay Calculator application to use a function:

START HERE

1. Use Windows to make a copy of the Gross Pay Solution-Sub folder. Rename the copy Gross Pay Solution-Function. Open the Gross Pay Solution (Gross Pay Solution.sln) file contained in the Gross Pay Solution-Function folder. Open the designer window.

2. Open the Code Editor window and then locate the btnCalc control's Click event procedure. Change the comment above the Call statement to the following:

   ' use a function to calculate the gross pay

3. The Call statement will need to be replaced with a statement that invokes the CalcGrossPay function (rather than the CalcGrossPay Sub procedure). The statement will assign the function's return value, which is the gross pay, to the **dblGrossPay** variable. Like the Sub procedure, the function will need the statement to pass the values stored in the **dblHoursWkd** and **dblRateOfPay** variables, because those values are needed to calculate the gross pay. However, the function will not need the statement to pass the address of the **dblGrossPay** variable, because the statement itself will store the gross pay in the variable. Change the Call statement to the following assignment statement and then click the **blank line** below the statement:

   dblGrossPay = CalcGrossPay(dblHoursWkd, dblRateOfPay)

4. Now you will change the CalcGrossPay Sub procedure to a function. Locate the CalcGrossPay Sub procedure in the Code Editor window. First, change the **Sub** keyword in the procedure header to **Function** and then click the **blank line** above the procedure. The Code Editor automatically changes the procedure's footer to End Function.

5. Next, delete the third line in the function header. The third line contains ByRef dblGross As Double). Now replace the comma in the second line of the function header with **)** (a closing parenthesis).

6. Recall that the data type of the function's return value is specified at the end of the function header. The insertion point should be located after the closing parenthesis in the function header. Press the **Spacebar**, type **As Double**, and then click the **blank line** below the first comment in the procedure.

7. Now that the function header no longer contains ByRef dblGross As Double, which creates the dblGross variable, a jagged line appears below each occurrence of dblGross in the function. The jagged line indicates that the variable has not been declared. In order to use the dblGross variable, the function will need to declare it in a Dim statement. The insertion point should be located below the ' calculates the gross pay comment. Press **Enter** to insert another blank line and then enter the following Dim statement:

Dim dblGross As Double

8. Finally, you need to tell the function to return the gross pay to the statement that invoked the function. Click **after the letter f** in the End If clause and then press **Enter**. Enter the following Return statement:

Return dblGross

9. Save the solution and then start the application. Locate and then click **43.0** in the Hours list box and **7.75** in the Rate list box. Click the **Calculate** button. The gross pay is $344.88, as shown earlier in Figure 7-7.

10. Click the **Exit** button. Close the Code Editor window and then close the solution.

Figure 7-16 shows the code entered in the CalcGrossPay function and btnCalc control's Click event procedure. The modified lines of code are shaded in the figure.

```
Private Function CalcGrossPay(ByVal dblHours As Double,
                        ByVal dblRate As Double) As Double
    ' calculates the gross pay

    Dim dblGross As Double

    dblGross = dblHours * dblRate
    ' add overtime, if necessary
```

Figure 7-16 CalcGrossPay function and btnCalc control's Click event procedure *(continues)*

(continued)

```
    If dblHours > 40 Then
        dblGross = dblGross +
            (dblHours - 40) * dblRate / 2
    End If
    Return dblGross

End Function

Private Sub btnCalc_Click(ByVal sender As Object,
ByVal e As System.EventArgs) Handles btnCalc.Click
    ' calculates and displays a gross pay amount

    Dim dblHoursWkd As Double
    Dim dblRateOfPay As Double
    Dim dblGrossPay As Double

    Double.TryParse(lstHours.SelectedItem.ToString, dblHoursWkd)
    Double.TryParse(lstRate.SelectedItem.ToString, dblRateOfPay)

    ' use a function to calculate the gross pay
    dblGrossPay = CalcGrossPay(dblHoursWkd, dblRateOfPay)

    lblGross.Text = dblGrossPay.ToString("C2")
End Sub
```

> invokes the function and assigns the return value to the dblGrossPay variable

Figure 7-16   CalcGrossPay function and btnCalc control's Click event procedure

YOU DO IT 3!

Create a Visual Basic Windows application named YouDoIt 3. Save the application in the VB2010\Chap07 folder. Add a text box, a label, and a button to the form. The button's Click event procedure should assign the text box value to an Integer variable and then pass a copy of the variable's value to a function named GetBonus. The GetBonus function should multiply the integer it receives by 10% and then return the result. The button's Click event procedure should display the function's return value in the label control. Code the GetBonus function and the button's Click event procedure. Save the solution and then start and test the application. Close the solution.

Lesson A Summary

- To create an independent Sub procedure:

  Refer to the syntax shown in Figure 7-2.

- To call an independent Sub procedure:

  Use the syntax **Call** *procedureName*(*[argumentList]*).

- To pass information to a Sub or Function procedure:

  Include the information in the Call statement's argumentList. In the parameterList in the procedure header, include the names of memory locations that will store the information. The number, data type, and sequence of the arguments in the argumentList should agree with the number, data type, and sequence of the parameters in the parameterList.

- To pass a variable *by value* to a procedure:

  Include the ByVal keyword before the parameter name in the procedure header's parameterList. Because only a copy of the value stored in the variable is passed, the receiving procedure cannot access the variable.

- To pass a variable *by reference*:

  Include the ByRef keyword before the parameter name in the procedure header's parameterList. Because the address of the variable is passed, the receiving procedure can change the contents of the variable.

- To create a Function procedure:

  Refer to the syntax and steps shown in Figure 7-14.

Lesson A Key Terms

Function procedure—a procedure that returns a value after performing its assigned task

Functions—another name for Function procedures

Passing by reference—the process of passing a variable's address to a procedure so that the value in the variable can be changed

Passing by value—the process of passing a copy of a variable's value to a procedure

Return statement—the Visual Basic statement that returns a function's value to the statement that invoked the function

Lesson A Review Questions

1. Which of the following is false?

   a. A function can return one or more values to the statement that invoked it.

   b. A procedure can accept one or more items of data passed to it.

   c. The parameterList in a procedure header is optional.

   d. At times, a memory location inside the computer's internal memory may have more than one name.

2. The items listed in the Call statement are referred to as _____.

    a. arguments

    b. parameters

    c. passers

    d. none of the above

3. Each memory location listed in the parameterList in the procedure header is referred to as _____.

    a. an address

    b. a constraint

    c. a parameter

    d. a value

4. To determine whether a variable is being passed to a procedure *by value* or *by reference*, you will need to examine _____.

    a. the Call statement

    b. the procedure header

    c. the statements entered in the procedure

    d. either a or b

5. Which of the following statements invokes the GetArea Sub procedure, passing it two variables *by value*?

    a. `Call GetArea(dblLength, dblWidth)`

    b. `Call GetArea(ByVal dblLength, ByVal dblWidth)`

    c. `Invoke GetArea(dblLength, dblWidth)`

    d. `GetArea(dblLength, dblWidth) As Double`

6. Which of the following is a valid header for a procedure that receives only a copy of the value stored in a String variable?

    a. `Private Sub DisplayName(ByContents strName As String)`

    b. `Private Sub DisplayName(ByValue strName As String)`

    c. `Private Sub DisplayName ByVal(strName As String)`

    d. none of the above

7. Which of the following is a valid header for a procedure that receives an integer followed by a number with a decimal place?

   a. `Private Sub GetFee(intBase As Integer, decRate As Decimal)`

   b. `Private Sub GetFee(ByRef intBase As Integer, ByRef decRate As Decimal)`

   c. `Private Sub GetFee(ByVal intBase As Integer, ByVal decRate As Decimal)`

   d. none of the above

8. Which of the following is false?

   a. The sequence of the arguments listed in the Call statement should agree with the sequence of the parameters listed in the receiving procedure's header.

   b. The data type of each argument in the Call statement should match the data type of its corresponding parameter in the procedure header.

   c. The name of each argument in the Call statement should be identical to the name of its corresponding parameter in the procedure header.

   d. When you pass information to a procedure *by value*, the procedure stores a copy of each value it receives in a separate memory location.

9. Which of the following instructs a function to return the contents of the **decStateTax** variable?

   a. `Return decStateTax`

   b. `Return ByVal decStateTax`

   c. `Send decStateTax`

   d. `SendBack decStateTax`

10. Which of the following is a valid header for a procedure that receives an integer followed by the address of a Decimal variable?

   a. `Private Sub GetFee(ByVal intBase As Integer, ByAdd decRate As Decimal)`

   b. `Private Sub GetFee(intBase As Integer, decRate As Decimal)`

   c. `Private Sub GetFee(ByVal intBase As Integer, ByRef decRate As Decimal)`

   d. none of the above

11. Which of the following is a valid header for a procedure that is passed the number 15?

    a. `Private Function GetTax(ByVal intRate As Integer)`
       `As Decimal`

    b. `Private Function GetTax(ByAdd intRate As Integer)`
       `As Decimal`

    c. `Private Sub CalcTax(ByVal intRate As Integer)`

    d. both a and c

12. If the statement `Call CalcNet(decNetPay)` passes the variable's address, the variable is said to be passed _____.

    a. *by address*

    b. *by content*

    c. *by reference*

    d. *by value*

13. Which of the following is false?

    a. When you pass a variable *by reference*, the receiving procedure can change its contents.

    b. To pass a variable *by reference* in Visual Basic, you include the `ByRef` keyword before the variable's name in the Call statement.

    c. When you pass a variable *by value*, the receiving procedure creates a procedure-level variable that it uses to store a copy of the value passed to it.

    d. Unless you specify otherwise, a variable in Visual Basic will be passed *by value*.

14. A Sub procedure named GetEndingInventory is passed four Integer variables named `intBegin`, `intSales`, `intPurchases`, and `intEnding`. The procedure should calculate the ending inventory using the beginning inventory, sales, and purchase amounts passed to the procedure. The result should be stored in the `intEnding` variable. Which of the following procedure headers is correct?

    a. `Private Sub GetEndingInventory(ByVal intB As`
       `Integer, ByVal intS As Integer, ByVal intP As`
       `Integer, ByRef intFinal As Integer)`

    b. `Private Sub GetEndingInventory(ByVal intB As`
       `Integer, ByVal intS As Integer, ByVal intP As`
       `Integer, ByVal intFinal As Integer)`

    c. `Private Sub GetEndingInventory(ByRef intB As`
       `Integer, ByRef intS As Integer, ByRef intP As`
       `Integer, ByVal intFinal As Integer)`

    d. `Private Sub GetEndingInventory(ByRef intB As`
       `Integer, ByRef intS As Integer, ByRef intP As`
       `Integer, ByRef intFinal As Integer)`

15. Which of the following statements should you use to call the GetEndingInventory procedure from Review Question 14?

    a. `Call GetEndingInventory(intBegin, intSales, intPurchases, intEnding)`

    b. `Call GetEndingInventory(ByVal intBegin, ByVal intSales, ByVal intPurchases, ByRef intEnding)`

    c. `Call GetEndingInventory(ByRef intBegin, ByRef intSales, ByRef intPurchases, ByRef intEnding)`

    d. `Call GetEndingInventory(ByVal intBegin, ByVal intSales, ByVal intPurchases, ByVal intEnding)`

16. The memory locations listed in the parameterList in a procedure header have procedure scope and are removed from the computer's internal memory when the procedure ends.

    a. True

    b. False

17. Which of the following statements invokes the GetDiscount function, passing it the contents of two Decimal variables named **decSales** and **decRate**? The statement should assign the function's return value to the **decDiscount** variable.

    a. `decDiscount = Call GetDiscount(decSales, decRate)`

    b. `Call GetDiscount(decSales, decRate, decDiscount)`

    c. `decDiscount = GetDiscount(decSales, decRate)`

    d. none of the above

18. Explain the difference between a Sub procedure and a Function procedure.

19. Explain the difference between passing a variable *by value* and passing it *by reference*.

20. Explain the difference between invoking a Sub procedure and invoking a function.

Lesson A Exercises

INTRODUCTORY

1. Write the code for a Sub procedure that receives an integer passed to it. The procedure should divide the integer by 2 and then display the result in the lblNum control. Name the procedure DivideByTwo. Then write a statement to invoke the procedure, passing it the number 87.

INTRODUCTORY

2. Write the code for a Sub procedure that prompts the user to enter the name of a city and then stores the user's response in the String variable whose address is passed to the procedure. Name the procedure GetCity and use **strName** as the parameter's name. Then write a statement to invoke the procedure, passing it the **strCity** variable.

3. Write the code for a function that prompts the user to enter the name of a state and then returns the user's response. Name the function GetState. Then write a statement to invoke the GetState function. Display the function's return value in a message box.

4. Write the code for a Sub procedure that receives three Double variables: the first two *by value* and the last one *by reference*. The procedure should divide the first variable by the second variable and then store the result in the third variable. Name the procedure CalcQuotient.

5. Write the code for a function that receives a copy of the value stored in an Integer variable. The function should divide the value by 2 and then return the result, which may contain a decimal place. Name the function GetQuotient. Then write an appropriate statement to invoke the function, passing it the `intNumber` variable. Assign the function's return value to the `dblAnswer` variable.

6. In this exercise, you experiment with passing variables *by value* and *by reference*. Open the Passing Solution (Passing Solution.sln) file contained in the VB2010\Chap07\Passing Solution folder. If necessary, open the designer window.

   a. Open the Code Editor window and review the existing code. Notice that the `strMyName` variable is passed *by value* to the GetName procedure. Start the application. Click the Display Name button. When prompted to enter a name, type your name and press Enter. Explain why the btnDisplay control's Click event procedure does not display your name in the lblName control. Stop the application.

   b. Modify the btnDisplay control's Click event procedure so that it passes the `strMyName` variable *by reference* to the GetName procedure. Save the solution and then start the application. Click the Display Name button. When prompted to enter a name, type your name and press Enter. This time, your name appears in the lblName control. Explain why the btnDisplay control's Click event procedure now works correctly. Close the Code Editor window and then close the solution.

7. Write the Visual Basic code for a function that receives a copy of the contents of four Integer variables. The function should calculate the average of the four integers and then return the result, which may contain a decimal place. Name the function CalcAverage. Then write a statement to invoke the function, passing it the `intNum1`, `intNum2`, `intNum3`, and `intNum4` variables. Assign the function's return value to the `dblAverage` variable.

8. Write the code for a Sub procedure that receives four Integer variables: the first two *by value* and the last two *by reference*. The procedure should calculate the sum of and the difference between the two variables passed *by value*, and then store the results in the variables passed *by reference*. When calculating the difference, subtract the

contents of the second variable from the contents of the first variable. Name the procedure GetSumAndDiff. Then write an appropriate statement to invoke the procedure, passing it the `intFirst`, `intSecond`, `intSum`, and `intDifference` variables.

INTERMEDIATE   9. Open the Temperature Solution (Temperature Solution.sln) file contained in the VB2010\Chap07\Temperature Solution-Sub folder. If necessary, open the designer window. Code the application so that it uses two independent Sub procedures: one to convert a temperature from Fahrenheit to Celsius, and the other to convert a temperature from Celsius to Fahrenheit. Save the solution and then start and test the application. Close the Code Editor window and then close the solution.

INTERMEDIATE   10. Open the Temperature Solution (Temperature Solution.sln) file contained in the VB2010\Chap07\Temperature Solution-Function folder. If necessary, open the designer window. Code the application so that it uses two functions: one to convert a temperature from Fahrenheit to Celsius, and the other to convert a temperature from Celsius to Fahrenheit. Save the solution and then start and test the application. Close the Code Editor window and then close the solution.

INTERMEDIATE   11. The owner of Pine Lodge wants an application that calculates an employee's new hourly pay, given the employee's current hourly pay and raise rate. Create a Visual Basic Windows application. Use the following names for the solution, project, and form file, respectively: Pine Lodge Solution, Pine Lodge Project, and Main Form.vb. Save the application in the VB2010\Chap07 folder. Create the interface shown in Figure 7-17. The lstPay control should display amounts from 7.00 through 12.00 in increments of .50. The lstRate control should display rates from 2 through 11 in increments of 1. The label that displays the new pay should be cleared when a change is made to either list box. The Calculate button's Click event procedure should use a function to calculate and return the new pay. Code the application. Save the solution and then start the application. Calculate the new pay based on a current pay of 8.00 and a raise rate of 5. The answer should be $8.40. Test the application using your own data. Close the Code Editor window and then close the solution.

Figure 7-17   Interface for Exercise 11

12. In this exercise, you modify the application from Exercise 11. Use Windows to make a copy of the Pine Lodge Solution folder. Rename the copy Modified Pine Lodge Solution. Open the Pine Lodge Solution (Pine Lodge Solution.sln) file contained in the Modified Pine Lodge Solution folder. Open the designer and Code Editor windows. Change the function to a Sub procedure and then make the necessary modifications to the Calculate button's Click event procedure. Save the solution and then start and test the application. Close the Code Editor window and then close the solution.

13. Create a Visual Basic Windows application. Use the following names for the solution, project, and form file, respectively: Rainfall Solution, Rainfall Project, and Main Form.vb. Save the application in the VB2010\Chap07 folder. Create the interface shown in Figure 7-18. The user will enter a monthly rainfall amount and then click the Calculate button. The button's Click event procedure should calculate and display both the total and average of the rainfall amounts entered so far. The event procedure should use a Sub procedure named CalcTotalAndAverage to make the necessary calculations. Code the application. Save the solution and then start and test the application. Close the Code Editor window and then close the solution.

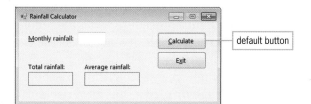

Figure 7-18 Interface for Exercise 13

14. In this exercise, you modify the Rainfall Calculator application from Exercise 13. Use Windows to make a copy of the Rainfall Solution folder. Rename the copy Modified Rainfall Solution. Open the Rainfall Solution (Rainfall Solution.sln) file contained in the Modified Rainfall Solution folder. Open the designer and Code Editor windows. Modify the code to use two Function procedures (rather than one Sub procedure) to calculate the total and average rainfall amounts. Save the solution and then start and test the application. Close the Code Editor window and then close the solution.

Discovery

15. In this exercise, you learn how to specify that one or more arguments are optional in a Call statement. Open the Optional Solution (Optional Solution.sln) file contained in the VB2010\Chap07\ Optional Solution folder. If necessary, open the designer window.

   a. Open the Code Editor window and review the existing code. The btnCalc control's Click event procedure contains two Call statements. The first Call statement passes three variables to the CalcBonus procedure. The second call statement, however, passes only two variables to the procedure. (Do not be concerned about the jagged line that appears below the second Call statement.) Notice that the `dblRate` variable is omitted from the second Call statement. You indicate that the `dblRate` variable is optional in the Call statement by including the keyword `Optional` before the variable's corresponding parameter in the procedure header; you enter the `Optional` keyword before the `ByVal` keyword. You also assign a default value that the procedure will use for the missing parameter when the procedure is called. You assign the default value by entering the assignment operator and the default value after the corresponding parameter in the procedure header. In this case, you will assign the number .1 as the default value for the `dblRate` variable. (Optional parameters must be listed at the end of the procedure header.)

b. Change the `ByVal dblBonusRate As Double` in the procedure header appropriately. Save the solution and then start the application. Enter a and 1000 in the Code and Sales boxes, respectively. Click the Calculate button. Type .05 and press Enter. The `Call CalcBonus(dblSales, dblBonus, dbl-Rate)` statement calls the CalcBonus procedure, passing it the number 1000, the address of the `dblBonus` variable, and the number .05. The CalcBonus procedure stores the number 1000 in the `dblTotalSales` variable. It also assigns the name `dblBonusAmount` to the `dblBonus` variable and stores the number .05 in the `dblBonusRate` variable. The procedure then multiplies the contents of the `dblTotalSales` variable (1000) by the contents of the `dblBonusRate` variable (.05), assigning the result (50) to the `dblBonusAmount` variable. The `lblBonus.Text = dblBonus.ToString("C2")` statement then displays $50.00 in the lblBonus control.

c. Now enter b and 2000 in the Code and Sales boxes, respectively. Click the Calculate button. The `Call CalcBonus(dblSales, dblBonus)` statement calls the CalcBonus procedure, passing it the number 2000 and the address of the `dblBonus` variable. The CalcBonus procedure stores the number 2000 in the `dblTotalSales` variable and assigns the name `dblBonusAmount` to the `dblBonus` variable. Because the Call statement did not supply a value for the `dblBonusRate` parameter, the default value (.1) is assigned to the variable. The procedure then multiplies the contents of the `dblTotalSales` variable (2000) by the contents of the `dblBonusRate` variable (.1), assigning the result (200) to the `dblBonusAmount` variable. The `lblBonus.Text = dblBonus.ToString("C2")` statement then displays $200.00 in the lblBonus control. Close the Code Editor window and then close the solution.

▌ LESSON B

After studying Lesson B, you should be able to:

- Include a combo box in an interface
- Add items to a combo box
- Select a combo box item from code
- Determine the item either selected or entered in a combo box
- Code a combo box's TextChanged event procedure

Including a Combo Box in an Interface

In many interfaces, combo boxes are used in place of list boxes. You use the ComboBox tool in the toolbox to add a combo box to an interface. A **combo box** is similar to a list box in that it allows the user to select from a list of choices. However, unlike a list box, the full list of choices in a combo box can be hidden, allowing you to save space on the form. Also unlike a list box, a combo box contains a text field. Depending on the style of the combo box, the text field may or may not be editable by the user.

Three styles of combo boxes are available in Visual Basic. The style is controlled by the combo box's **DropDownStyle property**, which can be set to Simple, DropDown (the default), or DropDownList. Each style of combo box contains a text portion and a list portion. When the DropDownStyle property is set to either Simple or DropDown, the text portion of the combo box is editable. However, in a Simple combo box the list portion is always displayed, while in a DropDown combo box the list portion appears only when the user clicks the combo box's list arrow. When the DropDownStyle property is set to the third style, DropDownList, the text portion of the combo box is not editable and the user must click the combo box's list arrow to display the list of choices.

Figure 7-19 shows an example of each combo box style. You should use a label control to provide keyboard access to the combo box, as shown in the figure. For the access key to work correctly, you must set the label's TabIndex property to a value that is one less than the combo box's TabIndex value. Like the items in a list box, the items in the list portion of a combo box are either arranged by use, with the most used entries listed first, or sorted in ascending order. To sort the items in the list portion of a combo box, you set the combo box's Sorted property to True.

You can use the Items collection's Count property to determine the number of items in the list portion of a combo box, like this: `cboName.Items.Count`.

Like the first item in a list box, the first item in a combo box has an index of 0.

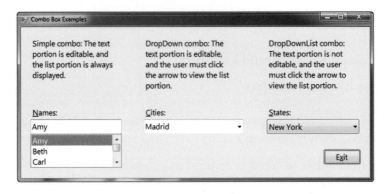

Figure 7-19   Examples of the combo box styles

Figure 7-20 shows the code used to fill the combo boxes in Figure 7-19 with values. As you do with a list box, you use the Items collection's Add method to add an item to a combo box. You can use any of the following properties to select a default item, which will appear in the text portion of the combo box: SelectedIndex, SelectedItem, or Text. If no item is selected, the SelectedItem and Text properties contain the empty string, and the SelectedIndex property contains –1 (negative one).

```
Private Sub frmMain_Load(ByVal sender As Object,
ByVal e As System.EventArgs) Handles Me.Load
    ' fills the combo boxes with values

    cboName.Items.Add("Amy")
    cboName.Items.Add("Beth")
    cboName.Items.Add("Carl")
    cboName.Items.Add("Dan")
    cboName.Items.Add("Jan")
    cboName.SelectedIndex = 0

    cboCity.Items.Add("London")
    cboCity.Items.Add("Madrid")
    cboCity.Items.Add("Paris")
    cboCity.SelectedItem = "Madrid"

    cboState.Items.Add("Alabama")
    cboState.Items.Add("Maine")
    cboState.Items.Add("New York")
    cboState.Items.Add("South Dakota")
    cboState.Text = "New York"
End Sub
```

you can use any of these three properties to select the default item in a combo box

Figure 7-20   Code associated with the combo boxes in Figure 7-19

GUI DESIGN TIP   Combo Box Standards

- Use a label control to provide keyboard access to a combo box. Set the label's TabIndex property to a value that is one less than the combo box's TabIndex value.

- Combo box items are either arranged by use, with the most used entries appearing first in the list, or sorted in ascending order.

It is easy to confuse a combo box's SelectedItem property with its Text property. The SelectedItem property contains the value of the item selected in the list portion of the combo box, whereas the Text property contains the value that appears in the text portion. A value can appear in the text portion as a result of the user either selecting an item in the list portion of the control or typing an entry in the text portion itself. It also can appear in the text portion as a result of a statement that assigns a value to the control's SelectedIndex, SelectedItem, or Text property. If the combo box is a DropDownList style, where the text portion is not editable, you can use the SelectedItem and Text properties interchangeably. However, if the combo box is either a Simple or DropDown style, where the user can type an entry in the text portion, you should use the Text property; this is because the Text property contains the value either selected or entered by the user. When the value in the text portion of a combo box changes, the combo box's TextChanged event occurs. In the next set of steps, you will modify one of the Gross Pay Calculator applications from Lesson A. The modified application will use a combo box rather than a list box.

To modify one of the Gross Pay Calculator applications from Lesson A:

START HERE

1. Use Windows to make a copy of the Gross Pay Solution-Function folder from Lesson A. Rename the copy Modified Gross Pay Solution-Function.

2. If necessary, start Visual Studio 2010 or Visual Basic 2010 Express. Open the Gross Pay Solution (Gross Pay Solution.sln) file contained in the Modified Gross Pay Solution-Function folder. Open the designer window.

3. First, you will replace the Rate list box with a DropDownList combo box. Unlock the controls on the form. Click the **lstRate** control on the form and then press **Delete**. Click the **ComboBox** tool in the toolbox and then drag the mouse pointer to the form. Position the mouse pointer below the Rate label and then release the mouse button. Change the combo box's DropDownStyle property to **DropDownList**.

4. The three-character ID used when naming combo boxes is cbo. Change the combo box's name to **cboRate** and then size the control to match Figure 7-21.

5. Lock the controls on the form and then use the information shown in Figure 7-21 to set the TabIndex values.

Figure 7-21 Correct TabIndex values

6. Press **Esc** to remove the TabIndex boxes from the form.

7. Open the Code Editor window. Locate the form's Load event procedure. Change `lstRate` in the second For...Next loop to **cboRate**. Also change `lstRate` in the `lstRate.SelectedIndex = 0` statement to **cboRate**. In addition, change `list boxes` in the first comment to **a list box and combo box**.

8. Locate the btnCalc control's Click event procedure. Replace `lstRate.SelectedItem.ToString` in the second TryParse method with **cboRate.Text**.

9. Locate the lstRate_SelectedValueChanged procedure and then delete the entire procedure from the Code Editor window. Open the code template for the cboRate control's TextChanged event procedure and then enter the following assignment statement:

lblGross.Text = String.Empty

10. Save the solution and then start the application. Click the **list arrow** in the Rate combo box and then click **9.00** in the list. Click the **Calculate** button. The Gross Pay box shows $360.00. See Figure 7-22.

Figure 7-22   Gross pay amount shown in the interface

11. Click the **Exit** button. Close the Code Editor window and then close the solution.

Figure 7-23 shows the code entered in the btnCalc control's Click event procedure, the form's Load event procedure, and the cboRate control's TextChanged event procedure . The modified lines of code are shaded in the figure.

```
Private Sub btnCalc_Click(ByVal sender As Object,
ByVal e As System.EventArgs) Handles btnCalc.Click
    ' calculates and displays a gross pay amount

    Dim dblHoursWkd As Double
    Dim dblRateOfPay As Double
    Dim dblGrossPay As Double
```

Figure 7-23   Modified code for the Gross Pay Calculator application (continues)

(continued)

```
        Double.TryParse(lstHours.SelectedItem.ToString, dblHoursWkd)
        Double.TryParse(cboRate.Text, dblRateOfPay)

        ' use a function to calculate the gross pay
        dblGrossPay = CalcGrossPay(dblHoursWkd, dblRateOfPay)

        lblGross.Text = dblGrossPay.ToString("C2")
End Sub

Private Sub frmMain_Load(ByVal sender As Object,
ByVal e As System.EventArgs) Handles Me.Load
        ' fills a list box and combo box with values, then
        ' selects a default item

        For dblHours As Double = 0.5 To 50 Step 0.5
            lstHours.Items.Add(dblHours.ToString("N1"))
        Next dblHours

        For dblRates As Double = 7.25 To 10.5 Step 0.25
            cboRate.Items.Add(dblRates.ToString("N2"))
        Next dblRates

        lstHours.SelectedItem = "40.0"
        cboRate.SelectedIndex = 0
End Sub

Private Sub cboRate_TextChanged(ByVal sender As Object,
ByVal e As System.EventArgs) Handles cboRate.TextChanged
        lblGross.Text = String.Empty

End Sub
```

Figure 7-23 Modified code for the Gross Pay Calculator application

Lesson B Summary

- To add a combo box to a form:

  Use the ComboBox tool in the toolbox.

- To specify the style of a combo box:

  Set the combo box's DropDownStyle property.

- To add items to a combo box:

  Use the Items collection's Add method. The method's syntax is
  object.**Items.Add**(*item*), where *object* is the name of the combo box, and
  item is the text you want added to the control.

- To automatically sort the items in the list portion of a combo box:

  Set the combo box's Sorted property to True.

- To select a combo box item from code:

  Use the combo box's SelectedIndex, SelectedItem, or Text property.

- To determine the item either selected in the list portion of a combo box or entered in the text portion:

  Use the combo box's Text property. However, if the combo box is a DropDownList style, you also can use the SelectedIndex or SelectedItem property.

- To process code when the value in a combo box's Text property changes:

  Enter the code in the combo box's TextChanged event procedure.

Lesson B Key Terms

Combo box—a control that allows the user to select from a list of choices and also has a text field that may or may not be editable

DropDownStyle property—determines the style of a combo box

Lesson B Review Questions

1. Which property is used to specify a combo box's style?

    a. ComboBoxStyle

    b. DropDownStyle

    c. DropStyle

    d. Style

2. The items in a combo box belong to which collection?

    a. Items

    b. List

    c. ListBox

    d. Values

3. Which of the following selects the Cat item, which appears third in the cboAnimal control?

    a. `cboAnimal.SelectedIndex = 2`

    b. `cboAnimal.SelectedItem = "Cat"`

    c. `cboAnimal.Text = "Cat"`

    d. all of the above

4. The item that appears in the text portion of a combo box is stored in which property?

   a. SelectedText

   b. SelectedValue

   c. Text

   d. TextItem

5. The _____ event occurs when the user either types a value in the text portion of a combo box or selects a different item in the list portion.

   a. ChangedItem

   b. ChangedValue

   c. SelectedItemChanged

   d. TextChanged

Lesson B Exercises

1. Use Windows to make a copy of the Gross Pay Solution-Sub folder from Lesson A. Rename the copy Modified Gross Pay Solution-Sub. Open the Gross Pay Solution (Gross Pay Solution.sln) file contained in the Modified Gross Pay Solution-Sub folder. Open the designer window. Replace the Hours list box with a DropDownList combo box. Make the necessary modifications to the code. Save the solution and then start and test the application. Close the Code Editor window and then close the solution.

   INTRODUCTORY

2. In this exercise, you modify the Shoppers Haven application that you created in Chapter 6's Lesson C. Use Windows to make a copy of the Shoppers Haven Solution folder, which is contained in the VB2010\Chap06 folder. Save the copy in the VB2010\Chap07 folder. Open the Shoppers Haven Solution (Shoppers Haven Solution.sln) file contained in the VB2010\Chap07\Shoppers Haven Solution folder. Open the designer window. Replace the Discount rate list box with a DropDown combo box. Make the necessary modifications to the code. Save the solution and then start and test the application. Close the Code Editor window and then close the solution.

   INTRODUCTORY

3. Create a Visual Basic Windows application. Use the following names for the solution, project, and form file, respectively: Car Shoppers Solution, Car Shoppers Project, and Main Form.vb. Save the application in the VB2010\Chap07 folder. Create the interface shown in Figure 7-24. The Interest rate combo box should have the DropDown style and contain rates from .02 through .1 in increments of .01. The Term combo box should have the DropDownList style and contain terms of 2, 3, 4, and 5 years. The Calculate Payment button's Click event procedure should invoke a function that calculates and returns

   INTERMEDIATE

the monthly payment on a car loan. (Hint: Use the Financial.Pmt method, which you learned about in Chapter 4, to calculate the monthly payment.) The event procedure should display the return value in the Monthly payment box. The application should use a Sub procedure to clear the Monthly payment box when a change is made to any of the text boxes or combo boxes. Code the application. Save the solution and then start and test the application. Close the Code Editor window and then close the solution.

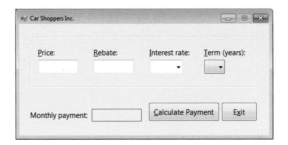

Figure 7-24   Interface for Exercise 3

LESSON C

After studying Lesson C, you should be able to:

- Prevent a form from closing
- Round a number

Creating the Harvey Industries Application

Recall that your task is to create an application that calculates an employee's weekly gross pay, federal withholding tax (FWT), Social Security and Medicare (FICA) tax, and net pay. Figure 7-25 shows the application's TOE chart.

The Ch07CVideo file demonstrates all of the steps contained in Lesson C. You can view the video either before or after completing the lesson.

427

Task	Object	Event
End the application	btnExit	Click
1. Calculate gross pay, FWT, FICA, and net pay 2. Display calculated amounts in appropriate labels	btnCalc	Click
Display calculated amounts (from btnCalc)	lblGross, lblFwt, lblFica, lblNet	None
Clear lblGross, lblFwt, lblFica, and lblNet	txtName, cboAllowances	TextChanged
	lstHours, lstRate	SelectedValueChanged
	radMarried, radSingle	Click
Select the existing text	txtName	Enter
Allow only numbers and the Backspace key	cboAllowances	KeyPress
Get and display the name, hours worked, pay rate, marital status, and withholding allowances	txtName, lstHours, lstRate, radMarried, radSingle, cboAllowances	None
Fill lstHours, lstRate, and cboAllowances with values and then select a default item	frmMain	Load
Verify that the user wants to close the application, and then take the appropriate action based on the user's response		FormClosing

Figure 7-25 TOE chart for the Harvey Industries application

START HERE

To open the Harvey Industries application:

1. If necessary, start Visual Studio 2010 or Visual Basic 2010 Express.

2. Open the Harvey Industries Solution (Harvey Industries Solution.sln) file contained in the VB2010\Chap07\Harvey Industries Solution folder. If necessary, open the designer window. See Figure 7-26.

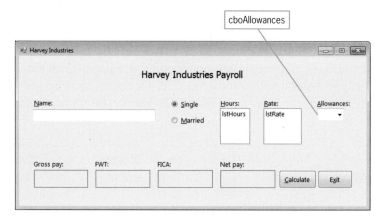

Figure 7-26   User interface for the Harvey Industries application

The interface in Figure 7-26 provides a text box for entering the employee's name, and radio buttons for entering his or her marital status. It also provides list boxes for specifying the hours worked and rate of pay. The combo box in the interface allows the user to either select the number of withholding allowances from the list portion of the control or type a number in the text portion. To complete the Harvey Industries application, you will need to code the btnCalc control's Click event procedure and the form's FormClosing event procedure.

Coding the FormClosing Event Procedure

A form's **FormClosing event** occurs when a form is about to be closed. In most cases, this happens when the computer processes the `Me.Close()` statement in the application's code. However, it also occurs when the user clicks the Close button on the form's title bar. According to the TOE chart shown earlier in Figure 7-25, the FormClosing event procedure is responsible for verifying that the user wants to close the application, and then taking the appropriate action based on the user's response. Figure 7-27 shows the procedure's pseudocode.

---

frmMain FormClosing event procedure
1. use a message box to ask the user whether he or she wants to exit the application
2. if the user does not want to exit the application
                prevent the form from closing
          end if

Figure 7-27   Pseudocode for the FormClosing event procedure

To begin coding the FormClosing event procedure:

1. Open the Code Editor window. Click the **Class Name** list arrow and then click **(frmMain Events)** in the list. Click the **Method Name** list arrow and then click **FormClosing** in the list. The code template for the FormClosing event procedure appears above the Load event procedure in the Code Editor window.

2. Type the following comment and then press **Enter** twice:

    ' verify that the user wants to exit the application

3. The procedure will use the MessageBox.Show method to display the appropriate message in a message box. The method's return value will be assigned to a variable named `dlgButton`. Enter the following Dim statement:

    Dim dlgButton As DialogResult

4. The message box will contain the "Do you want to exit?" message, Yes and No buttons, and the Exclamation icon. The Yes button will be designated as the default button. Enter the following statement. Press **Enter** twice after typing the last line in the statement.

    dlgButton =
    MessageBox.Show("Do you want to exit?",
    "Harvey Industries", MessageBoxButtons.YesNo,
    MessageBoxIcon.Exclamation,
    MessageBoxDefaultButton.Button1)

If the user selects the No button in the message box, the FormClosing procedure should stop the computer from closing the form. You prevent the computer from closing a form by setting the **Cancel property** of the FormClosing event procedure's **e** parameter to True.

To complete the FormClosing event procedure and then test it:

1. Enter the following comment and selection structure:

    ' if the No button was selected, don't close the form
    If dlgButton = DialogResult.No Then
    e.Cancel = True
    End If

2. Save the solution and then start the application. Click the **Close** button on the form's title bar. Doing this invokes the FormClosing event procedure, which displays the message box shown in Figure 7-28.

Figure 7-28   Message box displayed by the code in the FormClosing event procedure

3. Click the **No** button in the message box. Notice that the form remains on the screen.

4. Click the **Exit** button. This time, click the **Yes** button in the message box. The application ends.

Coding the btnCalc Control's Click Event Procedure

According to the application's TOE chart, the btnCalc control's Click event procedure is responsible for calculating and displaying the gross pay, FWT (federal withholding tax), FICA tax, and net pay. The procedure's pseudocode is shown in Figure 7-29.

---

btnCalc Click event procedure
1.   store user input (hours, pay rate, and allowances) in variables
2.   if the Single radio button is selected
       assign "S" as the marital status
    else
       assign "M" as the marital status
    end if
3.   if the number of hours is less than or equal to 40
      calculate the gross pay = hours * pay rate
    else
      calculate the gross pay = 40 * pay rate + (hours – 40) * pay rate * 1.5
    end if
4.   invoke a function named GetFwt to calculate and return the FWT
5.   calculate the FICA tax = gross pay * 7.65%
6.   round the gross pay, FWT, and FICA tax to two decimal places
7.   calculate the net pay = gross pay – FWT – FICA tax
8.   display the gross pay, FWT, FICA tax, and net pay in the appropriate labels

---

Figure 7-29   Pseudocode for the btnCalc control's Click event procedure

To begin coding the btnCalc control's Click event procedure:

1. Open the code template for the btnCalc control's Click event procedure. Type the following comment and then press **Enter** twice:

   ' displays gross pay, taxes, and net pay

2. First, determine the variables and named constants (if any) the procedure will use. In this case, the procedure will use a named constant for the FICA tax rate (7.65%). It also will use eight variables. The `strStatus` variable will store either the letter S or the letter M, depending on the radio button selected in the interface. The `dblHours` variable will store the number of hours worked, which is selected in the lstHours control. The `dblPayRate` variable will store the pay rate selected in the lstRate control. The `intAllowances` variable will store the number of withholding allowances, which is either selected or entered in the cboAllowances control. The `dblGross`, `dblFwt`, `dblFica`, and `dblNet` variables will store the gross pay, FWT, FICA, and net pay, respectively. Enter the following nine declaration statements. Press **Enter** twice after typing the last declaration statement.

   Const dblFICA_RATE As Double = .0765
   Dim strStatus As String
   Dim dblHours As Double
   Dim dblPayRate As Double
   Dim intAllowances As Integer
   Dim dblGross As Double
   Dim dblFwt As Double
   Dim dblFica As Double
   Dim dblNet As Double

3. Step 1 in the procedure's pseudocode is to store the user input in variables. Enter the following statements. Press **Enter** twice after typing the last statement.

   dblHours = Convert.ToDouble(lstHours.SelectedItem.ToString)
   dblPayRate = Convert.ToDouble(lstRate.SelectedItem.ToString)
   intAllowances = Convert.ToInt32(cboAllowances.Text)

4. Step 2 in the pseudocode is a selection structure whose condition determines the employee's marital status. Type the selection structure shown in Figure 7-30 and then position the insertion point as indicated in the figure.

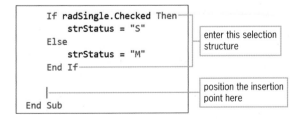

Figure 7-30   Selection structure entered in the procedure

5. The next step in the pseudocode is a selection structure whose condition compares the number of hours worked with the number 40. If the number of hours worked is less than or equal to 40, the selection structure's true path should calculate the gross pay by multiplying the number of hours worked by the pay rate. Enter the following comment, If clause, and assignment statement:

' calculate gross pay
If dblHours <= 40 Then
    dblGross = dblHours * dblPayRate

6. If the number of hours worked is greater than 40, the employee is entitled to his or her regular pay rate for the hours worked up to and including 40, and then time and one-half for the hours worked over 40. Enter the Else clause and assignment statement shown in Figure 7-31, and then save the solution.

enter the Else clause and the assignment statement

```
' calculate gross pay
If dblHours <= 40 Then
     dblGross = dblHours * dblPayRate
Else
     dblGross = 40 * dblPayRate +
       (dblHours - 40) * dblPayRate * 1.5
End If
End Sub
```

Figure 7-31 Selection structure's false path entered in the procedure

Step 4 in the procedure's pseudocode uses a function named GetFwt to calculate and return the FWT (federal withholding tax). Before entering the appropriate instruction, you will create the function.

Creating the GetFwt Function

The amount of federal withholding tax (FWT) to deduct from an employee's weekly gross pay is based on the employee's weekly taxable wages and his or her filing status, which is either single (including head of household) or married. You calculate the weekly taxable wages by first multiplying the number of withholding allowances by $70.19 (the value of a withholding allowance in 2010), and then subtracting the result from the weekly gross pay. For example, if your weekly gross pay is $400 and you have two withholding allowances, your weekly taxable wages are $259.62. The $259.62 is calculated by multiplying 70.19 by 2 and then subtracting the result (140.38) from 400. You use the weekly taxable wages, along with the filing status and the appropriate weekly Federal Withholding Tax table, to determine the amount of FWT to withhold. The weekly tax tables for the year 2010 are shown in Figure 7-32.

FWT Tables – Weekly Payroll Period				

Single person (including head of household)

If the taxable
wages are: The amount of income tax to withhold is:

Over	But not over	Base amount	Percentage	Of excess over
	$ 116	0		
$ 116	$ 200	0	10%	$ 116
$ 200	$ 693	$ 8.40 plus	15%	$ 200
$ 693	$1,302	$ 82.35 plus	25%	$ 693
$1,302	$1,624	$ 234.60 plus	27%	$1,302
$1,624	$1,687	$ 321.54 plus	30%	$1,624
$1,687	$3,344	$ 340.44 plus	28%	$1,687
$3,344	$7,225	$ 804.40 plus	33%	$3,344
$7,225		$2,085.13 plus	35%	$7,225

Married person

If the taxable
wages are: The amount of income tax to withhold is

Over	But not over	Base amount	Percentage	Of excess over
	$ 264	0		
$ 264	$ 471	0	10%	$ 264
$ 471	$1,457	$ 20.70 plus	15%	$ 471
$1,457	$1,809	$ 168.80 plus	25%	$1,457
$1,809	$2,386	$ 256.60 plus	27%	$1,809
$2,386	$2,789	$ 412.39 plus	25%	$2,386
$2,789	$4,173	$ 513.14 plus	28%	$2,789
$4,173	$7,335	$ 900.66 plus	33%	$4,173
$7,335		$1,944.12 plus	35%	$7,335

Figure 7-32   Weekly FWT tables

Each table in Figure 7-32 contains five columns of information. The first two columns list various ranges, also called brackets, of taxable wage amounts. The first column (Over) lists the amount that a taxable wage in that bracket must be over, and the second column (But not over) lists the maximum amount included in the bracket. The remaining three columns (Base amount, Percentage, and Of excess over) tell you how to calculate the tax for each range. For example, assume that you are married and your weekly taxable wages are $388.46. Before you can calculate the amount of your tax, you need to locate your taxable wages in the first two columns of the Married table. Taxable wages of $388.46 fall within the $264 through $471 bracket. After locating the bracket that contains your taxable wages, you then use the remaining three columns in the table to calculate your tax. In this case, you calculate the tax by first subtracting 264 (the amount shown in the Of excess over column) from your taxable wages of 388.46, giving 124.46. You then multiply 124.46 by 10% (the amount shown in the Percentage column), giving 12.45. You add the amount shown in the Base amount column—in this case, 0—to that result, giving $12.45 as your tax. The calculations are shown in Figure 7-33.

Taxable wages	$388.46
Of excess over	−264.00
	124.46
Percentage	* .10
	12.45
Base amount	+ 0.00
Tax	$ 12.45

Figure 7-33   FWT calculation for a married taxpayer whose weekly taxable wages are $388.46

Now calculate the tax for a single taxpayer whose weekly taxable wages are $600. Figure 7-34 shows how the tax amount is calculated.

Taxable wages	$600.00
Of excess over	−200.00
	400.00
Percentage	* .15
	60.00
Base amount	+ 8.40
Tax	$ 68.40

Figure 7-34   FWT calculation for a single taxpayer whose weekly taxable wages are $600

To calculate the federal withholding tax, the GetFwt function needs to know the employee's gross pay amount, the number of his or her withholding allowances, and his or her marital status. The gross pay amount and number of withholding allowances are necessary to calculate the taxable wages, and the marital status indicates the appropriate FWT table to use when calculating the tax. The function will receive the necessary information from the btnCalc control's Click event procedure, which will pass the information when it invokes the function. Recall that the information is stored in the procedure's `dblGross`, `intAllowances`, and `strStatus` variables. Figure 7-35 shows the function's pseudocode.

GetFwt function
1. calculate the taxable wages = gross pay − number of withholding allowances * 70.19
2. if the marital status is Single
    calculate the FWT using the Single FWT table
   else
    calculate the FWT using the Married FWT table
   end if
3. return the FWT

Figure 7-35   Pseudocode for the GetFwt function

To create the GetFwt function:

START HERE

1. Scroll to the top of the Code Editor window. Click the **blank line** below the `Public Class frmMain` clause and then press **Enter** to insert another blank line.

2. When it invokes the GetFwt function, the btnCalc control's Click event procedure will need to pass the values stored in its `strStatus`, `intAllowances`, and `dblGross` variables. You do not want the GetFwt function to change the contents of the variables, so you will pass a copy of each variable's value (rather than its address). You will store the values passed to the function in three parameters named `strMarital`, `intNumAllow`, and `dblWeekPay`. The GetFwt function will use the information it receives to calculate and return the FWT as a Double number. Type the function header and comment shown in Figure 7-36 and then position the insertion point as indicated in the figure. (Notice that the Code Editor automatically enters the procedure footer for you.)

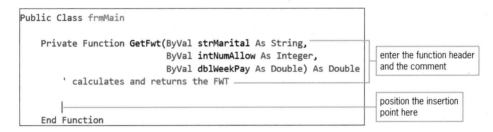

```
Public Class frmMain

    Private Function GetFwt(ByVal strMarital As String,
                            ByVal intNumAllow As Integer,
                            ByVal dblWeekPay As Double) As Double
        ' calculates and returns the FWT

    End Function
```

enter the function header and the comment

position the insertion point here

Figure 7-36   GetFwt function header and footer

3. The function will use a named constant for the withholding allowance amount ($70.19). It also will use two additional variables: one to store the taxable wages and the other to store the FWT. Enter the following declaration statements. Press **Enter** twice after typing the last declaration statement.

   Const dblONE_ALLOW As Double = 70.19
   Dim dblTaxWages As Double
   Dim dblTax As Double

4. The first step in the function's pseudocode calculates the taxable wages. Enter the following comment and assignment statement. Press **Enter** twice after typing the assignment statement.

   ' calculate taxable wages
   dblTaxWages =
   dblWeekPay – intNumAllow * dblONE_ALLOW

5. The second step in the pseudocode is a selection structure whose condition determines the marital status. Enter the following comment and If clause:

   ' determine marital status and then calculate FWT
   If strMarital = "S" Then

435

6. If the `strMarital` variable contains the letter S, the selection structure's true path should calculate the federal withholding tax using the information from the Single tax table. You will find the appropriate code in the Single.txt file. Click **File** on the menu bar and then click **Open File**. If necessary, open the Harvey Industries Project folder. Click **Single.txt** in the list of filenames and then click the **Open** button. Click **Edit** on the menu bar and then click **Select All**. Press **Ctrl+c** to copy the selected text to the Windows Clipboard, and then close the Single.txt window.

7. The insertion point should be in the blank line below the If clause in the GetFwt function. Press **Ctrl+v** to paste the copied text into the selection structure's true path.

8. If the `strMarital` variable does not contain the letter S, the selection structure's false path should calculate the federal withholding tax using the information from the Married tax table. You will find the appropriate code in the Married.txt file. Click **File** and then click **Open File**. Click **Married.txt** in the list of filenames and then click the **Open** button. Click **Edit** and then click **Select All**. Press **Ctrl+c** to copy the selected text to the Windows Clipboard, and then close the Married.txt window.

9. The insertion point should be in the blank line below the End Select clause. Type **Else** and then press **Tab** twice. Type **' strMarital = "M"** and then press **Enter**. Press **Ctrl+v** to paste the copied text into the selection structure's false path.

10. The last step in the function's pseudocode returns the federal withholding tax amount to the statement that invoked the function. The tax amount is stored in the `dblTax` variable. Click **after the letter f** in the End If clause and then press **Enter** twice. Type **Return dblTax** and then click the **blank line** above the Return statement. Save the solution. (You can look ahead to Figure 7-38 to view the function's code.)

Completing the btnCalc Control's Click Event Procedure

Now that you have created the GetFwt function, you can invoke the function from the btnCalc control's Click event procedure. Invoking the GetFwt function is the fourth step listed in the event procedure's pseudocode (shown earlier in Figure 7-29).

START HERE   **To continue coding the btnCalc control's Click event procedure:**

1. Locate the btnCalc control's Click event procedure. Click **after the letter f** in the second End If clause and then press **Enter** twice.

2. Recall that the procedure needs to pass to the GetFwt function a copy of the values stored in the `strStatus`, `intAllowances`, and `dblGross` variables. The value returned by the function will be

assigned to the `dblFwt` variable. Enter the following comment and assignment statement. Press **Enter** twice after typing the assignment statement.

' call a function to calculate the FWT
dblFwt = GetFwt(strStatus, intAllowances, dblGross)

3. The next step in the procedure's pseudocode calculates the FICA tax by multiplying the gross pay amount by the FICA rate. Enter the following comment and assignment statement. Press **Enter** twice after typing the assignment statement.

' calculate FICA tax
dblFica = dblGross * dblFICA_RATE

4. Save the solution.

Next, the procedure should round the gross pay, FWT, and FICA tax amounts to two decimal places. Rounding these amounts before making the net pay calculation will prevent the "penny off" error from occurring. (You can observe the "penny off" error by completing Exercise 1 at the end of this lesson.) You can use the **Math.Round function** to return a number rounded to a specific number of decimal places. The function's syntax is **Math.Round(*value*[, *digits*])**. In the syntax, *value* is a numeric expression, and *digits* (which is optional) is an integer indicating how many places to the right of the decimal point are included in the rounding. For example, `Math.Round(3.235, 2)` returns the number 3.24, and `Math.Round(3.234, 1)` returns the number 3.2. If the *digits* argument is omitted, the Math.Round function returns an integer.

To complete the btnCalc control's Click event procedure and then test the application:

START HERE

1. Enter the following comment and assignment statements. Press **Enter** twice after typing the last assignment statement.

' round gross pay, FWT, and FICA tax
dblGross = Math.Round(dblGross, 2)
dblFwt = Math.Round(dblFwt, 2)
dblFica = Math.Round(dblFica, 2)

2. Next, the procedure should calculate the net pay by subtracting the two tax amounts from the gross pay amount. Enter the following comment and assignment statement. Press **Enter** twice after typing the assignment statement.

' calculate net pay
dblNet = dblGross – dblFwt – dblFica

3. The last step in the procedure's pseudocode displays the calculated amounts in the appropriate label controls. Enter the following comment and assignment statements:

' display calculated amounts
lblGross.Text = dblGross.ToString("N2")
lblFwt.Text = dblFwt.ToString("N2")
lblFica.Text = dblFica.ToString("N2")
lblNet.Text = dblNet.ToString("N2")

4. Save the solution and then start the application. First, calculate the weekly gross pay, taxes, and net pay for Kate Kaufman. Last week, Kate worked 40 hours. She earns $10 per hour and her marital status is Single. She claims one withholding allowance. Type **Kate Kaufman** in the Name box. Locate and then click **10.00** in the Rate list box. Click the **list arrow** in the Allowances combo box and then click **1** in the list. Click the **Calculate** button. See Figure 7-37.

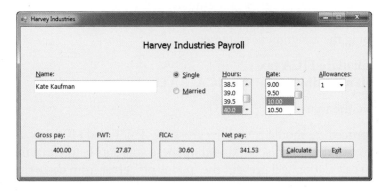

Figure 7-37   Payroll calculations shown in the interface

5. Now calculate the weekly gross pay, taxes, and net pay for Carl Schmidt. Last week, Carl worked 39.5 hours. He earns $11.50 per hour and his marital status is Married. He claims two withholding allowances. Change the name entered in the Name box to **Carl Schmidt**. Click the **Married** radio button and then click **39.5** in the Hours list box. Locate and then click **11.50** in the Rate list box. Press **Tab** to move the focus to the Allowances combo box. In addition to selecting the number of allowances in the list portion of the combo box, the user also can type the number in the text portion. Type **2** and then click the **Calculate** button. The application displays 454.25, 4.99, 34.75, and 414.51 as Carl's gross pay, FWT, FICA tax, and net pay amounts, respectively.

6. Click the **Exit** button and then click the **Yes** button. Close the Code Editor window and then close the solution.

Figure 7-38 shows the application's code.

```
1 ' Name:      Harvey Industries Project
2 ' Purpose:  Displays gross pay, taxes, and net pay
3 ' Programmer:   <your name> on <current date>
4
5 Option Explicit On
6 Option Strict On
7 Option Infer Off
8
9 Public Class frmMain
10
11   Private Function GetFwt(ByVal strMarital As String,
12              ByVal intNumAllow As Integer,
13              ByVal dblWeekPay As Double) As Double
```

Figure 7-38   Harvey Industries application's code (*continues*)

(continued)

```
14        ' calculates and returns the FWT
15
16        Const dblONE_ALLOW As Double = 70.19
17        Dim dblTaxWages As Double
18        Dim dblTax As Double
19
20        ' calculate taxable wages
21        dblTaxWages =
22            dblWeekPay - intNumAllow * dblONE_ALLOW
23
24        ' determine marital status and then calculate FWT
25        If strMarital = "S" Then
26            Select Case dblTaxWages
27                Case Is <= 116D
28                    dblTax = 0D
29                Case Is <= 200D
30                    dblTax = 0.1D * (dblTaxWages - 116D)
31                Case Is <= 693D
32                    dblTax = 8.4D + 0.15D * (dblTaxWages - 200D)
33                Case Is <= 1302D
34                    dblTax = 82.35D + 0.25D * (dblTaxWages - 693D)
35                Case Is <= 1624D
36                    dblTax = 234.6D + 0.27D * (dblTaxWages - 1302D)
37                Case Is <= 1687D
38                    dblTax = 321.54D + 0.3D * (dblTaxWages - 1624D)
39                Case Is <= 33447D
40                    dblTax = 340.44D + 0.28D * (dblTaxWages - 1687D)
41                Case Is <= 7225D
42                    dblTax = 804.4D + 0.33D * (dblTaxWages - 3344D)
43                Case Else
44            End Select
45        Else    ' strMarital = "M"
46            Select Case dblTaxWages
47                Case Is <= 264D
48                    dblTax = 0D
49                Case Is <= 471D
50                    dblTax = 0.1D * (dblTaxWages - 264D)
51                Case Is <= 1457D
52                    dblTax = 20.7D + 0.15D * (dblTaxWages - 471D)
53                Case Is <= 1809D
54                    dblTax = 168.8D + 0.25D * (dblTaxWages - 1457D)
55                Case Is <= 2386D
56                    dblTax = 256.6D + 0.27D * (dblTaxWages - 1809D)
57                Case Is <= 2789D
58                    dblTax = 412.39D + 0.25D * (dblTaxWages - 2386D)
59                Case Is <= 4173D
60                    dblTax = 513.14D + 0.28D * (dblTaxWages - 2789D)
61                Case Is <= 7335D
62                    dblTax = 900.66D + 0.33D * (dblTaxWages - 4173D)
63                Case Else
64                    dblTax = 1944.12D + 0.35D * (dblTaxWages - 7335D)
65            End Select
66        End If
67
68        Return dblTax
69    End Function
70
```

Figure 7-38 Harvey Industries application's code *(continues)*

(continued)

```
71    Private Sub txtName_Enter(ByVal sender As Object,
      ByVal e As System.EventArgs) Handles txtName.Enter
72      ' select the existing text
73
74      txtName.SelectAll()
75    End Sub
76
77    Private Sub cboAllowances_KeyPress(ByVal sender As Object,
      ByVal e As System.Windows.Forms.KeyPressEventArgs
      ) Handles cboAllowances.KeyPress
78      ' allow only numbers and the Backspace key
79
80      If (e.KeyChar < "0" OrElse e.KeyChar > "9") AndAlso
        e.KeyChar <> ControlChars.Back Then
81        e.Handled = True
82      End If
83    End Sub
84
85    Private Sub ClearLabels(ByVal sender As Object,
      ByVal e As System.EventArgs
      ) Handles lstHours.SelectedValueChanged,
86    lstRate.SelectedValueChanged, radSingle.Click,
      radMarried.Click, txtName.TextChanged,
      cboAllowances.TextChanged
87
88      lblGross.Text = String.Empty
89      lblFwt.Text = String.Empty
90      lblFica.Text = String.Empty
91      lblNet.Text = String.Empty
92    End Sub
93
94    Private Sub frmMain_FormClosing(ByVal sender As Object,
      ByVal e As System.Windows.Forms.FormClosingEventArgs
      ) Handles Me.FormClosing
95      ' verify that the user wants to exit the application
96
97      Dim dlgButton As DialogResult
98      dlgButton =
99        MessageBox.Show("Do you want to exit?",
100       "Harvey Industries", MessageBoxButtons.YesNo,
101       MessageBoxIcon.Exclamation,
102       MessageBoxDefaultButton.Button1)
103
104     ' if the No button was selected, don't close the form
105     If dlgButton = DialogResult.No Then
106       e.Cancel = True
107     End If
108   End Sub
109
110   Private Sub frmMain_Load(ByVal sender As Object,
      ByVal e As System.EventArgs) Handles Me.Load
111     ' fills the list boxes with values, then selects
        a default value
112
113     For dblHours As Double = 0 To 55 Step 0.5
114       lstHours.Items.Add(dblHours.ToString("N1"))
115     Next dblHours
```

Figure 7-38   Harvey Industries application's code *(continues)*

(continued)

```
116
117     For dblRates As Double = 7.5 To 15.5 Step 0.5
118         lstRate.Items.Add(dblRates.ToString("N2"))
119     Next dblRates
120
121     For intAllow As Integer = 0 To 10
122         cboAllowances.Items.Add(intAllow.ToString)
123     Next intAllow
124
125     lstHours.SelectedItem = "40.0"
126     lstRate.SelectedItem = "9.50"
127     cboAllowances.SelectedIndex = 0
128 End Sub
129
130 Private Sub btnExit_Click(ByVal sender As Object,
    ByVal e As System.EventArgs) Handles btnExit.Click
131     Me.Close()
132 End Sub
133
134 Private Sub btnCalc_Click(ByVal sender As Object,
    ByVal e As System.EventArgs) Handles btnCalc.Click
135     ' displays gross pay, taxes, and net pay
136
137     Const dblFICA_RATE As Double = 0.0765
138     Dim strStatus As String
139     Dim dblHours As Double
140     Dim dblPayRate As Double
141     Dim intAllowances As Integer
142     Dim dblGross As Double
143     Dim dblFwt As Double
144     Dim dblFica As Double
145     Dim dblNet As Double
146
147     dblHours = Convert.ToDouble(lstHours.SelectedItem.ToString)
148     dblPayRate = Convert.ToDouble(lstRate.SelectedItem.ToString)
149     intAllowances = Convert.ToInt32(cboAllowances.Text)
150
151     If radSingle.Checked Then
152         strStatus = "S"
153     Else
154         strStatus = "M"
155     End If
156
157     ' calculate gross pay
158     If dblHours <= 40 Then
159         dblGross = dblHours * dblPayRate
160     Else
161         dblGross = 40 * dblPayRate +
162             (dblHours - 40) * dblPayRate * 1.5
163     End If
164
165     ' call a function to calculate the FWT
166     dblFwt = GetFwt(strStatus, intAllowances, dblGross)
167
168     ' calculate FICA tax
```

Figure 7-38 Harvey Industries application's code *(continues)*

441

(continued)

```
169      dblFica = dblGross * dblFICA_RATE
170
171      ' round gross pay, FWT, and FICA tax
172      dblGross = Math.Round(dblGross, 2)
173      dblFwt = Math.Round(dblFwt, 2)
174      dblFica = Math.Round(dblFica, 2)
175
176      ' calculate net pay
177      dblNet = dblGross - dblFwt - dblFica
178
179      ' display calculated amounts
180      lblGross.Text = dblGross.ToString("N2")
181      lblFwt.Text = dblFwt.ToString("N2")
182      lblFica.Text = dblFica.ToString("N2")
183      lblNet.Text = dblNet.ToString("N2")
184
185   End Sub
186 End Class
```

Figure 7-38   Harvey Industries application's code

Lesson C Summary

- To process code when a form is about to be closed:

  Enter the code in the form's FormClosing event procedure, which occurs when the user clicks the Close button on a form's title bar or when the computer processes the `Me.Close()` statement.

- To prevent a form from being closed:

  Set the Cancel property of the FormClosing event procedure's **e** parameter to True.

- To round a number to a specific number of decimal places:

  Use the Math.Round function. The function's syntax is **Math.Round(***value*[, *digits*]**)**, where *value* is a numeric expression and *digits* (which is optional) is an integer indicating how many places to the right of the decimal point are included in the rounding. If the *digits* argument is omitted, the Math.Round function returns an integer.

Lesson C Key Terms

Cancel property—a property of the **e** parameter in the form's FormClosing event procedure; when set to True, it prevents the form from closing

FormClosing event—occurs when a form is about to be closed, which can happen as a result of the computer processing the `Me.Close()` statement or the user clicking the Close button on the form's title bar

Math.Round function—used to round a number to a specific number of decimal places

Lesson C Review Questions

1. A form's _____ event is triggered when you click the Close button on its title bar.

    a. Close

    b. CloseForm

    c. FormClose

    d. FormClosing

2. A form's _____ event is triggered when the computer processes the `Me.Close()` statement.

    a. Close

    b. Closing

    c. FormClose

    d. FormClosing

3. Which of the following statements prevents a form from being closed?

    a. `e.Cancel = False`

    b. `e.Cancel = True`

    c. `e.Close = False`

    d. `sender.Close = False`

4. Which of the following rounds the contents of the `intNum` variable to three decimal places?

    a. `Math.Round(3, intNum)`

    b. `Math.Round(intNum, 3)`

    c. `Round.Math(intNum, 3)`

    d. `Round.Math(3, intNum)`

Lesson C Exercises

1. In this exercise, you will remove the Math.Round function from the payroll application created in the lesson; doing this will allow you to observe the "penny off" error. Use Windows to make a copy of the Harvey Industries Solution folder. Rename the copy No Rounding Harvey Industries Solution. Open the Harvey Industries Solution (Harvey Industries Solution.sln) file contained in the No Rounding Harvey Industries Solution folder. Open the designer and Code Editor windows. The Math.Round function appears in three statements in the btnCalc control's Click event procedure. Type an apostrophe at the beginning of each of the three statements, making them

INTRODUCTORY

comments. Save the solution and then start the application. Test the application by clicking 38.5 in the Hours list box and 10.50 in the Rate list box. Click the Calculate button. What is wrong with the calculated amounts? Close the Code Editor window and then close the solution.

INTRODUCTORY

2. In this exercise, you modify one of the Gross Pay applications completed in Lesson A. Use Windows to make a copy of the Gross Pay Solution-Sub folder. Rename the copy FormClosing Gross Pay Solution-Sub. Open the Gross Pay Solution (Gross Pay Solution.sln) file contained in the FormClosing Gross Pay Solution-Sub folder. Open the designer and Code Editor windows. Code the form's FormClosing event procedure so that it asks the user whether he or she wants to exit the application. Take the appropriate action based on the user's response. Save the solution and then start and test the application. Close the Code Editor window and then close the solution.

INTERMEDIATE

3. In this exercise, you modify the Harvey Industries application from this lesson. Use Windows to make a copy of the Harvey Industries Solution folder. Rename the copy Harvey Industries Solution-Sub. Open the Harvey Industries Solution (Harvey Industries Solution.sln) file contained in the Harvey Industries Solution-Sub folder. Open the designer and Code Editor windows. Change the GetFwt function to an independent Sub procedure and then modify the statement that calls the procedure. Save the solution and then start and test the application. Close the Code Editor window and then close the solution.

INTERMEDIATE

4. In this exercise, you modify the Harvey Industries application from this lesson. Use Windows to make a copy of the Harvey Industries Solution folder. Rename the copy Modified Harvey Industries Solution. Open the Harvey Industries Solution (Harvey Industries Solution.sln) file contained in the Modified Harvey Industries Solution folder. Open the designer and Code Editor windows. Modify the code so that the GetFwt function (rather than the btnCalc control's Click event procedure) determines the selected radio button. Save the solution and then start and test the application. Close the Code Editor window and then close the solution.

ADVANCED

5. Create a Visual Basic Windows application. Use the following names for the solution, project, and form file, respectively: Cable Direct Solution, Cable Direct Project, and Main Form.vb. Save the application in the VB2010\Chap07 folder. Create the interface shown in Figure 7-39. The list boxes are named lstPremium and lstConnections. Display numbers from 0 through 20 in the lstPremium control. Display numbers from 0 through 100 in the lstConnections control. The Calculate Total Due button's Click event procedure should calculate and display a customer's cable bill. The cable rates are shown in Figure 7-40. Business customers must have

at least one connection. Use two functions: one to calculate and return the total due for business customers, and the other to calculate and return the total due for residential customers. The form's FormClosing event procedure should verify that the user wants to close the application. Code the application. Save the solution and then start and test the application. Close the Code Editor window and then close the solution.

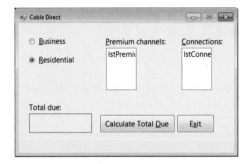

Figure 7-39   User interface for Exercise 5

Residential customers:	
Processing fee:	$4.50
Basic service fee:	$30
Premium channels:	$5 per channel
Business customers:	
Processing fee:	$16.50
Basic service fee:	$80 for the first 10 connections; $4 for each additional connection
Premium channels:	$50 per channel for any number of connections

Figure 7-40   Cable rates for Exercise 5

 ## Swat The Bugs

6. The purpose of this exercise is to demonstrate a common error made when using functions. Open the Debug Solution (Debug Solution.sln) file contained in the VB2010\Chap07\Debug Solution-Lesson C folder. If necessary, open the designer window. Open the Code Editor window and review the existing code. Start the application. Click 20 in the Length list box and then click 30 in the Width list box. Click the Calculate Area button, which should display the area of a rectangle having a length of 20 feet and a width of 30 feet. Notice that the application is not working properly. Correct the application's code. Save the solution and then start and test the application again. Close the Code Editor window and then close the solution.

CHAPTER 8

String Manipulation

Creating the Hangman Game Application

Mr. Mitchell teaches second grade at Hinsbrook School. On days when the weather is bad and the students cannot go outside to play, he spends recess time playing a simplified version of the Hangman game with his class. The game requires two people to play. Currently, Mr. Mitchell thinks of a word that has five letters. He then draws five dashes on the chalkboard—one for each letter in the word. One student then is chosen to guess the word, letter by letter. When the student guesses a correct letter, Mr. Mitchell replaces the appropriate dash or dashes with the letter. For example, if the original word is moose and the student guesses the letter o, Mr. Mitchell changes the five dashes on the chalkboard to –oo––. If the student's letter does not appear in the word, Mr. Mitchell begins drawing the Hangman image, which contains nine lines and one circle. The game is over when the student either guesses all of the letters in the word or makes 10 incorrect guesses, whichever comes first.

Previewing the Hangman Game Application

Before you start the first lesson in this chapter, you will preview the completed application. The application is contained in the VB2010\Chap08 folder.

To preview the completed application:

START HERE

447

1. Use the Run dialog box to run the Hangman (Hangman.exe) file contained in the VB2010\Chap08 folder. The application's user interface appears on the screen. As indicated in Figure 8-1, the interface contains a File menu. Menus are covered in Lesson B.

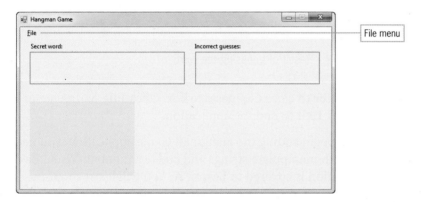

Figure 8-1 Hangman Game application's interface

2. Click **File** on the menu bar and then click **New Game**. The Hangman Game dialog box opens and prompts you to enter a five-letter word.

3. Type **puppy** and then press **Enter**. Five dashes (hyphens) appear in the Secret word box. Each dash represents a letter in the word "puppy". In addition, the Letter dialog box opens and prompts you to enter a letter.

4. Type **y** and then press **Enter**. The application replaces the last dash in the Secret word box with the letter Y. This indicates that the letter Y is the last letter in the word.

5. Type **x** and then press **Enter**. The letter x does not appear in the word "puppy", so the application displays the letter X in the Incorrect guesses box. It also displays the bottom line of the Hangman image. Recall that the image contains nine lines and one circle.

6. Type **a** and then press **Enter**. The letter a does not appear in the word "puppy", so the application displays the letter A in the Incorrect guesses box. It also displays another line in the Hangman image.

7. Type **u** and then press **Enter**. The application replaces the second dash in the Secret word box with the letter U.

8. Next, you will guess the letters d, g, and b. Type **d** and then press **Enter**. Type **g** and then press **Enter**. Type **b** and then press **Enter**. The letters you entered do not appear in the word "puppy", so the application displays the letters in the Incorrect guesses box. It also displays two additional lines and a circle in the Hangman image.

9. Type **p** and then press **Enter**. The application replaces the remaining dashes in the Secret word box with the letter P. It then displays the "Great guessing!" message in a message box. See Figure 8-2.

Figure 8-2   Result of guessing the word

10. Press **Enter** to close the message box. Click **File** on the menu bar and then click **Exit** to end the application.

Before you can begin coding the Hangman Game application, you need to learn how to both manipulate strings and create a menu in Visual Basic. String manipulation is covered in Lesson A. You will learn about the MenuStrip tool in Lesson B, and then use it to add a menu to the Hangman Game application's interface. You will code the application in Lessons B and C. Be sure to complete each lesson in full and do all of the end-of-lesson questions and several exercises before continuing to the next lesson.

LESSON A

After studying Lesson A, you should be able to:

- Determine the number of characters in a string
- Remove characters from a string
- Insert characters in a string
- Align the characters in a string
- Search a string
- Access characters in a string
- Compare strings using pattern-matching

Working with Strings

Many times, an application will need to manipulate (process) string data in some way. For example, it may need to look at the first character in an inventory part number to determine the part's location in the warehouse. Or, it may need to search an address to determine the street name. In this lesson, you will learn several ways of manipulating strings in Visual Basic. You will begin by learning how to determine the number of characters in a string.

Determining the Number of Characters in a String

If an application expects the user to enter a seven-digit phone number or a five-digit ZIP code, you should verify that the user entered the required number of characters. The number of characters contained in a string is stored as an integer in the string's **Length property**. Figure 8-3 shows the syntax of the Length property and includes examples of using the property. In the syntax, *string* can be a String variable, a String named constant, or the Text property of a control. Example 1 assigns the number 16 to the `intNumChars` variable, because there are 16 characters in the `strName` variable. Example 2 assigns the number of characters in the txtZip control's Text property to the `intNumChars` variable. Example 3 continues prompting the user for a ZIP code until the user enters exactly five characters.

Determining the number of characters in a string

Syntax
string.**Length**

Example 1
```
strName = "Veronica Yardley"
intNumChars = strName.Length
```
assigns the number 16 to the `intNumChars` variable

Example 2
```
intNumChars = txtZip.Text.Length
```
assigns the number of characters in the txtZip control's Text property to the
`intNumChars` variable

Example 3
```
Do
     strZip = InputBox("5-digit ZIP code", "ZIP")
Loop Until strZip.Length = 5
```
continues prompting the user for a ZIP code until the user enters exactly five characters

---

Figure 8-3   Syntax and examples of the Length property

Removing Characters from a String

The Trim method also can remove other characters from the beginning and end of a string. To learn more about the Trim method, as well as its companion TrimStart and TrimEnd methods, complete Exercises 17 and 18 at the end of this lesson.

Visual Basic provides the Trim and Remove methods for removing characters from a string. You can use the **Trim method** to remove (trim) any space characters from both the beginning and end of a string. You can use the **Remove method**, on the other hand, to remove a specified number of characters located anywhere in a string. Figure 8-4 shows the syntax of both methods and includes examples of using the methods. In each syntax, *string* can be a String variable, a String named constant, or the Text property of a control. When processing the Trim and Remove methods, the computer first makes a temporary copy of the *string* in memory. It then performs the specified removal on the copy only. In other words, neither method removes any characters from the original *string*. Both methods return a string with the appropriate characters removed.

The *startIndex* argument in the Remove method is the index of the first character you want removed from the copy of the *string*. A character's index is an integer that indicates the character's position in the string. The first character in a string has an index of 0; the second character has an index of 1, and so on. The optional *numCharsToRemove* argument is the number of characters you want removed. To remove only the first character from a string, you use 0 as the startIndex and 1 as the numCharsToRemove. To remove the fourth through eighth characters, you use 3 as the startIndex and 5 as the numCharsToRemove. If the numCharsToRemove argument is omitted, the Remove method removes all of the characters from the startIndex position through the end of the string, as shown in Example 3 in Figure 8-4.

Removing characters from a string

Syntax
string.**Trim**
string.**Remove**(*startIndex*[, *numCharsToRemove*])

Example 1
```
strCity = txtCity.Text.Trim
```
assigns the contents of the txtCity control's Text property, excluding any leading and trailing spaces, to the `strCity` variable

Example 2
```
strName = "Joanne Hashem"
txtLast.Text = strName.Remove(0, 7)
```
assigns the string "Hashem" to the txtLast control's Text property

Example 3
```
strName = "Penny Swanson"
txtFirst.Text = strName.Remove(5)
```
assigns the string "Penny" to the txtFirst control's Text property; you also can write the assignment statement as `txtFirst.Text = strName.Remove(5, 8)`

Example 4
```
strFirst = "John"
strFirst = strFirst.Remove(2, 1)
```
assigns the string "Jon" to the `strFirst` variable

Figure 8-4 Syntax and examples of the Trim and Remove methods

The Product ID Application

You will use both the Length property and the Trim method in the Product ID application. The application displays a listing of the product IDs entered by the user. Each product ID must contain exactly five characters.

To code and then test the Product ID application: ◄ START HERE

1. If necessary, start Visual Studio 2010 or Visual Basic 2010 Express. Open the Product Solution (Product Solution.sln) file contained in the VB2010\Chap08\Product Solution folder. If necessary, open the designer window. The interface provides a text box for entering the product ID.

2. Open the Code Editor window. Replace <your name> and <current date> in the comments with your name and the current date, respectively.

3. Locate the btnAdd control's Click event procedure. Before verifying the product ID's length, you will remove any leading and trailing spaces from the ID. Click the **blank line** below the ` ' remove any leading and trailing spaces` comment and then enter the following assignment statement:

   strId = txtId.Text.Trim

4. Now you will determine whether the ID contains exactly five characters. Click the **blank line** below the `' verify length` comment and then enter the following If clause:

If strId.Length = 5 Then

5. If the ID contains exactly five characters, the selection structure's true path should add the ID to the lstId control; otherwise, its false path should display an appropriate message. Enter the five lines of code indicated in Figure 8-5.

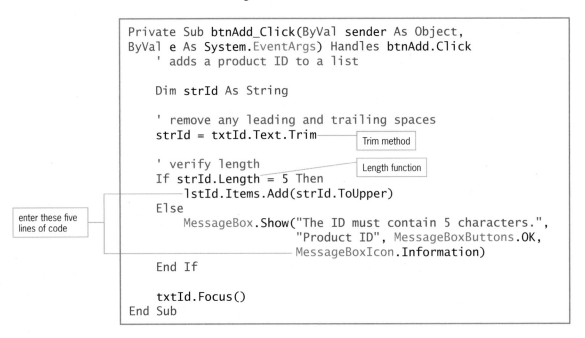

```
Private Sub btnAdd_Click(ByVal sender As Object,
ByVal e As System.EventArgs) Handles btnAdd.Click
    ' adds a product ID to a list

    Dim strId As String

    ' remove any leading and trailing spaces
    strId = txtId.Text.Trim              Trim method

    ' verify length                      Length function
    If strId.Length = 5 Then
        lstId.Items.Add(strId.ToUpper)
    Else
        MessageBox.Show("The ID must contain 5 characters.",
                        "Product ID", MessageBoxButtons.OK,
                        MessageBoxIcon.Information)
    End If

    txtId.Focus()
End Sub
```

enter these five lines of code

Figure 8-5 btnAdd control's Click event procedure

6. Save the solution and then start the application. First, you will enter an ID that contains four characters. Type **bcd2** as the product ID and then click the **Add to List** button. A message box opens and displays the message "The ID must contain 5 characters." Close the message box.

7. Now you will include two leading spaces in the ID. Click **immediately before the letter b** in the text box. Press the **Spacebar** twice and then type the letter **a**. The text box now contains two space characters followed by abcd2. Click the **Add to List** button. ABCD2 appears in the listing of product IDs.

8. On your own, test the application using an ID that contains nine characters. Also test it using an ID that contains both leading and trailing spaces. When you are finished testing the application, click the **Exit** button. Close the Code Editor window and then close the solution.

YOU DO IT 1!

Create a Visual Basic Windows application named YouDoIt 1. Save the application in the VB2010\Chap08 folder. Add a text box, a label, and a button to the form. The button's Click event procedure should remove any leading or trailing spaces from the text entered in the text box. If the remaining text contains more than four characters, the button's Click event procedure should display only the first four characters in the label; otherwise, it should display the remaining text in the label. Code the procedure. Save the solution and then start and test the application. Close the solution.

Inserting Characters in a String

Visual Basic's **Insert method** allows you to insert characters anywhere in a string. The method's syntax is shown in Figure 8-6 along with examples of using the method. In the syntax, *string* can be a String variable, a String named constant, or the Text property of a control. When processing the Insert method, the computer first makes a temporary copy of the *string* in memory. It then performs the specified insertion on the copy only. In other words, the method does not affect the original *string*. The *startIndex* argument in the Insert method is an integer that specifies where in the string's copy you want the *value* inserted. The integer represents the character's index—in other words, its position in the string. To insert the value at the beginning of a string, you use a startIndex of 0, as shown Example 1 in Figure 8-6. To insert the value beginning with the eighth character in the string, you use a startIndex of 7, as shown in Example 2. The Insert method returns a string with the appropriate characters inserted.

Inserting characters in a string

<u>Syntax</u>
string.**Insert**(*startIndex*, *value*)

<u>Example 1</u>
```
strPhone = "111-2222"
txtPhone.Text = strPhone.Insert(0, "(877) ")
```
assigns the string "(877) 111-2222" to the txtPhone control's Text property

<u>Example 2</u>
```
strName = "Joanne Hashem"
strName = strName.Insert(7, "C. ")
```
assigns the string "Joanne C. Hashem" to the strName variable

---

Figure 8-6 Syntax and examples of the Insert method

Aligning the Characters in a String

You can use Visual Basic's PadLeft and PadRight methods to align the characters in a string. The methods do this by inserting (padding) the string with zero or more characters until the string is a specified length; each method then returns the padded string. Figure 8-7 shows the syntax of both methods. In each syntax, *string* can be a String variable, a String named constant, or the Text property of a control. When processing the PadLeft and PadRight methods, the computer first makes a temporary copy of the *string* in memory; it then pads the copy only. The *totalChars* argument in each syntax is an integer that represents the total number of characters you want the string's copy to contain. The optional *padCharacter* argument is the character that each method uses to pad the string until it reaches the desired number of characters. If the padCharacter argument is omitted, the default padding character is the space character.

The **PadLeft method** pads the string on the left, which means it inserts the padded characters at the beginning of the string; doing this right-aligns the characters within the string. The **PadRight method**, on the other hand, pads the string on the right, which means it inserts the padded characters at the end of the string and left-aligns the characters within the string. Examples of using both methods are included in Figure 8-7. Notice that Example 3's expression contains the ToString and PadLeft methods. Recall that when an expression contains more than one method, the computer processes the methods from left to right. In this case, the computer will process the ToString method before processing the PadLeft method. Also notice the letter c that appears at the end of the *padCharacter* argument in Example 3. The letter c is one of the literal type characters in Visual Basic. As you learned in Chapter 3, a literal type character forces a literal constant to assume a data type other than the one its form indicates. In this case, the letter c forces the "*" string in the padCharacter argument to assume the Char (character) data type.

Aligning the characters in a string

Syntax
string.**PadLeft**(*totalChars*[, *padCharacter*])
string.**PadRight**(*totalChars*[, *padCharacter*])

Example 1
```
strNumber = "73"
txtNum.Text = strNumber.PadLeft(5)
```
assigns the string "   73" to the txtNum control's Text property

└── three space characters

Example 2
```
strFirst = "Joe"
strFirst = strFirst.PadRight(10)
```
assigns the string "Joe   " to the strFirst variable

└── seven space characters

Example 3
```
dblNet = 543.65
strFormattedNet =
    dblNet.ToString("C2").PadLeft(10, "*"c)
```
assigns the string "***$543.65" to the strFormattedNet variable (Many companies use this type of formatting on their employee paychecks, because it makes it more difficult for someone to change the amount.)

You learned about another literal type character in Chapter 3: the letter D. Recall that the letter D forces a number to assume the Decimal data type.

Figure 8-7   Syntax and examples of the PadLeft and PadRight methods

The Net Pay Application

You will use the Insert and PadLeft methods in the Net Pay application. The application allows the user to enter the amount of an employee's net pay. It then displays the net pay with a leading dollar sign, asterisks, and two decimal places. For example, if the net pay is 500, the application will display the net pay as $****500.00.

START HERE

455

To code and then test the Net Pay application:

1. Open the Net Pay Solution (Net Pay Solution.sln) file contained in the VB2010\Chap08\Net Pay Solution folder. If necessary, open the designer window. The interface provides a text box for entering the net pay.

2. Open the Code Editor window. Replace <your name> and <current date> in the comments with your name and the current date, respectively.

3. Locate the btnFormat control's Click event procedure. First, you will format the net pay to include two decimal places. Click the **blank line** below the ' format the net pay with two decimal places comment and then enter the following assignment statement:

   strFormatted = decNet.ToString("N2")

4. Next, you will use the PadLeft method to pad the net pay with asterisks until it contains 10 characters. Click the **blank line** below the ' pad the net pay with asterisks until its length is 10 comment and then enter the following assignment statement:

   strFormatted = strFormatted.PadLeft(10, "*"c)

5. Finally, you will insert a dollar sign at the beginning of the formatted net pay. Click the **blank line** below the ' insert a dollar sign as the first character comment and then enter the assignment statement indicated in Figure 8-8.

```
Private Sub btnFormat_Click(ByVal sender As Object,
ByVal e As System.EventArgs) Handles btnFormat.Click
    ' format the net pay with two decimal places, then pad with
    ' asterisks and insert a dollar sign as the first character

    Dim decNet As Decimal
    Dim strFormatted As String

    Decimal.TryParse(txtNetPay.Text, decNet)

    ' format the net pay with two decimal places
    strFormatted = decNet.ToString("N2")

    ' pad the net pay with asterisks until its length is 10
    strFormatted = strFormatted.PadLeft(10, "*"c)
```

Figure 8-8 btnFormat control's Click event procedure *(continues)*

(continued)

enter this assignment
statement

```
    ' insert a dollar sign as the first character
    strFormatted = strFormatted.Insert(0, "$")

    ' display the net pay, then set the focus
    lblFormatted.Text = strFormatted
    txtNetPay.Focus()
End Sub
```

456

Figure 8-8   btnFormat control's Click event procedure

6. Save the solution and then start the application. Type **1256** as the net pay and then click the **Format** button. The button's Click event procedure displays $\$**1,256.00$ in the interface, as shown in Figure 8-9. Click the **Exit** button. Close the Code Editor window and then close the solution.

Figure 8-9   Interface showing the formatted net pay

YOU DO IT 2!

Create a Visual Basic Windows application named YouDoIt 2. Save the application in the VB2010\Chap08 folder. Add a text box, a label, and a button to the form. Set the text box's MaxLength property to 5. The button's Click event procedure should assign the contents of the text box to a String variable; it then should remove any leading or trailing spaces from the string stored in the variable. If the variable contains more than three characters, the procedure should insert a number sign (#) as the second character and then pad the variable's value with asterisks until the variable contains 10 characters. Insert the asterisks at the end of the string stored in the variable. Finally, the procedure should display the variable's contents in the label. Code the procedure. Save the solution and then start and test the application. Close the solution.

Searching a String

If you need to determine whether a string contains a specific sequence of characters, you can use either the Contains method or the IndexOf method. Figure 8-10 shows the syntax of both methods. In each syntax, *string* can be a String variable, a String named constant, or the Text property of a control. When processing the Contains and IndexOf methods, the computer first makes a temporary copy of the *string* in memory. It then performs the specified search on the copy only. The *subString* argument in each syntax represents the sequence of characters for which you are searching. Both methods perform a case-sensitive search, which means the case of the subString must match the case of the string in order for both to be considered equal.

The **Contains method** returns the Boolean value True when the subString is contained anywhere in the string; otherwise, it returns the Boolean value False. The Contains method always begins the search with the first character in the string. The Contains method is used in Examples 1 through 3 in Figure 8-10. The **IndexOf method**, on the other hand, returns an integer— either −1 if the subString is not contained in the string or the character index that represents the starting position of the subString in the string. Unless you specify otherwise, the IndexOf method starts the search with the first character in the string. To specify a different starting location, you use the optional *startIndex* argument. The IndexOf method is used in Examples 4 through 6 in Figure 8-10. Notice that two methods appear in the expression in Example 3: ToUpper and Contains. Two methods also appear in the expression in Example 6: ToLower and IndexOf. Recall that when an expression contains more than one method, the computer processes the methods from left to right. In this case, the computer will process the ToUpper method before the Contains method in Example 3, and process the ToLower method before the IndexOf method in Example 6.

457

Searching a string

Syntax
string.**Contains**(*subString*)
string.**IndexOf**(*subString*[, *startIndex*])

Example 1
```
strCityState = "Nashville, TN"
blnIsContained = strCityState.Contains("TN")
```
assigns True to the `blnIsContained` variable because the string "TN" appears in the `strCityState` variable

Example 2
```
strCityState = "Nashville, TN"
blnIsContained = strCityState.Contains("Tn")
```
the Contains method performs a case-sensitive search

assigns False to the `blnIsContained` variable because the string "Tn" does not appear in the `strCityState` variable

Figure 8-10   Syntax and examples of the Contains and IndexOf methods *(continues)*

458

(continued)

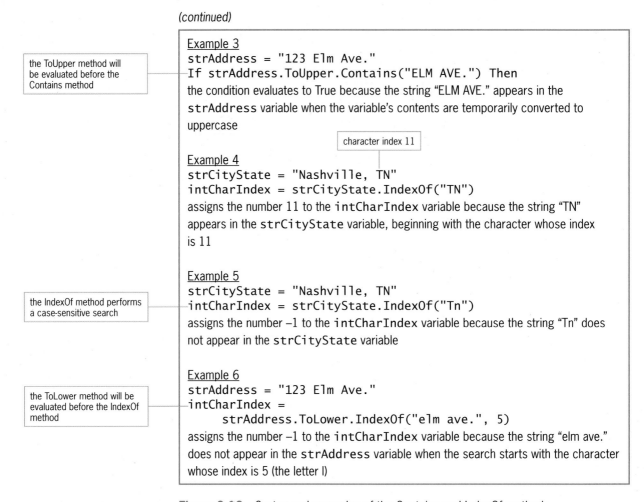

the ToUpper method will be evaluated before the Contains method

Example 3
```
strAddress = "123 Elm Ave."
If strAddress.ToUpper.Contains("ELM AVE.") Then
```
the condition evaluates to True because the string "ELM AVE." appears in the strAddress variable when the variable's contents are temporarily converted to uppercase

character index 11

Example 4
```
strCityState = "Nashville, TN"
intCharIndex = strCityState.IndexOf("TN")
```
assigns the number 11 to the intCharIndex variable because the string "TN" appears in the strCityState variable, beginning with the character whose index is 11

the IndexOf method performs a case-sensitive search

Example 5
```
strCityState = "Nashville, TN"
intCharIndex = strCityState.IndexOf("Tn")
```
assigns the number –1 to the intCharIndex variable because the string "Tn" does not appear in the strCityState variable

the ToLower method will be evaluated before the IndexOf method

Example 6
```
strAddress = "123 Elm Ave."
intCharIndex =
      strAddress.ToLower.IndexOf("elm ave.", 5)
```
assigns the number –1 to the intCharIndex variable because the string "elm ave." does not appear in the strAddress variable when the search starts with the character whose index is 5 (the letter l)

Figure 8-10   Syntax and examples of the Contains and IndexOf methods

The City and State Application

You will use the IndexOf method in the City and State application. The application allows the user to enter a string composed of a city name, followed by a comma, a space, and a state name. It then displays the index of the comma contained in the string.

START HERE

To code and then test the City and State application:

1. Open the City State Solution (City State Solution.sln) file contained in the VB2010\Chap08\City State Solution folder. If necessary, open the designer window. The interface provides a text box for entering the string.

2. Open the Code Editor window. Replace <your name> and <current date> in the comments with your name and the current date, respectively.

3. Locate the btnLocate control's Click event procedure. Click the **blank line** below the ' determine the comma's index comment.

4. To begin the search with the first character in the string, you can use either strCityState.IndexOf(",", 0) or strCityState. IndexOf(","). You will assign the IndexOf method's return value to the intCommaIndex variable. Enter the additional assignment statement shown in Figure 8-11.

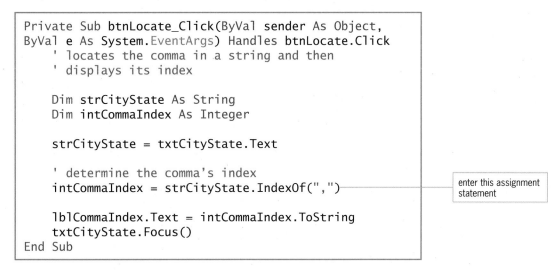

```
Private Sub btnLocate_Click(ByVal sender As Object,
ByVal e As System.EventArgs) Handles btnLocate.Click
    ' locates the comma in a string and then
    ' displays its index

    Dim strCityState As String
    Dim intCommaIndex As Integer

    strCityState = txtCityState.Text

    ' determine the comma's index
    intCommaIndex = strCityState.IndexOf(",")          enter this assignment
                                                        statement

    lblCommaIndex.Text = intCommaIndex.ToString
    txtCityState.Focus()
End Sub
```

Figure 8-11 btnLocate control's Click event procedure

5. Save the solution and then start the application. Type **Nashville, TN** in the text box and then click the **Locate the Comma** button. As Figure 8-12 shows, the comma's index is 9. Click the **Exit** button. Close the Code Editor window and then close the solution.

Figure 8-12 Interface showing the comma's index

YOU DO IT 3!

Create a Visual Basic Windows application named YouDoIt 3. Save the application in the VB2010\Chap08 folder. Add a text box, a label, and a button to the form. The button's Click event procedure should determine whether the number 9 appears anywhere in the text box and then display the result (either True or False) in the label. Code the procedure. Save the solution and then start and test the application. Close the solution.

Accessing the Characters in a String

Visual Basic provides the **Substring method** for accessing any number of characters in a string. Figure 8-13 shows the method's syntax and includes examples of using the method. In the syntax, *string* can be a String variable, a String named constant, or the Text property of a control. When processing the Substring method, the computer first makes a temporary copy of the *string* in memory. It then accesses the specified number of characters in the copy only. The *startIndex* argument in the syntax is the index of the first character you want to access in the string's copy. As you already know, the first character in a string has an index of 0. The optional *numCharsToAccess* argument specifies the number of characters you want to access. The Substring method returns a string that contains the number of characters specified in the numCharsToAccess argument, beginning with the character whose index is startIndex. If you omit the numCharsToAccess argument, the Substring method returns all characters from the startIndex position through the end of the string.

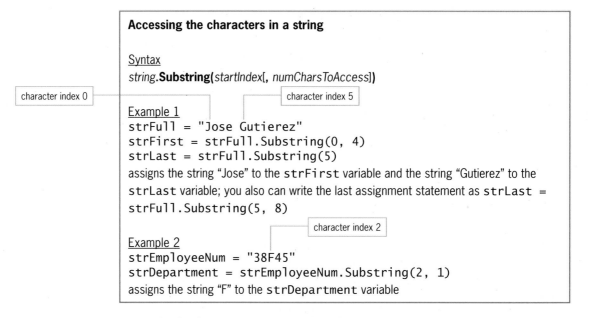

Accessing the characters in a string

Syntax
string.**Substring**(*startIndex*[, *numCharsToAccess*])

character index 0

character index 5

Example 1
```
strFull = "Jose Gutierez"
strFirst = strFull.Substring(0, 4)
strLast = strFull.Substring(5)
```
assigns the string "Jose" to the `strFirst` variable and the string "Gutierez" to the `strLast` variable; you also can write the last assignment statement as `strLast = strFull.Substring(5, 8)`

character index 2

Example 2
```
strEmployeeNum = "38F45"
strDepartment = strEmployeeNum.Substring(2, 1)
```
assigns the string "F" to the `strDepartment` variable

Figure 8-13   Syntax and examples of the Substring method

The Rearrange Name Application

You will use the Substring method in the Rearrange Name application. The application's user interface provides a text box for entering a person's first name followed by a space and the person's last name. The application rearranges the name so that the last name comes first, followed by a comma, a space, and the first name.

To code and then test the Rearrange Name application:

START HERE

1. Open the Rearrange Name Solution (Rearrange Name Solution.sln) file contained in the VB2010\Chap08\Rearrange Name Solution folder. If necessary, open the designer window.

2. Open the Code Editor window. Replace <your name> and <current date> in the comments with your name and the current date, respectively.

3. Locate the btnRearrange control's Click event procedure. The procedure assigns the name entered by the user, excluding any leading or trailing spaces, to the `strName` variable.

4. Before you can rearrange the name stored in the `strName` variable, you need to separate the first name from the last name. To do this, you first search for the space character that appears between the names. Click the **blank line** below the `' search for the space in the name` comment and then enter the following assignment statement, being sure to include a space character between the quotation marks:

   intIndex = strName.IndexOf(" ")

5. If the value in the `intIndex` variable is not −1, it means that the IndexOf method found a space character in the `strName` variable. In that case, the selection structure's true path should continue rearranging the name; otherwise, its false path should display the "Invalid name format" message. Notice that the statement to display the message is already entered in the selection structure's false path. Change the If clause in the procedure to the following:

   If intIndex <> −1 Then

6. Now you will use the value stored in the `intIndex` variable to separate the first name from the last name. Click the **blank line** below the `' separate the first and last names` comment. All of the characters to the left of the space character represent the first name, and all of the characters to the right of the space character represent the last name. Enter the following assignment statements:

   strFirstName = strName.Substring(0, intIndex)
   strLastName = strName.Substring(intIndex + 1)

7. Finally, you will display the rearranged name in the interface. Click the **blank line** above the Else clause. Enter the additional assignment statement indicated in Figure 8-14. Be sure to include a space character after the comma.

```vb
Private Sub btnRearrange_Click(ByVal sender As Object,
ByVal e As System.EventArgs) Handles btnRearrange.Click
    ' rearranges and then displays a name

    Dim strName As String
    Dim strFirstName As String
    Dim strLastName As String
    Dim intIndex As Integer

    ' assign the input to a variable
    strName = txtName.Text.Trim

    ' search for the space in the name
    intIndex = strName.IndexOf(" ")

    ' if the input contains a space
    If intIndex <> -1 Then
        ' separate the first and last names
        strFirstName = strName.Substring(0, intIndex)
        strLastName = strName.Substring(intIndex + 1)

        ' display last name, comma, space, and first name
        lblRearrangedName.Text =
            strLastName & ", " & strFirstName

    Else    ' the name does not contain a space
        MessageBox.Show("Invalid name format",
                    "Rearrange Name",
                    MessageBoxButtons.OK,
                    MessageBoxIcon.Information)
    End If
End Sub
```

enter this assignment statement

Figure 8-14   btnRearrange control's Click event procedure

8. Save the solution and then start the application. Type **Suman Patel**
    as the name and then click the **Rearrange Name** button. The rear-
    ranged name appears in the interface, as shown in Figure 8-15.
    Click the **Exit** button. Close the Code Editor window and then close
    the solution.

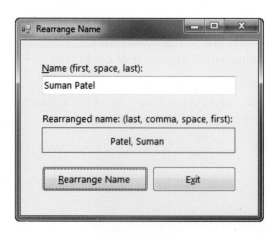

Figure 8-15   Interface showing the rearranged name

YOU DO IT 4!

Create a Visual Basic Windows application named YouDoIt 4. Save the application in the VB2010\Chap08 folder. Add a label and a button to the form. The button's Click event procedure should declare a String variable named `strMessage` and initialize it to the 26 uppercase letters of the alphabet. It then should use the Substring method to display only the letters K, L, M, N, and O in the label. Code the procedure. Save the solution and then start and test the application. Close the solution.

Using Pattern-Matching to Compare Strings

The **Like operator** allows you to use pattern-matching characters to determine whether one string is equal to another string. Figure 8-16 shows the Like operator's syntax. In the syntax, *string* can be a String variable, a String named constant, or the Text property of a control. *Pattern* is a String expression containing one or more of the pattern-matching characters listed in the figure. As the figure indicates, the question mark (?) character in a pattern represents one character only, whereas the asterisk (*) character represents zero or more characters. To represent a single digit in a pattern, you use the number sign (#) character. The last two pattern-matching characters listed in Figure 8-16 contain a *characterList*, which is simply a listing of characters. "[A9M]" is a characterList that contains three characters: A, 9, and M. You also can include a range of values in a characterList. You do this using a hyphen to separate the lowest value in the range from the highest value in the range. For example, to include all lowercase letters in a characterList, you use "[a-z]". To include both lowercase and uppercase letters in the characterList, you use "[a-zA-Z]".

The Like operator compares the string to the pattern; the comparison is case-sensitive. If the string matches the pattern, the Like operator returns the Boolean value True; otherwise, it returns the Boolean value False. Examples of using the Like operator are included in Figure 8-16.

Using pattern-matching to compare strings

<u>Syntax</u>
string **Like** *pattern*

Pattern-matching characters	Matches in *string*
?	any single character
*	zero or more characters
#	any single digit (0 through 9)
[*characterList*]	any single character in the *characterList* (for example, "[A5T]" matches A, 5, or T, whereas "[a-z]" matches any lowercase letter)
[!*characterList*]	any single character *not* in the *characterList* (for example, "[!A5T]" matches any character other than A, 5, or T, whereas "[!a-z]" matches any character that is not a lowercase letter)

Figure 8-16 Syntax and examples of the Like operator *(continues)*

(continued)

Example 1
```
If strFirst.ToUpper Like "B?LL" Then
```
The condition evaluates to True when the string stored in the `strFirst` variable (converted to uppercase) begins with the letter B followed by one character and then the two letters LL; otherwise, it evaluates to False. Examples of strings that would make the condition evaluate to True include "Bill", "Ball", "bell", and "bull". Examples of strings for which the condition would evaluate to False include "BPL", "BLL", and "billy".

Example 2
```
If txtState.Text Like "K*" Then
```
The condition evaluates to True when the value in the txtState control's Text property begins with the letter K followed by zero or more characters; otherwise, it evaluates to False. Examples of strings that would make the condition evaluate to True include "KANSAS", "Ky", and "Kentucky". Examples of strings for which the condition would evaluate to False include "kansas" and "ky".

Example 3
```
Do While strId Like "###*"
```
The condition evaluates to True when the string stored in the `strId` variable begins with three digits followed by zero or more characters; otherwise, it evaluates to False. Examples of strings that would make the condition evaluate to True include "178" and "983Ab". Examples of strings for which the condition would evaluate to False include "X34" and "34Z5".

Example 4
```
If strFirst.ToUpper Like "T[OI]M" Then
```
The condition evaluates to True when the string stored in the `strFirst` variable (converted to uppercase) is either "TOM" or "TIM". When the variable does not contain "TOM" or "TIM"—for example, when it contains "Tam" or "Tommy"—the condition evaluates to False.

Example 5
```
If strLetter Like "[a-z]" Then
```
The condition evaluates to True when the string stored in the `strLetter` variable is one lowercase letter; otherwise, it evaluates to False.

Example 6
```
For intIndex As Integer = 0 To strInput.Length - 1
    strChar = strInput.Substring(intIndex, 1)
    If strChar Like "[!a-zA-Z]" Then
        intNonLetter = intNonLetter + 1
    End If
Next intIndex
```
Compares each character contained in the `strInput` variable with the lowercase and uppercase letters of the alphabet, and counts the number of characters that are not letters.

Example 7
```
If strInput Like "*.*" Then
```
The condition evaluates to True when a period appears anywhere in the `strInput` variable; otherwise, it evaluates to False.

Figure 8-16   Syntax and examples of the Like operator *(continues)*

(continued)

Example 8
```
If strInput.ToUpper Like "[A-Z][A-Z]##" Then
```
The condition evaluates to True when the value in the `strInput` variable (converted to uppercase) is two letters followed by two numbers; otherwise, it evaluates to False.

Figure 8-16　Syntax and examples of the Like operator

Modifying the Product ID Application

Earlier in this lesson, you coded the Product ID application, which displayed a listing of the product IDs entered by the user. As you may remember, each product ID contained exactly five characters. In the following set of steps, you will modify the application to ensure that the five characters are three letters followed by two numbers.

To modify and then test the Product ID application:

START HERE

1. Use Windows to make a copy of the Product Solution folder. Save the copy in the VB2010\Chap08 folder. Rename the copy Modified Product Solution.

2. Open the Product Solution (Product Solution.sln) file contained in the Modified Product Solution folder. Open the designer window.

3. Open the Code Editor window and locate the btnAdd control's Click event procedure. Change the `' remove any leading and trailing spaces` comment to the following:

   **' remove any leading and trailing spaces and
   ' then convert to uppercase**

4. Change the `strId = txtId.Text.Trim` statement to the following:

   strId = txtId.Text.Trim.ToUpper

5. Replace the `' verify length` comment with the following comments:

   **' verify that the ID contains 3 letters
   ' followed by 2 numbers**

6. Change the If clause to the following:

   If strId Like "[A-Z][A-Z][A-Z]##" Then

7. In the statement below the If clause, change `strId.ToUpper` to **strId**. Finally, change the message in the MessageBox.Show method to **"Invalid product ID"**. Figure 8-17 shows the modified Click event procedure. The modified comments and code are shaded in the figure.

466

```
Private Sub btnAdd_Click(ByVal sender As Object,
ByVal e As System.EventArgs) Handles btnAdd.Click
    ' adds a product ID to a list

    Dim strId As String

    ' remove any leading and trailing spaces and
    ' then convert to uppercase
    strId = txtId.Text.Trim.ToUpper

    ' verify that the ID contains 3 letters
    ' followed by 2 numbers
    If strId Like "[A-Z][A-Z][A-Z]##" Then
        lstId.Items.Add(strId)
    Else
        MessageBox.Show("Invalid product ID",
                    "Product ID", MessageBoxButtons.OK,
                    MessageBoxIcon.Information)

    End If

    txtId.Focus()
End Sub
```

Figure 8-17   Modified Click event procedure for the btnAdd control

8. Save the solution and then start the application. First, you will test the application using an invalid ID. Type **abc2f** as the product ID and then click the **Add to List** button. The "Invalid product ID" message appears in a message box. Close the message box.

9. Now you will enter a valid ID. Change the product ID to **abc23** and then click the **Add to List** button. ABC23 appears in the listing of product IDs.

10. On your own, test the application using different valid and invalid IDs. When you are finished testing the application, click the **Exit** button. Close the Code Editor window and then close the solution.

YOU DO IT 5!

Create a Visual Basic Windows application named YouDoIt 5. Save the application in the VB2010\Chap08 folder. Add a text box, a label, and a button to the form. The button's Click event procedure should display the message "OK" when the text box contains two numbers followed by zero or more characters; otherwise, it should display the message "Not OK". Display the message in the label control. Code the procedure. Save the solution and then start and test the application. Close the solution.

Lesson A Summary

- To manipulate strings in Visual Basic:

Use one of the string manipulation techniques listed in Figure 8-18.

Technique	Syntax	Purpose
Length property	*string*.**Length**	stores an integer that represents the number of characters contained in a string
Trim method	*string*.**Trim**	removes any spaces from both the beginning and end of a string
Remove method	*string*.**Remove(**startIndex[, numCharsToRemove]**)**	removes characters from a string
Insert method	*string*.**Insert(**startIndex, value**)**	inserts characters in a string
Contains method	*string*.**Contains(**subString**)**	determines whether a string contains a specific sequence of characters; returns a Boolean value
IndexOf method	*string*.**IndexOf(**subString[, startIndex]**)**	determines whether a string contains a specific sequence of characters; returns either –1 or an integer that indicates the starting position of the characters in the string
Substring method	*string*.**Substring(**startIndex[, numCharsToAccess]**)**	accesses one or more characters in a string
PadLeft method	*string*.**PadLeft(**totalChars[, padCharacter]**)**	pads the beginning of a string with a character until the string has the specified number of characters; right-aligns the string
PadRight method	*string*.**PadRight(**totalChars[, padCharacter]**)**	pads the end of a string with a character until the string has the specified number of characters; left-aligns the string
Like operator	*string* **Like** *pattern*	uses pattern-matching to compare strings

Important note: The following additional techniques are covered in the Discovery Exercises at the end of this lesson: the StartsWith and EndsWith methods, the Replace method, the full syntax of the Trim method, the TrimStart and TrimEnd methods, and the Mid statement.

Figure 8-18   String manipulation techniques

Lesson A Key Terms

Contains method—determines whether a string contains a specific sequence of characters; returns a Boolean value

IndexOf method—determines whether a string contains a specific sequence of characters; returns either −1 (if the string does not contain the sequence of characters) or an integer that represents the starting position of the sequence of characters

Insert method—inserts characters anywhere in a string

Length property—stores an integer that represents the number of characters contained in a string

Like operator—uses pattern-matching characters to determine whether one string is equal to another string

PadLeft method—right-aligns a string by inserting characters at the beginning of the string

PadRight method—left-aligns a string by inserting characters at the end of the string

Remove method—removes a specified number of characters located anywhere in a string

Substring method—used to access any number of characters contained in a string

Trim method—removes spaces from both the beginning and end of a string

Lesson A Review Questions

1. The **strState** variable contains the string "MI   " (the letters M and I followed by three spaces). Which of the following statements removes the three spaces from the variable's contents?

    a. strState = strState.Trim

    b. strState = Trim(strState)

    c. strState = Trim(strState, String.Empty)

    d. none of the above

2. Which of the following statements assigns the first three characters in the **strPart** variable to the **strCode** variable?

    a. strCode = strPart.Assign(0, 3)

    b. strCode = strPart.Sub(0, 3)

    c. strCode = strPart.Substring(0, 3)

    d. strCode = strPart.Assign(3, 1)

3. The `strWord` variable contains the string "Bells". Which of the following statements changes the contents of the variable to "Bell"?

   a. `strWord = strWord.Trim(4)`

   b. `strWord = strWord.Trim(5)`

   c. `strWord = strWord.Remove(4)`

   d. `strWord = strWord.Remove(5, 1)`

4. Which of the following statements changes the contents of the `strZip` variable from 60521 to 60721?

   a. `strZip = strZip.Insert(2, "7")`
      `strZip = strZip.Remove(3, 1)`

   b. `strZip = strZip.Insert(3, "7")`
      `strZip = strZip.Remove(2, 1)`

   c. `strZip = strZip.Remove(2, 1)`
      `strZip = strZip.Insert(2, "7")`

   d. all of the above

5. Which of the following methods can be used to determine whether the `strAmount` variable contains the dollar sign?

   a `blnResult = strAmount.Contains("$")`

   b. `intResult = strAmount.IndexOf("$")`

   c. `intResult = strAmount.IndexOf("$", 0)`

   d. all of the above

6. Which of the following statements changes the contents of the `strWord` variable from "men" to "mean"?

   a. `strWord = strWord.AddTo(2, "a")`

   b. `strWord = strWord.Insert(2, "a")`

   c. `strWord = strWord.Insert(3, "a")`

   d. `strWord = strWord.Insert(3, "a"c)`

7. If the `strMsg` variable contains the string "Happy holidays", what value will the `strMsg.IndexOf("day")` method return?

   a. −1

   b. 0

   c. 10

   d. 11

8. If the `strWord` variable contains the string "window", which of the following statements assigns the fifth character in the variable to the `strLetter` variable?

   a. `strLetter = strWord.Substring(4)`

   b. `strLetter = strWord.Substring(4, 1)`

   c. `strLetter = strWord(5).Substring`

   d. none of the above

9. Which of the following expressions evaluates to True when the `strPart` variable contains the string "123X45"?

   a. `strPart Like "999[A-Z]99"`

   b. `strPart Like "######"`

   c. `strPart Like "###[A-Z]##"`

   d. none of the above

10. Which of the following changes the contents of the `strCityState` variable from Boise Idaho to Boise, Idaho?

    a. `strCityState = strCityState.Insert(5, ",")`

    b. `strCityState = strCityState.Insert(6, ",")`

    c. `strCityState = strCityState.Insert(7, ",")`

    d. none of the above

11. If the `strMsg` variable contains the string "Today is Monday", which of the following assigns the number 9 to the `intNum` variable?

    a. `intNum = strMsg.Substring(0, "M")`

    b. `intNum = strMsg.Contains("M")`

    c. `intNum = strMsg.IndexOf("M")`

    d. `intNum = strMsg.IndexOf(0, "M")`

12. If the `strName` variable contains the string "John Jones", which of the following changes the contents of the variable to "John K. Jones"?

    a. `strName = strName.Insert(5, "K. ")`

    b. `strName = strName.Insert(4, " K.")`

    c. `strName = strName.InsertInto(4, " K.")`

    d. both a and b

13. The `strAmount` variable contains the string "76.89". Which of the following statements changes the contents of the variable to "76.89!!!!"?

    a. `strAmount = strAmount.PadRight(4, "!"c)`

    b. `strAmount = strAmount.PadRight(9, "!"c)`

c. `strAmount= strAmount.PadLeft(4, "!"c)`

d. none of the above

14. If the `strAddress` variable contains the string "34 Elm Street", what will the `strAddress.IndexOf("Elm")` method return?

    a. −1

    b. 3

    c. 4

    d. True

15. If the `strAddress` variable contains the string "34 Elm Street", what will the `strAddress.IndexOf("Elm", 4)` method return?

    a. −1

    b. 3

    c. 4

    d. False

Lesson A Exercises

1. Write a Visual Basic statement that removes the leading and trailing spaces from the txtAddress control.   `INTRODUCTORY`

2. Write a Visual Basic statement that uses the Insert method to change the contents of the `strWord` variable from "men" to "women".   `INTRODUCTORY`

3. Using the Insert and Remove methods, write the Visual Basic statements to change the contents of the `strWord` variable from "dog" to "frog".   `INTRODUCTORY`

4. The `strPartNum` variable contains the string "ABCD34G". Write a Visual Basic statement that assigns the string "CD34" from the `strPartNum` variable to the `strCode` variable.   `INTRODUCTORY`

5. Write the Visual Basic statements to accomplish the following tasks: `INTRODUCTORY`

    a. Display in the lblSize control the number of characters contained in the `strMsg` variable.

    b. Remove the leading and trailing spaces from the `strCity` variable.

    c. Use the Insert and Remove methods to change the contents of the `strWord` variable from "mouse" to "mouth".

    d. Use the Insert method to change the contents of the `strWord` variable from "mend" to "amend".

    e. Change the contents of the `strPay` variable from "235.67" to "****235.67".

INTRODUCTORY

6. The **strAmount** variable contains the string "3,123,560". Write the Visual Basic statements to change the contents of the variable to "3123560"; use the Remove method.

INTRODUCTORY

7. Write the Visual Basic statement that uses the Contains method to determine whether the **strAddress** variable contains the string "Maple Street" (entered in uppercase, lowercase, or a combination of uppercase and lowercase). Assign the method's return value to a Boolean variable named **blnIsContained**.

INTRODUCTORY

8. Open the City Names Solution (City Names Solution.sln) file contained in the VB2010\Chap08\City Names Solution folder. If necessary, open the designer window. The interface allows the user to enter a city name. Code the Add Name button's Click event procedure so that it removes any leading and/or trailing spaces from the city name. If the city name contains at least one character, add the name to the combo box. The procedure also should send the focus to the combo box. Save the solution and then start the application. Test the application by entering spaces before and after the following city names: New York and Miami. Close the Code Editor window and then close the solution.

INTRODUCTORY

9. Open the Item Prices Solution (Item Prices Solution.sln) file contained in the VB2010\Chap08\Item Prices Solution folder. If necessary, open the designer window. Open the Code Editor window. Modify the form's Load event procedure so that it right-aligns the prices listed in the cboRight control and then selects the first price. Save the solution and then start the application. (The prices listed in the cboLeft control should still be left-aligned.) Close the Code Editor window and then close the solution.

INTRODUCTORY

10. Open the Date Solution (Date Solution.sln) file contained in the VB2010\Chap08\Date Solution folder. If necessary, open the designer window. The interface allows the user to enter a date. Code the Change Date button's Click event procedure so that it uses the Insert method to change the year number from *yy* to 20*yy* before displaying the year number in the lblDate control. Save the solution and then start and test the application. Close the Code Editor window and then close the solution.

INTERMEDIATE

11. The **strAmount** variable contains the string "3123560" . Write the Visual Basic statements to change the variable's contents to "$3,123,560".

INTERMEDIATE

12. Open the Sales Tax Solution (Sales Tax Solution.sln) file contained in the VB2010\Chap08\Sales Tax Solution folder. The interface allows the user to enter a sales amount and a tax rate. Open the Code Editor window. The btnCalc control's Click event procedure should determine whether the tax rate ends with a percent sign. If it does, the procedure should remove the percent sign from the rate. Make the appropriate modifications to the code. Save the solution and then start the application. Test the application using the following

data: a sales amount of 1000 and a tax rate of 5%, and then a sales amount of 5000 and a tax rate of 7. Close the Code Editor window and then close the solution.

473

13. Open the Zip Solution (Zip Solution.sln) file contained in the VB2010\Chap08\Zip Solution folder. The Display Shipping Charge button's Click event procedure should display the appropriate shipping charge based on the ZIP code entered by the user. To be valid, the ZIP code must contain exactly five digits and the first three digits must be either "605" or "606". The shipping charge for "605" ZIP codes is $25. The shipping charge for "606" ZIP codes is $30. Display an appropriate message if the ZIP code is invalid. Code the procedure. Save the solution and then start the application. Test the application using the following ZIP codes: 60677, 60511, 60344, and 7130. Close the Code Editor window and then close the solution.

INTERMEDIATE

14. Open the Social Security Solution (Social Security Solution.sln) file contained in the VB2010\Chap08\Social Security Solution-Remove folder. The interface allows the user to enter a Social Security number. Code the Remove Dashes button's Click event procedure so that it first verifies that the Social Security number contains three numbers followed by a hyphen, two numbers, a hyphen, and four numbers. If the Social Security number is in the correct format, the procedure should remove the dashes from the number before displaying the number in the lblNumber control. Save the solution and then start and test the application. Close the Code Editor window and then close the solution.

INTERMEDIATE

Discovery

15. Visual Basic provides the StartsWith and EndsWith methods for determining whether a specific sequence of characters occurs at the beginning or end, respectively, of a string. The StartsWith method's syntax is *string*.**StartsWith**(*subString*), and the EndsWith method's syntax is *string*.**EndsWith**(*subString*). Open the City Solution (City Solution.sln) file contained in the VB2010\Chap08\City Solution folder. The interface provides a text box for the user to enter the name of a city. The Add to List button's Click event procedure should add the city name to the list box, but only if the city name begins with either the letter L or the letters Ch. The letters can be entered in uppercase, lowercase, or a combination of uppercase and lowercase. Code the procedure. Save the solution and then start and test the application. Close the Code Editor window and then close the solution.

16. Visual Basic provides the Replace method for replacing a sequence of characters in a string with another sequence of characters. The method's syntax is *string*.**Replace**(*oldValue*, *newValue*). When processing the Replace method, the computer makes a temporary copy of the *string* in memory; it then replaces the characters in the copy only. The Replace method returns a string with all occurrences of *oldValue* replaced with *newValue*. Open the Social Security Solution (Social

Security Solution.sln) file contained in the VB2010\Chap08\Social Security Solution-Replace folder. The interface allows the user to enter a Social Security number. Code the Remove Dashes button's Click event procedure so that it first verifies that the Social Security number contains at least one dash (hyphen). If it does, the procedure should remove all of the dashes from the number before displaying the number in the lblNumber control. Save the solution and then start and test the application. Close the Code Editor window and then close the solution.

17. In this lesson, you learned how to use the Trim method to remove space characters from both the beginning and end of a string. You also can use the Trim method to remove other characters. The syntax for doing this is *string*.**Trim**[(*trimChars*)]. The optional *trimChars* argument is a comma-separated list of characters that you want removed (trimmed). For example, if the txtInput control contains the string "#$456#", you can remove the number signs and dollar sign from the control's Text property using the statement `txtInput.Text = txtInput.Text.Trim("#"c, "$"c)`. Open the Trim Method Solution (Trim Method Solution.sln) file contained in the VB2010\Chap08\Trim Method Solution folder. Open the Code Editor window and code the btnTrim control's Click event procedure. Save the solution and then start and test the application. Close the Code Editor window and then close the solution.

18. Visual Basic provides the TrimStart and TrimEnd methods for removing one or more characters from the beginning or end, respectively, of a string. The TrimStart method's syntax is *string*.**TrimStart**[(*trimChars*)], and the TrimEnd method's syntax is *string*.**TrimEnd**[(*trimChars*)]. The optional *trimChars* argument is a comma-separated list of characters that you want removed (trimmed). For example, if the txtSales control contains the string "$56.80", you can remove the dollar sign from the control's Text property using the statement `txtSales.Text = txtSales.Text.TrimStart("$"c)`. The default value for the *trimChars* argument is the space character (" "c). When processing the TrimStart and TrimEnd methods, the computer makes a temporary copy of the string in memory; it then removes the characters from the copy only. Open the Tax Calculator Solution (Tax Calculator Solution.sln) file contained in the VB2010\Chap08\Tax Calculator Solution folder. The Calculate button's Click event procedure should calculate and display the sales tax, using the amount entered in the text box and the rate selected in the list box. Code the procedure. Save the solution and then start and test the application. Close the Code Editor window and then close the solution.

19. Visual Basic provides the Mid statement for replacing a specified number of characters in a string with another string. The statement's syntax is **Mid**(*targetString*, *start*[, *count*]) = *replacementString*. In the syntax, the *targetString* argument is the string in which you want characters replaced, and *replacementString* contains the replacement characters. The *start* argument is the position of the first character you want replaced in the targetString. The first character in the targetString is in position 1; the second is in position 2, and so on. The optional *count* argument specifies the number of characters to replace in the targetString. If the count argument is omitted, the Mid statement replaces the lesser of either the number of characters in the replacementString or the number of characters in the targetString from position *start* through the end of the targetString. Open the Area Code Solution (Area Code Solution.sln) file contained in the VB2010\Chap08\Area Code Solution folder. The interface allows the user to enter a phone number, including the area code. Code the Change Area Code button's Click event procedure so that it first verifies whether the phone number is in the proper format. If the format is valid, the procedure should use the Mid statement to change the area code to 800 before displaying the phone number in the lblNew control. Save the solution and then start and test the application. Close the Code Editor window and then close the solution.

▌ LESSON B

After studying Lesson B, you should be able to:

- Include a MenuStrip control on a form

- Add elements to a menu

- Assign access keys to menu elements

- Assign shortcut keys to commonly used menu items

- Code a menu item's Click event procedure

Adding a Menu to a Form

The Menus and Toolbars section of the toolbox contains a MenuStrip tool for instantiating a menu strip control. You use a **menu strip control** to include one or more menus on a Windows form. Each menu contains a menu title, which appears on the menu bar at the top of the form. When you click a menu title, its corresponding menu opens and displays a list of options, called menu items. The menu items can be commands (such as Open or Exit), separator bars, or submenu titles. As in all Windows applications, clicking a command on a menu executes the command, and clicking a submenu title opens an additional menu of options. Each of the options on a submenu is referred to as a submenu item. You can use a separator bar to visually group together related items on a menu or submenu. Figure 8-19 identifies the location of these menu elements. Although you can create many levels of submenus, it is best to use only one level in your application, because too many layers of submenus can be confusing to the user.

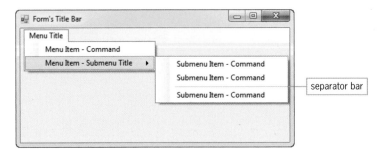

Figure 8-19   Location of menu elements

Each menu element is considered an object; therefore, each has a set of properties associated with it. The most commonly used properties for a menu element are the Name and Text properties. The programmer uses the Name property to refer to the menu element in code. The Text property stores the menu element's caption, which is the text that the user sees when he or she is working with the menu. The caption indicates the purpose of the menu element. Examples of familiar captions for menu elements include Edit, Save As, Copy, and Exit.

Menu title captions should be one word only, with the first letter capitalized. Each menu title should have a unique access key. The access key allows the user to open the menu by pressing the Alt key in combination with the access key. Unlike the captions for menu titles, the captions for menu items typically consist of one to three words. The Windows standard is to use book title capitalization for the menu item captions. Each menu item should have an access key that is unique within its menu. The access key allows the user to select the item by pressing the access key when the menu is open. If a menu item requires additional information from the user, the Windows standard is to place an ellipsis (...) at the end of the caption. The ellipsis alerts the user that the menu item requires more information before it can perform its task.

The menus included in your application should follow the standard Windows conventions. For example, if your application uses a File menu, it should be the first menu on the menu bar. File menus typically contain commands for opening, saving, and printing files, as well as exiting the application. If your application requires Cut, Copy, and Paste commands, the commands should be placed on an Edit menu, which typically is the second menu on the menu bar.

Recall that your task in this chapter is to create an application that simulates the Hangman game. Most of the application's interface has been created for you. To complete the interface, you just need to add a File menu to it. The File menu will contain three menu items: a New Game command, a separator bar, and an Exit command.

The Ch08BVideo file demonstrates all of the steps contained in Lesson B. You can view the video either before or after completing the lesson.

START HERE

To complete the Hangman Game application's interface:

1. If necessary, start Visual Studio 2010 or Visual Basic 2010 Express. Open the Hangman Game Solution (Hangman Game Solution.sln) file contained in the VB2010\Chap08\Hangman Game Solution folder. If necessary, open the designer, Toolbox, and Properties windows. The interface contains four label controls, 10 picture boxes, and a panel control. You create a panel control using the Panel tool, which is located in the Containers section of the toolbox.

2. Click the **MenuStrip** tool, which is located in the Menus & Toolbars section of the toolbox. Drag the mouse pointer to the form and then release the mouse button. A MenuStrip control named MenuStrip1 appears in the component tray, and the words "Type Here" appear in a box on the form's title bar. See Figure 8-20.

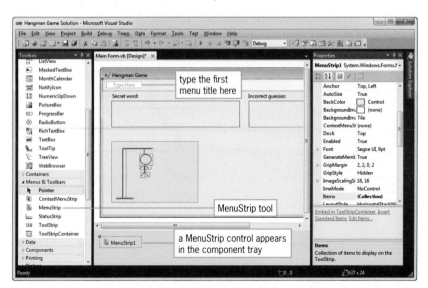

Figure 8-20 MenuStrip control added to the form

477

3. Auto-hide the toolbox. Click the **Type Here** box on the menu bar and then type **&File**. See Figure 8-21. You use the Type Here box that appears below the menu title to add a menu item to the File menu. You use the Type Here box that appears to the right of the menu title to add another menu title to the menu bar.

478

Figure 8-21   Menu title included on the form

4. Press **Enter** and then click the **File** menu title. Scroll the Properties window until you see the Text property; notice that the property contains &File.

5. Scroll to the top of the Properties window and then click **(Name)**. Type **mnuFile** and then press **Enter**.

6. Click the **Type Here** box that appears below the File menu title. Type **&New Game** and then press **Enter**.

7. Click the **New Game** menu item. Change the menu item's name to **mnuFileNew**.

8. Next, you will add a separator bar to the File menu. Place your mouse pointer on the Type Here box that appears below the New Game menu item, but don't click the box. Instead, click the **list arrow** that appears inside the box. See Figure 8-22.

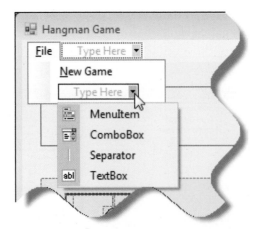

Figure 8-22   Drop-down list

9. Click **Separator** in the list. A horizontal line, called a separator bar, appears below the New Game menu item.

10. Click the **Type Here** box that appears below the separator bar. Type **E&xit** and then press **Enter**. Click the **Exit** menu item. Change the menu item's name to **mnuFileExit**.

11. Save the solution and then start the application. Click **File** on the menu bar. The File menu opens and offers two options separated by a separator bar. See Figure 8-23.

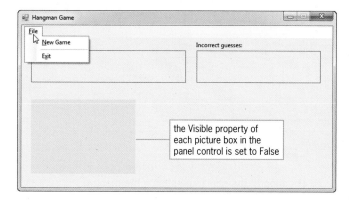

Figure 8-23 File menu opened during run time

12. Click the **Close** button on the form's title bar.

Assigning Shortcut Keys to Menu Items

Commonly used menu items should be assigned shortcut keys. The **shortcut keys** appear to the right of a menu item and allow the user to select the item without opening the menu. Examples of familiar shortcut keys include Ctrl+X and Ctrl+V. In Windows applications that have an Edit menu, Ctrl+X and Ctrl+V are used to select the Cut and Paste commands, respectively, when the Edit menu is closed. In the Hangman Game application, you will assign shortcut keys to the New Game option on the File menu.

> A menu item's access key can be used only when the menu is open. A menu item's shortcut key can be used only when the menu is closed.

To assign shortcut keys to the New Game menu item:

START HERE

1. Click the **New Game** menu item on the File menu. Click **ShortcutKeys** in the Properties window and then click the **list arrow** in the Settings box. A box opens and allows you to specify a modifier and a key. In this case, the modifier and key will be Ctrl and N, respectively. Click the **Ctrl** check box to select it, and then click the **list arrow** that appears in the Key combo box. An alphabetical list of keys appears. Scroll the list until you see the letter N, and then click **N** in the list. See Figure 8-24.

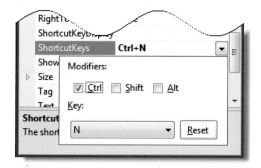

Figure 8-24 Shortcut key specified in the ShortcutKeys box

2. Press **Enter**. Ctrl+N appears in the ShortcutKeys property in the Properties list. It also appears to the right of the New Game menu item.

3. Auto-hide the Properties window. Save the solution and then start the application. Click **File** on the menu bar. See Figure 8-25.

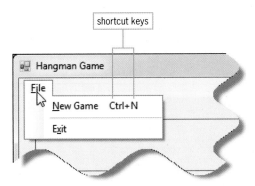

Figure 8-25   Location of the shortcut keys on the menu

4. Click the **Close** button on the form's title bar.

GUI DESIGN TIP   Menu Standards

*   Menu title captions should begin with a capital letter and be one word only. Each menu title should have a unique access key.

*   Menu item captions can be from one to three words. Use book title capitalization and assign a unique access key to each menu item on the same menu.

*   Assign unique shortcut keys to commonly used menu items.

*   If a menu item requires additional information from the user, place an ellipsis (...) at the end of the item's caption, which is entered in the item's Text property.

*   Follow the Windows standards for the placement of menu titles and items.

*   Use a separator bar to separate groups of related menu items.

Coding the Exit Menu Item

When the user clicks the Exit option on the Hangman Game application's File menu, the option's Click event procedure should end the application.

START HERE   **To code and then test the Exit menu item:**

1. Open the Code Editor window. Replace <your name> and <current date> in the comments with your name and the current date, respectively.

2. Open the code template for the mnuFileExit item's Click event procedure. Enter the following statement:

Me.Close()

3. Save the solution and then start the application. Click **File** on the Hangman Game application's menu bar and then click **Exit** to end the application. Close the Code Editor window and then close the solution.

Lesson B Summary

- To add a MenuStrip control to a form:

  Use the MenuStrip tool, which is located in the Menus & Toolbars section of the toolbox.

- To create a menu:

  Replace the words "Type Here" with the menu element's caption. Assign a meaningful name and a unique access key to each menu element, with the exception of separator bars.

- To include a separator bar on a menu:

  Place your mouse pointer on a Type Here box and then click the list arrow that appears inside the box. Click Separator on the list.

- To assign shortcut keys to a menu item:

  Set the menu item's ShortcutKeys property.

Lesson B Key Terms

Menu strip control—used to include one or more menus on a form

Shortcut keys—appear to the right of a menu item and allow the user to select the item without opening the menu

Lesson B Review Questions

1. The horizontal line in a menu is called _____ .

   a. a menu bar

   b. a separator bar

   c. an item separator

   d. none of the above

2. The underlined letter in a menu element's caption is called _____ .

   a. an access key

   b. a menu key

   c. a shortcut key

   d. none of the above

3. Which of the following allows the user to access a menu item without opening the menu?

   a. an access key

   b. a menu key

   c. shortcut keys

   d. none of the above

4. Which of the following is false?

   a. Menu titles should be one word only.

   b. Each menu title should have a unique access key.

   c. You should assign shortcut keys to commonly used menu titles.

   d. Menu items should be entered using book title capitalization.

5. Explain the difference between a menu item's access key and its shortcut keys.

Lesson B Exercises

INTRODUCTORY

1. Open the Bonus Solution (Bonus Solution.sln) file contained in the VB2010\Chap08\Bonus Solution folder. If necessary, open the designer window. Add a File menu to the form. The File menu should contain an Exit menu item that ends the application. Enter the appropriate code in the menu item's Click event procedure. Save the solution and then start the application. Use the Exit option on the File menu to end the application. Close the Code Editor window and then close the solution.

INTERMEDIATE

2. Open the Commission Solution (Commission Solution.sln) file contained in the VB2010\Chap08\Commission Solution folder. If necessary, open the designer window. Add a File menu and a Calculate menu to the form. Include an Exit menu item on the File menu. Include two menu items on the Calculate menu: 2% Commission and 5% Commission. Assign shortcut keys to the Calculate menu's items. When the user clicks the Exit menu item, the application should end. When the user clicks the 2% Commission menu item, the application should calculate and display a 2% commission on the sales entered by the user. When the user clicks the 5% Commission menu item, the application should calculate and display a 5% commission on the sales entered by the user. Enter the appropriate code in each menu item's Click event procedure. Save the solution and then start and test the application. Close the Code Editor window and then close the solution.

LESSON C

After studying Lesson C, you should be able to:

- Include the Length property in a procedure
- Include the Substring method in a procedure
- Include the Like operator in a procedure
- Include the Remove method in a procedure
- Include the Insert method in a procedure
- Include the Contains method in a procedure

Completing the Hangman Game Application

Figure 8-26 shows the Hangman Game application's TOE chart. You coded the mnuFileExit object's Click event procedure in Lesson B. In this lesson, you will complete the application by coding the mnuFileNew object's Click event procedure.

Task	Object	Event
1.　Hide the 10 picture boxes	mnuFileNew	Click
2.　Get a five-letter word from player 1		
3.　Determine whether the word contains exactly 5 letters		
4.　Display 5 dashes in lblWord		
5.　Clear lblIncorrect		
6.　Get a letter from player 2		
7.　Search the word for the letter		
8.　If the letter is contained in the word, replace the appropriate dashes		
9.　If the letter is not contained in the word, display the letter in lblIncorrect, add 1 to the number of incorrect guesses, and show the appropriate picture box		
10.　If all of the dashes have been replaced, the game is over, so display the message "Great guessing!" in a message box		
11.　If the user makes 10 incorrect guesses, the game is over, so display an appropriate message and the word in a message box		
End the application	mnuFileExit	Click
Display the Hangman images	picBottom, picPost, picTop, picRope, picHead, picBody, picRightArm, picLeftArm, picRightLeg, picLeftLeg	None
Display dashes and letters (from mnuFileNew)	lblWord	None
Display the incorrect letters (from mnuFileNew)	lblIncorrect	None

Figure 8-26　TOE chart for the Hangman Game application

 The Ch08CVideo file demonstrates all of the steps contained in Lesson C. You can view the video either before or after completing the lesson.

START HERE **To open the Hangman Game application from Lesson B:**

1. If necessary, start Visual Studio 2010 or Visual Basic 2010 Express.

2. Open the Hangman Game Solution (Hangman Game Solution.sln) file contained in the VB2010\Chap08\Hangman Game Solution folder. If necessary, open the designer window. See Figure 8-27.

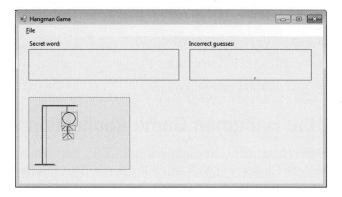

Figure 8-27   Interface for the Hangman Game application from Lesson B

Coding the mnuFileNew Object's Click Event Procedure

The mnuFileNew object's Click event procedure is invoked when the user clicks the New Game option on the File menu. The procedure should allow player 1 to enter a five-letter word and then allow player 2 to guess the word, letter by letter. The game is over when player 2 either guesses all of the letters in the word or makes 10 incorrect guesses, whichever comes first. The procedure's pseudocode is shown in Figure 8-28.

<u>mnuFileNew Click event procedure</u>
1. hide the 10 picture boxes
2. get a 5-letter word from player 1 and convert it to uppercase
3. if the word does not contain exactly 5 letters
       assign False to blnValidWord variable
  else
      if the word does not contain only letters
        assign False to blnValidWord variable
      end if
  end if
4. if the blnValidWord variable contains False
       display an appropriate message
  else
      display 5 dashes in lblWord
      clear lblIncorrect

      get a letter from player 2 and convert it to uppercase
      repeat while the user entered a letter and the game is not over
        repeat for each letter in the word
          if the current letter is the same as the letter entered by player 2

Figure 8-28   Pseudocode for the mnuFileNew object's Click event procedure *(continues)*

(continued)

```
                        replace the appropriate dash in lblWord
                        assign True to blnDashReplaced variable
                    end if
                end repeat

                if the blnDashReplaced variable contains True
                    if lblWord does not contain any dashes
                        assign True to the blnGameOver variable
                        display the "Great guessing!" message
                    else
                        assign False to the blnDashReplaced variable
                    end if
                else
                        display the incorrect letter in lblIncorrect
                        add 1 to the number of incorrect guesses counter

                        value of the number of incorrect guesses counter:
                        1    show picBottom
                        2    show picPost
                        3    show picTop
                        4    show picRope
                        5    show picHead
                        6    show picBody
                        7    show picRightArm
                        8    show picLeftArm
                        9    show picRightLeg
                        10   show picLeftLeg
                            assign True to the blnGameOver variable
                            display the "Sorry, the word is" message and the word
                end if

                if the blnGameOver variable contains False
                        get another letter from the user
                end if
            end repeat
        end if
```

Figure 8-28   Pseudocode for the mnuFileNew object's Click event procedure

To code the mnuFileNew object's Click event procedure:

START HERE

1. Open the Code Editor window and then open the code template for the mnuFileNew object's Click event procedure. Type the following comment and then press **Enter** twice:

    ' simulates the Hangman game

2. The procedure will use six variables: two String variables, three Boolean variables, and one Integer variable. The `strWord` and `strLetter` variables will store the word entered by player 1 and the letter entered by player 2, respectively. The `blnValidWord` variable will store a Boolean value that indicates whether the word entered

by player 1 is valid. To be valid, the word must contain exactly five letters. The `blnDashReplaced` variable will keep track of whether a dash was replaced in the word, and the `blnGameOver` variable will indicate whether the game is over. The `intIncorrect` variable will keep track of the number of incorrect guesses made by player 2. Enter the following Dim statements. Press **Enter** twice after typing the last Dim statement.

Dim strWord As String
Dim strLetter As String
Dim blnValidWord As Boolean
Dim blnDashReplaced As Boolean
Dim blnGameOver As Boolean
Dim intIncorrect As Integer

3. The first step in the pseudocode is to hide the 10 picture boxes. Enter the following comment and assignment statements. Press **Enter** twice after typing the last assignment statement.

' hide the picture boxes
picBottom.Visible = False
picPost.Visible = False
picTop.Visible = False
picRope.Visible = False
picHead.Visible = False
picBody.Visible = False
picRightArm.Visible = False
picLeftArm.Visible = False
picRightLeg.Visible = False
picLeftLeg.Visible = False

4. The next step is to get a five-letter word from player 1 and convert it to uppercase. Enter the following comment and lines of code. Press **Enter** twice after typing the last line.

' get a 5-letter word from player 1 and convert to uppercase
strWord = InputBox("Enter a 5-letter word:",
                    "Hangman Game").ToUpper

5. Now you need to verify that the word contains exactly five letters. Enter the comments and code indicated in Figure 8-29, and then position the insertion point as shown in the figure. Be sure to include the exclamation point in the "[!A-Z]" *characterList*.

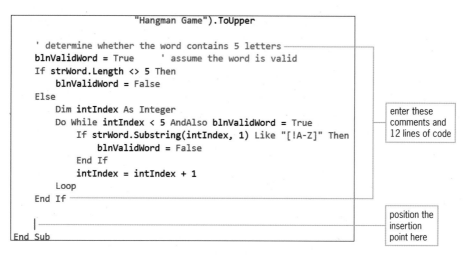

Figure 8-29   Additional comments and code entered in the procedure

6. If the word does not contain exactly five letters, the `blnValidWord` variable will contain False. In that case, you should display an appropriate message. Enter the comment and code indicated in Figure 8-30, and then position the insertion point as shown in the figure.

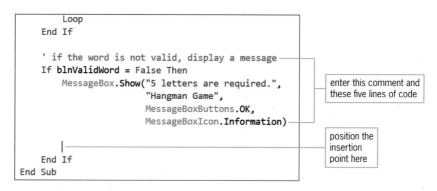

Figure 8-30   Comment and selection structure's true path

7. However, if the word does contain exactly five letters, you should display five dashes in the lblWord control and then clear the lblIncorrect control. Enter the following Else clause, comment, and assignment statement. (The first assignment statement assigns five hyphens to the lblWord control's Text property.) Press **Enter** twice after typing the last assignment statement.

Else
    ' display five dashes in lblWord and clear lblIncorrect
    lblWord.Text = "-----"
    lblIncorrect.Text = String.Empty

8. Save the solution. Next, you need to get a letter from player 2 and then convert it to uppercase. Enter the following comment and lines of code. Press **Enter** twice after typing the last line.

' get a letter from player 2 and convert to uppercase
strLetter = InputBox("Enter a letter:",
                "Letter", "", 600, 400).ToUpper

9. The next task in the pseudocode is a pretest loop that repeats its instructions as long as both of the following conditions are true: player 2 entered a letter and the game is not over. Enter the following comments and Do clause:

**' verify that player 2 entered a letter
' and that the game is not over
Do While strLetter <> String.Empty AndAlso
　　　　blnGameOver = False**

10. If the user entered a letter and the game is not over, you need to determine whether the letter appears in the word. You can accomplish this using a counter-controlled loop that compares the letter with each character in the word, character by character. Enter the following comment and For clause:

**' search the word for the letter
For intIndex As Integer = 0 To 4**

11. Change the Next clause to **Next intIndex**.

12. According to the pseudocode, the loop should use a selection structure to compare the current letter in the word with the letter entered by player 2. If both letters are the same, the selection structure's true path should replace the appropriate dash in the lblWord control. It also should assign the Boolean value True to the `blnDashReplaced` variable to indicate that a dash was replaced in the label control. Enter the comments and selection structure shown in Figure 8-31, and then position the insertion point as shown in the figure.

```
' verify that player 2 entered a letter
' and that the game is not over
Do While strLetter <> String.Empty AndAlso
        blnGameOver = False
    ' search the word for the letter
    For intIndex As Integer = 0 To 4
        ' if the letter appears in the word, then
        ' replace the dash in lblWord and
        ' indicate that a replacement was made
        If strWord.Substring(intIndex, 1) = strLetter Then
            lblWord.Text = lblWord.Text.Remove(intIndex, 1)
            lblWord.Text = lblWord.Text.Insert(intIndex, strLetter)
            blnDashReplaced = True
        End If
    Next intIndex

    Loop
End If
```

enter these comments and five lines of code

position the insertion point here

Figure 8-31 Additional comments and selection structure entered in the procedure

13. If a dash was replaced in the lblWord control, you need to determine whether the control contains any more dashes. If there are no more dashes in the control, it means that the user has guessed the word and the game is over. In that case, you should assign True to the `blnGameOver` variable and then display the "Great guessing!" message. However, if the lblWord control contains at least one dash,

you should reset the `blnDashReplaced` variable's value to False. Enter the comments and selection structures shown in Figure 8-32, and then position the insertion point as shown in the figure.

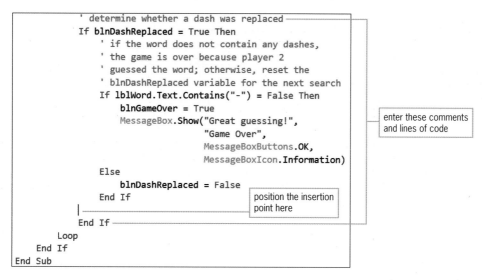

```
' determine whether a dash was replaced
If blnDashReplaced = True Then
    ' if the word does not contain any dashes,
    ' the game is over because player 2
    ' guessed the word; otherwise, reset the
    ' blnDashReplaced variable for the next search
    If lblWord.Text.Contains("-") = False Then
        blnGameOver = True
        MessageBox.Show("Great guessing!",
                        "Game Over",
                        MessageBoxButtons.OK,
                        MessageBoxIcon.Information)
    Else
        blnDashReplaced = False
    End If
    |
End If
Loop
End If
End Sub
```

enter these comments and lines of code

position the insertion point here

Figure 8-32   Additional comments and selection structures entered in the procedure

14. On the other hand, if no dash was replaced, it means that player 2's letter does not appear in the word. Therefore, you should perform the following tasks: display the incorrect letter in the lblIncorrect control, update the `intIncorrect` variable by 1, and use the variable's value to display the appropriate picture box. Enter the following comments and lines of code. Be sure to include a space between the quotation marks in the statement that assigns a value to the lblIncorrect control's Text property.

```
Else    ' processed when no dash was replaced
    ' display the incorrect letter, then update
    ' the intIncorrect variable, then show
    ' the appropriate picture box
    lblIncorrect.Text = _
        lblIncorrect.Text & " " & strLetter
    intIncorrect = intIncorrect + 1
    Select Case intIncorrect
        Case 1
            picBottom.Visible = True
        Case 2
            picPost.Visible = True
        Case 3
            picTop.Visible = True
        Case 4
            picRope.Visible = True
        Case 5
            picHead.Visible = True
        Case 6
            picBody.Visible = True
        Case 7
            picRightArm.Visible = True
```

Case 8
     picLeftArm.Visible = True
Case 9
     picRightLeg.Visible = True
Case 10
     picLeftLeg.Visible = True
     blnGameOver = True
     MessageBox.Show("Sorry, the word is " &
         strWord & ".", "Game Over",
         MessageBoxButtons.OK,
         MessageBoxIcon.Information)
End Select

15. Save the solution. As the pseudocode shown earlier in Figure 8-28 indicates, the last task determines whether you need to get another letter from the user. Another letter is necessary only when the game is not over. Insert two blank lines above the Loop clause and then enter the comment and selection structure shown in Figure 8-33.

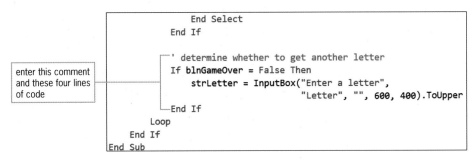

enter this comment and these four lines of code

Figure 8-33   Final comment and selection structure entered in the procedure

START HERE

To test the application's code:

1. Save the solution and then start the application. Click **File** on the application's menu bar and then click **New Game**. The Hangman Game dialog box opens and prompts you to enter a five-letter word. Type **cat** in the dialog box and then press **Enter**. A message box opens and informs you that five letters are required. Press **Enter** to close the message box.

2. Press **Ctrl+n**, which are the New Game option's shortcut keys. Type **cats4** and then press **Enter**. A message box opens and informs you that five letters are required. Close the message box.

3. Click **File** and then click **New Game**. Type **puppy** and press **Enter**. The Letter dialog box opens and prompts you to enter a letter. Type **p** and press **Enter**. Three of the dashes in the Secret word box are replaced with the letter P. See Figure 8-34.

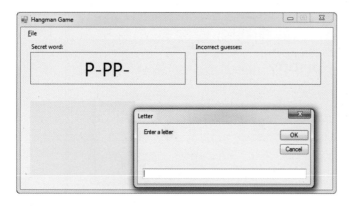

Figure 8-34   Dashes replaced with the letter P

491

4. Type **a** in the Letter dialog box and press **Enter**. The mnuFileNew object's Click event procedure displays the letter A in the Incorrect guesses box and also makes the picBottom control visible. See Figure 8-35.

Figure 8-35   Result of entering the first incorrect letter

5. Type **b** in the Letter dialog box and press **Enter**. The letter B is added to the contents of the Incorrect guesses box and the picPost control is now visible.

6. Type **u** in the Letter dialog box and press **Enter**. Now, type **y** and press **Enter**. The "Great guessing!" message appears in a message box. If necessary, drag the message box down and to the right until you can see the entire contents of the Secret word and Incorrect guesses boxes. See Figure 8-36.

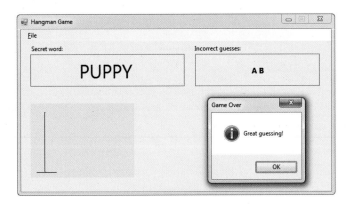

Figure 8-36 Result of guessing the word

7. Close the message box. Now you will observe what happens when you make 10 incorrect guesses. Press **Ctrl+n**. Type **basic** and press **Enter**. Now type the following 12 letters, pressing **Enter** after typing each letter: **d, c, e, f, g, h, a, j, k, x, y, z**. The mnuFileNew object's Click event procedure displays the 10 incorrect letters and 10 picture boxes, as well as a message box. Drag the message box to the location shown in Figure 8-37.

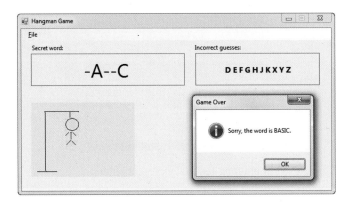

Figure 8-37 Result of making 10 incorrect guesses

8. Close the message box. Click **File** on the application's menu bar and then click **Exit**. Close the Code Editor window and then close the solution. Figure 8-38 shows the application's code.

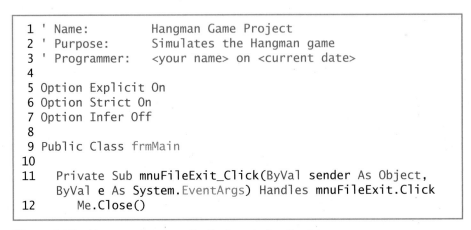

```
1 ' Name:          Hangman Game Project
2 ' Purpose:       Simulates the Hangman game
3 ' Programmer:    <your name> on <current date>
4
5 Option Explicit On
6 Option Strict On
7 Option Infer Off
8
9 Public Class frmMain
10
11    Private Sub mnuFileExit_Click(ByVal sender As Object,
      ByVal e As System.EventArgs) Handles mnuFileExit.Click
12        Me.Close()
```

Figure 8-38 Hangman Game application's code *(continues)*

(continued)

```
13
14       End Sub
15
16       Private Sub mnuFileNew_Click(ByVal sender As Object,
         ByVal e As System.EventArgs) Handles mnuFileNew.Click
17           ' simulates the Hangman game
18
19           Dim strWord As String
20           Dim strLetter As String
21           Dim blnValidWord As Boolean
22           Dim blnDashReplaced As Boolean
23           Dim blnGameOver As Boolean
24           Dim intIncorrect As Integer
25
26           ' hide the picture boxes
27           picBottom.Visible = False
28           picPost.Visible = False
29           picTop.Visible = False
30           picRope.Visible = False
31           picHead.Visible = False
32           picBody.Visible = False
33           picRightArm.Visible = False
34           picLeftArm.Visible = False
35           picRightLeg.Visible = False
36           picLeftLeg.Visible = False
37
38           ' get a 5-letter word from player 1 and
             convert to uppercase
39           strWord = InputBox("Enter a 5-letter word:",
40                               "Hangman Game").ToUpper
41
42           ' determine whether the word contains 5 letters
43           blnValidWord = True       ' assume the word is valid
44           If strWord.Length <> 5 Then
45               blnValidWord = False
46           Else
47               Dim intIndex As Integer
48               Do While intIndex < 5 AndAlso blnValidWord = True
49                   If strWord.Substring(intIndex, 1) Like
                            "[!A-Z]" Then
50                       blnValidWord = False
51                   End If
52                   intIndex = intIndex + 1
53               Loop
54           End If
55
56           ' if the word is not valid, display a message
57           If blnValidWord = False Then
58               MessageBox.Show("5 letters are required.",
59                               "Hangman Game",
60                               MessageBoxButtons.OK,
61                               MessageBoxIcon.Information)
62
63           Else
64                   ' display five dashes in lblWord and
                     clear lblIncorrect
```

Figure 8-38   Hangman Game application's code *(continues)*

(continued)

```
65              lblWord.Text = "-----"
66              lblIncorrect.Text = String.Empty
67
68          ' get a letter from player 2 and
            convert to uppercase
69          strLetter = InputBox("Enter a letter:",
70                      "Letter", "", 600, 400).ToUpper
71
72          ' verify that player 2 entered a letter
73          ' and that the game is not over
74          Do While strLetter <> String.Empty AndAlso
75                  blnGameOver = False
76            ' search the word for the letter
77            For intIndex As Integer = 0 To 4
78              ' if the letter appears in the word, then
79              ' replace the dash in lblWord and
80              ' indicate that a replacement was made
81              If strWord.Substring(intIndex, 1) =
                    strLetter Then
82                lblWord.Text =
                    lblWord.Text.Remove(intIndex, 1)
83                lblWord.Text =
                    lblWord.Text.Insert(intIndex, strLetter)
84                blnDashReplaced = True
85              End If
86            Next intIndex
87
88            ' determine whether a dash was replaced
89            If blnDashReplaced = True Then
90                ' if the word does not contain any dashes,
91                ' the game is over because player 2
92                ' guessed the word; otherwise, reset the
93                ' blnDashReplaced variable for
                  the next search
94                If lblWord.Text.Contains("-") = False Then
95                    blnGameOver = True
96                    MessageBox.Show("Great guessing!",
97                            "Game Over",
98                            MessageBoxButtons.OK,
99                            MessageBoxIcon.Information)
100               Else
101                   blnDashReplaced = False
102               End If
103           Else       ' processed when no dash was
                          replaced
104               ' display the incorrect letter, then update
105               ' the intIncorrect variable, then show
106               ' the appropriate picture box
107               lblIncorrect.Text =
108                   lblIncorrect.Text & " " & strLetter
109               intIncorrect = intIncorrect + 1
110               Select Case intIncorrect
111                   Case 1
112                       picBottom.Visible = True
113                   Case 2
114                       picPost.Visible = True
```

Figure 8-38   Hangman Game application's code *(continues)*

(continued)

```
115                         Case 3
116                             picTop.Visible = True
117                         Case 4
118                             picRope.Visible = True
119                         Case 5
120                             picHead.Visible = True
121                         Case 6
122                             picBody.Visible = True
123                         Case 7
124                             picRightArm.Visible = True
125                         Case 8
126                             picLeftArm.Visible = True
127                         Case 9
128                             picRightLeg.Visible = True
129                         Case 10
130                             picLeftLeg.Visible = True
131                             blnGameOver = True
132                             MessageBox.Show("Sorry,
                                the word is " &
133                                 strWord & ".", "Game Over",
134                                 MessageBoxButtons.OK,
135                                 MessageBoxIcon.Information)
136                     End Select
137                 End If
138
139                 ' determine whether to get another letter
140                 If blnGameOver = False Then
141                     strLetter = InputBox("Enter a letter",
142                         "Letter", "", 600, 400).ToUpper
143                 End If
144             Loop
145         End If
146     End Sub
147 End Class
```

Figure 8-38   Hangman Game application's code

Lesson C Summary

- To determine the length of a string:

  Use the string's Length property.

- To access one or more characters in a string:

  Use the Substring method.

- To use pattern-matching to compare two strings:

  Use the Like operator.

- To remove a specified number of characters located anywhere in a string:

  Use the Remove method.

- To insert characters anywhere in a string:

  Use the Insert method.

- To determine whether a specific character is contained in a string:

  Use the Contains method.

Lesson C Key Terms

There are no key terms in Lesson C.

Lesson C Review Questions

1. The `strName` variable contains 10 characters. Which of the following For clauses will access each character contained in the variable, character by character?

   a. `For intIndex As Integer = 0 To 10`

   b. `For intIndex As Integer = 0 To strName.Length - 1`

   c. `For intIndex As Integer = 1 To 10`

   d. `For intIndex As Integer = 1 To strName.Length - 1`

2. Which of the following changes the contents of the `strName` variable from Carl to Carla?

   a. `strName = strName.Append(4, "a")`

   b. `strName = strName.Append(5, "a")`

   c. `strName = strName.Insert(4, "a")`

   d. `strName = strName.Insert(5, "a")`

3. If the `strWord` variable contains the string "Irene Turner", what value will the `strWord.Contains("r")` method return?

   a. True

   b. False

   c. 1

   d. 2

4. The `strItem` variable contains uppercase letters only. Which of the following determines whether the variable contains either the word "SHIRT" or the word "SKIRT"?

   a. `If strItem = "SHIRT" AndAlso strItem = "SKIRT" Then`

   b. `If strItem = "S[HK]IRT" Then`

   c. `If strItem Like "S[HK]IRT" Then`

   d. `If strItem Like "S[H-K]IRT" Then`

5. Which of the following returns the Boolean value True when the
    `strPetName` variable contains the string "Micki"?

    a. `strPetName.Contains("k")`

    b. `strPetName Like "M*"`

    c. `strPetName.Substring(2, 1) = "c"`

    d. all of the above

Lesson C Exercises

1. Open the Item Number Solution (Item Number Solution.sln) file con-
    tained in the VB2010\Chap08\Item Number Solution folder. If neces-
    sary, open the designer window. Open the Code Editor window. The
    btnVerify control's Click event procedure should determine whether
    the user entered the item number in the required format: three digits,
    a hyphen, a letter, a hyphen, and two digits. Display an appropriate
    message indicating whether the format is correct or incorrect. Code
    the procedure. Save the solution and then start and test the applica-
    tion. Close the Code Editor window and then close the solution.

    INTRODUCTORY

2. Open the Color Solution (Color Solution.sln) file contained in
    the VB2010\Chap08\Color Solution folder. If necessary, open the
    designer window. The Display Color button's Click event procedure
    should display the color of the item whose item number is entered by
    the user. All item numbers contain exactly seven characters. All items
    are available in four colors: blue, green, red, and white. The fourth
    character in the item number indicates the item's color, as follows: a B
    or b indicates Blue, a G or g indicates Green, an R or r indicates Red,
    and a W or w indicates White. If the item number does not contain
    exactly seven characters, or if the fourth character is not one of the
    valid color characters, the procedure should display an appropriate
    message. Code the procedure. Save the solution and then start and
    test the application. Close the Code Editor window and then close the
    solution.

    INTRODUCTORY

3. In this exercise, you modify the Hangman Game application com-
    pleted in Lesson C. Use Windows to make a copy of the Hangman
    Game Solution folder. Rename the copy Modified Hangman Game
    Solution. Open the Hangman Game Solution (Hangman Game
    Solution.sln) file contained in the Modified Hangman Game Solution
    folder. Open the designer and Code Editor windows. Modify the code
    to allow player 1 to enter a word that contains any number of letters,
    up to a maximum of 10 letters. Also verify that the character entered
    by player 2 is a letter of the alphabet. Save the solution and then start
    and test the application. Close the Code Editor window and then
    close the solution.

    INTERMEDIATE

4. Open the Reverse Letters Solution (Reverse Letters Solution.sln) file
    contained in the VB2010\Chap08\Reverse Letters Solution folder.
    The interface provides a text box for the user to enter a word. The

    INTERMEDIATE

Reverse Letters button's Click event procedure should display the letters in reverse order. In other words, if the user enters the word "Programming", the procedure should display "gnimmargorP". Code the procedure. Save the solution and then start and test the application. Close the Code Editor window and then close the solution.

INTERMEDIATE

5. Open the Proper Case Solution (Proper Case Solution.sln) file contained in the VB2010\Chap08\Proper Case Solution folder. The interface provides a text box for the user to enter a person's first and last names. The Proper Case button's Click event procedure should display the first and last names in the proper case. In other words, the first and last names should begin with an uppercase letter and the remaining letters should be lowercase. Code the procedure. Save the solution and then start and test the application. Close the Code Editor window and then close the solution.

INTERMEDIATE

6. Open the Part Number Solution (Part Number Solution.sln) file contained in the VB2010\Chap08\Part Number Solution folder. The interface allows the user to enter a part number, which will consist of two numbers followed by either one or two letters. The letter or letters represent the delivery method, as follows: MS represents Mail – Standard, MP represents Mail – Priority, FS represents FedEx – Standard, FO represents FedEx – Overnight, and U represents UPS. Code the Select Delivery button's Click event procedure so that it uses the Like operator to select the appropriate delivery method in the list box. Display an appropriate message when the part number does not contain two numbers followed by one or two letters, or when the letters do not represent a valid delivery method. Save the solution and then start the application. Test the application using the following data: 73mp, 34fs, 12u, 78h, 9FO, and 34ms. Close the Code Editor window and then close the solution.

INTERMEDIATE

7. Before completing this exercise, you should complete Lesson A's Discovery Exercise 16. Open the Jacobson Solution (Jacobson Solution.sln) file contained in the VB2010\Chap08\Jacobson Solution folder. The interface provides a text box for entering a password. The password can contain five, six, or seven characters (but no spaces). The Display New Password button should create and display a new password using the following three rules. First, replace all vowels (A, E, I, O, and U) with the letter X. Second, replace all numbers with the letter Z. Third, reverse the characters in the password. Code the procedure. Save the solution and then start and test the application. Close the Code Editor window and then close the solution.

ADVANCED

8. Each salesperson at BobCat Motors is assigned an ID number that consists of four characters. The first character is either the letter F or the letter P. The letter F indicates that the salesperson is a full-time employee. The letter P indicates that he or she is a part-time employee. The middle two characters are the salesperson's initials, and the last character is either a 1 or a 2. A 1 indicates that the

salesperson sells new cars, and a 2 indicates that the salesperson sells used cars. Create a Visual Basic Windows application. Use the following names for the solution, project, and form file, respectively: BobCat Motors Solution, BobCat Motors Project, and Main Form. vb. Save the application in the VB2010\Chap08 folder. Create the interface shown in Figure 8-39. The application should allow the sales manager to enter the ID and number of cars sold for as many salespeople as needed. The application should calculate and display the total number of cars sold by each of the following four categories of employees: full-time employees, part-time employees, employees selling new cars, and employees selling used cars. Code the application. Save the solution and then start and test the application. Close the Code Editor window and then close the solution.

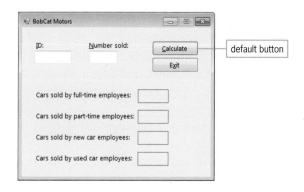

Figure 8-39   Sample interface for Exercise 8

9. Create a Visual Basic Windows application. Use the following names for the solution, project, and form file, respectively: Pig Latin Solution, Pig Latin Project, and Main Form.vb. Save the application in the VB2010\Chap08 folder. Create an interface that allows the user to enter a word. The application should display the word in pig latin form. The rules for converting a word into pig latin form are shown in Figure 8-40. Code the application. Save the solution and then start and test the application. Close the Code Editor window and then close the solution.

ADVANCED

> 1. If the word begins with a vowel (A, E, I, O, or U), then add the string "-way" (a dash followed by the letters w, a, and y) to the end of the word. For example, the pig latin form of the word "ant" is "ant-way".
> 2. If the word does not begin with a vowel, first add a dash to the end of the word. Then continue moving the first character in the word to the end of the word until the first character is the letter A, E, I, O, U, or Y. Then add the string "ay" to the end of the word. For example, the pig latin form of the word "Chair" is "air-Chay".
> 3. If the word does not contain the letter A, E, I, O, U, or Y, then add the string "-way" to the end of the word. For example, the pig latin form of "56" is "56-way".

Figure 8-40   Pig latin rules for Exercise 9

499

ADVANCED

10. Credit card companies typically assign a special digit, called a check digit, to the end of each customer's credit card number. Many methods for creating the check digit have been developed. One simple method is to multiply every other digit in the credit card number by two. You then add the products to the remaining digits to get the total. Finally, you take the last digit in the total and append it to the end of the credit card number, as illustrated in Figure 8-41. Create a Visual Basic Windows application. Use the following names for the solution, project, and form file, respectively: Georgetown Solution, Georgetown Project, and Main Form.vb. Save the application in the VB2010\Chap08 folder. Create the interface shown in Figure 8-42. The interface allows the user to enter a five-digit credit card number, with the fifth digit being the check digit. The Verify button's Click event procedure should use the method illustrated in Figure 8-41 to verify that the credit card number is valid. The procedure should display appropriate messages indicating whether the credit card number is valid or invalid. Code the procedure. Save the solution and then start and test the application. Close the Code Editor window and then close the solution.

Check Digit Algorithm								
First four digits in credit card number:	1	3	5	7				
Step 1: Multiply the second and fourth digits by 2:		*2		*2				
Result	1	6	5	14				
Step 2: Add the numbers together:	1	+	6	+	5	+	14	= 26
Step 3: Take the last digit in the sum and append it to the first four digits, resulting in the final credit card number:							13576	

Figure 8-41   Illustration of a check digit algorithm

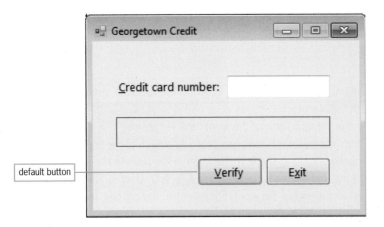

Figure 8-42 Sample interface for Exercise 10

11. Open the Count Solution (Count Solution.sln) file contained in the VB2010\Chap08\Count Solution folder. The interface allows the user to enter a string. Code the Search button's Click event procedure so that it prompts the user to enter the sequence of characters for which he or she wants to search. The procedure should determine the number of times the sequence of characters appears in the string. Use the IndexOf method to search the string for the sequence of characters. Save the solution and then start the application. Enter the string "The weather is beautiful!" (without the quotes) and then click the Search button. Search for the two characters "ea" (without the quotes). The two characters appear twice in the string. On your own, test the application using other data. Close the Code Editor window and then close the solution.

 Swat The Bugs

12. Open the Debug Solution (Debug Solution.sln) file contained in the VB2010\Chap08\Debug Solution-Lesson C folder. If necessary, open the designer window. Open the Code Editor window and review the existing code. Start and then test the application. Notice that the application is not working correctly. Correct the application's code. Save the solution and then start and test the application again. Close the Code Editor window and then close the solution.

ADVANCED

501

CHAPTER 9

Arrays

Creating the Treasures Gift Shop Application

In this chapter, you will create an application for Takoda Tapahe, the owner of a small gift shop named Treasures. The application will allow Takoda to enter a product ID. It then will display the product's price. A portion of the gift shop's price list is shown below.

Product ID	Price
BX35	13
CR20	10
FE15	12
KW10	24
MM67	4

Previewing the Treasures Gift Shop Application

Before you start the first lesson in this chapter, you will preview the completed application. The application is contained in the VB2010\Chap09 folder.

To preview the completed application:

START HERE

503

1. Use the Run dialog box to run the Treasures (Treasures.exe) file contained in the VB2010\Chap09 folder. The application's user interface appears on the screen.

2. Type **bx35** in the Product ID box. The text box's CharacterCasing property is set to Upper, so the letters you enter appear in uppercase. Click the **Display Price** button. The product's price appears in the Price box. See Figure 9-1.

Figure 9-1   Interface showing the product's price

3. Try typing **tr678** in the Product ID box. The text box's MaxLength property is set to 4, so the text box accepts only the first four characters (tr67). Click the **Display Price** button. TR67 is not a valid ID, so the application displays the message "Invalid ID" in a message box.

4. Close the message box and then click the **Exit** button.

Before you can begin coding the Treasures Gift Shop application, you need to learn about arrays. One-dimensional arrays are covered in Lesson A, and parallel one-dimensional arrays are covered in Lesson B. Lesson C covers two-dimensional arrays. You will code two versions of the Treasures Gift Shop application: one in Lesson B and the other in Lesson C. Be sure to complete each lesson in full and do all of the end-of-lesson questions and several exercises before continuing to the next lesson.

■ LESSON A

After studying Lesson A, you should be able to:

- Declare and initialize a one-dimensional array
- Store data in a one-dimensional array
- Determine the number of array elements and the highest subscript
- Traverse a one-dimensional array
- Code a loop using the For Each...Next statement
- Compute the total and average of a one-dimensional array's contents
- Find the highest value in a one-dimensional array
- Associate a list box with a one-dimensional array
- Use a one-dimensional array as an accumulator or a counter
- Sort a one-dimensional array

Arrays

All of the variables you have used so far have been simple variables. A **simple variable**, also called a **scalar variable**, is one that is unrelated to any other variable in memory. At times, however, you will encounter situations in which some of the variables *are* related to each other. In those cases, it is easier and more efficient to treat the related variables as a group. You already are familiar with the concept of grouping. The clothes in your closet probably are separated into groups, such as coats, sweaters, shirts, and so on. Grouping your clothes in this manner allows you to easily locate your favorite sweater, because you just need to look through the sweater group rather than through the entire closet. You also probably have your CD (compact disc) collection grouped by either music type or artist. If your collection is grouped by artist, it will take only a few seconds to find all of your Garth Brooks CDs and, depending on the number of Garth Brooks CDs you own, only a short time after that to locate a particular CD.

When you group together related variables, the group is referred to as an array of variables or, more simply, an **array**. You might use an array of 50 variables to store the population of each U.S. state. Or, you might use an array of eight variables to store the sales made in each of your company's eight sales regions. As you will learn in this lesson, the variables in an array can be used just like any other variables. You can assign values to them, use them in calculations, display their contents, and so on.

Storing data in an array increases the efficiency of a program, because data can be both stored in and retrieved from the computer's internal memory much faster than it can be written to and read from a file on a disk. In addition, after the data is entered into an array, which typically is done at the beginning of a program, the program can use the data as many times as necessary without having to enter the data again. Your company's sales program, for example, can use the sales amounts stored in an array to calculate the total company sales and the percentage that each region contributed to the

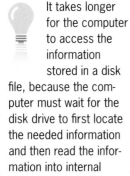

It takes longer for the computer to access the information stored in a disk file, because the computer must wait for the disk drive to first locate the needed information and then read the information into internal memory.

total sales. It also can use the sales amounts in the array either to calculate the average sales amount or to simply display the sales made in a specific region.

The most commonly used arrays in business applications are one-dimensional and two-dimensional. You will learn about one-dimensional arrays in this lesson, as well as in Lesson B. Two-dimensional arrays are covered in Lesson C. Arrays having more than two dimensions are used mostly in scientific and engineering applications and are beyond the scope of this book. At this point, it is important to point out that arrays are one of the more challenging topics for beginning programmers. Therefore, it is important for you to read and study each section in each lesson thoroughly before moving on to the next section. If you still feel overwhelmed by the end of the chapter, try reading each lesson again, paying particular attention to the examples and procedures shown in the figures.

One-Dimensional Arrays

The variables in an array are stored in consecutive locations in the computer's internal memory. Each variable in an array has the same name and data type. You distinguish one variable in a **one-dimensional array** from another variable in the same array using a unique number. The unique number, which is always an integer, is called a subscript. The **subscript** indicates the variable's position in the array and is assigned by the computer when the array is created in internal memory. The first variable in a one-dimensional array is assigned a subscript of 0, the second a subscript of 1, and so on. You refer to each variable in an array by the array's name and the variable's subscript, which is specified in a set of parentheses immediately following the array name. To refer to the first variable in a one-dimensional array named `strCities`, you use `strCities(0)`—read "`strCities` sub zero." Similarly, to refer to the second variable in the `strCities` array, you use `strCities(1)`. If the `strCities` array contains four variables, you refer to the fourth (and last) variable using `strCities(3)`. Notice that the last subscript in an array is always one number less than the total number of variables in the array; this is because array subscripts start at 0. Figure 9-2 illustrates the variables contained in the one-dimensional `strCities` array.

 A subscript is also called an index.

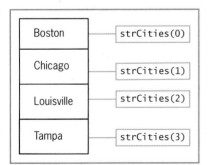

Figure 9-2   Illustration of the one-dimensional `strCities` array

Before you can use an array, you first must declare (create) it. Figure 9-3 shows two versions of the syntax for declaring a one-dimensional array in Visual Basic. The {Dim | Private | Static} portion in each version indicates

506

that you can select only one of the keywords appearing within the braces. The appropriate keyword depends on whether you are creating a procedure-level array or a class-level array. *ArrayName* is the name of the array, and *dataType* is the type of data the array variables, referred to as **elements**, will store. In Version 1 of the syntax, *highestSubscript* is an integer that specifies the highest subscript in the array. When the array is created, it will contain one element more than the number specified in the highestSubscript argument. This is because the first element in a one-dimensional array has a subscript of 0. In Version 2 of the syntax, *initialValues* is a comma-separated list of values you want assigned to the array elements. Also included in Figure 9-3 are examples of using both versions of the syntax.

Declaring a one-dimensional array

Syntax – Version 1
{**Dim** | **Private** | **Static**} *arrayName*(*highestSubscript*) **As** *dataType*

Syntax – Version 2
{**Dim** | **Private** | **Static**} *arrayName*() **As** *dataType* = {*initialValues*}

Example 1
`Dim strNames(3) As String`
declares a four-element procedure-level array named `strNames`; each element is automatically initialized using the keyword `Nothing`

Example 2
`Static intNumbers(5) As Integer`
declares a static, six-element procedure-level array named `intNumbers`; each element is automatically initialized to 0

Example 3
`Dim strCities() As String = {"Boston", "Chicago",`
`                                "Louisville", "Tampa"}`
declares and initializes a four-element procedure-level array named `strCities`

Example 4
`Private dblSales() As Double = {75.33, 9.65,`
`                                 23.55, 6.89, 4.5}`
declares and initializes a five-element class-level array named `dblSales`

Figure 9-3 Syntax versions and examples of declaring a one-dimensional array

 Like class-level variables, class-level arrays are declared in the form's Declarations section.

When you use Version 1 of the syntax, the computer automatically initializes each array element when the array is created. If the array's data type is String, each element in the array is initialized using the keyword `Nothing`. As you learned in Chapter 3, variables initialized to `Nothing` do not actually contain the word "Nothing"; rather, they contain no data at all. Elements in a numeric array are initialized to the number 0, and elements in a Boolean array are initialized using the Boolean keyword `False`. Date array elements are initialized to 12:00 AM January 1, 0001.

Rather than having the computer use a default value to initialize each array element, you can use Version 2 of the syntax to specify each element's initial value when the array is declared. Assigning initial values to an array is often referred to as **populating the array**. You list the initial values in the initialValues section of the syntax, using commas to separate the values, and you enclose the list of values in braces ({}). Notice that Version 2's syntax does not include the highestSubscript argument; instead, an empty set of parentheses follows the array name. The computer automatically calculates the highest subscript based on the number of values listed in the initialValues section. Because the first subscript in a one-dimensional array is the number 0, the highest subscript is always one number less than the number of values listed in the initialValues section. The Dim statement in Example 3 in Figure 9-3, for instance, creates a four-element array with subscripts of 0, 1, 2, and 3. The computer assigns the string "Boston" to the `strCities(0)` element, "Chicago" to the `strCities(1)` element, "Louisville" to the `strCities(2)` element, and "Tampa" to the `strCities(3)` element, as illustrated earlier in Figure 9-2. Similarly, the Private statement in Example 4 in Figure 9-3 creates a five-element array with subscripts of 0, 1, 2, 3, and 4. It then uses the numbers in the initialValues section to populate the array.

After an array is declared, you can use another statement to store a different value in an array element. Examples of such statements include assignment statements and statements that contain the TryParse method. Figure 9-4 shows examples of both types of statements.

Storing data in a one-dimensional array

Example 1
```
strCities(0) = "Madrid"
```
assigns the string "Madrid" to the first element in the `strCities` array

Example 2
```
For intX As Integer = 1 To 6
      intNumbers(intX - 1) = intX ^ 2
Next intX
```
assigns the squares of the numbers from 1 through 6 to the `intNumbers` array

Example 3
```
Dim intSubscript As Integer
Do While intSubscript <= 5
      intNumbers(intSubscript) = 0
      intSubscript += 1
Loop
```
assigns the number 0 to each element in the `intNumbers` array

Example 4
```
dblSales(1) = dblSales(1) * .1
```
multiplies the contents of the second element in the `dblSales` array by .1 and then assigns the result to the element; you also can write this statement as
```
dblSales(1) *= .1
```

Example 5
```
Double.TryParse(txtSales.Text, dblSales(2))
```
assigns either the value entered in the txtSales control (converted to Double) or the number 0 to the third element in the `dblSales` array

---

Figure 9-4 Examples of statements used to store data in a one-dimensional array

Determining the Number of Elements and the Highest Subscript

The number of elements in a one-dimensional array is stored, as an integer, in the array's **Length property**. Figure 9-5 shows the property's syntax and includes an example of using the property.

Using a one-dimensional array's Length property

<u>Syntax</u>
arrayName.**Length**

<u>Example</u>
```
Dim strNames(3) As String
Dim intNumElements As Integer
intNumElements = strNames.Length
```
assigns the number 4 to the `intNumElements` variable

Figure 9-5 Syntax and an example of a one-dimensional array's Length property

You can determine the highest subscript in a one-dimensional array by subtracting the number 1 from the array's Length property. This is because the highest subscript in a one-dimensional array is always one number less than the number of array elements. You also can use the array's GetUpperBound method. Figure 9-6 shows the method's syntax and includes an example of using the method. The **GetUpperBound method** returns an integer that represents the highest subscript in the specified dimension in the array. When used with a one-dimensional array, the specified dimension (which appears between the parentheses after the method's name) is always 0.

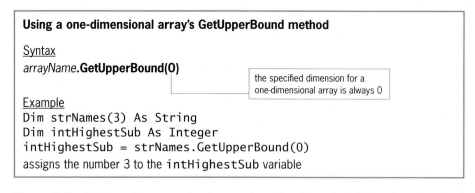

Using a one-dimensional array's GetUpperBound method

<u>Syntax</u>
arrayName.**GetUpperBound(0)**

the specified dimension for a one-dimensional array is always 0

<u>Example</u>
```
Dim strNames(3) As String
Dim intHighestSub As Integer
intHighestSub = strNames.GetUpperBound(0)
```
assigns the number 3 to the `intHighestSub` variable

Figure 9-6 Syntax and an example of a one-dimensional array's GetUpperBound method

YOU DO IT 1!

Create a Visual Basic Windows application named YouDoIt 1. Save the application in the VB2010\Chap09 folder. Add two labels and a button to the form. The button's Click event procedure should declare and initialize an Integer array named `intNums`. Use the following numbers to initialize the array: 2, 4, 6, 8, 10, and 12. The procedure should use the Length property to display the number of array elements in one of the label controls. It should use the GetUpperBound method to display the number of array elements in the other label control. Code the procedure. Save the solution and then start and test the application. Close the solution.

Traversing a One-Dimensional Array

At times, you may need to traverse an array, which means to look at each array element, one by one, beginning with the first element and ending with the last element. You traverse an array using a loop. Figure 9-7 shows two examples of loops that traverse the **strCities** array, displaying each element's value in the lstCities control. The loop in Example 1 is coded using the For...Next statement; Example 2's loop uses the Do...Loop statement.

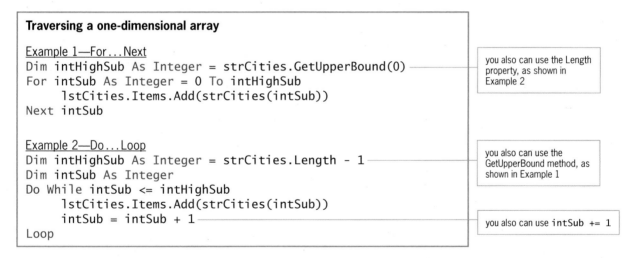

Traversing a one-dimensional array

Example 1—For...Next
```
Dim intHighSub As Integer = strCities.GetUpperBound(0)
For intSub As Integer = 0 To intHighSub
    lstCities.Items.Add(strCities(intSub))
Next intSub
```
you also can use the Length property, as shown in Example 2

Example 2—Do...Loop
```
Dim intHighSub As Integer = strCities.Length - 1
Dim intSub As Integer
Do While intSub <= intHighSub
    lstCities.Items.Add(strCities(intSub))
    intSub = intSub + 1
Loop
```
you also can use the GetUpperBound method, as shown in Example 1

you also can use `intSub += 1`

Figure 9-7 Examples of loops used to traverse a one-dimensional array

To code and then test the Cities application:

START HERE

1. If necessary, start Visual Studio 2010 or Visual Basic 2010 Express. Open the Cities Solution (Cities Solution.sln) file contained in the VB2010\Chap09\Cities Solution folder. If necessary, open the designer window.

2. Open the Code Editor window. Replace <your name> and <current date> in the comments with your name and the current date, respectively.

3. Locate the code template for the form's Load event procedure. Click the **blank line** above the End Sub clause. Type the following array declaration statement and then press **Enter** twice:

Dim strCities() As String = {"Boston", "Chicago",
                                       "Louisville", "Tampa"}

4. Next, you will fill the lstCities control with values. Enter the lines of code shown in either Example 1 or Example 2 in Figure 9-7.

5. Now you will select the first item in the list box. Insert a blank line above the End Sub clause and then enter the following assignment statement:

lstCities.SelectedIndex = 0

6. Save the solution and then start the application. The computer processes the code contained in the form's Load event procedure, which creates and initializes the **strCities** array. The first time the procedure's loop is processed, the **intSub** variable contains the number 0. Therefore, the Add method in the loop adds the contents of the **strCities(0)** element, which is Boston, to the lstCities control. The computer then increases the **intSub** variable's value by 1, giving 2. When the loop is processed the second time, the Add method in the loop adds the contents of the **strCities(1)** element (Chicago) to the lstCities control, and so on. The computer repeats the loop instructions for each element in the **strCities** array. The computer stops processing the loop when the **intSub** variable contains the number 4, which is one number more than the highest subscript in the array. See Figure 9-8.

Figure 9-8 Result of starting the Cities application

7. Click **Louisville** in the list box. Louisville appears in the You selected box.

8. Click the **Exit** button. Close the Code Editor window and then close the solution.

Recall that Visual Basic provides three statements for coding a loop: Do...Loop, For...Next, and For Each...Next. You already know how to use the Do...Loop and For...Next statements. You will learn about the For Each...Next statement in the next section.

The For Each...Next Statement

Visual Basic provides the **For Each...Next statement** for coding a loop whose instructions you want processed for each element in a group, such as for each variable in an array. An advantage of using the For Each...Next statement to process an array is that your code does not need to keep track of the array subscripts or even know the number of array elements. However, unlike the loop instructions in a Do...Loop or For...Next statement, the instructions in a For Each...Next statement can only read the array values; they cannot permanently modify the values.

Figure 9-9 shows the For Each...Next statement's syntax. The *element-VariableName* that appears in the For Each and Next clauses is the name of a variable that the computer can use to keep track of each element in the *group*. The variable's data type is specified in the **As** *dataType* portion of the For Each clause and must be the same as the group's data type. A variable declared in the For Each clause has block scope and is recognized only by the instructions within the For Each...Next loop. You enter the loop body, which contains the instructions you want the computer to repeat, between the For Each and Next clauses. The example in Figure 9-9 shows how to write the loops from Figure 9-7 using the For Each...Next statement.

Although you do not need to specify the *element-VariableName* in the Next clause, doing so is highly recommended because it makes your code more self-documenting.

You learned about block scope in Chapter 4.

For Each...Next statement

Syntax
For Each *elementVariableName* **As** *dataType* **In** *group*
    loop body instructions
Next *elementVariableName*

Example
```
For Each strCityElement As String In strCities
    lstCities.Items.Add(strCityElement)
Next strCityElement
```

Figure 9-9   Syntax and an example of the For Each...Next statement

To use the For Each...Next statement in the Cities application: START HERE

1. Open the Cities Solution (Cities Solution.sln) file contained in the VB2010\Chap09\Cities Solution-ForEachNext folder. If necessary, open the designer window.

2. Open the Code Editor window. Replace <your name> and <current date> in the comments with your name and the current date, respectively.

3. Locate the code template for the form's Load event procedure. Click the **blank line** above the assignment statement and then enter the lines of code shown in the example in Figure 9-9.

4. Save the solution and then start the application. The four city names appear in the list box, as shown earlier in Figure 9-8.

5. Click the **Exit** button. Close the Code Editor window and then close the solution.

512

YOU DO IT 2!

Create a Visual Basic Windows application named YouDoIt 2. Save the application in the VB2010\Chap09 folder. Add a button to the form. The button's Click event procedure should declare and initialize a one-dimensional String array. Use any four names to initialize the array. The procedure should display the contents of the array three times. First, it should use the For Each...Next statement to display the four names in message boxes. Second, it should use the Do...Loop statement to display the four names in message boxes. Third, it should use the For...Next statement to display the four names in message boxes. (Hint: The procedure will display 12 message boxes.) Code the procedure. Save the solution and then start and test the application. Close the solution.

Calculating the Total and Average Values

Figure 9-10 shows the problem specification for the Sweet Tooth Chocolate application. The application displays the total number of pounds of chocolate sold during a six-month period and the average number of pounds sold each month.

The store manager at Sweet Tooth Chocolate wants an application that displays two items: the total number of pounds of chocolate sold during a six-month period and the average number of pounds sold each month. Last year, the monthly amounts were as follows: 150.75, 300.5, 200, 225.5, 268.5, and 325.75. The application will store the monthly amounts in a six-element one-dimensional array. It then will calculate the total number of pounds sold during the six months and the average number of pounds sold each month. The total number of pounds sold is calculated by accumulating the array values. The average number of pounds sold each month is calculated by dividing the total number of pounds sold by the number of array elements.

Figure 9-10   Problem specification for the Sweet Tooth Chocolate application

START HERE   **To begin coding the Sweet Tooth Chocolate application:**

1. Open the Sweet Tooth Solution (Sweet Tooth Solution.sln) file contained in the VB2010\Chap09\Sweet Tooth Solution folder. If necessary, open the designer window.

2. Open the Code Editor window. Replace <your name> and <current date> in the comments with your name and the current date, respectively.

3. Locate the btnCalc control's Click event procedure. First, you will declare a one-dimensional array to store the amounts sold during the six-month period. Click the **blank line** above the End Sub clause. Type the following Dim statement and then press **Enter** twice:

    Dim dblMthlyPounds() As Double = {150.75, 300.5,
    200, 225.5,
    268.5, 325.75}

Figure 9-11 shows three examples of code for the Calculate button's Click event procedure. In each example, a loop is used to traverse the array, adding each array element's value to the **dblTotal** variable. The loop in Example 1 is coded using the Do...Loop statement. Example 2's loop is coded using the For...Next statement, and Example 3's loop is coded using the For Each...Next statement. The code pertaining to each loop is shaded in the figure. Notice that you need to specify the highest array subscript in the Do...Loop and For...Next statements, but not in the For Each...Next statement. The Do...Loop and For...Next statements also must keep track of the array subscripts; this task is not necessary in the For Each...Next statement. When each loop has finished processing, the **dblTotal** variable contains the total number of pounds sold during the six-month period. After accumulating the array values, the code in each example calculates the average monthly usage. The calculation is made by dividing the value stored in the **dblTotal** variable by the number of array elements. The code in each example then displays the total and average amounts on the form.

```vb
Example 1—Do...Loop
Dim intHighSub As Integer =
        dblMthlyPounds.GetUpperBound(0)
Dim dblTotal As Double
Dim dblAvg As Double
Dim intSub As Integer

' accumulate pounds sold
Do While intSub <= intHighSub
    dblTotal += dblMthlyPounds(intSub)
    intSub += 1
Loop

' calculate average
dblAvg = dblTotal / dblMthlyPounds.Length
' display total and average
lblTotal.Text = dblTotal.ToString("N1")
lblAvg.Text = dblAvg.ToString("N2")

Example 2—For...Next
Dim intHighSub As Integer =
        dblMthlyPounds.GetUpperBound(0)
Dim dblTotal As Double
Dim dblAvg As Double

' accumulate pounds sold
For intSub As Integer = 0 To intHighSub
    dblTotal += dblMthlyPounds(intSub)
Next intSub

' calculate average
dblAvg = dblTotal / dblMthlyPounds.Length
' display total and average
lblTotal.Text = dblTotal.ToString("N1")
lblAvg.Text = dblAvg.ToString("N2")

Example 3—For Each...Next
Dim dblTotal As Double
Dim dblAvg As Double
```

Figure 9-11   Examples of code for the btnCalc_Click procedure *(continues)*

(continued)

```
' accumulate pounds sold
For Each dblMonth As Double In dblMthlyPounds
    dblTotal += dblMonth
Next dblMonth

' calculate average
dblAvg = dblTotal / dblMthlyPounds.Length
' display total and average
lblTotal.Text = dblTotal.ToString("N1")
lblAvg.Text = dblAvg.ToString("N2")
```

514

Figure 9-11   Examples of code for the btnCalc_Click procedure

START HERE

To continue coding the Sweet Tooth Chocolate application:

1. In the btnCalc control's Click event procedure, enter the comments and code shown in any of the three examples from Figure 9-11.

2. Save the solution and then start the application. Click the **Calculate** button. See Figure 9-12.

Figure 9-12   Total and average amounts shown in the interface

 The Ch09AVideo file reviews what you have learned so far about one-dimensional arrays.

YOU DO IT 3!

Create a Visual Basic Windows application named YouDoIt 3. Save the application in the VB2010\Chap09 folder. Add three labels and a button to the form. The button's Click event procedure should declare and initialize a one-dimensional Integer array. Use any five integers to initialize the array. The procedure should total the five integers and then display the result in the labels. Use the Do...Loop statement to calculate the total to display in the first label. Use the For Each...Next statement to calculate the total to display in the second label. Use the For...Next statement to calculate the total to display in the third label. Code the procedure. Save the solution and then start and test the application. Close the solution.

Finding the Highest Value

Figure 9-13 shows the problem specification for the Cycles Galore application. The application displays the highest bonus amount earned during the month and the number of salespeople who earned that amount.

> The sales manager at Cycles Galore wants an application that displays two items: the highest bonus amount earned during the month and the number of salespeople who earned that amount. Last month, the following bonus amounts were paid to the 10 salespeople: 500, 400, 1000, 400, 1000, 400, 850, 500, 780, and 890. The application will store the bonus amounts in a 10-element one-dimensional array. It then will examine each element in the array, looking for the highest bonus amount. It will use a counter variable to keep track of the number of salespeople earning that amount.

Figure 9-13   Problem specification for the Cycles Galore application

To begin coding the Cycles Galore application:

START HERE

1. Open the Cycles Galore Solution (Cycles Galore Solution.sln) file contained in the VB2010\Chap09\Cycles Galore Solution folder. If necessary, open the designer window.

2. Open the Code Editor window. Replace <your name> and <current date> in the comments with your name and the current date, respectively.

3. Locate the btnGetHighest control's Click event procedure. The procedure already contains the statement to declare and initialize the 10-element array. It also contains the statements to display the highest bonus and the number of salespeople who earned that bonus.

4. First, you will declare a variable named intHighSub and initialize it to the highest subscript in the array. The intHighSub variable will be used by the For...Next statement to traverse the array. Click the **blank line** below the array declaration statement and then enter the following Dim statement:

   **Dim intHighSub As Integer =
      intBonusAmts.GetUpperBound(0)**

5. The procedure will use a variable named intHighBonus to keep track of the highest bonus amount in the array. When searching an array for the highest (or lowest) value, it's a common programming practice to initialize the variable to the value stored in the first array element. In this case, you will initialize it to the value stored in the intBonusAmts(0) element. Enter the following Dim statement:

   Dim intHighBonus As Integer = intBonusAmts(0)

6. Next, you will declare and initialize a counter variable named intSalespeople. The counter variable will keep track of the number of salespeople whose bonus amount matches the value stored in the intHighBonus variable. You will initialize the intSalespeople variable to 1 because, at this point, one salesperson (the first one) has earned the bonus amount currently stored in the intHighBonus variable. Type the following Dim statement and then press **Enter** twice:

   Dim intSalespeople As Integer = 1

516

7. Now you will use the For...Next statement to traverse the second through the last elements in the `intBonusAmts` array. Each element's value will be compared, one at a time, to the value stored in the `intHighBonus` variable. You don't need to look at the first element because its value is already contained in the `intHighBonus` variable. Enter the following For clause:

For intX As Integer = 1 To intHighSub

8. Change the `Next` clause to **Next intX**.

9. The first instruction in the loop will determine whether the value stored in the current array element is equal to the value stored in the `intHighBonus` variable. Click the **blank line** below the For clause and then enter the following If clause:

If intBonusAmts (intX) = intHighBonus Then

10. If both bonus amounts are equal, the selection structure's true path will add 1 to the `intSalespeople` counter variable. Enter the following assignment statement:

intSalespeople += 1

11. If both bonus amounts are not equal, the selection structure's false path will determine whether the value stored in the current array element is greater than the value stored in the `intHighBonus` variable. Enter the following Else and If clauses:

Else
    If intBonusAmts(intX) > intHighBonus Then

12. If the value in the current array element is greater than the value in the `intHighBonus` variable, the nested selection structure's true path should assign the higher value to the `intHighBonus` variable. It also should reset the number of salespeople to 1 because, at this point, only one salesperson has earned that bonus amount. Enter the assignment statements indicated in Figure 9-14.

```
If intBonusAmts(intX) > intHighBonus Then
      intHighBonus = intBonusAmts(intX)
      intSalespeople = 1
End If
```

enter these two assignment statements

Figure 9-14 Additional assignment statements entered in the procedure

13. Save the solution and then start the application. Click the **Get Highest Bonus** button. See Figure 9-15.

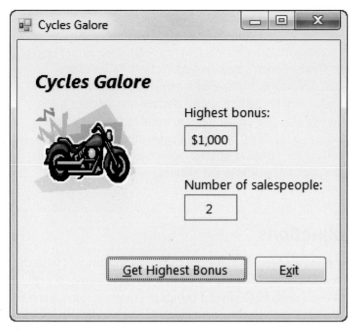

Figure 9-15 Calculated amounts shown in the interface

Figure 9-16 shows the code entered in the Get Highest Bonus button's Click event procedure.

```
Private Sub btnGetHighest_Click(ByVal sender As Object,
ByVal e As System.EventArgs) Handles btnGetHighest.Click
    ' displays the highest bonus and the
    ' number who earned that amount

    Dim intBonusAmts() As Integer = {500, 400, 1000,
                                     400, 1000, 400,
                                     850, 500, 780, 890}
    Dim intHighSub As Integer =
        intBonusAmts.GetUpperBound(0)
    Dim intHighBonus As Integer = intBonusAmts(0)
    Dim intSalespeople As Integer = 1

    For intX As Integer = 1 To intHighSub
        If intBonusAmts(intX) = intHighBonus Then
            intSalespeople += 1
        Else
            If intBonusAmts(intX) > intHighBonus Then
                intHighBonus = intBonusAmts(intX)
                intSalespeople = 1
            End If
        End If
    Next intX

    lblHighest.Text = intHighBonus.ToString("C0")
    lblSalespeople.Text = intSalespeople.ToString
End Sub
```

> assign the first element's value and the number 1 to the intHighBonus and intSalespeople variables, respectively

> search the second through the last array elements

Figure 9-16 Get Highest Bonus button's Click event procedure

YOU DO IT 4!

Create a Visual Basic Windows application named YouDoIt 4. Save the application in the VB2010\Chap09 folder. Add a label and a button to the form. The button's Click event procedure should declare and initialize a one-dimensional Double array. Use any six numbers to initialize the array. The procedure should display (in the label) the lowest value stored in the array. Code the procedure using the For...Next statement. Save the solution and then start and test the application. Close the solution.

Arrays and Collections

Recall that the items in a list box belong to the Items collection.

It's not uncommon for programmers to associate the items in a list box with the values stored in an array. This is because the items in a list box belong to a collection, and collections and arrays have several things in common. First, each is a group of individual objects treated as one unit. Second, each individual object in the group is identified by a unique number. The unique number is called an index when referring to a collection, but a subscript when referring to an array. Third, both the first index in a collection and the first subscript in an array are 0. These commonalities allow you to associate the list box items and array elements by their positions within their respective groups. In other words, you can associate the first item in a list box with the first element in an array, the second item with the second element, and so on. To associate a list box with an array, you first add the appropriate items to the list box. You then store each item's related value in its corresponding position in the array. You will use a list box and a one-dimensional array in the Prairie Auditorium application, which you code next. Figure 9-17 shows the application's problem specification.

The theater manager at Prairie Auditorium wants an application that displays the price of a ticket. The price is based on the seating section, as shown in the chart below. The application's interface will provide a list box from which the user can select the seating section. The application will store the prices in a four-element one-dimensional array. It will use the index of the item selected in the list box to access the appropriate price from the array.

Section	Price ($)
A	92.00
B	85.00
C	67.50
D	32.50

Figure 9-17   Problem specification for the Prairie Auditorium application

START HERE

To begin coding the Prairie Auditorium application:

1. Open the Prairie Solution (Prairie Solution.sln) file contained in the VB2010\Chap09\Prairie Solution folder. If necessary, open the designer window.

2. Open the Code Editor window. Replace <your name> and <current date> in the comments with your name and the current date, respectively.

3. First, you will fill the list box with values and then select the first item in the list. Open the code template for the form's Load event procedure and then enter the following lines of code:

lstSection.Items.Add("A")
lstSection.Items.Add("B")
lstSection.Items.Add("C")
lstSection.Items.Add("D")
lstSection.SelectedIndex = 0

4. As the problem specification states, the ticket prices should be stored in a one-dimensional array. You can declare the array in the list box's SelectedIndexChanged or SelectedValueChanged procedures, making it a procedure-level array. Or, you can declare it in the form's Declarations section, making it a class-level array. In this case, you will use a class-level array so that the array will not need to be created each time the user clicks a different item in the list box. Click the **blank line** below the `Public Class frmMain` clause and then press **Enter** to insert another blank line. Enter the following array declaration statement:

Private dblPrices() As Double = {92, 85, 67.5, 32.5}

Notice that the array declaration statement initializes the first array element to 92, which is the price associated with the first item in the list box (A). The remaining array elements are initialized to the prices corresponding to their list box items. The relationship between the list box items and the array elements is illustrated in Figure 9-18.

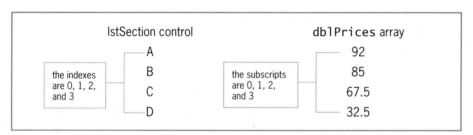

Figure 9-18 Illustration of the relationship between the list box and array

To continue coding the Prairie Auditorium application: START HERE

1. When the user clicks an item in the list box, the application should display the appropriate price in the Price box. You can accomplish this task by coding either the list box's SelectedIndexChanged procedure or its SelectedValueChanged procedure. Open the code template for the lstSection control's SelectedIndexChanged procedure. Type the following comment and then press **Enter** twice:

' displays the corresponding price from the array

2. The procedure will use the index of the item selected in the list box to access the appropriate price from the `dblPrices` array. Enter the following Dim statement:

Dim intSub As Integer = lstSection.SelectedIndex

3. If the first item is selected in the list box, the Dim statement you entered in Step 2 will initialize the **intSub** variable to 0. If the second item is selected, it will initialize the variable to 1, and so on. You can use the **intSub** variable to access the appropriate price from the array. Enter the following assignment statement:

lblPrice.Text = dblPrices(intSub).ToString("C2")

Figure 9-19 shows most of the code for the Prairie Auditorium application.

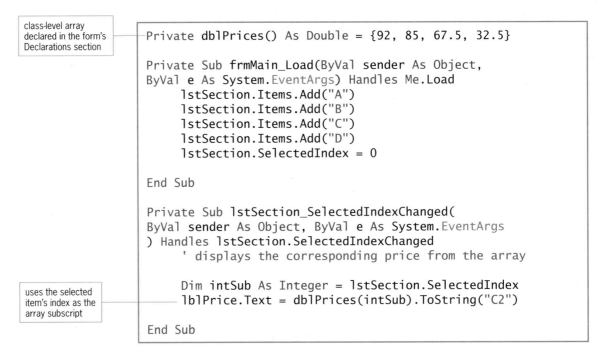

```
Private dblPrices() As Double = {92, 85, 67.5, 32.5}

Private Sub frmMain_Load(ByVal sender As Object,
ByVal e As System.EventArgs) Handles Me.Load
    lstSection.Items.Add("A")
    lstSection.Items.Add("B")
    lstSection.Items.Add("C")
    lstSection.Items.Add("D")
    lstSection.SelectedIndex = 0

End Sub

Private Sub lstSection_SelectedIndexChanged(
ByVal sender As Object, ByVal e As System.EventArgs
) Handles lstSection.SelectedIndexChanged
    ' displays the corresponding price from the array

    Dim intSub As Integer = lstSection.SelectedIndex
    lblPrice.Text = dblPrices(intSub).ToString("C2")

End Sub
```

class-level array declared in the form's Declarations section

uses the selected item's index as the array subscript

Figure 9-19   Most of the code for the Prairie Auditorium application

START HERE

To test the Prairie Auditorium application's code:

1. Save the solution and then start the application. $92.00 appears in the Price box, as shown in Figure 9-20.

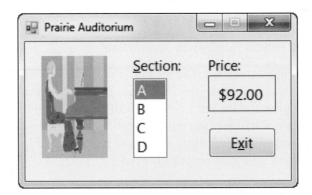

Figure 9-20   Price displayed in the interface

2. On your own, test the application by clicking the remaining items in the list box.

3. Click the **Exit** button.

Before closing the Prairie Auditorium application, you will observe the run time error that occurs when the computer tries to access a memory location that is outside the bounds of the array. A **run time error** is an error that occurs while an application is running.

To modify and then test the Prairie Auditorium application:

START HERE

521

1. In the form's Declarations section, delete **, 32.50** from the array declaration statement. The initialValues section of the statement now contains only three values.

2. Save the solution and then start the application. Click **D** in the Section list box. Because this seat section does not have a corresponding price in the **dblPrices** array, a run time error occurs. An arrow points to the statement where the error was encountered, and the statement is highlighted. In addition, a help box opens; the help box provides information pertaining to the error. In this case, the help box indicates that the statement is trying to access an element that is outside the bounds of the array.

3. Place your mouse pointer on **intSub** in the highlighted statement, as shown in Figure 9-21. The **intSub** variable contains the number 3, which is not a valid subscript for the modified array. The valid subscripts for the modified array are 0, 1, and 2.

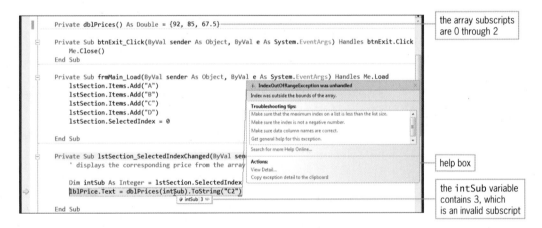

Figure 9-21   Result of the run time error caused by an invalid subscript

4. Click **Debug** on the menu bar and then click **Stop Debugging**.

Before accessing an individual array element, you should verify that the subscript you are using is valid. You can do this using a selection structure whose condition verifies that the subscript is within the acceptable range. The acceptable range would be a number that is greater than or equal to 0 but less than or equal to the highest subscript in the array.

START HERE ▶ **To continue modifying and testing the Prairie Auditorium application:**

1. Modify the lstSection control's SelectedIndexChanged procedure by adding the selection structure shown in Figure 9-22. Be sure to move the `lblPrice.Text = dblPrices(intSub).ToString("C2")` statement into the selection structure's true path.

```
Private Sub lstSection_SelectedIndexChanged(ByVal sender
        ' displays the corresponding price from the array

    Dim intSub As Integer = lstSection.SelectedIndex
    If intSub <= dblPrices.GetUpperBound(0) Then
        lblPrice.Text = dblPrices(intSub).ToString("C2")
    Else
        lblPrice.Text = "N/A"
    End If

End Sub
```

add this selection structure

Figure 9-22   Modified SelectedIndexChanged procedure

2. Save the solution and then start the application. Click **D** in the Section list box. This time, N/A appears in the Price box. Click the **Exit** button.

3. In the form's Declarations section, click immediately before } in the array declaration statement and then type **, 32.5**. The initialValues section of the statement now contains four values.

4. Save the solution and then start the application. Click **D** in the Section list box. $32.50 appears in the Price box.

5. Click the **Exit** button. Close the Code Editor window and then close the solution.

Accumulator and Counter Arrays

One-dimensional arrays are often used to either accumulate or count related values; such arrays are commonly referred to as accumulator arrays and counter arrays, respectively. You will use an accumulator array in the Warren School application, which you finish coding next. The application's problem specification is shown in Figure 9-23.

Warren School is having its annual Chocolate Fund Raiser event. Students sell the following five candies: Chocolate Bar, Chocolate Bar-Peanuts, Kit Kat, Peanut Butter Cups, and Take 5 Bar. The school principal wants an application that she can use to enter the amount of each candy sold by each student. The application should display the total number sold for each candy. The interface will provide a list box for the user to select the candy, and a text box for entering the amount sold by a student. The application will use a five-element one-dimensional array to accumulate the amounts sold.

Figure 9-23   Problem specification for the Warren School application

To open the Warren School application:

START HERE

1. Open the Warren Solution (Warren Solution.sln) file contained in the VB2010\Chap09\Warren Solution folder. If necessary, open the designer window.

2. Open the Code Editor window, which already contains some code. Replace <your name> and <current date> in the comments with your name and the current date, respectively.

The form's Load event procedure fills the list box with the five candy types and then selects the first item in the list. To complete the application, you just need to finish coding the btnAdd control's Click event procedure, which should accumulate the amounts sold by candy type. The procedure will accomplish its task using an accumulator array: a one-dimensional array named `intCandiesSold`. The array will have five elements, each corresponding to an item listed in the list box. The first array element will correspond to the Chocolate Bar item, the second array element to the Chocolate Bar-Peanuts item, and so on. Each array element will be used to accumulate the sales of its corresponding list box item.

To complete the btnAdd control's Click event procedure:

START HERE

1. Locate the btnAdd control's Click event procedure. Click the **blank line** below the ` ' declare array and variables` comment.

2. First, you will declare the `intCandiesSold` array. The array will need to retain its values until the application ends. You can accomplish this by declaring the array in either the form's Declarations section (using the `Private` keyword to make it a class-level array) or in the btnAdd control's Click event procedure (using the `Static` keyword to make it a static procedure-level array); you will use the latter approach. Like static variables, which you learned about in Chapter 3, static arrays remain in memory and retain their values until the application ends. Enter the following declaration statement:

   Static intCandiesSold(4) As Integer

3. The event procedure will also use two Integer variables: one to store the amount sold and the other to store the index of the item selected in the list box. Enter the following Dim statements. Press **Enter** twice after typing the last Dim statement.

   Dim intSold As Integer
   Dim intSub As Integer

4. Now you will convert the contents of the txtSold control to Integer and then store the result in the `intSold` variable. Enter the following TryParse method:

   Integer.TryParse(txtSold.Text, intSold)

5. Next, you will assign the index of the item selected in the list box to the `intSub` variable. Enter the following assignment statement:

   intSub = lstCandy.SelectedIndex

6. Now you will use the number stored in the `intSub` variable to update the appropriate array element. Click the blank line below the `' update array value` comment and then enter the following assignment statement. (If you prefer, you can enter the `intCandiesSold(intSub) = intCandiesSold(intSub) + intSold` statement instead.)

intCandiesSold(intSub) += intSold

7. Finally, you will enter the code to display the array values in the interface. Enter the following five assignment statements:

lblChocBar.Text = intCandiesSold(0).ToString
lblChocBarPeanuts.Text = intCandiesSold(1).ToString
lblKitKat.Text = intCandiesSold(2).ToString
lblPeanutButCups.Text = intCandiesSold(3).ToString
lblTake5Bar.Text = intCandiesSold(4).ToString

Figure 9-24 shows the code entered in the btnAdd control's Click event procedure.

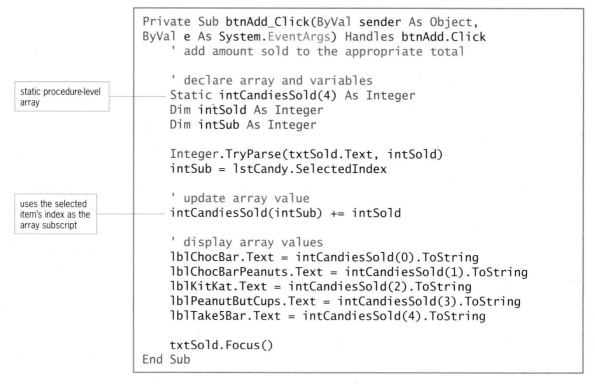

static procedure-level array

uses the selected item's index as the array subscript

```
Private Sub btnAdd_Click(ByVal sender As Object,
ByVal e As System.EventArgs) Handles btnAdd.Click
    ' add amount sold to the appropriate total

    ' declare array and variables
    Static intCandiesSold(4) As Integer
    Dim intSold As Integer
    Dim intSub As Integer

    Integer.TryParse(txtSold.Text, intSold)
    intSub = lstCandy.SelectedIndex

    ' update array value
    intCandiesSold(intSub) += intSold

    ' display array values
    lblChocBar.Text = intCandiesSold(0).ToString
    lblChocBarPeanuts.Text = intCandiesSold(1).ToString
    lblKitKat.Text = intCandiesSold(2).ToString
    lblPeanutButCups.Text = intCandiesSold(3).ToString
    lblTake5Bar.Text = intCandiesSold(4).ToString

    txtSold.Focus()
End Sub
```

Figure 9-24   btnAdd control's Click event procedure

START HERE

To test the Warren School application:

1. Save the solution and then start the application. Click the **Sold** box, type **100**, and then press **Enter** to select the Add to Total button. The number 100 appears in the Chocolate Bar label.

2. Click **Kit Kat** in the Candy list box. Change the 100 in the Sold box to **45** and then click the **Add to Total** button. Now change the 45 in the Sold box to **36** and then press **Enter**. See Figure 9-25.

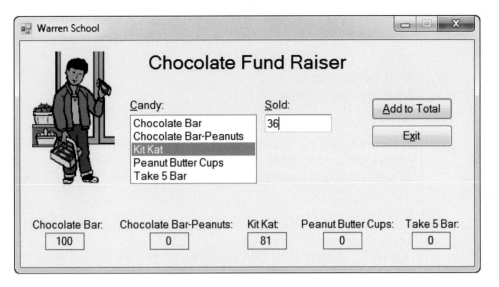

Figure 9-25   Array values displayed in the interface

3. On your own, test the application using different candy types and sales amounts.

4. Click the **Exit** button. Close the Code Editor window and then close the solution.

YOU DO IT 5!

Create a Visual Basic Windows application named YouDoIt 5. Save the application in the VB2010\Chap09 folder. Add two list boxes and a button to the form. The button's Click event procedure should declare and initialize a one-dimensional Integer array. Use any 10 numbers to initialize the array. The procedure should use the For Each...Next statement to display the contents of the array in the first list box. The procedure should then use the For...Next statement to increase each array element's value by 2. Finally, it should use the Do...Loop statement to display the results in the second list box. Code the procedure. Save the solution and then start and test the application. Close the solution.

Sorting a One-Dimensional Array

In some applications, you might need to arrange the contents of an array in either ascending or descending order. Arranging data in a specific order is called **sorting**. When an array is sorted in ascending order, the first element in the array contains the smallest value and the last element contains the largest value. When an array is sorted in descending order, on the other hand, the first element contains the largest value and the last element contains the smallest value. You can use the **Array.Sort method** to sort a one-dimensional array's values in ascending order. To sort the values in descending order, you first use the Array.Sort method to sort the values in ascending order, and then use the **Array.Reverse method** to reverse the values. Figure 9-26 shows the syntax of both methods. In each syntax, *arrayName* is the name of a one-dimensional array.

Array.Sort and Array.Reverse methods

<u>Syntax</u>
Array.Sort(*arrayName***)**
Array.Reverse(*arrayName***)**

<u>Example 1</u>
```
Dim intScores As Integer = {78, 83, 75, 90}
Array.Sort(intScores)
```
sorts the contents of the array in ascending order, as follows: 75, 78, 83, and 90

<u>Example 2</u>
```
Dim intScores As Integer = {78, 83, 75, 90}
Array.Reverse(intScores)
```
reverses the contents of the array, placing the values in the following order: 90, 75, 83, and 78

<u>Example 3</u>
```
Dim intScores As Integer = {78, 83, 75, 90}
Array.Sort(intScores)
Array.Reverse(intScores)
```
sorts the contents of the array in ascending order and then reverses the contents, placing the values in descending order as follows: 90, 83, 78, and 75

Figure 9-26   Syntax and examples of the Array.Sort and Array.Reverse methods

You will use the Array.Sort and Array.Reverse methods in the State application, which you finish coding in the next set of steps. The application stores the names of five states in a one-dimensional array named strStates. The application allows the user to display the names in either ascending or descending order.

START HERE ▶ **To code the State application:**

1. Open the State Solution (State Solution.sln) file contained in the VB2010\Chap09\State Solution folder. If necessary, open the designer window.

2. Open the Code Editor window. Replace <your name> and <current date> in the comments with your name and the current date, respectively.

3. The array in this application needs to be accessed by more than one procedure. Therefore, you will declare the array as a class-level array. Click the **blank line** below the ' class-level array comment in the form's Declarations section. Enter the following array declaration statement:

Private strStates(4) As String

4. Next, locate the btnEnter control's Click event procedure. Click the **blank line** below the lstStates.Items.Clear() statement, which clears the contents of the list box in the interface. You will use a loop and the InputBox function to get five state names from the user,

storing each state name in an array element. Press **Enter** to insert a blank line, and then enter the following lines of code:

For intSub As Integer = 0 To strStates.GetUpperBound(0)
    strStates(intSub) =
        InputBox("State name", "State Names")
Next intSub

5. Now locate the btnAscending control's Click event procedure. Click the **blank line** below the `lstStates.Items.Clear()` statement and then press **Enter**. The procedure should sort the array values in ascending order and then display the values in the lstStates control. Enter the following lines of code:

Array.Sort(strStates)
For Each strName As String In strStates
    lstStates.Items.Add(strName)
Next strName

6. Finally, locate the btnDescending control's Click event procedure. Click the **blank line** below the `lstStates.Items.Clear()` statement and then press **Enter**. The procedure should sort the array values in descending order and then display the values in the lstStates control. Enter the following lines of code:

Array.Sort(strStates)
Array.Reverse(strStates)
For Each strName As String In strStates
    lstStates.Items.Add(strName)
Next strName

Figure 9-27 shows the State application's code.

```
Public Class frmMain

    ' class-level array
    Private strStates(4) As String

    Private Sub btnExit_Click(ByVal sender As Object,
    ByVal e As System.EventArgs) Handles btnExit.Click
        Me.Close()
    End Sub

    Private Sub btnEnter_Click(ByVal sender As Object,
    ByVal e As System.EventArgs) Handles btnEnter.Click
        ' stores five state names in the class-level
        ' strStates array

        lstStates.Items.Clear()

        For intSub As Integer = 0 To strStates.GetUpperBound(0)
            strStates(intSub) =
                InputBox("State name", "State Names")
        Next intSub
    End Sub
```

Figure 9-27   State application's code *(continues)*

(continued)

```
    Private Sub btnAscending_Click(ByVal sender As Object,
    ByVal e As System.EventArgs) Handles btnAscending.Click
        ' displays the array values in ascending order

        lstStates.Items.Clear()

        Array.Sort(strStates)
        For Each strName As String In strStates
            lstStates.Items.Add(strName)
        Next strName
    End Sub

    Private Sub btnDescending_Click(ByVal sender As Object,
    ByVal e As System.EventArgs) Handles btnDescending.Click
        ' displays the array values in descending order

        lstStates.Items.Clear()

        Array.Sort(strStates)
        Array.Reverse(strStates)
        For Each strName As String In strStates
            lstStates.Items.Add(strName)
        Next strName
    End Sub
End Class
```

Figure 9-27 State application's code

START HERE

To test the State application:

1. Save the solution and then start the application. Click the **Enter State Names** button. Type the following state names in the State Names dialog box, pressing **Enter** after typing each name: **Kentucky**, **Tennessee**, **Alaska**, **New York**, and **Idaho**.

2. Click the **Ascending Sort** button. The application displays the state names in ascending order. See Figure 9-28.

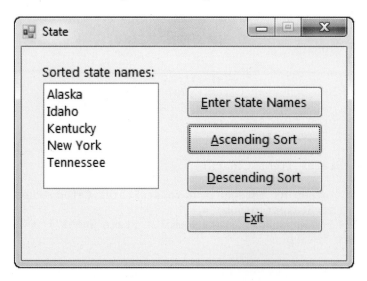

Figure 9-28 State names displayed in ascending order

3. Click the **Descending Sort** button. The application displays the state names in descending order.

4. Click the **Exit** button. Close the Code Editor window and then close the solution.

Lesson A Summary

- To refer to an element in a one-dimensional array:

  Use the array's name followed by the element's subscript, which is specified in a set of parentheses immediately following the array name.

- To declare a one-dimensional array:

  Use either of the syntax versions shown below. The *highestSubscript* argument in Version 1 is an integer that specifies the highest subscript in the array. Using Version 1's syntax, the computer automatically initializes the array elements. The *initialValues* section in Version 2 is a list of values separated by commas and enclosed in braces. The values are used to initialize each element in the array.

  Version 1: {**Dim** | **Private** | **Static**} *arrayName*(*highestSubscript*) **As** *dataType*

  Version 2: {**Dim** | **Private** | **Static**} *arrayName*() **As** *dataType* = {*initialValues*}

- To determine the number of elements in a one-dimensional array:

  Use the array's Length property in the following syntax: *arrayName*.**Length**.

- To determine the highest subscript in a one-dimensional array:

  Use the array's GetUpperBound method in the following syntax: *arrayName*.**GetUpperBound(0)**. Alternatively, you can subtract the number 1 from the value stored in the array's Length property.

- To traverse (or look at) each element in a one-dimensional array:

  Use a loop coded with one of the following statements: Do...Loop, For...Next, or For Each...Next.

- To process instructions for each element in a group:

  Use the For Each...Next statement. The statement's syntax is shown in Figure 9-9.

- To associate the items in a list box with the elements in an array:

  Use each list box item's index and each array element's subscript.

- To sort the elements in a one-dimensional array in ascending order:

  Use the Array.Sort method. The method's syntax is **Array.Sort(***arrayName***)**.

- To reverse the order of the elements in a one-dimensional array:

  Use the Array.Reverse method. The method's syntax is **Array.Reverse(***arrayName***)**.

Lesson A Key Terms

Array—a group of related variables that have the same name and data type

Array.Reverse method—reverses the order of the elements in a one-dimensional array

Array.Sort method—sorts the elements in a one-dimensional array in ascending order

Elements—the variables in an array

For Each...Next statement—used to code a loop whose instructions you want processed for each element in a group

GetUpperBound method—returns an integer that represents the highest subscript in a specified dimension, which is 0 for a one-dimensional array

Length property—one of the properties of an array; stores an integer that represents the number of array elements

One-dimensional array—an array whose elements are identified by a unique subscript

Populating the array—refers to the process of initializing the elements in an array

Run time error—an error that occurs while an application is running

Scalar variable—another name for a simple variable

Simple variable—a variable that is unrelated to any other variable in the computer's internal memory; also called a scalar variable

Sorting—the process of arranging data in a specific order

Subscript—a unique integer that identifies the position of an element in an array

Lesson A Review Questions

1. Which of the following declares a five-element one-dimensional array?

   a. `Dim dblAmounts(4) As Double`

   b. `Dim dblAmounts(5) As Double`

   c. `Dim dblAmounts(4) As Double =`
      `{3.55, 6.70, 8, 4, 2.34}`

   d. both a and c

2. The `strItems` array is declared as follows: `Dim strItems(20) As String`. The `intSub` variable keeps track of the array subscripts and is initialized to 0. Which of the following Do clauses will process the loop instructions for each element in the array?

   a. `Do While intSub > 20`

   b. `Do While intSub < 20`

   c. `Do While intSub >= 20`

   d. `Do While intSub <= 20`

3. The `intSales` array is declared as follows: `Dim intSales() As Integer = {10000, 12000, 900, 500, 20000}`. The statement `intSales(3) = intSales(3) + 10` will _____.

   a. replace the 500 amount with 10

   b. replace the 500 amount with 510

   c. replace the 900 amount with 10

   d. replace the 900 amount with 910

4. The `intSales` array is declared as follows: `Dim intSales() As Integer = {10000, 12000, 900, 500, 20000}`. Which of the following If clauses determines whether the `intSub` variable contains a valid subscript for the array?

   a. `If intSales(intSub) >= 0 AndAlso`
      `      intSales(intSub) < 4 Then`

   b. `If intSales(intSub) >= 0 AndAlso`
      `      intSales(intSub) <= 4 Then`

   c. `If intSub >= 0 AndAlso intSub < 4 Then`

   d. `If intSub >= 0 AndAlso intSub <= 4 Then`

5. The `intSales` array is declared as follows: `Dim intSales() As Integer = {10000, 12000, 900, 500, 20000}`. Which of the following loops will correctly add 100 to each array element? The `intSub` variable contains the number 0 before the loops are processed.

   a. `Do While intSub <= 4`
      `      intSub = intSub + 100`
      `Loop`

   b. `Do While intSub <= 4`
      `      intSales = intSales + 100`
      `Loop`

   c. `Do While intSub < 5`
      `      intSales(intSub) =`
      `            intSales(intSub) + 100`
      `Loop`

   d. none of the above

6. The intNums array is declared as follows: Dim intNums() As Integer = {10, 5, 7, 2}. Which of the following blocks of code correctly calculates the average value stored in the array? The intTotal, intSub, and dblAvg variables contain the number 0 before the loops are processed.

a.
```
Do While intSub < 4
      intNums(intSub) = intTotal + intTotal
      intSub = intSub + 1
Loop
dblAvg = intTotal / intSub
```

b.
```
Do While intSub < 4
      intTotal = intTotal + intNums(intSub)
      intSub = intSub + 1
Loop
dblAvg = intTotal / intSub
```

c.
```
Do While intSub < 4
      intTotal = intTotal + intNums(intSub)
      intSub = intSub + 1
Loop
dblAvg = intTotal / intSub - 1
```

d.
```
Do While intSub < 4
      intTotal = intTotal + intNums(intSub)
      intSub = intSub + 1
Loop
dblAvg = intTotal / (intSub - 1)
```

7. What will the code in Review Question 6's answer a assign to the dblAvg variable?

   a. 0

   b. 5

   c. 6

   d. 8

8. What will the code in Review Question 6's answer b assign to the dblAvg variable?

   a. 0

   b. 5

   c. 6

   d. 8

9. What will the code in Review Question 6's answer c assign to the dblAvg variable?

   a. 0

   b. 5

   c. 6

   d. 8

10. What will the code in Review Question 6's answer d assign to the dblAvg variable?

    a. 0

    b. 5

    c. 6

    d. 8

11. Which of the following statements sorts the intQuantities array in ascending order?

    a. Array.Sort(intQuantities)

    b. intQuantities.Sort

    c. Sort(intQuantities)

    d. SortArray(intQuantities)

12. Which of the following statements assigns (to the intElements variable) the number of elements contained in the intNums array?

    a. intElements = Len(intNums)

    b. intElements = Length(intNums)

    c. intElements = intNums.Len

    d. intElements = intNums.Length

13. Which of the following assigns the string "Rover" to the fifth element in a one-dimensional array named strPetNames?

    a. strPetNames(4) = "Rover"

    b. strPetNames[4] = "Rover"

    c. strPetNames(5) = "Rover"

    d. strPetNames.Items.Add(5) = "Rover"

14. Which of the following assigns the number 1 to each element in a five-element, one-dimensional Integer array named `intCounters`?

a.
```
For intSub As Integer = 0 To 4
        intCounters(intSub) = 1
Next intSub
```

b.
```
Dim intSub As Integer
Do While intSub < 5
        intCounters(intSub) = 1
        intSub += 1
Loop
```

c.
```
For intSub As Integer = 1 To 5
        intCounters(intSub - 1) = 1
Next intSub
```

d. all of the above

Lesson A Exercises

INTRODUCTORY   1. Write the statement to declare a procedure-level one-dimensional array named `intNumbers`. The array should be able to store 20 integers. Then write the statement to store the number 7 in the second element.

INTRODUCTORY   2. Write the statement to declare a class-level one-dimensional array named `strProducts`. The array should be able to store 10 strings. Then write the statement to store the string "Paper" in the third element.

INTRODUCTORY   3. Write the statement to declare and initialize a procedure-level one-dimensional array named `dblRates`. Use the following numbers to initialize the array: 6.5, 8.3, 4, 2, 10.5.

INTRODUCTORY   4. Write the code to display the contents of the `dblRates` array from Exercise 3 in the lstRates control. Use the For…Next statement.

INTRODUCTORY   5. Rewrite the code from Exercise 4 using the Do…Loop statement.

INTRODUCTORY   6. Rewrite the code from Exercise 4 using the For Each…Next statement.

INTRODUCTORY   7. Write the statement to sort the `dblRates` array in ascending order.

INTRODUCTORY   8. Write the statement to reverse the contents of the `dblRates` array.

INTRODUCTORY   9. Open the Months Solution (Months Solution.sln) file contained in the VB2010\Chap09\Months Solution-Introductory folder. If necessary, open the designer window. Declare and initialize a one-dimensional String array. Use the names of the 12 months to initialize the array. Use the For Each…Next statement to display the contents of the array in the list box. Code the list box so that it displays (in the You selected box) the name of the month selected in the list box. Save the solution and then start and test the application. Close the Code Editor window and then close the solution.

10. Open the Salary Code Solution (Salary Code Solution.sln) file contained in the VB2010\Chap09\Salary Code Solution folder. If necessary, open the designer window. The application should allow the user to select a salary code from the list box; it then should display the salary associated with the code. The salary codes and salaries are listed in Figure 9-29. Code the application. Save the solution and then start and test the application. Close the Code Editor window and then close the solution.

INTRODUCTORY

Salary code	Salary
101	25000
102	35000
103	55000
104	75000
105	80500
106	83000
107	90500

Figure 9-29   Salary codes and salaries for Exercise 10

11. In this exercise, you modify the Cycles Galore application coded in the lesson. Use Windows to make a copy of the Cycles Galore Solution folder. Rename the copy Modified Cycles Galore Solution. Open the Cycles Galore Solution (Cycles Galore Solution.sln) file contained in the Modified Cycles Galore Solution folder. Open the designer window. In addition to displaying the highest bonus amount and the number of salespeople earning that amount, the modified application should display the lowest bonus amount and the number of salespeople earning that amount. Make the appropriate modifications to the interface and code. Save the solution and then start and test the application. Close the Code Editor window and then close the solution.

INTRODUCTORY

12. Open the Sales Solution (Sales Solution.sln) file contained in the VB2010\Chap09\Sales Solution folder. If necessary, open the designer window. The interface allows the user to enter a sales amount. The application should display the number of salespeople earning at least that amount. Open the Code Editor window. The sales amounts are stored in the `intSales` array. Finish coding the application. Save the solution and then start and test the application. Close the Code Editor window and then close the solution.

INTERMEDIATE

536

INTERMEDIATE

13. Open the Months Solution (Months Solution.sln) file contained in the VB2010\Chap09\Months Solution-Intermediate folder. If necessary, open the designer window. Display the names of the 12 months in the list box. Declare and initialize a one-dimensional Integer array named `intDaysInTheMonth`. Use the following 12 integers to initialize the array: 31, 28, 31, 30, 31, 30, 31, 31, 30, 31, 30, and 31. Code the list box so that it displays (in the Days box) the number of days in the selected month. Save the solution and then start and test the application. Close the Code Editor window and then close the solution.

INTERMEDIATE

14. Write the code to multiply by 3 the number stored in the first element in a one-dimensional array named `intNumbers`. Store the result in the `intResult` variable.

INTERMEDIATE

15. Write the code to add together the numbers stored in the first and second elements in a one-dimensional array named `intNumbers`. Display the sum in the lblSum control.

INTERMEDIATE

16. Write two versions of the code to subtract the number 1 from each element in a one-dimensional Integer array named `intQuantities`. Use the Do...Loop statement in the first version. Use the For...Next statement in the second version.

INTERMEDIATE

17. Open the Test Scores Solution (Test Scores Solution.sln) file contained in the VB2010\Chap09\Test Scores Solution folder. If necessary, open the designer window. The Average button's Click event procedure should display the number of test scores contained in a one-dimensional array and also the average test score. Code the procedure. Save the solution and then start and test the application. Close the Code Editor window and then close the solution.

INTERMEDIATE

18. Open the Update Prices Solution (Update Prices Solution.sln) file contained in the VB2010\Chap09\Update Prices Solution folder. If necessary, open the designer window. The Increase button's Click event procedure should ask the user for a percentage amount by which each price stored in an array should be increased. It then should increase each price by that amount, displaying each increased price (right-aligned with two decimal places) in the list box. (Hint: You can clear the contents of a list box using the Items collection's Clear method.) Save the solution and then start the application. Click the Increase button. Increase each price by 5%. Close the Code Editor window and then close the solution.

INTERMEDIATE

19. Open the Car Sales Solution (Car Sales Solution.sln) file contained in the VB2010\Chap09\Car Sales Solution folder. If necessary, open the designer window. The interface allows the user to enter the number of each car type sold by each salesperson. The Add to Total button should use an array to accumulate the numbers sold by car type. It also should display (in the labels) the total number sold for each car type. Save the solution and then start and test the application. Close the Code Editor window and then close the solution.

20. In this exercise, you modify the application from Exercise 18. The modified application allows the user to update a specific price. Use Windows to make a copy of the Update Prices Solution folder. Rename the folder Modified Update Prices Solution. Open the Update Prices Solution (Update Prices Solution.sln) file contained in the Modified Update Prices Solution folder. Open the designer window. Modify the Increase button's Click event procedure so it also asks the user to enter a number from 1 through 10. If the user enters the number 1, the procedure should update the first price in the array. If the user enters the number 2, the procedure should update the second price in the array, and so on. Save the solution and then start the application. Click the Increase button. Increase the second price by 10%. Click the Increase button again. This time, increase the tenth price by 5%. (The second price in the list box should still reflect the 10% increase.) Close the Code Editor window and then close the solution.

ADVANCED

537

21. Open the Scores Solution (Scores Solution.sln) file contained in the VB2010\Chap09\Scores Solution folder. If necessary, open the designer window. Open the Code Editor window and then open the code template for the btnDisplay control's Click event procedure. Declare a 20-element, one-dimensional Integer array named `intScores`. Assign the following 20 numbers to the array: 88, 72, 99, 20, 66, 95, 99, 100, 72, 88, 78, 45, 57, 89, 85, 78, 75, 88, 72, and 88. The procedure should prompt the user to enter a score from 0 through 100. It then should display (in a message box) the number of students who earned that score. Code the procedure. Save the solution and then start the application. Use the application to answer the following questions, and then close the Code Editor window and the solution:

ADVANCED

How many students earned a score of 72?
How many students earned a score of 88?
How many students earned a score of 20?
How many students earned a score of 99?

22. In this exercise, you modify the application from Exercise 21. The modified application allows the user to display the number of students earning a score within a specific range. Use Windows to make a copy of the Scores Solution folder. Rename the folder Modified Scores Solution. Open the Scores Solution (Scores Solution.sln) file contained in the Modified Scores Solution folder. Open the designer and Code Editor windows. Modify the btnDisplay control's Click event procedure to prompt the user to enter both a minimum score and a maximum score. The procedure then should display (in a message box) the number of students who earned a score within that range. Save the solution and then start the application. Use the application to answer the following questions, and then close the Code Editor window and the solution:

ADVANCED

How many students earned a score from 70 through 79?
How many students earned a score from 65 through 85?
How many students earned a score from 0 through 50?

ADVANCED

23. In this exercise, you code an application that generates and displays six unique random numbers for a lottery game. Each lottery number can range from 1 through 54 only. Open the Lottery Game Solution (Lottery Game Solution.sln) file contained in the VB2010\Chap09\ Lottery Game Solution folder. If necessary, open the designer window. Code the Display Lottery Numbers button's Click event procedure so that it displays six unique random numbers in the interface. (Hint: Store the numbers in a one-dimensional array.) Save the solution and then start the application. Click the Display Lottery Numbers button several times. Each time you click the button, six unique random numbers between 1 and 54 (inclusive) should appear in the interface. Close the Code Editor window and then close the solution.

 Discovery

24. In this exercise, you learn about the ReDim statement.

a. Research the Visual Basic ReDim statement. What is the purpose of the statement? What is the purpose of the **Preserve** keyword?

b. Open the ReDim Solution (ReDim Solution.sln) file contained in the VB2010\Chap09\ReDim Solution folder. If necessary, open the designer window. Open the Code Editor window and locate the btnDisplay control's Click event procedure. Study the existing code, and then modify the procedure so that it stores any number of sales amounts in the **intSales** array. (Hint: Declare the array using empty sets of parentheses and braces. Use the ReDim statement to add an element to the array.)

c. Save the solution and then start the application. Click the Display Sales button and then enter the following sales amounts, one at a time: 700, 550, and 800. Click the Cancel button in the input box. The three sales amounts should appear in the list box.

d. Click the Display Sales button again and then enter the following sales amounts, one at a time: 5, 9, 45, 67, 8, and 0. Click the Cancel button in the input box. This time, six sales amounts should appear in the list box. Close the Code Editor window and then close the solution.

LESSON B

After studying Lesson B, you should be able to:

- Explain the relationship between the elements in parallel one-dimensional arrays

- Create parallel one-dimensional arrays

- Locate information in two parallel one-dimensional arrays

Parallel One-Dimensional Arrays

Recall that your task in this chapter is to create an application for Takoda Tapahe, the owner of a small gift shop named Treasures. The application should allow Takoda to enter a product ID. It then should display the product's price. Figure 9-30 shows a portion of the gift shop's price list.

Product ID	Price
BX35	13
CR20	10
FE15	12
KW10	24
MM67	4

Figure 9-30   A portion of the gift shop's price list

Recall that all of the variables in an array have the same data type. So how can you store a price list that includes a string (the product ID) and a number (the price) in an array? One solution is to use two one-dimensional arrays: a String array to store the product IDs and an Integer array to store the prices. Both arrays, referred to as parallel arrays, are illustrated in Figure 9-31.

Parallel arrays are two or more arrays whose elements are related by their position in the arrays; in other words, they are related by their subscripts. The `strIds` and `intPrices` arrays in Figure 9-31 are parallel because each element in the `strIds` array corresponds to the element located in the same position in the `intPrices` array. For example, the item whose product ID is BX35 [`strIds(0)`] has a price of $13 [`intPrices(0)`]. Likewise, the item whose product ID is CR20 [`strIds(1)`] has a price of $10 [`intPrices(1)`]. The same relationship is true for the remaining elements in both arrays. To determine an item's price, you locate the item's ID in the `strIds` array and then view its corresponding element in the `intPrices` array.

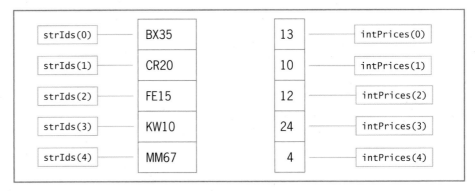

Figure 9-31   Illustration of two parallel one-dimensional arrays

START HERE ▶

To use parallel one-dimensional arrays to code the Treasures Gift Shop application:

1. If necessary, start Visual Studio 2010 or Visual Basic 2010 Express. Open the Treasures Solution (Treasures Solution.sln) file contained in the VB2010\Chap09\Treasures Solution-Parallel folder. If necessary, open the designer window. The text box's CharacterCasing and MaxLength properties are set to Upper and 4, respectively. Recall that when a text box's CharacterCasing property is set to Upper, any letters the user types will appear in uppercase. When a text box's MaxLength property is set to 4, the user can enter a maximum of four characters in the text box.

2. Open the Code Editor window. Replace <your name> and <current date> in the comments with your name and the current date, respectively.

3. Locate the btnDisplay control's Click event procedure. First, you will declare and initialize the two parallel one-dimensional arrays. Click the **blank line** above the `' assign the ID to a variable` comment and then enter the following array declaration statements:

   Dim strIds() As String =
   {"BX35", "CR20", "FE15", "KW10", "MM67"}
   Dim intPrices() As Integer = {13, 10, 12, 24, 4}

4. The procedure will use a String variable to store the product ID entered by the user. It also will use an Integer variable to keep track of the array subscripts while the array is being searched. Enter the following two declaration statements:

   Dim strSearchForId As String
   Dim intSub As Integer

5. Now you will assign the product ID entered by the user to the `strSearchForId` variable. Click the **blank line** below the `' assign the ID to a variable` comment and then enter the following assignment statement:

   strSearchForId = txtId.Text

6. Next, you will use a loop to search each element in the `strIds` array, stopping either when the end of the array is reached or when the ID is located in the array. Click the **blank line** below the `' the array or the ID is found` comment and then enter the following lines of code:

> **Do Until intSub = strIds.Length OrElse**
> > **strSearchForId = strIds(intSub)**
> > **intSub = intSub + 1**
> **Loop**

7. Now you need to determine why the loop ended. You can do this using a selection structure whose condition compares the value stored in the `intSub` variable with the value stored in the `strIds` array's Length property. If the variable's value is less than the number of array elements, the loop ended because the ID was located in the array. In that case, the selection structure's true path should display the price located in the same position in the `intPrices` array. On the other hand, if the variable's value is not less than the number of array elements, the loop ended because it reached the end of the array without finding the ID. In that case, the selection structure's false path should display the "Invalid ID" message in a message box. Click the **blank line** below the `' determine whether the ID was found` comment and then enter the following lines of code:

> **If intSub < strIds.Length Then**
> > **lblPrice.Text = intPrices(intSub).ToString("C0")**
> **Else**
> > **MessageBox.Show("Invalid ID",**
> > > **"Treasures Gift Shop",**
> > > **MessageBoxButtons.OK,**
> > > **MessageBoxIcon.Information)**
> **End If**

Figure 9-32 shows the btnDisplay control's Click event procedure.

```
Private Sub btnDisplay_Click(ByVal sender As Object,
ByVal e As System.EventArgs) Handles btnDisplay.Click
    ' displays the price associated with an ID

    Dim strIds() As String =
        {"BX35", "CR20", "FE15", "KW10", "MM67"}
    Dim intPrices() As Integer = {13, 10, 12, 24, 4}
    Dim strSearchForId As String
    Dim intSub As Integer

    ' assign the ID to a variable
    strSearchForId = txtId.Text

    ' search the strIds array for the ID
    ' continue searching until the end of
    ' the array or the ID is found
```

parallel one-dimensional arrays

Figure 9-32 btnDisplay control's Click event procedure using parallel one-dimensional arrays *(continues)*

542

(continued)

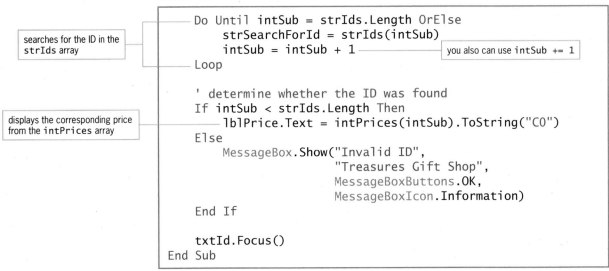

searches for the ID in the strIds array

displays the corresponding price from the intPrices array

```
      Do Until intSub = strIds.Length OrElse
          strSearchForId = strIds(intSub)
          intSub = intSub + 1                    you also can use intSub += 1
      Loop

      ' determine whether the ID was found
      If intSub < strIds.Length Then
          lblPrice.Text = intPrices(intSub).ToString("C0")
      Else
          MessageBox.Show("Invalid ID",
                          "Treasures Gift Shop",
                          MessageBoxButtons.OK,
                          MessageBoxIcon.Information)
      End If

      txtId.Focus()
  End Sub
```

Figure 9-32 btnDisplay control's Click event procedure using parallel one-dimensional arrays

START HERE

To test the Treasures Gift Shop application:

1. Save the solution and then start the application. Type **cr20** in the Product ID box and then click the **Display Price** button. $10 appears in the Price box. See Figure 9-33.

Figure 9-33 Interface showing the price for product ID CR20

2. Type **xx44** in the Product ID box and then click the **Display Price** button. The "Invalid ID" message appears in a message box. Close the message box.

3. On your own, test the application using other valid and invalid IDs. When you are finished testing the application, click the **Exit** button.

4. Close the Code Editor window and then close the solution.

Lesson B Summary

- To create parallel one-dimensional arrays:

Create two or more one-dimensional arrays. When assigning values to the arrays, be sure that the value stored in each element in the first array corresponds to the values stored in the same elements in the other arrays.

Lesson B Key Term

Parallel arrays—two or more arrays whose elements are related by their subscripts (position) in the arrays

Lesson B Review Questions

1. If the elements in two arrays are related by their subscripts, the arrays are called _____ arrays.

   a. associated

   b. coupled

   c. matching

   d. parallel

2. The `strStates` and `strCapitals` arrays are parallel arrays. If Illinois is stored in the second element in the `strStates` array, where is its capital (Springfield) stored?

   a. `strCapitals(1)`

   b. `strCapitals(2)`

Lesson B Exercises

1. Open the State Capitals Solution (State Capitals Solution.sln) file contained in the VB2010\Chap09\State Capitals Solution folder. If necessary, open the designer window. Open the Code Editor window. Locate the btnDisplay control's Click event procedure. The procedure declares and initializes parallel one-dimensional arrays named `strStates` and `strCaps`. The procedure should display the contents of the arrays in the list box. Display the information in the following format: the capital name followed by a comma, a space, and the state name. Code the procedure. Save the solution and then start and test the application. Close the Code Editor window and then close the solution.

   INTRODUCTORY

2. In this exercise, you code an application that allows Professor Carver to display a grade based on the number of points he enters. The grading scale is shown in Figure 9-34. Open the Carver Solution

   INTERMEDIATE

(Carver Solution.sln) file contained in the VB2010\Chap09\Carver Solution-Parallel folder. If necessary, open the designer window. Open the Code Editor window and then open the code template for the btnDisplay control's Click event procedure. Store the minimum points in a one-dimensional Integer array named `intPoints`. Store the grades in a one-dimensional String array named `strGrades`. The arrays should be parallel arrays. The procedure should search the `intPoints` array for the number of points entered by the user. It then should display the corresponding grade from the `strGrades` array. Save the solution and then start and test the application. Close the Code Editor window and then close the solution.

Minimum points	Maximum points	Grade
0	299	F
300	349	D
350	399	C
400	449	B
450	500	A

Figure 9-34   Grading scale for Exercise 2

INTERMEDIATE

3. In this exercise, you modify the application from Exercise 2. The modified application will allow the user to change the grading scale when the application is started. Use Windows to make a copy of the Carver Solution-Parallel folder. Rename the folder Modified Carver Solution-Parallel. Open the Carver Solution (Carver Solution.sln) file contained in the Modified Carver Solution-Parallel folder. Open the designer and Code Editor windows.

a. When the form is loaded into the computer's memory, the application should use the InputBox function to prompt the user to enter the total number of possible points—in other words, the total number of points a student can earn in the course. Modify the application's code to perform this task.

b. Modify the application's code to use the grading scale shown in Figure 9-35. For example, if the user enters the number 500 in response to the InputBox function, the code should enter 450 (90% of 500) as the minimum number of points for an A. If the user enters the number 300, the code should enter 270 (90% of 300) as the minimum number of points for an A.

c. Save the solution and then start the application. Enter 300 as the number of possible points, and then enter 185 in the Points text box. Click the Display Grade button. A grade of D should appear in the interface. Stop the application.

d. Start the application again. Enter 500 as the number of possible points, and then enter 363 in the Points text box. Click the Display Grade button. A grade of C should appear in the interface. Close the Code Editor window and then close the solution.

Minimum points	Grade
0	F
60% of the possible points	D
70% of the possible points	C
80% of the possible points	B
90% of the possible points	A

Figure 9-35   Grading scale for Exercise 3

4. Open the Laury Solution (Laury Solution.sln) file contained in the VB2010\Chap09\Laury Solution-Parallel folder. If necessary, open the designer window. Open the Code Editor window and then open the code template for the btnDisplay control's Click event procedure. The procedure should display a shipping charge that is based on the number of items a customer orders. The order amounts and shipping charges are listed in Figure 9-36. Code the procedure. Store the minimum order amounts and shipping charges in parallel arrays. Display the appropriate shipping charge with a dollar sign and two decimal places. Save the solution and then start and test the application. Close the Code Editor window and then close the solution.

INTERMEDIATE

Minimum order	Maximum order	Shipping charge
1	10	15
11	50	10
51	100	5
101	No maximum	0

Figure 9-36   Order amounts and shipping charges for Exercise 4

LESSON C

After studying Lesson C, you should be able to:

- Declare and initialize a two-dimensional array
- Store data in a two-dimensional array
- Sum the values in a two-dimensional array
- Search a two-dimensional array

Two-Dimensional Arrays

As you learned in Lesson A, the most commonly used arrays in business applications are one-dimensional and two-dimensional. You can visualize a one-dimensional array as a column of variables in memory. A **two-dimensional array**, on the other hand, resembles a table in that the variables (elements) are in rows and columns. You can determine the number of elements in a two-dimensional array by multiplying the number of its rows by the number of its columns. An array that has four rows and three columns, for example, contains 12 elements.

Each element in a two-dimensional array is identified by a unique combination of two subscripts that the computer assigns to the element when the array is created. The subscripts specify the element's row and column positions in the array. Elements located in the first row in a two-dimensional array are assigned a row subscript of 0. Elements in the second row are assigned a row subscript of 1, and so on. Similarly, elements located in the first column in a two-dimensional array are assigned a column subscript of 0. Elements in the second column are assigned a column subscript of 1, and so on.

You refer to each element in a two-dimensional array by the array's name and the element's row and column subscripts, with the row subscript listed first and the column subscript listed second. The subscripts are separated by a comma and specified in a set of parentheses immediately following the array name. For example, to refer to the element located in the first row, first column in a two-dimensional array named `strProducts`, you use `strProducts(0, 0)`—read "`strProducts` sub zero comma zero." Similarly, to refer to the element located in the second row, third column, you use `strProducts(1, 2)`. Notice that the subscripts are one number less than the row and column in which the element is located. This is because the row and column subscripts start at 0 rather than at 1. You will find that the last row subscript in a two-dimensional array is always one number less than the number of rows in the array. Likewise, the last column subscript is always one number less than the number of columns in the array. Figure 9-37 illustrates the elements contained in the two-dimensional `strProducts` array.

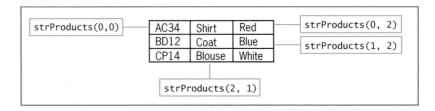

Figure 9-37 Names of some of the elements in the `strProducts` array

546

Figure 9-38 shows two versions of the syntax for declaring a two-dimensional array in Visual Basic. In each version, *arrayName* is the name of the array and *dataType* is the type of data the array variables will store. In Version 1's syntax, *highestRowSubscript* and *highestColumnSubscript* are integers that specify the highest row and column subscripts, respectively, in the array. When the array is created, it will contain one row more than the number specified in the highestRowSubscript argument and one column more than the number specified in the highestColumnSubscript argument. This is because the first row and column subscripts in a two-dimensional array are 0. When you declare a two-dimensional array using the syntax shown in Version 1, the computer automatically initializes each element in the array when the array is created.

You would use Version 2's syntax when you want to specify each variable's initial value. You do this by including a separate *initialValues* section, enclosed in braces, for each row in the array. If the array has two rows, then the statement that declares and initializes the array should have two initial-Values sections. If the array has five rows, then the declaration statement should have five initialValues sections. Within the individual initialValues sections, you enter one or more values separated by commas. The number of values to enter corresponds to the number of columns in the array. If the array contains 10 columns, then each individual initialValues section should contain 10 values. In addition to the set of braces enclosing each individual initialValues section, Version 2's syntax also requires all of the initialValues sections to be enclosed in a set of braces.

When using Version 2's syntax, be sure to include a comma within the parentheses that follow the array's name. The comma indicates that the array is a two-dimensional array. (Recall that a comma is used to separate the row subscript from the column subscript in a two-dimensional array.) Also included in Figure 9-38 are examples of using both syntax versions.

Declaring a two-dimensional array

Syntax – Version 1
{**Dim** | **Private** | **Static**} *arrayName*(*highestRowSubscript*, *highestColumnSubscript*) **As** *dataType*

Syntax – Version 2
{**Dim** | **Private** | **Static**} *arrayName*(,) **As** *dataType* = {{*initialValues*}, . . . {*initialValues*}}

Example 1
```
Dim strNames(5, 2) As String
```
declares a six-row, three-column procedure-level array named `strNames`; each element is automatically initialized using the keyword `Nothing`

Example 2
```
Static intNumbers(4, 3) As Integer
```
declares a static, five-row, four-column procedure-level array named `intNumbers`; each element is automatically initialized to 0

Figure 9-38 Syntax versions and examples of declaring a two-dimensional array *(continues)*

(continued)

Example 3
```
Dim strProducts(,) As String =
          {{"AC34", "Shirt", "Red"},
           {"BD12", "Coat", "Blue"},
           {"CP14", "Blouse", "White"}}
```
declares and initializes a three-row, three-column procedure-level array named
strProducts (the array is illustrated in Figure 9-37)

Example 4
```
Private dblSales(,) As Double = {{75.33, 9.65},
                                 {23.55, 6.89},
                                 {4.5, 89.3}}
```
declares and initializes a three-row, two-column class-level array named dblPrices

Figure 9-38   Syntax versions and examples of declaring a two-dimensional array

After an array is declared, you can use another statement to store a different value in an array element. Examples of such statements include assignment statements and statements that contain the TryParse method. Figure 9-39 shows examples of both types of statements.

Storing data in a two-dimensional array

Example 1
```
strNames(0, 1) = "Sarah"
```
assigns the string "Sarah" to the element located in the first row, second column in the strNames array

Example 2
```
For intRow As Integer = 0 To 4
    For intColumn As Integer = 0 To 3
        intNumbers(intRow, intColumn) += 1
    Next intColumn
Next intRow
```
adds the number 1 to the contents of each element in the intNumbers array

Example 3
```
Dim intRow As Integer
Dim intCol As Integer
Do While intRow <= 2
    intCol = 0
    Do While intCol <= 1
        dblSales(intRow, intCol) = 100
        intCol = intCol + 1
    Loop
    intRow = intRow + 1
Loop
```
assigns the number 100 to each element in the dblSales array

Figure 9-39   Examples of statements used to store data in a two-dimensional array
(continues)

(continued)

> Example 4
> ```
> dblSales(2, 1) = dblSales(2, 1) * .1
> ```
> multiplies the value contained in the third row, second column in the dblSales array by .1 and then assigns the result to the element; you also can write this statement as
> ```
> dblSales(2, 1) *= .1
> ```
>
> Example 5
> ```
> Double.TryParse(txtSales.Text, dblSales(0, 0))
> ```
> assigns either the value entered in the txtSales control (converted to Double) or the number 0 to the element located in the first row, first column in the dblSales array

Figure 9-39   Examples of statements used to store data in a two-dimensional array

549

Earlier, you learned how to use the GetUpperBound method to determine the highest subscript in a one-dimensional array. You also can use the GetUpperBound method to determine the highest row and column subscripts in a two-dimensional array, as shown in Figure 9-40.

> **Using a two-dimensional array's GetUpperBound method**
>
> Syntax to determine the highest row subscript
> *arrayName*.**GetUpperBound(0)**
>
> the row dimension is always 0
>
> Syntax to determine the highest column subscript
> *arrayName*.**GetUpperBound(1)**
>
> the column dimension is always 1
>
> Example
> ```
> Dim strOrders(10, 3) As String
> Dim intHighestRowSub As Integer
> Dim intHighestColumnSub As Integer
> intHighestRowSub = strOrders.GetUpperBound(0)
> intHighestColumnSub = strOrders.GetUpperBound(1)
> ```
> assigns the numbers 10 and 3 to the intHighestRowSub and
> intHighestColumnSub variables, respectively

Figure 9-40   Syntax and an example of a two-dimensional array's GetUpperBound method

Traversing a Two-Dimensional Array

Recall that you use a loop to traverse a one-dimensional array. To traverse a two-dimensional array, you typically use two loops: an outer loop and a nested loop. One of the loops keeps track of the row subscript and the other keeps track of the column subscript. You can code the loops using either the For…Next statement or the Do…Loop statement. Rather than using two loops, you also can traverse a two-dimensional array using one For Each…Next loop. However, recall that the instructions in a For Each…Next loop can only read the array values; they cannot permanently modify the values. Figure 9-41 shows examples of loops that traverse the strMonths array, displaying each element's value in the lstMonths control.

Traversing a two-dimensional array

```
Private strMonths(,) As String =
                        {{"Jan", "31"},
                         {"Feb", "28"},
                         {"Mar", "31"},
                         {"Apr", "30"}}
```

Example 1
```
Dim intHighRow As Integer = strMonths.GetUpperBound(0)
Dim intHighCol As Integer = strMonths.GetUpperBound(1)
For intR As Integer = 0 To intHighRow
    For intC As Integer = 0 To intHighCol
        lstMonths.Items.Add(strMonths(intR, intC))
    Next intC
Next intR
```
displays the contents of the strMonths array in the lstMonths control; the contents are displayed row by row, as follows: Jan, 31, Feb, 28, Mar, 31, Apr, and 30

Example 2
```
Dim intHighRow As Integer = strMonths.GetUpperBound(0)
Dim intHighCol As Integer = strMonths.GetUpperBound(1)
Dim intR As Integer
Dim intC As Integer
Do While intC <= intHighCol
    intR = 0
    Do While intR <= intHighRow
        lstMonths.Items.Add(strMonths(intR, intC))
        intR += 1
    Loop
    intC += 1
Loop
```
displays the contents of the strMonths array in the lstMonths control; the contents are displayed column by column, as follows: Jan, Feb, Mar, Apr, 31, 28, 31, and 30

Example 3
```
For Each strElement As String In strMonths
    lstMonths.Items.Add(strElement)
Next strElement
```
displays the contents of the strMonths array in the lstMonths control; the contents are displayed as follows: Jan, 31, Feb, 28, Mar, 31, Apr, and 30

Figure 9-41   Examples of loops used to traverse a two-dimensional array

Totaling the Values Stored in a Two-Dimensional Array

Figure 9-42 shows the problem specification for the Jenko Booksellers application. The application displays the total of the sales stored in a two-dimensional array.

Jenko Booksellers sells paperback and hardcover books in each of its three stores. The sales manager wants an application that displays the total sales made in the previous month. The sales amounts for the previous month are shown in the chart below. The application will store the sales amounts in a two-dimensional array that has three rows and two columns. Each row will contain the data pertaining to one of the three stores. The sales amounts for paperback books will be stored in the first column. The second column will contain the sales amounts for hardcover books. The application will need to total the values stored in the array.

	Paperback sales ($)	Hardcover sales ($)
Store 1	1200.33	2350.75
Store 2	3677.80	2456.05
Store 3	750.67	1345.99

Figure 9-42 Problem specification for the Jenko Booksellers application

To code and then test the Jenko Booksellers application:

START HERE

1. If necessary, start Visual Studio 2010 or Visual Basic 2010 Express. Open the Jenko Booksellers Solution (Jenko Booksellers Solution.sln) file contained in the VB2010\Chap09\Jenko Booksellers Solution folder. If necessary, open the designer window.

2. Open the Code Editor window. Replace <your name> and <current date> in the comments with your name and the current date, respectively.

3. Locate the btnCalc control's Click event procedure. First, you will declare and initialize a two-dimensional array to store the sales amounts. The array will contain three rows (one for each store) and two columns. The first column in the array will contain the paperback book sales, and the second column will contain the hardcover book sales. Click the **blank line** immediately above the ' total the sales amounts stored in the array comment and then enter the following array declaration statement:

   Dim dblSales(,) As Double = {{1200.33, 2350.75},
   {3677.8, 2456.05},
   {750.67, 1345.99}}

4. Now you will declare a Double variable named dblTotal. The dblTotal variable will be an accumulator variable; it will accumulate the sales amounts stored in the array. Enter the following declaration statement:

   Dim dblTotal As Double

5. Next, you will enter a loop that totals the values stored in the array. Click the **blank line** below the ' total the sales amounts stored in the array comment and then enter the following lines of code:

   For Each dblElement As Double in dblSales
   dblTotal = dblTotal + dblElement
   Next dblElement

6. Finally, you will display the total sales, which is stored in the `dblTotal` variable. Insert a blank line below the `Next dblElement` clause and then enter the additional assignment statement shown in Figure 9-43.

```
Private Sub btnCalc_Click(ByVal sender As Object, ByV
    ' displays the total sales

    Dim dblSales(,) As Double = {{1200.33, 2350.75},
                                 {3677.8, 2456.05},
                                 {750.67, 1345.99}}
    Dim dblTotal As Double

    ' total the sales amounts stored in the array
    For Each dblElement As Double In dblSales
        dblTotal = dblTotal + dblElement
    Next dblElement
    lblTotal.Text = dblTotal.ToString("C2")

End Sub
```

you also can use
`dblTotal += dblElement`

enter this additional assignment statement

Figure 9-43   btnCalc control's Click event procedure

7. Save the solution and then start the application. Click the **Calculate** button. $11,781.59 appears in the Total sales box, as shown in Figure 9-44.

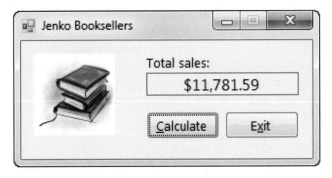

Figure 9-44   Total sales displayed in the interface

Searching a Two-Dimensional Array

In Lesson B, you coded the Treasures Gift Shop application. As you may remember, the application stores the gift shop's price list in two parallel one-dimensional arrays: a String array for the product IDs and an Integer array for the prices. It then searches the String array for the ID entered by the user. If the ID is in the array, the application displays its corresponding price from the Integer array; otherwise, it displays an appropriate message in a message box. Instead of using two parallel one-dimensional arrays for the price list, you can use a two-dimensional array. To do this, you store the product IDs in the first column of the array, and store the prices in the second column. However, you will need to treat the prices as strings, because all of the data in a two-dimensional array must have the same data type.

To use a two-dimensional array to code the Treasures Gift Shop application:

START HERE

1. Open the Treasures Solution (Treasures Solution.sln) file contained in the VB2010\Chap09\Treasures Solution-Two-Dimensional folder. If necessary, open the designer window. The text box's CharacterCasing and MaxLength properties are set to Upper and 4, respectively. Recall that when a text box's CharacterCasing property is set to Upper, any letters the user types will appear in uppercase. When a text box's MaxLength property is set to 4, the user can enter a maximum of four characters in the text box.

2. Open the Code Editor window. Replace <your name> and <current date> in the comments with your name and the current date, respectively.

3. Locate the btnDisplay control's Click event procedure. First, you will declare and initialize the two-dimensional array. Click the **blank line** above the ` ' assign the ID to a variable` comment and then enter the following array declaration statement:

   Dim strProducts(,) As String = {{"BX35", "13"},
   {"CR20", "10"},
   {"FE15", "12"},
   {"KW10", "24"},
   {"MM67", "4"}}

4. The procedure will use a String variable to store the product ID entered by the user. It also will use an Integer variable to keep track of the row subscripts while the array is being searched. Enter the following two declaration statements:

   Dim strSearchForId As String
   Dim intRowSub As Integer

5. Now you will assign the product ID entered by the user to the `strSearchForId` variable. Click the **blank line** below the ` ' assign the ID to a variable` comment and then enter the following assignment statement:

   strSearchForId = txtId.Text

6. Next, you will use a loop to search each element in the first column in the `strProducts` array, stopping either when the end of the array is reached or when the ID is located in the array. Click the **blank line** below the ` ' the array or the ID is found` comment and then enter the following lines of code:

   Do Until intRowSub > strProducts.GetUpperBound(0) OrElse
   strSearchForId = strProducts(intRowSub, 0)
   intRowSub = intRowSub + 1
   Loop

7. Now you need to determine why the loop ended. You can do this using a selection structure whose condition determines whether the value stored in the `intRowSub` variable is less than or equal to the highest row subscript in the array. Click the **blank line**

below the ' determine whether the ID was found comment and then enter the following If clause:

If intRowSub <= strProducts.GetUpperBound(0) Then

8. If the value in the intRowSub variable is less than or equal to the highest row subscript, the loop ended because the ID was located in the first column in the array. In that case, the selection structure's true path should display the price contained in the same row as the ID, but in the second column in the array. For example, if the ID is contained in the strProducts(3, 0) element, then its associated price is contained in the strProducts(3, 1) element. However, recall that the price is stored as a string in the strProducts array. In order to use the ToString method to format the price with a dollar sign and zero decimal places, you first need to convert the price to a numeric data type. (Recall that the ToString method is used with numeric variables.) Enter the following lines of code:

Dim intPrice As Integer
Integer.TryParse(strProducts(intRowSub, 1), intPrice)
lblPrice.Text = intPrice.ToString("C0")

9. On the other hand, if the value in the intRowSub variable is greater than the highest row subscript, the loop ended because it reached the end of the array without finding the ID. In that case, the selection structure's false path should display the "Invalid ID" message in a message box. Enter the following five lines of code:

Else
    MessageBox.Show("Invalid ID",
           "Treasures Gift Shop",
           MessageBoxButtons.OK,
           MessageBoxIcon.Information)

10. If necessary, delete the blank line above the End If clause.

Figure 9-45 shows the btnDisplay control's Click event procedure.

```
Private Sub btnDisplay_Click(ByVal sender As Object,
ByVal e As System.EventArgs) Handles btnDisplay.Click
    ' displays the price associated with an ID

    Dim strProducts(,) As String = {{"BX35", "13"},
                                    {"CR20", "10"},
                                    {"FE15", "12"},
                                    {"KW10", "24"},
                                    {"MM67", "4"}}
    Dim strSearchForId As String
    Dim intRowSub As Integer

    ' assign the ID to a variable
    strSearchForId = txtId.Text

    ' search the strProducts array for the ID
    ' continue searching until the end of
    ' the array or the ID is found
```

two-dimensional array (label pointing to the Dim strProducts(,) declaration)

Figure 9-45 btnDisplay control's Click event procedure using a two-dimensional array *(continues)*

(continued)

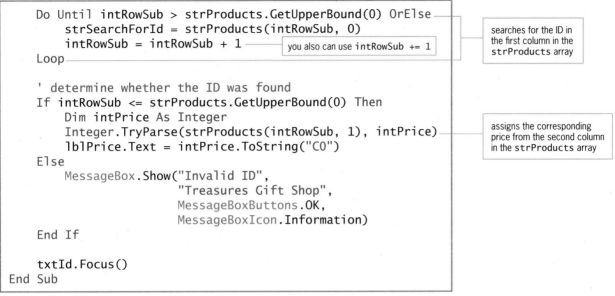

```
        Do Until intRowSub > strProducts.GetUpperBound(0) OrElse
            strSearchForId = strProducts(intRowSub, 0)
            intRowSub = intRowSub + 1        you also can use intRowSub += 1
        Loop

        ' determine whether the ID was found
        If intRowSub <= strProducts.GetUpperBound(0) Then
            Dim intPrice As Integer
            Integer.TryParse(strProducts(intRowSub, 1), intPrice)
            lblPrice.Text = intPrice.ToString("C0")
        Else
            MessageBox.Show("Invalid ID",
                            "Treasures Gift Shop",
                            MessageBoxButtons.OK,
                            MessageBoxIcon.Information)
        End If

        txtId.Focus()
    End Sub
```

searches for the ID in the first column in the strProducts array

assigns the corresponding price from the second column in the strProducts array

555

Figure 9-45   btnDisplay control's Click event procedure using a two-dimensional array

To test the Treasures Gift Shop application: START HERE

1. Save the solution and then start the application. Type **kw10** in the Product ID box and then click the **Display Price** button. $24 appears in the Price box. See Figure 9-46.

Figure 9-46   Interface showing the price for product ID KW10

2. Type **xx44** in the Product ID box and then click the **Display Price** button. The "Invalid ID" message appears in a message box. Close the message box.

3. On your own, test the application using other valid and invalid IDs. When you are finished testing the application, click the **Exit** button.

4. Close the Code Editor window and then close the solution.

Lesson C Summary

- To declare a two-dimensional array:

Use either of the syntax versions shown below. The *highestRowSubscript* and *highestColumnSubscript* arguments in Version 1 are integers that specify the highest row and column subscripts, respectively, in the array. Using Version 1's syntax, the computer automatically initializes the array elements. The *initialValues* section in Version 2 is a list of values separated by commas and enclosed in braces. You include a separate initialValues section for each row in the array. Each initialValues section should contain the same number of values as there are columns in the array.

Version 1: {**Dim** | **Private** | **Static**} *arrayName*(*highestRowSubscript,* *highestColumnSubscript*) **As** *dataType*

Version 2: {**Dim** | **Private** | **Static**} *arrayName*(,) **As** *dataType* = {{*initialValues*},…{*initialValues*}}

- To refer to an element in a two-dimensional array:

    Use the syntax *arrayName*(*rowSubscript, columnSubscript*).

- To determine the highest row subscript in a two-dimensional array:

    Use the GetUpperBound method as follows: *arrayName*.**GetUpperBound(0)**.

- To determine the highest column subscript in a two-dimensional array:

    Use the GetUpperBound method as follows: *arrayName*.**GetUpperBound(1)**.

Lesson C Key Term

Two-dimensional array—an array made up of rows and columns; each element has the same data type and is identified by a unique combination of two subscripts: a row subscript and a column subscript

Lesson C Review Questions

1. Which of the following declares a two-dimensional array that has three rows and four columns?

    a. `Dim decNums(2, 3) As Decimal`

    b. `Dim decNums(3, 4) As Decimal`

    c. `Dim decNums(3, 2) As Decimal`

    d. `Dim decNums(4, 3) As Decimal`

2. The `intSales` array is declared as follows: `Dim intSales(,) As Integer = {{1000, 1200, 900, 500, 2000}, {350, 600, 700, 800, 100}}`. The `intSales(1, 3) = intSales(1, 3) + 10` statement will _____ .

   a. replace the 900 amount with 910

   b. replace the 500 amount with 510

   c. replace the 700 amount with 710

   d. replace the 800 amount with 810

3. The `intSales` array is declared as follows: `Dim intSales(,) As Integer = {{1000, 1200, 900, 500, 2000}, {350, 600, 700, 800, 100}}`. The `intSales(0, 4) = intSales (0, 4 - 2)` statement will _____ .

   a. replace the 500 amount with 1200

   b. replace the 2000 amount with 900

   c. replace the 2000 amount with 1998

   d. result in an error

4. The `intSales` array is declared as follows: `Dim intSales(,) As Integer = {{1000, 1200, 900, 500, 2000}, {350, 600, 700, 800, 100}}`. Which of the following If clauses determines whether the `intRow` and `intCol` variables contain valid row and column subscripts, respectively, for the array?

   a. `If intSales(intRow, intCol) >= 0 AndAlso`
      `    intSales(intRow, intCol) < 5 Then`

   b. `If intSales(intRow, intCol) >= 0 AndAlso`
      `    intSales(intRow, intCol) <= 5 Then`

   c. `If intRow >= 0 AndAlso intRow < 3 AndAlso`
      `    intCol >= 0 AndAlso intCol < 6 Then`

   d. `If intRow >= 0 AndAlso intRow < 2 AndAlso`
      `    intCol >= 0 AndAlso intCol < 5 Then`

5. Which of the following statements assigns the string "California" to the element located in the third column, fifth row in the two-dimensional `strStates` array?

   a. `strStates(3, 5) = "California"`

   b. `strStates(5, 3) = "California"`

   c. `strStates(4, 2) = "California"`

   d. `strStates(2, 4) = "California"`

6. Which of the following assigns the number 0 to each element in a two-row, four-column Integer array named `intSums`?

a.
```
For intRow As Integer = 0 To 1
    For intCol As Integer = 0 To 3
        intSums(intRow, intCol) = 0
    Next intCol
Next intRow
```

b.
```
Dim intRow As Integer
Dim intCol As Integer
Do While intRow < 2
    intCol = 0
    Do While intCol < 4
        intSums(intRow, intCol) = 0
        intCol = intCol + 1
    Loop
    intRow = intRow + 1
Loop
```

c.
```
For intX As Integer = 1 To 2
    For intY As Integer = 1 To 4
        intSums(intX - 1, intY - 1) = 0
    Next intY
Next intX
```

d. all of the above

7. Which of the following returns the highest column subscript in a two-dimensional array named `decPays`?

a. `decPays.GetUpperBound(1)`

b. `decPays.GetUpperBound(0)`

c. `decPays.GetUpperSubscript(0)`

d. `decPays.GetHighestColumn(0)`

Lesson C Exercises

INTRODUCTORY

1. Write the statement to declare a procedure-level two-dimensional array named `intBalances`. The array should have four rows and six columns. Then write the statement to store the number 100 in the element located in the second row, fourth column.

INTRODUCTORY

2. Write the code to store the number 10 in each element in the `intBalances` array from Exercise 1. Use the For...Next statement.

INTRODUCTORY

3. Rewrite the code from Exercise 2 using a Do...Loop statement.

INTRODUCTORY

4. Write the statement to assign the Boolean value True to the variable located in the third row, first column of a two-dimensional Boolean array named `blnAnswers`.

5. Write the Private statement to declare a two-dimensional Integer array named `intOrders` that has three rows and two columns. Use the following values to initialize the array: 1, 2, 10, 20, 100, 200.

INTRODUCTORY

6. Write the code to display the contents of a two-dimensional String array named `strParts` in the lstParts control. Use the For Each...Next statement. Then rewrite the code using two For...Next statements to display the array's contents, row by row.

INTERMEDIATE

7. Write the statements that determine the highest row and highest column subscripts in a two-dimensional array named `strTypes`. The statements should assign the subscripts to the `intHighRow` and `intHighCol` variables, respectively.

INTERMEDIATE

8. Write the statement that determines the number of elements in a two-dimensional array named `strTypes`. The statement should assign the number to the `intNumTypes` variable.

INTERMEDIATE

9. The `dblBonus` array is a two-dimensional array. Write the statement to total the numbers stored in the following three array elements: the first row, first column; the second row, third column; and the third row, fourth column. Assign the sum to the `dblTotal` variable.

INTERMEDIATE

10. The `intQuantities` array is a two-dimensional array. Write the code to multiply each array element by 2. Use two For...Next statements.

INTERMEDIATE

11. Open the Laury Solution (Laury Solution.sln) file contained in the VB2010\Chap09\Laury Solution-TwoDimensional folder. If necessary, open the designer window. Open the Code Editor window and then open the code template for the btnDisplay control's Click event procedure. The procedure should display a shipping charge that is based on the number of items a customer orders. The order amounts and shipping charges are listed in Figure 9-47. Code the procedure. Store the minimum order amounts and shipping charges in a two-dimensional array. Display the appropriate shipping charge with a dollar sign and two decimal places. Save the solution and then start and test the application. Close the Code Editor window and then close the solution.

ADVANCED

Minimum order	Maximum order	Shipping charge
1	10	15
11	50	10
51	100	5
101	No maximum	0

Figure 9-47   Order amounts and shipping charges for Exercise 11

ADVANCED

12. In this exercise, you code an application that allows Professor Carver to display a grade based on the number of points he enters. The grading scale is shown in Figure 9-48. Open the Carver Solution (Carver Solution.sln) file contained in the VB2010\Chap09\Carver Solution-TwoDimensional folder. If necessary, open the designer window. Open the Code Editor window and then open the code template for the btnDisplay control's Click event procedure. Store the minimum points and grades in a two-dimensional array. The procedure should search the array for the number of points entered by the user. It then should display the corresponding grade from the array. Save the solution and then start and test the application. Close the Code Editor window and then close the solution.

Minimum points	Maximum points	Grade
0	299	F
300	349	D
350	399	C
400	449	B
450	500	A

Figure 9-48   Grading scale for Exercise 12

ADVANCED

13. The sales manager at Conway Enterprises wants an application that she can use to display the total domestic, total international, and total company sales made during a six-month period. The sales amounts are shown in Figure 9-49. Create a Visual Basic Windows application. Use the following names for the solution, project, and form file, respectively: Conway Solution, Conway Project, and Main Form.vb. Save the application in the VB2010\Chap09 folder. Create the interface shown in Figure 9-50. Code the application. Store the sales amounts in a two-dimensional array. Save the solution and then start and test the application. Close the Code Editor window and then close the solution.

Month	Domestic sales ($)	International sales ($)
1	100,000	150,000
2	90,000	120,000
3	75,000	210,000
4	88,000	50,000
5	125,000	220,000
6	63,000	80,000

Figure 9-49   Sales amounts for Exercise 13

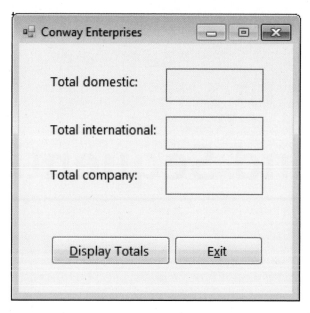

Figure 9-50   Interface for Exercise 13

14. Open the Harrison Solution (Harrison Solution.sln) file contained in the VB2010\Chap09\Harrison Solution folder. Open the Code Editor window. The btnDisplay control's Click event procedure should display the largest number stored in the first column of the `intQuantities` array. Code the procedure using the For...Next statement. Save the solution and then start and test the application. Close the Code Editor window and then close the solution.

ADVANCED

15. Open the Count Solution (Count Solution.sln) file contained in the VB2010\Chap09\Count Solution folder. Code the Display button's Click event procedure so that it displays the number of times each of the numbers from 1 through 9 appears in the `intNumbers` array. (Hint: Store the counts in a one-dimensional array.) Save the solution and then start the application. Click the Display button to display the nine counts. Close the Code Editor window and then close the solution.

ADVANCED

 ## Swat The Bugs

16. Open the Debug Solution (Debug Solution.sln) file contained in the VB2010\Chap09\Debug Solution-Lesson C folder. Open the Code Editor window and review the existing code. The first column in the `strNames` array contains first names, and the second column contains last names. The btnDisplay control's Click event procedure should display the first and last names in the lstFirst and lstLast controls, respectively. Correct the code to remove the jagged lines. Save the solution and then start the application. Click the Display button. Notice that the application is not working correctly. Correct the errors in the application's code. Save the solution and then start and test the application. Close the Code Editor window and then close the solution.

CHAPTER 10

Structures and Sequential Access Files

Creating the CD Collection Application

In this chapter, you will create an application that keeps track of a person's CD collection. More specifically, the application will save each CD's name, the artist's name, and the CD price in a sequential access file named CDs.txt. When the application is started, it will display the contents of the file in a list box. The application will allow the user to add information to the file and also remove information from the file.

Previewing the CD Collection Application

Before you start the first lesson in this chapter, you will preview the completed application. The application is contained in the VB2010\Chap10 folder.

To preview the completed application:

START HERE

1. Use the Run dialog box to run the CD (CD.exe) file contained in the VB2010\Chap10 folder. The application's user interface appears on the screen, with the contents of the CDs.txt file displayed in the list box. Notice that the list box contains three columns. You will learn how to align columnar information in Lesson C.

2. First, you will add a new CD to the list box. Click the **Add** button. Type **Breakout** as the CD name and then press **Enter**. Type **Miley Cyrus** as the artist name and then press **Enter**. Type **9** as the price and then press **Enter**. The information you entered appears in the list box. See Figure 10-1.

the CD information you entered

Figure 10-1 CD information added to the list box

3. Now you will remove the Covers CD from the list box. Click **Covers** in the list box and then click the **Remove** button. The information pertaining to the Covers CD is removed from the list box.

4. Click the **Exit** button to end the application. The application saves the contents of the list box in the CDs.txt sequential access file. You will learn about sequential access files in Lesson B.

5. Use Windows to open the VB2010\Chap10 folder. Right-click **CDs.txt** in the list of filenames. Point to **Open with** and then click **Notepad**. The information contained in the CDs.txt file appears in a window. See Figure 10-2.

```
CDs.txt - Notepad
File  Edit  Format  View  Help
A Little Bit Longer               Jonas Brothers      12.50
At Folsom Prison                  Johnny Cash         11.99
Breakout                          Miley Cyrus          9.00
Funhouse                          Pink                 8.99
High School Musical 3: Senior Year  Original Soundtrack 12.99
Jennifer Hudson                   Jennifer Hudson     12.99
Lucky Old Sun                     Kenny Chesney        9.99
Soul                              Seal                10.99
```

Figure 10-2 Contents of the CDs.txt file

6. Close the CDs.txt window. Start the application again. The list box displays the current contents of the CDs.txt file, which includes the Breakout CD information added in Step 2 but does not include the Covers CD information removed in Step 3.

7. Click the **Exit** button to end the application.

In Lesson A, you will learn how to create a structure in Visual Basic. Lesson B covers sequential access files. You will code the CD Collection application in Lesson C. Be sure to complete each lesson in full and do all of the end-of-lesson questions and several exercises before continuing to the next lesson.

LESSON A

After studying Lesson A, you should be able to:

- Create a structure
- Declare and use a structure variable
- Pass a structure variable to a procedure
- Create an array of structure variables

Structures

The data types used in previous chapters, such as the Integer and Double data types, are built into the Visual Basic language. You also can create your own data types in Visual Basic using the **Structure statement**. Data types created by the Structure statement are referred to as **user-defined data types** or **structures**. Figure 10-3 shows the statement's syntax. Between the Structure and End Structure clauses, you define the members included in the structure. The members can be variables, constants, or procedures. However, in most cases the members will be variables; such variables are referred to as **member variables**.

Each member variable's definition contains the keyword `Public` followed by the variable's name, which typically is entered using Pascal case. Following the variable's name is the keyword `As` and the variable's *dataType*. The dataType identifies the type of data the member variable will store and can be any of the standard data types available in Visual Basic; it also can be another structure (user-defined data type). The Employee structure shown in the example in Figure 10-3 contains four member variables: three String variables and one Double variable. In most applications, you enter the Structure statement in the form's Declarations section, which begins with the Public Class clause and ends with the End Class clause.

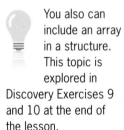 Most programmers use the Class statement (rather than the Structure statement) to create data types that contain procedures. You will learn about the Class statement in Chapter 11.

You also can include an array in a structure. This topic is explored in Discovery Exercises 9 and 10 at the end of the lesson.

Structure statement

Syntax
Structure *structureName*
      Public *memberVariableName1* **As** *dataType*
      [**Public** *memberVariableNameN* **As** *dataType*]
End Structure

Example
```
Structure Employee
    Public strId As String
    Public strFirstName As String
    Public strLastName As String
    Public dblPay As Double
End Structure
```

Figure 10-3 Syntax and an example of the Structure statement

The Structure statement allows the programmer to group related items into one unit: a structure. However, keep in mind that the Structure statement merely defines the structure members; it does not reserve any memory locations inside the computer. You reserve memory locations by declaring a structure variable.

Declaring and Using a Structure Variable

After entering the Structure statement in the Code Editor window, you then can use the structure to declare a variable. Variables declared using a structure are often referred to as **structure variables**. The syntax for creating a structure variable is shown in Figure 10-4. The figure also includes examples of declaring structure variables using the Employee structure from Figure 10-3.

Declaring a structure variable

<u>Syntax</u>
{**Dim** | **Private**} *structureVariableName* **As** *structureName*

<u>Example 1</u>
`Dim hourly As Employee`
declares a procedure-level Employee structure variable named `hourly`

<u>Example 2</u>
`Private salaried As Employee`
declares a class-level Employee structure variable named `salaried`

Figure 10-4   Syntax and examples of declaring a structure variable

Similar to the way the `Dim intAge As Integer` instruction declares an Integer variable named `intAge`, the `Dim hourly As Employee` instruction in Example 1 declares an Employee variable named `hourly`. However, unlike the `intAge` variable, the `hourly` variable contains four member variables. In code, you refer to the entire structure variable by its name—in this case, `hourly`. You refer to a member variable by preceding its name with the name of the structure variable in which it is defined. You use the dot member access operator (a period) to separate the structure variable's name from the member variable's name. For instance, to refer to the member variables within the `hourly` structure variable, you use `hourly.strId`, `hourly.strFirstName`, `hourly.strLastName`, and `hourly.dblPay`. The `Private salaried As Employee` instruction in Example 2 in Figure 10-4 declares a class-level Employee variable named `salaried`. The names of the member variables within the `salaried` variable are `salaried.strId`, `salaried.strFirstName`, `salaried.strLastName`, and `salaried.dblPay`.

The member variables in a structure variable can be used just like any other variables. You can assign values to them, use them in calculations, display their contents, and so on. Figure 10-5 shows various ways of using the member variables created by the statements shown in Figure 10-4.

> The dot member access operator indicates that `strId`, `strFirstName`, `strLastName`, and `dblPay` are members of the `hourly` and `salaried` variables.

Using a member variable

Example 1
`hourly.strLastName = "Yardley"`
assigns the string "Yardley" to the `hourly.strLastName` member variable

Example 2
`hourly.dblPay = hourly.dblPay * 1.05`
multiplies the contents of the `hourly.dblPay` member variable by 1.05 and then
assigns the result to the member variable; you also can write the statement as
`hourly.dblPay *= 1.05`

Example 3
`lblSalary.Text = salaried.dblPay.ToString("C2")`
formats the value contained in the `salaried.dblPay` member variable and then
displays the result in the lblSalary control

Figure 10-5   Examples of using a member variable

Programmers use structure variables when they need to pass a group of
related items to a procedure for further processing, because it's easier to pass
one structure variable rather than many individual variables. Programmers
also use structure variables to store related items in an array, even when the
members have different data types. In the next two sections, you will learn
how to pass a structure variable to a procedure and also store a structure
variable in an array.

Passing a Structure Variable to a Procedure

The sales manager at Willow Pools wants an application that determines the
amount of water required to fill a rectangular pool. To perform this task, the
application will need to calculate the volume of the pool. You calculate the
volume by first multiplying the pool's length by its width and then multiplying the result by the pool's depth. Assuming the length, width, and depth are
measured in feet, this gives you the volume in cubic feet. To determine the
number of gallons of water, you multiply the number of cubic feet by 7.48,
because there are 7.48 gallons in one cubic foot.

To open and then test the Willow Pools application:

START HERE

1. If necessary, start Visual Studio 2010 or Visual Basic 2010 Express.
    Open the Willow Pools Solution (Willow Pools Solution.sln) file
    contained in the VB2010\Chap10\Willow Pools Solution folder. If
    necessary, open the designer window.

2. Start the application. Type **100** in the Length box, **30** in the Width
    box, and **4** in the Depth box. Click the **Calculate** button. The
    required number of gallons appears in the interface. See Figure 10-6.

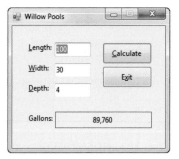

Figure 10-6 Interface showing the required number of gallons

3. Click the **Exit** button to end the application, and then open the Code Editor window.

Figure 10-7 shows the GetGallons function and the btnCalc control's Click event procedure. The event procedure calls the GetGallons function, passing it three variables *by value.* The GetGallons function uses the values to calculate the number of gallons required to fill the pool. The function returns the number of gallons as a Double number to the event procedure, which assigns the value to the **dblGallons** variable.

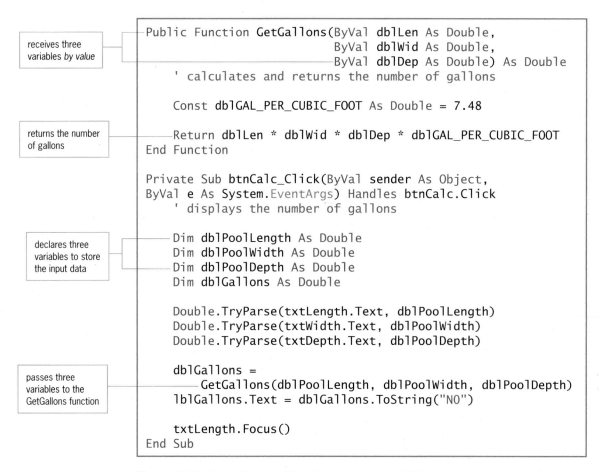

```
Public Function GetGallons(ByVal dblLen As Double,
                           ByVal dblWid As Double,
                           ByVal dblDep As Double) As Double
    ' calculates and returns the number of gallons

    Const dblGAL_PER_CUBIC_FOOT As Double = 7.48

    Return dblLen * dblWid * dblDep * dblGAL_PER_CUBIC_FOOT
End Function

Private Sub btnCalc_Click(ByVal sender As Object,
ByVal e As System.EventArgs) Handles btnCalc.Click
    ' displays the number of gallons

    Dim dblPoolLength As Double
    Dim dblPoolWidth As Double
    Dim dblPoolDepth As Double
    Dim dblGallons As Double

    Double.TryParse(txtLength.Text, dblPoolLength)
    Double.TryParse(txtWidth.Text, dblPoolWidth)
    Double.TryParse(txtDepth.Text, dblPoolDepth)

    dblGallons =
        GetGallons(dblPoolLength, dblPoolWidth, dblPoolDepth)
    lblGallons.Text = dblGallons.ToString("N0")

    txtLength.Focus()
End Sub
```

- receives three variables *by value*
- returns the number of gallons
- declares three variables to store the input data
- passes three variables to the GetGallons function

Figure 10-7 Code for the Willow Pools application (without a structure)

A more convenient way of coding the Willow Pools application is to use a structure to group together the input items: length, width, and depth. It's logical to group the three items because they are related; each represents one of the three dimensions of a rectangular pool. A descriptive name for the structure would be Dimensions.

To use a structure in the Willow Pools application:
START HERE

1. Replace <your name> and <current date> in the comments with your name and the current date, respectively.

2. First, you will declare the structure in the form's Declarations section. Click the **blank line** immediately below the `Public Class frmMain` clause and then press **Enter** to insert another blank line. Enter the following Structure statement:

    Structure Dimensions
        Public dblLength As Double
        Public dblWidth As Double
        Public dblDepth As Double
    End Structure

3. Locate the btnCalc control's Click event procedure. The procedure will use a structure variable (rather than three separate variables) to store the input items. Replace the first three Dim statements with the following Dim statement:

    Dim poolSize As Dimensions

4. Now you will store each input item in its corresponding member in the structure variable. In the three TryParse methods, change `dblPoolLength`, `dblPoolWidth`, and `dblPoolDepth` to **poolSize.dblLength**, **poolSize.dblWidth**, and **poolSize.dblDepth**, respectively.

5. Next, consider the changes you will need to make to the statement that invokes the GetGallons function. Instead of sending three separate variables to the function, you now need to send only one variable: the structure variable. When you pass a structure variable to a procedure, all of its members are passed automatically. Although passing one structure variable rather than three separate variables may not seem like a huge advantage, consider the convenience of passing one structure variable rather than 10 separate variables! Change the statement that invokes the GetGallons function to **dblGallons = GetGallons(poolSize)**. Don't be concerned about the jagged line that appears below `GetGallons(poolSize)` in the statement. It will disappear when you modify the GetGallons function in the next step.

6. Locate the GetGallons function in the Code Editor window. The function will now receive a Dimensions structure variable rather than three Double variables. Like the Double variables, the structure variable will be passed *by value*, because the function does not need to change any member's value. Change the function's header to the following:

    Public Function GetGallons(ByVal pool As Dimensions) As Double

7. Now you will use the members of the structure variable to calculate the number of gallons. Change the Return statement as follows:

    Return pool.dblLength * pool.dblWidth *
        pool.dblDepth * dblGAL_PER_CUBIC_FOOT

Figure 10-8 shows the Structure statement, the GetGallons function, and the btnCalc control's Click event procedure. The event procedure calls the GetGallons function, passing it a structure variable *by value*. The GetGallons function uses the values contained in the structure variable to calculate the number of gallons required to fill the pool. The function returns the number of gallons as a Double number to the event procedure, which assigns the value to the `dblGallons` variable.

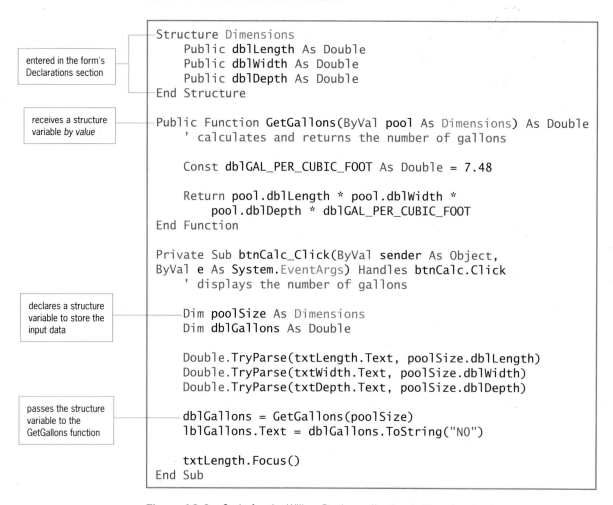

entered in the form's Declarations section

receives a structure variable *by value*

declares a structure variable to store the input data

passes the structure variable to the GetGallons function

```
Structure Dimensions
    Public dblLength As Double
    Public dblWidth As Double
    Public dblDepth As Double
End Structure

Public Function GetGallons(ByVal pool As Dimensions) As Double
    ' calculates and returns the number of gallons

    Const dblGAL_PER_CUBIC_FOOT As Double = 7.48

    Return pool.dblLength * pool.dblWidth *
        pool.dblDepth * dblGAL_PER_CUBIC_FOOT
End Function

Private Sub btnCalc_Click(ByVal sender As Object,
ByVal e As System.EventArgs) Handles btnCalc.Click
    ' displays the number of gallons

    Dim poolSize As Dimensions
    Dim dblGallons As Double

    Double.TryParse(txtLength.Text, poolSize.dblLength)
    Double.TryParse(txtWidth.Text, poolSize.dblWidth)
    Double.TryParse(txtDepth.Text, poolSize.dblDepth)

    dblGallons = GetGallons(poolSize)
    lblGallons.Text = dblGallons.ToString("N0")

    txtLength.Focus()
End Sub
```

Figure 10-8   Code for the Willow Pools application (with a structure)

START HERE   **To test the modified code:**

1. Save the solution and then start the application. Type **100** in the Length box, **30** in the Width box, and **4** in the Depth box. Press **Enter** to select the Calculate button. The required number of gallons appears in the interface, as shown earlier in Figure 10-6.

2. Click the **Exit** button. Close the Code Editor window and then close the solution.

YOU DO IT 1!

Create a Visual Basic Windows application named YouDoIt 1. Save the application in the VB2010\Chap10 folder. Add two text boxes, a label, and a button to the form. Open the Code Editor window. Create a structure named Rectangle. The structure should have two members: one for the rectangle's length and the other for its width. The button's Click event procedure should declare a Rectangle variable named `myRectangle`. It then should assign the text box values to the variable's members. Next, the procedure should pass the `myRectangle` variable to a function that calculates and returns the area of the rectangle. Finally, the procedure should display the function's return value in the label. Code the procedure. Save the solution and then start and test the application. Close the solution.

Creating an Array of Structure Variables

As mentioned earlier, another advantage of using a structure is that a structure variable can be stored in an array, even when its members have different data types. The Treasures Gift Shop application from Chapter 9 can be used to illustrate this concept. As you may remember, you coded the application in two different ways. In Chapter 9's Lesson B, you coded the application using two parallel one-dimensional arrays (one having the String data type and the other having the Integer data type). In Chapter 9's Lesson C, you coded it using a two-dimensional String array. In this chapter, you will code the application using a one-dimensional array of structure variables. (Notice that there are many different ways of solving the same problem.) Each structure variable will contain two member variables: a String variable for the ID and an Integer variable for the price.

To open the Treasures Gift Shop application:

START HERE

1. Open the Treasures Solution (Treasures Solution.sln) file contained in the VB2010\Chap10\Treasures Solution-Structure folder. If necessary, open the designer window. The text box's CharacterCasing and MaxLength properties are set to Upper and 4, respectively.

2. Open the Code Editor window. Replace <your name> and <current date> in the comments with your name and the current date, respectively.

Figure 10-9 shows the code entered in the btnDisplay control's Click event procedure. The code does not use a structure.

```
Private Sub btnDisplay_Click(ByVal sender As Object,
ByVal e As System.EventArgs) Handles btnDisplay.Click
    ' displays the price associated with an ID

    Dim strIds() As String =
        {"BX35", "CR20", "FE15", "KW10", "MM67"}
    Dim intPrices() As Integer = {13, 10, 12, 24, 4}
    Dim strSearchForId As String
    Dim intSub As Integer
```

parallel one-dimensional arrays

Figure 10-9 Code for the Treasures Gift Shop application (without a structure)
(continues)

(continued)

```
         ' assign the ID to a variable
         strSearchForId = txtId.Text

         ' search the strIds array for the ID
         ' continue searching until the end of
         ' the array or the ID is found
         Do Until intSub = strIds.Length OrElse
             strSearchForId = strIds(intSub)
             intSub = intSub + 1
         Loop

         ' determine whether the ID was found
         If intSub < strIds.Length Then
             lblPrice.Text = intPrices(intSub).ToString("C0")
         Else
             MessageBox.Show("Invalid ID",
                             "Treasures Gift Shop",
                             MessageBoxButtons.OK,
                             MessageBoxIcon.Information)
         End If

         txtId.Focus()
     End Sub
```

Figure 10-9   Code for the Treasures Gift Shop application (without a structure)

START HERE **To begin modifying the code to use a structure:**

1. First, you will declare the structure in the form's Declarations section. A descriptive name for the structure would be ProductInfo. Click the **blank line** immediately below the `Public Class frmMain` clause and then press **Enter** to insert another blank line. Enter the following Structure statement:

   Structure ProductInfo
       Public strId As String
       Public intPrice As Integer
   End Structure

2. Locate the btnDisplay control's Click event procedure. Rather than using two parallel one-dimensional arrays to store the price list, the procedure will use a one-dimensional array of ProductInfo structure variables. Replace the two Dim statements that declare the `strIds` and `intPrices` arrays with the following Dim statement:

   Dim priceList(4) As ProductInfo

Next, you need to store the five product IDs and prices in the `priceList` array. Keep in mind that each element in the array is a structure variable, and each structure variable contains two member variables: `strId` and `intPrice`. You refer to a member variable in an array element using the syntax *arrayName*(*subscript*).*memberVariableName*. For example, `priceList(0).strId` refers to the `strId` member contained in the first element in the `priceList` array. Likewise, `priceList(4).intPrice` refers to the `intPrice` member contained in the last element in the `priceList` array. Figure 10-10 illustrates this naming convention.

Figure 10-10   Names of some of the member variables in the `priceList` array

To continue modifying the code:

◀ START HERE

1. Click the **blank line** below the `Dim intSub As Integer` instruction, and then press **Enter** to insert another blank line. Enter the following 10 assignment statements:

   priceList(0).strId = "BX35"
   priceList(0).intPrice = 13
   priceList(1).strId = "CR20"
   priceList(1).intPrice = 10
   priceList(2).strId = "FE15"
   priceList(2).intPrice = 12
   priceList(3).strId = "KW10"
   priceList(3).intPrice = 24
   priceList(4).strId = "MM67"
   priceList(4).intPrice = 4

2. The loop in the procedure now needs to search the `priceList` array (rather than the `strIds` array). Change `strIds` in the `' search the strIds array for the ID` comment to **priceList**.

3. The loop should search each element in the `priceList` array, comparing the value contained in the current element's `strId` member with the value stored in the `strSearchForId` variable. The loop should stop searching either when the end of the array is reached or when the ID is found. Change the Do clause to the following:

   Do Until intSub = priceList.Length OrElse
   **   strSearchForId = priceList(intSub).strId**

4. The If...Then...Else statement in the procedure determines why the loop ended and then takes the appropriate action. Currently, the statement's condition compares the value contained in the `intSub` variable with the value stored in the `strIds` array's Length property. Recall that a one-dimensional array's Length property stores an integer that represents the number of elements in the array. You will need to modify the condition so that it compares the value contained

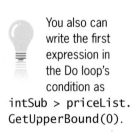

You also can write the first expression in the Do loop's condition as `intSub > priceList.GetUpperBound(0)`.

574

in the `intSub` variable with the value stored in the `priceList` array's Length property. Change `strIds.Length` in the If clause to **priceList.Length**.

5. If the value contained in the `intSub` variable is less than the number of array elements, the loop ended because the ID was located in the array; in that case, the selection structure's true path should display the corresponding price. Change the assignment statement below the If clause as follows:

**lblPrice.Text =
    priceList(intSub).intPrice.ToString("C0")**

6. On the other hand, if the value in the `intSub` variable is not less than the number of array elements, the loop ended because it reached the end of the array without finding the ID. In that case, the selection structure's false path should display the "Invalid ID" message in a message box. The appropriate code is already entered in the selection structure's false path.

Figure 10-11 shows the Structure statement and the btnDisplay control's Click event procedure.

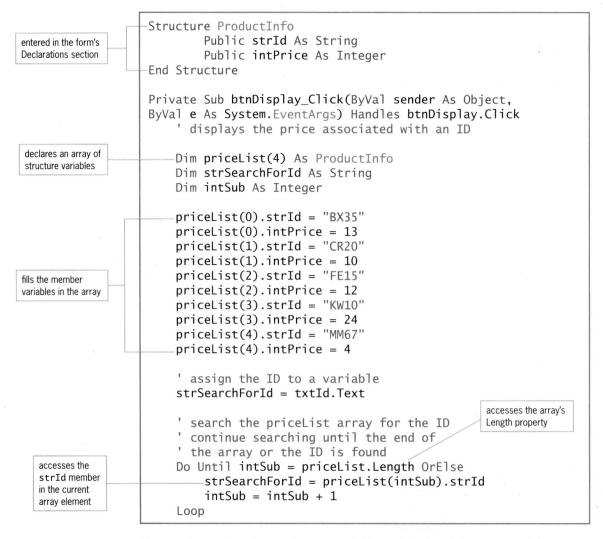

```
                    ┌─Structure ProductInfo
entered in the form's│      Public strId As String
Declarations section │      Public intPrice As Integer
                    └─End Structure

                     Private Sub btnDisplay_Click(ByVal sender As Object,
                     ByVal e As System.EventArgs) Handles btnDisplay.Click
                         ' displays the price associated with an ID

declares an array of ──Dim priceList(4) As ProductInfo
structure variables    Dim strSearchForId As String
                       Dim intSub As Integer

                       priceList(0).strId = "BX35"
                       priceList(0).intPrice = 13
                       priceList(1).strId = "CR20"
                       priceList(1).intPrice = 10
                       priceList(2).strId = "FE15"
fills the member       priceList(2).intPrice = 12
variables in the array priceList(3).strId = "KW10"
                       priceList(3).intPrice = 24
                       priceList(4).strId = "MM67"
                      ─priceList(4).intPrice = 4

                       ' assign the ID to a variable
                       strSearchForId = txtId.Text
                                                            accesses the array's
                       ' search the priceList array for the ID   Length property
                       ' continue searching until the end of
                       ' the array or the ID is found
accesses the           Do Until intSub = priceList.Length OrElse
strId member          ─── strSearchForId = priceList(intSub).strId
in the current         intSub = intSub + 1
array element       Loop
```

Figure 10-11 Code for the Treasures Gift Shop application (with a structure) *(continues)*

(continued)

```
    ' determine whether the ID was found
    If intSub < priceList.Length Then
        lblPrice.Text =
            priceList(intSub).intPrice.ToString("C0")
    Else
        MessageBox.Show("Invalid ID",
                        "Treasures Gift Shop",
                        MessageBoxButtons.OK,
                        MessageBoxIcon.Information)
    End If

    txtId.Focus()
End Sub
```

accesses the intPrice member in the current array element

575

Figure 10-11 Code for the Treasures Gift Shop application (with a structure)

To test the application's code: ► START HERE

1. Save the solution and then start the application. Type **fe15** in the Product ID box and then click the **Display Price** button. $12 appears in the Price box, as shown in Figure 10-12.

Figure 10-12 Interface showing the price for product ID FE15

2. Click the **Exit** button. Close the Code Editor window and then close the solution.

Lesson A Summary

- To create a structure (user-defined data type):

  Use the Structure statement. The statement's syntax is shown in Figure 10-3. In most applications, you enter the Structure statement in the form's Declarations section.

- To declare a structure variable:

  Use the following syntax: {**Dim** | **Private**} *structureVariableName* **As** *structureName*.

- To refer to a member within a structure variable:

  Use the syntax *structureVariableName.memberVariableName.*

- To create an array of structure variables:

  Declare the array using the structure as the data type.

- To refer to a member within a structure variable stored in an array:

  Use the syntax *arrayName*(*subscript*)*.memberVariableName.*

Lesson A Key Terms

Member variables—the variables contained in a structure

Structure statement—used to create user-defined data types, called structures

Structure variables—variables declared using a structure as the data type

Structures—data types created by the Structure statement; allow the programmer to group related items into one unit; also called user-defined data types

User-defined data types—data types created by the Structure statement; also called structures

Lesson A Review Questions

1. Which statement is used to create a user-defined data type?

   a. Declare

   b. Define

   c. Structure

   d. UserType

2. In most applications, the code to define a user-defined data type is entered in the form's _____.

   a. Declarations section

   b. Definition section

   c. Load event procedure

   d. User-defined section

3. A structure variable named `address` contains a member variable named `strStreet`. Which of the following statements assigns the string "Maple" to the member variable?

   a. `address&strStreet = "Maple"`

   b. `address.strStreet = "Maple"`

   c. `strStreet.address = "Maple"`

   d. none of the above

4. An array is declared using the statement `Dim inventory(4) As Product`. Which of the following statements assigns the number 100 to the `intQuantity` member variable contained in the last array element?

   a. `inventory.intQuantity(4) = 100`

   b. `inventory(4).Product.intQuantity = 100`

   c. `inventory(3).intQuantity = 100`

   d. none of the above

5. An application uses a structure named Employee. Which of the following statements declares a five-element array of Employee structure variables?

   a. `Dim workers(4) As Employee`

   b. `Dim workers(5) As Employee`

   c. `Dim workers As Employee(4)`

   d. `Dim workers As Employee(5)`

Lesson A Exercises

1. Write a Structure statement that defines a structure named Book. The structure contains three member variables named `strTitle`, `strAuthor`, and `decPrice`. Then write a Dim statement that declares a Book variable named `fiction`.

   INTRODUCTORY

2. Write a Structure statement that defines a structure named Tape. The structure contains four member variables named `strName`, `strArtist`, `strSongLength`, and `intSongNum`. Then write a Private statement that declares a Tape variable named `blues`.

   INTRODUCTORY

3. An application contains the Structure statement shown here. Write a Dim statement that declares a Computer variable named `homeUse`. Then, write an assignment statement that assigns the string "IB-50" to the `strModel` member. Finally, write an assignment statement that assigns the number 2400 to the `dblCost` member.

   INTRODUCTORY

   ```
   Structure Computer
       Public strModel As String
       Public dblCost As Double
   End Structure
   ```

4. An application contains the Structure statement shown here. Write a Dim statement that declares a MyFriend variable named `school`. Then, write assignment statements that assign the value in the txtFirst control to the `strFirst` member and assign the value in the txtLast control to the `strLast` member. Finally, write assignment

   INTRODUCTORY

statements that assign the value in the **strLast** member to the lblLast control and assign the value in the **strFirst** member to the lblFirst control.

```
Structure MyFriend
    Public strLast As String
    Public strFirst As String
End Structure
```

INTERMEDIATE

5. An application contains the Structure statement shown here. Write a Private statement that declares a 10-element one-dimensional array of Computer variables. Name the array **business**. Then, write an assignment statement that assigns the string "HPP405" to the **strModel** member contained in the first array element. Finally, write an assignment statement that assigns the number 3600 to the **decCost** member contained in the first array element.

```
Structure Computer
    Public strModel As String
    Public decCost As Decimal
End Structure
```

INTERMEDIATE

6. An application contains the Structure statement shown here. Write a Dim statement that declares a five-element one-dimensional array of MyFriend variables. Name the array **home**. Then, write an assignment statement that assigns the value in the txtName control to the **strName** member contained in the last array element. Finally, write an assignment statement that assigns the value in the txtBirthday control to the **strBirthday** member contained in the last array element.

```
Structure MyFriend
    Public strName As String
    Public strBirthday As String
End Structure
```

INTERMEDIATE

7. In this exercise, you modify the Treasures Gift Shop application completed in the lesson. Use Windows to make a copy of the Treasures Solution-Structure folder. Rename the folder Modified Treasures Solution-Structure. Open the Treasures Solution (Treasures Solution. sln) file contained in the Modified Treasures Solution-Structure folder. Open the designer window. The modified application should display both the name and price corresponding to the product ID entered by the user. Make the appropriate modifications to the interface and the code (including the Structure statement). The names of the products are shown in Figure 10-13. Save the solution and then start and test the application. Close the Code Editor window and then close the solution.

Product ID	Name
BX35	Necklace
CR20	Bracelet
FE15	Jewelry box
KW10	Doll
MM67	Ring

Figure 10-13   Product information for Exercise 7

8. Open the Carver Solution (Carver Solution.sln) file contained in the VB2010\Chap10\Carver Solution folder. If necessary, open the designer window. The application should display a grade based on the number of points entered by the user. The grading scale is shown in Figure 10-14. Open the Code Editor window. Create a structure that contains two members: an Integer variable for the minimum points and a String variable for the grades. Use the structure to declare a five-element one-dimensional array. Store the minimum points and grades in the array. The application should search the array for the number of points earned and then display the appropriate grade from the array. Code the application. Save the solution and then start and test the application. Close the Code Editor window and then close the solution.

INTERMEDIATE

Minimum points	Maximum points	Grade
0	299	F
300	349	D
350	399	C
400	449	B
450	500	A

Figure 10-14   Grade information for Exercise 8

Discovery

9. Open the Average Solution (Average Solution.sln) file contained in the VB2010\Chap10\Average Solution folder. If necessary, open the designer window. The application should display a student's name and the average of five test scores entered by the user.

   a. Open the Code Editor window. Create a structure named StudentInfo. The structure should contain two members: a String variable for the student's name and a Double array for the test scores. An array contained in a structure cannot be assigned an initial size, so you will need to include an empty set of parentheses after the array name, like this: `Dim dblScores() As Double`.

b.   Open the code template for the btnCalc control's Click event procedure. First, use the StudentInfo structure to declare a structure variable. Next, research the Visual Basic ReDim statement. Use the ReDim statement to declare the array's size. The array should have five elements.

c.   The btnCalc control's Click event procedure should use the InputBox function to get the student's name. It also should use a repetition structure and the InputBox function to get the five test scores from the user, storing each in the array. The procedure should display the student's name and average test score in the lblAverage control.

d.   Save the solution and then start and test the application. Close the Code Editor window and then close the solution.

10.   In this exercise, you modify the application from Exercise 9. Use Windows to make a copy of the Average Solution folder. Rename the folder Modified Average Solution. Open the Average Solution (Average Solution.sln) file contained in the Modified Average Solution folder. Open the designer window. Change the font used in the lblAverage control to Courier New. Change the control's TextAlign property to TopLeft and then resize the control to display four lines of text. Open the Code Editor window. Modify the application to calculate the average of five test scores for each of four students. (Hint: You will need to use an array of structure variables.) Display each student's name and average test score in the lblAverage control. Save the solution and then start and test the application. Close the Code Editor window and then close the solution.

LESSON B

After studying Lesson B, you should be able to:

- Open and close a sequential access file
- Write data to a sequential access file
- Read data from a sequential access file
- Determine whether a sequential access file exists
- Test for the end of a sequential access file

The Ch10BVideo file demonstrates all of the steps contained in Lesson B. You can view the video either before or after completing the lesson.

Sequential Access Files

In addition to getting data from the keyboard and sending data to the computer screen, an application also can get data from and send data to a file on a disk. Getting data from a file is referred to as "reading the file," and sending data to a file is referred to as "writing to the file." Files to which data is written are called **output files**, because the files store the output produced by an application. Files that are read by the computer are called **input files**, because an application uses the data in these files as input. Most input and output files are composed of lines of text that are both read and written sequentially. In other words, they are read and written in consecutive order, one line at a time, beginning with the first line in the file and ending with the last line in the file. Such files are referred to as **sequential access files**, because of the manner in which the lines of text are accessed. They also are called **text files**, because they are composed of lines of text. Examples of text stored in sequential access files include an employee list, a memo, or a sales report.

Writing Data to a Sequential Access File

An item of data—such as the string "Harriet"—is viewed differently by a human being and a computer. To a human being, the string represents a person's name; to a computer, it is merely a sequence of characters. Programmers refer to a sequence of characters as a **stream of characters**. In Visual Basic, you use a **StreamWriter object** to write a stream of characters to a sequential access file. Before you create the StreamWriter object, you first declare a variable to store the object in the computer's internal memory. Figure 10-15 shows the syntax and an example of declaring a StreamWriter variable. The IO in the syntax stands for Input/Output.

Declaring a StreamWriter variable

Syntax
{**Dim** | **Private**} *streamWriterVariableName* **As IO.StreamWriter**

Example
```
Dim outFile As IO.StreamWriter
```
declares a StreamWriter variable named `outFile`

Figure 10-15 Syntax and an example of declaring a StreamWriter variable

You will use a StreamWriter variable in the Game Show Contestants application, which you code in this lesson. The application will write the names of contestants to a sequential access file. It also will subsequently read the names and display them in a list box.

START HERE

To begin coding the Game Show Contestants application:

1. If necessary, start Visual Studio 2010 or Visual Basic 2010 Express. Open the Contestant Solution (Contestant Solution.sln) file contained in the VB2010\Chap10\Contestant Solution folder. If necessary, open the designer window. See Figure 10-16.

Figure 10-16   Interface for the Game Show Contestants application

2. Open the Code Editor window. Replace <your name> and <current date> in the comments with your name and the current date, respectively.

3. Locate the code template for the btnWrite control's Click event procedure. Click the **blank line** below the ` ' declare a StreamWriter variable` comment and then enter the following declaration statement:

Dim outFile As IO.StreamWriter

After declaring a StreamWriter variable, you can use the syntax shown in Figure 10-17 to create a StreamWriter object. As the figure indicates, creating a StreamWriter object involves opening a sequential access file using one of two methods: CreateText or AppendText. You use the **CreateText method** to open a sequential access file for output. When you open a file for output, the computer creates a new, empty file to which data can be written. If the file already exists, the computer erases the contents of the file before writing any data to it. You use the **AppendText method** to open a sequential access file for append. When a file is opened for append, new data is written after any existing data in the file. If the file does not exist, the computer creates the file for you. In addition to opening the file, both methods automatically create a StreamWriter object to represent the file in the application. You assign the StreamWriter object to a StreamWriter variable, which you use to refer to the file in code.

Also included in Figure 10-17 are examples of using the CreateText and AppendText methods. When processing the statement in Example 1, the computer searches for the employee.txt file in the Chap10 folder on the F drive. If the file exists, its contents are erased and the file is opened for output; otherwise, a new, empty file is created and opened for output.

The statement creates a StreamWriter object and assigns it to the `outFile` variable. Unlike the *fileName* argument in Example 1, the *fileName* argument in Example 2 does not contain a folder path. Therefore, the computer will search for the file in the default folder, which is the current project's bin\ Debug folder. In this case, if the computer locates the report.txt file in the default folder, it opens the file for append. If it does not find the file, it creates a new, empty file and then opens the file for append. Like the statement in Example 1, the statement in Example 2 creates a StreamWriter object and assigns it to the `outFile` variable.

Only specify the folder path in the fileName argument when you are sure that the folder path will not change. Keep in mind that a USB drive may have a different letter designation on another computer.

583

Creating a StreamWriter object

Syntax
IO.File.*method*(*fileName*)

method	Description
CreateText	opens a sequential access file for output
AppendText	opens a sequential access file for append

Example 1
`outFile = IO.File.CreateText("F:\Chap10\employee.txt")`
opens the employee.txt file for output; creates a StreamWriter object and assigns it to the `outFile` variable

Example 2
`outFile = IO.File.AppendText("report.txt")`
opens the report.txt file for append; creates a StreamWriter object and assigns it to the `outFile` variable

---

Figure 10-17   Syntax and examples of the CreateText and AppendText methods

When the user clicks the Write to File button in the Game Show Contestants interface, the name entered in the Name box should be added to the end of the existing names in the file. Therefore, you will need to open the sequential access file for append. A descriptive name for a file that stores the names of contestants is contestants.txt. Although it is not a requirement, the "txt" (short for "text") filename extension is commonly used when naming sequential access files; this is because the files contain text.

To continue coding the btnWrite control's Click event procedure:

START HERE

1. Click the **blank line** below the `' open the file for append` comment and then enter the following statement:

    outFile = IO.File.AppendText("contestants.txt")

After opening a file for either output or append, you can begin writing data to it. You can write data to a sequential access file using either the **Write method** or the **WriteLine method**; however, in most cases you will use the WriteLine method. The difference between both methods is that the WriteLine method writes a newline character after the data. Figure 10-18 shows the syntax and an example of both methods. As the figure indicates, when using the Write method, the next character written to the file will appear immediately after the letter o in the string "Hello". When using the

WriteLine method, however, the next character written to the file will appear on the line immediately below the string. You do not need to include the file's name in either method's syntax, because the data will be written to the file associated with the StreamWriter variable.

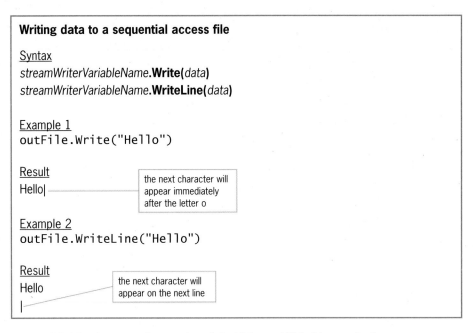

Writing data to a sequential access file

Syntax
streamWriterVariableName.**Write**(*data*)
streamWriterVariableName.**WriteLine**(*data*)

Example 1
`outFile.Write("Hello")`

Result
Hello| ——————— the next character will appear immediately after the letter o

Example 2
`outFile.WriteLine("Hello")`

Result
Hello
| ——— the next character will appear on the next line

Figure 10-18   Syntax and examples of the Write and WriteLine methods

Each contestant's name should appear on a separate line in the file, so you will use the WriteLine method to write each name to the file.

START HERE   **To continue coding the btnWrite control's Click event procedure:**

1. Click the **blank line** below the `' write the name on a separate line in the file` comment and then enter the following statement:

    outFile.WriteLine(txtName.Text)

Closing an Output Sequential Access File

You should use the **Close method** to close an output sequential access file as soon as you are finished using it. This ensures that the data is saved and it makes the file available for use elsewhere in the application. The syntax to close an output sequential access file is shown in Figure 10-19 along with an example of using the method. Here again, notice that you use the StreamWriter variable to refer to the file in code.

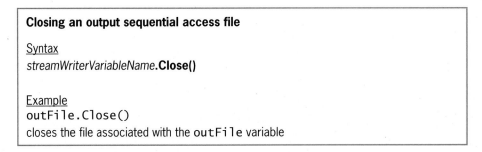

Closing an output sequential access file

Syntax
streamWriterVariableName.**Close()**

Example
`outFile.Close()`
closes the file associated with the `outFile` variable

Figure 10-19   Syntax and an example of closing an output sequential access file

To finish coding and then test the btnWrite control's Click event procedure: ◀ START HERE

1. Click the **blank line** below the `' close the file` comment and then enter the following statement:

   outFile.Close()

2. Save the solution and then start the application. Type **Inez Harrison** in the Name box and then click the **Write to File** button. Use the application to write the following four names to the file:

   Clark Smith
   Khalid Shaw
   Joe Mendez
   Sue Chang

3. Click the **Exit** button to end the application. Now you will open the contestants.txt file to verify its contents. Click **File** on the menu bar and then click **Open File**. Open the project's bin\Debug folder. Click **contestants.txt** in the list of filenames and then click the **Open** button. The contestants.txt window opens and shows the five names contained in the file. See Figure 10-20.

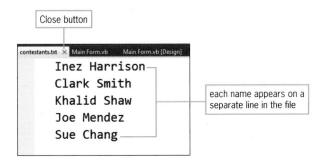

Figure 10-20 Names contained in the contestants.txt file

4. Close the contestants.txt window by clicking its **Close** button.

Reading Data from a Sequential Access File

In Visual Basic, you use a **StreamReader object** to read data from a sequential access file. Before creating the StreamReader object, you first declare a variable to store the object in the computer's internal memory. Figure 10-21 shows the syntax and an example of declaring a StreamReader variable. As mentioned earlier, the IO in the syntax stands for Input/Output.

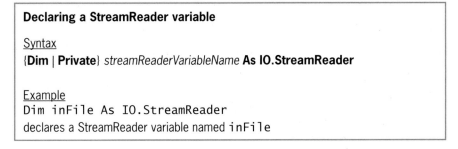

Declaring a StreamReader variable

Syntax
{**Dim** | **Private**} *streamReaderVariableName* **As IO.StreamReader**

Example
```
Dim inFile As IO.StreamReader
```
declares a StreamReader variable named `inFile`

Figure 10-21 Syntax and an example of declaring a StreamReader variable

START HERE **To begin coding the Read from File button's Click event procedure:**

1. Locate the code template for the btnRead control's Click event procedure.

2. Click the **blank line** below the `' declare variables` comment and then enter the following declaration statement:

   Dim inFile As IO.StreamReader

After declaring a StreamReader variable, you can use the **OpenText method** to open a sequential access file for input; doing this automatically creates a StreamReader object. When a file is opened for input, the computer can read the lines of text stored in the file. Figure 10-22 shows the OpenText method's syntax along with an example of using the method. The *fileName* argument in the example does not include a folder path, so the computer will search for the report.txt file in the current project's bin\Debug folder. If the computer finds the file, it opens the file for input; otherwise, a run time error occurs, causing the application to end abruptly. You assign the StreamReader object created by the OpenText method to a StreamReader variable, which you use to refer to the file in code.

Creating a StreamReader object

<u>Syntax</u>
IO.File.OpenText(*fileName* **)**

<u>Example</u>
```
inFile = IO.File.OpenText("report.txt")
```
opens the report.txt file for input; creates a StreamReader object and assigns it to the `inFile` variable

---

Figure 10-22 Syntax and an example of the OpenText method

You can use the Exists method to avoid the run time error that occurs when the computer cannot locate the file you want opened for input. Figure 10-23 shows the method's syntax and includes an example of using the method. If the *fileName* argument does not include a folder path, the computer searches for the file in the current project's bin\Debug folder. The **Exists method** returns the Boolean value True if the file exists; otherwise, it returns the Boolean value False.

Determining whether a sequential access file exists

<u>Syntax</u>
IO.File.Exists(*fileName* **)**

<u>Example</u>
```
If IO.File.Exists("report.txt") Then
```
determines whether the report.txt file exists in the current project's bin\Debug folder; you also can write the If clause as `If IO.File.Exists("report.txt") = True Then`

Figure 10-23 Syntax and an example of the Exists method

To continue coding the btnRead control's Click event procedure:

START HERE

1. Click the **blank line** below the `' determine whether the file exists` comment and then enter the following If clause:

   If IO.File.Exists("contestants.txt") Then

2. If the file exists, you will use the OpenText method to open the file. Enter the following comment and assignment statement. Press **Enter** twice after typing the assignment statement.

   ' open the file for input
   inFile = IO.File.OpenText("contestants.txt")

3. If the file does not exist, you will display an appropriate message. Enter the additional lines of code shown in Figure 10-24.

```
' determine whether the file exists
If IO.File.Exists("contestants.txt") Then
    ' open the file for input
    inFile = IO.File.OpenText("contestants.txt")

Else
    MessageBox.Show("Can't find the file",
                    "Game Show Contestants",
                    MessageBoxButtons.OK,
                    MessageBoxIcon.Information)
End If
```

enter these five lines of code

Figure 10-24   Additional code entered in the procedure

After opening a file for input, you can use the **ReadLine method** to read the file's contents, one line at a time. A **line** is defined as a sequence (stream) of characters followed by the newline character. The ReadLine method returns a string that contains only the sequence of characters in the current line; the string does not include the newline character at the end of the line. In most cases, you assign the string returned by the ReadLine method to a String variable. Figure 10-25 shows the ReadLine method's syntax and includes an example of using the method. The ReadLine method does not require you to provide the file's name, because it uses the file associated with the StreamReader variable.

Reading a line of text from a sequential access file

Syntax
streamReaderVariableName.**ReadLine**

Example
```
Dim strMessage As String
strMessage = inFile.ReadLine
```
reads a line of text from the sequential access file associated with the `inFile` variable and assigns the line, excluding the newline character, to the `strMessage` variable

---

Figure 10-25   Syntax and an example of the ReadLine method

In most cases, an application will need to read each line of text contained in a sequential access file, one line at a time. You can do this using a loop along with the Peek method. The **Peek method** "peeks" into the file to determine whether the file contains another character to read. If the file contains another character, the Peek method returns the character; otherwise, it returns the number –1 (a negative 1). The Peek method's syntax is shown in Figure 10-26 along with an example of using the method. The Do clause in the example tells the computer to process the loop instructions until the Peek method returns the number –1, which indicates that there are no more characters to read. In other words, the Do clause tells the computer to process the loop instructions until it reaches the end of the file.

Determining the end of the file

Syntax
streamReaderVariableName.**Peek**

Example
```
Dim strLineOfText As String
Do Until inFile.Peek = -1
    strLineOfText = inFile.ReadLine
    MessageBox.Show(strLineOfText)
Loop
```
reads each line of text from the sequential access file associated with the `inFile` variable, line by line; each line (excluding the newline character) is assigned to the `strLineOfText` variable and is then displayed in a message box

---

Figure 10-26   Syntax and an example of the Peek method

START HERE ▶   **To continue coding the btnRead control's Click event procedure:**

1. First, you will declare a variable to store the string returned by the ReadLine method. Click the **blank line** below the Dim statement. Each line in the contestants.txt file represents a name, so you will call the variable `strName`. Enter the following declaration statement:

   Dim strName As String

2. The Do clause is next. Click the **blank line** below the statement that opens the contestants.txt file. Enter the following comment and Do clause, being sure to type the minus sign before the number 1:

   ' process loop instructions until end of file
   Do Until inFile.Peek = –1

3. Now you will tell the computer to read a line of text and assign it (excluding the newline character) to the `strName` variable. Enter the following comment and assignment statement:

   ' read a name
   strName = inFile.ReadLine

4. Next, you will add the name to the Contestants list box. Enter the following comment and statement:

   ' add name to list box
   lstContestants.Items.Add(strName)

5. If necessary, delete the blank line above the Loop clause.

Closing an Input Sequential Access File

Just as you do with an output sequential access file, you should use the Close method to close an input sequential access file as soon as you are finished using it. Doing this makes the file available for use elsewhere in the application. The syntax to close an input sequential access file is shown in Figure 10-27 along with an example of using the method. Notice that you use the StreamReader variable to refer to the file in code.

Closing an input sequential access file

Syntax
streamReaderVariableName.**Close()**

Example
```
inFile.Close()
```
closes the file associated with the `inFile` variable

Figure 10-27   Syntax and an example of closing an input sequential access file

To finish coding the btnRead control's Click event procedure: ◁ START HERE

1. Click **after the letter p** in the Loop clause and then press **Enter** to insert a blank line.

2. Enter the following comment and statement:

   ' close the file
   inFile.Close()

Figure 10-28 shows the code entered in the Click event procedures for the btnWrite and btnRead controls.

```
Private Sub btnWrite_Click(ByVal sender As Object,
ByVal e As System.EventArgs) Handles btnWrite.Click
    ' writes a name to a sequential access file

    ' declare a StreamWriter variable
    Dim outFile As IO.StreamWriter

    ' open the file for append
    outFile = IO.File.AppendText("contestants.txt")

    ' write the name on a separate line in the file
    outFile.WriteLine(txtName.Text)

    ' close the file
    outFile.Close()

    ' clear the list box and then set the focus
    lstContestants.Items.Clear()
    txtName.Focus()
End Sub
```

Figure 10-28   Click event procedures for the btnWrite and btnRead controls *(continues)*

(continued)

```
Private Sub btnRead_Click(ByVal sender As Object,
ByVal e As System.EventArgs) Handles btnRead.Click
    ' reads names from a sequential access file
    ' and displays them in the interface

    ' declare variables
    Dim inFile As IO.StreamReader
    Dim strName As String

    ' clear previous names from the list box
    lstContestants.Items.Clear()

    ' determine whether the file exists
    If IO.File.Exists("contestants.txt") Then
        ' open the file for input
        inFile = IO.File.OpenText("contestants.txt")
        ' process loop instructions until end of file
        Do Until inFile.Peek = -1
            ' read a name
            strName = inFile.ReadLine
            ' add name to list box
            lstContestants.Items.Add(strName)
        Loop
        ' close the file
        inFile.Close()

    Else
        MessageBox.Show("Can't find the file",
                        "Game Show Contestants",
                        MessageBoxButtons.OK,
                        MessageBoxIcon.Information)
    End If
End Sub
```

Figure 10-28   Click event procedures for the btnWrite and btnRead controls

START HERE

To test the application's code:

1. Save the solution and then start the application. Click the **Read from File** button. The five names contained in the contestants.txt file appear in the Contestants box. See Figure 10-29.

Figure 10-29   Five contestant names listed in the Contestants box

2. Type **Opal Jones** in the Name box and then click the **Write to File** button.

3. On your own, add the following three names to the file:

   Willow Smith
   Hank Padito
   Charize Baker

4. Click the **Read from File** button to display the nine names in the list box. See Figure 10-30.

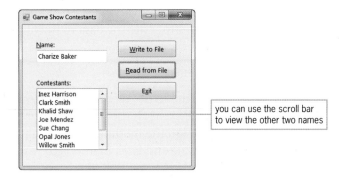

you can use the scroll bar to view the other two names

Figure 10-30   Nine contestant names listed in the list box

5. Click the **Exit** button.

6. Next, you will modify the If clause in the btnRead control's Click event procedure. More specifically, you will change the filename in the If clause from contestants.txt to contestant.txt. Doing this will allow you to test the code entered in the selection structure's false path. Change `contestants.txt` in the If clause to **contestant.txt**.

7. Save the solution and then start the application. Click the **Read from File** button. Because the contestant.txt file does not exist, the Exists method in the If clause returns the Boolean value False. As a result, the instruction in the selection structure's false path is processed. The instruction displays the "Can't find the file" message in a message box. Close the message box and then click the **Exit** button.

8. Change `contestant.txt` in the If clause to **contestants.txt**. Save the solution and then start the application. Click the **Read from File** button, which displays the nine names in the list box.

9. Click the **Exit** button. Close the Code Editor window and then close the solution.

YOU DO IT 2!

Create a Visual Basic Windows application named YouDoIt 2. Save the application in the VB2010\Chap10 folder. Add a label and two buttons to the form. The first button's Click event procedure should allow the user to enter one or more numbers, saving each to a sequential access file. The second button's Click event procedure should total the numbers contained in the sequential access file and then display the total in the label control. Code the procedures. Save the solution and then start and test the application. Close the solution.

Lesson B Summary

- To write data to a sequential access file:

  Declare a StreamWriter variable and then use either the CreateText method or the AppendText method to open a sequential access file. Assign the method's return value to the StreamWriter variable. Use either the Write method or the WriteLine method to write the data to the file. Close the file using the Close method.

- To read data from a sequential access file:

  Declare a StreamReader variable. Use the Exists method to determine whether the sequential access file exists. If the file exists, use the OpenText method to open the file. Assign the method's return value to the StreamReader variable. Use the ReadLine and Peek methods to read the data from the file. Close the file using the Close method.

- To determine whether a sequential access file exists:

  Use the Exists method. The method's syntax is **IO.File.Exists(***fileName***)**. The method returns the Boolean value True if the file exists; otherwise, it returns the Boolean value False.

- To determine whether the end of a sequential access file has been reached:

  Use the Peek method. The method's syntax is *streamReaderVariableName.***Peek**. The method returns the number −1 when the end of the file has been reached; otherwise, it returns the next character in the file.

Lesson B Key Terms

AppendText method—used with a StreamWriter variable to open a sequential access file for append

Close method—used with either a StreamWriter variable or a StreamReader variable to close a sequential access file

CreateText method—used with a StreamWriter variable to open a sequential access file for output

Exists method—used to determine whether a file exists

Input files—files from which an application reads data

Line—a sequence (stream) of characters followed by the newline character

OpenText method—used with a StreamReader variable to open a sequential access file for input

Output files—files to which an application writes data

Peek method—used with a StreamReader variable to determine whether a file contains another character to read

ReadLine method—used with a StreamReader variable to read a line of text from a sequential access file

Sequential access files—files composed of lines of text that are both read and written sequentially; also called text files

Stream of characters—a sequence of characters

StreamReader object—used to read a sequence (stream) of characters from a sequential access file

StreamWriter object—used to write a sequence (stream) of characters to a sequential access file

Text files—another name for sequential access files

Write method—used with a StreamWriter variable to write data to a sequential access file; differs from the WriteLine method in that it does not write a newline character after the data

WriteLine method—used with a StreamWriter variable to write data to a sequential access file; differs from the Write method in that it writes a newline character after the data

Lesson B Review Questions

1. Which of the following opens the states.txt file and allows the computer to write new data to the end of the file's existing data?

    a. `outFile = IO.File.AddText("states.txt")`

    b. `outFile = IO.File.AppendText("states.txt")`

    c. `outFile = IO.File.InsertText("states.txt")`

    d. `outFile = IO.File.OpenText("states.txt")`

2. If the file to be opened exists, the _____ method erases the file's contents.

    a. AppendText

    b. CreateText

    c. InsertText

    d. OpenText

3. Which of the following reads a line of text from a sequential access file and assigns the line (excluding the newline character) to the `strText` variable?

    a. `inFile.Read(strText)`

    b. `inFile.ReadLine(strText)`

    c. `strText = inFile.ReadLine`

    d. `strText = inFile.Read(line)`

4. The Peek method returns _____ when the end of the file is reached.

    a.   −1

    b.   0

    c.   the last character in the file

    d.   the newline character

5. Which of the following can be used to determine whether the employ.txt file exists?

    a.   `If IO.File.Exists("employ.txt") Then`

    b.   `If IO.File("employ.txt").Exists Then`

    c.   `If IO.Exists("employ.txt") = True Then`

    d.   `If IO.Exists.File("employ.txt") = True Then`

6. The OpenText method creates a _____ object.

    a.   File

    b.   SequenceReader

    c.   StreamWriter

    d.   none of the above

7. The AppendText method creates a _____ object.

    a.   File

    b.   SequenceReader

    c.   StreamWriter

    d.   none of the above

Lesson B Exercises

INTRODUCTORY

1. Write the code to declare a variable named **outFile** that can be used to write data to a sequential access file. Then write the statement to open a sequential access file named sales.txt for output.

INTRODUCTORY

2. Write the code to declare a variable named **inFile** that can be used to read data from a sequential access file. Then write the statement to open a sequential access file named sales.txt for input.

INTRODUCTORY

3. Write the code to close the sequential access file associated with a StreamWriter variable named **outFile**.

INTRODUCTORY

4. Write an If clause that determines whether a sequential access file exists. The file's name is sales.txt.

5. Write a Do clause that determines whether the end of a sequential access file has been reached. The file is associated with a StreamReader variable named inFile.

6. Open the Gross Pay Solution (Gross Pay Solution.sln) file contained in the VB2010\Chap10\Gross Pay Solution folder. If necessary, open the designer window. The interface provides a text box for entering a gross pay amount. The Save button should write the gross pay amount to a sequential access file named gross.txt. Save the file in the project's bin\Debug folder. The Display button should read the gross pay amounts from the gross.txt file and display each (formatted with a dollar sign and two decimal places) in the list box. Right-align the numbers in the list box. Open the Code Editor window. Code the Click event procedures for the btnSave and btnDisplay controls. Save the solution and then start the application. Write the following 10 gross pay amounts to the file: 600, 1250, 750.67, 350.75, 2000, 450, 125.89, 560, 1400, and 555.78. Click the Display button to display the gross pay amounts in the interface. Close the Code Editor window and then close the solution.

7. Open the Name Solution (Name Solution.sln) file contained in the VB2010\Chap10\Name Solution folder. If necessary, open the designer window. Open the Code Editor window. Open the names.txt file contained in the project's bin\Debug folder. The sequential access file contains five names. Close the names.txt window. The btnDisplay control's Click event procedure should read the five names contained in the names.txt file, storing each in a five-element one-dimensional array. The procedure should sort the array in descending order and then display the contents of the array in the list box. Code the procedure. Save the solution and then start and test the application. Close the Code Editor window and then close the solution. (If you need to recreate the names.txt file, open the file in a window in the IDE. Delete the contents of the file and then type the following five names, pressing Enter after typing each name: Joanne, Zelda, Abby, Ben, and Linda.)

8. Open the Salary Solution (Salary Solution.sln) file contained in the VB2010\Chap10\Salary Solution folder. If necessary, open the designer window. Open the Code Editor window and study the existing code. The btnDisplay control's Click event procedure stores six salary amounts in a one-dimensional array named intSalaries. Each salary amount corresponds to a salary code from 1 through 6. Code 1's salary is stored in the intSalaries(0) element in the array, code 2's salary is stored in the intSalaries(1) element, and so on. After storing the salary amounts in the array, the procedure prompts the user to enter a salary code. It then displays the amount associated with the code. Currently, the Dim statement assigns the six salary amounts to the array. Modify the procedure so that it reads the salary amounts from the salary.txt file and stores each in the array. The salary.txt file is contained in the project's bin\Debug folder. Save the solution and then start and test the application. Close the Code Editor window and then close the solution.

INTERMEDIATE

9. Open the Test Scores Solution (Test Scores Solution.sln) file contained in the VB2010\Chap10\Test Scores Solution folder. If necessary, open the designer window. Open the Code Editor window. The btnSave control's Click event procedure should allow the user to enter an unknown number of test scores, saving each score in a sequential access file. The btnCount control's Click event procedure should display (in a message box) the number of scores stored in the file. Code both procedures. Save the solution and then start and test the application. Close the Code Editor window and then close the solution.

INTERMEDIATE

10. In this exercise, you code an application that reads five numbers from a sequential access file and stores the numbers in a one-dimensional array. The application then increases each number by 1 and writes the numbers to the file. The application also displays the current contents of the sequential access file. Open the Numbers Solution (Numbers Solution.sln) file contained in the VB2010\Chap10\Numbers Solution folder. If necessary, open the designer window. Open the Code Editor window. Code the btnDisplay control's Click event procedure so it reads the five numbers stored in the numbers.txt file and displays the numbers in the list box. The numbers.txt file is contained in the project's bin\Debug folder. Currently, the file contains the numbers 1 through 5. Code the btnUpdate control's Click event procedure so it reads the five numbers from the numbers.txt file and stores the numbers in an array. It then should increase each number in the array by 1 and write the array contents to an empty numbers.txt file. Save the solution and then start the application. Click the Display button. The numbers 1 through 5 appear in the interface. Click the Update button and then click the Display button. The numbers 2 through 6 appear in the interface. Close the Code Editor window and then close the solution. (If you need to recreate the numbers.txt file, open the file in a window in the IDE. Delete the contents of the file and then type the numbers 1 through 5, pressing Enter after typing each number.)

ADVANCED

11. During July and August of each year, the Political Awareness Organization (PAO) sends a questionnaire to the voters in its district. The questionnaire asks the voter for his or her political party (Democratic, Republican, or Independent) and age. From the returned questionnaires, the organization's secretary tabulates the number of Democrats, Republicans, and Independents in the district. The secretary wants an application that she can use to save each respondent's information (political party and age) to a sequential access file. The application also should calculate and display the number of voters in each political party. Create a new Visual Basic Windows application. Use the following names for the solution, project, and form file, respectively: PAO Solution, PAO Project, and Main Form.vb. Save the application in the VB2010\Chap10 folder. Create the interface shown in Figure 10-31. The Party list box should contain three items: Democratic, Republican, and Independent. The Age text box should accept only numbers and the Backspace key. Code the Click event procedures for the Write to File and Display Totals buttons without using a structure. Save the solution and then start and test the application. Close the Code Editor window and then close the solution.

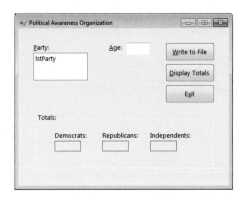

Figure 10-31 Interface for Exercise 11

12. In this exercise, you modify the application from Exercise 11. Use
Windows to make a copy of the PAO Solution folder. Rename
the folder Modified PAO Solution. Open the PAO Solution (PAO
Solution.sln) file contained in the Modified PAO Solution folder.
Open the designer window and then open the Code Editor window.
Modify the code to use a structure in the btnDisplay control's Click
event procedure. Save the solution and then start and test the applica-
tion. Close the Code Editor window and then close the solution.

ADVANCED

 Swat The Bugs

13. Open the Debug Solution (Debug Solution.sln) file contained in the
VB2010\Chap10\Debug Solution-Lesson B folder. Open the Code
Editor window and study the existing code. Start the application. Test
the application using Sue and 1000, and then using Pete and 5000.
A run time error occurs. Read the error message. Click Debug on
the menu bar and then click Stop Debugging. Open the bonus.txt
file contained in the project's bin\Debug folder. Notice that the file
is empty. Close the bonus.txt window. Locate and correct the error
in the code. Save the solution and then start and test the application
again. Close the Code Editor window and then close the solution.

▍LESSON C

After studying Lesson C, you should be able to:

- Add an item to a list box while an application is running
- Align columns of information
- Remove an item from a list box while an application is running
- Save list box items in a sequential access file
- Write records to a sequential access file

The Ch10CVideo file demonstrates all of the steps contained in Lesson C. You can view the video either before or after completing the lesson.

Coding the CD Collection Application

Recall that your task in this chapter is to create an application that uses a sequential access file to keep track of a person's CD collection. The application's user interface is shown in Figure 10-32, and its TOE chart is shown in Figure 10-33.

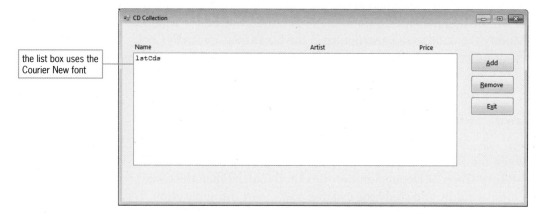

the list box uses the Courier New font

Figure 10-32   Interface for the CD Collection application

Task	Object	Event
Read the CDs.txt file and assign its contents to lstCds Save the contents of lstCds in the CDs.txt file	frmMain	Load FormClosing
End the application	btnExit	Click
1. Get CD name, artist name, and price 2. Add CD name, artist name, and price to lstCds	btnAdd	Click
Remove the selected line from lstCds	btnRemove	Click
Display the CD name, artist name, and price	lstCds	None

Figure 10-33   TOE chart for the CD Collection application

START HERE ▸ **To open the CD Collection application and then view the CDs.txt file:**

1. If necessary, start Visual Studio 2010 or Visual Basic 2010 Express. Open the CD Collection Solution (CD Collection Solution.sln) file contained in the VB2010\Chap10\CD Collection Solution folder. If necessary, open the designer window.

2. Open the Code Editor window. Replace <your name> and <current date> in the comments with your name and the current date, respectively.

3. Click **File** on the menu bar and then click **Open File**. Open the project's bin\Debug folder. Click **CDs.txt** in the list of filenames and then click the **Open** button. The CDs.txt window shows the information contained in the file. See Figure 10-34. The CD names are listed in the first column, the artist names in the second column, and the CD prices in the third column.

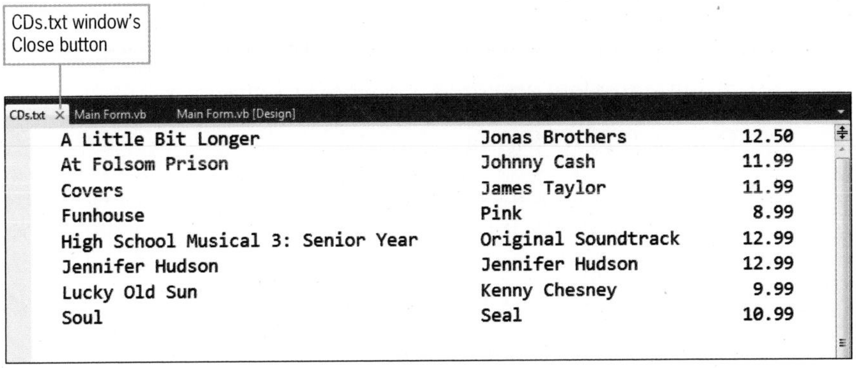

CDs.txt window's
Close button

```
CDs.txt  ×  Main Form.vb     Main Form.vb [Design]
    A Little Bit Longer                   Jonas Brothers      12.50
    At Folsom Prison                      Johnny Cash         11.99
    Covers                                James Taylor        11.99
    Funhouse                              Pink                 8.99
    High School Musical 3: Senior Year    Original Soundtrack 12.99
    Jennifer Hudson                       Jennifer Hudson     12.99
    Lucky Old Sun                         Kenny Chesney        9.99
    Soul                                  Seal                10.99
```

Figure 10-34 CDs.txt window

4. Close the CDs.txt window by clicking its **Close** button.

The TOE chart indicates that five procedures need to be coded. The Code Editor window already contains the code for the btnExit control's Click event procedure. So you will need to code only the form's Load and FormClosing event procedures and the Click event procedures for the btnAdd and btnRemove controls. You will code the form's Load event procedure first.

Coding the Form's Load Event Procedure

Figure 10-35 shows the pseudocode for the form's Load event procedure.

```
frmMain Load event procedure
if the CDs.txt sequential access file exists
    open the file for input
    repeat until the end of the file
        read a line from the file
        add the line to the lstCds control
    end repeat
    close the file
    select the first line in the lstCds control
else
    display the "Can't find the CDs.txt file" message
end if
```

Figure 10-35 Pseudocode for the form's Load event procedure

START HERE **To code and then test the form's Load event procedure:**

1. As you learned in Lesson B, you use a StreamReader object to read data from a sequential access file. Before creating the StreamReader object, you first declare a variable to store the object in the computer's internal memory. Locate the form's Load event procedure. Click the **blank line** below the `' declare variables` comment and then enter the following declaration statement:

   Dim inFile As IO.StreamReader

2. The procedure also will need a variable to store the string returned by the ReadLine method when reading the file. Type the following declaration statement and then press **Enter** twice:

   Dim strInfo As String

3. According to its pseudocode, the procedure needs to verify that the CDs.txt file exists. If the file does not exist, the procedure should display an appropriate message. Enter the comment and selection structure shown in Figure 10-36, and then position the insertion point as shown in the figure.

```
      Dim strInfo As String

      ' verify that the file exists
      If IO.File.Exists("CDs.txt") Then
                                                  ◄── position the insertion
                                                      point here
      Else
          MessageBox.Show("Can't find the CDs.txt file",
                          "CD Collection",
                          MessageBoxButtons.OK,
                          MessageBoxIcon.Information)
      End If
  End Sub
```

enter this comment and selection structure

Figure 10-36 Additional comment and code entered in the Load event procedure

4. If the file exists, the procedure should open the file for input. Enter the following comment and assignment statement:

   ' open the file for input
   inFile = IO.File.OpenText("CDs.txt")

5. Next, the procedure should use a loop to read each line from the file, adding each to the list box. Enter the following comments and lines of code:

   ' process loop instructions until end of file
   Do Until inFile.Peek = −1
       ' read a line from the file
       strInfo = inFile.ReadLine
       ' add the line to the list box
       lstCds.Items.Add(strInfo)
   Loop

6. After the loop ends, the procedure should close the file. Click **after the letter p** in the Loop clause and then press **Enter** twice to insert two blank lines. Enter the following comment and line of code:

   ' close the file
   inFile.Close()

7. The last task in the selection structure's true path is to select the first line in the list box. Enter the following comment and line of code:

   ' select the first line in the list box
   lstCds.SelectedIndex = 0

8. Save the solution and then start the application. The information contained in the CDs.txt file appears in the list box, as shown in Figure 10-37.

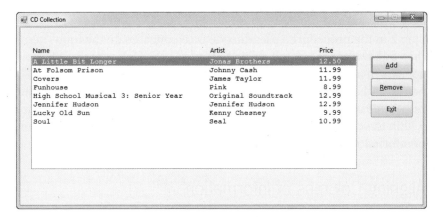

Figure 10-37   Contents of the CDs.txt file shown in the list box

9. Click the **Exit** button.

Coding the btnAdd Control's Click Event Procedure

According to the application's TOE chart, the btnAdd control's Click event procedure should get a CD name, an artist name, and a price from the user, and then display that information in the list box. Figure 10-38 shows the procedure's pseudocode.

---

btnAdd Click event procedure
1. use the InputBox function to get the CD name, artist name, and price
2. concatenate the CD name, artist name, and price, and then add the concatenated string to the lstCds control

---

Figure 10-38   Pseudocode for the btnAdd control's Click event procedure

To begin coding the btnAdd control's Click event procedure:

START HERE

1. Locate the btnAdd control's Click event procedure and then click the **blank line** below the ' declare variables comment. The procedure will use four String variables: three to store the input items and one to store the concatenated string. It also will use a Double variable

to store the numeric equivalent of the CD price. Enter the following five declaration statements:

Dim strName As String
Dim strArtist As String
Dim strPrice As String
Dim strConcatenatedInfo As String
Dim dblPrice As Double

2. Now you will use the InputBox function to get the CD information from the user. Click the **blank line** below the `' get the CD information` comment and then enter the following assignment statements:

strName = InputBox("CD name:", "CD Collection")
strArtist = InputBox("Artist:", "CD Collection")
strPrice = InputBox("Price:", "CD Collection")

Step 2 in the procedure's pseudocode is to concatenate the input items and then add the concatenated string to the list box. Notice that each input item appears in a separate column in the list box shown in Figure 10-37. The CD names and artist names in the first two columns are left-aligned within their respective column. The prices in the third column, however, are right-aligned within the column. In the next section, you will learn how to align columns of information.

Aligning Columns of Information

In Chapter 8, you learned how to use the PadLeft and PadRight methods to pad a string with a character until the string is a specified length. Each method's syntax is shown in Figure 10-39. Recall that when processing the methods, the computer first makes a temporary copy of the *string* in memory; it then pads the copy only. The *totalChars* argument in each syntax is an integer that represents the total number of characters you want the string's copy to contain. The optional *padCharacter* argument is the character that each method uses to pad the string until it reaches the desired number of characters. If the padCharacter argument is omitted, the default padding character is the space character.

You can use the PadLeft and PadRight methods to align columns of information, as shown in the examples in Figure 10-39. Example 1 aligns a column of numbers by the decimal point. Notice that you first format each number in the column to ensure that each has the same number of digits to the right of the decimal point. You then use the PadLeft method to insert spaces at the beginning of the number (if necessary); this right-aligns the number within the column. Because each number has the same number of digits to the right of the decimal point, aligning each number on the right will align each by its decimal point.

Example 2 in Figure 10-39 shows how you can align the second column of information when the first column contains strings with varying lengths. First, you use either the PadRight or PadLeft method to ensure that each string in the first column contains the same number of characters. You then concatenate the padded string to the information in the second column. The code in Example 2, for instance, uses the PadRight method to ensure that each name in the first column contains exactly 15 characters. It then concatenates the 15 characters with the string stored in the **strCity** variable before writing the concatenated string to a sequential access file. Because each name has 15 characters, each city entry will automatically appear beginning in character position 16 in the file. Example 2 also shows how you can use the **Strings.Space method** to include a specific number of space characters in a string. The method's syntax is **Strings.Space(*number*)**, in which *number* is an integer representing the number of spaces to include.

Aligning columns of information

Syntax
string.**PadLeft(***totalChars*[, *padCharacter*]**)**
string.**PadRight(***totalChars*[, *padCharacter*]**)**

Example 1
```
Dim strPrice As String
For dblPrice As Double = 9 To 11 Step 0.5
    strPrice = dblPrice.ToString("N2").PadLeft(5)
    lstPrices.Items.Add(strPrice)
Next dblPrice
```

Result
```
 9.00
 9.50
10.00
10.50
11.00
```

Example 2
```
Dim outFile As IO.StreamWriter
Dim strHeading As String =
    "Name" & Strings.Space(11) & "City"          contains the
                                                 Strings.Space
                                                 method
Dim strName As String
Dim strCity As String

outFile = IO.File.CreateText("Example2.txt")
outFile.WriteLine(strHeading)

strName = InputBox("Enter name:", "Name")
Do While strName <> String.Empty
    strCity = InputBox("Enter city:", "City")
    outFile.WriteLine(strName.PadRight(15) & strCity)
    strName = InputBox("Enter name:", "Name")
Loop
outFile.Close()
```

Result (when the user enters the following: Janice, Paris, Sue, Rome)
```
Name           City
Janice         Paris
Sue            Rome
```

In Example 1, you also need to set the lstPrices control's Font property to a fixed-spaced font, such as Courier New. A fixed-spaced font uses the same amount of space to display each character.

Figure 10-39 Examples of aligning columns of information

START HERE

To complete and then test the btnAdd control's Click event procedure:

1. Click the **blank line** below the `' and 5 spaces for the price` comment. First, you will format the price to ensure that it contains two decimal places. Enter the following lines of code:

   Double.TryParse(strPrice, dblPrice)
   strPrice = dblPrice.ToString("N2")

2. Now you will concatenate the three input items, reserving 40 characters for the CD name, 25 characters for the artist name, and 5 characters for the price. You will left-align the first two columns but right-align the last column. Enter the following assignment statement:

   strConcatenatedInfo = strName.PadRight(40) &
   strArtist.PadRight(25) & strPrice.PadLeft(5)

3. Now you will add the concatenated string to the list box. Click the **blank line** below the `' add the information to the list box` comment and then enter the following line of code:

   lstCds.Items.Add(strConcatenatedInfo)

4. Save the solution and then start the application. Click the **Add** button. Type **Breakout** as the CD name and then press **Enter**. Type **Miley Cyrus** as the artist name and then press **Enter**. Type **8** as the price and then press **Enter**. The Add button's Click event procedure adds the CD information to the list box. The list box's Sorted property is set to True, so the information you entered appears in the third line of the list box. See Figure 10-40.

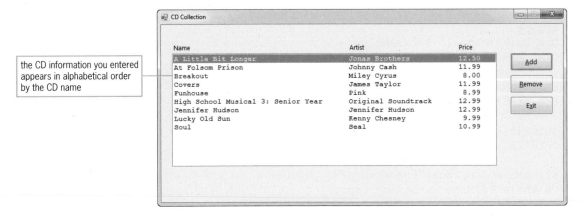

the CD information you entered appears in alphabetical order by the CD name

Figure 10-40   CD information added to the list box

5. Click the **Exit** button.

Coding the btnRemove Control's Click Event Procedure

According to the application's TOE chart, the btnRemove control's Click event procedure should remove the selected line from the lstCds control. The procedure's pseudocode is shown in Figure 10-41.

> btnRemove Click event procedure
> if a line is selected in the lstCds control
>   remove the line from the control
> end if

Figure 10-41   Pseudocode for the btnRemove control's Click event procedure

You remove an item from a list box using either the Items collection's Remove method or its RemoveAt method. Figure 10-42 shows each method's syntax and includes an example of using each method. In each syntax, *object* is the name of the list box control. The **Remove method** removes the item whose value is specified in its *item* argument. The **RemoveAt method** removes the item whose index is specified in its *index* argument.

Remove and RemoveAt methods (Items collection)

Syntax
object.**Items.Remove**(*item*)
object.**Items.RemoveAt**(*index*)

Example 1 – Remove
lstAnimal.Items.Remove("Cat")
removes the Cat item from the lstAnimal control

Example 2 – RemoveAt
lstAnimal.Items.RemoveAt(0)
removes the first item from the lstAnimal control

Figure 10-42   Syntax and examples of the Items collection's Remove and RemoveAt methods

To code and then test the btnRemove control's Click event procedure: <START HERE

1. Locate the btnRemove control's Click event procedure and then click the **blank line** below the second comment.

2. If a line is selected in the list box, the list box's SelectedIndex property will contain the line's index; otherwise, it will contain −1. Therefore, if the SelectedIndex property does not contain the number −1, the procedure should remove the selected line from the list box. Enter the following selection structure:

   If lstCds.SelectedIndex <> −1 Then
   **   lstCds.Items.RemoveAt(lstCds.SelectedIndex)**
   End If

3. Save the solution and then start the application. Click **Funhouse** in the list box and then click the **Remove** button. The button's Click event procedure removes the Funhouse CD from the list box.

4. Click the **Exit** button.

Coding the Form's FormClosing Event Procedure

The last procedure you need to code is the form's FormClosing event procedure. According to the application's TOE chart, the procedure is responsible for saving the contents of the lstCds control in the CDs.txt file. Figure 10-43 shows the procedure's pseudocode.

---

frmMain FormClosing event procedure
1. open the CDs.txt file for output
2. repeat for each line in the list box
      write the line to the file
  end repeat
3. close the file

Figure 10-43   Pseudocode for the form's FormClosing event procedure

START HERE   **To code and then test the form's FormClosing event procedure:**

1. Locate the form's FormClosing event procedure and then click the **blank line** below the `' declare a StreamWriter variable` comment. As you learned in Lesson B, you use a StreamWriter object to write data to a sequential access file. Before creating the StreamWriter object, you first declare a variable to store the object in the computer's internal memory. Enter the following declaration statement:

   Dim outFile As IO.StreamWriter

2. Step 1 in the pseudocode is to open the CDs.txt file for output. Click the **blank line** below the `' open the file for output` comment and then enter the following line of code:

   outFile = IO.File.CreateText("CDs.txt")

3. The next step in the pseudocode is a loop that will write each line from the list box to the file. Click the **blank line** below the `' write each line in the list box` comment and then enter the following loop:

   For intIndex As Integer = 0 To lstCds.Items.Count – 1
       outFile.WriteLine(lstCds.Items(intIndex))
   Next intIndex

4. The last step in the pseudocode is to close the file. Click the **blank line** below the `' close the file` comment and then enter the following line of code:

   outFile.Close()

5. Save the solution and then start the application. Click the **Add** button. Use the input boxes to enter the following CD name, artist, and price: **Breakout**, **Miley Cyrus**, and **8**. The Add button's Click event procedure adds the CD information to the list box.

6. Click the **Exit** button. The computer processes the `Me.Close()` statement in the Exit button's Click event procedure; doing this

invokes the form's FormClosing event. The FormClosing event procedure saves the contents of the list box to the CDs.txt file.

7. Now you will verify that the CD information you entered was saved to the CDs.txt file. Click **File** on the menu bar and then click **Open File**. Open the project's bin\Debug folder. Click **CDs.txt** in the list of filenames and then click the **Open** button. The CD information you entered appears in the third line in the file. Close the CDs.txt window by clicking its **Close** button.

8. Start the application again. Click **Breakout** in the list box and then click the **Remove** button. The button's Click event procedure removes the CD information from the list box.

9. Click the **Exit** button. Now you will verify that the CDs.txt file does not contain the CD information you removed from the list box. Open the CDs.txt file. Notice that the Breakout CD's information does not appear in the file. Close the CDs.txt window.

10. Close the Code Editor window and then close the solution.

Figure 10-44 shows the application's code.

```
1 ' Name:      CD Collection Project
2 ' Purpose: Allows the user to add and delete list box entries
3 '            Reads CD information from a sequential access file
4 '            Writes CD information to a sequential access file
5 ' Programmer:   <your name> on <current date>
6
7 Option Explicit On
8 Option Strict On
9 Option Infer Off
10
11 Public Class frmMain
12
13    Private Sub btnExit_Click(ByVal sender As Object,
      ByVal e As System.EventArgs) Handles btnExit.Click
14       Me.Close()
15    End Sub
16
17    Private Sub frmMain_FormClosing(ByVal sender As Object,
      ByVal e As System.Windows.Forms.FormClosingEventArgs
      ) Handles Me.FormClosing
18       ' save the list box information
19
20       ' declare a StreamWriter variable
21       Dim outFile As IO.StreamWriter
22
23       ' open the file for output
24       outFile = IO.File.CreateText("CDs.txt")
25
26       ' write each line in the list box
27       For intIndex As Integer = 0 To lstCds.Items.Count - 1
28          outFile.WriteLine(lstCds.Items(intIndex))
29       Next intIndex
30
31       ' close the file
```

Figure 10-44   Code for the CD Collection application *(continues)*

(continued)

```
32        outFile.Close()
33
34    End Sub
35
36    Private Sub frmMain_Load(ByVal sender As Object,
      ByVal e As System.EventArgs) Handles Me.Load
37        ' fills the list box with data
38        ' stored in a sequential access file
39
40        ' declare variables
41        Dim inFile As IO.StreamReader
42        Dim strInfo As String
43
44        ' verify that the file exists
45        If IO.File.Exists("CDs.txt") Then
46            ' open the file for input
47            inFile = IO.File.OpenText("CDs.txt")
48            ' process loop instructions until end of file
49            Do Until inFile.Peek = -1
50                ' read a line from the file
51                strInfo = inFile.ReadLine
52                ' add the line to the list box
53                lstCds.Items.Add(strInfo)
54            Loop
55
56            ' close the file
57            inFile.Close()
58            ' select the first line in the list box
59            lstCds.SelectedIndex = 0
60
61        Else
62            MessageBox.Show("Can't find the CDs.txt file",
63                            "CD Collection",
64                            MessageBoxButtons.OK,
65                            MessageBoxIcon.Information)
66        End If
67    End Sub
68
69    Private Sub btnAdd_Click(ByVal sender As Object,
      ByVal e As System.EventArgs) Handles btnAdd.Click
70        ' adds CD information to the list box
71
72        ' declare variables
73        Dim strName As String
74        Dim strArtist As String
75        Dim strPrice As String
76        Dim strConcatenatedInfo As String
77        Dim dblPrice As Double
78
79        ' get the CD information
80        strName = InputBox("CD name:", "CD Collection")
81        strArtist = InputBox("Artist:", "CD Collection")
82        strPrice = InputBox("Price:", "CD Collection")
83
84        ' format the price, then concatenate the
85        ' input items, using 40 spaces for the
86        ' CD name, 25 spaces for the artist name,
```

Figure 10-44   Code for the CD Collection application *(continues)*

(continued)

```
87        ' and 5 spaces for the price
88        Double.TryParse(strPrice, dblPrice)
89        strPrice = dblPrice.ToString("N2")
90        strConcatenatedInfo = strName.PadRight(40) &
91           strArtist.PadRight(25) & strPrice.PadLeft(5)
92
93        ' add the information to the list box
94        lstCds.Items.Add(strConcatenatedInfo)
95
96    End Sub
97
98    Private Sub btnRemove_Click(ByVal sender As Object,
      ByVal e As System.EventArgs) Handles btnRemove.Click
99        ' removes the selected line from the list box
100
101       ' if a line is selected, remove the line
102       If lstCds.SelectedIndex <> -1 Then
103           lstCds.Items.RemoveAt(lstCds.SelectedIndex)
104       End If
105   End Sub
106 End Class
```

Figure 10-44   Code for the CD Collection application

Lesson C Summary

- To align columns of information:

  Use the PadLeft and PadRight methods.

- To align a column of numbers by the decimal point:

  Format each number in the column to ensure that each has the same number of digits to the right of the decimal point, and then use the PadLeft method to right-align the numbers.

- To include a specific number of spaces in a string:

  Use the Strings.Space method. The method's syntax is **Strings. Space(***number***)**, in which *number* is an integer that represents the number of spaces to include.

- To remove an item from a list box:

  Use either the Items collection's Remove method or its RemoveAt method. The Remove method's syntax is *object*.**Items.Remove(***item***)**, where *item* is the value of the item you want to remove. The RemoveAt method's syntax is *object*.**Items.RemoveAt(***index***)**, where *index* is the index of the item you want removed.

Lesson C Key Terms

Remove method—used to specify the value of the item to remove from a list box

RemoveAt method—used to specify the index of the item to remove from a list box

Strings.Space method—used to include a specific number of spaces in a string

Lesson C Review Questions

1. Which of the following opens a sequential access file named "MyFriends.txt" for input?

   a. `inFile = IO.File.Input("MyFriends.txt")`

   b. `inFile = IO.InputFile("MyFriends.txt")`

   c. `inFile = IO.File.InputText("MyFriends.txt")`

   d. `inFile = IO.File.OpenText("MyFriends.txt")`

2. Which of the following right-aligns the contents of the `strNumbers` variable?

   a. `strNumbers = strNumbers.PadLeft(10)`

   b. `strNumbers = strNumbers.PadRight(10)`

   c. `strNumbers = strNumbers.AlignLeft(10)`

   d. `strNumbers = strNumbers.RightAlign(10)`

3. Which of the following removes the fourth item from the lstFriends control?

   a. `lstFriends.Items.Remove(4)`

   b. `lstFriends.Items.RemoveAt(4)`

   c. `lstFriends.Items.RemoveIndex(3)`

   d. none of the above

4. Which of the following determines whether an item is selected in the lstFriends control?

   a. `If lstFriends.SelectedIndex >= 0`

   b. `If lstFriends.SelectedItem <> -1`

   c. `If lstFriends.IndexSelected = -1`

   d. none of the above

5. The lstFriends control contains five items. Which of the following writes the last item to the file associated with the `outFile` variable?

a. `outFile.WriteLine(lstFriends.Items(5))`

b. `outFile.WriteLine(lstFriends.Items(4))`

c. `outFile.WriteLine(lstFriends.Index(4))`

d. none of the above

Lesson C Exercises

1. In this exercise, you modify the CD Collection application coded in the lesson. Use Windows to make a copy of the CD Collection Solution folder. Rename the copy CD Collection Solution-Verify Save. Open the CD Collection Solution (CD Collection Solution.sln) file contained in the CD Collection Solution-Verify Save folder. Open the designer and Code Editor windows. The FormClosing event procedure should verify that the user wants to save the changes made to the list box. It then should take the appropriate action based on the user's response. Modify the code accordingly. Save the solution and then start and test the application. Close the Code Editor window and then close the solution.

   INTRODUCTORY

2. In this exercise, you modify the CD Collection application coded in the lesson. Use Windows to make a copy of the CD Collection Solution folder. Rename the copy CD Collection Solution-Verify Remove. Open the CD Collection Solution (CD Collection Solution.sln) file contained in the CD Collection Solution-Verify Remove folder. Open the designer and Code Editor windows. The btnRemove control's Click event procedure should verify that the user wants to remove the selected CD information from the list box. Use the message "Do you want to remove the x CD?", where x is the name of the CD. The procedure should take the appropriate action based on the user's response. Modify the code accordingly. Save the solution and then start and test the application. Close the Code Editor window and then close the solution.

   INTERMEDIATE

3. Open the Friends Solution (Friends Solution.sln) file contained in the VB2010\Chap10\Friends Solution folder. If necessary, open the designer window. The Add button should add the name entered in the text portion of the combo box to the list portion, but only if the name is not already in the list. The Remove button should remove (from the list portion of the combo box) the name either entered in the text portion or selected in the list portion. The form's FormClosing event procedure should save the combo box items in a sequential access file named MyFriends.txt. The form's Load event procedure should read the names from the MyFriends.txt file and add each to the combo box. Code the application. Save the solution and then start and test the application. Close the Code Editor window and then close the solution.

   INTERMEDIATE

4. In this exercise, you modify the CD Collection application coded in the lesson. Use Windows to make a copy of the CD Collection Solution folder. Rename the copy CD Collection Solution-No

   INTERMEDIATE

Duplicate. Open the CD Collection Solution (CD Collection Solution.sln) file contained in the CD Collection Solution-No Duplicate folder. Open the designer and Code Editor windows. Before getting the artist name and price, the btnAdd control's Click event procedure should determine whether the CD name is already included in the list box. If the list box contains the CD name, the procedure should display an appropriate message and then not add the CD to the list. Save the solution and then start and test the application. Close the Code Editor window and then close the solution.

INTERMEDIATE

5. In this exercise, you modify the CD Collection application coded in the lesson. Use Windows to make a copy of the CD Collection Solution folder. Rename the copy CD Collection Solution-Undo. Open the CD Collection Solution (CD Collection Solution.sln) file contained in the CD Collection Solution-Undo folder. Open the designer window. Add an Undo Remove button to the form. The Undo Remove button's Click event procedure should restore the last line removed by the Remove button. Open the Code Editor window and make the necessary modifications to the code. Save the solution and then start and test the application. Close the Code Editor window and then close the solution.

INTERMEDIATE

6. In this exercise, you modify the CD Collection application coded in the lesson. Use Windows to make a copy of the CD Collection Solution folder. Rename the copy CD Collection Solution-Structure. Open the CD Collection Solution (CD Collection Solution.sln) file contained in the CD Collection Solution-Structure folder. Open the designer and Code Editor windows. Create a structure for the input information and then use the structure in the btnAdd control's Click event procedure. Save the solution and then start and test the application. Close the Code Editor window and then close the solution.

INTERMEDIATE

7. Glovers Industries stores the item numbers and prices of its products in a sequential access file named ItemInfo.txt. The company's sales manager wants an application that displays the price corresponding to the item selected in a list box.

a. Open the Glovers Solution (Glovers Solution.sln) file contained in the VB2010\Chap10\Glovers Solution folder. If necessary, open the designer window.

b. Open the Code Editor window. Open the ItemInfo.txt file, which is contained in the project's bin\Debug folder. Notice that the item number and price appear on separate lines in the file. Close the ItemInfo.txt window.

c. Define a structure named Product. The structure should contain two member variables: a String variable to store the item number and a Double variable to store the price.

d. Declare a class-level array that contains five Product structure variables.

e. The form's Load event procedure should read the item numbers and prices from the ItemInfo.txt file and store them in the class-level array. It also should add the item numbers to the list box. Code the procedure.

f. When the user selects an item in the list box, the item's price should appear in the lblPrice control. Code the appropriate procedure.

g. Save the solution and then start and test the application. Close the Code Editor window and then close the solution.

8. Each year, WKRK-Radio polls its audience to determine the best Super Bowl commercial. The choices are as follows: Budweiser, FedEx, E"Trade, and Pepsi. The station manager wants an application that allows him to enter a caller's choice. The choice should be saved in a sequential access file. The application also should display the number of votes for each commercial. Create a Visual Basic Windows application. Use the following names for the solution, project, and form file, respectively: WKRK Solution, WKRK Project, and Main Form.vb. Create the interface shown in Figure 10-45, and then code the application. Save the solution and then start and test the application. Close the Code Editor window and then close the solution.

ADVANCED

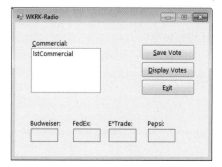

Figure 10-45   Interface for Exercise 8

9. Carlton Industries stores the item numbers and prices of the items it sells in a sequential access file named ItemInfo.txt. The company's sales manager wants an application that displays the price corresponding to the item selected in a list box.

ADVANCED

a. Create a Visual Basic Windows application. Use the following names for the solution, project, and form file, respectively: Carlton Solution, Carlton Project, and Main Form.vb. Create the interface shown in Figure 10-46.

b. Use Windows to copy the ItemInfo.txt file from the VB2010\Chap10 folder to the project's bin\Debug folder. Open the Code Editor window and then open the ItemInfo.txt file contained in the project's bin\Debug folder. Each line contains an item's number followed by a comma and the price. Close the ItemInfo.txt window.

c. Define a structure named Item. The structure should contain two member variables: a String variable to store the item number and a Decimal variable to store the price.

d. Declare a class-level array that contains five Item structure variables.

e. Code the form's Load event procedure so that it reads the item numbers and prices from the ItemInfo.txt file. The procedure should store the item numbers and prices in the class-level array. It also should add the item numbers to the list box.

f. When the user selects an item in the list box, the item's price should appear in the lblPrice control. Code the appropriate procedure.

g. Save the solution and then start and test the application. Close the Code Editor window and then close the solution.

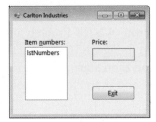

Figure 10-46   Interface for Exercise 9

CHAPTER 11

Classes and Objects

Creating the ABC Company Application

In this chapter, you will create an application that calculates and displays the gross pay for salaried and hourly employees. Salaried employees are paid twice per month. Therefore, each salaried employee's gross pay is calculated by dividing his or her annual salary by 24. Hourly employees are paid weekly. The gross pay for an hourly employee is calculated by multiplying the number of hours the employee worked during the week by his or her hourly pay rate. The application also will display a report showing each employee's number, name, and gross pay.

Previewing the ABC Company Application

Before you start the first lesson in this chapter, you will preview the completed application. The application is contained in the VB2010\Chap11 folder.

START HERE

To preview the completed application:

1. Use the Run dialog box to run the ABC (ABC.exe) file contained in the VB2010\Chap11 folder. The application's user interface appears on the screen.

2. First, you will calculate the gross pay for Sarah Lopez. Sarah worked 38 hours and earns $9 per hour. Her employee number is 1234. Type **1234** in the Number box, press **Tab**, and then type **Sarah Lopez** in the Name box. Click **38.0** in the Hours list box and then click **9.00** in the Rate list box. Click the **Calculate** button. $342.00 appears in the Gross pay box, and Sarah's information appears in the Report box. See Figure 11-1.

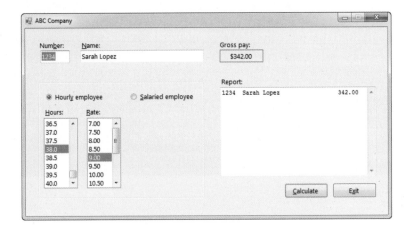

Figure 11-1   Interface showing Sarah's gross pay and information

3. Now you will calculate the gross pay for a salaried employee earning $30,000 per year. Type **9999** in the Number box, press **Tab**, and then type **Henry Jacoby** in the Name box. Click the **Salaried employee** radio button. Scroll the Annual salary list box and then click **30000** in the list. Click the **Calculate** button. $1,250.00 appears in the Gross pay box, and Henry's information appears below Sarah's information in the Report box.

4. Click the **Exit** button to end the application.

In Lesson A, you will learn about object-oriented programming (OOP). More specifically, you will learn how to define a class and how to use the class to instantiate an object. You also will learn how to utilize the instantiated object in an application. Lesson B will teach you how to include ReadOnly and auto-implemented properties in a class. You also will learn how to overload a class method. You will code the ABC Company application in Lesson B. Lesson C covers an advanced OOP topic: inheritance. Be sure to complete each lesson in full and do all of the end-of-lesson questions and several exercises before continuing to the next lesson.

LESSON A

After studying Lesson A, you should be able to:

- Explain the terminology used in object-oriented programming
- Create a class

- Instantiate an object
- Add Property procedures to a class
- Include data validation in a class
- Create a default constructor
- Create a parameterized constructor
- Include methods other than constructors in a class

Object-Oriented Programming Terminology

As you learned in the Overview, Visual Basic 2010 is an **object-oriented programming language**, which is a language that allows the programmer to use objects to accomplish a program's goal. Recall that an object is anything that can be seen, touched, or used. In other words, an object is nearly any *thing*. The objects used in an object-oriented program can take on many different forms. The text boxes, list boxes, and buttons included in most Windows applications are objects, and so are the application's named constants and variables. An object also can represent something found in real life, such as a wristwatch or a car.

Every object used in an object-oriented program is created from a **class**, which is a pattern that the computer uses to create the object. Using object-oriented programming (**OOP**) terminology, objects are **instantiated** (created) from a class, and each object is referred to as an **instance** of the class. A button control, for example, is an instance of the Button class. The button is instantiated when you drag the Button tool from the toolbox to the form. A String variable, on the other hand, is an instance of the String class and is instantiated the first time you refer to the variable in code. Keep in mind that the class itself is not an object. Only an instance of a class is an object.

Every object has **attributes**, which are the characteristics that describe the object. Attributes are also called properties. Included in the attributes of buttons and text boxes are the Name and Text properties. List boxes have a Name property as well as a Sorted property. In addition to attributes, every object also has behaviors. An object's **behaviors** include methods and events. **Methods** are the operations (actions) that the object is capable of performing. For example, a button can use its Focus method to send the focus to itself. **Events** are the actions to which an object can respond. A button's Click event, for instance, allows it to respond to a mouse click. A class contains—or, in OOP terms, it **encapsulates**—all of the attributes and behaviors of the object it instantiates. The term "encapsulate" means "to enclose in a capsule." In the context of OOP, the "capsule" is a class.

Creating a Class

In previous chapters, you instantiated objects using classes that are built into Visual Basic, such as the TextBox and Label classes. You used the instantiated objects in a variety of ways in many different applications. In some applications, you used a text box to enter a name, while in other applications you used it to enter a sales tax rate. Similarly, you used label controls to identify text boxes and also to display the result of calculations. The ability to use an object for more than one purpose saves programming time and money—an advantage that contributes to the popularity of object-oriented programming. You also can define your own classes in Visual Basic and then create instances (objects) from those classes. Like the Visual Basic classes, your classes must specify the attributes and behaviors of the objects they create.

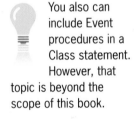

The creation of a good class, which is one whose objects can be used in a variety of ways by many different applications, requires a lot of planning.

You define a class using the **Class statement**, which you enter in a class file. Figure 11-2 shows the statement's syntax and lists the steps for adding a class file to an open project. Although it is not a requirement, the convention is to use Pascal case for the class name. The names of Visual Basic classes (for example, Integer and TextBox) also follow this naming convention. Within the Class statement, you define the attributes and behaviors of the objects the class will create. In most cases, the attributes are represented by Private variables and Public properties. The behaviors are represented by methods, which can be Sub or Function procedures. Figure 11-3 shows an example of the Class statement entered in a class file. The three Option statements included in the figure have the same meaning in a class file as they have in a form file.

You also can include Event procedures in a Class statement. However, that topic is beyond the scope of this book.

Class statement

<u>Syntax</u>
Public Class *className*
    attributes section
    behaviors section
End Class

<u>Adding a class file to an open project</u>
1. Click Project on the menu bar and then click Add Class. The Add New Item dialog box opens with Class selected in the middle column of the dialog box.
2. Type the name of the class followed by a period and the letters vb in the Name box, and then click the Add button.

Figure 11-2   Syntax of the Class statement

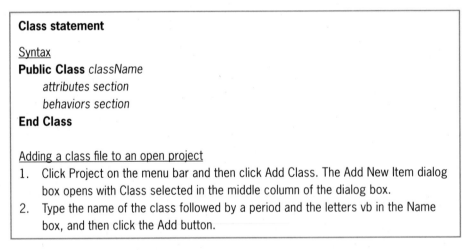

you enter the attributes and behaviors sections here

Figure 11-3   Class statement entered in the TimeCard.vb class file

618

After you define a class, it then can be used to instantiate one or more objects. Figure 11-4 shows two versions of the syntax for instantiating an object. In both versions, *className* is the name of the class, and *variableName* is the name of a variable that will represent the object. The difference between both versions relates to when the object is actually created. The computer creates the object only when it processes the statement containing the New keyword. (You will learn more about the New keyword later in this lesson.) Also included in Figure 11-4 is an example of using each version of the syntax. In Example 1, the `Private hoursInfo As TimeCard` instruction creates a class-level variable that can represent a TimeCard object; however, it does not create the object. The object isn't created until the computer processes the `hoursInfo = New TimeCard` statement, which uses the TimeCard class to instantiate a TimeCard object. The statement assigns the object to the `hoursInfo` variable. In Example 2, the `Dim hoursInfo As New TimeCard` instruction creates a procedure-level variable named `hoursInfo`. It also instantiates a TimeCard object and assigns it to the variable.

Instantiating an object from a class

Syntax – Version 1
{**Dim | Private**} *variableName* **As** *className*
variableName = **New** *className*

Syntax – Version 2
{**Dim | Private**} *variableName* **As New** *className*

Example 1 (using syntax version 1)
```
Private hoursInfo As TimeCard
hoursInfo = New TimeCard
```
the Private instruction creates a TimeCard variable named `hoursInfo`; the assignment statement instantiates a TimeCard object and assigns it to the `hoursInfo` variable

Example 2 (using syntax version 2)
```
Dim hoursInfo As New TimeCard
```
the Dim instruction creates a TimeCard variable named `hoursInfo` and also instantiates a TimeCard object, which it assigns to the `hoursInfo` variable

---

Figure 11-4 Syntax and examples of instantiating an object from a class

In the remainder of this lesson, you will view examples of class definitions, as well as examples of code in which objects are instantiated and used. The first example is a class that contains attributes only, with each attribute represented by a Public variable.

Example 1—A Class that Contains Public Variables Only

In its simplest form, the Class statement can be used in place of the Structure statement, which you learned about in Chapter 10. Like the Structure statement, the Class statement groups related items into one unit. However, the unit is called a class rather than a structure. In the following set of steps, you will modify the Willow Pools application from Chapter 10 to use a class instead of a structure.

START HERE ▶ **To open the Willow Pools application:**

1. If necessary, start Visual Studio 2010 or Visual Basic 2010 Express. Open the Willow Pools Solution (Willow Pools Solution.sln) file contained in the VB2010\Chap11\Willow Pools Solution folder. If necessary, open the designer window.

2. Open the Code Editor window. Figure 11-5 shows the Structure statement, the GetGallons function, and the btnCalc control's Click event procedure. The Structure statement groups together the three dimensions of a rectangular pool: length, width, and depth. The event procedure declares a structure variable and then fills the variable's members with values. It then passes the structure variable to the GetGallons function, which calculates and returns the number of gallons required to fill the pool. The event procedure displays the returned value in the lblGallons control.

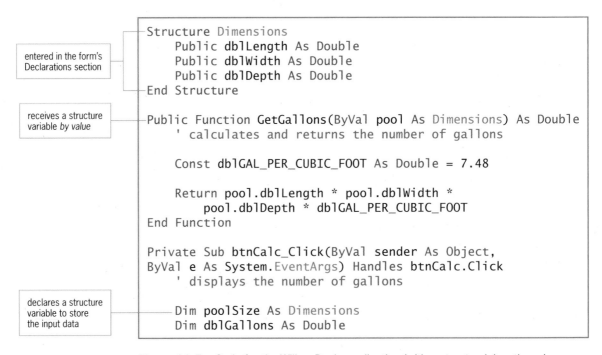

entered in the form's Declarations section

receives a structure variable *by value*

declares a structure variable to store the input data

```
Structure Dimensions
    Public dblLength As Double
    Public dblWidth As Double
    Public dblDepth As Double
End Structure

Public Function GetGallons(ByVal pool As Dimensions) As Double
    ' calculates and returns the number of gallons

    Const dblGAL_PER_CUBIC_FOOT As Double = 7.48

    Return pool.dblLength * pool.dblWidth *
        pool.dblDepth * dblGAL_PER_CUBIC_FOOT
End Function

Private Sub btnCalc_Click(ByVal sender As Object,
ByVal e As System.EventArgs) Handles btnCalc.Click
    ' displays the number of gallons

    Dim poolSize As Dimensions
    Dim dblGallons As Double
```

Figure 11-5   Code for the Willow Pools application (with a structure) *(continues)*

Example 1—A Class that Contains Public Variables Only **LESSON A**

(continued)

```
    Double.TryParse(txtLength.Text, poolSize.dblLength)
    Double.TryParse(txtWidth.Text, poolSize.dblWidth)
    Double.TryParse(txtDepth.Text, poolSize.dblDepth)

    dblGallons = GetGallons(poolSize)
    lblGallons.Text = dblGallons.ToString("N0")

    txtLength.Focus()
End Sub
```

> passes the structure variable to the GetGallons function

Figure 11-5 Code for the Willow Pools application (with a structure)

To add a class file to the project:

START HERE

1. Click **Project** on the menu bar and then click **Add Class**. The Add New Item dialog box opens with Class selected in the middle column of the dialog box. Type **RectangularPool.vb** in the Name box. As you learned in Chapter 1, the .vb in a filename indicates that the file contains Visual Basic code.

2. Click the **Add** button. The computer adds the RectangularPool.vb file to the project. It also opens the file, which contains the Class statement, in the Code Editor window. Temporarily display the Solution Explorer window, if necessary, to verify that the class file's name appears in the window.

3. Insert a blank line above the Class statement and then enter the comments and Option statements shown in Figure 11-6. (Replace <your name> and <current date> in the comments with your name and the current date, respectively.) Also, position the insertion point as shown in the figure.

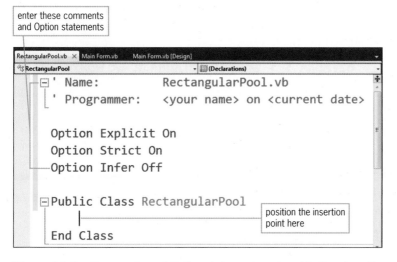

Figure 11-6 Comments and Option statements entered in the class file

A RectangularPool object has three attributes: length, width, and depth. In the Class statement, each attribute will be represented by a Public variable. When a variable in a class is declared using the `Public` keyword, it can be accessed by any application that contains an instance of the class.

The convention is to use Pascal case for the names of the Public variables in a class, and to omit the three-character ID that indicates the variable's data type. This is because Public variables represent properties that will be seen by anyone using an object created from the class. The properties of Visual Basic objects—such as the Text and StartPosition properties—also follow this naming convention.

START HERE

To enter the Public variables in the class definition:

1. Enter the following three Public statements:

    Public Length As Double
    Public Width As Double
    Public Depth As Double

2. Save the solution.

Now you will modify the application's code to use the RectangularPool class rather than the Dimensions structure.

START HERE

To modify the code to use the RectangularPool class:

1. Click the **Main Form.vb** tab to return to the form's Code Editor window. Replace <your name> and <current date> in the comments with your name and the current date, respectively.

2. First, delete the Structure statement from the form's Declarations section.

3. Next, locate the btnCalc control's Click event procedure. The procedure will instantiate a RectangularPool object. Replace the `Dim poolSize As Dimensions` instruction with the following instruction:

    Dim customerPool As New RectangularPool

4. Now you will modify the three TryParse methods to use the object's Public variables. Highlight (select) `poolSize.dblLength` in the first TryParse method. Type **customerPool.** and then click the **Common** tab (if necessary). The Public variables appear in the IntelliSense list, as shown in Figure 11-7.

Figure 11-7 Public variables included in the IntelliSense list

5. Click **Length** and then press **Tab**. Now change `poolSize.dblWidth` and `poolSize.dblDepth` in the remaining TryParse methods to **customerPool.Width** and **customerPool.Depth**, respectively.

Example 1—A Class that Contains Public Variables Only **LESSON A**

6. The procedure needs to pass the customerPool object (rather than the poolSize structure) to the GetGallons function. Change `poolSize` in the `dblGallons = GetGallons(poolSize)` statement to **customerPool**.

7. Locate the GetGallons function. The function will need to receive a RectangularPool object rather than a Dimensions structure. Change `Dimensions` in the function header to **RectangularPool**.

8. Finally, change `dblLength`, `dblWidth`, and `dblDepth` in the Return statement to **Length**, **Width**, and **Depth**, respectively.

Figure 11-8 shows the Class statement, the GetGallons function, and the btnCalc control's Click event procedure. The changes made to the original function and procedure (both of which are shown earlier in Figure 11-5) are shaded in the figure.

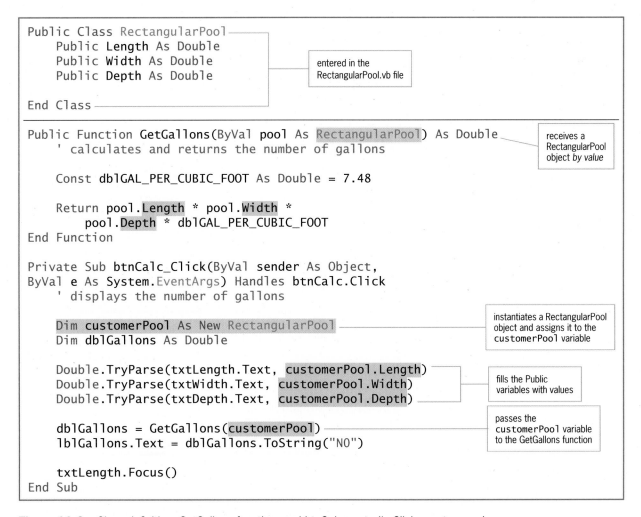

```
Public Class RectangularPool
    Public Length As Double          entered in the
    Public Width As Double           RectangularPool.vb file
    Public Depth As Double

End Class

Public Function GetGallons(ByVal pool As RectangularPool) As Double      receives a
    ' calculates and returns the number of gallons                       RectangularPool
                                                                         object by value
    Const dblGAL_PER_CUBIC_FOOT As Double = 7.48

    Return pool.Length * pool.Width *
        pool.Depth * dblGAL_PER_CUBIC_FOOT
End Function

Private Sub btnCalc_Click(ByVal sender As Object,
ByVal e As System.EventArgs) Handles btnCalc.Click
    ' displays the number of gallons
                                                    instantiates a RectangularPool
    Dim customerPool As New RectangularPool         object and assigns it to the
    Dim dblGallons As Double                        customerPool variable

    Double.TryParse(txtLength.Text, customerPool.Length)
    Double.TryParse(txtWidth.Text, customerPool.Width)     fills the Public
    Double.TryParse(txtDepth.Text, customerPool.Depth)     variables with values

    dblGallons = GetGallons(customerPool)           passes the
    lblGallons.Text = dblGallons.ToString("N0")     customerPool variable
                                                    to the GetGallons function
    txtLength.Focus()
End Sub
```

Figure 11-8 Class definition, GetGallons function, and btnCalc control's Click event procedure

623

START HERE
To test the modified code:

1. Save the solution and then start the application. Type **60** in the Length box, **30** in the Width box, and **5** in the Depth box. Click the **Calculate** button to display the required number of gallons of water. See Figure 11-9.

Figure 11-9   Interface showing the number of gallons

2. Click the **Exit** button to stop the application. Close the Main Form.vb and RectangularPool.vb windows and then close the solution.

Example 2—A Class that Contains Private Variables, Public Properties, and Methods

Although you can define a class that contains only attributes represented by Public variables—like the RectangularPool class shown in Figure 11-8—that is rarely done. The disadvantage of using Public variables in a class is that a class cannot control the values assigned to its Public variables. As a result, the class cannot validate the values to ensure they are appropriate for the variables. Furthermore, most classes contain not only attributes, but behaviors as well. This is because the purpose of a class in OOP is to encapsulate the properties that describe an object, the methods that allow the object to perform tasks, and the events that allow the object to respond to actions. In this section, you will create a class that contains data validation code and methods. (Including events in a class is beyond the scope of this book.) The class will be used in the Carpet Haven application, which calculates and displays the number of square yards of carpeting required to carpet a rectangular floor. It also calculates and displays the cost of the carpet.

START HERE
To add a class file to the Carpet Haven application:

1. Open the Carpet Haven Solution (Carpet Haven Solution.sln) file contained in the VB2010\Chap11\Carpet Haven Solution folder. If necessary, open the designer window. The interface allows the user to enter the length and width of a room's floor and the price of a square yard of carpet. See Figure 11-10.

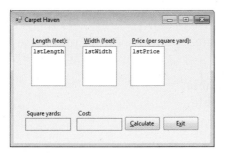

Figure 11-10 Interface for the Carpet Haven application

2. Click **Project** on the menu bar and then click **Add Class**. Type **Rectangle.vb** in the Name box and then click the **Add** button. Insert a blank line above the Class statement and then enter the comments and Option statements shown in Figure 11-11. (Replace <your name> and <current date> in the comments with your name and the current date, respectively.) Also, position the insertion point as shown in the figure.

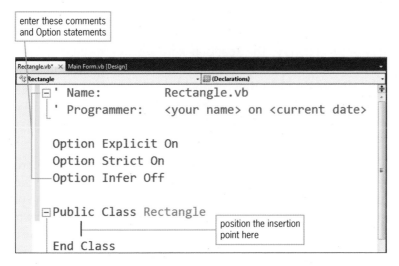

Figure 11-11 Comments and Option statements entered in the class file

A room's floor is an object. More specifically, it is a rectangular object that has two attributes: length and width. Rather than using Public variables to represent both attributes, the Rectangle class will use Private variables and Property procedures.

Private Variables and Property Procedures

Unlike a class's Public variables, its Private variables are not visible to applications that contain an instance of the class. Because of this, the names of the Private variables will not appear in the IntelliSense list as you are coding, nor will they be recognized within the application's code. A class's Private variables can be used only by instructions within the class itself. The naming convention for a class's Private variables is to use the underscore as the first character in the name and then camel case for the remainder of the name. Following this naming convention, you will use the names `_dblLength` and `_dblWidth` for the Private variables in the Rectangle class.

START HERE **To include Private variables in the Rectangle class:**

1. Enter the following two Private statements. Press **Enter** twice after typing the last statement.

    Private _dblLength As Double
    Private _dblWidth As Double

2. Save the solution.

When an application instantiates an object, only the Public members of the object's class are visible to the application; the application cannot access the Private members of the class. Using OOP terminology, the Public members are "exposed" to the application, whereas the Private members are "hidden" from the application. For an application to assign data to or retrieve data from a Private variable in a class, it must use a Public property. In other words, an application cannot directly refer to a Private variable in a class. Rather, it must refer to the variable indirectly, through the use of a Public property.

You create a Public property using a **Property procedure**. Figure 11-12 shows the syntax of a Property procedure. In most cases, a Property procedure header begins with the keywords `Public Property`. However, as the syntax indicates, the header also can include one of the following keywords: `ReadOnly` or `WriteOnly`. The **ReadOnly keyword** indicates that the property's value can be retrieved (read) by an application, but the application cannot set (write to) the property. The property would get its value from the class itself rather than from the application. The **WriteOnly keyword** indicates that an application can set the property's value, but it cannot retrieve the value. In this case, the value would be set by the application for use within the class.

A one-dimensional array's Length property is an example of a ReadOnly property. You learned about the Length property in Chapter 9.

Following the `Property` keyword in the header is the name of the property. You should use nouns and adjectives to name a property and enter the name using Pascal case, as in Side, Bonus, and AnnualSales. Following the property name is an optional *parameterList* enclosed in parentheses, the keyword **As**, and the property's *dataType*. The dataType must match the data type of the Private variable associated with the Property procedure.

Between a Property procedure's header and footer, you include a Get block of code, a Set block of code, or both Get and Set blocks of code. The appropriate block or blocks of code to include depends on the keywords contained in the procedure header. If the header contains the `ReadOnly` keyword, you include only a Get block of code in the Property procedure. The code contained in the **Get block** allows an application to retrieve the contents of the Private variable associated with the property. In the Property procedure shown in Example 2 in Figure 11-12, the `ReadOnly` keyword indicates that an application can retrieve the contents of the Bonus property, but it cannot set the property's value. If the header contains the `WriteOnly` keyword, on the other hand, you include only a Set block of code in the procedure. The code in the **Set block** allows an application to assign a value to the Private variable associated with the property. In the Property procedure shown in Example 3 in Figure 11-12, the `WriteOnly` keyword indicates that an application can assign a value to the AnnualSales property, but it cannot retrieve the property's contents. If the Property procedure header does not contain the `ReadOnly` or `WriteOnly` keywords, you include both a Get block of code and a Set block of code in the procedure, as shown in Example 1 in

Figure 11-12. In this case, an application can both retrieve and set the Side property's value. A Public Property procedure creates a property that is visible to any application that contains an instance of the class.

Property procedure

<u>Syntax</u>
Public [ReadOnly | WriteOnly] Property *propertyName*[**(***parameterList***)**] **As** *dataType*
   Get
      [*instructions*]
      Return *privateVariable*
   End Get
   Set(ByVal value As *dataType***)**
      [*instructions*]
      privateVariable = {**value** | *defaultValue*}
   End Set
End Property

<u>Example 1 – an application can both retrieve and set the Side property's value</u>
```
Private _intSide As Integer

Public Property Side As Integer
     Get
          Return _intSide
     End Get
     Set(ByVal value As Integer)
          If value > 0 Then
               _intSide = value
          Else
               _intSide = 0
          End If
     End Set
End Property
```

<u>Example 2 – an application can retrieve, but not set, the Bonus property's value</u>
```
Private _dblBonus As Double

Public ReadOnly Property Bonus As Double
     Get
          Return _dblBonus
     End Get
End Property
```

<u>Example 3 – an application can set, but not retrieve, the AnnualSales property's value</u>
```
Private _decAnnualSales As Decimal

Public WriteOnly Property AnnualSales As Decimal
     Set(ByVal value As Decimal)
          _decAnnualSales = value
     End Set
End Property
```

Figure 11-12   Syntax and examples of a Property procedure

The Get block contains the **Get statement**, which begins with the keyword `Get` and ends with the keywords `End Get`. Most times, you will enter only the `Return` *privateVariable* instruction within the Get statement. The instruction directs the computer to return the contents of the Private variable associated with the property. In Example 1 in Figure 11-12, the `Return _intSide` statement tells the computer to return the contents of the `_intSide` variable, which is the Private variable associated with the Side property. Similarly, the `Return _dblBonus` statement in Example 2 tells the computer to return the contents of the `_dblBonus` variable, which is the Private variable associated with the Bonus property. Example 3 does not contain a Get statement, because the AnnualSales property is designated as a `WriteOnly` property.

The Set block contains the **Set statement**, which begins with the keyword `Set` and ends with the keywords `End Set`. Following the `Set` keyword is a parameter enclosed in parentheses. The parameter begins with the keywords `ByVal value As`. The keywords are followed by a *dataType*, which must match the data type of the Private variable associated with the Property procedure. The `value` parameter temporarily stores the value that is passed to the property by the application. You can enter one or more instructions within the Set statement. One of the instructions should assign the contents of the `value` parameter to the Private variable associated with the property. In Example 3 in Figure 11-12, the `_decAnnualSales = value` statement assigns the contents of the property's `value` parameter to the Private `_decAnnualSales` variable.

In the Set statement, you often will include instructions to validate the value received from the application before assigning it to the Private variable. The Set statement in Example 1 in Figure 11-12 includes a selection structure that determines whether the side measurement received from the application is valid. In this case, a valid side measurement is an integer that is greater than 0. If the side measurement is valid, the `_intSide = value` instruction assigns the integer stored in the `value` parameter to the Private `_intSide` variable. Otherwise, the `_intSide = 0` instruction assigns a default value (in this case, 0) to the variable. The Property procedure in Example 2 in Figure 11-12 does not contain a Set statement, because the Bonus property is designated as a `ReadOnly` property.

START HERE

To enter a Property procedure for each Private variable in the Rectangle class:

1. The insertion point should be positioned in the blank line above the End Class clause. Enter the following Property procedure header and Get clause. When you press Enter after typing the Get clause, the Code Editor automatically enters the End Get clause, the Set statement, and the End Property clause.

   Public Property Length As Double
   Get

2. Recall that, in most cases, the Get statement simply returns the contents of the Private variable associated with the Property procedure. Type the following statement, but don't press Enter:

   Return _dblLength

3. The Set statement should assign either the contents of its `value` parameter or a default value to the Private variable associated with the Property procedure. In this case, you will assign the integer stored

in the **value** parameter only when the integer is greater than 0; otherwise, you will assign the number 0. Click the **blank line** above the End Set clause and then enter the following selection structure:

If value > 0 Then
   _dblLength = value
Else
   _dblLength = 0
End If

4. Save the solution. Figure 11-13 shows the Length Property procedure associated with the **_dblLength** variable.

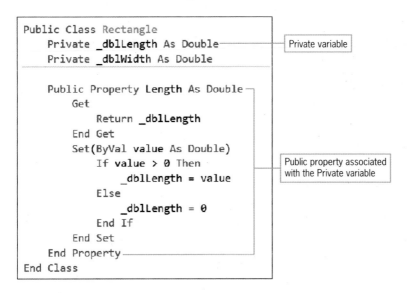

```
Public Class Rectangle
     Private _dblLength As Double ──────── Private variable
     Private _dblWidth As Double

     Public Property Length As Double ─┐
         Get
                Return _dblLength
         End Get
         Set(ByVal value As Double)
              If value > 0 Then          Public property associated
                  _dblLength = value      with the Private variable
              Else
                  _dblLength = 0
              End If
         End Set
     End Property ─────────────────────┘
End Class
```

Figure 11-13   Length Property procedure entered in the class

5. Now you will enter a Property procedure for the **_dblWidth** variable. Insert two blank lines below the End Property clause. Enter the following Property procedure header and Get clause:

Public Property Width As Double
Get

6. Now type the following Return statement in the line below the Get clause, but don't press Enter:

Return _dblWidth

7. Click the **blank line** above the End Set clause and then enter the following selection structure:

If value > 0 Then
   _dblWidth = value
Else
   _dblWidth = 0
End If

8. Save the solution.

You have finished entering the class's Private variables and Property procedures. The class's methods are next. The first method you will learn about is a constructor.

629

Constructors

Most classes contain at least one constructor. A **constructor** is a class method, always named New, whose sole purpose is to initialize the class's Private variables. Constructors never return a value, so they are always Sub procedures rather than Function procedures. The syntax for creating a constructor is shown in Figure 11-14. Notice that a constructor's *parameterList* is optional. A constructor that has no parameters, like the constructor in Example 1 in Figure 11-14, is called the **default constructor**. A class can have only one default constructor. A class that contains one or more parameters, like the constructor in Example 2, is called a **parameterized constructor**. A class can have as many parameterized constructors as needed; however, the parameterList in each parameterized constructor must be unique within the class. The method name (in this case, New) combined with its optional parameterList is called the method's **signature**.

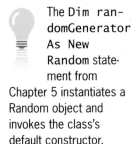

The Dim ran-domGenerator As New Random statement from Chapter 5 instantiates a Random object and invokes the class's default constructor.

When an object is instantiated, the computer uses one of the class's constructors to initialize the class's Private variables. If a class contains more than one constructor, the computer determines the appropriate constructor by matching the number, data type, and position of the arguments in the statement that instantiates the object with the number, data type, and position of the parameters listed in each constructor's parameterList. Examples of statements that will invoke the default constructor in Figure 11-14 include `Dim floor As New Rectangle` and `floor = New Rectangle`. (Recall that the `New` keyword tells the computer to instantiate the object.) The default constructor is used because neither of the statements contains any arguments. Examples of statements that will invoke the parameterized constructor in Figure 11-14 include `Dim floor As New Rectangle(10.5, 12.5)` and `floor = New Rectangle(dblRoomLen, dblRoomWid)`. In this case, the parameterized constructor is used because both statements contain two arguments whose data type is Double.

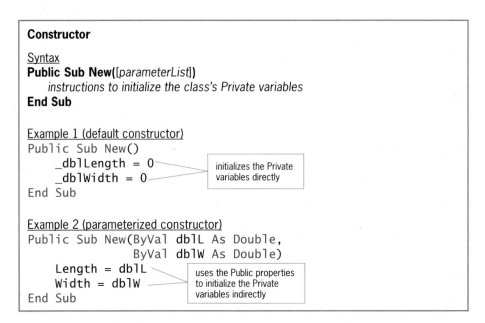

Figure 11-14   Syntax and examples of a constructor

As Figure 11-14 shows, a default constructor is allowed to initialize the class's Private variables directly. The default constructor in Example 1, for instance, assigns the number 0 to the class's Private `_dblLength` and `_dblWidth` variables. Parameterized constructors, on the other hand, should use the class's Public properties to access the Private variables indirectly. This is because the values passed to a parameterized constructor come from the application rather than from the class itself. Values that originate outside of the class should always be assigned to the Private variables indirectly, through the Public properties. Doing this ensures that the Property procedure's Set block, which typically contains validation code, is processed. The parameterized constructor in Example 2 in Figure 11-14, for instance, uses the Public Length property to initialize the Private `_dblLength` variable, thereby invoking the validation code in the Length property.

START HERE

To include a default constructor in the Rectangle class:

1. Insert two blank lines below the Width property's End Property clause.

2. Enter the following default constructor:

    Public Sub New()
    _dblLength = 0
    _dblWidth = 0
    End Sub

Methods Other than Constructors

Except for constructors, which must be Sub procedures, the other methods in a class can be either Sub procedures or Function procedures. Recall from Chapter 7 that the difference between these two types of procedures is that a Function procedure returns a value after performing its assigned task, whereas a Sub procedure does not return a value. Figure 11-15 shows the syntax for a method that is not a constructor. Like property names, method names should be entered using Pascal case. However, unlike property names, the first word in a method name should be a verb, and any subsequent words should be nouns and adjectives. Figure 11-15 also includes two examples of a method that allows a Rectangle object to calculate its area. Notice that you can write the method as either a Function procedure or a Sub procedure.

631

Method that is not a constructor

Syntax
Public {Sub | Function} *methodName***(**[*parameterList*]**)** **[As** *dataType*]
    instructions
End {Sub | Function}

Example 1 (coded as a Function procedure)
```
Public Function GetArea() As Double
    Return _dblLength * _dblWidth
End Function
```


Example 2 (coded as a Sub procedure)
```
Public Sub GetArea(ByRef dblA As Double)
    dblA = _dblLength * _dblWidth
End Sub
```

Figure 11-15   Syntax and examples of a method that is not a constructor

START HERE

To enter the GetArea method from Example 1:

1. Insert two blank lines below the default constructor's End Sub clause and then enter the following GetArea method:

   Public Function GetArea() As Double
       Return _dblLength * _dblWidth
   End Function

2. The Rectangle class definition is now complete. Save the solution.

Coding the Carpet Haven Application

The Calculate button's Click event procedure is the only procedure you need to code in the Carpet Haven application. Figure 11-16 shows the procedure's pseudocode.

---

btnCalc Click event procedure
1. instantiate a Rectangle object to represent the floor
2. declare variables to store the price per square yard, required number of square yards, and carpet cost
3. assign the input data to the appropriate properties and variable
4. calculate the required number of square yards by dividing the floor's area by 9
5. calculate the carpet cost by multiplying the price per square yard by the required number of square yards
6. display the required number of square yards and the carpet cost

Figure 11-16   Pseudocode for the Calculate button's Click event procedure

To code the Calculate button's Click event procedure:

START HERE

1. Click the **designer window's tab** and then open the Code Editor window. Replace <your name> and <current date> in the comments with your name and the current date, respectively.

2. Open the code template for the btnCalc control's Click event procedure. Type the following comment and then press **Enter** twice:

   ' displays square yards and cost of carpet

3. The first step in the pseudocode is to instantiate a Rectangle object to represent the room's floor. Type the following Dim statement and then press **Enter** twice:

   Dim floor As New Rectangle

4. Now you will declare variables to store the following items: the price of a square yard of carpet, the number of square yards needed, and the cost of the carpet. You won't need variables to store the floor's length and width measurements, because the procedure will assign those values to the Rectangle object's Length and Width properties, respectively. Enter the following three Dim statements. Press **Enter** twice after typing the last Dim statement.

   Dim dblPriceSqYd As Double
   Dim dblSqYards As Double
   Dim dblCost As Double

5. Next, you will assign the length and width entries to the Rectangle object's Length and Width properties, respectively. You also will assign the price entry to the **dblPriceSqYd** variable. Enter the three TryParse methods shown in Figure 11-17, and then position the insertion point as shown in the figure. Notice that when you press the period after typing **floor** in the first two TryParse methods, the **floor** object's Length and Width properties appear in the IntelliSense list.

```
    Dim dblCost As Double

    Double.TryParse(lstLength.SelectedItem.ToString, floor.Length)
    Double.TryParse(lstWidth.SelectedItem.ToString, floor.Width)
    Double.TryParse(lstPrice.SelectedItem.ToString, dblPriceSqYd)

    |          position the insertion
               point here
End Sub
```

enter these TryParse methods

Figure 11-17 TryParse methods entered in the procedure

6. The fourth step in the pseudocode is to calculate the required number of square yards by dividing the floor's area (which is in square feet) by the number 9. You need to divide by 9 because there are 9 square feet in a square yard. You can use the Rectangle object's GetArea method to calculate and return the area of the floor. Enter the following comment and assignment statement. Here again, notice that when you

press the period after typing **floor**, the **floor** object's GetArea method appears in the IntelliSense list.

' calculate the required square yards
dblSqYards = floor.GetArea / 9

7. The next step is to calculate the cost of the carpet by multiplying the price per square yard by the required number of square yards. Enter the following comment and assignment statement. Press **Enter** twice after typing the assignment statement.

' calculate the carpet cost
dblCost = dblPriceSqYd * dblSqYards

8. The last step in the pseudocode is to display the required number of square yards and the carpet cost. Enter the following comment and assignment statements:

' display square yards and carpet cost
lblSquareYards.Text = dblSqYards.ToString("N1")
lblCost.Text = dblCost.ToString("C2")

Figure 11-18 shows the Rectangle class definition contained in the Rectangle.vb file. It also shows the btnCalc control's Click event procedure contained in the Main Form.vb. file.

beginning of the class definition (entered in the Rectangle.vb file)

```
Public Class Rectangle
    Private _dblLength As Double
    Private _dblWidth As Double

    Public Property Length As Double
        Get
            Return _dblLength
        End Get
        Set(ByVal value As Double)
            If value > 0 Then
                _dblLength = value
            Else
                _dblLength = 0
            End If
        End Set
    End Property

    Public Property Width As Double
        Get
            Return _dblWidth
        End Get
        Set(ByVal value As Double)
            If value > 0 Then
                _dblWidth = value
```

Figure 11-18 Rectangle class definition and btnCalc control's Click event procedure
(continues)

(continued)

```
            Else
                _dblWidth = 0
            End If
        End Set
    End Property

    Public Sub New()
        _dblLength = 0
        _dblWidth = 0
    End Sub

    Public Function GetArea() As Double
        Return _dblLength * _dblWidth
    End Function
End Class

Private Sub btnCalc_Click(ByVal sender As Object,
ByVal e As System.EventArgs) Handles btnCalc.Click
    ' displays square yards and cost of carpet

    Dim floor As New Rectangle

    Dim dblPriceSqYd As Double
    Dim dblSqYards As Double
    Dim dblCost As Double

    Double.TryParse(lstLength.SelectedItem.ToString, floor.Length)
    Double.TryParse(lstWidth.SelectedItem.ToString, floor.Width)
    Double.TryParse(lstPrice.SelectedItem.ToString, dblPriceSqYd)

    ' calculate the required square yards
    dblSqYards = floor.GetArea / 9
    ' calculate the carpet cost
    dblCost = dblPriceSqYd * dblSqYards

    ' display square yards and carpet cost
    lblSquareYards.Text = dblSqYards.ToString("N1")
    lblCost.Text = dblCost.ToString("C2")

End Sub
```

- beginning of the Calculate button's Click event procedure (entered in the Main Form.vb file)
- instantiates a Rectangle object
- assigns values to the object's Public properties
- invokes the object's GetArea method

635

Figure 11-18　Rectangle class definition and btnCalc control's Click event procedure

To test the Carpet Haven application:

START HERE

1. Save the solution and then start the application. Click **9.0** in the Length list box and then click **8.0** in the Width list box. Click **7.50** in the Price list box and then click the **Calculate** button. The Dim floor As New Rectangle instruction in the button's Click event procedure instantiates a Rectangle object. At this point, the computer processes the class's default constructor, which initializes the object's Private variables (_dblLength and _dblWidth) to the number 0.

The next three Dim statements in the procedure create and initialize three Double variables. Next, the TryParse methods assign the appropriate values to the Rectangle object's Public properties and to the `dblPriceSqYd` variable. The procedure then calculates the required number of square yards of carpet, using the Rectangle object's GetArea method to calculate and return the area of the floor. Finally, the procedure calculates the cost of the carpet and then displays both the required number of square yards and the cost. See Figure 11-19.

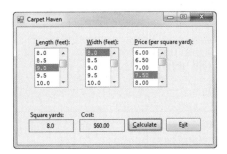

Figure 11-19   Square yards and cost displayed in the interface

2. On your own, test the application using different lengths, widths, and prices. When you are finished, click the **Exit** button. Close the Main Form.vb and Rectangle.vb windows and then close the solution.

YOU DO IT 1!

Create a Visual Basic Windows application named YouDoIt 1. Save the application in the VB2010\Chap11 folder. Add a text box, a label, and a button to the form. Add a class file named Circle.vb to the project. Define a class named Circle. The class should contain one attribute: the circle's radius. It also should contain a default constructor and a method that calculates and returns the circle's area. Use the following formula to calculate the area: $3.141592 * radius^2$. Open the form's Code Editor window. The button's Click event procedure should display the circle's area, using the radius entered by the user. Code the procedure. Save the solution and then start and test the application. Close the solution.

Example 3—A Class that Contains a Parameterized Constructor

In this example, you will add a parameterized constructor to the Rectangle class created in Example 2. Recall that a parameterized constructor is simply a constructor that has parameters. You then will modify the Carpet Haven application to use the parameterized constructor.

START HERE ▶ **To add a parameterized constructor to the Rectangle.vb file:**

1. Use Windows to make a copy of the Carpet Haven Solution folder from Example 2. Rename the copy **Modified Carpet Haven Solution**. Open the Carpet Haven Solution (Carpet Haven Solution.sln) file contained in the Modified Carpet Haven Solution folder. Open the designer window.

Example 3—A Class that Contains a Parameterized Constructor   LESSON A

2. Right-click **Rectangle.vb** in the Solution Explorer window and then click **View Code**.

3. Locate the default constructor. Click the **blank line** below the default constructor's End Sub clause and then press **Enter** twice to insert two blank lines. Press the **up arrow** key on your keyboard and then enter the following parameterized constructor:

Public Sub New(ByVal dblL As Double, ByVal dblW As Double)
    Length = dblL
    Width = dblW
End Sub

4. Save the solution and then close the Rectangle.vb window.

Figure 11-20 shows the Rectangle class's default and parameterized constructors. Unlike the default constructor, which automatically initializes the Private variables to 0 when a Rectangle object is created, a parameterized constructor allows an application to specify the object's initial values. In this case, the initial values must have the Double data type because the constructor's parameterList contains two Double variables. You include the initial values, enclosed in a set of parentheses, in the statement that instantiates the object. In other words, you include them in the statement that contains the **New** keyword, such as the `Dim floor As New Rectangle(10.5, 12.5)` statement or the `floor = New Rectangle(dblRoomLen, dblRoomWid)` statement.

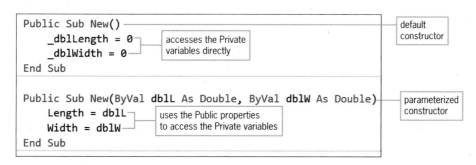

```
Public Sub New()
    _dblLength = 0          accesses the Private        default
    _dblWidth = 0           variables directly          constructor
End Sub


Public Sub New(ByVal dblL As Double, ByVal dblW As Double)   parameterized
    Length = dblL           uses the Public properties          constructor
    Width = dblW            to access the Private variables
End Sub
```

Figure 11-20   Default and parameterized constructors

To use the parameterized constructor in the modified Carpet Haven application: START HERE

1. Open the form's Code Editor window. Locate the btnCalc control's Click event procedure.

2. Delete the **New** keyword from the first Dim statement. The statement should now say `Dim floor As Rectangle`.

3. Click the **blank line** below the `Dim floor As Rectangle` statement and then enter the following two declaration statements:

Dim dblRoomLen As Double
Dim dblRoomWid As Double

4. In the first TryParse method, replace `floor.Length` with **dblRoomLen**. Then, in the second TryParse method, replace `floor.Width` with **dblRoomWid**.

5. Click the **blank line** below the last TryParse method and then press **Enter**. Enter the following comment and assignment statement:

' instantiate and initialize a Rectangle object
floor = New Rectangle(dblRoomLen, dblRoomWid)

Figure 11-21 shows the modified Rectangle class definition and modified btnCalc control's Click event procedure. The modifications made to the original code (shown earlier in Figure 11-18) are shaded in Figure 11-21. When the user clicks the Calculate button, the `Dim floor As Rectangle` instruction in the button's Click event procedure creates a variable that can store a Rectangle object; but it does not create the object. The remaining Dim statements create and initialize five Double variables. Next, the TryParse methods assign the input values to the `dblRoomLen`, `dblRoomWid`, and `dblPriceSqYd` variables.

The next statement in the procedure, `floor = New Rectangle(dblRoomLen, dblRoomWid)`, instantiates a Rectangle object. The two Double arguments in the statement tell the computer to use the class's parameterized constructor (rather than its default constructor) to initialize the class's Private variables. In this case, the computer passes the two Double arguments (*by value*) to the parameterized constructor, which stores them in its `dblL` and `dblW` variables. The `Length = dblL` and `Width = dblW` instructions in the constructor assign the values stored in the `dblL` and `dblW` parameters to the Public Length and Width properties, respectively. When you assign a value to a property, the computer passes the value to the property's Set statement, where it is stored in the Set statement's `value` parameter. In this case, the selection structure in the Length property's Set statement compares the value stored in the `value` parameter with the number 0. If the value is greater than 0, the selection structure's true path assigns the value to the Private `_dblLength` variable; otherwise, its false path assigns the number 0 to the variable. Similarly, the selection structure in the Width property's Set statement compares the value stored in the `value` parameter with the number 0. If the value is greater than 0, the selection structure's true path assigns the value to the Private `_dblWidth` variable; otherwise, its false path assigns the number 0 to the variable. Notice that a parameterized constructor uses the class's Public properties to access the Private variables indirectly. This is because the values passed to a parameterized constructor come from the application rather than from the class itself. As mentioned earlier, values that originate outside of the class should always be assigned to the Private variables indirectly, through the Public properties. Doing this ensures that the Property procedure's Set block, which typically contains validation code, is processed.

After the Rectangle object is instantiated and its Private variables are initialized, the Click event procedure uses the object's GetArea method to calculate and return the area of the floor. The procedure uses the area to calculate the required number of square yards of carpet. Finally, the procedure calculates the cost of the carpet and then displays both the required number of square yards and the cost.

Example 3—A Class that Contains a Parameterized Constructor   LESSON A

```
Public Class Rectangle
    Private _dblLength As Double
    Private _dblWidth As Double

    Public Property Length As Double
        Get
            Return _dblLength
        End Get
        Set(ByVal value As Double)
            If value > 0 Then
                _dblLength = value
            Else
                _dblLength = 0
            End If
        End Set
    End Property

    Public Property Width As Double
        Get
            Return _dblWidth
        End Get
        Set(ByVal value As Double)
            If value > 0 Then
                _dblWidth = value
            Else
                _dblWidth = 0
            End If
        End Set
    End Property

    Public Sub New()
        _dblLength = 0
        _dblWidth = 0
    End Sub

    Public Sub New(ByVal dblL As Double, ByVal dblW As Double)
        Length = dblL
        Width = dblW
    End Sub

    Public Function GetArea() As Double
        Return _dblLength * _dblWidth
    End Function
End Class

Private Sub btnCalc_Click(ByVal sender As Object,
ByVal e As System.EventArgs) Handles btnCalc.Click
    ' displays square yards and cost of carpet
```

parameterized
constructor

639

Figure 11-21   Modified Rectangle class definition and modified btnCalc control's Click event procedure *(continues)*

(continued)

declares a variable that can
store a Rectangle object

```
Dim floor As Rectangle
Dim dblRoomLen As Double
Dim dblRoomWid As Double

Dim dblPriceSqYd As Double
Dim dblSqYards As Double
Dim dblCost As Double

Double.TryParse(lstLength.SelectedItem.ToString, dblRoomLen)
Double.TryParse(lstWidth.SelectedItem.ToString, dblRoomWid)
Double.TryParse(lstPrice.SelectedItem.ToString, dblPriceSqYd)
```

uses the parameterized
constructor to instantiate and
initialize a Rectangle object

```
' instantiate and initialize a Rectangle object
floor = New Rectangle(dblRoomLen, dblRoomWid)

' calculate the required square yards
dblSqYards = floor.GetArea / 9
' calculate the carpet cost
dblCost = dblPriceSqYd * dblSqYards

' display square yards and carpet cost
lblSquareYards.Text = dblSqYards.ToString("N1")
lblCost.Text = dblCost.ToString("C2")

End Sub
```

Figure 11-21   Modified Rectangle class definition and modified btnCalc control's Click event procedure

START HERE

To test the modified Carpet Haven application:

1. Save the solution and then start the application. Click **9.0** in the Length list box and then click **8.0** in the Width list box. Click **7.50** in the Price list box and then click the **Calculate** button. The required number of square yards and the cost appear in the interface, as shown earlier in Figure 11-19.

2. On your own, test the application using different lengths, widths, and prices. When you are finished, click the **Exit** button. Close the Main Form.vb and Rectangle.vb windows and then close the solution.

Example 4—Reusing a Class

In Examples 2 and 3, you used the Rectangle class to create an object that represented the floor in a room. In this example, you will use the Rectangle class to represent a square pizza. A square is simply a rectangle that has four equal sides. As mentioned earlier, the ability to use an object—in this case, a Rectangle object—for more than one purpose saves programming time and money, which contributes to the popularity of object-oriented programming.

Example 4—Reusing a Class   LESSON A

To add the Rectangle.vb file to the Pizza Roma application:

1. Open the Pizza Roma Solution (Pizza Roma Solution.sln) file contained in the VB2010\Chap11\Pizza Roma Solution folder. If necessary, open the designer window. The interface provides text boxes for entering the side measurement of the entire pizza, as well as the side measurement of a slice of pizza. The application will use both measurements to calculate the number of pizza slices that can be cut from the entire pizza. See Figure 11-22.

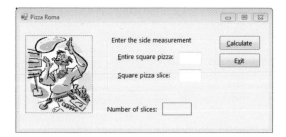

Figure 11-22 Pizza Roma application's interface

2. First, you will copy the Rectangle.vb class file from the modified Carpet Haven application to the Pizza Roma application. Use Windows to copy the Rectangle.vb file from the VB2010\Chap11\Modified Carpet Haven Solution\Carpet Haven Project folder to the Pizza Roma Solution\Pizza Roma Project folder. (If you did not complete the Carpet Haven application, you can copy the Rectangle.vb file contained in the VB2010\Chap11 folder.)

3. Next, you will add the Rectangle.vb file to the Pizza Roma project. Click **Project** on the menu bar and then click **Add Existing Item**. Open the Pizza Roma Project folder (if necessary) and then click **Rectangle.vb** in the list of filenames. Click the **Add** button. Temporarily display the Solution Explorer window (if necessary) to verify that the Rectangle.vb file was added to the project.

4. Open the Code Editor window. Replace <your name> and <current date> in the comments with your name and the current date, respectively.

5. Open the code template for the btnCalc control's Click event procedure and then enter the following two comments. Press **Enter** twice after typing the last comment.

   ' displays the number of square pizza slices
   ' that can be cut from a square pizza

Figure 11-23 shows the pseudocode for the btnCalc control's Click event procedure.

btnCalc Click event procedure
1. instantiate a Rectangle object to represent the entire square pizza
2. instantiate a Rectangle object to represent a square pizza slice
3. declare variables to store the area of the entire pizza, the area of a pizza slice, and the number of slices
4. assign the input data to the properties of the appropriate Rectangle object
5. calculate the area of the entire pizza
6. calculate the area of a pizza slice
7. if the area of a pizza slice is > 0 then
        calculate the number of pizza slices by dividing the area of the
          entire pizza by the area of a pizza slice
    else
        assign 0 as the number of pizza slices
    end if
8. display the number of pizza slices

Figure 11-23   Pseudocode for the btnCalc control's Click event procedure

START HERE ▶

To code the btnCalc control's Click event procedure:

1. The first two steps in the pseudocode are to instantiate two Rectangle objects to represent the entire pizza and a pizza slice. Enter the following Dim statements:

    Dim entirePizza As New Rectangle
    Dim pizzaSlice As New Rectangle

2. The third step in the pseudocode is to declare variables to store the area of the entire pizza, the area of a pizza slice, and the number of slices. You won't need variables to store the side measurements entered by the user, because the procedure will assign those values to each Rectangle object's Length and Width properties. Enter the following three Dim statements. Press **Enter** twice after typing the last Dim statement.

    Dim dblEntireArea As Double
    Dim dblSliceArea As Double
    Dim dblSlices As Double

3. The fourth step in the pseudocode is to assign the side measurements to the properties of the appropriate Rectangle object. Enter the following four lines of code. Notice that when you press the period after typing either `entirePizza` or `pizzaSlice`, the object's Length and Width properties appear in the IntelliSense list. Press **Enter** twice after typing the last line.

    Double.TryParse(txtEntirePizza.Text, entirePizza.Length)
    Double.TryParse(txtEntirePizza.Text, entirePizza.Width)
    Double.TryParse(txtPizzaSlice.Text, pizzaSlice.Length)
    Double.TryParse(txtPizzaSlice.Text, pizzaSlice.Width)

Example 4—Reusing a Class   LESSON A

4. The fifth and sixth steps in the pseudocode are to calculate the area of the entire pizza and the area of a slice of pizza, respectively. You can accomplish both tasks using the Rectangle object's GetArea method. Because the method already contains the code needed to calculate the area of a rectangle, you do not need to waste time planning and then reentering the code. Enter the following comment and assignment statement:

' calculate area of entire pizza and pizza slice
dblEntireArea = entirePizza.GetArea
dblSliceArea = pizzaSlice.GetArea

5. The seventh step in the pseudocode is a selection structure that determines whether the pizza slice area is greater than 0. You need to make this determination because the pizza slice area is used as the divisor when calculating the number of pizza slices. If the area is greater than 0, the selection structure's true path should calculate the number of pizza slices; otherwise, its false path should assign 0 as the number of pizza slices. Enter the following comment and selection structure:

' calculate number of slices
If dblSliceArea > 0 Then
**   dblSlices = dblEntireArea / dblSliceArea**
Else
**   dblSlices = 0**
End If

6. The last step in the pseudocode is to display the number of pizza slices. Insert a blank line below the End If clause and then enter the following comment and assignment statement:

' display number of slices
lblSlices.Text = dblSlices.ToString("N1")

The btnCalc control's Click event procedure is shown in Figure 11-24.

```
Private Sub btnCalc_Click(ByVal sender As Object,
ByVal e As System.EventArgs) Handles btnCalc.Click
    ' displays the number of square pizza slices
    ' that can be cut from a square pizza

    Dim entirePizza As New Rectangle          instantiates two
    Dim pizzaSlice As New Rectangle           Rectangle objects
    Dim dblEntireArea As Double
    Dim dblSliceArea As Double
    Dim dblSlices As Double

    Double.TryParse(txtEntirePizza.Text, entirePizza.Length)
    Double.TryParse(txtEntirePizza.Text, entirePizza.Width)    assigns values to each
    Double.TryParse(txtPizzaSlice.Text, pizzaSlice.Length)     object's Public properties
    Double.TryParse(txtPizzaSlice.Text, pizzaSlice.Width)
```

Figure 11-24   btnCalc control's Click event procedure *(continues)*

(continued)

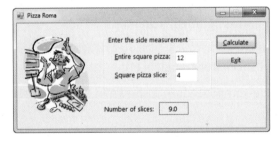

invokes each object's GetArea method

```
        ' calculate area of entire pizza and pizza slice
        dblEntireArea = entirePizza.GetArea
        dblSliceArea = pizzaSlice.GetArea
        ' calculate number of slices
        If dblSliceArea > 0 Then
            dblSlices = dblEntireArea / dblSliceArea
        Else
            dblSlices = 0
        End If
        ' display number of slices
        lblSlices.Text = dblSlices.ToString("N1")

End Sub
```

Figure 11-24   btnCalc control's Click event procedure

START HERE   **To test the application's code:**

1. Save the solution and then start the application. First, you will determine the number of 4-inch slices that can be cut from a 12-inch pizza. Type **12** in the Entire square pizza box and then type **4** in the Square pizza slice box. Click the **Calculate** button. As Figure 11-25 indicates, nine 4-inch square pizza slices can be cut from a 12-inch square pizza.

Figure 11-25   Number of pizza slices shown in the interface

2. On your own, test the application using different side measurements. When you are finished, click the **Exit** button. Close the Code Editor window and then close the solution.

Lesson A Summary

- To define a class:

  Use the Class statement. The statement's syntax is shown in Figure 11-2.

- To add a class file to a project:

  Click Project on the menu bar and then click Add Class. In the Name box, type the name of the class followed by a period and the letters vb, and then click the Add button.

644

- To instantiate (create) an object from a class:

  Use either of the syntax versions shown in Figure 11-4.

- To create a Property procedure:

  Use the syntax shown in Figure 11-12. The Get block allows an application to retrieve the contents of the Private variable associated with the Property procedure. The Set block allows an application to assign a value to the Private variable associated with the Property procedure.

- To create a constructor:

  Use the syntax shown in Figure 11-14. A constructor that has no parameters is called the default constructor. A class can have only one default constructor. A constructor that has one or more parameters is called a parameterized constructor. A class can have as many parameterized constructors as needed. All constructors are Sub procedures that are named New. Each constructor must have a unique parameterList (if any) within the class.

- To create a method other than a constructor:

  Use the syntax shown in Figure 11-15.

Lesson A Key Terms

Attributes—the characteristics that describe an object

Behaviors—an object's methods and events

Class—a pattern that the computer follows when instantiating (creating) an object

Class statement—the statement used to define a class in Visual Basic

Constructor—a method whose instructions are automatically processed each time the class is used to instantiate an object; its purpose is to initialize the class's Private variables; always a Sub procedure named New

Default constructor—a constructor that has no parameters; a class can have only one default constructor

Encapsulates—an OOP term that means "contains"

Events—the actions to which an object can respond

Get block—the section of a Property procedure that contains the Get statement

Get statement—appears in a Get block in a Property procedure; contains the code that allows an application to retrieve the contents of the Private variable associated with the property

Instance—an object created from a class

Instantiated—the process of creating an object from a class

Methods—the actions that an object is capable of performing

Object-oriented programming language—a programming language that allows the use of objects to accomplish a program's goal

OOP—an acronym for object-oriented programming

Parameterized constructor—a constructor that contains one or more parameters

Property procedure—creates a Public property that an application can use to access a Private variable in a class

ReadOnly keyword—used when defining a Property procedure; indicates that the property's value can only be retrieved (read) by an application

Set block—the section of a Property procedure that contains the Set statement

Set statement—appears in a Set block in a Property procedure; contains the code that allows an application to assign a value to the Private variable associated with the property; may also contain validation code

Signature—a method's name combined with its optional parameterList

WriteOnly keyword—used when defining a Property procedure; indicates that an application can only set the property's value

Lesson A Review Questions

1. The name of a class file ends with _____.

    a. .cla

    b. .cls

    c. .vb

    d. none of the above

2. A constructor is _____.

    a. a Function procedure

    b. a Property procedure

    c. a Sub procedure

    d. either a Function procedure or a Sub procedure

3. The Product class contains a Private variable named _intPrice. The variable is associated with the Public Price property. An application instantiates a Product object and assigns it to a variable named item. Which of the following can be used by the application to assign the number 45 to the _intPrice variable?

    a. `_intPrice = 45`

    b. `Price = 45`

    c. `item._intPrice = 45`

    d. `item.Price = 45`

4. The Product class in Review Question 3 also contains a Public method named GetNewPrice. The method is a Function procedure. Which of the following can be used by the application from Review Question 3 to invoke the GetNewPrice method?

   a. `intNewPrice = Call GetNewPrice`

   b. `intNewPrice = Price.GetNewPrice`

   c. `intNewPrice = item.GetNewPrice`

   d. `intNewPrice = item.GetNewPrice(_intPrice)`

5. Which of the following statements is false?

   a. A class can contain only one constructor.

   b. An example of a behavior is the `SetTime` method in a Time class.

   c. An object created from a class is referred to as an instance of the class.

   d. An instance of a class is considered an object.

6. A Private variable in a class can be accessed directly by a Public method in the same class.

   a. True

   b. False

7. An application can access the Private variables in a class _____.

   a. directly

   b. using properties created by Public Property procedures

   c. through Private procedures contained in the class

   d. none of the above

8. To expose a variable or method contained in a class, you declare the variable or method using the keyword _____.

   a. `Exposed`

   b. `Private`

   c. `Public`

   d. `Viewable`

9. Which of the following is the name of the Animal class's default constructor?

   a. Animal

   b. AnimalConstructor

   c. Default

   d. none of the above

10. Which of the following instantiates an Animal object and assigns it to the **dog** variable?

    a. `Dim dog As Animal`

    b. `Dim dog As New Animal`

    c. `Dim dog As Animal`
       `dog = New Animal`

    d. both b and c

11. If you need to validate a value before assigning it to a Private variable, you enter the validation code in the _____ block in a Property procedure.

    a. Assign

    b. Get

    c. Set

    d. Validate

12. The Return statement is entered in the _____ statement in a Property procedure.

    a. Get

    b. Set

13. A class contains a Private variable named `_strCapital`. The variable is associated with a Public property named Capital. Which of the following is the best way for a parameterized constructor to assign the value stored in its `strCapName` parameter to the variable?

    a. `_strCapital = strCapName`

    b. `Capital = strCapName`

    c. `_strCapital.Capital = strCapName`

    d. none of the above

Lesson A Exercises

INTRODUCTORY

1. A class contains more than one constructor. Explain how the computer determines the appropriate constructor to use when instantiating an object.

INTRODUCTORY

2. Write a Class statement that defines a class named Book. The class contains three Public variables named `Title`, `Author`, and `Cost`. The `Title` and `Author` variables are String variables. The `Cost` variable is a Decimal variable. Then use the syntax shown in Version 1 in Figure 11-4 to declare a variable that can store a Book object; name the variable **fiction**. Also write a statement that instantiates the Book object and assigns it to the **fiction** variable.

3. Rewrite the Class statement from Exercise 2 so that it uses Private variables rather than Public variables. Be sure to include the Property procedures and default constructor.

INTRODUCTORY

4. Write a Class statement that defines a class named Tape. The class contains four Private String variables named _strName, _strArtist, _strSongNumber, and _strLength. Name the corresponding properties TapeName, Artist, SongNumber, and Length. Then, use the syntax shown in Version 2 in Figure 11-4 to create a Tape object, assigning it to a variable named blues.

INTRODUCTORY

649

5. The Computer class definition is shown in Figure 11-26. Write a Dim statement that uses the default constructor to instantiate a Computer object in an application. The Dim statement should assign the object to a variable named homeUse. Next, write assignment statements that the application can use to assign the string "IB-50" and the number 2400 to the Model and Cost properties, respectively. Finally, write an assignment statement that the application can use to invoke the GetNewPrice function. Assign the function's return value to a variable named dblNewPrice.

INTRODUCTORY

```
Public Class Computer
    Private _strModel As String
    Private _dblCost As Double

    Public Property Model As String
        Get
            Return _strModel
        End Get
        Set(ByVal value As String)
            _strModel = value
        End Set
    End Property

    Public Property Cost As Double
        Get
            Return _dblCost
        End Get
        Set(ByVal value As Double)
            _dblCost = value
        End Set
    End Property

    Public Sub New()
        _strModel = String.Empty
        _dblCost = 0
    End Sub
```

Figure 11-26 Computer class definition *(continues)*

(continued)

```
        Public Sub New(ByVal strM As String, ByVal dblC As Double)
            Model = strM
            Cost = dblC
        End Sub

        Public Function GetNewPrice() As Double
            Return _dblCost * 1.2
        End Function
    End Class
```

Figure 11-26   Computer class definition

INTRODUCTORY

6. Using the Computer class shown in Figure 11-26, write a Dim statement that uses the parameterized constructor to instantiate a Computer object. Pass the parameterized constructor the string "JK-75" and the number 899.99. The Dim statement should assign the object to a variable named **companyUse**.

INTRODUCTORY

7. An application contains the statement **Dim gaming As Computer**. Using the Computer class shown in Figure 11-26, write an assignment statement that instantiates a Computer object and initializes it using the **strName** and **dblPrice** variables. The statement should assign the object to the **gaming** variable.

INTRODUCTORY

8. In this exercise, you modify the Pizza Roma application completed in the lesson. Use Windows to make a copy of the Pizza Roma Solution folder. Rename the copy Modified Pizza Roma Solution. Open the Pizza Roma Solution (Pizza Roma Solution.sln) file contained in the Modified Pizza Roma Solution folder. Open the designer and Code Editor windows. Modify the btnCalc control's Click event procedure to use the Rectangle class's parameterized constructor. Save the solution and then start and test the application. Close the Code Editor window and then close the solution.

INTRODUCTORY

9. In this exercise, you modify the Willow Pools application completed in the lesson. Use Windows to make a copy of the Willow Pools Solution folder. Rename the copy Modified Willow Pools Solution-Introductory. Open the Willow Pools Solution (Willow Pools Solution.sln) file contained in the Modified Willow Pools Solution-Introductory folder. Open the designer window and then open the RectangularPool.vb file. Modify the RectangularPool class so that it uses Private variables and Public Property procedures rather than Public variables. Include both a default constructor and a parameterized constructor in the class. Save the solution and then start and test the application. Close the Code Editor window and then close the solution.

INTERMEDIATE

10. In this exercise, you modify the Willow Pools application from Exercise 9. Use Windows to make a copy of the Modified Willow Pools Solution-Introductory folder. Rename the copy Modified Willow Pools Solution-Intermediate. Open the Willow Pools Solution

(Willow Pools Solution.sln) file contained in the Modified Willow Pools Solution-Intermediate folder.

a. Open the designer window. Add two labels to the form. Position one of the labels below the Gallons: label, and then change its Text property to Cost:. Position the other label below the lblGallons control and then change its Name and TextAlign properties to lblCost and MiddleCenter, respectively.

b. Open the RectangularPool.vb file. Add a method named GetVolume to the RectangularPool class. The method should calculate and return the volume of a RectangularPool object. The formula for calculating the volume is *length * width * depth*. Save the solution and then close the RectangularPool.vb window.

c. Open the form's Code Editor window. The btnCalc control's Click event procedure should use the RectangularPool object's GetVolume method to determine the pool's volume. It then should pass only the pool's volume to the GetGallons function. The Click event procedure also should calculate and display the cost of filling the pool with water. The charge for water is $1.75 per 1000 gallons (or .00175 per gallon). Make the necessary modifications to the code.

d. Save the solution and then start and test the application. Close the Code Editor window and then close the solution.

11. In this exercise, you create an application that can be used to estimate the cost of laying sod on a rectangular piece of property. **INTERMEDIATE**

a. Create a Visual Basic Windows application. Use the following names for the solution, project, and form file, respectively: Kessler Solution, Kessler Project, and Main Form.vb, respectively. Save the application in the VB2010\Chap11 folder.

b. Use Windows to copy the Rectangle.vb file from the VB2010\Chap11 folder to the Kessler Solution\Kessler Project folder. Use the Project menu to add the Rectangle.vb class file to the project.

c. Create the interface shown in Figure 11-27.

d. Open the form's Code Editor window and then code the application. Save the solution and then start and test the application. Close the Code Editor window and then close the solution.

Figure 11-27 Interface for Exercise 11

INTERMEDIATE

12. In this exercise, you create an application that can be used to calculate the cost of installing a fence around a rectangular area.

a. Create a Visual Basic Windows application. Use the following names for the solution, project, and form file, respectively: Fence Solution, Fence Project, and Main Form.vb. Save the application in the VB2010\Chap11 folder.

b. Use Windows to copy the Rectangle.vb file from the VB2010\Chap11 folder to the Fence Solution\Fence Project folder. Use the Project menu to add the Rectangle.vb class file to the project. Add a method named GetPerimeter to the Rectangle class. The GetPerimeter method should calculate and return the perimeter of a rectangle. To calculate the perimeter, the method will need to add together the length and width measurements and then multiply the sum by 2.

c. Create the interface shown in Figure 11-28.

d. Open the form's Code Editor window and then code the application, which should calculate and display the cost of installing the fence.

e. Save the solution and then start the application. Test the application using 120 feet as the length, 75 feet as the width, and 10 as the cost per linear foot of fencing. The installation cost should be $3,900.00. Close the Main Form.vb and Rectangle.vb windows and then close the solution.

Figure 11-28 Interface for Exercise 12

ADVANCED

13. In this exercise, you define a Triangle class. You also create an application that allows the user to display either a Triangle object's area or its perimeter. The formula for calculating the area of a triangle is $1/2 * base * height$. The formula for calculating the perimeter of a triangle is $a + b + c$, where a, b, and c are the lengths of the sides.

a. Create a Visual Basic Windows application. Use the following names for the solution, project, and form file, respectively: Math Triangle Solution, Math Triangle Project, and Main Form.vb. Save the application in the VB2010\Chap11 folder.

b. Create the interface shown in Figure 11-29.

c. Add a class file to the project. Name the class file Triangle.vb. The Triangle class should verify that the dimensions are greater than zero before assigning the values to the Private variables. The class also should include a method to calculate the area of a triangle and a method to calculate the perimeter of a triangle. Save the solution and then close the Triangle.vb window.

d. Open the form's Code Editor window. Use the InputBox function to get the appropriate data from the user. Save the solution and then start and test the application. Close the Code Editor window and then close the solution.

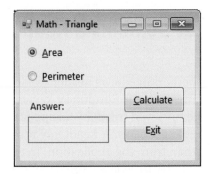

Figure 11-29 Interface for Exercise 13

■ LESSON B

After studying Lesson B, you should be able to:

- Include a ReadOnly property in a class

- Create an auto-implemented property

- Overload a method in a class

Example 5—A Class that Contains a ReadOnly Property

In Lesson A, you learned that a Property procedure's header can include the `ReadOnly` keyword. As you may remember, the `ReadOnly` keyword indicates that the property's value can be retrieved (read) by an application, but the application cannot set (write to) the property. A ReadOnly property gets its value from the class itself rather than from the application. In the next set of steps, you will add a ReadOnly property to a class named CourseGrade. You also will add the default constructor and a method that will assign the appropriate grade to the Private variable associated with the ReadOnly property. You will use the ReadOnly property and the method in the Grade Calculator application, which you will finish coding in the second set of steps. The application displays a grade based on two test scores entered by the user.

START HERE ▶ **To modify the CourseGrade class:**

1. If necessary, start Visual Studio 2010 or Visual Basic 2010 Express. Open the Grade Solution (Grade Solution.sln) file contained in the VB2010\Chap11\Grade Solution folder. If necessary, open the designer window. The interface provides list boxes for entering two test scores, which can range from 0 to 100 points each. See Figure 11-30.

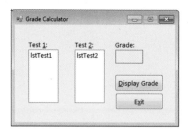

Figure 11-30 Interface for the Grade Calculator application

2. Right-click **CourseGrade.vb** in the Solution Explorer window and then click **View Code**. Replace <your name> and <current date> in the comments with your name and the current date, respectively.

3. The CourseGrade class should contain three attributes: two test scores and a letter grade. The Private variable for the letter grade is missing from the code. Click the **blank line** below the `Private _intScore2 As Integer` statement and then enter the following Private statement:

Private _strGrade As String

Example 5—A Class that Contains a ReadOnly Property **LESSON B**

4. Now you will create a Public property for the Private `_strGrade` variable. You will make the property ReadOnly so that the class (rather than the Grade Calculator application) determines the appropriate grade. By making the property ReadOnly, the application will only be able to retrieve the grade; it will not be able to change the grade. Click the **blank line** immediately above the End Class clause and then enter the following Property procedure header. Notice that when you press Enter after typing the header, the Code Editor automatically includes the Get block of code and the End Property clause in the procedure. This is because the header contains the `ReadOnly` keyword.

    Public ReadOnly Property Grade As String

5. Type the following Return statement in the blank line below the Get clause, but don't press Enter:

    Return _strGrade

6. Next, you will enter the default constructor in the class. The default constructor will initialize the Private variables when a CourseGrade object is instantiated. Insert two blank lines above the End Class clause. Click the **blank line** immediately above the clause (if necessary) and then enter the following default constructor:

    Public Sub New()
        _intScore1 = 0
        _intScore2 = 0
        _strGrade = String.Empty
    End Sub

7. Finally, you will enter the DetermineGrade method, which will assign the appropriate letter grade to the `_strGrade` variable. The method will be a Sub procedure, because it will not need to return a value to the application that calls it. Insert two blank lines below the default constructor's End Sub clause. Click the **blank line** immediately above the clause (if necessary) and then enter the following procedure header:

    Public Sub DetermineGrade()

8. Now enter the following Select Case statement:

    Select Case _intScore1 + _intScore2
        Case Is >= 180
          _strGrade = "A"
        Case Is >= 160
          _strGrade = "B"
        Case Is >= 140
          _strGrade = "C"
        Case Is >= 120
          _strGrade = "D"
        Case Else
          _strGrade = "F"
    End Select

9. Save the solution. (The completed class definition is shown in Figure 11-32.)

Now that you have finished defining the class, you can use the class to instantiate a CourseGrade object in the Grade Calculator application.

START HERE   **To complete the Grade Calculator application:**

1. Click the **designer window's tab** and then open the form's Code Editor window. Replace <your name> and <current date> in the comments with your name and the current date, respectively.

2. Locate the btnDisplay control's Click event procedure. First, you will instantiate a CourseGrade object. Click the **blank line** above the second comment in the procedure and then enter the following Dim statement:

   Dim studentGrade As New CourseGrade

3. Now you will assign the test scores, which are selected in the list boxes, to the object's properties. Click the **blank line** below the second comment in the procedure and then enter the following TryParse methods:

   Integer.TryParse(lstTest1.SelectedItem.ToString, studentGrade.Score1)
   Integer.TryParse(lstTest2.SelectedItem.ToString, studentGrade.Score2)

4. Next, you will use the object's DetermineGrade method to determine the appropriate grade. Click the **blank line** below the `' object's DetermineGrade method` comment and then enter the following Call statement:

   Call studentGrade.DetermineGrade()

5. Finally, you will display the grade, which is stored in the object's ReadOnly Grade property. Click the **blank line** below the `' object's ReadOnly property` comment. Type the following code, but don't press Enter:

   lblGrade.Text = studentGrade.

6. Click **Grade** in the IntelliSense list. If necessary, click the **Common** tab. See Figure 11-31. The message that appears next to the IntelliSense list indicates that the Grade property is ReadOnly.

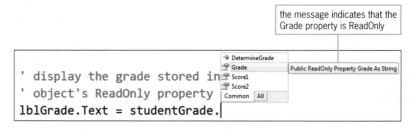

Figure 11-31   ReadOnly property message

7. Press **Tab** to include the Grade property in the assignment statement.

Figure 11-32 shows the CourseGrade class definition and the btnDisplay control's Click event procedure.

Example 5—A Class that Contains a ReadOnly Property   **LESSON B**

```
Public Class CourseGrade
    Private _intScore1 As Integer
    Private _intScore2 As Integer
    Private _strGrade As String

    Public Property Score1 As Integer
        Get
            Return _intScore1
        End Get
        Set(ByVal value As Integer)
            _intScore1 = value
        End Set
    End Property

    Public Property Score2 As Integer
        Get
            Return _intScore2
        End Get
        Set(ByVal value As Integer)
            _intScore2 = value
        End Set
    End Property

    Public ReadOnly Property Grade As String
        Get
            Return _strGrade
        End Get
    End Property

    Public Sub New()
        _intScore1 = 0
        _intScore2 = 0
        _strGrade = String.Empty
    End Sub

    Public Sub DetermineGrade()
        Select Case _intScore1 + _intScore2
            Case Is >= 180
                _strGrade = "A"
            Case Is >= 160
                _strGrade = "B"
            Case Is >= 140
                _strGrade = "C"
            Case Is >= 120
                _strGrade = "D"
            Case Else
                _strGrade = "F"
        End Select
    End Sub
End Class

Private Sub btnDisplay_Click(ByVal sender As Object,
ByVal e As System.EventArgs) Handles btnDisplay.Click
    ' calculates and displays a letter grade

    Dim studentGrade As New CourseGrade

    ' assign test scores to object's properties
```

the class definition begins here

the btnDisplay control's Click event procedure begins here

Figure 11-32 CourseGrade class definition and btnDisplay control's Click event procedure *(continues)*

(continued)

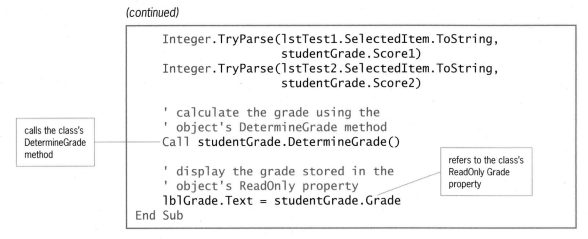

```
        Integer.TryParse(lstTest1.SelectedItem.ToString,
                         studentGrade.Score1)
        Integer.TryParse(lstTest2.SelectedItem.ToString,
                         studentGrade.Score2)

        ' calculate the grade using the
        ' object's DetermineGrade method
        Call studentGrade.DetermineGrade()

        ' display the grade stored in the
        ' object's ReadOnly property
        lblGrade.Text = studentGrade.Grade
    End Sub
```

calls the class's DetermineGrade method

refers to the class's ReadOnly Grade property

Figure 11-32   CourseGrade class definition and btnDisplay control's Click event procedure

START HERE

To test the Grade Calculator application:

1. Save the solution and then start the application. Scroll the Test 1 list box and then click **86** in the list. Scroll the Test 2 list box and then click **95** in the list. Click the **Display Grade** button. The letter A appears in the Grade box, as shown in Figure 11-33.

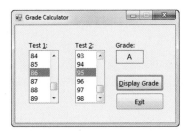

Figure 11-33   Grade displayed in the interface

2. On your own, test the application using different test scores. When you are finished, click the **Exit** button. Close the Main Form.vb and CourseGrade.vb windows and then close the solution.

Example 6—A Class that Contains Auto-Implemented Properties

A new feature in Visual Basic 2010, called **auto-implemented properties**, enables you to specify the property of a class in one line of code, as shown in Figure 11-34. When you enter the line of code in the Code Editor window, Visual Basic automatically creates a hidden Private variable that it associates with the property; it also automatically creates hidden Get and Set blocks. The Private variable's name will be the same as the property's name, but it will be preceded by an underscore. For example, if you create an auto-implemented property named City, Visual Basic will create a hidden Private variable named `_City`. The auto-implemented properties feature provides a shorter syntax for you to use when creating a class: You don't need to create the Private variable associated with a property, nor do you need to enter the

Example 6—A Class that Contains Auto-Implemented Properties   LESSON B

property's Get and Set blocks of code. However, keep in mind that you will need to use the standard syntax if you want to add validation code to the Set block, or if you want the property to be either ReadOnly or WriteOnly.

Auto-implemented property

Syntax
Public Property *propertyName* **As** *dataType*

Example 1
`Public Property City As Integer`
creates a Public property named City, a hidden Private variable named _City, and hidden Get and Set blocks

Example 2
`Public Property Sales As Integer`
creates a Public property named Sales, a hidden Private variable named _Sales, and hidden Get and Set blocks

---

Figure 11-34   Syntax and examples of creating an auto-implemented property

In the next set of steps, you will modify the CourseGrade class from Example 5 to use two auto-implemented properties.

To modify the CourseGrade class: ◀ START HERE

1. Use Windows to make a copy of the Grade Solution folder from Example 5. Rename the copy Modified Grade Solution. Open the Grade Solution (Grade Solution.sln) file contained in the Modified Grade Solution folder. Open the designer window.

2. Right-click **CourseGrade.vb** in the Solution Explorer window and then click **View Code**.

3. First, replace the `Private _intScore1 As Integer` and `Private _intScore2 As Integer` statements with the following statements:

    Public Property Score1 As Integer
    Public Property Score2 As Integer

4. Next, delete the Score1 and Score2 Property procedures. (Don't delete the Grade property procedure.)

5. Now change `_intScore1` and `_intScore2` in the default constructor to **_Score1** and **_Score2**, respectively. (Recall that the name of the Private variable associated with an auto-implemented property is the property's name preceded by an underscore.)

6. Finally, change `_intScore1` and `_intScore2` in the DetermineGrade method to **_Score1** and **_Score2**, respectively.

Figure 11-35 shows the modified class definition. The code pertaining to the two auto-implemented properties (Score1 and Score2) is shaded in the figure. You cannot use the auto-implemented properties feature for the Grade property because that property is ReadOnly.

auto-implemented
properties

a ReadOnly
property cannot
be an auto-
implemented
property

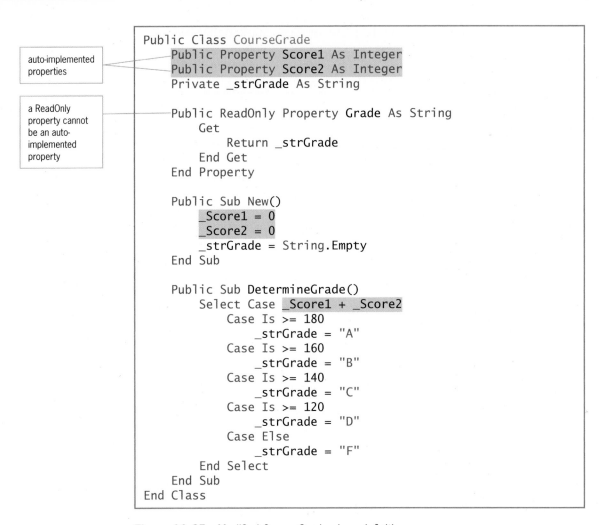

```
Public Class CourseGrade
    Public Property Score1 As Integer
    Public Property Score2 As Integer
    Private _strGrade As String

    Public ReadOnly Property Grade As String
        Get
            Return _strGrade
        End Get
    End Property

    Public Sub New()
        _Score1 = 0
        _Score2 = 0
        _strGrade = String.Empty
    End Sub

    Public Sub DetermineGrade()
        Select Case _Score1 + _Score2
            Case Is >= 180
                _strGrade = "A"
            Case Is >= 160
                _strGrade = "B"
            Case Is >= 140
                _strGrade = "C"
            Case Is >= 120
                _strGrade = "D"
            Case Else
                _strGrade = "F"
        End Select
    End Sub
End Class
```

Figure 11-35   Modified CourseGrade class definition

START HERE

To test the modified Grade Calculator application:

1. Save the solution and then start the application. Scroll the Test 1 list box and then click **86** in the list. Scroll the Test 2 list box and then click **95** in the list. Click the **Display Grade** button. The letter A appears in the Grade box, as shown earlier in Figure 11-33.

2. On your own, test the application using different test scores. When you are finished, click the **Exit** button. Close the CourseGrade.vb window and then close the solution.

Example 7—A Class that Contains Overloaded Methods   LESSON B

YOU DO IT 2!

Create a Visual Basic Windows application named YouDoIt 2. Save the application in the VB2010\Chap11 folder. Add a text box, a label, and a button to the form. Add a class file named Square.vb to the project. Define a class named Square. The class should contain an auto-implemented property that will store the side measurement of a square. It also should contain a default constructor and a method that calculates and returns the square's perimeter. Use the following formula to calculate the perimeter: 4 * *side*. Open the form's Code Editor window. The button's Click event procedure should display the square's perimeter, using the side measurement entered by the user. Code the procedure. Save the solution and then start and test the application. Close the solution.

Example 7—A Class that Contains Overloaded Methods

In this example, you will use a class named Employee to instantiate an object. Employee objects have the attributes and behaviors shown in Figure 11-36.

<u>Attributes</u>
employee number
employee name

<u>Behaviors</u>
1. An employee object can initialize its attributes using values provided by the class.
2. An employee object can initialize its attributes using values provided by the application in which it is instantiated.
3. An employee object can calculate and return the gross pay for salaried employees. The gross pay is calculated by dividing the salaried employee's annual salary by 24, because the salaried employees are paid twice per month.
4. An employee object can calculate and return the gross pay for hourly employees. The gross pay is calculated by multiplying the number of hours the employee worked during the week by his or her pay rate.

Figure 11-36   Attributes and behaviors of an Employee object

Figure 11-37 shows the Employee class defined in the Employee.vb file. The class contains two auto-implemented properties and four methods. The two New methods are the class's constructors. The first New method is the default constructor and the second is a parameterized constructor. Notice that the default constructor initializes the class's Private variables directly, while the parameterized constructor uses the class's Public properties to initialize the Private variables indirectly. As you learned in Lesson A, using a Public property in this manner ensures that the computer processes any validation code associated with the property. Even though the Number and EmpName properties in Figure 11-37 do not have any validation code, it's a good programming practice to use the properties in the parameterized constructor in case validation code is added to the class in the future.

When two or more methods have the same name but different parameters, the methods are referred to as **overloaded methods**. The two constructors in Figure 11-37 are considered overloaded methods, because each is named New and each has a different parameterList. You can overload any of the methods contained in a class, not just constructors. The two GetGross methods in the figure also are overloaded methods, because they have the same name but a different parameterList.

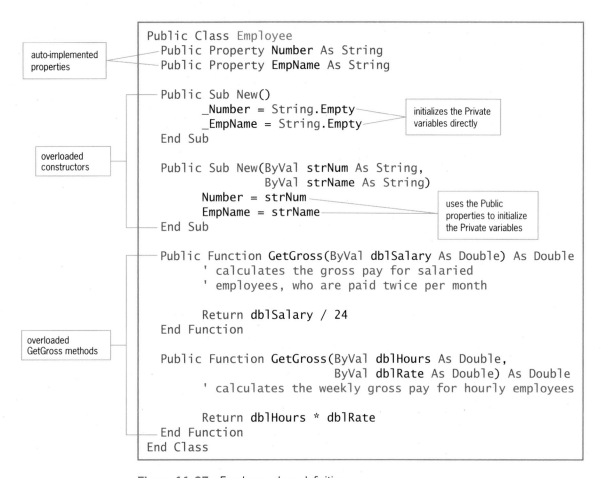

Figure 11-37 Employee class definition

You already are familiar with overloaded methods, as you have used several of the overloaded methods built into Visual Basic. Examples of such methods include ToString, TryParse, Convert.ToDecimal, and MessageBox.Show. The Code Editor's IntelliSense feature displays a box that allows you to view a method's signatures, one signature at a time. Recall that a method's signature includes its name and optional parameterList. The box shown in Figure 11-38 displays the first of the ToString method's four signatures. You use the up and down arrows in the box to display the other signatures. The IntelliSense feature also will display the signatures of the overloaded methods contained in the classes you create.

Example 7—A Class that Contains Overloaded Methods **LESSON B**

663

Figure 11-38   First of the ToString method's signatures

Overloading is useful when two or more methods require different parameters to perform essentially the same task. Both overloaded constructors in the Employee class, for example, initialize the class's Private variables. However, the default constructor does not need to be passed any information to perform the task, whereas the parameterized constructor requires two items of information (the employee number and name). Similarly, both GetGross methods in the Employee class calculate and return a gross pay amount. However, the first GetGross method performs its task for salaried employees and requires an application to pass it one item of information: the employee's annual salary. The second GetGross method performs its task for hourly employees and requires two items of information: the number of hours the employee worked and his or her rate of pay. Rather than using two overloaded GetGross methods, you could have used two methods having different names, such as GetSalariedGross and GetHourlyGross. The advantage of overloading the GetGross method is that you need to remember the name of only one method.

You will use the Employee class when coding the ABC Company application. As mentioned at the beginning of the chapter, the application displays the gross pay for salaried and hourly employees. Salaried employees are paid twice per month. Therefore, each salaried employee's gross pay is calculated by dividing his or her annual salary by 24. Hourly employees are paid weekly. The gross pay for an hourly employee is calculated by multiplying the number of hours the employee worked during the week by his or her hourly pay rate. The application also displays a report showing each employee's number, name, and gross pay.

The Ch11BVideo file demonstrates all of the steps for coding the ABC Company application. You can view the video either before or after completing the lesson.

To view the class file contained in the ABC Company application:

START HERE

1. Open the ABC Solution (ABC Solution.sln) file contained in the VB2010\Chap11\ABC Solution folder. If necessary, open the designer window. See Figure 11-39.

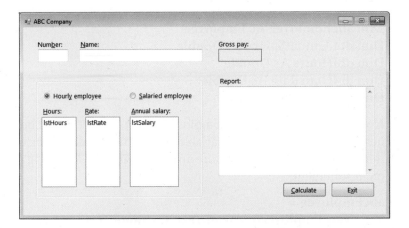

Figure 11-39   Interface for the ABC Company application

2. Right-click **Employee.vb** in the Solution Explorer window and then click **View Code**. The class definition from Figure 11-37 appears in the Employee.vb window.

3. Replace <your name> and <current date> in the comments with your name and the current date, respectively. Save the solution and then close the Employee.vb window.

You will need to code only the Calculate button's Click event procedure. The procedure's pseudocode is shown in Figure 11-40.

---

btnCalc Click event procedure
1. declare variables to store an Employee object, the annual salary, hours worked, hourly pay rate, and gross pay
2. instantiate an Employee object to represent an employee; initialize the object's variables using the number and name entered in the text boxes
3. if the Hourly employee radio button is selected
        assign the hours worked and hourly pay rate to the appropriate variables
        use the Employee object's GetGross method to calculate the gross pay for an hourly employee
    else
        assign the annual salary to the appropriate variable
        use the Employee object's GetGross method to calculate the gross pay for a salaried employee
    end if
4. display the gross pay and the report
5. send the focus to the txtNum control

Figure 11-40   Pseudocode for the Calculate button's Click event procedure

START HERE

To code the Calculate button's Click event procedure:

1. Open the form's Code Editor window. Replace <your name> and <current date> in the comments with your name and the current date, respectively.

2. Locate the btnCalc control's Click event procedure. First, you will declare the necessary variables. Click the **blank line** below the second comment in the procedure and then enter the following five Dim statements:

    Dim abcEmployee As Employee
    Dim dblAnnualSalary As Double
    Dim dblHours As Double
    Dim dblHourRate As Double
    Dim dblGross As Double

3. Now you will instantiate an Employee object, using the text box values to initialize the object's variables. Click the **blank line** below the third comment in the procedure and then enter the following assignment statement:

    abcEmployee =
        New Employee(txtNum.Text, txtName.Text)

Example 7—A Class that Contains Overloaded Methods   LESSON B

4. The third step in the pseudocode determines the selected radio button and then takes the appropriate action. Click the **blank line** below the ` ' determine the selected radio button ` comment and then enter the following If clause:

If radHourly.Checked Then

5. If the Hourly employee radio button is selected, the selection structure's true path should use the Employee object's GetGross method to calculate the gross pay for an hourly employee. Enter the following comment and lines of code:

' calculate the gross pay for an hourly employee
Double.TryParse(lstHours.SelectedItem.ToString, dblHours)
Double.TryParse(lstRate.SelectedItem.ToString, dblHourRate)
dblGross = abcEmployee.GetGross(dblHours, dblHourRate)

6. If the Salaried employee radio button is selected, the selection structure's false path should use the Employee object's GetGross method to calculate the gross pay for a salaried employee. Enter the additional comment and lines of code indicated in Figure 11-41.

```
        dblGross = abcEmployee.GetGross(dblHours, dblHourRate)
    Else
        ' calculate the gross pay for a salaried employee
        Double.TryParse(lstSalary.SelectedItem.ToString,
                        dblAnnualSalary)
        dblGross = abcEmployee.GetGross(dblAnnualSalary)
    End If
```

enter this comment and these lines of code

Figure 11-41   Additional comment and code entered in the false path

7. Next, you need to display the gross pay and the report. Click the **blank line** below the ` ' display the gross pay and report ` comment and then enter the following lines of code:

lblGross.Text = dblGross.ToString("C2")
txtReport.Text = txtReport.Text &
      abcEmployee.Number.PadRight(6) &
      abcEmployee.EmpName.PadRight(25) &
      dblGross.ToString("N2").PadLeft(9) & ControlChars.NewLine

8. The last step in the pseudocode is to set the focus. The code for this step has already been entered in the Code Editor window.

Figure 11-42 shows the btnCalc control's Click event procedure.

666

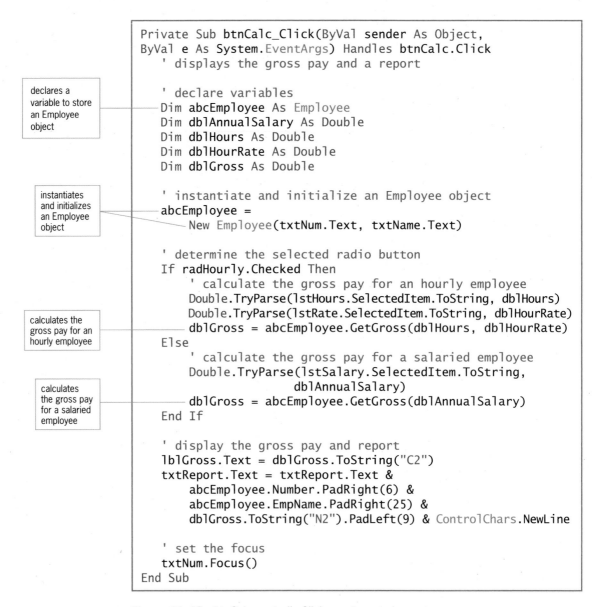

declares a variable to store an Employee object

instantiates and initializes an Employee object

calculates the gross pay for an hourly employee

calculates the gross pay for a salaried employee

```vb
Private Sub btnCalc_Click(ByVal sender As Object,
ByVal e As System.EventArgs) Handles btnCalc.Click
    ' displays the gross pay and a report

    ' declare variables
    Dim abcEmployee As Employee
    Dim dblAnnualSalary As Double
    Dim dblHours As Double
    Dim dblHourRate As Double
    Dim dblGross As Double

    ' instantiate and initialize an Employee object
    abcEmployee =
        New Employee(txtNum.Text, txtName.Text)

    ' determine the selected radio button
    If radHourly.Checked Then
        ' calculate the gross pay for an hourly employee
        Double.TryParse(lstHours.SelectedItem.ToString, dblHours)
        Double.TryParse(lstRate.SelectedItem.ToString, dblHourRate)
        dblGross = abcEmployee.GetGross(dblHours, dblHourRate)
    Else
        ' calculate the gross pay for a salaried employee
        Double.TryParse(lstSalary.SelectedItem.ToString,
                        dblAnnualSalary)
        dblGross = abcEmployee.GetGross(dblAnnualSalary)
    End If

    ' display the gross pay and report
    lblGross.Text = dblGross.ToString("C2")
    txtReport.Text = txtReport.Text &
        abcEmployee.Number.PadRight(6) &
        abcEmployee.EmpName.PadRight(25) &
        dblGross.ToString("N2").PadLeft(9) & ControlChars.NewLine

    ' set the focus
    txtNum.Focus()
End Sub
```

Figure 11-42　btnCalc control's Click event procedure

START HERE

To test the ABC Company application:

1. Save the solution and then start the application. Type **120** in the Number box, press **Tab**, and then type **Peggy Milas** in the Name box. Click **8.00** in the Rate list box and then click the **Calculate** button. $320.00 appears in the Gross pay box, and Peggy's information appears in the Report box. See Figure 11-43.

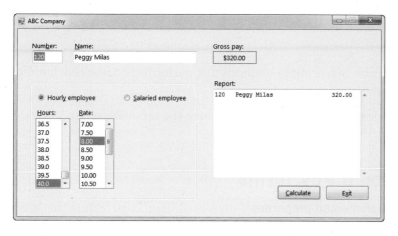

Figure 11-43 Peggy's gross pay and information shown in the interface

667

2. Type **9336** in the Number box, press **Tab**, and then type **Jackie Smith** in the Name box. Click the **Salaried employee** radio button. Scroll the Annual salary list box and then click **27000** in the list. Click the **Calculate** button. The button's Click event procedure displays the gross pay amount ($1,125.00) in the Gross pay box. It also adds Jackie's information to the Report box. See Figure 11-44.

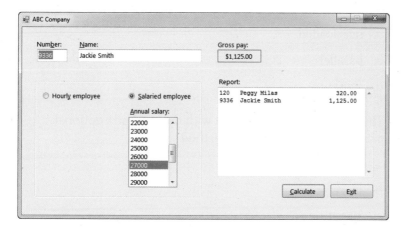

Figure 11-44 Jackie's gross pay and information shown in the interface

3. Click the **Exit** button. Close the Code Editor window and then close the solution.

Lesson B Summary

- To create a property whose value can only be retrieved by an application:

  Include the **ReadOnly** keyword in the Property procedure's header.

- To specify the property of a class in one line:

  Create an auto-implemented property using the following syntax: **Public Property** *propertyName* **As** *dataType*.

- To include a parameterized method in a class:

  Enter the parameters between the parentheses that follow the method's name.

- To create two or more methods that perform the same task but require different parameters:

  Overload the methods by giving them the same name but different parameterLists.

Lesson B Key Terms

Auto-implemented properties—the Visual Basic 2010 feature that enables you to specify the property of a class in one line

Overloaded methods—two or more class methods that have the same name but different parameterLists

Lesson B Review Questions

1. Two or more methods that have the same name but different parameterLists are referred to as _____ methods.

   a. loaded

   b. overloaded

   c. parallel

   d. signature

2. The method name combined with the method's optional parameterList is called the method's _____.

   a. autograph

   b. inscription

   c. signature

   d. statement

3. A class contains an auto-implemented property named Location. Which of the following is the correct way for the default constructor to assign the string "Unknown" to the variable associated with the property?

   a. `_Location = "Unknown"`

   b. `_Location.strLocation = "Unknown"`

   c. `Location = "Unknown"`

   d. none of the above

4. A ReadOnly property can be an auto-implemented property.

   a. True

   b. False

5. The Salesperson class contains a ReadOnly property named Bonus. The property is associated with the Private `_dblBonus` variable. A button's Click event procedure instantiates a Salesperson object and assigns it to the `ourSalesperson` variable. Which of the following is valid in the Click event procedure?

a. `lblBonus.Text =`
   `ourSalesperson.Bonus.ToString("C2")`

b. `ourSalesperson.Bonus = dblSales * .1`

c. `ourSalesperson._dblBonus = 500`

d. none of the above

Lesson B Exercises

1. What are overloaded methods and why are they used?   INTRODUCTORY

2. Write the Property procedure for a ReadOnly property named BonusRate. The property is associated with the `_decBonusRate` variable.   INTRODUCTORY

3. Write the code for an auto-implemented property named Commission. The property's data type is Double.   INTRODUCTORY

4. Write the class definition for a class named Worker. The class should include Private variables and Property procedures for a Worker object's name and salary. The salary may contain a decimal place. The class also should contain two constructors: the default constructor and a parameterized constructor.   INTRODUCTORY

5. Rewrite the code from Exercise 4 using auto-implemented properties.   INTRODUCTORY

6. Add a method named GetNewSalary to the Worker class from Exercise 5. The method should calculate a Worker object's new salary, which is based on a raise percentage provided by the application using the object. Before calculating the new salary, the method should verify that the raise percentage is greater than or equal to zero. If the raise percentage is less than zero, the method should assign the number 0 as the new salary.   INTRODUCTORY

7. Open the Willow Pools Solution (Willow Pools Solution.sln) file contained in the VB2010\Chap11\Willow Pools Solution-Auto-Implemented folder. Modify the RectangularPool class so that it uses Public auto-implemented properties rather than Public variables. Include a default constructor in the class. Save the solution and then start and test the application. Close the Code Editor window and then close the solution.   INTRODUCTORY

8. Open the Hire Date Solution (Hire Date Solution.sln) file contained in the VB2010\Chap11\Hire Date Solution folder. Open the designer window.   INTRODUCTORY

a. Open the FormattedDate.vb file. Add a default constructor and a parameterized constructor to the class. Also add a method that returns the month and day numbers, separated by a slash (/).

b. Open the form's Code Editor window. The Click event procedures for the btnDefault and btnParameterized controls should display the hire date in the following format: *month/day*. For example, if the numbers 3 and 2 are selected in the Month and Day list boxes, respectively, the Click event procedures should display 3/2 in the Hire date box. Code the btnDefault control's Click event procedure using the FormattedDate class's default constructor. Code the btnParameterized control's Click event procedure using the class's parameterized constructor.

c. Save the solution and then start and test the application. Close the Main Form.vb and FormattedDate.vb windows and then close the solution.

INTERMEDIATE

9. Open the Salary Solution (Salary Solution.sln) file contained in the VB2010\Chap11\Salary Solution folder. Open the Worker.vb class file and then enter the Worker class definition from Exercises 5 and 6. Save the solution and then close the Worker.vb window. Open the form's Code Editor window. Use the comments in the btnCalc control's Click event procedure to enter the missing instructions. Save the solution and then start the application. Test the application by entering your name, a current salary amount of 54000, and a raise percentage of 10 (for 10%). The new salary should be $59,400.00. Close the Code Editor window and then close the solution.

INTERMEDIATE

10. In this exercise, you modify the Grade Calculator application coded in the lesson. Use Windows to make a copy of the Grade Solution folder. Rename the copy Modified Grade Solution-Intermediate. Open the Grade Solution (Grade Solution.sln) file contained in the Modified Grade Solution-Intermediate folder. Open the designer window.

a. Open the CourseGrade.vb file. Modify the DetermineGrade method so that it accepts the maximum number of points that can be earned on both tests. (Currently, the maximum number of points is 200: 100 points per test.) For an A grade, the student must earn at least 90% of the total number of points. For a B, C, and D grade, the student must earn at least 80%, 70%, and 60%, respectively. If the student earns less than 60% of the total points, the grade is F. Make the appropriate modifications to the class and then save the solution.

b. Add a label control and a text box to the form. Change the label control's Text property to "&Maximum points". Change the text box's name to txtMax.

c. Open the form's Code Editor window. The maximum number allowed in the text box should be 400. Each list box should display numbers from 0 through 200. Make the necessary modifications to the code.

d. Save the solution and then start and test the application. Close the CourseGrade.vb and Main Form.vb windows and then close the solution.

11. Each member of Glasgow Health Club must pay monthly dues that consist of a basic fee and one or more optional charges. The basic monthly fee for a single membership is $50; for a family membership, it is $90. If the member has a single membership, the additional monthly charges are $30 for tennis, $25 for golf, and $20 for racquetball. If the member has a family membership, the additional monthly charges are $50 for tennis, $35 for golf, and $30 for racquetball. The application should display the member's basic fee, additional charges, and monthly dues. Create a Visual Basic Windows application. Use the following names for the solution, project, and form file, respectively: Glasgow Health Solution, Glasgow Health Project, and Main Form.vb. Save the application in the VB2010\Chap11 folder. Create the interface shown in Figure 11-45 and then code the application. Be sure to use a class in your code. Save the solution and then start and test the application. Close the Code Editor windows and then close the solution.

ADVANCED

671

Figure 11-45   Interface for Exercise 11

12. Jeremiah Carter, the manager of the Accounts Payable department at Franklin Calendars, wants an application that keeps track of the checks written by his department. More specifically, he wants to record (in a sequential access file) the check number, date, payee, and amount of each check. Create a Visual Basic Windows application. Use the following names for the solution, project, and form file, respectively: Franklin Calendars Solution, Franklin Calendars Project, and Main Form.vb. Save the application in the VB2010\Chap11 folder. Create the interface shown in Figure 11-46 and then code the application. Be sure to use a class in your code. Save the solution and then start and test the application. Close the Code Editor windows and then close the solution.

ADVANCED

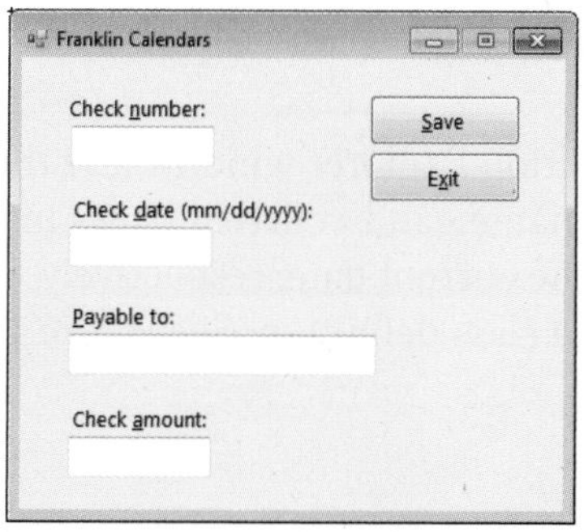

Figure 11-46   Interface for Exercise 12

LESSON C

After studying Lesson C, you should be able to:

- Create a derived class
- Refer to the base class using the `MyBase` keyword
- Override a method in the base class

Example 8—Using a Base Class and a Derived Class

You can create one class from another class; in OOP, this is referred to as **inheritance**. The new class is called the **derived class** and it inherits the attributes and behaviors of the original class, called the **base class**. You indicate that a class is a derived class by including the Inherits clause in the derived class's Class statement. The **Inherits clause** is simply the keyword `Inherits` followed by the name of the class whose attributes and behaviors you want the derived class to inherit. You enter the Inherits clause immediately below the Public Class clause in the derived class. You will use a base class named Square and a derived class named Cube to code the Area Calculator application. The application calculates and displays either the area of a square or the surface area of a cube.

START HERE   **To open the Area Calculator application and then view the class file:**

1. If necessary, start Visual Studio 2010 or Visual Basic 2010 Express. Open the Area Solution (Area Solution.sln) file contained in the VB2010\Chap11\Area Solution folder. If necessary, open the designer window. The interface provides a text box for entering the side measurement. See Figure 11-47.

Figure 11-47   Interface for the Area Calculator application

2. Right-click **Shapes.vb** in the Solution Explorer window and then click **View Code**. Replace <your name> and <current date> in the comments with your name and the current date, respectively. The Shapes.vb file contains the Square class definition. See Figure 11-48.

Example 8—Using a Base Class and a Derived Class   LESSON C

```
' Name:           Shapes.vb
' Programmer:     <your name> on <current date>

Option Explicit On
Option Strict On
Option Infer Off

' base class
Public Class Square
    Public Property Side As Double

    Public Sub New()
        _Side = 0
    End Sub

    Public Sub New(ByVal dblS As Double)        Square class
        Side = dblS                             definition
    End Sub

    Public Function GetArea() As Double
        ' returns the area of a square
        Return _Side ^ 2
    End Function
End Class

' derived class
```

Figure 11-48 Contents of the Shapes.vb file

The Square class contains one Public property named Side, two constructors, and a method named GetArea. The Side property represents an attribute of a Square object: its side measurement. Each time a Square object is
instantiated, the computer will use one of the two constructors to initialize
the object. An application can use the class's GetArea method to calculate
the area of a Square object. Notice that you calculate the area by raising the
Square object's side measurement to the second power. The GetArea method
will return the area to the statement that invoked the method.

In this section, you will create a derived class from the Square class. The
derived class will inherit only the base class's Side attribute and GetArea
method. It will not inherit the two constructors, because constructors are
never inherited. You will name the derived class Cube.

To create a derived class named Cube: ◄ START HERE

1. Click the **blank line** below the ' derived class comment and
    then enter the following two lines of code. Press **Enter** twice after
    typing the Inherits clause.

    Public Class Cube
    Inherits Square

2. As already mentioned, the Cube class will not inherit the Square
    class's constructors. Therefore, it will need its own constructors. Enter
    the following procedure header for the default constructor:

    Public Sub New()

3. Insert two blank lines below the default constructor's End Sub clause in the Cube class. Click the **blank line** above the End Class clause (if necessary) and then enter the following procedure header for the parameterized constructor:

Public Sub New(ByVal dblS As Double)

Recall that when a Square object is instantiated, the computer uses one of the Square class's constructors to initialize the object. When a Cube object is instantiated, its constructors will call upon the base class's constructors to initialize the object. You refer to the base class using the **MyBase** keyword. For example, the `MyBase.New()` statement tells the computer to process the code contained in the base class's default constructor. Similarly, the `MyBase.New(dblS)` statement tells the computer to process the code contained in the base class's parameterized constructor.

START HERE   **To finish coding the Cube class's constructors:**

1. Click the **blank line** below the default constructor's procedure header and then type the following statement, but don't press Enter:

MyBase.New()

2. Click the **blank line** below the parameterized constructor's procedure header and then type the following statement, but don't press Enter:

MyBase.New(dblS)

Recall that the Square (base) class contains a method that calculates and returns the area of a Square object; the method's name is GetArea. You also will include a GetArea method in the Cube (derived) class. However, the Cube class's GetArea method will calculate and return the surface area of a Cube object. The formula for calculating the surface area is $sideMeasurement^2 * 6$. The GetArea method in the Cube class will use the Square class's GetArea method to calculate and return the first part of the formula: $sideMeasurement^2$. It then will simply multiply the return value by 6 to get the surface area of a Cube object.

In order to use the same method name—in this case, GetArea—in both a base class and a derived class, the method's procedure header in the base class will need to contain the Overridable keyword, and the method's procedure header in the derived class will need to contain the Overrides keyword. The **Overridable** keyword in the base class indicates that the method can be overridden by any class that is derived from the base class. In other words, classes derived from the Square (base) class will provide their own GetArea method. The **Overrides** keyword in the derived class indicates that the method overrides (replaces) the same method contained in the base class. In this case, for example, the GetArea method in the Cube class replaces the GetArea method in the Square class.

START HERE   **To finish coding the Cube class:**

1. Locate the GetArea function in the Square class. Replace the procedure header with the following:

Public Overridable Function GetArea() As Double

Example 8—Using a Base Class and a Derived Class LESSON C

2. Locate the parameterized constructor in the Cube class. Insert two blank lines below the parameterized constructor's End Sub clause. Click the **blank line** above the End Class clause (if necessary) and then enter the following GetArea method:

Public Overrides Function GetArea() As Double
　　　　Return MyBase.GetArea * 6
End Function

3. Save the solution.

Figure 11-49 shows the Square and Cube class definitions contained in the Shapes.vb file.

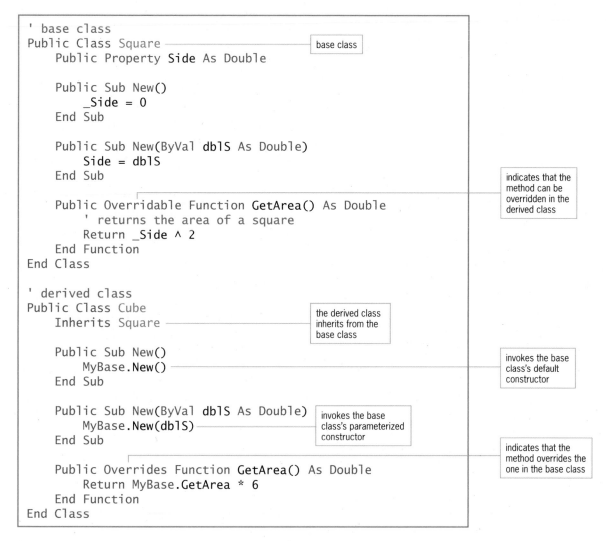

```
' base class
Public Class Square                          base class
    Public Property Side As Double

    Public Sub New()
        _Side = 0
    End Sub

    Public Sub New(ByVal dblS As Double)
        Side = dblS
    End Sub                                   indicates that the
                                              method can be
                                              overridden in the
                                              derived class
    Public Overridable Function GetArea() As Double
        ' returns the area of a square
        Return _Side ^ 2
    End Function
End Class

' derived class
Public Class Cube
    Inherits Square          the derived class
                             inherits from the
                             base class
    Public Sub New()
        MyBase.New()                          invokes the base
    End Sub                                    class's default
                                              constructor

    Public Sub New(ByVal dblS As Double)   invokes the base
        MyBase.New(dblS)                    class's parameterized
    End Sub                                 constructor
                                           indicates that the
                                           method overrides the
                                           one in the base class
    Public Overrides Function GetArea() As Double
        Return MyBase.GetArea * 6
    End Function
End Class
```

Figure 11-49　Modified Square class and Cube class definitions

To complete the Area Calculator application, you still need to code the Click event procedures for the Square Area and Cube Surface Area buttons in the interface. The Square Area button's Click event procedure will calculate and display the area of a square. Similarly, the Cube Surface Area button's Click event procedure will calculate and display the surface area of a cube. You will code the Square Area button's Click event procedure first.

START HERE **To code and then test the Square Area button's Click event procedure:**

1. Click the **designer window's tab** and then open the form's Code Editor window.

2. Locate the btnSquare control's Click event procedure and then click the **blank line** immediately above the End Sub clause. First, you will instantiate a Square object. Enter the following Dim statement:

   Dim mySquare As New Square

3. Next, you will declare a variable to store the mySquare object's area. Type the following Dim statement and then press **Enter** twice:

   Dim dblArea As Double

4. Now you will assign the side measurement, which is entered by the user, to the mySquare object's Side property. Type the following TryParse method and then press **Enter** twice:

   Double.TryParse(txtSide.Text, mySquare.Side)

5. Next, you will use the mySquare object's GetArea method to calculate the area. You will assign the method's return value to the `dblArea` variable. Enter the following comment and assignment statement:

   ' calculate the area
   dblArea = mySquare.GetArea

6. Finally, you will display the area in the lblArea control. Enter the following comment and assignment statement:

   ' display the area
   lblArea.Text = "Square: " & dblArea.ToString("N1")

7. Save the solution and then start the application. Type **10** in the Side measurement box and then click the **Square Area** button. The message "Square: 100.0" appears in the Area box. See Figure 11-50.

Figure 11-50   Interface showing the square's area

8. Click the **Exit** button.

Finally, you will code the Cube Surface Area button's Click event procedure.

Example 8—Using a Base Class and a Derived Class   LESSON C

To code and then test the Cube Surface Area button's Click event procedure:

1. Locate the btnCube control's Click event procedure and then click the **blank line** immediately above the End Sub clause. First, you will instantiate a Cube object. Enter the following Dim statement:

   Dim myCube As New Cube

2. Next, you will declare a variable to store the myCube object's area. Type the following Dim statement and then press **Enter** twice:

   Dim dblArea As Double

3. Now you will assign the side measurement to the myCube object's Side property. Type the following TryParse method and then press **Enter** twice:

   Double.TryParse(txtSide.Text, myCube.Side)

4. Next, you will use the myCube object's GetArea method to calculate the area. You will assign the method's return value to the `dblArea` variable. Enter the following comment and assignment statement:

   ' calculate the area
   dblArea = myCube.GetArea

5. Finally, you will display the area in the lblArea control. Enter the following comment and assignment statement:

   ' display the area
   lblArea.Text = "Cube: " & dblArea.ToString("N1")

6. Save the solution and then start the application. Type **10** in the Side measurement box and then click the **Cube Surface Area** button. The message "Cube: 600.0" appears in the Area box.

7. Click the **Exit** button. Close the form's Code Editor window and the Shapes.vb window, and then close the solution.

Figure 11-51 shows the Click event procedures for the btnSquare and btnCube controls.

```
Private Sub btnSquare_Click(ByVal sender As Object,
ByVal e As System.EventArgs) Handles btnSquare.Click
    ' displays the area of a square

    Dim mySquare As New Square
    Dim dblArea As Double

    Double.TryParse(txtSide.Text, mySquare.Side)

    ' calculate the area
    dblArea = mySquare.GetArea
    ' display the area
    lblArea.Text = "Square: " & dblArea.ToString("N1")

End Sub
```

Figure 11-51 btnSquare and btnCube controls' Click event procedures *(continues)*

(continued)

```
Private Sub btnCube_Click(ByVal sender As Object,
ByVal e As System.EventArgs) Handles btnCube.Click
    ' displays the surface area of a cube

    Dim myCube As New Cube
    Dim dblArea As Double

    Double.TryParse(txtSide.Text, myCube.Side)

    ' calculate the area
    dblArea = myCube.GetArea
    ' display the area
    lblArea.Text = "Cube: " & dblArea.ToString("N1")

End Sub
```

Figure 11-51   btnSquare and btnCube controls' Click event procedures

Lesson C Summary

- To allow a derived class to inherit the attributes and behaviors of a base class:

  Enter the Inherits clause immediately below the Public Class clause in the derived class. The Inherits clause is the keyword `Inherits` followed by the name of the base class.

- To refer to the base class:

  Use the `MyBase` keyword.

- To indicate that a method in the base class can be overridden (replaced) in the derived class:

  Use the `Overridable` keyword in the method's header in the base class.

- To indicate that a method in the derived class overrides (replaces) a method in the base class:

  Use the `Overrides` keyword in the method's header in the derived class.

Lesson C Key Terms

Base class—the original class from which another class is derived

Derived class—a class that inherits the attributes and behaviors of a base class

Inheritance—the ability to create one class from another class

Inherits clause—entered immediately below the Public Class clause in a derived class; specifies the name of the base class associated with the derived class

MyBase—a keyword used in a derived class to refer to the base class

Overridable—a keyword that can appear in a method's header in a base class; indicates that the method can be overridden by any class that is derived from the base class

Overrides—a keyword that can appear in a method's header in a derived class; indicates that the method overrides the method with the same name in the base class

Lesson C Review Questions

1. Which of the following clauses allows a derived class named Dog to have the same attributes and behaviors as its base class, which is named Animal?

   a. `Inherits Animal`

   b. `Inherits Dog`

   c. `Overloads Dog`

   d. `Overrides Animal`

2. A base class contains a method named GetBonus. Which of the following procedure headers can be used in the base class to indicate that a derived class can provide its own code for the method?

   a. `Public Inherits Sub GetBonus()`

   b. `Public Overloads Sub GetBonus()`

   c. `Public Overridable Sub GetBonus()`

   d. `Public Overrides Sub GetBonus()`

3. A base class contains a method named GetBonus. Which of the following procedure headers can be used in the derived class to indicate that it is providing its own code for the method?

   a. `Public Inherits Sub GetBonus()`

   b. `Public Overloads Sub GetBonus()`

   c. `Public Overridable Sub GetBonus()`

   d. `Public Overrides Sub GetBonus()`

4. The Salaried class is derived from a base class named Employee. Which of the following statements can be used by the Salaried class to invoke the Employee class's default constructor?

   a. `MyBase.New()`

   b. `MyEmployee.New()`

   c. `Call Employee.New`

   d. none of the above

Lesson C Exercises

1. Open the Formula Solution (Formula Solution.sln) file contained in the VB2010\Chap11\Formula Solution folder. If necessary, open the designer window. Double-click Areas.vb in the Solution Explorer window. The file contains the Parallelogram class definition. The class

INTRODUCTORY

contains two Public properties and two constructors. It also contains a method that calculates the area of a parallelogram. The method's name is GetArea.

a. Create a derived class named Triangle. The derived class should inherit the properties and GetArea method from the Parallelogram class. However, the Triangle class's GetArea method should calculate the area of a triangle. The formula for calculating the area of a triangle is *base * height* / 2. Be sure to include a default constructor and a parameterized constructor in the derived class.

b. The Calculate button's Click event procedure should display either the area of a parallelogram or the area of a triangle. The appropriate area to display depends on the radio button selected in the interface. Code the button's Click event procedure.

c. Save the solution and then start and test the application. Close the form's Code Editor window and the Areas.vb window, and then close the solution.

INTERMEDIATE

2. Open the Kerry Sales Solution (Kerry Sales Solution.sln) file contained in the VB2010\Chap11\Kerry Sales Solution folder. If necessary, open the designer window. Double-click Payroll.vb in the Solution Explorer window.

a. Create a base class named Commission. The class should contain two Public properties: a String property named SalesId and a Double property named Sales. Include a default constructor and a parameterized constructor in the class. Also include a GetCommission method (function) that calculates a salesperson's commission using the following formula: *sales * .05*.

b. Create a derived class named BonusCommission. The derived class's GetCommission method should calculate the commission as follows: *sales * .05 + (sales − 2500) * .01*. Be sure to include a default constructor and a parameterized constructor in the derived class.

c. Open the form's Code Editor window and locate the btnCalc control's Click event procedure. Finish coding the procedure, using the comments as a guide.

d. Save the solution and then start and test the application. Close the form's Code Editor window and the Payroll.vb window, and then close the solution.

 ## Swat The Bugs

3. Open the Debug Solution (Debug Solution.sln) file contained in the VB2010\Chap11\Debug Solution-Lesson C folder. If necessary, open the designer window. Open the Code Editor windows for the form and class file. Review the existing code. Correct the code to remove the jagged lines in the Shape and Circle class definitions. Save the solution and then start and test the application. Notice that the application is not working correctly. Locate and correct the errors in the code. Save the solution and then start and test the application again. Close the Code Editor windows and then close the solution.

CHAPTER 12

Web Applications

Creating the DJ Tom Application

In this chapter, you will create a Web application for DJ (disc jockey) Tom. Although DJ Tom can be hired for any event, his specialty is weddings. Therefore, he has requested a Web page that allows the user to enter the names of the bride and groom, the wedding date, an e-mail address, and the name of the first song to be danced by the newly married couple. The Web page will provide a Submit button that, when clicked, displays a message on the page. The message will contain the information entered by the user.

Previewing the DJ Tom Application

Before you start the first lesson in this chapter, you will preview the completed application. The application is contained in the VB2010\Chap12 folder.

START HERE ▶ **To preview the completed application:**

1. If necessary, start Visual Studio 2010 or Visual Web Developer 2010 Express.

2. Click **File** on the menu bar and then click **Open Web Site**. The Open Web Site dialog box appears. If necessary, click the **File System** button. Click the **DJTom-Preview** folder contained in the VB2010\ Chap12 folder and then click the **Open** button. If the Default.aspx Web page does not appear in the Document window, right-click **Default.aspx** in the Solution Explorer window and then click **View Designer**.

3. Press **Ctrl+F5** to start the application. The Web page appears in a browser window.

4. Click the **Bride** box and then type **Melinda**. Press **Tab** and then type **Pierre** as the groom's name.

5. Click **any date** in the calendar.

6. Click the **E-mail box** and then type **anyEmail@domain.com**.

7. Click the **down arrow** in the First song box and then click **The Way You Look Tonight**.

8. Click the **Submit** button. A message appears in a purple box on the Web page. See Figure 12-1. (The top of your browser window may look slightly different from the one shown in Figure 12-1.)

a message appears in a purple box

Figure 12-1   Result of clicking the Submit button

9. Close the **browser** window. Click **File** on the Visual Studio 2010 (Visual Web Developer 2010 Express) menu bar and then click **Close Solution**. If you are asked whether you want to save the changes to the DJTom-Preview.sln file, click the **No** button.

10. Click **File** and then click **Exit** to close Visual Studio 2010 (Visual Web Developer 2010 Express).

In Lesson A, you will learn how to create static Web pages. Dynamic Web pages are covered in Lessons B and C. You will code the DJ Tom application in Lesson C. Be sure to complete each lesson in full and do all of the end-of-lesson questions and several exercises before continuing to the next lesson.

LESSON A

After studying Lesson A, you should be able to:

- Define basic Web terminology

- Create a Web application

- Add Web pages to an application

- Customize a Web page

- Add static text to a Web page

- Format a Web page's static text

- View a Web page in full screen view

- Add a link button and an image to a Web page

- Start a Web application

- Close and open a Web application

- Reposition a control on a Web page

Web Applications

The Internet is the world's largest computer network, connecting millions of computers located all around the world. One of the most popular features of the Internet is the World Wide Web, often referred to simply as the Web. The Web consists of documents called **Web pages** that are stored on Web servers. A **Web server** is a computer that contains special software that "serves up" Web pages in response to requests from client computers. A **client computer** is a computer that requests information from a Web server. The information is requested and subsequently viewed through the use of a program called a Web browser or, more simply, a **browser.** Currently, the two most popular browsers are Microsoft Internet Explorer and Mozilla Firefox.

Many Web pages are static. A **static Web page** is a document whose purpose is merely to display information to the viewer. Static Web pages are not interactive. The only interaction that can occur between static Web pages and the user is through links that allow the user to "jump" from one Web page to another. Figures 12-2 and 12-3 show examples of static Web pages created for the Greenview Toy Store. The Web page in Figure 12-2 shows the store's name, address, and telephone number. The page also provides a link to the Web page shown in Figure 12-3. That page shows the store's business hours and provides a link for returning to the first Web page. You will create both Web pages in this lesson.

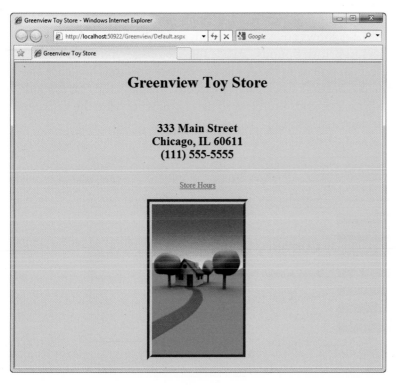

Figure 12-2   Example of a static Web page

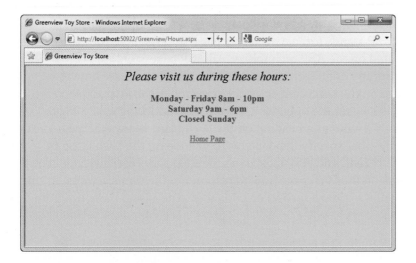

Figure 12-3   Another example of a static Web page

Although static Web pages provide a means for a store to list its location and hours, a company wanting to do business on the Web must be able to do more than just list information: It must be able to interact with customers through its Web site. The Web site should allow customers to submit inquiries, select items for purchase, and submit payment information. It also should allow the company to track customer inquiries and process customer orders. Tasks such as these can be accomplished using dynamic Web pages.

Unlike a static Web page, a **dynamic Web page** is interactive in that it can accept information from the user and also retrieve information for the user. Examples of dynamic Web pages that you might have already encountered include forms for purchasing merchandise online and for submitting online resumes. Figure 12-4 shows an example of a dynamic Web page that converts American dollars to British pounds. To use the Web page, you enter the number of American dollars in the American dollars box and then click the Submit button. The button's Click event procedure displays the corresponding number of British pounds on the Web page. You will create the Currency Converter Web page in Lesson B.

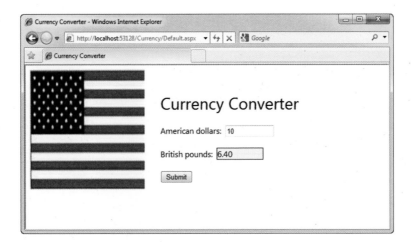

Figure 12-4   Example of a dynamic Web page

The Web applications created in this chapter use a technology called ASP.NET 4.0. **ASP** stands for "active server page" and refers to the type of Web page created by the ASP technology. All ASP pages contain HTML (Hypertext Markup Language) tags that tell the client's browser how to render the page on the computer screen. For example, the instruction `<h1>Hello</h1>` uses the opening `<h1>` tag and its closing `</h1>` tag to display the word "Hello" as a heading on the Web page. Many ASP pages also contain ASP tags that specify the controls to include on the Web page. In addition to the HTML and ASP tags, dynamic ASP pages contain code that tells the objects on the Web page how to respond to the user's actions. In this chapter, you will write the appropriate code using the Visual Basic programming language.

When a client computer's browser sends a request for an ASP page, the Web server locates the page and then sends the appropriate HTML instructions to the client. The client's browser uses the instructions to render the Web page on the computer screen. If the Web page is a dynamic one, like the Currency Converter page shown in Figure 12-4, the user can interact with the page by entering data. In most cases, the user then clicks a button on the Web page to submit the data to the server for processing. When the server receives the data, it executes the Visual Basic code associated with the Web page. It then sends back the appropriate HTML, which now includes the result of processing the code and data, to the client for rendering in the browser window. Using the Currency Converter Web page as an example, the user first enters the number of American dollars and then clicks the Submit button, which submits the user's entry to the Web server.

The server executes the Visual Basic code to convert the American dollars to British pounds and then sends back the HTML, which now includes the number of British pounds. Notice that the Web page's HTML is interpreted and executed by the client computer, whereas the program code is executed by the Web server. Figure 12-5 illustrates the relationship between the client computer and the Web server.

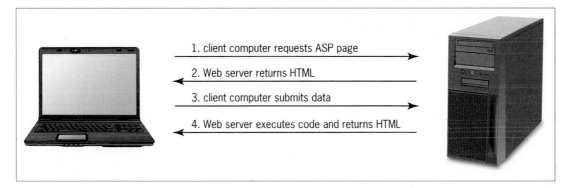

1. client computer requests ASP page

2. Web server returns HTML

3. client computer submits data

4. Web server executes code and returns HTML

Figure 12-5   Illustration of the relationship between a client computer and a Web server

In this lesson, you will create a Web application that contains static Web pages. You will create applications containing dynamic Web pages in Lessons B and C.

Creating a Web Application

You create a Web application in Visual Basic using Visual Web Developer 2010, which is available either as a stand-alone product (called Visual Web Developer 2010 Express) or as part of Visual Studio 2010. You can download a free copy of Visual Web Developer 2010 Express from Microsoft's Web site. At the time of this writing, the address is *http://www.microsoft.com/express/Downloads/#2010-Visual-Web-Developer*. The following steps show you how to configure Visual Web Developer 2010 Express. You should perform these steps only if you are using Visual Web Developer 2010 Express.

To configure Visual Web Developer 2010 Express: START HERE

1. Click the **Start** button on the Windows 7 taskbar and then point to **All Programs**.

2. Click **Microsoft Visual Studio 2010 Express** and then click **Microsoft Visual Web Developer 2010 Express**.

3. Click **Tools** on the menu bar, and then click **Options** to open the Options dialog box. If necessary, select the **Show all settings** check box. Click the **Projects and Solutions** node. Use the information shown in Figure 12-6 to select and deselect the appropriate check boxes.

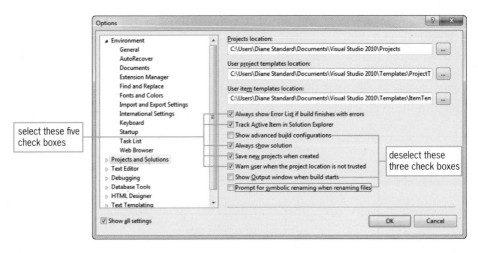

select these five
check boxes

deselect these
three check boxes

Figure 12-6   Options dialog box

4. Click the **OK** button to close the Options dialog box.

5. Click **Tools** on the menu bar and then point to **Settings**. If necessary, click **Expert Settings** to select it.

In the next set of steps, you begin creating the Greenview Toy Store Web application.

START HERE

To begin creating the Web application:

1. If necessary, start Visual Studio 2010 or Visual Web Developer 2010 Express.

2. If necessary, open the Solution Explorer and Properties windows and auto-hide the Toolbox window.

3. Click **File** on the menu bar and then click **New Web Site** to open the New Web Site dialog box. If necessary, click **Visual Basic** in the Installed Templates list. Click **ASP.NET Empty Web Site** in the middle column of the dialog box.

4. If necessary, change the entry in the Web location box to **File System**. The File System selection allows you to store your Web application in any folder on either your computer or a network drive.

5. In this chapter, you will be instructed to store your Web applications in the F:\VB2010\Chap12 folder; however, you can use any location. In the box that appears next to the Web location box, replace the existing text with **F:\VB2010\Chap12\Greenview**. Figure 12-7 shows the completed New Web Site dialog box. Your New Web Site dialog box will look slightly different if you are using Visual Web Developer 2010 Express.

Figure 12-7 New Web Site dialog box

6. Click the **OK** button to close the New Web Site dialog box. The computer creates an empty Web application named Greenview.

Adding the Default.aspx Web Page to the Application

After creating an empty Web application, you need to add a Web page to it. The first Web page added to an application is usually named Default.aspx.

To add the Default.aspx Web page to the application:

START HERE

1. Click **Website** on the menu bar and then click **Add New Item** to open the Add New Item dialog box. (If Website does not appear on the menu bar, click the Web application's location and name in the Solution Explorer window.)

2. If necessary, click **Visual Basic** in the Installed Templates list and then (if necessary) click **Web Form** in the middle column of the dialog box. Verify that the Place code in separate file check box is selected, and that the Select master page check box is not selected. As indicated in Figure 12-8, the Web page will be named Default.aspx.

Figure 12-8 Add New Item dialog box

3. Click the **Add** button to display the Default.aspx page in the Document window. If necessary, click the **Design** tab that appears at the bottom of the IDE. When the Design tab is selected, the Web page appears in Design view in the Document window, as shown in Figure 12-9. You can use Design view to add text and controls to the Web page. If the Formatting toolbar does not appear on your screen, click **View** on the menu bar, point to **Toolbars**, and then click **Formatting**. If the div tag does not appear in the Document window, click either the **<div>** button at the bottom of the IDE or the **rectangle** below the body tag.

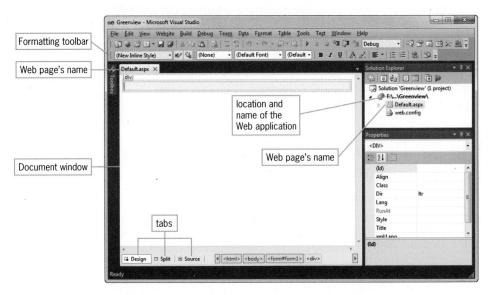

Figure 12-9 Default.aspx Web page shown in Design view

4. Click the **Source** tab to display the Web page in Source view. This view shows the HTML and ASP tags that tell a browser how to render the Web page. The tags are automatically generated for you as you are creating the Web page in Design view. Currently, the Web page contains only HTML tags.

5. Click the **Split** tab to split the Document window into two parts. The upper half displays the Web page in Source view, and the lower half displays it in Design view.

6. Click the **Design** tab to return to Design view, and then auto-hide the Solution Explorer window.

Customizing a Web Page

You can use the Properties window to customize a Web page. The properties appear in the Properties window when you select DOCUMENT in the window's Object box. A Web page's Title property, for example, determines the value that appears in the browser's title bar and also on the page's tab in the browser window. Its BgColor property controls the page's background color.

To change the Title and BgColor properties:

1. Click the **down arrow** button in the Properties window's Object box and then click **DOCUMENT** in the list. (If DOCUMENT does not appear in the Object box, click the Design tab.) The DOCUMENT object represents the Web page.

2. If necessary, click the **Alphabetical** button in the Properties window to display the properties in alphabetical order. Click **Title** in the Properties list. Type **Greenview Toy Store** in the Settings box and then press **Enter**.

3. Click **BgColor** in the Properties list and then click the **...** (ellipsis) button to open the More Colors dialog box. Click the **hexagon** indicated in Figure 12-10.

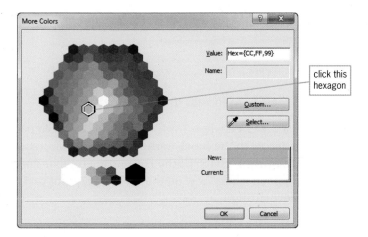

Figure 12-10   More Colors dialog box

4. Click the **OK** button to close the More Colors dialog box. The page's background color changes from white to a pale green.

5. Auto-hide the Properties window. Save the application by clicking either the **Save All** button on the Standard toolbar or the **Save All** option on the File menu.

Adding Static Text to a Web Page

All Web pages contain some text that the user is not allowed to edit, such as a company name or the caption that identifies a text box. Text that cannot be changed by the user is referred to as **static text**. You can add static text to a Web page by simply typing the text on the page itself; or, you can use a label control that you dragged to the Web page from the Toolbox window. In this lesson, you will type the static text on the Web page.

To add static text to the Web page:

1. If necessary, click **inside the rectangle** that appears below the div tag at the top of the Document window. The div tag defines a division in a Web page. (If the div tag does not appear in the Document window, click the <div> button at the bottom of the IDE.)

2. Enter the following four lines of text. Press **Enter** twice after typing the last line.

Greenview Toy Store
333 Main Street
Chicago, IL 60611
(111) 555-5555

3. Save the application.

You can use either the Format menu or the Formatting toolbar to format the static text on a Web page. Figure 12-11 indicates some of the tools available on the Formatting toolbar.

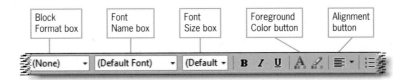

Figure 12-11   Formatting toolbar

START HERE

To use the Formatting toolbar to format the static text:

1. Select (highlight) the Greenview Toy Store text on the Web page. Click the **down arrow** in the Block Format box on the Formatting toolbar. Click **Heading 1 <h1>**. (If the Formatting toolbar does not appear on your screen, click View on the menu bar, point to Toolbars, and then click Formatting.)

2. Select the address and phone number text on the Web page. Click the **down arrow** in the Block Format box and then click **Heading 2 <h2>**.

3. Now, you will use the Formatting toolbar's Alignment button to center all of the static text. Select all of the static text on the Web page and then click the **down arrow** on the Alignment button. See Figure 12-12.

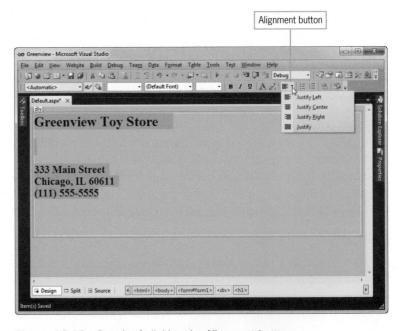

Figure 12-12   Result of clicking the Alignment button

4. Click **Justify Center**. The selected text appears centered, horizontally, on the Web page. Click **anywhere below the phone number** to deselect the text, and then save the application.

Viewing a Web Page in Full Screen View

While you are designing a Web page, you can periodically view the page in full screen view to determine how it will appear to the user. You do this using the Full Screen option on the View menu.

To view the Web page using the Full Screen option:

START HERE

1. Click **View** on the menu bar and then click **Full Screen** on the menu. See Figure 12-13. Although not identical to viewing in a browser window, full screen view provides a quick and easy way to verify the placement of controls and text on the Web page.

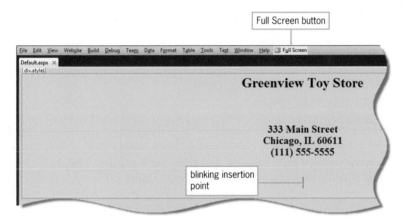

Figure 12-13   Default.aspx Web page displayed in full screen view

2. Click the **Full Screen** button to return to the standard view. (If you mistakenly clicked the window's Close button, click the Full Screen button, right-click Default.aspx in the Solution Explorer window, and then click View Designer.)

Adding Another Web Page to the Application

In the next set of steps, you will add a second Web page to the Greenview Toy Store application. The Web page will display the store's hours of operation.

To add another Web page to the application:

START HERE

1. Click **Website** on the menu bar and then click **Add New Item** to open the Add New Item dialog box. (If Website does not appear on the menu bar, click the Web application's location and name in the Solution Explorer window.)

2. If necessary, click **Visual Basic** in the Installed Templates list and then (if necessary) click **Web Form** in the middle column of the dialog box. Change the filename in the Name box to **Hours** and then click the **Add** button. The computer appends the .aspx extension on the filename and then displays the Hours.aspx Web page in the Document window.

693

3. Temporarily display the Solution Explorer window. Notice that the window now contains the Hours.aspx filename.

4. Temporarily display the Properties window. Click the **down arrow** button in the Properties window's Object box and then click **DOCUMENT** in the list. (If DOCUMENT does not appear in the Object box, click the Design tab.) Change the Web page's Title property to **Greenview Toy Store**. Also change its BgColor property to the same color as the Default.aspx page. (If necessary, refer back to Figure 12-10.) Click the **OK** button to close the More Colors dialog box.

5. If necessary, click the **Design** tab and then click **inside the rectangle** that appears below the div tag at the top of the Document window. (If the div tag does not appear in the Document window, click either the <div> button at the bottom of the IDE or the rectangle below the body tag.) Type **Please visit us during these hours:** and press **Enter** twice.

6. Now, enter the following three lines of text. Press **Enter** twice after typing the last line.

   Monday – Friday 8am – 10pm
   Saturday 9am – 6pm
   Closed Sunday

7. Select the **Please visit us during these hours:** text. Click the **down arrow** in the Font Size box and then click **x-large (24pt)**. Also click the *I* (Italic) button on the Formatting toolbar.

8. Select the three lines of text that contain the store hours. Click the **down arrow** in the Font Size box and then click **large (18pt)**. Also click the **B** (Bold) button on the Formatting toolbar.

9. Now, you will change the color of the selected text. Click the **Foreground Color** button on the Formatting toolbar to open the More Colors dialog box. Click **any dark green hexagon** and then click the **OK** button.

10. Select all of the static text on the Web page. Click the **down arrow** on the Alignment button and then click **Justify Center**.

11. Click the **blank line** below the store hours to deselect the text, and then save the application.

Adding a Link Button Control to a Web Page

In addition to customizing a Web page by changing its properties and formatting its static text, you also can add controls to the Web page. You do this using the tools provided in the Toolbox window. In the next set of steps, you will add a **link button control** to both Web pages. The link button control on the Default.aspx page will display the Hours.aspx page. The link button control on the Hours.aspx page will return the user to the Default.aspx page.

To add a link button control to both Web pages: START HERE

1. First, you will add a link button control to the Hours.aspx page.
    Permanently display the Toolbox window and then click the
    LinkButton tool. Drag your mouse pointer to the location shown
    in Figure 12-14 and then release the mouse button.

Figure 12-14   Link button control added to the Hours.aspx Web page

2. Temporarily display the Properties window. Change the control's Text
    property to **Home Page** and press **Enter**. Click **PostBackUrl** in the
    Properties list and then click the **...** (ellipsis) button to open the Select
    URL dialog box. Click **Default.aspx** in the Contents of folder list. See
    Figure 12-15.

Figure 12-15   Select URL dialog box

3. Click the **OK** button to close the dialog box and then click the **Web page**.

4. Now, you will add a link button control to the Default.aspx page. Click
    the **Default.aspx** tab. Click the **LinkButton** tool. Drag your mouse
    pointer to the location shown in Figure 12-16 and then release the
    mouse button.

Figure 12-16   Link button control added to the Default.aspx Web page

5. Temporarily display the Properties window. Change the control's Text property to **Store Hours** and press **Enter**. Change its PostBackUrl property to **Hours.aspx**.

6. Click the **OK** button to close the dialog box and then click the **Web page**. Save the application.

Starting a Web Application

Typically, you start a Web application either by pressing Ctrl+F5 or by clicking the Start Without Debugging option on the Debug menu. The method you use—the shortcut keys or the menu option—is a matter of personal preference. If you prefer to use a menu option, you might need to add the Start Without Debugging option to the Debug menu, because the option is not automatically included on the menu in either Visual Studio or Visual Web Developer Express. You can add the option to the menu by performing the next set of steps. If you prefer to use the Ctrl+F5 shortcut keys, you can skip the next set of steps.

START HERE ▶ **To add the Start Without Debugging option to the Debug menu:**

1. First, you will determine whether your Debug menu already contains the Start Without Debugging option. Click **Debug** on the menu bar. If the Debug menu contains the Start Without Debugging option, close the menu by clicking **Debug** again, and then skip the remaining steps in this set of steps.

2. If the Debug menu does not contain the Start Without Debugging option, close the menu by clicking **Debug** again. Click **Tools** on the menu bar and then click **Customize** to open the Customize dialog box.

3. Click the **Commands** tab. The Menu bar radio button should be selected. Click the **down arrow** in the Menu bar list box. Scroll down the list until you see Debug, and then click **Debug**.

4. Click the **Add Command** button to open the Add Command dialog box, and then click **Debug** in the Categories list. Scroll down the Commands list until you see Start Without Debugging, and then click **Start Without Debugging**. Click the **OK** button to close the Add Command dialog box.

5. Click the **Move Down** button three times. The completed Customize dialog box is shown in Figure 12-17. After viewing the figure, click the **Close** button to close the Customize dialog box.

Figure 12-17   Customize dialog box

When you start a Web application in either Visual Studio 2010 or Visual Web Developer 2010 Express, the computer creates a temporary Web server that allows you to view your Web page in a browser. However, keep in mind that your Web page will need to be placed on an actual Web server for others to view it.

To start the Greenview Toy Store Web application:

START HERE

1. Start the Web application either by pressing **Ctrl+F5** or by clicking the **Start Without Debugging** option on the Debug menu. Your browser requests the Default.aspx page from the server. The server locates the page and then sends the appropriate HTML instructions to your browser for rendering on the screen. Notice that the value in the page's Title property appears in the browser's title bar and on the page's tab in the browser window. See Figure 12-18.

the Title property's value appears here

Figure 12-18   Default.aspx Web page displayed in a browser window

2. Click **Store Hours** to display the Hours.aspx page. See Figure 12-19.

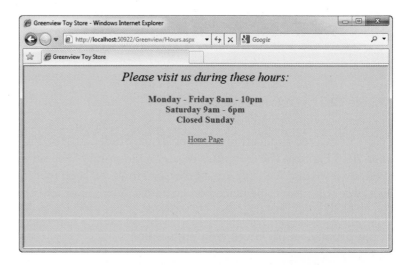

Figure 12-19   Hours.aspx Web page displayed in a browser window

3. Click **Home Page** to display the Default.aspx page, and then close the browser window.

Adding an Image to a Web Page

In the next set of steps, you will add an image to the Default.aspx page. The image is stored in the Small_house.jpg file, which is contained in the VB2010\ Chap12 folder. The image file was downloaded from the Stock.XCHNG site and was generously contributed by photographer Gerrit Schneider. (You can browse and optionally download other free images at *www.sxc.hu*. However, be sure to read the Web site's copyright policies before downloading any images.)

To add an image to the Web page:

START HERE

1. First, you will need to add the image file to the application. Click **Website** on the menu bar and then click **Add Existing Item**. Open the VB2010\Chap12 folder. Click the **down arrow** in the box that controls the file types and then click **All Files (*.*)** in the list. Click **Small_house.jpg** in the list of filenames and then click the **Add** button.

2. If necessary, insert a blank line below the Store Hours link button control. Click the **blank line** below the control and then press **Enter** to insert another blank line. Click the **Image** tool in the toolbox. Drag your mouse pointer to the location shown in Figure 12-20 and then release the mouse button.

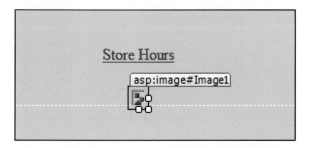

Figure 12-20   Image control added to the Default.aspx Web page

3. Temporarily display the Properties window. Click **ImageUrl** in the Properties list and then click the **...** (ellipsis) button to open the Select Image dialog box. Click **Small_house.jpg** in the Contents of folder section and then click the **OK** button.

4. Next, you will put a colored border around the image control and also change the border's width to 10 pixels. Change the image control's BorderStyle property to **Groove**, and then change its BorderWidth property to **10**. Press **Enter** after typing the number 10.

5. Now, you will change the color of the image's border to match the Web page's color. Click **BorderColor** in the Properties list and then click the **...** (ellipsis) button. When the More Colors dialog box opens, click the same hexagon as you did for the DOCUMENT's BgColor. (If necessary, refer back to Figure 12-10.) Click the **OK** button to close the dialog box and then click the **Web page**.

6. Auto-hide the toolbox. Save and then start the application. See Figure 12-21.

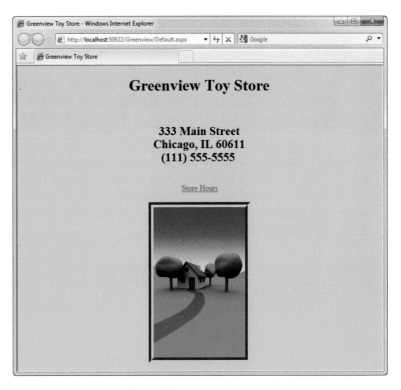

Figure 12-21   Default.aspx Web page

7. Verify that the browser window is not maximized. Place your mouse pointer on the window's right border and then drag the border to the left to make the window narrower. Notice that the text and image remain centered in the visible portion of the window. Now, drag the right border to the right to make the window wider. Here again, the text and image remain centered in the visible portion of the window.

8. Close the browser window.

Closing and Opening an Existing Web Application

You can use the File menu to close and also open an existing Web application.

START HERE   **To close and then open the Greenview Toy Store application:**

1. Click **File** on the menu bar and then click **Close Solution** to close the application.

2. Now, you will open the application. Click **File** on the menu bar and then click **Open Web Site**. The Open Web Site dialog box appears. If necessary, click the **File System** button. Click the **Greenview** folder, which is contained in the VB2010\Chap12 folder, and then click the **Open** button. (If you need to open the Web page in the Document window, right-click the Web page's name in the Solution Explorer window and then click View Designer.)

Repositioning a Control on a Web Page

At times, you may want to reposition a control on a Web page. In this section, you will move the image and link button controls to different locations on the Default.aspx Web page. First, however, you will create a new Web application and then copy the Greenview files to the application.

To create a new Web application and then copy files to the application:

START HERE

1. Close the Greenview application. Use the New Web Site option on the File menu to create an empty Web application named **Greenview2**. Save the application in the VB2010\Chap12 folder.

2. Close the Greenview2 application.

3. Use Windows to open the Greenview2 folder. Delete the web.config file.

4. Use Windows to open the Greenview folder. Select the folder's contents, which include six files (Default.aspx, Default.aspx.vb, Hours.aspx, Hours.aspx.vb, Small_house.jpg, and web.config). Copy the six files to the Greenview2 folder.

Now, you will open the Greenview2 application and move the two controls to different locations on the Default.aspx Web page.

To open the Greenview2 application and then move the controls:

START HERE

1. Open the Greenview2 Web application. Right-click **Default.aspx** in the Solution Explorer window and then click **View Designer**.

2. First, you will move the image control from the bottom of the Web page to the top of the Web page. If necessary, click **immediately before the letter G** in the Greenview Toy Store heading. Press **Enter** to insert a blank line above the heading.

3. Click the **image control** on the Web page. Drag the image control to the blank line immediately above the heading, and then release the mouse button.

4. Next, you will move the link button control to the empty area below the store's name. Click the **link button control**. Drag the control to the empty area below the store's name, and then release the mouse button.

5. Save and then start the application. See Figure 12-22.

Figure 12-22   Modified Default.aspx Web page

6. Close the browser window and then close the application.

YOU DO IT 1!

Create an empty Web application named YouDoIt 1. Save the application in the VB2010\Chap12 folder. Add two Web pages to the application: one named Default.aspx and the other named Address.aspx. The Default.aspx page should contain your name and a link button control. Change the link button control's Text property to Address. The control should display the Address.aspx page. The Address.aspx page should contain your address and a link button control. Change this link button control's Text property to Name. The control should display the Default.aspx page. Save the application and then start and test it. Close the browser window and then close the application.

Lesson A Summary

- To create an empty Web application:

Start Visual Studio 2010 or Visual Web Developer 2010 Express. Click File on the menu bar and then click New Web Site to open the New Web Site dialog box. If necessary, click Visual Basic in the Installed Templates list.

Click ASP.NET Empty Web Site in the middle column of the dialog box. If necessary, change the entry in the Web location box to File System. In the box that appears next to the Web location box, enter the location where you want the Web application saved. Also enter the application's name. Click the OK button to close the New Web Site dialog box.

- To add a Web page to a Web application:

  Open the Web application. Click Website on the menu bar and then click Add New Item to open the Add New Item dialog box. (If Website does not appear on the menu bar, click the Web application's location and name in the Solution Explorer window.) If necessary, click Visual Basic in the Installed Templates list and then click Web Form in the middle column of the dialog box. Verify that the Place code in separate file check box is selected, and that the Select master page check box is not selected. Enter an appropriate name in the Name box. Click the Add button to display the Web page in the Document window. If necessary, click the Design tab that appears at the bottom of the IDE.

- To add a title to a Web page:

  Set the DOCUMENT object's Title property.

- To change the background color of a Web page:

  Set the DOCUMENT object's BgColor property.

- To add static text to a Web page:

  Either type the text on the Web page or use a label control that you dragged to the Web page from the Toolbox window.

- To format the static text on a Web page:

  Use either the Format menu or the Formatting toolbar.

- To display a Web page in full screen view:

  Click View on the menu bar and then click Full Screen on the menu.

- To add a link button control to a Web page:

  Use the LinkButton tool in the toolbox to drag a link button control to the Web page, and then set the control's Text and PostBackUrl properties.

- To display a Web page in a browser window:

  Start the Web application either by pressing Ctrl+F5 or by clicking the Start Without Debugging option on the Debug menu.

- To add an image file to an application:

  Click Website on the menu bar and then click Add Existing Item. Open the appropriate folder and then click the image filename. Click the Add button.

- To add an image control to a Web page:

  Use the Image tool in the toolbox to drag an image control to the Web page, and then set the image control's ImageUrl property.

- To close a Web application:

  Click File on the menu bar and then click Close Solution.

- To open an existing Web application:

  Click File on the menu bar and then click Open Web Site. If necessary, click the File System button in the Open Web Site dialog box. Click the name of the Web site and then click the Open button. If necessary, right-click the Web page's name in the Solution Explorer window and then click View Designer.

- To reposition a control on a Web page:

  Drag the control to the new location.

Lesson A Key Terms

ASP—stands for "active server page"

Browser—a program that allows a client computer to request and view Web pages

Client computer—a computer that requests information from a Web server

Dynamic Web page—an interactive document that can accept information from the user and also retrieve information for the user

Link button control—allows the user to "jump" from one Web page to another

Static text—text that the user is not allowed to edit

Static Web page—a non-interactive document whose purpose is merely to display information to the viewer

Web pages—the documents stored on Web servers

Web server—a computer that contains special software that "serves up" Web pages in response to requests from client computers

Lesson A Review Questions

1. A computer that requests an ASP page from a Web server is called a _____ computer.

   a. browser

   b. client

   c. requesting

   d. none of the above

2. A _____ is a program that uses HTML to render a Web page on the computer screen.

   a. browser

   b. client

   c. server

   d. none of the above

3. An online form used to purchase a product is an example of a _____ Web page.

   a. dynamic

   b. static

4. The first Web page in an empty Web application is automatically assigned the name _____.

   a. Default.aps

   b. Default1.vb

   c. WebForm1.aspx

   d. none of the above

5. The HTML instructions in a Web page are processed by the _____.

   a. client computer

   b. Web server

6. The background color of a Web page is determined by the _____ property.

   a. BackColor

   b. BackgroundColor

   c. BgColor

   d. none of the above

Lesson A Exercises

1. Create an empty Web application named Johansen. Save the application in the VB2010\Chap12 folder. Add a new Web page named Default.aspx to the application. Change the DOCUMENT object's Title property to Johansen Pet Supplies. Create a Web page similar to the one shown in Figure 12-23. The static text should be centered, horizontally, on the page. Save and then start the application. Close the browser window and then close the application.

INTRODUCTORY

Figure 12-23   Web page for Johansen Pet Supplies

INTRODUCTORY

2. Create an empty Web application named Winterland. Save the application in the VB2010\Chap12 folder. Add a new Web page named Default.aspx to the application. Change the DOCUMENT object's Title property to Winterland Farms. Change the DOCUMENT object's BgColor property to a light blue. Create a Web page similar to the one shown in Figure 12-24. The winterland.jpg file is contained in the VB2010\Chap12 folder. Save and then start the application. Close the browser window and then close the application.

Figure 12-24   Web page for Winterland Farms

INTERMEDIATE

3. Create an empty Web application named Gutierrez. Save the application in the VB2010\Chap12 folder. Add two new Web pages named Default.aspx and Message.aspx to the application. Change the DOCUMENT object's Title property to Gutierrez Heating and Cooling. Create Web pages similar to the ones shown in Figures 12-25 and 12-26. The static text and link button control on the Default.aspx page should be centered, horizontally, on the page. As you are creating the Web pages, periodically view them in full screen view. Save and then start the application. Close the browser window and then close the application.

Figure 12-25   Default.aspx Web page for Gutierrez Heating and Cooling

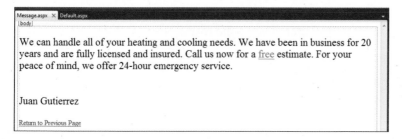

Figure 12-26   Message.aspx Web page for Gutierrez Heating and Cooling

LESSON B

After studying Lesson B, you should be able to:

- Add a text box, a label, and a button to a Web page
- Code a control on a Web page
- Use a RequiredFieldValidator control

Dynamic Web Pages

A dynamic Web page contains controls with which the user can interact. It also contains code that tells the controls how to respond to the user's actions. In this lesson, you will create a dynamic Web page that allows the user to enter the number of American dollars. When the user clicks the page's Submit button, the button's Click event procedure will convert the dollars to British pounds and then display the result.

START HERE ▶ **To create the Currency Converter Web application:**

1. If necessary, start Visual Studio 2010 or Visual Web Developer 2010 Express.

2. If necessary, open the Solution Explorer, Properties, and Toolbox windows.

3. Use the New Web Site option on the File menu to create an empty Web application named **Currency**. Save the application in the VB2010\Chap12 folder.

4. Use the Add New Item option on the Website menu to add a Web page named Default.aspx to the application. (If Website does not appear on the menu bar, click the Web application's location and name in the Solution Explorer window.)

5. If necessary, click the **Design** tab. Change the DOCUMENT object's Title property to **Currency Converter**.

Before you add any text or controls to a Web page, you should plan the page's layout. Figure 12-27 shows a sketch of the Web page for the Currency Converter application. The Web page will contain static text. It also will contain the following controls: an image, a text box, a label, and a button.

Figure 12-27 Sketch of the Currency Converter application's Web page

To begin creating the Web page:

1. Click **inside the rectangle** that appears below the div (or body) tag at the top of the Document window. Recall that the div tag defines a division in a Web page. All of the text in this division will use the Segoe UI font. If necessary, use the View menu to display the Formatting toolbar. Click the **down arrow** in the Font Name box and then scroll the list until you see Segoe UI. Click **Segoe UI** in the list.

2. Before dragging an image control to the Web page, you will add the American flag image file to the application. Click **Website** on the menu bar and then click **Add Existing Item**. Open the VB2010\ Chap12 folder. Click the **down arrow** in the box that controls the file types and then click **All Files (*.*)** in the list. Click **USflag.jpg** in the list of filenames and then click the **Add** button.

3. Drag an image control into the rectangle that appears below the div tag and then release the mouse button. Change the image control's ImageUrl property to **USflag.jpg** and then click the **OK** button to close the Select Image dialog box.

4. Click an **empty area** to the right of the flag to deselect the image control, and then press **Enter** twice.

5. Next, you will enter the Web page's static text. Press **Tab** twice. Type **Currency Converter** and then press **Enter** twice.

6. Press **Tab** twice. Type **American dollars:**, press the **Spacebar** twice, and then press **Enter** twice.

7. Press **Tab** twice. Type **British pounds:**, press the **Spacebar** twice, and then press **Enter** twice.

8. Press **Tab** twice. Figure 12-28 shows the image control and static text on the Web page.

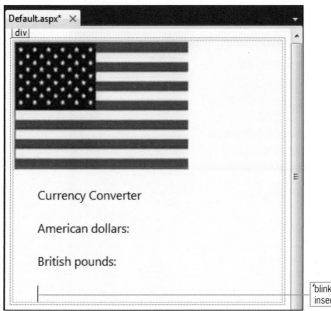

Figure 12-28 Image control and static text on the Web page

In addition to the image control and static text, the Web page will contain a text box, a label, and a button. You will add those controls next.

START HERE   **To add a text box, a label, and a button to the page:**

1. Drag a text box control to the Web page. Position the control immediately after the two spaces that follow the "American dollars:" text, and then release the mouse button.

2. Unlike Windows controls, Web controls have an ID property rather than a Name property. Use the Properties window to set the TextBox1 control's ID property (which appears at the top of the Properties list) to **txtDollars**. Also set its Width property to **90px**.

3. Drag a label control to the Web page. Position the control immediately after the two spaces that follow the "British pounds:" text, and then release the mouse button. Set the following properties for the Label1 control:

ID	**lblPounds**
BorderStyle	**Solid**
BorderWidth	**1px**
Text	**0**
Width	**90px**

4. Change the label control's BackColor property to a pale yellow.

5. Finally, drag a button control to the Web page. Position the control two blank lines below the letter B in the "British pounds:" text, and then release the mouse button. Set the following properties for the Button1 control:

ID	**btnSubmit**
Text	**Submit**

6. Click a **blank area** on the Web page and then save the application. See Figure 12-29.

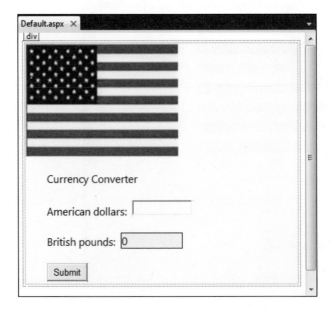

Figure 12-29   Current status of the Web page

Looking back at the sketch shown earlier in Figure 12-27, you will notice that the heading text (Currency Converter) is larger than the other text on the page. Also, the image control is positioned to the left of the static text and other controls. You will make these modifications in the next set of steps.

To complete the Web page's interface:

START HERE

1. Auto-hide the Solution Explorer, Properties, and Toolbox windows.

2. Select (highlight) the Currency Converter text. Use the Font Size box on the Formatting toolbar to change the font size to **xx-large (36pt)**. (You also can use the Font option on the Format menu to change the font size.)

3. Click the **image control**. Click **Format** on the menu bar and then click **Position** to open the Position dialog box. See Figure 12-30.

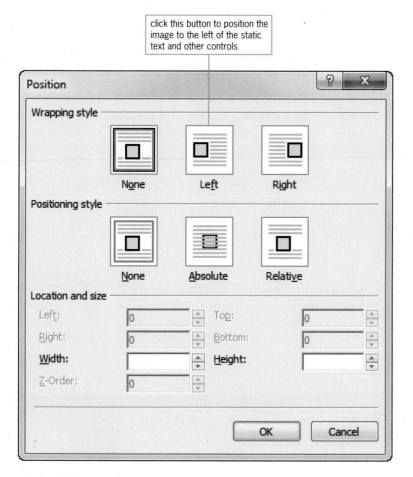

click this button to position the image to the left of the static text and other controls

Figure 12-30   Position dialog box

4. The image control should appear on the left side of the static text and other controls. Click **Left** in the Wrapping style section, and then click the **OK** button.

5. Position your mouse pointer on the image control's lower-right sizing handle, as shown in Figure 12-31. Drag the sizing handle until the control is approximately the size shown in the figure. (The number of pixels may be different on your screen. Just be sure that all of the static text and other controls appear to the right of the image control.)

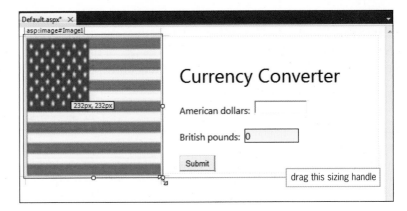

Figure 12-31   Size and position of the image control

6. Click an **empty area** on the Web page to deselect the image control. Save the application and then start it by pressing **Ctrl+F5**. The Web page appears in a browser window. Close the browser window.

Coding the Submit Button's Click Event Procedure

In the following set of steps, you will code the Submit button's Click event procedure so that it converts the number of American dollars to British pounds and then displays the result on the Web page. At the time of this writing, an American dollar was equivalent to approximately .64 British pounds. As you do when coding a control on a Windows form, you enter the code for a control on a Web page in the Code Editor window.

START HERE

To code the Submit button's Click event procedure:

1. Right-click the **Web page** and then click **View Code** on the context menu. The Default.aspx.vb window opens. Recall that the .vb extension on a filename indicates that the file contains Visual Basic code. In this case, the file is referred to as the code-behind file, because it contains code that supports the Web page. Temporarily display the Solution Explorer window. See Figure 12-32.

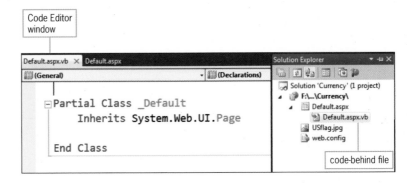

Figure 12-32   Code Editor and Solution Explorer windows

2. Enter the following comments above the Partial Class clause. Replace <your name> and <current date> with your name and the current date, respectively. Press **Enter** twice after typing the last comment.

```
' Name:          Currency
' Purpose:       Convert dollars to pounds
' Programmer:    <your name> on <current date>
```

3. Now, enter the following Option statements:

   Option Explicit On
   Option Strict On
   Option Infer Off

4. Open the btnSubmit control's Click event procedure. Type the following comment and then press **Enter** twice:

   ' converts dollars to pounds

5. The procedure will use a Double named constant to store the conversion rate of .64. Enter the following Const statement:

   Const dblPOUND_RATE As Double = .64

6. The procedure will use two Double variables to store the number of American dollars and the number of British pounds. Enter the following Dim statements. Press **Enter** twice after typing the second Dim statement.

   Dim dblDollars As Double
   Dim dblPounds As Double

7. The procedure will store the user's entry in the `dblDollars` variable. Enter the following TryParse method:

   Double.TryParse(txtDollars.Text, dblDollars)

8. Next, the procedure will convert the dollars to pounds and then store the result in the `dblPounds` variable. Enter the following assignment statement:

   dblPounds = dblDollars * dblPOUND_RATE

9. Finally, the procedure will display the number of pounds in the lblPounds control. Enter the following assignment statement:

   lblPounds.Text = dblPounds.ToString("N2")

Figure 12-33 shows the code entered in the btnSubmit control's Click event procedure.

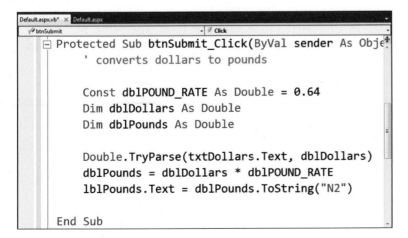

```
Default.aspx.vb*  X  Default.aspx
btnSubmit                          Click
  Protected Sub btnSubmit_Click(ByVal sender As Obje
      ' converts dollars to pounds

      Const dblPOUND_RATE As Double = 0.64
      Dim dblDollars As Double
      Dim dblPounds As Double

      Double.TryParse(txtDollars.Text, dblDollars)
      dblPounds = dblDollars * dblPOUND_RATE
      lblPounds.Text = dblPounds.ToString("N2")

  End Sub
```

Figure 12-33 btnSubmit control's Click event procedure

Now you will test the Currency Converter application to verify that it is working correctly.

START HERE **To test the Currency Converter application:**

1. Save and then start the application. Your browser requests the Default.aspx page from the server. The server locates the page and then sends the appropriate HTML instructions to your browser for rendering on the screen.

2. Click the **American dollars** box and then type **10**. Click the **Submit** button; doing this submits your entry to the server, along with a request for additional services. The server processes the code contained in the button's Click event procedure and then sends the appropriate HTML to the browser for rendering on the screen. See Figure 12-34.

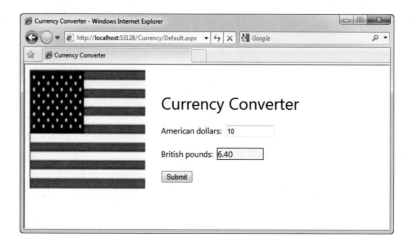

Figure 12-34   Result of clicking the Submit button

3. Close the browser window and then close the Code Editor window.

Validating User Input

The Validation section of the toolbox provides several tools for validating user input. The tools are referred to as **validator tools**. The name, purpose, and important properties of each validator tool are listed in Figure 12-35. In the Currency Converter application, you will use a RequiredFieldValidator control to verify that the user entered the number of American dollars.

Name	Purpose	Properties
CompareValidator	compare an entry with a constant value or the property stored in a control	ControlToCompare ControlToValidate ErrorMessage Type ValueToCompare
CustomValidator	verify that an entry passes the specified validation logic	ClientValidationFunction ControlToValidate ErrorMessage
RangeValidator	verify that an entry is within the specified minimum and maximum values	ControlToValidate ErrorMessage MaximumValue MinimumValue Type
RegularExpressionValidator	verify that an entry matches a specific pattern	ControlToValidate ErrorMessage ValidationExpression
RequiredFieldValidator	verify that a control contains data	ControlToValidate ErrorMessage
ValidationSummary	display all of the validation error messages in a single location on a Web page	DisplayMode HeaderText

Figure 12-35 Validator tools

To verify that the user entered the number of American dollars: START HERE

1. If necessary, maximize the Visual Studio (Visual Web Developer) window.

2. Click **to the immediate right of the txtDollars control** and then press the **Spacebar** three times.

3. Temporarily display the Toolbox window. If necessary, expand the Validation section. Click the **RequiredFieldValidator** tool and then drag your mouse pointer to the Web page. Position your mouse pointer to the right of the txtDollars control and then release the mouse button.

4. Temporarily display the Properties window. Set the following properties for the RequiredFieldValidator1 control:

   ControlToValidate   **txtDollars**
   ErrorMessage   **Required entry**
   ForeColor   choose a red hexagon

5. Click an **empty area** of the Web page. Save the application and then start it by pressing **Ctrl+F5**.

6. Click the **Submit** button without entering a value in the txtDollars control. The RequiredFieldValidator control displays the "Required entry" message, as shown in Figure 12-36.

Figure 12-36   Result of clicking the Submit button when the American dollars box is empty

7. Click the **American dollars** box and then type **20**. Click the **Submit** button. The error message is removed from the Web page and the number 12.80 appears in the lblPounds control.

8. Close the browser window and then close the application.

YOU DO IT 2!

Create an empty Web application named YouDoIt 2. Save the application in the VB2010\Chap12 folder. Add a Web page named Default.aspx to the application. The Web page should contain a text box, a label, and a button. When the user clicks the button, the application should multiply the number entered in the text box by 2 and then display the result in the label. Include a RequiredFieldValidator control on the Web page. Save the application and then start and test it. Close the application.

Lesson B Summary

- To wrap text and other controls around an image control:

  Click the image control. Click Format on the menu bar and then click Position. Click the Left button in the Wrapping style section to place the image control on the left side of the text or controls. Click the Right button to place the image control on the right side of the text or controls.

- To code a control on a Web page:

  Enter the code in the Code Editor window.

- To validate user input on a Web page:

  Use one or more of the validator tools contained in the Validation section of the toolbox. The tools are listed in Figure 12-35.

Lesson B Key Term

Validator tools—the tools contained in the Validation section of the toolbox; used to validate user input on a Web page

Lesson B Review Questions

1. In code, you refer to a control on a Web page using the control's
   _____ property.

   a. Caption

   b. ID

   c. Name

   d. Text

2. If you want text to appear to the left of the selected image control on a Web form, you would need to click the _____ button in the Position dialog box.

   a. Align

   b. AlignLeft

   c. Left

   d. Right

3. The Visual Basic code in a Web page is processed by the _____.

   a. client computer

   b. Web server

4. You can use a _____ control to verify that a control on a Web page contains data.

   a. RequiredFieldValidator

   b. RequiredField

   c. RequiredValidator

   d. none of the above

5. You can use a(n) _____ control to verify that an entry on a Web page is within a minimum and maximum value.

   a. MinMaxValidation

   b. MaxMinValidation

   c. EntryValidator

   d. RangeValidator

Lesson B Exercises

INTRODUCTORY

1. In this exercise, you modify the Currency Converter application from this lesson.

   a. Create an empty Web application named CurrencyRangeValidator. Save the application in the VB2010\Chap12 folder. Close the CurrencyRangeValidator application.

   b. Use Windows to open the CurrencyRangeValidator folder. Delete the web.config file.

   c. Use Windows to open the Currency folder. Select the folder's contents. Copy the selected contents to the CurrencyRangeValidator folder.

   d. Open the CurrencyRangeValidator Web site. Right-click Default.aspx in the Solution Explorer window and then click View Designer.

   e. Add a RangeValidator control to the Web page. Change the control's Type property to Double. The control should display an appropriate message when the number of American dollars is either less than 1 or greater than 100,000.

   f. Save the application and then start and test it. Close the browser window and then close the application.

INTRODUCTORY

2. Create an empty Web application named Multiplication. Save the application in the VB2010\Chap12 folder.

   a. Add a new Web page named Default.aspx to the application. Change the DOCUMENT object's Title property to Multiplication Calculator. Create a Web page similar to the one shown in Figure 12-37. The X image is contained in the VB2010\Chap12\Times.jpg file.

   b. Add two RequiredFieldValidator controls to the Web page. The controls should verify that their respective text boxes contain data.

   c. Open the Code Editor window. Use comments to document the application's name and purpose, as well as your name and the current date. Also enter the appropriate Option statements. Code the Submit button's Click event procedure so it multiplies the value entered in the txtMultiplier control by the value entered in the txtMultiplicand control and then displays the result in the lblProduct control.

   d. Save the application and then start and test it. Close the browser window. Close the Code Editor window and then close the application.

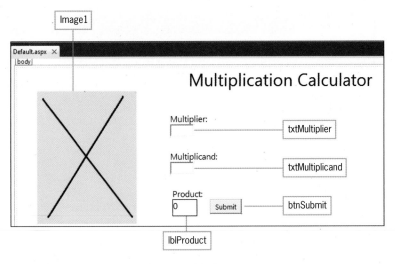

Figure 12-37   Web page for Exercise 2

INTRODUCTORY

3. In this exercise, you create an application that displays the result of converting British pounds to American dollars. Create an empty Web application named PoundsToDollars. Save the application in the VB2010\Chap12 folder. Add a new Web page named Default. aspx to the application. Change the DOCUMENT object's Title property to Pounds to Dollars. The Default.aspx page should look similar to the Currency Converter page from this lesson; however, it should display the BritishFlag.jpg image file in the image control. The image file is contained in the VB2010\Chap12 folder. Open the Code Editor window. Use comments to document the application's name and purpose, as well as your name and the current date. Also enter the appropriate Option statements. Code the Submit button's Click event procedure. Use 1.56 as the number of American dollars for each British pound. Save the application and then start and test it. Close the browser window. Close the Code Editor window and then close the application.

INTERMEDIATE

4. Create an empty Web application named ZipCode. Save the application in the VB2010\Chap12 folder. Add a new Web page named Default.aspx to the application. Change the DOCUMENT object's Title property to ZIP Code Verifier. Create a Web page similar to the one shown in Figure 12-38. Use labels for the static text. Also, use the Segoe UI font for the static text and controls. Verify that the user entered the ZIP code and that the ZIP code is in the appropriate format. (Hint: Use a RegularExpressionValidator control to verify the format.) If the ZIP code is valid, the Submit button's Click event procedure should display the message "Your ZIP code is " followed by the ZIP code and a period. Save and then start the application. Test the application by clicking the Submit button without entering a ZIP code. Then test it using the following ZIP codes: 60611, 606123, 60611-3456, and 60611-5. Close the browser window. Close the Code Editor window and then close the application.

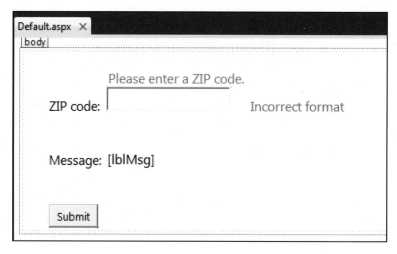

Figure 12-38   Web page for Exercise 4

INTERMEDIATE

5. In this exercise, you modify the Currency Converter application from this lesson.

   a. Create an empty Web application named CurrencyPesos. Save the application in the VB2010\Chap12 folder. Close the CurrencyPesos application.

   b. Use Windows to open the CurrencyPesos folder. Delete the web.config file.

   c. Use Windows to open the Currency folder. Select the folder's contents. Copy the selected contents to the CurrencyPesos folder.

   d. Open the CurrencyPesos Web site. Right-click Default.aspx in the Solution Explorer window and then click View Designer.

   e. The Default.aspx page also should display the result of converting the number of American dollars to Mexican pesos. Make the appropriate modifications to the Web page and its code. Use 12.46 as the number of pesos for each American dollar.

   f. Save the application and then start and test it. Close the browser window. Close the Code Editor window and then close the application.

LESSON C

After studying Lesson C, you should be able to:

- Make changes to the Web page in Source view

- Create columns using the <div> tag

- Utilize an ASP table in a Web page

- Add a calendar to a Web page

- Add a drop-down list box to a Web page

- Create a new line using the <br /> tag

Creating the DJ Tom Application

Recall that your task is to create a Web application for DJ (disc jockey) Tom. The application's Web page should allow the user to enter the names of the bride and groom, the wedding date, an e-mail address, and the name of the first song to be danced by the newly married couple. The Web page should provide a Submit button that, when clicked, displays a message on the page. The message should contain the names of the bride and groom, the wedding date, the e-mail address, and the name of the first song. A sketch of the Web page is shown in Figure 12-39.

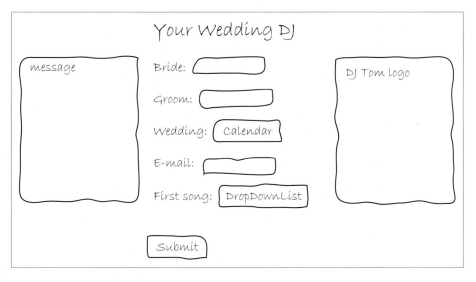

Figure 12-39 Sketch of the DJ Tom application's Web page

To create the DJ Tom Web application: ◀ START HERE

1. If necessary, start Visual Studio 2010 or Visual Web Developer 2010 Express.

2. If necessary, auto-hide the Solution Explorer, Properties, and Toolbox windows.

3. Use the New Web Site option on the File menu to create an empty Web application named **DJTom**. Save the application in the VB2010\Chap12 folder.

4. Use the Add New Item option on the Website menu to add a Web page named Default.aspx to the application. (If Website does not appear on the menu bar, click the Web application's location and name in the Solution Explorer window.)

5. If necessary, click the **Design** tab. Change the DOCUMENT object's Title property to **DJ Tom**.

First, you will set the font for the text in the Web page. You can do this by switching to Source view and then setting one of the style attribute's properties in the <body> tag. More specifically, you set the style attribute's **font-family property**.

START HERE **To set the font for the text, and then continue creating the Web page:**

1. Click the **Source** tab at the bottom of the IDE and then locate the <body> tag.

2. You can use the style attribute's font-family property to specify one or more fonts to use for the Web page's text. For example, the `style="font-family:Segoe UI, Arial, Sans-Serif"` attribute tells the browser to use the Segoe UI font when displaying text. However, if the Segoe UI font is not available, the browser should use the Arial font. If neither of those two fonts is available, the browser should use an available sans serif font. Modify the <body> tag as shown in Figure 12-40. The modifications are shaded in the figure.

```
  </head>
<body style="font-family:Segoe UI, Arial, Sans-Serif">
    <form id="form1" runat="server">
```

Figure 12-40   Modified <body> tag

3. Click the **Design** tab at the bottom of the IDE. If necessary, click **inside the rectangle** that appears below the div tag at the top of the Document window. (If the div tag does not appear on the Web page, click the <div> button at the bottom of the IDE.) Type **Your Wedding DJ** and press **Enter**.

4. If necessary, use the View menu to display the Formatting toolbar. Select (highlight) the **Your Wedding DJ** text.

5. Click the **down arrow** in the Block Format box and then click **Heading 1 <h1>** in the list. Click the **Alignment** button on the Formatting toolbar and then click **Justify Center**. Click **an empty area** of the Web page to deselect the text.

Creating a Columnar Layout

The content in many Web pages is laid out in a columnar format, similar to a newspaper. The sketch of DJ Tom's Web page (shown earlier in Figure 12-39) indicates that the page contains three columns. The first column displays a message, the second column displays the data entry controls, and the third column displays DJ Tom's logo. You can divide a Web page into columns using the **<div> tag**.

To divide DJ Tom's Web page into three columns:

1. Click the **Source** tab and then click the **blank line** below the **
** tag. If necessary, press **Tab** to align the insertion point with the tag.

2. The first column, which you will name "MessageColumn", will occupy 30% of the page. You will change the column's background color to purple and then specify that the column should appear on the left side of the page. Type **<div>**. The Source view editor automatically enters the closing </div> tag for you. Click **immediately after the letter v** in the <div> tag and then press the **Spacebar**. Complete the tag by entering the text shaded in Figure 12-41, and then position the insertion point as shown in the figure.

```
        Your Wedding DJ</h1>
    <br />
    <div id="MessageColumn"
        style="width:30%; background-color:Purple;
        float:left"></div>
    |                              ┌──────────────────────┐
    |------------------------------│ position the insertion │
</div>                             │ point here             │
                                   └──────────────────────┘
```

Figure 12-41   Completed <div> tag for the first column

3. Now you will use another <div> tag to create the second column. This column will occupy 39% of the Web page and appear next to the first column. Type the following <div> tag:

   <div id="ContentColumn" style="width:39%; float:left"></div>

4. Click **immediately after the </div> tag** from Step 3 and then press **Enter**. The third column will occupy 30% of the Web page and appear on the right side of the page. Type the following <div> tag:

   <div id="LogoColumn" style="width:30%; float:right"></div>

5. Click the **Design** tab. Three columns appear in the Web page. See Figure 12-42.

Figure 12-42   Web page showing the three columns

6. Permanently display the Toolbox and Properties windows. Drag a label control into the MessageColumn. Set the control's ID and ForeColor properties to **lblMsg** and **White**, respectively. Also remove the contents of its Text property.

7. Before dragging an image control to the Web page, you will add the DJ Tom image file to the application. Click **Website** on the menu bar and then click **Add Existing Item**. Open the VB2010\Chap12 folder. Click the **down arrow** in the box that controls the file types and then click **All Files** (*.*) in the list. Click **DJ.jpg** in the list of filenames and then click the **Add** button.

8. Now drag an image control into the LogoColumn. Set the control's ImageUrl property to **DJ.jpg** and then click an **empty area** on the Web page to deselect the control.

Using an ASP Table

The Table tool in the Standard section of the toolbox creates an **ASP table control**. The control displays information in a row and column format, similar to a spreadsheet, and is often used to align the information on a Web page. The ASP table control you will use in DJ Tom's Web page will have six rows and two columns. The intersection of a row and a column in a table is called a **cell**.

START HERE

To add an ASP table to the Web page:

1. Click the **Table** tool located in the Standard section of the toolbox and then drag a table control to the ContentColumn. (The HTML section of the toolbox also has a Table tool. Be sure to use the Table tool listed in the Standard section.) See Figure 12-43.

Figure 12-43   ASP table control added to the ContentColumn

2. Set the table control's CellSpacing property to **40**. The CellSpacing property controls the spacing between the table cells. Set the table control's HorizontalAlign property to **Center**.

3. Now you will begin defining the table rows. Click **Rows** in the Properties window and then click the **...** (ellipsis) button in the Settings box. The TableRow Collection Editor dialog box opens. Click the **Add** button and then click **(ID)** in the list of TableRow properties. Type **tblRow1** and press **Enter**. See Figure 12-44.

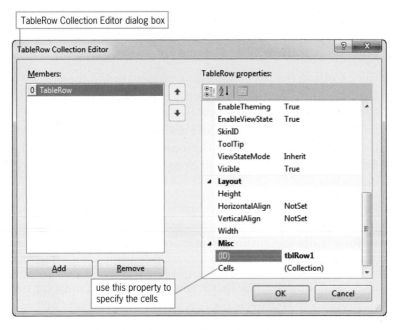

TableRow Collection Editor dialog box

use this property to specify the cells

Figure 12-44 TableRow Collection Editor dialog box

4. The row will have two cells: one will contain the text "Bride:" and the other will contain a text box for entering the bride's name. Click **Cells** in the list of TableRow properties and then click the **...** (ellipsis) button in the Settings box. The TableCell Collection Editor dialog box opens.

5. Click the **Add** button. Change the cell's Text property to **Bride:** and press **Enter**. Change its ID property to **tblRow1Col1** and press **Enter**. See Figure 12-45.

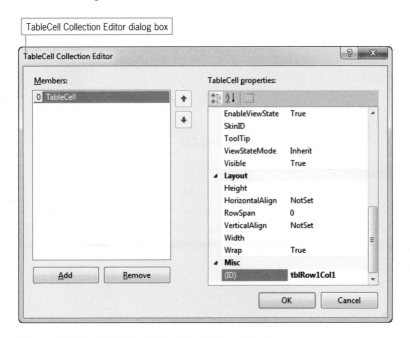

TableCell Collection Editor dialog box

Figure 12-45 TableCell Collection Editor dialog box

6. Click the **Add** button again. Change the cell's ID property to **tblRow1Col2** and press **Enter**. Click the **OK** button. The TableCell Collection Editor dialog box closes and you are returned to the TableRow Collection Editor dialog box.

7. Now you will define the second row in the table. Click the **Add** button in the TableRow Collection Editor dialog box. Set the row's ID property to **tblRow2** and press **Enter**.

8. Click **Cells** in the list of TableRow properties and then click the **...** (ellipsis) button in the Settings box. Click the **Add** button. Change the cell's Text property to **Groom:** and press **Enter**. Change its ID property to **tblRow2Col1** and press **Enter**. Click the **Add** button again. Change the cell's ID property to **tblRow2Col2** and press **Enter**. Click the **OK** button to close the TableCell Collection Editor dialog box.

9. On your own, define the third row in the table. Change the row's ID property to **tblRow3**. The row should have two cells named **tblRow3Col1** and **tblRow3Col2**. The tblRow3Col1 cell should contain the text **Wedding:**. Close the TableCell Collection Editor dialog box.

10. On your own, define the fourth row in the table. Change the row's ID property to **tblRow4**. The row should have two cells named **tblRow4Col1** and **tblRow4Col2**. The tblRow4Col1 cell should contain the text **E-mail:**. Close the TableCell Collection Editor dialog box.

11. On your own, define the fifth row in the table. Change the row's ID property to **tblRow5**. The row should have two cells named **tblRow5Col1** and **tblRow5Col2**. The tblRow5Col1 cell should contain the text **First song:**. Close the TableCell Collection Editor dialog box.

12. Finally, define the last row in the table. Change the row's ID property to **tblRow6**. The row should have one cell named **tblRow6Col1**.

13. Click the **OK** button to close the TableCell Collection Editor dialog box, and then click the **OK** button to close the TableRow Collection Editor dialog box.

14. Auto-hide the Toolbox and Properties windows and then save the application.

Figure 12-46 shows the table on the Web page.

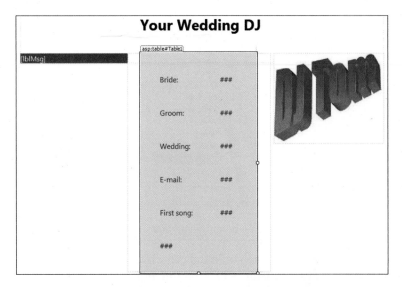

Figure 12-46 Table containing six rows and two columns

Dragging Controls in Source View

In the next set of steps, you will open the Web page in Source view. You then will drag the controls to the appropriate cells in the table.

To drag controls to the table in Source view:

START HERE

1. Click the **Your Wedding DJ** text to deselect the table control and then click the **Source** tab at the bottom of the IDE.

2. Permanently display the Toolbox window. First, you will drag a text box into the cell located next to the Bride: text. That cell is located in the second column of the first row in the table. Locate the opening tag for the tblRow1Col2 cell. The opening tag says `<asp:TableCell ID="tblRow1Col2" runat="server"></asp:TableCell>`. Click **immediately before the cell's closing tag** (which says `</asp:TableCell>`) and then press **Enter**. Click the **TextBox** tool in the toolbox. Press and hold down the left mouse button as you drag your mouse pointer to the location shown in Figure 12-47.

```
<asp:Table ID="Table1" runat="server" CellSpacing="40" Height="466px"
    HorizontalAlign="Center" Width="251px">
    <asp:TableRow ID="tblRow1" runat="server">
        <asp:TableCell ID="tblRow1Col1" runat="server">Bride:</asp:TableCell>
        <asp:TableCell ID="tblRow1Col2" runat="server">
        </asp:TableCell>
    </asp:TableRow>
```

drag the text box to this location

the text box will be placed in the cell located in row 1, column 2

Figure 12-47   Text box control being dragged in Source view

3. Release the mouse button. See Figure 12-48.

```
        <asp:TableCell ID="tblRow1Col1" runat="server">Bride:</asp:TableCell>
        <asp:TableCell ID="tblRow1Col2" runat="server">
            <asp:TextBox ID="TextBox1" runat="server"></asp:TextBox></asp:TableCell>
    </asp:TableRow>
```

text box tags

Figure 12-48   Opening and closing text box tags added to the table instructions

4. In the <asp:TextBox> tag, change the text box control's ID property from **"TextBox1"** to **"txtBride"**.

5. Click the **Design** tab. A text box control appears in the second cell in row 1. See Figure 12-49.

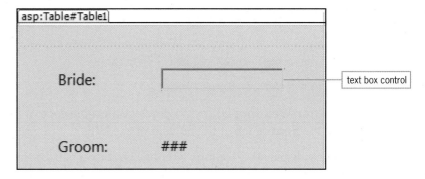

Figure 12-49   Text box control shown in the table

6. Click the **Your Wedding DJ** text to deselect the table control and then click the **Source** tab.

7. Now you will place a text box in the cell located in the second row, second column in the table. Locate the opening tag for the tblRow2Col2 cell. In this case, the opening tag will say `<asp:TableCell ID="tblRow2Col2" runat="server">` `</asp:TableCell>`. Click **immediately before the cell's closing tag** and then press **Enter**. Drag a text box control to the immediate left of the closing tag and then release the mouse button. Change the text box control's ID property to **"txtGroom"**.

8. Next, you will add a calendar control to the cell located in the second column of the table's third row. Locate the opening tag for the tblRow3Col2 cell. Click **immediately before the cell's closing tag** and then press **Enter**. Click the **Calendar** tool in the toolbox. Drag a calendar control to the immediate left of the closing tag and then release the mouse button. Change the calendar control's ID property to **"calWedding"**.

9. Now you will add a text box to the cell located in the second column of the fourth row. Locate the opening tag for the tblRow4Col2 cell. Click **immediately before the cell's closing tag** and then press **Enter**. Drag a text box control to the immediate left of the closing tag and then release the mouse button. Change the text box control's ID property to **"txtEmail"**.

10. Next, you will place a drop-down list control in the cell located in the second column of the fifth row. Locate the opening tag for the tblRow5Col2 cell. Click **immediately before the cell's closing tag** and then press **Enter**. Click the **DropDownList** tool in the toolbox. Drag a drop-down list control to the immediate left of the closing tag and then release the mouse button. Change the drop-down list control's ID property to **"ddlSongs"**.

11. Finally, you will add a button to the last row in the table. Locate the opening tag for the tblRow6Col1 cell. Click **immediately before the cell's closing tag** and then press **Enter**. Drag a button control to the immediate left of the closing tag and then release the mouse button. Change the button's ID property to **"btnSubmit"** and change its Text property to **"Submit"**.

12. Save the application. Auto-hide the toolbox and then click the **Design** tab.

Figure 12-50 shows the controls added to the table.

Figure 12-50   Controls added to the table

Adding Items to a DropDownList Control

Currently, the drop-down list control on DJ Tom's Web page does not contain any items. You add items to a drop-down list control using the **<asp:ListItem> tag**. In the next set of steps, you will add the following four song titles to the drop-down list control: From This Moment On, At Last, Because You Loved Me, and The Way You Look Tonight.

To add items to the drop-down list control:

START HERE

1. Click the **Source tab**. Locate the `<asp:DropDownList ID="ddlSongs" runat="server">` tag. Click **immediately after the > in the tag** and then press **Enter**.

2. Press **Tab** to indent the line and then type **<asp:ListItem Text="From This Moment On">**. When you type the > symbol, the Source view editor automatically enters the closing `</asp:ListItem>` tag for you. See Figure 12-51.

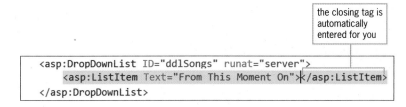

Figure 12-51   First song title added to the drop-down list control

3. Click **after the >** in the list item's closing tag and then press **Enter**. Enter the three additional <asp:ListItem> tags indicated in Figure 12-52.

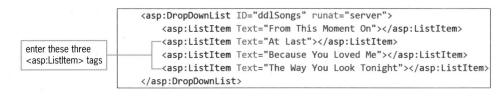

Figure 12-52   Remaining song titles added to the drop-down list control

4. Save the application and then click the **Design** tab. Start the application and then click the **down arrow** in the drop-down list control. The song titles appear as shown in Figure 12-53.

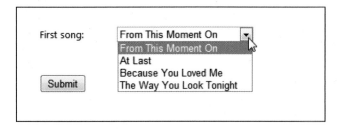

Figure 12-53   Song titles displayed in the drop-down list control

5. Close the browser window.

Coding DJ Tom's Web Page

Now that the interface is complete, you can code the Web page's Submit button. The button's Click event procedure will display a message in the lblMsg control. Recall that the control is contained in the MessageColumn on the Web page.

START HERE   **To code the Submit button's Click event procedure:**

1. Right-click the **Web page** and then click **View Code** to open the Code Editor window. Enter the following comments. Replace <your name> and <current date> with your name and the current date, respectively. Press **Enter** twice after typing the last comment.

```
' Name:          DJTom
' Purpose:       Display a message
' Programmer:    <your name> on <current date>
```

2. Now enter the following Option statements:

Option Explicit On
Option Strict On
Option Infer Off

3. Open the code template for the btnSubmit control's Click event procedure. Type the following comment and then press **Enter** twice:

' displays the user's input in a message

4. First, you will declare variables to store the five input items. Enter the following Dim statements. Press **Enter** twice after typing the last Dim statement.

Dim strBride As String
Dim strGroom As String
Dim strWedDate As String
Dim strEmail As String
Dim strSong As String

5. Now you will assign the names of the bride and groom to the appropriate variables. Enter the following assignment statements:

strBride = txtBride.Text.Trim
strGroom = txtGroom.Text.Trim

6. Next, you will assign the date selected in the Calendar control to the strWedDate variable. The selected date is stored in the control's SelectedDate property. You can use the ToShortDateString method to convert the date to the String data type and, at the same time, format it as follows: mm/dd/yyyy. Enter the following assignment statement:

strWedDate = calWedding.SelectedDate.ToShortDateString

7. Now you will assign the e-mail address to the strEmail variable. Enter the following assignment statement:

strEmail = txtEmail.Text.Trim

8. Next, you will assign the item selected in the drop-down list control to the strSong variable. The selected item is stored in the control's SelectedItem property. Type the following assignment statement and then press **Enter** twice:

strSong = ddlSongs.SelectedItem.ToString

9. Finally, you will display the user's input in the lblMsg control. Enter the following lines of code:

lblMsg.Text = "Thank you " & strBride & " and " &
**   strGroom & " for visiting my Web site. " &**
**   "Wedding date: " & strWedDate &**
**   "E-mail address: " & strEmail & "Song: " & strSong**

Next, you will test the Submit button's Click event procedure to verify that its code is working correctly.

The Calendar control also has a ToLongDateString method that formats the date as follows: day of the week, month name, day number, year number.

731

START HERE **To test the Submit button's Click event procedure:**

1. Save and then start the application. Click the **Bride** box and then type **Pam**. Press **Tab** and then type **Nathan** in the Groom box.

2. Click **any date** in the Calendar control. Click the **E-mail** box and then type **anyEmail@domain.com**. Click the **down arrow** in the drop-down list control and then click **Because You Loved Me** in the list.

3. Click the **Submit** button. The button's Click event procedure displays the message shown in Figure 12-54 in the lblMsg control. (Your message may contain a different date.) Notice that the message is difficult to read. It would be better if the "Thank you" message, the wedding date, the e-mail address, and the song title appeared on separate lines in the control. You will learn how to accomplish this in the next section.

lblMsg control ────

> Thank you Pam and Nathan for visiting my Web site. Wedding date: 8/6/2011E-mail address: anyEmail@domain.comSong: Because You Loved Me

Figure 12-54   Message displayed in the lblMsg control

4. Close the browser window.

Using the
 Tag

At times, you may need to break the text on a Web page in a specific location. You can do this using the <br /> tag. The "br" in the tag stands for "break." The **
 tag** in a Web page is similar to the ControlChars.NewLine constant in a Windows form; both are used to create a new line. In DJ Tom's Web page, you will use the <br /> tag to separate the wedding date information from the "Thank you" message. You also will use it to display the e-mail information and song information on separate lines in the lblMsg control.

START HERE **To use the <br /> tag to separate the text in the lblMsg control:**

1. Modify the assignment statement that displays the message in the lblMsg control. The modifications are shaded in Figure 12-55. (Although the <br /> tags appear at the beginning of the lines in Figure 12-55, they can appear anywhere within a line.)

```
Protected Sub btnSubmit_Click(ByVal sender As Object,
ByVal e As System.EventArgs) Handles btnSubmit.Click
    ' displays the user's input in a message

    Dim strBride As String
    Dim strGroom As String
    Dim strWedDate As String
    Dim strEmail As String
    Dim strSong As String
```

Figure 12-55   Modified Click event procedure for the btnSubmit control *(continues)*

(continued)

```
      strBride = txtBride.Text.Trim
      strGroom = txtGroom.Text.Trim
      strWedDate = calWedding.SelectedDate.ToShortDateString
      strEmail = txtEmail.Text.Trim
      strSong = ddlSongs.SelectedItem.ToString

      lblMsg.Text = "Thank you " & strBride & " and " &
          strGroom & " for visiting my Web site. " &
          "<br /><br />Wedding date: " & strWedDate &
          "<br />E-mail address: " & strEmail &
          "<br />Song: " & strSong

End Sub
```

Figure 12-55   Modified Click event procedure for the btnSubmit control

733

2. Save and then start the application. Click the **Bride** box and then type **Kristy**. Press **Tab** and then type **James** in the Groom box.

3. Click **any date** in the Calendar control. Click the **E-mail** box and then type **anyEmail@domain.com**. Click the **down arrow** in the drop-down list control and then click **At Last** in the list.

4. Click the **Submit** button. The button's Click event procedure displays the message shown in Figure 12-56 in the lblMsg control. (Your message may contain a different date.)

Figure 12-56   Message displayed on separate lines in the lblMsg control

5. Close the browser window. Close the Code Editor window and then close the application.

Lesson C Summary

- To set the font for the text on a Web page:

  Assign one or more fonts to the style attribute's font-family property in the <body> tag.

- To divide a Web page into columns:

  Use the <div> tag. Use the id attribute to assign a name to the column. Assign a percentage to the style attribute's width property. Assign either left or right to the style attribute's float property.

- To use an ASP table:

  Drag a table control from the Standard section of the toolbox. The table's CellSpacing property controls the spacing between the table cells. Its HorizontalAlign property controls its horizontal alignment on the Web page. Use the Rows property to add rows and columns (cells) to the table. It's helpful to set the ID property for each row and each cell.

- To place a control in an ASP table:

  Open the Web page in Source view. Drag the control to a location immediately before the desired cell's closing tag.

- To add items to a drop-down list control:

  Use a separate <asp:ListItem> tag for each item. In each tag, set the item's Text property. Place the tags between the opening <asp:DropDownList> and closing </asp:DropDownList> tags.

- To determine the date selected in a Calendar control:

  Use the control's SelectedDate property.

- To format the date selected in a Calendar control:

  Use the control's ToShortDateString method to format the date as follows: mm/dd/yyyy. Use the control's ToLongDateString method to format the date as follows: day of the week, month name, day number, year number.

- To determine the item selected in a drop-down list control:

  Use the control's SelectedItem property.

- To create a new line on a Web page from code:

  Use the <br /> tag.

Lesson C Key Terms

<asp:ListItem> tag—used to add items to a drop-down list control

**
 tag**—used to create a new line on a Web page or in a control

<div> tag—creates a division on a Web page; can be used to divide a Web page into columns

ASP table control—displays information in a row and column format; can be used to align information on a Web page

Cell—the intersection of a row and a column in a table

font-family property—a property of the style attribute in the <body> tag; assigns one or more fonts to be used for text

Lesson C Review Questions

1. Which of the following specifies the fonts to use for the text on a Web page?

   a. `style="font-family:Segoe UI, Arial, Sans-Serif"`

   b. `style="fonts:Segoe UI, Arial, Sans-Serif"`

   c. `style:"font-family=Segoe UI, Arial, Sans-Serif"`

   d. `style:"fonts=Segoe UI, Arial, Sans-Serif"`

2. Which of the following specifies that Col1 should occupy 15% of the Web page and be positioned on the right?

   a. `<div id="Col1" "width:15%; position:right">`

   b. `<div id="Col1" style="width:15%; float:right">`

   c. `<div id="Col1" "position:right; column:15%">`

   d. `<div id="Col1" style="width:15%; position:right">`

3. Which of the following adds the word "Dog" to a drop-down list control?

   a. `<asp:ListItem Caption="Dog">`

   b. `<asp:ListItem Item="Dog">`

   c. `<asp:Item Text="Dog">`

   d. none of the above

4. The item selected in a drop-down list control is stored in the control's _____ property.

   a. Item

   b. Selected

   c. SelectedItem

   d. none of the above

5. The date selected in a Calendar control is stored in the control's _____ property.

   a. Date

   b. SelectedDate

   c. DateSelection

   d. none of the above

6. You can use the _____ tag to display text on the next line in a control.

a.

b. <break>

c. <newline>

d. none of the above

Lesson C Exercises

INTRODUCTORY

1. In this exercise, you modify the DJ Tom application from this lesson.

a. Create an empty Web application named DJTomIntro1. Save the application in the VB2010\Chap12 folder. Close the DJTomIntro1 application.

b. Use Windows to open the DJTomIntro1 folder. Delete the web.config file.

c. Use Windows to open the DJTom folder. Select the folder's contents. Copy the selected contents to the DJTomIntro1 folder.

d. Open the DJTomIntro1 Web site. Right-click Default.aspx in the Solution Explorer window and then click View Designer.

e. Drag a RegularExpressionValidator control to the Web page. Don't be concerned about the control's location. The control will verify the format of the e-mail address entered by the user. Click ErrorMessage in the Properties window, press the Spacebar twice and then type Invalid. Now, change the ValidationExpression and ControlToValidate properties to Internet e-mail address and txtEmail, respectively. Click the Source tab. Cut the control's asp tag and then paste the tag before the txtEmail control's </asp:TableCell> closing tag. Click the Design tab.

f. Save and then start and test the application. Close the browser window and then close the application.

INTRODUCTORY

2. In this exercise, you modify the DJ Tom application from this lesson.

a. Create an empty Web application named DJTomIntro2. Save the application in the VB2010\Chap12 folder. Close the DJTomIntro2 application.

b. Use Windows to open the DJTomIntro2 folder. Delete the web.config file.

c. Use Windows to open the DJTom folder. Select the folder's contents. Copy the selected contents to the DJTomIntro2 folder.

d. Open the DJTomIntro2 Web site. Right-click Default.aspx in the Solution Explorer window and then click View Designer.

e. Open the Web page in Source view. Add the titles of any four additional songs to the drop-down list control.

f. Save and then start and test the application. Close the browser window and then close the application.

3. In this exercise, you modify the DJ Tom application from this lesson.   **INTERMEDIATE**

a. Create an empty Web application named DJTomIntermediate. Save the application in the VB2010\Chap12 folder. Close the DJTomIntermediate application.

b. Use Windows to open the DJTomIntermediate folder. Delete the web.config file.

c. Use Windows to open the DJTom folder. Select the folder's contents. Copy the selected contents to the DJTomIntermediate folder.

d. Open the DJTomIntermediate Web site. Right-click Default.aspx in the Solution Explorer window and then click View Designer.

e. Open the Web page in Source view. Locate the asp tag for the last table row. Change tblRow6 and tblRow6Col1 to tblRow8 and tblRow8Col1, respectively. Add two rows to the table. The rows should be added above the last row in the table. Both rows should contain two cells. In the first new row, enter the text "Father/ Daughter:" (without the quotes) in the first column and then place a drop-down list control in the second column. In the second new row, enter the text "Mother/Son:" (without the quotes) in the first column and then place a drop-down list control in the second column. Add the titles of any four songs to the drop-down list control in the first new row. Add the titles of any three songs to the drop-down list control in the second new row.

f. Save the application and then switch to Design view. Open the Code Editor window and modify the code to display the additional user input in the lblMsg control.

g. Save and then start and test the application. Close the browser window. Close the Code Editor window and then close the application.

4. Create an empty Web application named MarketFoods. Save the   **INTERMEDIATE**
application in the VB2010\Chap12 folder. Add a new Web page named Default.aspx to the application. Change the DOCUMENT object's Title property to Market Foods. Create a Web page similar to the sketch shown in Figure 12-57. The DropDownList control should contain the store numbers listed in Figure 12-58. When the user clicks the Submit button, the button's Click event procedure should display the names of the manager and assistant manager on the Web page. Open the Code Editor window. Enter the appropriate comments and Option statements. Code the Submit button's Click

event procedure. Save and then start and test the application. Close the browser window. Close the Code Editor window and then close the application.

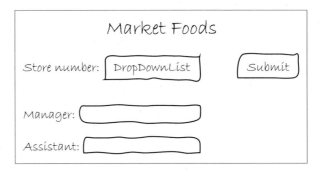

Figure 12-57   Sketch for Exercise 4

Store number	Manager	Assistant manager
1001	Jeffrey Jefferson	Paula Hendricks
1002	Barbara Millerton	Sung Lee
1003	Inez Baily	Homer Gomez
1004	Lou Chan	Jake Johansen
1005	Henry Abernathy	Ingrid Nadkarni

Figure 12-58   Store information for Exercise 4

INTERMEDIATE

5. Create an empty Web application named SalesTax. Save the application in the VB2010\Chap12 folder. Add a new Web page named Default.aspx to the application. Change the DOCUMENT object's Title property to Sales Tax Calculator. Create a Web page similar to the sketch shown in Figure 12-59. The application should allow the user to enter the sales. When the user clicks the Calculate button, the button's Click event procedure should calculate both a 5% sales tax and a 6% sales tax. It then should display the calculated amounts on the Web page. Code the procedure. Save and then start and test the application. Close the browser window. Close the Code Editor window and then close the application.

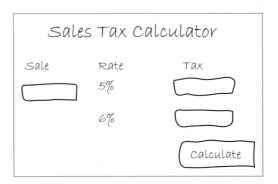

Figure 12-59   Sketch for Exercise 5

6. Create an empty Web application named SkateAway. Save the application in the VB2010\Chap12 folder. Add a new Web page named Default.aspx to the application. Change the DOCUMENT object's Title property to Skate-Away Sales. The Skate-Away Sales company sells skateboards by phone. The skateboards are priced at $100 each and are available in two colors: yellow and blue. The application should allow the salesperson to enter the customer's name and the number of blue and yellow skateboards ordered. It should calculate the total number of skateboards ordered and the total price of the order, including a 5% sales tax. Create a suitable Web page and then code the application. Save and then start and test the application. Close the browser window. Close the Code Editor window and then close the application.

ADVANCED

CHAPTER 13

Working with Access Databases and LINQ

Creating the Paradise Bookstore Application

In this chapter, you will create an application for the Paradise Bookstore. The application will display the records contained in a Microsoft Access database named Books. The bookstore manager also can use the application to display only the books written by the author whose name (or partial name) he or she enters. He or she also can use the application to display the total value of the books in the store.

Previewing the Paradise Bookstore Application

Before you start the first lesson in this chapter, you will preview the completed application. The application is contained in the VB2010\Chap13 folder.

To preview the completed application:

START HERE

1. Use the Run dialog box to run the Paradise (Paradise.exe) file contained in the VB2010\Chap13 folder. The application's user interface appears on the screen. The interface contains a DataGridView control that displays the 11 records stored in the Books database.

2. First, you will display only the books written by Carol Smith. Click the **Author** text box and then type **Smith, C** (be sure to include a space after the comma). Click the **Go** button. See Figure 13-1.

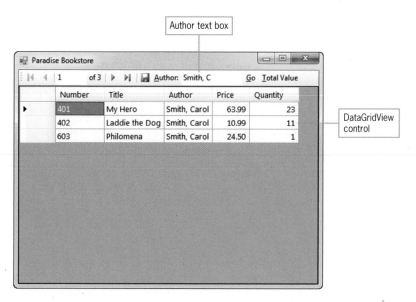

Figure 13-1 Books written by Carol Smith

3. Now you will display all of the records again. Delete the contents of the Author text box and then click the **Go** button. The 11 records appear in the DataGridView control.

4. Finally, you will display the total value of the books in the store. Click the **Total Value** button. The number $3,921.72 appears in a message box, as shown in Figure 13-2.

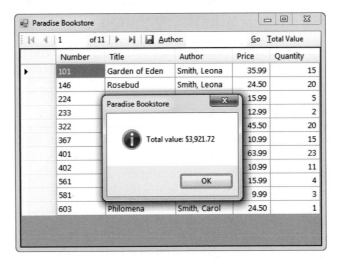

Figure 13-2   Total value of the inventory

5. Click the **OK** button to close the message box. Click the **Close** button
    on the form's title bar to stop the application.

In Lesson A, you will learn how to connect an application to a Microsoft
Access database. Lesson B will show you how to query a database using
LINQ, which stands for Language Integrated Query. You will complete the
Paradise Bookstore application in Lesson C. Be sure to complete each lesson
in full and do all of the end-of-lesson questions and several exercises before
continuing to the next lesson.

LESSON A

After studying Lesson A, you should be able to:

- Define basic database terminology

- Connect an application to a Microsoft Access database

- Bind table and field objects to controls

- Explain the purpose of the DataSet, BindingSource, TableAdapter, TableAdapterManager, and BindingNavigator objects

- Customize a DataGridView control

- Handle errors using the Try...Catch statement

- Position the record pointer in a dataset

Database Terminology

In order to maintain accurate records, most businesses store information about their employees, customers, and inventory in computer databases. A **computer database** is an electronic file that contains an organized collection of related information. Many products exist for creating computer databases; such products are called database management systems (or DBMS). Some of the most popular database management systems are Microsoft Access, Microsoft SQL Server, and Oracle. You can use Visual Basic to access the data stored in databases created by these database management systems. As a result, companies can use Visual Basic to create a standard interface that allows employees to access information stored in a variety of database formats. Instead of learning each DBMS's user interface, the employee needs to know only one interface. The actual format of the database is unimportant and will be transparent to the user.

You do not have to be a business to make use of a database. Many people use databases to keep track of their medical records, compact disc collections, and even golf scores.

In this chapter, you will learn how to access the data stored in Microsoft Access databases. Databases created using Microsoft Access are relational databases. A **relational database** is one that stores information in tables composed of columns and rows, similar to the format used in a spreadsheet. Each column in a table represents a field and each row represents a record. A **field** is a single item of information about a person, place, or thing—such as a name, a salary amount, a Social Security number, or a price. A **record** is a group of related fields that contain all of the necessary data about a specific person, place, or thing. The college you are attending keeps a student record on you. Examples of fields contained in your student record include your Social Security number, name, address, phone number, credits earned, and grades earned. A group of related records is called a **table**. Each record in a table pertains to the same topic and contains the same type of information. In other words, each record in a table contains the same fields.

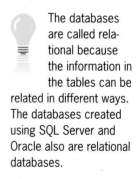

The databases are called relational because the information in the tables can be related in different ways. The databases created using SQL Server and Oracle also are relational databases.

A relational database can contain one or more tables. A one-table database would be a good choice for storing information about the college courses you have taken. An example of such a table is shown in Figure 13-3. Each record in the table contains four fields: an ID field that indicates the department name and course number, a course title field, a field listing the number of credit hours, and a grade field. Most tables have a **primary key**, which is a field that uniquely identifies each record. In the table shown in Figure 13-3, you could use either the ID field or the Title field as the primary key, because the data in those fields will be unique for each record.

ID	Title	Hours	Grade
CIS100	Intro to Computers	3	A
ENG100	English Composition	3	B
PHIL105	Philosophy Seminar	2	C
CIS201	Visual Basic 2010	3	A

Figure 13-3   Example of a one-table relational database

You might use a two-table database to store information about a CD (compact disc) collection. You would store the general information about each CD (such as the CD's name and the artist's name) in one table, and store the information about the songs on each CD (such as their title and track number) in the other table. You then would use a common field—for example, a CD number—to relate the records contained in both tables. Figure 13-4 shows an example of a two-table database that stores CD information. The first table is referred to as the **parent table**, and the second table is referred to as the **child table**. The CdNum field is the primary key in the parent table, because it uniquely identifies each record in the table. The CdNum field in the child table is used solely to link the song title and track information to the appropriate CD in the parent table. In the child table, the CdNum field is called the **foreign key**.

Parent and child tables are also referred to as master and detail tables, respectively.

CdNum	Name	Artist
01	Western Way	Dolly Draton
02	Midnight Blue	Paul Elliot

the two tables are related by the CdNum field

CdNum	SongTitle	Track
01	Country	1
01	Night on the Road	2
01	Old Times	3
02	Lovely Nights	1
02	Colors	2
02	Blue Clouds	3

Figure 13-4   Example of a two-table relational database

Storing data in a relational database offers many advantages. The computer can retrieve data stored in a relational format both quickly and easily, and the data can be displayed in any order. The information in the CD database, for example, can be arranged by artist name, song title, and so on. You also can control the amount of information you want to view from a relational database. You can view all of the information in the CD database, only the information pertaining to a certain artist, or only the names of the songs contained on a specific CD.

Connecting an Application to a Microsoft Access Database

In this lesson, you will use a Microsoft Access database named Employees. The Employees database is stored in the Employees.accdb file, which is located in the VB2010\Chap13\Access Databases folder. The .accdb filename extension stands for Access Database and indicates that the database was created using Microsoft Access. The Employees database contains one table, which is named tblEmploy. Figure 13-5 shows the table data displayed in a window in the IDE. The table contains seven fields and 14 records. The Emp_Number field is the primary key, because it uniquely identifies each record in the table. The Status field contains the employment status, which is either the letter F (for full-time) or the letter P (for part-time). The Code field identifies the employee's department: 1 for Accounting, 2 for Advertising, 3 for Personnel, and 4 for Inventory.

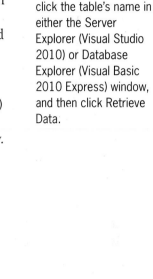
To open a database table in the IDE, first connect the database to an application, then right-click the table's name in either the Server Explorer (Visual Studio 2010) or Database Explorer (Visual Basic 2010 Express) window, and then click Retrieve Data.

745

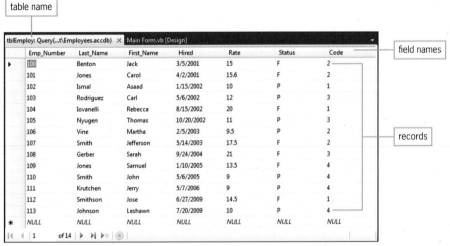

Figure 13-5   Data contained in the tblEmploy table

In order to access the data stored in a database, an application needs to be connected to the database. You can make the connection using the Data Source Configuration Wizard. The wizard allows you to specify the data you want to access. The computer makes a copy of the specified data and stores the copy in its internal memory. The copy of the data you want to access is called a **dataset**. In the following set of steps, you will connect the Morgan Industries application to the Employees database.

To connect the Morgan Industries application to the Employees database:

 START HERE

1. If necessary, start Visual Studio 2010 or Visual Basic 2010 Express. Auto-hide the Properties window and permanently display the Solution Explorer window.

2. Open the Morgan Industries Solution (Morgan Industries Solution. sln) file contained in the VB2010\Chap13\Morgan Industries Solution-DataGridView folder. If necessary, open the designer window.

3. If necessary, click **View** on the menu bar and then click either **Server Explorer** (Visual Studio) or **Database Explorer** (Visual Basic Express) to open the Server (Database) Explorer window, which lists the available connections.

In Visual Basic 2010 Express, the Server Explorer window is called the Database Explorer window.

4. Click **Data** on the menu bar and then click **Show Data Sources** to open the Data Sources window.

5. Click **Add New Data Source** in the Data Sources window to start the Data Source Configuration Wizard. If necessary, click **Database** on the Choose a Data Source Type screen.

6. Click the **Next** button to display the Choose a Database Model screen. If necessary, click **Dataset**.

7. Click the **Next** button to display the Choose Your Data Connection screen. Click the **New Connection** button to open the Add Connection dialog box. If Microsoft Access Database File (OLE DB) does not appear in the Data source box, click the **Change** button to open the Change Data Source dialog box, click **Microsoft Access Database File**, and then click the **OK** button.

8. Click the **Browse** button in the Add Connection dialog box. Open the VB2010\Chap13\Access Databases folder and then click **Employees. accdb** in the list of filenames. Click the **Open** button. Figure 13-6 shows the completed Add Connection dialog box. (The dialog box in the figure was widened to show the entire entry in the Database file name box. It is not necessary for you to widen the dialog box.)

Figure 13-6 Completed Add Connection dialog box

9. Click the **Test Connection** button. The "Test connection succeeded." message appears in a message box. Close the message box.

10. Click the **OK** button to close the Add Connection dialog box. Employees.accdb appears in the Choose Your Data Connection screen. Click the **Next** button. The message box shown in Figure 13-7

opens. The message asks whether you want to include the database file in the current project. By including the file in the current project, you can more easily copy the application and its database to another computer.

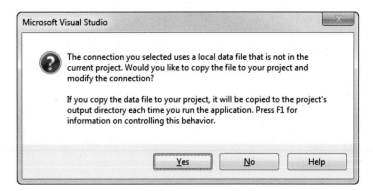

Figure 13-7 Message regarding copying the database file

11. Click the **Yes** button to add the Employees.accdb file to the application's project folder. The Save the Connection String to the Application Configuration File screen appears next. The name of the connection string, EmployeesConnectionString, appears on the screen. If necessary, select the **Yes, save the connection as** check box.

12. Click the **Next** button to display the Choose Your Database Objects screen. Expand the Tables node and then expand the tblEmploy node. You use this screen to select the table and/or field objects to include in the dataset, which is automatically named EmployeesDataSet.

13. In this application, you need the dataset to include all of the fields. Click the **empty box** next to tblEmploy. Doing this selects the table and field check boxes, as shown in Figure 13-8.

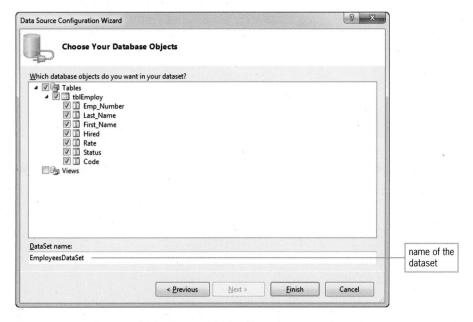

Figure 13-8 Objects selected in the Choose Your Database Objects screen

14. Click the **Finish** button. The computer adds the EmployeesDataSet to the Data Sources window. Expand the tblEmploy node in the Data Sources window. As shown in Figure 13-9, the dataset contains one table object and seven field objects.

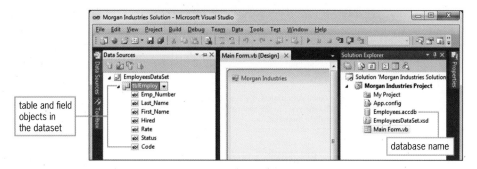

table and field objects in the dataset

database name

Figure 13-9   Result of running the Data Source Configuration Wizard

Previewing the Contents of a Dataset

After an application has been connected to a database, you can use the Preview Data option on the Data menu to view the fields and records in the dataset.

START HERE **To view the contents of the EmployeesDataSet:**

1. Click the **form** to make it the active window. Click **Data** on the menu bar and then click **Preview Data** to open the Preview Data dialog box.

2. Click the **Preview** button. As Figure 13-10 shows, the EmployeesDataSet contains 14 records (rows), each having seven fields (columns). Notice the information that appears in the Select an object to preview box in the figure. EmployeesDataSet is the name of the dataset in the application, and tblEmploy is the name of the table included in the dataset. Fill and GetData are methods. The Fill method populates an existing table with data, while the GetData method creates a new table and populates it with data.

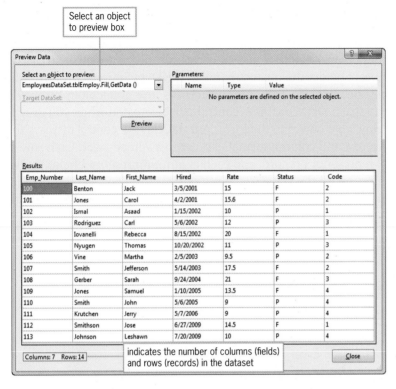

Select an object to preview box

Figure 13-10   Data displayed in the Preview Data dialog box

3. Click the **Close** button to close the Preview Data dialog box, and then auto-hide the Server (Database) Explorer, Solution Explorer, and (if necessary) Data Sources windows.

Binding the Objects in a Dataset

For the user to view the contents of a dataset while an application is running, you need to connect one or more objects in the dataset to one or more controls in the interface. Connecting an object to a control is called **binding**, and the connected controls are called **bound controls**. As indicated in Figure 13-11, you can bind the object to a control that the computer creates for you; or, you can bind it to an existing control in the interface. First, you will learn how to have the computer create a bound control.

Bound controls also are referred to as data-aware controls.

Binding an object in a dataset

<u>To have the computer create a control and then bind an object to it:</u>
In the Data Sources window, click the object you want to bind. If necessary, use the object's list arrow to change the control type. Drag the object to an empty area on the form and then release the mouse button.

<u>To bind an object to an existing control:</u>
In the Data Sources window, click the object you want to bind. Drag the object to the control on the form and then release the mouse button. Alternatively, you can click the control on the form and then use the Properties window to set the appropriate property or properties. (Refer to the *Binding to an Existing Control* section in this lesson.)

Figure 13-11   Ways to bind an object in a dataset

Having the Computer Create a Bound Control

When you drag an object from a dataset to an empty area on the form, the computer creates a control and automatically binds the object to it. The icon that appears before the object's name in the Data Sources window indicates the type of control the computer will create. The ⊞ icon in Figure 13-12 indicates that a DataGridView control will be created when you drag the tblEmploy table object to the form. A **DataGridView control** displays the table data in a row and column format, similar to a spreadsheet. Each row in the control represents a record, and each column represents a field. You will learn more about the DataGridView control in the next section. The abl icon shown in Figure 13-12 indicates that the computer will create a text box when you drag a field object to the form.

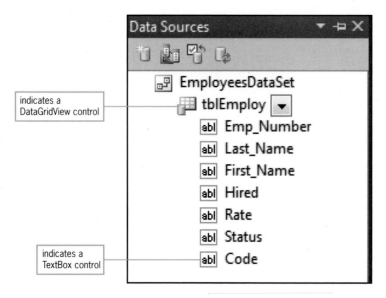

indicates a
DataGridView control

indicates a
TextBox control

Figure 13-12 Icons in the Data Sources window

When an object is selected in the Data Sources window, you can use the list arrow that appears next to the object's name to change the type of control the computer creates. For example, to display the table data in separate text boxes rather than in a DataGridView control, you click tblEmploy in the Data Sources window and then click the tblEmploy list arrow, as shown in Figure 13-13. Clicking Details in the list tells the computer to create a separate control for each field in the table.

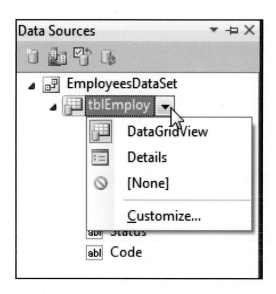

Figure 13-13 Result of clicking the tblEmploy object's list arrow

Similarly, to display the Last_Name field's data in a label control rather than
in a text box, you first click Last_Name in the Data Sources window. You
then click the field's list arrow, as shown in Figure 13-14, and then click Label
in the list.

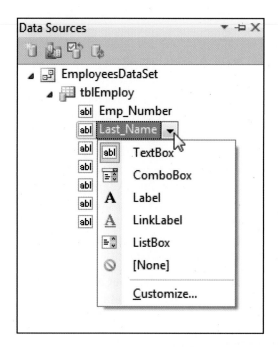

Figure 13-14 Result of clicking the Last_Name object's list arrow

In the following set of steps, you will drag the tblEmploy object from the
Data Sources window to the form, using the default control type for a table.

To bind the tblEmploy object to a DataGridView control:

1. If necessary, click **tblEmploy** in the Data Sources window to select the tblEmploy object.

2. Drag the tblEmploy object from the Data Sources window to the form and then release the mouse button. The computer adds a DataGridView control to the form, and it binds the tblEmploy object to the control. See Figure 13-15.

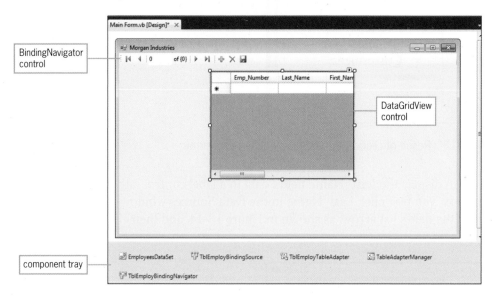

Figure 13-15 Result of dragging the table object to the form

As Figure 13-15 shows, besides adding a DataGridView control to the form, the computer also adds a BindingNavigator control. When an application is running, you can use the **BindingNavigator control** to move from one record to the next in the dataset, as well as to add or delete a record and save any changes made to the dataset. The computer also places five objects in the component tray: a DataSet, BindingSource, TableAdapter, TableAdapterManager, and BindingNavigator. As you learned in Chapter 1, the component tray stores objects that do not appear in the user interface while an application is running. An exception to this is the BindingNavigator object, which appears as the BindingNavigator control during both design time and run time.

The **TableAdapter object** connects the database to the **DataSet object**, which stores the information you want to access from the database. The TableAdapter is responsible for retrieving the appropriate information from the database and storing it in the DataSet. It also can be used to save to the database any changes made to the data contained in the DataSet. However, in most cases, you will use the **TableAdapterManager object** to save the changes, because it can handle saving data to multiple tables in the DataSet. The **BindingSource object** provides the connection between the DataSet and the bound controls on the form. The TblEmployBindingSource in Figure 13-15 connects the EmployeesDataSet to two bound controls: a DataGridView control and a BindingNavigator control. The TblEmployBindingSource allows the DataGridView control to display the data contained in the EmployeesDataSet. It also allows the BindingNavigator control to access the records stored in the EmployeesDataSet. Figure 13-16 illustrates the relationships among the database, the objects in the component tray, and the bound controls on the form.

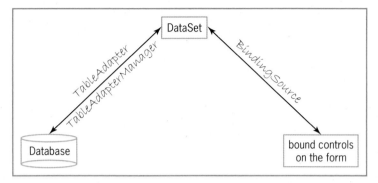

Figure 13-16   Illustration of the relationships among the database, the objects in the component tray, and the bound controls

If a table object's control type is changed from DataGridView to Details, the computer automatically provides the appropriate controls (such as text boxes, labels, and so on) when you drag the table object to the form. It also adds the BindingNavigator control to the form and the five objects to the component tray. The appropriate controls and objects are also automatically included when you drag a field object to an empty area on the form.

The DataGridView Control

The DataGridView control is one of the most popular controls for displaying table data, because it allows you to view a great deal of information at the same time. The control displays the data in a row and column format, similar to a spreadsheet. Each row represents a record, and each column represents a field. The intersection of a row and column in a DataGridView control is called a **cell**. Like the PictureBox control, which you learned about in Chapter 1, the DataGridView control has a task list. The task list is shown in Figure 13-17. The first three check boxes on the task list allow you to specify whether the user can add, edit, or delete records during run time. The fourth check box allows you to specify whether the user can reorder the columns in the DataGridView control during run time. Figure 13-18 explains the purpose of each task on the task list.

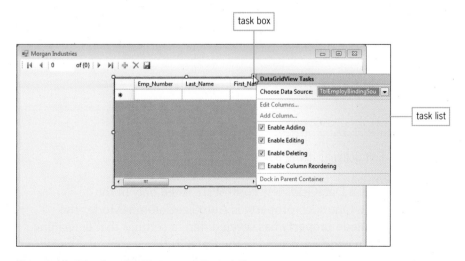

Figure 13-17   DataGridView control's task list

Task	Purpose
Choose Data Source	select a data source
Edit Columns	open the Edit Columns dialog box (see Figure 13-19)
Add Column	add a new column
Enable Adding	allow/disallow the user to add data
Enable Editing	allow/disallow the user to edit data
Enable Deleting	allow/disallow the user to delete data
Enable Column Reordering	allow/disallow the user to reorder the columns
Dock in Parent Container	bind the borders of the control to its container
Add Query	filter data from a dataset
Preview Data	view the data bound to the control

Figure 13-18 Purpose of each task in the DataGridView's task list

Figure 13-19 shows the Edit Columns dialog box, which opens when you click Edit Columns on the DataGridView control's task list. You can use the Edit Columns dialog box during design time to add columns to the DataGridView control, remove columns from the control, and reorder the columns. You also can use it to set the properties of the bound columns. For example, you can use the DefaultCellStyle property to format a column's data. You also can use the property to change the column's width and alignment. You can use the HeaderText property, on the other hand, to change a column's heading.

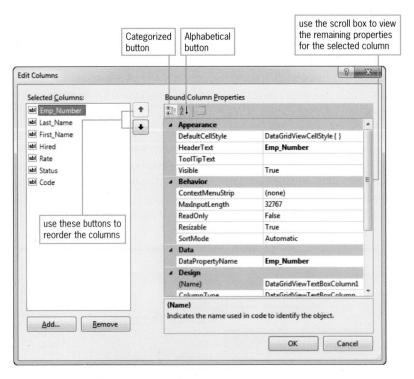

Figure 13-19 Edit Columns dialog box

Some properties of a DataGridView control are listed only in the Properties window. One such property is AutoSizeColumnsMode. The **AutoSizeColumnsMode property** has seven different settings that determine the way the column widths are sized in the DataGridView control. The Fill setting automatically adjusts the column widths so that all of the columns exactly fill the display area of the control. The ColumnHeader setting, on the other hand, automatically adjusts the column widths based on the header text.

To improve the appearance of the DataGridView control:

START HERE

1. Permanently display the Properties window, if necessary. Click **AutoSizeColumnsMode** in the Properties list and then set the property to **Fill**.

2. Click the **TblEmployDataGridView control's task box** and then click **Dock in Parent Container**. The DataGridView control expands to the size of the form. This is because the Dock in Parent Container option anchors the control's borders to the borders of its container, which (in this case) is the form.

3. Next, you will change the header text on several of the columns. Click **Edit Columns** in the task list. Click the **Alphabetical** button (shown in Figure 13-19) to display the property names in alphabetical order. Emp_Number is currently selected in the Selected Columns list. Click **HeaderText** in the Bound Column Properties list and then type **Employee Number** and press **Enter**.

4. Click **Last_Name** in the Selected Columns list and then change the HeaderText property to **Last Name**. On your own, change the First_Name column's HeaderText property to **First Name**. Also change the Rate column's HeaderText property to **Pay Rate**.

5. Now you will have the DataGridView control format the pay rates to show two decimal places. With Pay Rate selected in the Selected Columns list, click **DefaultCellStyle** and then click the **...** (ellipsis) button to open the CellStyle Builder dialog box. Click **Format** and then click the **...** (ellipsis) button to open the Format String Dialog box. Click **Numeric** in the Format type list and then verify that the number 2 appears in the Decimal places box. Click the **OK** button to close the Format String Dialog box. You are returned to the CellStyle Builder dialog box.

6. Next, you will have the DataGridView control align the pay rates in the Pay Rate column. Click **Alignment** and then set the property to **MiddleRight**. Figure 13-20 shows the completed CellStyle Builder dialog box.

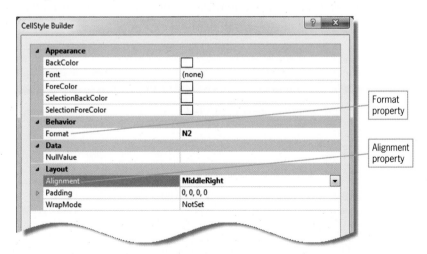

Figure 13-20   Completed CellStyle Builder dialog box

7. Click the **OK** button to close the CellStyle Builder dialog box and then click the **OK** button to close the Edit Columns dialog box.

8. Click the **DataGridView** control to close its task list. Auto-hide the Properties window and then save the solution.

Figure 13-21 shows the DataGridView control after completing the previous set of steps. You won't see the effect of the formatting and aligning until the application is started.

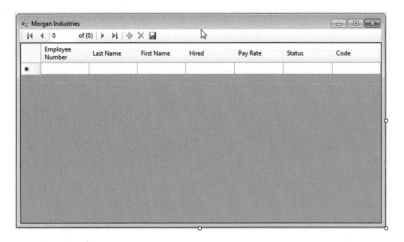

Figure 13-21 DataGridView control after setting some of its properties

Visual Basic Code

In addition to adding the appropriate controls and objects to the application when a table or field object is dragged to the form, the computer also enters some code in the Code Editor window.

START HERE

To view the code automatically entered in the Code Editor window:

1. Open the Code Editor window. Replace <your name> and <current date> in the comments with your name and the current date, respectively.

2. Locate the two procedures shown in Figure 13-22. Both procedures were automatically entered when the tblEmploy object was dragged to the form. (In your Code Editor window, the procedure headers and comments will appear on one line.)

```vb
Private Sub TblEmployBindingNavigatorSaveItem_Click(
        ByVal sender As System.Object, ByVal e As System.EventArgs
        ) Handles TblEmployBindingNavigatorSaveItem.Click
    Me.Validate()
    Me.TblEmployBindingSource.EndEdit()
    Me.TableAdapterManager.UpdateAll(Me.EmployeesDataSet)

End Sub

Private Sub frmMain_Load(ByVal sender As System.Object,
        ByVal e As System.EventArgs) Handles MyBase.Load
    'TODO: This line of code loads data into the
    'EmployeesDataSet.tblEmploy' table. You can move, or remove it, as needed.
    Me.TblEmployTableAdapter.Fill(Me.EmployeesDataSet.tblEmploy)

End Sub
```

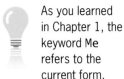

As you learned in Chapter 1, the keyword Me refers to the current form.

Figure 13-22 Code automatically entered in the Code Editor window

The first event procedure, TblEmployBindingNavigatorSaveItem_Click, is processed when you click the Save Data button (the disk) on the BindingNavigator control. The procedure's code validates the changes made to the data before saving the data to the database. Two methods are involved in the save operation: the BindingSource object's EndEdit method and the TableAdapterManager's UpdateAll method. The EndEdit method applies any pending changes (such as new records, deleted records, or changed records) to the dataset. The UpdateAll method commits the dataset changes to the database. The second event procedure in Figure 13-22 is the form's Load event procedure. This procedure uses the TableAdapter object's Fill method to retrieve the data from the database and store it in the DataSet object. In most applications, the code to fill a dataset belongs in the form's Load event procedure. However, as the comments in the Load event procedure indicate, you can either move or delete the code.

Because it is possible for an error to occur when saving data to a database, it is a good programming practice to add error handling code to the Save Data button's Click event procedure.

Handling Errors in the Code

An error that occurs while an application is running is called an **exception**. If you do not take deliberate steps in your code to handle the exceptions, Visual Basic handles them for you. Typically, it does this by displaying an error message and then abruptly terminating the application. You can prevent your application from behaving in such an unfriendly manner by taking control of the exception handling in your code; you can do this using the **Try...Catch statement**. Figure 13-23 shows the statement's basic syntax and includes examples of using the syntax. The basic syntax contains a Try block and a Catch block. Within the Try block, you place the code that could possibly generate an exception. When an exception occurs in the Try block's code, the computer processes the code contained in the Catch block; it then skips to the code following the End Try clause. A description of the exception that occurred is stored in the Message property of the Catch block's **ex** parameter. You can access the description using the code **ex.Message**, as shown in Example 2 in the figure.

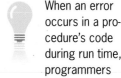

When an error occurs in a procedure's code during run time, programmers say that the procedure "threw an exception."

The Try...Catch statement also has a Finally block. The code in the Finally block is processed whether or not an exception is thrown within the Try block.

Try...Catch Statement

Basic syntax
Try
　　　　one or more statements that might generate an exception
Catch ex As Exception
　　　　one or more statements to execute when an exception occurs
End Try

Example 1
```
Private Sub btnDisplay_Click(ByVal sender As Object,
ByVal e As System.EventArgs) Handles btnDisplay.Click
```

Figure 13-23　Syntax and examples of the Try...Catch statement *(continues)*

(continued)

```
        Dim inFile As IO.StreamReader
        Dim strLine As String

        Try
            inFile = IO.File.OpenText("names.txt")
            Do Until inFile.Peek = -1
                strLine = inFile.ReadLine
                lstNames.Items.Add(strLine)
            Loop
            inFile.Close()
        Catch ex As Exception
            MessageBox.Show("File error", "JK's",
                MessageBoxButtons.OK,
                MessageBoxIcon.Information)
        End Try
End Sub


Example 2
Private Sub TblSalesBindingNavigatorSaveItem_Click(
ByVal sender As System.Object, ByVal e As System.EventArgs
) Handles TblSalesBindingNavigatorSaveItem.Click
        Try
            Me.Validate()
            Me.TblSalesBindingSource.EndEdit()
            Me.TableAdapterManager.UpdateAll(Me.SalesDataSet)
        Catch ex As Exception
            MessageBox.Show(ex.Message, "Sales Data",
                MessageBoxButtons.OK,
                MessageBoxIcon.Information)
        End Try
End Sub
```

Figure 13-23   Syntax and examples of the Try...Catch statement

START HERE   **To include a Try...Catch statement in the Save Data button's Click event procedure:**

1. Insert two blank lines above the `Me.Validate()` statement in the TblEmployBindingNavigatorSaveItem's Click event procedure.

2. In the blank line above the `Me.Validate()` statement, type **Try** and press **Enter**. The Code Editor automatically enters the `Catch ex As Exception` and `End Try` clauses for you.

3. Select (highlight) the three statements that appear below the `End Try` clause, as well as the blank line below the statements. Press **Ctrl+x** to place the selected lines on the Clipboard. Click the **blank line** below the `Try` clause and then press **Ctrl+v**.

4. If the three statements in the Try block do not produce (throw) an exception, the Try block should display the "Changes saved" message; otherwise, the Catch block should display a description of the exception. Enter the two MessageBox.Show methods shaded in Figure 13-24.

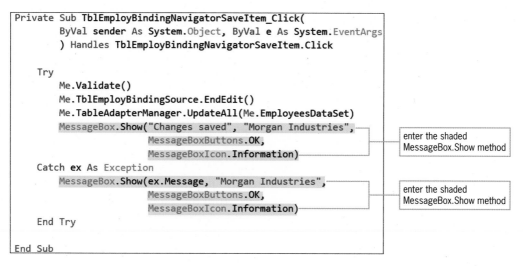

```
Private Sub TblEmployBindingNavigatorSaveItem_Click(
        ByVal sender As System.Object, ByVal e As System.EventArgs
        ) Handles TblEmployBindingNavigatorSaveItem.Click

    Try
        Me.Validate()
        Me.TblEmployBindingSource.EndEdit()
        Me.TableAdapterManager.UpdateAll(Me.EmployeesDataSet)
        MessageBox.Show("Changes saved", "Morgan Industries",
                    MessageBoxButtons.OK,
                    MessageBoxIcon.Information)
    Catch ex As Exception
        MessageBox.Show(ex.Message, "Morgan Industries",
                    MessageBoxButtons.OK,
                    MessageBoxIcon.Information)

    End Try

End Sub
```

enter the shaded MessageBox.Show method

enter the shaded MessageBox.Show method

Figure 13-24   Completed Click event procedure for the Save Data button

759

5. Save the solution and then start the application. The statement in the form's Load event procedure (shown earlier in Figure 13-22) retrieves the appropriate data from the Employees database and loads the data into the EmployeesDataSet. The data is displayed in the DataGridView control, which is bound to the tblEmploy table contained in the dataset. See Figure 13-25.

TblEmployBindingNavigator control

access a record

add, delete, and save

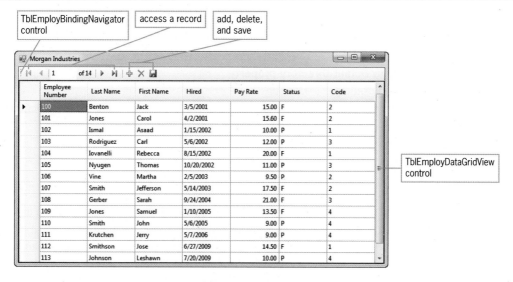

TblEmployDataGridView control

Figure 13-25   Dataset displayed in the DataGridView control

6. You can use the arrow keys on your keyboard to move the highlight to a different cell in the DataGridView control. When a cell is highlighted, you can modify its contents by simply typing the new data. Press the ↓ key to move the highlight to the next record, and then press the ↑ key to move it to the next field.

7. The BindingNavigator control provides buttons for accessing the first, last, previous, and next records in the dataset. Click the **Move next** button to move the highlight to the next record. Click the **Move**

A tooltip appears when you hover your mouse pointer over a button on the BindingNavigator control. The tooltip indicates the button's purpose.

last button ▶| to move the highlight to the last record, and then click the **Move first** button |◀ to move the highlight to the first record.

8. You also can use the BindingNavigator control to access a record by its record number. The record number for the first record in a dataset is 1; the record number for the second record is 2; and so on. Click the **Current position** box, which contains the number 1. Replace the 1 with a **6** and press **Enter**. The highlight moves to the sixth record.

9. Click the **Close** button on the form's title bar to stop the application.

The BindingNavigator control also provides buttons for adding a new record to the dataset, deleting a record from the dataset, and saving the changes made to the dataset. You can add additional items (such as buttons and text boxes) to a BindingNavigator control and also delete items from the control. You will learn how to add items to and delete items from a BindingNavigator control in the *Personalizing a BindingNavigator Control* section in Lesson B.

The Copy to Output Directory Property

When the Data Source Configuration Wizard connected the Morgan Industries application to the Employees database, it added the database file (Employees.accdb) to the application's project folder. (You can verify this in the Solution Explorer window.) A database file contained in a project is referred to as a local database file. The way Visual Basic saves changes to a local database file is determined by the file's **Copy to Output Directory property**. Figure 13-26 lists the values that can be assigned to the property.

Copy to Output Directory property	
Property setting	Meaning
Do not copy	the file in the project folder is not copied to the bin\Debug folder when the application is started
Copy always	the file in the project folder is copied to the bin\Debug folder each time the application is started
Copy if newer	when an application is started, the computer compares the date on the file in the project folder with the date on the file in the bin\Debug folder; the file from the project folder is copied to the bin\Debug folder only when its date is newer

Figure 13-26   Settings for the Copy to Output Directory property

When a file's Copy to Output Directory property is set to its default setting, Copy always, the file is copied from the project folder to the project folder's bin\Debug folder each time you start the application. In this case, the Employees.accdb file is copied from the Morgan Industries Project folder to the Morgan Industries Project\bin\Debug folder. As a result, the file will appear in two different folders in the solution. When you click the Save Data button on the BindingNavigator control, any changes made in the DataGridView control are recorded only in the file stored in the bin\Debug folder; the file stored in the project folder is not changed. The next time you start the application, the file in the project folder is copied to the bin\Debug folder, overwriting the file that contains the changes. One way to fix this problem is to set the database file's Copy to Output Directory property to "Copy if newer." The "Copy if newer" setting tells the computer to compare the dates on both files to determine which file has the newer (more current) date. If the database file in the project folder has the newer date, the computer should copy it to the bin\Debug folder; otherwise, it shouldn't copy it.

To change the Employees.accdb file's Copy to Output Directory property: START HERE

1. Right-click **Employees.accdb** in the Solution Explorer window and then click **Properties**. Change the Employees.accdb file's Copy to Output Directory property to **Copy if newer**.

2. Save the solution and then start the application.

3. Click the **Add new** button ✚ to add a new record to the end of the DataGridView control. Type **114** as the employee number, press **Tab**, and then type **Jacobs** as the last name. Press **Tab** and then type **Susan** as the first name. On your own, enter **8/9/2008**, **10**, **P**, and **3** in the Hired, Pay Rate, Status, and Code fields, respectively. Press **Enter** after typing the number 3.

4. Click the **Move first** button to move the highlight to the Code field in the first record. When a cell is highlighted, you can modify its existing data by simply typing the new data. Type **3** and press **Enter** to change the entry in Jack Benton's Code field.

5. Click the **Save Data** button 💾. The "Changes saved" message appears in a message box. Click the **OK** button to close the message box, and then click the **Close** button on the form's title bar to stop the application.

6. Start the application again. The DataGridView control now contains the record you added, as well as the change you made to Jack Benton's Code field. (You will need to scroll down the DataGridView control to see the new record.)

7. Change Jack Benton's Code field from 3 to **2**. Click the **Move last** button to move the highlight to the last record and then click the **Delete** button ✖ to delete the record. Click the **Save Data** button. The "Changes saved" message appears in a message box. Click the **OK** button to close the message box, and then click the **Close** button on the form's title bar to stop the application.

8. Start the application again to verify that your changes were saved, and then stop the application. Close the Code Editor window and then close the solution.

YOU DO IT 1!

Create a Visual Basic Windows application named YouDoIt 1. Save the application in the VB2010\Chap13 folder. Connect the application to the CD database. The database is stored in the CD.accdb file, which is contained in the VB2010\Chap13\Access Databases folder. The database contains one table named tblCds. The table contains 13 records. Each record contains three fields: CdName, Artist, and Price. Display the records in a DataGridView control. Include the Try...Catch statement in the Save Data button's Click event procedure. Also, change the database file's Copy to Output Directory property appropriately. Save the solution and then start and test the application. Close the Code Editor window and then close the solution.

Binding to an Existing Control

As indicated earlier in Figure 13-11, you can bind an object in a dataset to an existing control on a form. The easiest way to do this is by dragging the object from the Data Sources window to the control. However, you also can click the control and then set one or more properties in the Properties window. The appropriate property (or properties) to set depends on the control you are binding. For example, you use the DataSource property to bind a DataGridView control. However, you use the DataSource and DisplayMember properties to bind a ListBox control. To bind label and text box controls, you use the DataBindings/Text property.

When you drag an object from the Data Sources window to an existing control, the computer does not create a new control; instead, it binds the object to the existing control. Because a new control does not need to be created, the computer ignores the control type specified for the object in the Data Sources window. Therefore, it is not necessary to change the control type in the Data Sources window to match the existing control's type. In other words, you can drag an object that is associated with a text box in the Data Sources window to a label control on the form. The computer will bind the object to the label, but it will not change the label to a text box.

In the following set of steps, you will open a different version of the Morgan Industries application. You will connect the application to the Employees database and then bind objects from the dataset to existing label controls in the interface. In this version of the application, you will not need to change the database file's Copy to Output Directory property to "Copy if newer," because the user will not be adding, deleting, or editing the records in the dataset.

START HERE **To bind controls using a different version of the Morgan Industries application:**

1. Open the Morgan Industries Solution (Morgan Industries Solution. sln) file contained in the VB2010\Chap13\Morgan Industries Solution-Labels folder. If necessary, open the designer window. See Figure 13-27.

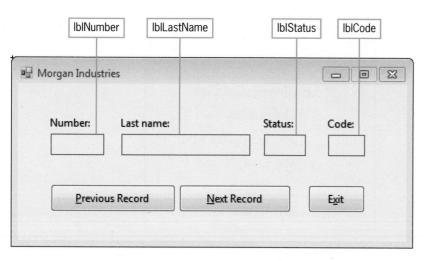

Figure 13-27   A different version of the Morgan Industries application

2. Temporarily display the Data Sources window and then click **Add New Data Source** to start the Data Source Configuration Wizard. If necessary, click **Database** on the Choose a Data Source Type screen.

3. Click the **Next** button to display the Choose a Database Model screen. If necessary, click **Dataset**.

4. Click the **Next** button to display the Choose Your Data Connection screen. Click the **New Connection** button to open the Add Connection dialog box. If Microsoft Access Database File (OLE DB) does not appear in the Data source box, click the **Change** button to open the Change Data Source dialog box, click **Microsoft Access Database File**, and then click the **OK** button.

5. Click the **Browse** button in the Add Connection dialog box. Open the VB2010\Chap13\Access Databases folder and then click **Employees. accdb** in the list of filenames. Click the **Open** button. Click the **Test Connection** button in the Add Connection dialog box. The "Test connection succeeded." message appears in a message box. Close the message box.

6. Click the **OK** button to close the Add Connection dialog box. Click the **Next** button on the Choose Your Data Connection screen and then click the **Yes** button to add the Employees.accdb file to the application's project folder.

7. If necessary, select the **Yes, save the connection as** check box on the Save the Connection String to the Application Configuration File screen. Click the **Next** button to display the Choose Your Database Objects screen.

8. Expand the Tables node and then expand the tblEmploy node. In this application, you will include only four fields in the dataset. Click the **empty box** that appears next to each of the following four field names: Emp_Number, Last_Name, Status, and Code. Click the **Finish** button. The computer adds the EmployeesDataSet to the Data Sources window. Expand the tblEmploy node in the Data Sources window. The dataset contains one table object and four field objects. See Figure 13-28.

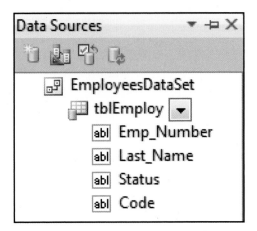

Figure 13-28   Dataset in this version of the Morgan Industries application

9. Click **Emp_Number** in the Data Sources window and then drag the field object to the lblNumber control. Release the mouse button. The computer binds the control and adds the DataSet, BindingSource, TableAdapter, and TableAdapterManager objects to the component tray. It also enters (in the Code Editor window) the Load event procedure shown earlier in Figure 13-22. Recall that the procedure uses the TableAdapter object's Fill method to retrieve the data from the database and store it in the DataSet object. Notice that when you drag an object from the Data Sources window to an existing control, the computer does not add a BindingNavigator object to the component tray, nor does it add a BindingNavigator control to the form. You can use the BindingNavigator tool in the toolbox to add a BindingNavigator control and object to the application. You then would set the control's DataSource property to the name of the BindingSource object (in this case, TblEmployBindingSource).

10. On your own, drag the Last_Name, Status, and Code field objects to the lblLastName, lblStatus, and lblCode controls, respectively.

11. Save the solution and then start the application. Only the first record in the dataset appears in the interface. Because the interface does not contain a BindingNavigator control, which would allow you to move from one record to the next, you will need to code the Next Record and Previous Record buttons to view the remaining records. Click the **Exit** button to stop the application.

Coding the Next Record and Previous Record Buttons

The BindingSource object uses an invisible record pointer to keep track of the current record in the dataset. It stores the position of the record pointer in its **Position property**. The first record is in position 0; the second is in position 1, and so on. Figure 13-29 shows the Position property's syntax and includes examples of using the property.

BindingSource object's Position property

Syntax
bindingSourceName.**Position**

Example 1
`intRecordNum = TblEmployBindingSource.Position`
assigns the current record's position to the `intRecordNum` variable

Example 2
`TblEmployBindingSource.Position = 4`
moves the record pointer to the fifth record in the dataset

Example 3
`TblEmployBindingSource.Position += 1`
moves the record pointer to the next record in the dataset

Figure 13-29   Syntax and examples of the BindingSource object's Position property

Rather than using the Position property to position the record pointer in a dataset, you also can use the BindingSource object's Move methods. The **Move methods** move the record pointer to the first, last, next, or previous record in the dataset. Figure 13-30 shows each Move method's syntax and includes examples of using two of the methods.

BindingSource object's Move methods

Syntax
bindingSourceName.**MoveFirst()**
bindingSourceName.**MoveLast()**
bindingSourceName.**MoveNext()**
bindingSourceName.**MovePrevious()**

Example 1
`TblEmployBindingSource.MoveFirst()`
moves the record pointer to the first record in the dataset

Example 2
`TblEmployBindingSource.MoveNext()`
moves the record pointer to the next record in the dataset

Figure 13-30   Syntax and examples of the BindingSource object's Move methods

To code the Next Record and Previous Record buttons: START HERE

1. Open the Code Editor window. Replace <your name> and <current date> in the comments with your name and the current date, respectively.

2. When the user clicks the Next Record button, the button's Click event procedure should move the record pointer to the next record in the

dataset. Open the code template for the btnNext control's Click event procedure. Type the following comment and then press **Enter** twice:

' moves the record pointer to the next record

3. Now enter the following line of code:

TblEmployBindingSource.MoveNext()

4. When the user clicks the Previous Record button, its Click event procedure should move the record pointer to the previous record in the dataset. Open the code template for the btnPrevious control's Click event procedure. Type the following comment and then press **Enter** twice:

' moves the record pointer to the previous record

5. Now enter the following line of code:

TblEmployBindingSource.MovePrevious()

Figure 13-31 shows the application's code.

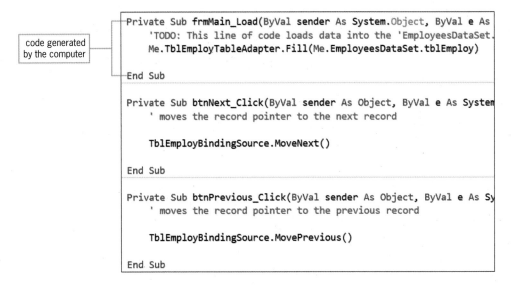

```
Private Sub frmMain_Load(ByVal sender As System.Object, ByVal e As
    'TODO: This line of code loads data into the 'EmployeesDataSet.
    Me.TblEmployTableAdapter.Fill(Me.EmployeesDataSet.tblEmploy)

End Sub

Private Sub btnNext_Click(ByVal sender As Object, ByVal e As System
    ' moves the record pointer to the next record

    TblEmployBindingSource.MoveNext()

End Sub

Private Sub btnPrevious_Click(ByVal sender As Object, ByVal e As Sy
    ' moves the record pointer to the previous record

    TblEmployBindingSource.MovePrevious()

End Sub
```

code generated by the computer

Figure 13-31   Application's code

START HERE   To test the application's code:

1. Save the solution and then start the application. Click the **Next Record** button to display the second record. Continue clicking the **Next Record** button until the last record appears in the interface.

2. Click the **Previous Record** button until the first record appears in the interface, and then click the **Exit** button. Close the Code Editor window and then close the solution.

YOU DO IT 2!

Create a Visual Basic Windows application named YouDoIt 2. Save the application in the VB2010\Chap13 folder. Connect the application to the CD database. The database is stored in the CD.accdb file, which is contained in the VB2010\Chap13\Access Databases folder. The database contains one table named tblCds. The table contains 13 records. Each record contains three fields: CdName, Artist, and Price. Display the records, one at a time, in label controls. Use a Next Record button and a Previous Record button (rather than a BindingNavigator control). Save the solution and then start and test the application. Close the Code Editor window and then close the solution.

Lesson A Summary

- To connect an application to a database:

  Use the Data Source Configuration Wizard. To start the wizard, click Data on the menu bar, click Show Data Sources, and then click Add New Data Source in the Data Sources window.

- To preview the data contained in a dataset:

  Click the form to make it the active window. Click Data on the menu bar and then click Preview Data. Click the Preview button in the Preview Data dialog box.

- To bind an object in a dataset:

  Use either of the ways shown in Figure 13-11.

- To have the columns exactly fill the display area in a DataGridView control:

  Set the DataGridView control's AutoSizeColumnsMode property to Fill.

- To anchor the DataGridView control to the borders of its container:

  Click the Dock in Parent Container option in the DataGridView control's task list. You also can set the DataGridView control's Dock property in the Properties window.

- To handle exceptions (errors) that occur during run time:

  Use the Try...Catch statement.

- To move the record pointer in a dataset during run time:

  You can use a BindingNavigator control. You also can use either the BindingSource object's Position property or one of its Move methods.

Lesson A Key Terms

AutoSizeColumnsMode property—determines the way the column widths are sized in a DataGridView control

Binding—the process of connecting an object in a dataset to a control on a form

BindingNavigator control—can be used to move the record pointer from one record to another in a dataset, as well as to add, delete, and save records

BindingSource object—connects a DataSet object to the bound controls on a form

Bound controls—the controls connected to an object in a dataset

Cell—the intersection of a row and column in a DataGridView control

Child table—a table linked to a parent table

Computer database—an electronic file that contains an organized collection of related information

Copy to Output Directory property—a property of a database file; determines when and if the file is copied from the project folder to the project folder's bin\Debug folder

DataGridView control—displays data in a row and column format

Dataset—a copy of the data (database fields and records) that can be accessed by an application

DataSet object—stores the information you want to access from a database

Exception—an error that occurs while an application is running

Field—a single item of information about a person, place, or thing

Foreign key—the field used to link a child table to a parent table

Move methods—methods of a BindingSource object; used to move the record pointer to the first, last, next, or previous record in a dataset

Parent table—a table linked to a child table

Position property—a property of a BindingSource object; stores the position of the record pointer

Primary key—a field that uniquely identifies each record in a table

Record—a group of related fields that contain all of the necessary data about a specific person, place, or thing

Relational database—a database that stores information in tables composed of columns (fields) and rows (records)

Table—a group of related records

TableAdapter object—connects a database to a DataSet object

TableAdapterManager object—handles saving data to multiple tables in a dataset

Try...Catch statement—used for exception handling in a procedure

Lesson A Review Questions

1. Which of the following objects connects a database to a DataSet object?

    a. BindingSource

    b. DataBase

    c. DataGridView

    d. TableAdapter

2. The _____ property stores an integer that represents the location of the record pointer in a dataset.

    a. BindingNavigator object's Position

    b. BindingSource object's Position

    c. TableAdapter object's Position

    d. none of the above

3. If the record pointer is positioned on record number 5 in a dataset, which of the following will move the record pointer to record number 4?

    a. `TblBooksBindingSource.GoPrevious`

    b. `TblBooksBindingSource.Move(4)`

    c. `TblBooksBindingSource.MovePrevious()`

    d. `TblBooksBindingSource.PositionPrevious`

4. A _____ is an organized collection of related information stored in a computer file.

    a. database

    b. dataset

    c. field

    d. record

5. The information in a _____ database is stored in tables.

    a. columnar

    b. relational

    c. sorted

    d. tabular

6. Which of the following objects provides the connection between a DataSet object and a control on a form?

   a. Bound

   b. Binding

   c. BindingSource

   d. Connecting

7. Which of the following statements retrieves data from the Friends database and stores it in the FriendsDataSet?

   a. `Me.FriendsDataSet.Fill(Friends.accdb)`

   b. `Me.TblNamesBindingSource.Fill(Me.FriendsDataSet)`

   c. `Me.TblNamesBindingNavigator.Fill(Me.FriendsDataSet.tblNames)`

   d. `Me.TblNamesTableAdapter.Fill(Me.FriendsDataSet.tblNames)`

8. If an application contains the `Catch ex As Exception` clause, which of the following can be used to access the exception's description?

   a. `ex.Description`

   b. `ex.Exception`

   c. `ex.Message`

   d. `Exception.Description`

9. If the current record is the second record in the dataset, which of the following statements will position the record pointer on the first record?

   a. `TblEmployBindingSource.Position = 0`

   b. `TblEmployBindingSource.Position = TblEmployBindingSource.Position - 1`

   c. `TblEmployBindingSource.MoveFirst()`

   d. all of the above

10. The field that links a child table to a parent table is called the _____.

    a. foreign key in the child table

    b. foreign key in the parent table

    c. link key in the parent table

    d. primary key in the child table

11. The process of connecting a control to an object in a dataset is called _____.

   a. assigning

   b. binding

   c. joining

   d. none of the above

12. Which of the following is true?

   a. Data stored in a relational database can be retrieved both quickly and easily by the computer.

   b. Data stored in a relational database can be displayed in any order.

   c. A relational database stores data in a column and row format.

   d. all of the above

Lesson A Exercises

1. In this exercise, you will learn how to open a database table in a window in the IDE. You also will modify one of the Morgan Industries applications from the lesson.

          INTRODUCTORY

   a. Use Windows to make a copy of the Morgan Industries Solution-Labels folder. Rename the copy Modified Morgan Industries Solution-Labels. Open the Morgan Industries Solution (Morgan Industries Solution.sln) file contained in the Modified Morgan Industries Solution-Labels folder. Open the designer window.

   b. Expand the Employees.accdb node in the Server (Database) Explorer window, and then expand the Tables node. Right-click tblEmploy and then click Retrieve Data. The table data appears in a window in the IDE, as shown earlier in Figure 13-5. Close the window.

   c. Modify the Next Record and Previous Record buttons' Click event procedures to use the Position property rather than the MoveNext and MovePrevious methods. Save the solution and then start and test the application. Close the Code Editor window and then close the solution.

2. Sydney Industries records the item number, name, and price of each of its products in a database named Products. The Products database is stored in the Products.accdb file, which is contained in the VB2010\Chap13\Access Databases folder. The database contains a table named tblProducts. The table contains 10 records, each composed of three fields. The ItemNum and ItemName fields contain text; the Price field contains numbers. Open the Sydney Solution (Sydney Solution.sln) file contained in the VB2010\Chap13\Sydney Solution-DataGridView folder. If necessary, open the designer window. Connect the

          INTRODUCTORY

application to the Products database. Change the database file's Copy to Output Directory property to "Copy if newer." Bind the table to a DataGridView control and then make the necessary modifications to the control. Open the Code Editor window and enter the Try...Catch statement in the Save Data button's Click event procedure. Include appropriate messages. Save the solution and then start and test the application. Close the Code Editor window and then close the solution.

INTRODUCTORY

3. Sydney Industries records the item number, name, and price of each of its products in a database named Products. The Products database is stored in the Products.accdb file, which is contained in the VB2010\ Chap13\Access Databases folder. The database contains a table named tblProducts. The table contains 10 records, each composed of three fields. The ItemNum and ItemName fields contain text; the Price field contains numbers. Open the Sydney Solution (Sydney Solution.sln) file contained in the VB2010\Chap13\Sydney Solution-Labels folder. If necessary, open the designer window. Connect the application to the Products database. Bind the appropriate objects to the existing label controls. Open the Code Editor window. Code the Click event procedures for the Next Record and Previous Record buttons. Save the solution and then start and test the application. Close the Code Editor window and then close the solution.

INTERMEDIATE

4. In this exercise, you modify one of the Morgan Industries applications from the lesson.

   a. Use Windows to make a copy of the Morgan Industries Solution-Labels folder. Rename the copy Morgan Industries Solution-ListBox. Open the Morgan Industries Solution (Morgan Industries Solution.sln) file contained in the Morgan Industries Solution-ListBox folder. Open the designer window.

   b. Unlock the controls and then delete the lblNumber control from the form. Add a list box to the form. Name the list box lstNumber. Modify the interface to make room for the list box. Lock the controls and then set the tab order appropriately.

   c. Set the lstNumber control's DataSource and DisplayMember properties to TblEmployBindingSource and Emp_Number, respectively. Save the solution and then start and test the application. Close the solution.

LESSON B

After studying Lesson B, you should be able to:

- Query a dataset using LINQ
- Customize a BindingNavigator control
- Use the LINQ aggregate operators

Creating a Query

You can arrange the records stored in a dataset in any order. The records in the EmployeesDataSet, for example, can be arranged by employee number, pay rate, status, and so on. You also can control the number of records you want to view at any one time. For example, you can view all of the records in the EmployeesDataSet; or, you can choose to view only the records for the part-time employees. You use a **query** to specify both the records to select in a dataset and the order in which to arrange the records. You can create a query in Visual Basic 2010 using a language feature called **Language Integrated Query** or, more simply, **LINQ**.

Figure 13-32 shows the basic syntax of LINQ when used to select and arrange records in a dataset. The figure also includes examples of using the syntax. In the syntax, *variableName* and *elementName* can be any names you choose, as long as the name follows the naming rules for variables. In other words, there is nothing special about the `records` and `employee` names used in the examples. The Where and Order By clauses are optional parts of the syntax. You use the **Where clause**, which contains a *condition*, to limit the records you want to view. Similar to the condition in the If…Then… Else and Do…Loop statements, the condition in a Where clause specifies a requirement that must be met for a record to be selected. The **Order By clause** is used to arrange (sort) the records in either ascending (the default) or descending order by one or more fields. Notice that the syntax does not require you to specify the data type of the variable in the Dim statement. Instead, the syntax allows the computer to infer the data type from the value being assigned to the variable. However, for this inference to take place, you must set Option Infer to On (rather than to Off, as you have been doing). You can do this by entering the `Option Infer On` statement in the General Declarations section of the Code Editor window.

The statement in Example 1 in Figure 13-32 selects all of the records in the dataset and assigns the records to the `records` variable. The statement in Example 2 performs the same task; however, the records are assigned in ascending order by the Code field. If you are sorting records in ascending order, you do not need to include the keyword `Ascending` in the Order By clause, because `Ascending` is the default. The statement in Example 3 assigns only the records for part-time employees to the `records` variable. The statement in Example 4 uses the Like operator and the asterisk pattern-matching character to select only records whose Last_Name field begins with the letter J. You learned about the Like operator and pattern-matching characters in Chapter 8.

When used to query a dataset, LINQ is referred to more specifically as LINQ to Datasets.

As you will learn later in this lesson, you also can use LINQ to perform arithmetic calculations (such as a sum or an average) on the data stored in a dataset.

774

Using LINQ to select and arrange records in a dataset

Basic syntax

Dim *variableName* = **From** *elementName* **In** *dataset.table*

    [**Where** *condition*]

    [**Order By** *elementName.fieldName1* [**Ascending** | **Descending**]

        [, *elementName.fieldNameN* [**Ascending** | **Descending**]]]

    Select *elementName*

Example 1

```
Dim records = From employee In EmployeesDataSet.tblEmploy
              Select employee
```
selects all of the records in the dataset

Example 2

```
Dim records = From employee In EmployeesDataSet.tblEmploy
              Order By employee.Code
              Select employee
```
selects all of the records in the dataset and arranges them in ascending order by the Code field

Example 3

```
Dim records = From employee In EmployeesDataSet.tblEmploy
              Where employee.Status.ToUpper = "P"
              Select employee
```
selects only the part-time employee records in the dataset

Example 4

```
Dim records = From employee In EmployeesDataSet.tblEmploy
              Where employee.Last_Name.ToUpper Like "J*"
              Order By employee.Code Descending
              Select employee
```
selects from the dataset only the employee records whose last name begins with the letter J, and arranges them in descending order by the Code field

You learned about the Like operator and the pattern-matching characters in Chapter 8.

Figure 13-32 Basic LINQ syntax and examples for selecting and arranging records in a dataset

The syntax and examples in Figure 13-32 merely select and/or arrange the appropriate records. To actually view the records, you need to assign the variable's contents to the DataSource property of a BindingSource object. The syntax for doing this is shown in Figure 13-33 along with an example of using the syntax.

Assigning a LINQ variable's contents to a BindingSource object

Basic syntax

bindingSource.**DataSource** = *variableName*.**AsDataView**

Example

```
TblEmployBindingSource.DataSource = records.AsDataView
```
assigns the contents of the `records` variable (from Figure 13-32) to the TblEmployBindingSource object

Figure 13-33 Syntax and an example of assigning a LINQ variable's contents to a BindingSource object

To use LINQ to select specific records in the Morgan Industries application:

START HERE

1. If necessary, start Visual Studio 2010 or Visual Basic 2010 Express. Open the Morgan Industries Solution (Morgan Industries Solution.sln) file contained in the VB2010\Chap13\Morgan Industries Solution-LINQ folder. If necessary, open the designer window. The Find Last Name button in the interface will display records whose Last_Name field begins with one or more characters entered by the user.

2. Open the Code Editor window. Replace <your name> and <current date> in the comments with your name and the current date, respectively.

3. The btnFind control's Click event procedure will use LINQ to select the appropriate records. Therefore, you will change the Option Infer setting from Off to On. Locate the `Option Infer Off` statement and then change `Off` to **On**. Press the **Tab** key and then type **' using LINQ**.

4. Locate the btnFind control's Click event procedure. The procedure uses the InputBox function to prompt the user to either enter one or more characters or leave the input area empty. The user's response is converted to uppercase and assigned to the `strFindName` variable.

5. First, you will enter the LINQ statement to select the appropriate records. The condition in the statement's Where clause will use the Like operator and the asterisk pattern-matching character to compare the contents of each record's Last_Name field with the user's entry followed by zero or more characters. Click the **blank line** below the last comment in the procedure and then enter the following lines of code:

   Dim records = From employee In EmployeesDataSet.tblEmploy Where employee.Last_Name.ToUpper Like strFindName & "*" Select employee

6. Now you will display the contents of the `records` variable in the DataGridView control. You do this by assigning the variable to the TblEmployBindingSource object's DataSource property. Press **Enter** and then enter the following assignment statement:

   TblEmployBindingSource.DataSource = records.AsDataView

Figure 13-34 shows the code entered in the General Declarations section and the btnFind control's Click event procedure.

set Option Infer to On in the General Declarations section

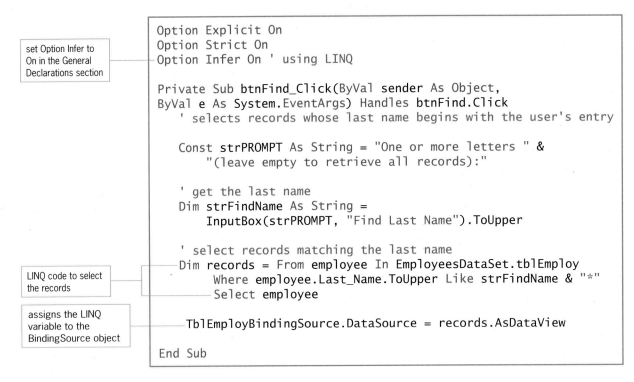

```
Option Explicit On
Option Strict On
Option Infer On ' using LINQ

Private Sub btnFind_Click(ByVal sender As Object,
ByVal e As System.EventArgs) Handles btnFind.Click
    ' selects records whose last name begins with the user's entry

    Const strPROMPT As String = "One or more letters " &
        "(leave empty to retrieve all records):"

    ' get the last name
    Dim strFindName As String =
        InputBox(strPROMPT, "Find Last Name").ToUpper

    ' select records matching the last name
    Dim records = From employee In EmployeesDataSet.tblEmploy
        Where employee.Last_Name.ToUpper Like strFindName & "*"
        Select employee

    TblEmployBindingSource.DataSource = records.AsDataView

End Sub
```

LINQ code to select the records

assigns the LINQ variable to the BindingSource object

Figure 13-34   Code entered in the General Declarations section and btnFind Click event procedure

START HERE

To test the btnFind control's code:

1. Save the solution and then start the application. The 14 records in the dataset appear in the DataGridView control.

2. Click the **Find Last Name** button. First, you will find all of the records whose Last_Name field begins with the letter S. Type **s** and press **Enter**. Three records appear in the DataGridView control, as shown in Figure 13-35.

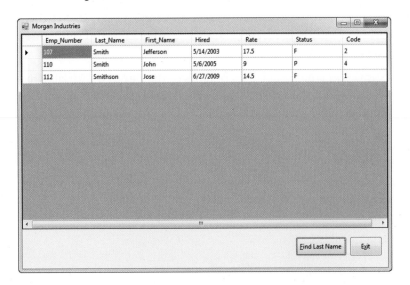

Figure 13-35   Employees whose last name begins with the letter S

3. Now you will display all of the records. Click the **Find Last Name** button and then press **Enter**.

4. You can click a column header to sort the records in order by the associated field. Click **Code** to sort the records in ascending order by the Code field. Now click **Code** again to sort the records in descending order by the Code field.

5. Click the **Exit** button. Close the Code Editor window and then close the solution.

Personalizing a BindingNavigator Control

As shown in Figure 13-25 in Lesson A, the BindingNavigator control contains buttons that allow you to move to a different record in the dataset, as well as to add or delete a record and save any changes made to the dataset. At times, you may want to include additional items—such as another button, a text box, or a drop-down button—on the BindingNavigator control. The steps for adding and deleting items are shown in Figure 13-36.

Adding items to and deleting items from a BindingNavigator control

To add an item to a BindingNavigator control:

1. Click the BindingNavigator control's task box and then click Edit Items to open the Items Collection Editor window.
2. If necessary, click the "Select item and add to list below" arrow.
3. Click the item you want to add to the BindingNavigator control and then click the Add button.
4. If necessary, you can use the up and down arrows to reposition the item.

To delete an item from a BindingNavigator control:

1. Click the BindingNavigator control's task box and then click Edit Items to open the Items Collection Editor window.
2. In the Members list, click the item you want to remove and then click the X button.

Figure 13-36   Manipulating the items on a BindingNavigator control

In the following set of steps, you will add a DropDownButton to the BindingNavigator control in the Morgan Industries application. The DropDownButton will display a menu that contains three options: All Employees, Part-time Employees, and Full-time Employees. The All Employees option will display the average pay rate for all employees. The Part-time Employees and Full-time Employees options will display the average pay rate for part-time and full-time employees, respectively.

To add a DropDownButton to the BindingNavigator control: ◀ START HERE

1. Open the Morgan Industries Solution (Morgan Industries Solution. sln) file contained in the VB2010\Chap13\Morgan Industries Solution-Aggregate folder. Open the designer window.

2. Click an **empty area** on the TblEmployBindingNavigator control and then click the control's **task box**.

3. Click **Edit Items** in the task list to open the Items Collection Editor dialog box. Click the **down arrow** in the "Select item and add to list below" box and then click **DropDownButton** in the list. Click the **Add** button. See Figure 13-37.

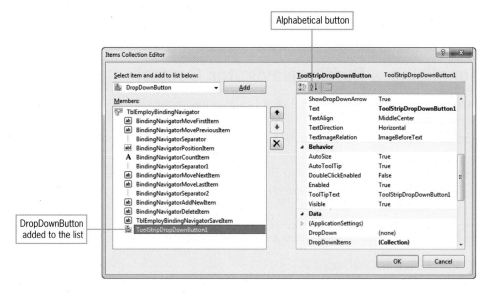

Figure 13-37   Items Collection Editor dialog box

4. Click the **Alphabetical** button to display the property names in alphabetical order. Click **(Name)** in the properties list and then type **ddbAverage** and press **Enter**. Change the DisplayStyle property to **Text** and then change the Text property to **Average Pay Rate**.

5. Click **DropDownItems** in the Properties list and then click the **...** (ellipsis) button. Click the **Add** button to add a menu item to the DropDownButton. Click the **Alphabetical** button to display the property names in alphabetical order. Click **(Name)** in the properties list and then type **mnuAverageAll** and press **Enter**. Change the DisplayStyle property to **Text** and then change the Text property to **All Employees**.

6. Click the **Add** button to add another menu item to the DropDownButton. Change the menu item's Name, DisplayStyle, and Text properties to **mnuAveragePart**, **Text**, and **Part-time Employees**, respectively.

7. Click the **Add** button to add another menu item to the DropDownButton. Change the menu item's Name, DisplayStyle, and Text properties to **mnuAverageFull**, **Text**, and **Full-time Employees**, respectively.

8. Click the **OK** button to close the Items Collection Editor (ddbAverage.DropDownItems) dialog box and then click the **OK** button to close the Items Collection Editor dialog box.

9. Save the solution. Click the **down arrow** on the Average Pay Rate button. See Figure 13-38.

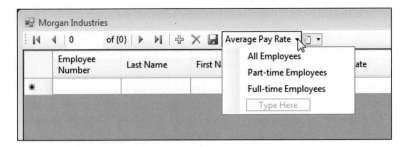

Figure 13-38   DropDownButton added to the TblEmployBindingNavigator control

779

Using the LINQ Aggregate Operators

LINQ provides several aggregate operators that you can use when querying a dataset. The most commonly used aggregate operators are Average, Count, Max, Min, and Sum. An **aggregate operator** returns a single value from a group of values. The Sum operator, for example, returns the sum of the values in the group, whereas the Min operator returns the smallest value in the group. You include an aggregate operator in a LINQ statement using the syntax shown in Figure 13-39. The figure also includes examples of using the syntax.

LINQ aggregate operators

<u>Syntax</u>
Dim *variableName* [**As** *dataType*] =
                          Aggregate *elementName* **In** *dataset.table*
                          [**Where** *condition*]
                          Select *elementName.fieldName*
                          Into *aggregateOperator***()**

<u>Example 1</u>
```
Dim dblAvgRate As Double =
    Aggregate employee In EmployeesDataSet.tblEmploy
    Select employee.Rate Into Average()
```
calculates the average of the pay rates in the dataset and assigns the result to the `dblAvgRate` variable

<u>Example 2</u>
```
Dim dblMaxRate As Double =
    Aggregate employee In EmployeesDataSet.tblEmploy
    Where employee.Status.ToUpper = "P"
    Select employee.Rate Into Max()
```
finds the highest pay rate for a part-time employee and assigns the result to the `dblMaxRate` variable

<u>Example 3</u>
```
Dim intCounter As Integer =
    Aggregate employee In EmployeesDataSet.tblEmploy
    Where employee.Code = 2
    Select employee.Emp_Number Into Count()
```
counts the number of employees whose department code is 2 and assigns the result to the `intCounter` variable

---

Figure 13-39   Syntax and examples of the LINQ aggregate operators

In the following set of steps, you will code the three menu items on the DropDownButton control. More specifically, you will use the Average aggregate operator to calculate the average pay rate for all employees, part-time employees, and full-time employees.

START HERE

To code the menu items on the DropDownButton control:

1. Open the Code Editor window. Replace <your name> and <current date> in the comments with your name and the current date, respectively.

2. Open the code template for the mnuAverageAll item's Click event procedure. Type the following comment and then press **Enter** twice:

   ' displays the average pay rate for all employees

3. Enter the following three lines of code. Press **Enter** twice after typing the last line.

   Dim dblAverage As Double =
   Aggregate employee In EmployeesDataSet.tblEmploy
   Select employee.Rate Into Average()

4. Next, enter the following five lines of code:

   MessageBox.Show("Average pay rate for all employees: " &
   dblAverage.ToString("C2"),
   "Morgan Industries",
   MessageBoxButtons.OK,
   MessageBoxIcon.Information)

5. Open the code template for the mnuAveragePart item's Click event procedure. Type the following comment and then press **Enter** twice:

   ' displays the average pay rate for part-time employees

6. Enter the following four lines of code. Press **Enter** twice after typing the last line.

   Dim dblAverage As Double =
   Aggregate employee In EmployeesDataSet.tblEmploy
   Where employee.Status.ToUpper = "P"
   Select employee.Rate Into Average()

7. Next, enter the following five lines of code:

   MessageBox.Show("Average pay rate for part-time employees: " &
   dblAverage.ToString("C2"),
   "Morgan Industries",
   MessageBoxButtons.OK,
   MessageBoxIcon.Information)

8. Open the code template for the mnuAverageFull item's Click event procedure. Type the following comment and then press **Enter** twice:

   ' displays the average pay rate for full-time employees

9. On your own, enter the appropriate LINQ statement and MessageBox.Show method.

Figure 13-40 shows the code entered in each menu item's Click event procedure.

```
Private Sub mnuAverageAll_Click(ByVal sender As Object,
ByVal e As System.EventArgs) Handles mnuAverageAll.Click
    ' displays the average pay rate for all employees

    Dim dblAverage As Double =
        Aggregate employee In EmployeesDataSet.tblEmploy
        Select employee.Rate Into Average()

    MessageBox.Show("Average pay rate for all employees: " &
                    dblAverage.ToString("C2"),
                    "Morgan Industries",
                    MessageBoxButtons.OK,
                    MessageBoxIcon.Information)

End Sub

Private Sub mnuAveragePart_Click(ByVal sender As Object,
ByVal e As System.EventArgs) Handles mnuAveragePart.Click
    ' displays the average pay rate for part-time employees

    Dim dblAverage As Double =
        Aggregate employee In EmployeesDataSet.tblEmploy
        Where employee.Status.ToUpper = "P"
        Select employee.Rate Into Average()

    MessageBox.Show("Average pay rate for part-time employees: " &
                    dblAverage.ToString("C2"),
                    "Morgan Industries",
                    MessageBoxButtons.OK,
                    MessageBoxIcon.Information)

End Sub

Private Sub mnuAverageFull_Click(ByVal sender As Object,
ByVal e As System.EventArgs) Handles mnuAverageFull.Click
    ' displays the average pay rate for full-time employees

    Dim dblAverage As Double =
        Aggregate employee In EmployeesDataSet.tblEmploy
        Where employee.Status.ToUpper = "F"
        Select employee.Rate Into Average()

    MessageBox.Show("Average pay rate for full-time employees: " &
                    dblAverage.ToString("C2"),
                    "Morgan Industries",
                    MessageBoxButtons.OK,
                    MessageBoxIcon.Information)

End Sub
```

calculates the average pay rate for all employees

calculates the average pay rate for part-time employees

calculates the average pay rate for full-time employees

Figure 13-40 Code entered in each menu item's Click event procedure

START HERE   **To test the code in each menu item's Click event procedure:**

1. Save the solution and then start the application. Click the **down arrow** on the Average Pay Rate button and then click **All Employees**. The average pay rate for all employees appears in a message box, as shown in Figure 13-41.

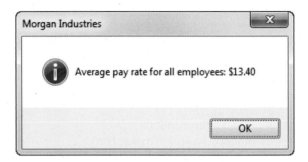

Morgan Industries

   Average pay rate for all employees: $13.40

OK

Figure 13-41   Message box showing the average pay rate for all employees

2. Close the message box. Click the **down arrow** on the Average Pay Rate button and then click **Part-time Employees**. The message indicates that the average pay rate for part-time employees is $10.07.

3. Close the message box. Click the **down arrow** on the Average Pay Rate button and then click **Full-time Employees**. The message indicates that the average pay rate for full-time employees is $16.73.

4. Close the message box and then click the **Close** button on the form's title bar. Close the Code Editor window and then close the solution.

Lesson B Summary

- To use LINQ to select and arrange records in a dataset:

  Use the syntax shown in Figure 13-32.

- To assign a LINQ variable's contents to a BindingSource object:

  Use the syntax shown in Figure 13-33.

- To either add items to or delete items from a BindingNavigator control:

  Follow the steps listed in Figure 13-36.

- To use the LINQ aggregate operators:

  Use the syntax shown in Figure 13-39.

Lesson B Key Terms

Aggregate operator—an operator that returns a single value from a group of values; LINQ provides the Average, Count, Max, Min, and Sum aggregate operators

Language Integrated Query—LINQ; the query language built into Visual Basic 2010

LINQ—an acronym for Language Integrated Query

Order By clause—used in LINQ to arrange the records in a dataset

Query—specifies the records to select in a dataset and the order in which to arrange the records

Where clause—used in LINQ to limit the records you want to view in a dataset

Lesson B Review Questions

1. Which of the following will select only records whose LastName field begins with an uppercase letter A?

   a. ```
      Dim records = From name In NamesDataSet.tblNames
          Where name.LastName Like "A*"
          Select name
      ```

   b. ```
      Dim records = From NamesDataSet.tblNames
          Select LastName Like "A*"
      ```

   c. ```
      Dim records = From tblNames
          Where tblName.LastName Like "A*"
          Select name
      ```

   d. ```
      Dim records = From name In NamesDataSet.tblNames
          Where tblName.LastName Like "A*"
          Select name
      ```

2. Which of the following calculates the sum of the values stored in a numeric field named JulySales?

   a. ```
      Dim dblTotal As Double =
          From sales In SalesDataSet.tblSales
          Select sales.JulySales
          Into Sum()
      ```

   b. ```
      Dim dblTotal As Double =
          Aggregate sales In SalesDataSet.tblSales
          Select sales.JulySales
          Into Sum()
      ```

   c. ```
      Dim dblTotal As Double =
          From sales In SalesDataSet.tblSales
          Aggregate sales.JulySales
          Into Sum()
      ```

   d. ```
      Dim dblTotal As Double =
          From sales In SalesDataSet.tblSales
          Sum sales.JulySales
      ```

3. Which of the following statements selects all of the records in the tblStates table?

a. ```
   Dim records =
       From state In StatesDataSet.tblStates
       Select All state
   ```

b. ```
   Dim records =
       From state In StatesDataSet.tblStates
       Select state
   ```

c. ```
   Dim records =
       Select state From StatesDataSet.tblStates
   ```

d. ```
   Dim records = From StatesDataSet.tblStates
       Select tblStates.state
   ```

4. The tblCities table contains a numeric field named Population. Which of the following statements selects all cities having a population that exceeds 15000?

a. ```
   Dim records =
       From city In CitiesDataSet.tblCities
       Where Population > 15000
       Select city
   ```

b. ```
   Dim records =
       From city In CitiesDataSet.tblCities
       Select city.Population > 15000
   ```

c. ```
   Dim records =
       From city In CitiesDataSet.tblCities
       Where city.Population > 15000
       Select city
   ```

d. ```
   Dim records =
       Select city.Population > 15000
       From tblCities
   ```

5. The tblCities table contains a numeric field named Population. Which of the following statements calculates the total population of all of the cities in the table?

a. ```
   Dim intTotal As Integer =
       Aggregate city In CitiesDataSet.tblCities
       Select city.Population
       Into Sum()
   ```

b. ```
   Dim intTotal As Integer =
       Sum city In CitiesDataSet.tblCities
       Select city.Population
       Into Total()
   ```

c. ```
Dim intTotal As Integer =
    Aggregate CitiesDataSet.tblCities.city
    Select city.Population
    Into Sum()
```

d. ```
Dim intTotal As Integer =
    Sum city In CitiesDataSet.tblCities.Population
```

6. In a LINQ statement, the _____ clause limits the records that will be selected.

a. Limit

b. Order By

c. Select

d. Where

Lesson B Exercises

1. The tblMagInfo table contains three fields. The Code and Cost fields are numeric. The Magazine field contains text. The dataset's name is MagsDataSet.

   INTRODUCTORY

   a. Write a LINQ statement that arranges the records in descending order by the Cost field.

   b. Write a LINQ statement that selects records having a code of 9.

   c. Write a LINQ statement that selects records having a cost of $3 or more.

   d. Write a LINQ statement that selects the Daily Food Guide magazine.

2. In this exercise, you modify one of the Morgan Industries applications from the lesson. Use Windows to make a copy of the Morgan Industries Solution-Aggregate folder. Rename the copy Modified Morgan Industries Solution-Aggregate. Open the Morgan Industries Solution (Morgan Industries Solution.sln) file contained in the Modified Morgan Industries Solution-Aggregate folder. Open the designer window.

   INTRODUCTORY

   a. Click an empty area on the TblEmployBindingNavigator control and then click the control's task box. Click Edit Items in the task list to open the Items Collection Editor dialog box. Add a DropDownButton to the control. Change the DropDownButton's name to ddbDepartment. Change its DisplayStyle and Text properties to Text and Department, respectively.

   b. Use the DropDownItems property to add four menu items to the DropDownButton: Accounting, Advertising, Personnel, and Inventory. Be sure to change each menu item's name, as well as its DisplayStyle and Text properties.

c. Each menu item should display (in a message box) the number of employees in the department. Code 1 is Accounting, Code 2 is Advertising, Code 3 is Personnel, and Code 4 is Inventory. Open the Code Editor window and code each menu item's Click event procedure.

d. Save the solution and then start and test the application. Close the Code Editor window and then close the solution.

INTRODUCTORY

3. Open the Magazine Solution (Magazine Solution.sln) file contained in the VB2010\Chap13\Magazine Solution-Introductory folder. If necessary, open the designer window. The application is connected to the Magazines database, which is stored in the Magazines.accdb file. The database contains a table named tblMagazine; the table has three fields. The Cost field is numeric. The Code and MagName fields contain text. Start the application to view the records contained in the dataset, and then stop the application. Open the Code Editor window. Code the btnCode control's Click event procedure so that it displays the record whose Code field contains PG24. Code the btnName control's Click event procedure so that it displays only the Java record. Code the btnAll control's Click event procedure to display all of the records. Save the solution and then start and test the application. Close the Code Editor window and then close the solution.

INTERMEDIATE

4. Using the information from Exercise 1, write a LINQ statement that selects magazines whose names begin with the letter G (in either uppercase or lowercase). Then write a LINQ statement that calculates the average cost of a magazine.

INTERMEDIATE

5. Open the Magazine Solution (Magazine Solution.sln) file contained in the VB2010\Chap13\Magazine Solution-Intermediate folder. If necessary, open the designer window. The application is connected to the Magazines database, which is stored in the Magazines.accdb file. The database contains a table named tblMagazine; the table has three fields. The Cost field is numeric. The Code and MagName fields contain text. Start the application to view the records contained in the dataset, and then stop the application. Open the Code Editor window. Code the btnAll control's Click event procedure so that it displays all of the records. Code the btnCost control's Click event procedure so that it displays records having a cost of $4 or more. Code the btnName control's Click event procedure so that it displays only magazines whose names begin with the letter C (in either uppercase or lowercase). Code the btnAverage control's Click event procedure so that it displays the average cost of a magazine. Display the average in a message box. Save the solution and then start and test the application. Close the Code Editor window and then close the solution.

LESSON C

After studying Lesson C, you should be able to:

- Prevent the user from adding and deleting records
- Remove buttons from a BindingNavigator control
- Add a label, a text box, and a button to a BindingNavigator control

Completing the Paradise Bookstore Application

As you may remember, your task in this chapter is to create an application for the Paradise Bookstore. The application will display the records contained in a Microsoft Access database named Books. It also will allow the store manager to enter an author's name (or part of a name) and then display only the books written by that author. You will accomplish this task using a label, a text box, and a button, which you will add to the application's BindingNavigator control. In addition, the application will allow the store manager to display the total value of the books in the store; you will provide a button on the BindingNavigator control for this purpose.

The Books database is stored in the Books.accdb file, which is contained in the VB2010\Chap13\Access Databases folder. The database contains one table named tblBooks. The table has five fields and 11 records. The BookNumber, Price, and QuantityInStock fields are numeric. The Title and Author fields contain text. The fields and records contained in the tblBooks table are shown in Figure 13-42.

BookNumber	Title	Author	Price	QuantityInStock
101	Garden of Eden	Smith, Leona	35.99	15
146	Rosebud	Smith, Leona	24.5	20
224	Cycle World	Russel, John	15.99	5
233	Motorcycle Ma...	Russel, John	12.99	2
322	Truthfully Yours	Staven, Harriet	45.5	20
367	Romance and Y...	Staven, Harriet	10.99	15
401	My Hero	Smith, Carol	63.99	23
402	Laddie the Dog	Smith, Carol	10.99	11
561	That Was the Day	Handel, Pat	15.99	4
581	Rusty the Robot	Handel, Pat	9.99	3
603	Philomena	Smith, Carol	24.5	1

Figure 13-42   tblBooks table in the Books database

To modify the DataGridView and BindingNavigator controls in the Paradise Bookstore application: `START HERE`

1. If necessary, start Visual Studio 2010 or Visual Basic 2010 Express. Open the Paradise Bookstore (Paradise Bookstore.sln) file contained in the VB2010\Chap13\Paradise Bookstore Solution folder. If necessary, open the designer window.

2. In this application, the user will not be allowed to add or delete records. Click the **TblBooksDataGridView** control. (Be sure

to click the TblBooksDataGridView control rather than the TblBooksBindingNavigator control.) Click the control's **task box** to open its task list. Click the **Enable Adding** and **Enable Deleting** check boxes to deselect both check boxes. Click the form's **title bar** to close the task list.

3. Click the **TblBooksBindingNavigator** control and then click its **task box**. Click **Edit Items** on the task list. Click **BindingNavigatorAddNewItem** in the Members list and then click the **X** button to remove the item from the list. This also removes the Add new button (the plus sign) from the TblBooksBindingNavigator control.

4. BindingNavigatorDeleteItem should be selected in the Members list. Click the **X** button to remove the item from the list. This also removes the Delete button (the letter **X**) from the TblBooksBindingNavigator control.

5. Now you will add a label, a text box, and a button for entering the author's name. Click the **down arrow** in the "Select item and add to list below" box and then click **Label** in the list. Click the **Add** button. Click the **Alphabetical** button to display the property names in alphabetical order. Click **Text** in the properties list (if necessary) and then type **&Author:** and press **Enter**.

6. Click the **down arrow** in the "Select item and add to list below" box and then click **TextBox** in the list. Click the **Add** button. Click **(Name)** in the properties list and then type **txtAuthor** and press **Enter**.

7. Click the **down arrow** in the "Select item and add to list below" box and then click **Button** in the list. Click the **Add** button. Change the button's name to **btnGo**. Also change its DisplayStyle and Text properties to **Text** and **&Go**, respectively.

8. Finally, you will add a button for displaying the total value of the books. Click the **Add** button again to add another button to the BindingNavigator control. Change the button's name to **btnTotal**. Also change its DisplayStyle and Text properties to **Text** and **&Total Value**, respectively. See Figure 13-43.

label, text box, and buttons added to the BindingNavigator control

Figure 13-43 Completed Items Collection Editor dialog box

9. Click the **OK** button to close the dialog box and then click the form's **title bar**. See Figure 13-44.

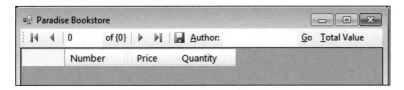

Figure 13-44   Completed TblBooksBindingNavigator control

Coding the Paradise Bookstore Application

The Go button's Click event procedure should display only records whose Author field begins with the one or more characters entered in the txtAuthor control. If the text box is empty, the Go button should display all of the records.

To code and then test the Go button's Click event procedure: START HERE

1. Open the Code Editor window. Replace <your name> and <current date> in the comments with your name and the current date, respectively.

2. Open the code template for the btnGo control's Click event procedure. Type the following comment and then press **Enter** twice:

   ' display records for a specific author

3. You can use LINQ to select the appropriate records. Enter the following lines of code. Press **Enter** twice after typing the last line.

   Dim records = From book In BooksDataSet.tblBooks
   Where book.Author.ToUpper Like
   txtAuthor.Text.ToUpper & "*"
   Select book

4. Now you will display the records in the DataGridView control. As you learned in Lesson B, you do this by assigning the `records` variable to the BindingSource object's DataSource property. Enter the following line of code:

   TblBooksBindingSource.DataSource = records.AsDataView

5. Save the solution and then start the application. Click the **Author** text box (or press Alt+a) and then type the letter **s**. Click the **Go** button (or press Alt+g). The DataGridView control shows only the books written by authors whose names begin with the letter s. See Figure 13-45.

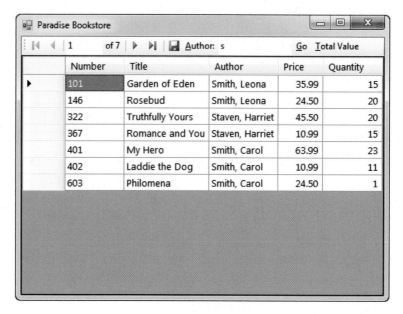

Figure 13-45 Books written by authors whose names begin with s

6. Remove the letter s from the Author text box and then click the **Go** button. All of the records appear in the DataGridView control.

7. Click the **Close** button on the form's title bar to stop the application.

The Total Value button's Click event procedure should display the total value of the books in the store. The total value is calculated by multiplying the quantity of each book by its price and then adding together the results.

START HERE ▶ **To code and then test the Total Value button's Click event procedure:**

1. Open the code template for the btnTotal control's Click event procedure. Type the following comment and then press **Enter** twice:

   ' display the total value of the inventory

2. You can use the Sum aggregate operator to accumulate the results of multiplying each book's quantity by its price. The quantity and price are stored in the QuantityInStock and Price fields, respectively. Enter the following lines of code. Press **Enter** twice after typing the last line.

   **Dim dblTotal As Double =
       Aggregate book In BooksDataSet.tblBooks
       Select book.QuantityInStock * book.Price
       Into Sum()**

3. Now display the total value in a message box. Enter the following lines of code:

   **MessageBox.Show("Total value: " &
           dblTotal.ToString("C2"),
           "Paradise Bookstore",
           MessageBoxButtons.OK,
           MessageBoxIcon.Information)**

4. Save the solution and then start the application. Click the **Total Value** button (or press Alt+t). The total value of the inventory appears in a message box. See Figure 13-46.

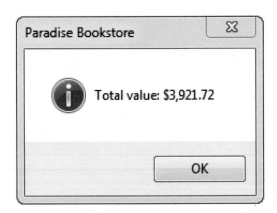

Figure 13-46   Message box showing the total value of the inventory

5. Close the message box and then click the **Close** button on the form's title bar to stop the application.

6. Close the Code Editor window and then close the solution.

Figure 13-47 shows the code entered in the btnGo and btnTotal Click event procedures.

```
Private Sub btnGo_Click(ByVal sender As Object,
ByVal e As System.EventArgs) Handles btnGo.Click
    ' display records for a specific author

    Dim records = From book In BooksDataSet.tblBooks
                  Where book.Author.ToUpper Like
                  txtAuthor.Text.ToUpper & "*"
                  Select book

    TblBooksBindingSource.DataSource = records.AsDataView

End Sub

Private Sub btnTotal_Click(ByVal sender As Object,
ByVal e As System.EventArgs) Handles btnTotal.Click
    ' display the total value of the inventory

    Dim dblTotal As Double =
        Aggregate book In BooksDataSet.tblBooks
        Select book.QuantityInStock * book.Price
        Into Sum()

    MessageBox.Show("Total value: " &
                dblTotal.ToString("C2"),
                "Paradise Bookstore",
                MessageBoxButtons.OK,
                MessageBoxIcon.Information)

End Sub
```

Figure 13-47   Click event procedures for the btnGo and btnTotal controls

Lesson C Summary

- To prevent the user from adding or deleting records in a DataGridView control:

  Click the DataGridView control's task box and then deselect the Enable Adding and Enable Deleting check boxes.

- To delete items from a BindingNavigator control:

  Click the BindingNavigator control's task box and then click Edit Items. In the Members list, click the item you want to remove. Click the X button.

- To add controls to a BindingNavigator control:

  Click the BindingNavigator control's task box and then click Edit Items. Use the "Select item and add to list below" box and Add button to add the appropriate control.

Lesson C Key Terms

There are no key terms in Lesson C.

Lesson C Review Questions

1. The Enable Adding check box in a _____ control's task list determines whether a record can be added to the control.

   a. BindingNavigator

   b. DataGridView

   c. BindingSource

   d. DataBindingNavigator

2. Using the Books database from the lesson, which of the following will select book number 224? The BookNumber field is numeric.

   a. ```
      Dim records = From book In BooksDataSet.tblBooks
          Where book.BookNumber = 224
          Select book
      ```

   b. ```
      Dim records = From book In BooksDataSet.tblBooks
          Select book.BookNumber = 224
      ```

   c. ```
      Dim records = From book In BooksDataSet.tblBooks
          Where book.BookNumber = "224"
          Select book
      ```

   d. none of the above
      ```

3. Using the Books database from the lesson, which of the following determines the number of records in the tblBooks table?

   a. ```
      Dim intNum As Integer =
          Aggregate book In BooksDataSet.tblBooks
          In Count()
      ```

   b. ```
      Dim intNum As Integer =
          Aggregate book In BooksDataSet.tblBooks
          Into Counter()
      ```

   c. ```
      Dim intNum As Integer =
          Aggregate book In BooksDataSet.tblBooks
          Into Sum()
      ```

   d. none of the above

## Lesson C Exercises

1. Open the Addison Playhouse Solution (Addison Playhouse Solution. sln) file contained in the VB2010\Chap13\Addison Playhouse Solution folder. If necessary, open the designer window. Connect the application to a Microsoft Access database named Play. The database is stored in the Play.accdb file, which is contained in the VB2010\ Chap13\Access Databases folder. The Play database contains one table named tblReservations. The table has 20 records. Each record has three fields: a numeric field named Seat and two text fields named Patron and Phone. The application should display the contents of the Play database in a DataGridView control. It also should allow the user to add, delete, modify, and save records. Enter the Try...Catch statement in the Save Data button's Click event procedure. Save the solution and then start and test the application. Close the Code Editor window and then close the solution.

   INTRODUCTORY

2. Open the Sports Action Solution (Sports Action Solution.sln) file contained in the VB2010\Chap13\Sports Action Solution folder. If necessary, open the designer window. Connect the application to a Microsoft Access database named Sports. The database is stored in the Sports.accdb file, which is contained in the VB2010\Chap13\ Access Databases folder. The database contains one table named tblScores. The table contains 10 records. Each record has five fields that store the following information: a unique number that identifies the game, the name of the opposing team, the date of the game, the home team's score, and the opposing team's score. The application should display each record contained in the Sports database, one at a time, in label controls. The user should not be allowed to add, delete, edit, or save records. Include a button on a BindingNavigator control to allow the user to display the average of the home team's scores. Open the Code Editor window and code the application. Save the solution and then start and test the application. Close the Code Editor window and then close the solution.

   INTRODUCTORY
      ```

INTERMEDIATE

3. The sales manager at JW Industries records the item number, name, and price of the company's products in a database named Items. The Items database is stored in the Items.accdb file, which is contained in the VB2010\Chap13\Access Databases folder. The database contains one table named tblItems. The table contains 10 records, each composed of three fields. The ItemNum and ItemName fields contain text, and the Price field contains numbers. The sales manager wants an application that displays the records in a DataGridView control. The application should not allow records to be added or deleted. The application should allow the sales manager to display records whose item number matches one or more characters he enters. In addition, it should allow him to display the average price.

    a. Create a Visual Basic Windows application. Use the following names for the solution, project, and form file, respectively: JW Solution, JW Project, and Main Form.vb. Save the application in the VB2010\Chap13 folder.

    b. Connect the application to the Items database and then drag the tblItems object to the form. Make the appropriate modifications to the DataGridView and BindingNavigator controls.

    c. Open the Code Editor window and code the application. Save the solution and then start and test the application. Close the Code Editor window and then close the solution.

INTERMEDIATE

4. In this exercise, you use a Microsoft Access database named Courses. The database is stored in the Courses.accdb file, which is contained in the VB2010\Chap13\Access Databases folder. The database contains one table named tblCourses. The table has 10 records. Each record has the following four fields: ID, Title, CreditHours, and Grade. The CreditHours field is numeric; the other fields contain text.

    a. Open the College Courses Solution (College Courses Solution.sln) file contained in the VB2010\Chap13\College Courses Solution folder. If necessary, open the designer window. Connect the application to the Courses database. Drag the table into the group box control and then dock the DataGridView control in its parent container. (In this case, the parent container is the group box control.) Use the task list to disable Adding, Editing, and Deleting. Change the DataGridView control's AutoSizeColumnsMode property to Fill. Change its RowHeadersVisible property to False.

    b. Remove the BindingNavigator control from the form by deleting the BindingNavigator object from the component tray.

    c. Open the Code Editor window. Delete the Save Data button's Click event procedure. Code the Next Record and Previous Record buttons. Code the Grade Display button so it allows the user to display either all the records or only the records matching a specific grade.

    d. Save the solution and then start and test the application. Close the Code Editor window and then close the solution.

5. In this exercise, you modify the College Courses application from Exercise 4. Use Windows to make a copy of the College Courses Solution folder. Rename the copy Modified College Courses Solution. Open the College Courses Solution (College Courses Solution.sln) file contained in the Modified College Courses Solution folder. Open the designer window. Add a Calculate GPA button to the form. Open the Code Editor window. Code the Calculate GPA button's Click event procedure so it displays the student's GPA. (An A grade is worth 4 points, a B is worth 3 points, and so on.) Display the GPA in a message box. Save the solution and then start and test the application. Close the Code Editor window and then close the solution.

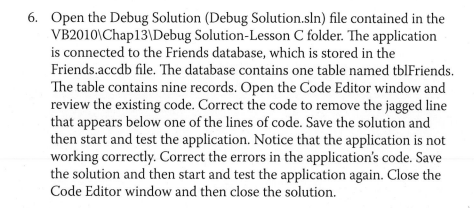

Swat The Bugs

6. Open the Debug Solution (Debug Solution.sln) file contained in the VB2010\Chap13\Debug Solution-Lesson C folder. The application is connected to the Friends database, which is stored in the Friends.accdb file. The database contains one table named tblFriends. The table contains nine records. Open the Code Editor window and review the existing code. Correct the code to remove the jagged line that appears below one of the lines of code. Save the solution and then start and test the application. Notice that the application is not working correctly. Correct the errors in the application's code. Save the solution and then start and test the application again. Close the Code Editor window and then close the solution.

CHAPTER 14

Access Databases and SQL

Creating the Academy Award Winners Application

In this chapter, you will create an application that uses a Microsoft Access database to keep track of the Academy Award winners for Best Picture of the Year. The Movies database will store the title of each movie, the year the movie won the award, and the name of the company that produced the movie. The application will allow the user to add records to the database and also delete records from the database.

Previewing the Academy Award Winners Application

Before you start the first lesson in this chapter, you will preview the completed application. The application is contained in the VB2010\Chap14 folder.

To preview the completed application:

START HERE

1. Use the Run dialog box to run the Award (Award.exe) file contained in the VB2010\Chap14 folder. The application's user interface appears on the screen. The interface contains a DataGridView control that displays the eight records stored in the Movies database. See Figure 14-1. Notice that the record for year number 2002 is missing from the movie listing.

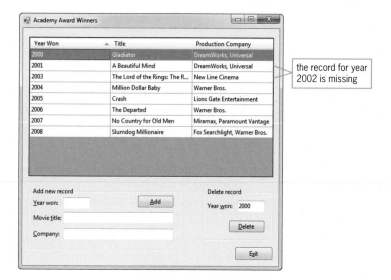

the record for year 2002 is missing

Figure 14-1 Academy Award Winners application

2. First, you will add the missing record to the database. Click the **Year won** text box in the Add new record section of the interface. Type **2002** and then press **Tab**. Type **Chicago** as the movie title and then press **Tab**. Type **Miramax** as the company name and then click the **Add** button. The record you added appears in numerical order by the year number. See Figure 14-2.

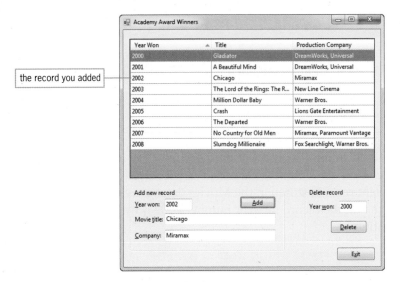

the record you added

Figure 14-2   Result of adding the missing record

3. Next, you'll verify that the record was saved to the database. Click the **Exit** button to end the application, and then run the Award (Award.exe) file again. The record for year number 2002 appears in the DataGridView control.

4. Now, you'll delete the record. Click **2002** in the first column of the DataGridView control; doing this highlights (selects) the entire record. Notice that the value in the record's YearWon field appears in the Year won box in the Delete record section. Click the **Delete** button. The "Delete winner from year 2002?" message appears in a message box. Click the **Yes** button to delete the record. The computer removes the record from the DataGridView control, the dataset, and the database.

5. Click **2000** in the first column of the DataGridView control, and then click the **Delete** button. This time, click the **No** button in the Confirm Delete message box. The record remains in the DataGridView control, the dataset, and the database.

6. Click the **Exit** button to end the application, and then run the Award (Award.exe) file again. Notice that the record you deleted in Step 4 does not appear in the DataGridView control.

7. Click the **Exit** button.

In Lesson A, you will learn how to add records to a dataset, delete records from a dataset, and sort the records in a dataset. You also will learn how to save (to a database) the changes made to a dataset. You will create the Academy Award Winners application in Lesson A. Lessons B and C cover SQL, which stands for Structured Query Language. Be sure to complete each lesson in full and do all of the end-of-lesson questions and several exercises before continuing to the next lesson.

LESSON A

After studying Lesson A, you should be able to:

- Add records to a dataset

- Delete records from a dataset

- Sort the records in a dataset

Adding Records to a Dataset

In Chapter 13, you learned how to use a BindingNavigator control to add records to a dataset and also delete records from a dataset. In this lesson, you will learn how to perform both tasks without using a BindingNavigator control. The records will be added to and deleted from a Microsoft Access database named Movies. The Movies database is stored in the Movies.accdb file. The database contains one table named tblMovies. As shown in Figure 14-3, the table contains nine records. Each record has three fields. The YearWon field is numeric; the Title and ProductionCo fields contain text. The database keeps track of the movies that won an Academy Award for Best Picture of the Year.

Figure 14-3   Data contained in the tblMovies table

To open the Academy Award Winners application:

START HERE

1. If necessary, start Visual Studio 2010 or Visual Basic 2010 Express. Open the Academy Award Solution (Academy Award Solution.sln) file contained in the VB2010\Chap14\Academy Award Solution folder. If necessary, open the designer window. The Academy Award Winners application is already connected to the Movies database. Notice that the interface contains a DataGridView control named TblMoviesDataGridView. The control is bound to the tblMovies table in the dataset. The application also contains four objects in its component tray. See Figure 14-4.

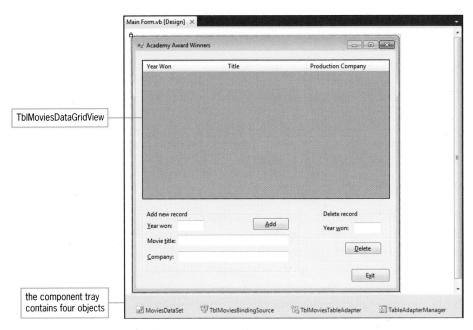

TblMoviesDataGridView

the component tray contains four objects

Figure 14-4   Interface for the Academy Award Winners application

2. Start the application. The records in the dataset appear in the TblMoviesDataGridView control. The control's AutoSizeColumnsMode, ReadOnly, and SelectionMode properties are set to Fill, True, and FullRowSelect, respectively. Its AllowUserToAddRows, AllowUserToDeleteRows, and RowHeadersVisible properties are set to False. Notice that the number 2000 appears in the txtDeleteYear control. This is because the control is bound to the YearWon field in the dataset. See Figure 14-5.

txtAddYear

txtTitle

txtCompany

txtDeleteYear

Figure 14-5   Records displayed in the TblMoviesDataGridView control

3. Press the **down arrow** key on your keyboard, slowly, several times. Each time the highlight moves to a different row in the DataGridView control, the value in the current row's YearWon field appears in the txtDeleteYear control.

4. Click the **Exit** button to end the application.

The first procedure you will code is the Add button's Click event procedure. The procedure should add the record entered in the txtAddYear, txtTitle, and txtCompany controls to the MoviesDataSet. Visual Basic provides several ways of adding records to a dataset. In this lesson, you will use the syntax shown in Figure 14-6. The figure also includes examples of using the syntax.

Adding a record to a dataset

Syntax
dataSetName.*tableName*.**Add***tableName***Row**(*valueField1*[,
                        valueField2..., *valueFieldN*]**)**

Example 1
```
BooksDataSet.tblBooks.AddtblBooksRow(txtTitle.Text,
txtAuthor.Text)
```
adds a record to the BooksDataSet

Example 2
```
CDDataSet.tblCds.AddtblCdsRow("02", "Colors", 12.99)
```
adds a record to the CDDataSet

Figure 14-6   Syntax and examples of adding a record to a dataset

To begin coding the Add button's Click event procedure: ◄ START HERE

1. Open the Code Editor window. Replace <your name> and <current date> in the comments with your name and the current date, respectively.

2. Locate the btnAdd control's Click event procedure. Click the **blank line** below the ' add a record to the dataset comment and then press **Enter**.

3. Recall that the YearWon field in the dataset is numeric. Therefore, you will need to convert the year entered in the txtAddYear control to a number before storing it in the field. Enter the following two statements. Press **Enter** twice after typing the second statement.

   Dim intYear As Integer
   Integer.TryParse(txtAddYear.Text, intYear)

4. Now, you will use the syntax shown in Figure 14-6 to add the record to the MoviesDataSet. Enter the following statement:

   MoviesDataSet.tblMovies.AddtblMoviesRow(intYear,
   **   txtTitle.Text,**
   **   txtCompany.Text)**

5. Save the solution and then start the application. In the Add new record section of the interface, type **2009** in the Year won box, **The Hurt Locker** in the Movie title box, and **Summit Entertainment** in the Company box. Click the **Add** button. The new record appears in the DataGridView control, as shown in Figure 14-7.

802

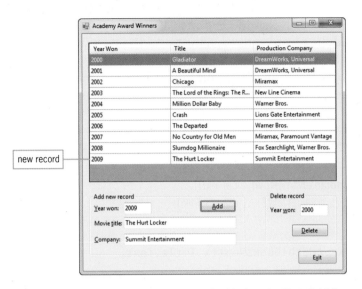

new record

Figure 14-7   New record added to the DataGridView control

6. Click the **Exit** button and then start the application again. Notice that the new record is missing from the DataGridView control. This is because the Add button's Click event procedure contains only the code for adding a record to a dataset. It does not yet contain the code for actually saving the record to the Movies database. You will add that code in the next set of steps. Click the **Exit** button.

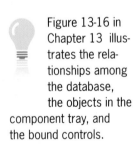

Figure 13-16 in Chapter 13 illustrates the relationships among the database, the objects in the component tray, and the bound controls.

For the changes made to a dataset to be permanent, you need to save the changes to the database associated with the dataset. Here too, Visual Basic provides several ways of performing this task. In this lesson, you will use the TableAdapter object's **Update method**. As you learned in Chapter 13, the TableAdapter object connects the database to the DataSet object. The Update method's syntax is shown in Figure 14-8 along with examples of using the syntax. Because it is possible for an error to occur when saving data to a database, it's a good programming practice to place the Update method within the Try block of a Try…Catch statement, as shown in the examples.

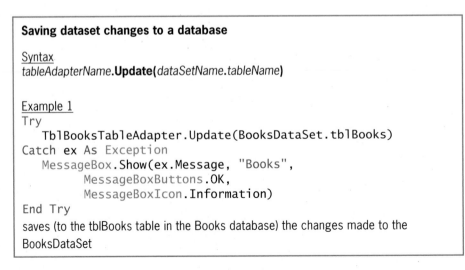

Saving dataset changes to a database

Syntax
tableAdapterName.**Update(***dataSetName.tableName***)**

Example 1
```
Try
    TblBooksTableAdapter.Update(BooksDataSet.tblBooks)
Catch ex As Exception
    MessageBox.Show(ex.Message, "Books",
        MessageBoxButtons.OK,
        MessageBoxIcon.Information)
End Try
```
saves (to the tblBooks table in the Books database) the changes made to the BooksDataSet

Figure 14-8   Syntax and examples of saving dataset changes to a database *(continues)*

(continued)

```
Example 2
Try
    TblCdsTableAdapter.Update(CDDataSet.tblCds)
Catch ex As Exception
    MessageBox.Show(ex.Message, "CDs",
            MessageBoxButtons.OK,
            MessageBoxIcon.Information)
End Try
saves (to the tblCds table in the CD database) the changes made to the CDDataSet
```

Figure 14-8 Syntax and examples of saving dataset changes to a database

To finish coding the Add button's Click event procedure:

◀ START HERE

1. Enter the additional lines of code indicated in Figure 14-9.

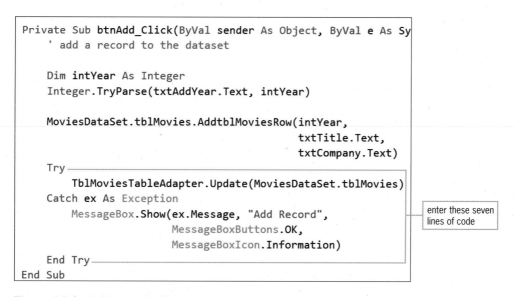

```
Private Sub btnAdd_Click(ByVal sender As Object, ByVal e As Sy
    ' add a record to the dataset

    Dim intYear As Integer
    Integer.TryParse(txtAddYear.Text, intYear)

    MoviesDataSet.tblMovies.AddtblMoviesRow(intYear,
                                    txtTitle.Text,
                                    txtCompany.Text)
    Try
        TblMoviesTableAdapter.Update(MoviesDataSet.tblMovies)
    Catch ex As Exception
        MessageBox.Show(ex.Message, "Add Record",
                    MessageBoxButtons.OK,
                    MessageBoxIcon.Information)
    End Try
End Sub
```

enter these seven lines of code

Figure 14-9 Add button's Click event procedure

2. Save the solution and then start the application. In the Add new record section of the interface, type **2009** in the Year won box, **The Hurt Locker** in the Movie title box, and **Summit Entertainment** in the Company box. Click the **Add** button. The new record appears in the DataGridView control, as shown earlier in Figure 14-7.

3. Now, enter the following record: **1999**, **American Beauty**, **DreamWorks**. Click the **Add** button. Notice that the record for the year 1999 appears as the last record in the DataGridView control. See Figure 14-10.

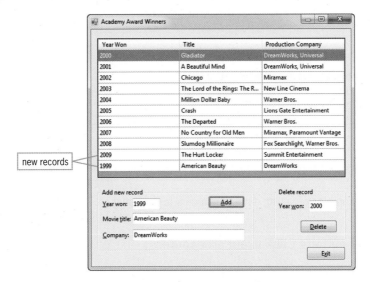

Figure 14-10   New records displayed in the DataGridView control

4. Click the **Year Won** header in the DataGridView control. The records now appear in numerical order by the YearWon field.

5. Click the **Exit** button and then start the application again. The two new records appear in the DataGridView control. However, the record for the year 1999 appears, once again, at the bottom of the list. This is because the records are displayed in the order they appear in the tblMovies table. The record for the year 1999 was the last record entered into the table, so it appears as the last record in the DataGridView control. You will fix this problem in the next section. Click the **Exit** button.

Sorting the Records in a Dataset

As you observed in the previous set of steps, you can sort the records in a DataGridView control by clicking the appropriate header while the application is running. You also can use the BindingSource object's **Sort method**. The method's syntax is shown in Figure 14-11 along with examples of using the syntax. If you want the records in a dataset to appear in a particular order when the application is started, you enter the Sort method in the form's Load event procedure.

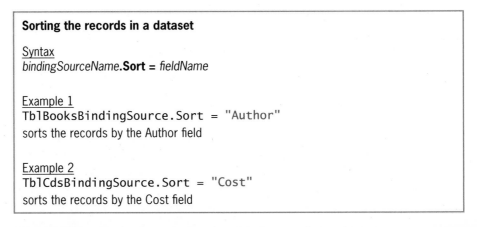

Sorting the records in a dataset

Syntax
bindingSourceName.**Sort** = *fieldName*

Example 1
`TblBooksBindingSource.Sort = "Author"`
sorts the records by the Author field

Example 2
`TblCdsBindingSource.Sort = "Cost"`
sorts the records by the Cost field

Figure 14-11   Syntax and examples of sorting the records in a dataset

To sort the records by the YearWon field:

1. Locate the form's Load event procedure in the Code Editor window. Click the **blank line** above the End Sub clause and then enter the following line of code:

   TblMoviesBindingSource.Sort = "YearWon"

2. Save the solution and then start the application. The records appear in numerical order by the YearWon field, as shown in Figure 14-12.

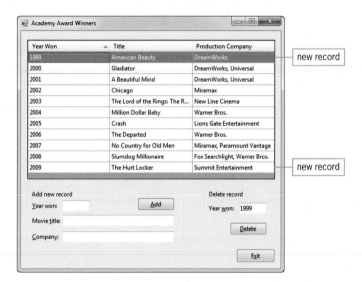

Figure 14-12   Records sorted by the YearWon field

3. Click the **Exit** button.

YOU DO IT 1!

Open the YouDoIt 1 (YouDoIt 1.sln) file contained in the VB2010\Chap14\ YouDoIt 1 folder. The application is connected to the Names database. The database contains one table named tblNames. The table contains five records. Each record contains two fields: FirstName and LastName. When the application starts, the records should be displayed in order by the LastName field. Add two text boxes and a button to the form. The button's Click event procedure should add the information entered in the text boxes to the dataset, and then save the record in the database. Don't add a record unless both text boxes contain data. Save the solution and then start and test the application. Close the Code Editor window and then close the solution.

Deleting Records from a Dataset

The last procedure you will code is the Delete button's Click event procedure. The procedure should search the dataset for the record whose YearWon field contains the value entered in the txtDeleteYear control. Before deleting the record, the procedure should display a message that asks the user to confirm the deletion. You will use the MessageBox.Show method to both display the message and get the user's response.

START HERE

To begin coding the Delete button's Click event procedure:

1. Locate the btnDelete control's Click event procedure. Click the **blank line** below the `' delete a record from the dataset` comment and then press **Enter**.

2. The procedure will use a DialogResult variable to store the value returned by the MessageBox.Show method. Enter the following statement:

   Dim dlgButton As DialogResult

3. Now, enter the MessageBox.Show method shown in Figure 14-13, and then position the insertion point as indicated in the figure. Notice that the message box will have Yes and No buttons.

```
Dim dlgButton As DialogResult
dlgButton =
    MessageBox.Show("Delete winner from year " &
                    txtDeleteYear.Text & "?", "Confirm Delete",
                    MessageBoxButtons.YesNo,
                    MessageBoxIcon.Exclamation)

End Sub
```

enter these five lines of code

position the insertion point here

Figure 14-13   MessageBox.Show method entered in the btnDelete control's Click event procedure

4. The procedure will delete the record only when the user selects the Yes button in the message box. Enter the following If clause:

   If dlgButton = DialogResult.Yes Then

5. Save the solution.

Before the Delete button's Click event procedure can delete the record from the dataset, it first must locate the record. Visual Basic provides several ways of locating records in a dataset. In this lesson, you will use the syntax shown in Figure 14-14. The figure also includes examples of using the syntax.

Locating a record in a dataset

Syntax
dataRowVariable =
        dataSetName.*tableName*.**FindBy***fieldName*(*value*)

Example 1
```
Dim row As DataRow
row = BooksDataSet.tblBooks.FindById(123)
```
The assignment statement searches the dataset for the record whose Id field contains 123, and then assigns the record to the `row` variable.

Figure 14-14   Syntax and examples of locating a record in a dataset *(continues)*

(continued)

> Example 2
> ```
> Dim findRow As DataRow
> findRow = CDDataSet.tblCds.FindByArtist("Cher")
> ```
> The assignment statement searches the dataset for the record whose Artist field contains "Cher", and then assigns the record to the **findRow** variable.

Figure 14-14 Syntax and examples of locating a record in a dataset

To continue coding the Delete button's Click event procedure: ◄ START HERE

1. First, enter the following declaration statement below the If clause:

   Dim row As DataRow

2. As mentioned earlier, the YearWon field in the dataset is numeric. Therefore, you will need to convert the year contained in the txtDeleteYear control to a number before searching for the record in the dataset. Enter the following statements:

   Dim intYear As Integer
   Integer.TryParse(txtDeleteYear.Text, intYear)

3. Now, you will use the syntax shown in Figure 14-14 to locate the appropriate record. Enter the following statement:

   row =
   MoviesDataSet.tblMovies.FindByYearWon(intYear)

4. Save the solution.

After locating the appropriate record and assigning it to a DataRow variable, you can use the variable's **Delete method** to delete the record. Figure 14-15 shows the syntax of the Delete method and includes an example of using the method.

Deleting a record from a dataset

Syntax
dataRowVariable.**Delete()**

Example
```
Dim row As DataRow
row = BooksDataSet.tblBooks.FindByTitle("Money")
row.Delete()
```
The Delete method deletes the record associated with the **row** variable.

Figure 14-15 Syntax and an example of deleting a record from a dataset

START HERE   **To finish coding the Delete button's Click event procedure:**

1. Enter the following statement:

   row.Delete()

2. As you learned earlier, the changes made to a dataset are not permanent until they are saved to the database associated with the dataset. Recall that you can save the changes using the TableAdapter object's Update method. Also recall that it's a good programming practice to enter the Update method within the Try block of a Try...Catch statement. Enter the additional code shown in Figure 14-16.

```
                         MessageBoxIcon.Exclamation)
If dlgButton = DialogResult.Yes Then
    Dim row As DataRow
    Dim intYear As Integer
    Integer.TryParse(txtDeleteYear.Text, intYear)
    row =
        MoviesDataSet.tblMovies.FindByYearWon(intYear)
    row.Delete()
    Try
        TblMoviesTableAdapter.Update(MoviesDataSet.tblMovies)
    Catch ex As Exception
        MessageBox.Show(ex.Message, "Delete Record",
                        MessageBoxButtons.OK,
                        MessageBoxIcon.Information)
    End Try
End If
```

enter these seven lines of code

Figure 14-16   Additional code entered in the btnDelete control's Click event procedure

3. Save the solution and then start the application. The first record is highlighted in the DataGridView control, and the value of the record's YearWon field—in this case, 1999—appears in the txtDeleteYear control.

4. Click the **Delete** button. The message box shown in Figure 14-17 appears on the screen.

Figure 14-17   Message box displayed by the btnDelete control's Click event procedure

5. Click the **Yes** button in the message box. The computer deletes the record from the dataset, the DataGridView control, and the database.

6. Next, click **2005** in the Year Won column. The record for the year 2005 is highlighted in the DataGridView control, and 2005 appears in the txtDeleteYear control. Click the **Delete** button, and then click the

No button in the message box. The record remains in the dataset, the DataGridView control, and the database.

7. Click the **Exit** button and then start the application again. Notice that the 2005 record remains in the dataset, but the 1999 record was deleted.

8. Click the **Exit** button to end the application. Close the Code Editor window and then close the solution.

Figure 14-18 shows the form's Load event procedure, the btnAdd control's Click event procedure, and the btnDelete control's Click event procedure. Keep in mind that the Click event procedures will produce a run time error if the user tries to either add a duplicate record or delete a non-existent record. To learn how to handle the run time error, complete Exercise 5 at the end of this lesson.

```
Private Sub frmMain_Load(ByVal sender As System.Object,
ByVal e As System.EventArgs) Handles MyBase.Load
    'TODO: This line of code loads data into the
    'MoviesDataSet.tblMovies' table. You can move,
    or remove it, as needed.
    Me.TblMoviesTableAdapter.Fill(Me.MoviesDataSet.tblMovies)
    TblMoviesBindingSource.Sort = "YearWon"

End Sub

Private Sub btnAdd_Click(ByVal sender As Object,
ByVal e As System.EventArgs) Handles btnAdd.Click
    ' add a record to the dataset

    Dim intYear As Integer
    Integer.TryParse(txtAddYear.Text, intYear)

    MoviesDataSet.tblMovies.AddtblMoviesRow(intYear,
                                            txtTitle.Text,
                                            txtCompany.Text)
    Try
        TblMoviesTableAdapter.Update(MoviesDataSet.tblMovies)
    Catch ex As Exception
        MessageBox.Show(ex.Message, "Add Record",
                    MessageBoxButtons.OK,
                    MessageBoxIcon.Information)
    End Try
End Sub

Private Sub btnDelete_Click(ByVal sender As Object,
ByVal e As System.EventArgs) Handles btnDelete.Click
    ' delete a record from the dataset

    Dim dlgButton As DialogResult
    dlgButton =
        MessageBox.Show("Delete winner from year " &
                txtDeleteYear.Text & "?", "Confirm Delete",
                MessageBoxButtons.YesNo,
                MessageBoxIcon.Exclamation)
```

Figure 14-18 frmMain_Load, btnAdd_Click, and btnDelete_Click procedures *(continues)*

(continued)

```
     If dlgButton = DialogResult.Yes Then
         Dim row As DataRow
         Dim intYear As Integer
         Integer.TryParse(txtDeleteYear.Text, intYear)
         row =
             MoviesDataSet.tblMovies.FindByYearWon(intYear)
         row.Delete()
         Try
             TblMoviesTableAdapter.Update(MoviesDataSet.tblMovies)
         Catch ex As Exception
             MessageBox.Show(ex.Message, "Delete Record",
                             MessageBoxButtons.OK,
                             MessageBoxIcon.Information)

         End Try
     End If
 End Sub
```

Figure 14-18   frmMain_Load, btnAdd_Click, and btnDelete_Click procedures

Lesson A Summary

- To add a record to a dataset:

  Use the syntax shown in Figure 14-6.

- To save dataset changes to a database:

  Use the TableAdapter object's Update method. The method's syntax is shown in Figure 14-8.

- To sort the records in a dataset:

  Use the BindingSource object's Sort method. The method's syntax is shown in Figure 14-11.

- To locate a record in a dataset:

  Use the syntax shown in Figure 14-14.

- To delete a record from a dataset:

  Use a DataRow variable's Delete method. The syntax is shown in Figure 14-15.

Lesson A Key Terms

Delete method—a method of a DataRow variable; used to delete a record from a dataset

Sort method—a method of the BindingSource object; used to sort a dataset in order by a specific field

Update method—a method of the TableAdapter object; used to save a dataset's changes to its associated database

Lesson A Review Questions

1. The FriendsDataSet contains a table named tblFriends. The table contains two text fields named FName and LName. Which of the following will add a new record to the dataset?

   a. `FriendsDataSet.tblFriends.AddFriendsRow`
      `(strF, strL)`

   b. `FriendsDataSet.tblFriends.AddRowToFriends`
      `(strF, strL)`

   c. `FriendsDataSet.tblFriends.AddtblFriendsRow`
      `(strF, strL)`

   d. `FriendsDataSet.AddtblFriendsRow(strF, strL)`

2. Two records were added to the FriendsDataSet from Review Question 1. Which of the following will save the records in the Friends database?

   a. `TblFriendsBindingSource.Save(FriendsDataSet.`
      `tblFriends)`

   b. `TblFriendsBindingSource.Update(FriendsDataSet.`
      `tblFriends`

   c. `TblFriendsTableAdapter.Save(FriendsDataSet.`
      `tblFriends)`

   d. `TblFriendsTableAdapter.Update(FriendsDataSet.`
      `tblFriends)`

3. The FriendsDataSet from Review Question 1 is associated with the TblFriendsBindingSource and TblFriendsTableAdapter objects. Which of the following will sort the records by the LName field?

   a. `TblFriendsBindingSource.Sort = "LName"`

   b. `TblFriendsBindingSource.Sort("LName")`

   c. `TblFriendsTableAdapter.Sort = "LName"`

   d. none of the above

4. Using the FriendsDataSet from Review Question 1, which of the following will locate the record whose last name is Winkler, and then assign the record to the row variable?

   a. `row =`
      `    FriendsDataSet.tblFriends.FindLName("Winkler")`

   b. `row =`
      `    FriendsDataSet.tblFriends.FindByLName("Winkler")`

   c. `row =`
      `    FriendsDataSet.tblFriends.Find("Winkler")`

   d. `row =`
      `    FriendsDataSet.FindByLName("Winkler")`

5. Which of the following will delete the record associated with a DataRow variable named findRow?

   a. `findRow.Delete()`

   b. `findRow.Remove()`

   c. `delete(findRow)`

   d. none of the above

Lesson A Exercises

INTRODUCTORY

1. Open the HR Sales Solution (HR Sales Solution.sln) file contained in the VB2010\Chap14\HR Sales Solution folder. If necessary, open the designer window. The application is connected to the Sales database. The database contains one table, which is named tblSales. The table contains three fields and five records. The three fields (YearNum, MonthNum, and Sales) are numeric. The Add button's Click event procedure should allow the user to add records to the database, but only when the three text boxes contain data. The records should appear in numerical order by the year number. Code the application. Save the solution and then start and test the application. Close the Code Editor window and then close the solution.

INTRODUCTORY

2. Open the Sydney Solution (Sydney Solution.sln) file contained in the VB2010\Chap14\Sydney Solution folder. If necessary, open the designer window. The application is connected to the Products database. The database contains a table named tblProducts. The table contains 10 records, each composed of three fields. The ItemNum (primary key) and ItemName fields contain text; the Price field contains numbers. The Add button's Click event procedure should allow the user to add records to the database, but only when the three text boxes contain data. The Delete button's Click event procedure should allow the user to delete records from the database. The records should appear in order by the item number when the application is started. Code the application. Save the solution and then start and test the application. (Don't try to add a record that has a duplicate item number.) Close the Code Editor window and then close the solution.

INTERMEDIATE

3. Open the Morgan Industries Solution (Morgan Industries Solution.sln) file contained in the Morgan Industries Solution folder. The application is connected to the Employees database. The database contains one table, which is named tblEmploy. The table contains seven fields and 14 records. The Emp_Number field is the primary key. The Status field contains the employment status, which is either the letter F (for full-time) or the letter P (for part-time). The Code field identifies the employee's department: 1 for Accounting, 2 for Advertising, 3 for Personnel, and 4 for Inventory. The Add button's Click event procedure should allow the user to add records to the database, but only when the user provides all of the employee information. The Delete button's Click event procedure should allow the user to delete records from the

database. The records should appear in order by the employee number when the application is started. Code the application. Be sure to code each text box's Enter event procedure, as well as the KeyPress event procedures for the Rate, Status, and Code text boxes. Save the solution and then start and test the application. (Don't try to add a record that has a duplicate employee number.) Close the Code Editor window and then close the solution.

4. In this exercise, you modify the HR Sales application from Exercise 1. Use Windows to make a copy of the HR Sales Solution folder. Rename the copy HR Sales Solution-LINQ. Open the HR Sales Solution (HR Sales Solution.sln) file contained in the HR Sales Solution-LINQ folder. Open the designer window. Add a button to the form. Change the button's name to btnTotal. Change its Text property to &Total Sales. The button's Click event procedure should display the total sales amount in a message box. (Hint: Use one of the aggregate operators available in LINQ.) Save the solution and then start and test the application. Close the Code Editor window and then close the solution.   `INTERMEDIATE`

5. In this exercise, you modify the Academy Award Winners application from this lesson. Use Windows to make a copy of the Academy Award Solution folder. Rename the copy Modified Academy Award Solution. Open the Academy Award Solution (Academy Award Solution.sln) file contained in the Modified Academy Award Solution folder. Open the designer and Code Editor windows.   `ADVANCED`

   a. If the user attempts to add a record that has the same year number as an existing record, a run time error will occur when the computer processes the AddtblMoviesRow function in the btnAdd control's Click event procedure. Place the statement containing the function in the Try block of a Try...Catch statement. The Catch block should display a message alerting the user that the record for that year already exists.

   b. If the user attempts to delete a record that does not exist, a run time error will occur when the computer processes the `row.Delete()` statement. Before processing the statement, you will have the computer determine whether the `row` variable contains a data row. Insert a blank line above the `row.Delete()` statement. Type `If row Is Nothing Then`, press Enter twice, type `Else`, and then press Enter. In the selection structure's true path, enter a MessageBox.Show method that displays the "No record found." message. Move the remaining code into the selection structure's false path.

   c. Save the solution and then start the application. Test the application by attempting to add a duplicate record. Also test it by entering the number 0 in the txtDeleteYear control and then clicking the Delete button followed by the Yes button. Close the Code Editor window and then close the solution.

Discovery

6. In this exercise, you modify the HR Sales application from Exercise 1. Use Windows to make a copy of the HR Sales Solution folder. Rename the copy HR Sales Solution-Discovery. Open the HR Sales Solution (HR Sales Solution.sln) file contained in the HR Sales Solution-Discovery folder. Open the designer and Code Editor windows. Currently, the form's Load event procedure sorts the records in numerical order by the year number. Modify the procedure so that it sorts the records in numerical order by month number within year number. Save the solution and then start and test the application. Close the Code Editor window and then close the solution.

LESSON B

After studying Lesson B, you should be able to:

- Query a database using the SQL SELECT statement
- Create queries using the Query Builder dialog box

Structured Query Language

As you learned in Chapter 13, you use a query to specify both the records to select from a database and the order in which to arrange the records. In Chapter 13, you created the queries using LINQ (Language Integrated Query). In this chapter, you will use a different query language, called SQL. You can pronounce SQL either as *ess-cue-el* or as *sequel*. **SQL**, which stands for **Structured Query Language**, is a set of statements that allows you to access and manipulate the data stored in many database management systems on computers of all sizes, from large mainframes to small microcomputers. You can use SQL statements—such as SELECT, INSERT, and DELETE—to perform common database tasks. Examples of these tasks include storing, retrieving, updating, deleting, and sorting data.

In this lesson, you will use the SQL SELECT statement to query the Movies database from Lesson A. The database keeps track of the movies that won an Academy Award for Best Picture of the Year. The database, which is stored in the Movies.accdb file, contains one table named tblMovies. As shown in Figure 14-19, the table contains nine records, with each record having three fields. The YearWon field is numeric; the Title and ProductionCo fields contain text.

YearWon	Title	ProductionCo
2000	Gladiator	DreamWorks, Universal
2001	A Beautiful Mind	DreamWorks, Universal
2002	Chicago	Miramax
2003	The Lord of the Rings: The Return of the King	New Line Cinema
2004	Million Dollar Baby	Warner Bros.
2005	Crash	Lions Gate Entertainment
2006	The Departed	Warner Bros.
2007	No Country for Old Men	Miramax, Paramount Vantage
2008	Slumdog Millionaire	Fox Searchlight, Warner Bros.

Record: 1 of 9   No Filter   Search

Figure 14-19   tblMovies table in the Movies database

The SELECT Statement

The **SELECT statement** is the most commonly used statement in SQL. The statement allows you to specify the fields and records you want to view, as well as control the order in which the fields and records appear when they are displayed. Figure 14-20 shows the statement's basic syntax. In the syntax, *fieldList* is one or more field names separated by commas, and *tableName* is the name of the table containing the fields. The WHERE and ORDER BY clauses are optional parts of the syntax. You use the **WHERE clause**, which contains a *condition*, to limit the records you want to view. Similar to the condition in the If...Then...Else and Do...Loop statements, the condition in a WHERE clause specifies a requirement that must be met for a record to be selected. The **ORDER BY clause** is used to arrange the records in either ascending (the default) or descending order by one or more fields. Although you do not have to capitalize the keywords SELECT, FROM, WHERE, ORDER BY, and DESC in a SELECT statement, many programmers do so for clarity.

Also included in Figure 14-20 are examples of using the SELECT statement. The SELECT statement in Example 1 tells the computer to select all of the fields and records from the tblMovies table. The SELECT statement in Example 2 uses the WHERE clause to limit the records that will be selected. In this case, the statement tells the computer to select all of the fields, but only from records for the year 2006 and later. The SELECT statement in Example 3 tells the computer to select the YearWon field, but only from the Chicago record. At this point, you may be wondering why the word "Chicago" in Example 3 appears in single quotes, but the number 2006 in Example 2 does not. The single quotes around the value in the WHERE clause's condition are necessary only when you are comparing a text field with a literal constant. Recall that the Title field contains text, whereas the YearWon field contains numbers. Text comparisons in SQL are not case-sensitive. Therefore, you also can write the WHERE clause in Example 3 as WHERE Title = 'chicago'.

The SELECT statement in Example 4 in Figure 14-20 selects all of the fields and records from the tblMovies table and then sorts the records in ascending order by the Title field. The SELECT statement in Example 5 shows how you can use the **LIKE operator** along with the **%** (percent sign) wildcard character in the WHERE clause. The statement tells the computer to select the Title and ProductionCo fields from records whose title begins with the word "The" followed by a space and zero or more characters. The statement then sorts the records in descending order by the ProductionCo field.

SELECT statement

Basic syntax
SELECT *fieldList* **FROM** *tableName*
      [**WHERE** *condition*]
      [**ORDER BY** *fieldName* [**DESC**]]

Example 1
```
SELECT YearWon, Title, ProductionCo FROM tblMovies
```
selects all of the fields and records in the tblMovies table

Example 2
```
SELECT YearWon, Title, ProductionCo FROM tblMovies
      WHERE YearWon >= 2006
```
selects all of the fields from records for the year 2006 and later

Example 3
```
SELECT YearWon FROM tblMovies WHERE Title = 'Chicago'
```
selects the YearWon field from the Chicago record

Figure 14-20   Syntax and examples of the SELECT statement *(continues)*

(continued)

Example 4

```
SELECT YearWon, Title, ProductionCo FROM tblMovies
     ORDER BY Title
```

selects all of the fields and records in the tblMovies table and then sorts the records in ascending order by the Title field

Example 5

```
SELECT Title, ProductionCo FROM tblMovies
     WHERE Title LIKE 'The %'
     ORDER BY ProductionCo DESC
```

selects the Title and ProductionCo fields from records whose title begins with the word "The" followed by a space and zero or more characters, and then sorts the records in descending order by the ProductionCo field

Figure 14-20   Syntax and examples of the SELECT statement

Creating a Query

In the following set of steps, you will open the Academy Award Winners application and then use it to test the SELECT statements from Figure 14-20.

To test the SELECT statements from Figure 14-20:

START HERE

1. If necessary, start Visual Studio 2010 or Visual Basic 2010 Express. Open the Movie Awards Solution (Movie Awards Solution.sln) file contained in the VB2010\Chap14\Movie Awards Solution-SQL folder. If necessary, open the designer window. The application is already connected to the Movies database.

2. Start the application. The dataset appears in the DataGridView control. See Figure 14-21.

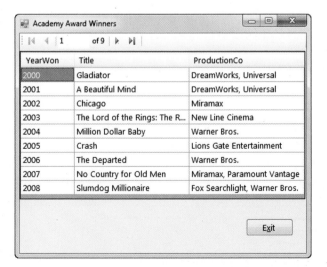

Figure 14-21   Contents of the dataset displayed in the DataGridView control

3. Click the **Exit** button to end the application. Right-click **MoviesDataSet.xsd** in the Solution Explorer window. The .xsd file is called the dataset's schema file. The file contains information about the tables, fields, records, and properties included in the MoviesDataSet. Click **Open** to open the DataSet Designer window. See Figure 14-22.

Figure 14-22   DataSet Designer window

4. Right-click **tblMoviesTableAdapter** in the DataSet Designer window. Point to **Add** on the shortcut menu and then click **Query**. (If Add does not appear on the shortcut menu, click Add Query instead.) Doing this starts the TableAdapter Query Configuration Wizard. The Use SQL statements radio button should be selected, as shown in Figure 14-23.

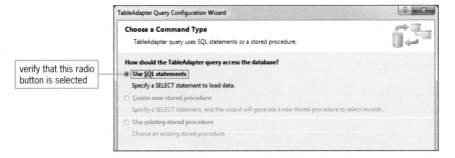

Figure 14-23   Choose a Command Type screen in the TableAdapter Query Configuration Wizard

5. Click the **Next** button to display the Choose a Query Type screen. The "SELECT which returns rows" radio button should be selected, as shown in Figure 14-24.

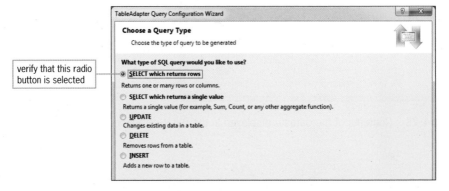

Figure 14-24   Choose a Query Type screen

6. Click the **Next** button to display the Specify a SQL SELECT statement screen. See Figure 14-25.

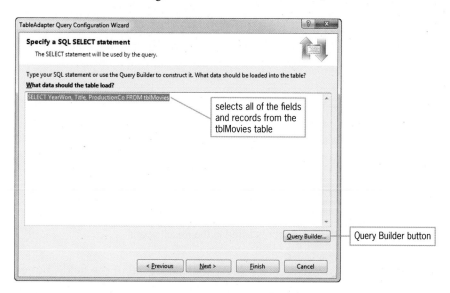

Figure 14-25 Specify a SQL SELECT statement screen

7. You can either type the SELECT statement yourself or use the Query Builder dialog box to construct the statement for you. In this case, you will use the Query Builder dialog box. Click the **Query Builder** button to open the Query Builder dialog box. See Figure 14-26. Notice that the table's primary key appears boldfaced in the Diagram pane.

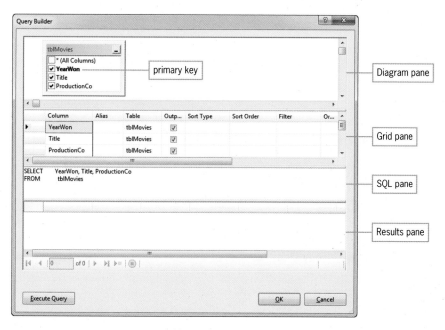

Figure 14-26 Query Builder dialog box

8. The SQL pane contains the same SELECT statement shown in Example 1 in Figure 14-20. Recall that the statement tells the computer to select all of the fields and records contained in the tblMovies table. Click the **Execute Query** button to run the query. The query results appear in the Results pane. See Figure 14-27. You can use the scroll bar to view the remaining records.

Figure 14-27   Records listed in the Results pane

9. Next, you will create a query that selects all of the fields, but only from records for the year 2006 and later. In the Grid pane, click the **blank cell** in the YearWon field's Filter column. Type **>= 2006** and press **Enter**. The Filter column entry tells the Query Builder to include the WHERE (YearWon >= 2006) clause in the SELECT statement. The funnel symbol that appears in the Diagram pane indicates that the YearWon field is used to filter the records. Notice the Query Changed message and icon that appear in the Results pane. The message and icon alert you that the information displayed in the Results pane is not from the current query. See Figure 14-28.

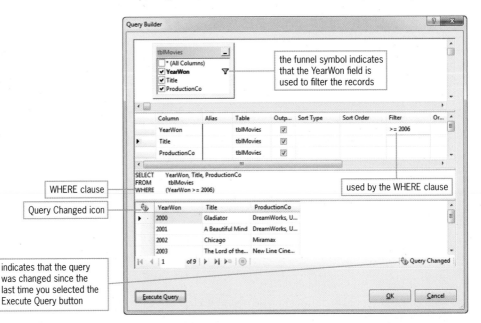

Figure 14-28   SELECT statement containing a WHERE clause

Important note: For clarity, the Query Builder places the WHERE clause's condition in parentheses; however, the parentheses are not required.

10. Click the **Execute Query** button to run the current query. If necessary, scroll the Results pane to verify that it contains only the records for the years 2006, 2007, and 2008.

11. Next, you will create a query that selects only the YearWon field for the Chicago record. Select (highlight) the **>= 2006** entry in the YearWon field's Filter column and then press **Delete**. Click the **blank cell** in the Title field's Filter column. Type **Chicago** and press **Enter**. The Query Builder changes the entry in the Filter column to = 'Chicago'. It also enters the WHERE (Title = 'Chicago') clause in the SELECT statement.

12. Now, click the **Title** and **ProductionCo** check boxes in the Diagram pane to remove the check marks. The Query Builder changes the first line in the SELECT statement to SELECT YearWon. Click the **Execute Query** button. See Figure 14-29.

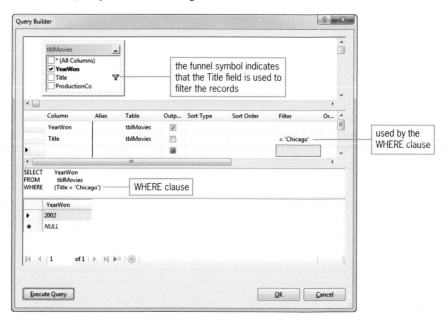

Figure 14-29 Result of executing the current query

13. Next, you will create a query that selects all of the fields and records in the tblMovies table and then sorts them in ascending order by the Title field. Select the **Title** and **ProductionCo** check boxes in the Diagram pane. The Query Builder changes the first line in the SELECT statement to SELECT YearWon, Title, ProductionCo. Delete the = 'Chicago' entry from the Filter column in the Grid pane and then press **Enter**. The Query Builder removes the WHERE clause from the SELECT statement.

14. Now, click the **blank cell** in the Title field's Sort Type column and then click the **list arrow** in the cell. Click **Ascending** and then press **Enter**. The word "Ascending" appears as the Title field's Sort Type, and the number 1 appears as its Sort Order. The number 1 indicates that the Title field is the primary field in the sort. As a result, the Query Builder adds the ORDER BY Title clause to the SELECT statement. Click the **Execute Query** button. See Figure 14-30.

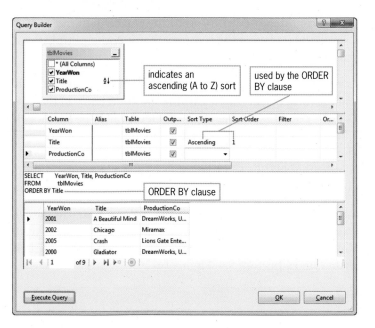

Figure 14-30   Records displayed in ascending order by the Title field

15. On your own, create a query that selects the Title and ProductionCo fields from records whose title begins with the word "The" followed by a space and zero or more characters. The query should sort the records in descending order by the ProductionCo field. Figure 14-31 shows the query along with the result of executing it.

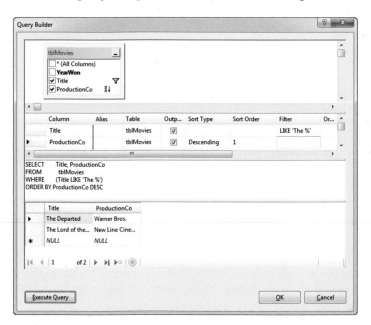

Figure 14-31   Records displayed by the current query

16. Click the **Cancel** button in the Query Builder dialog box and then click the **Cancel** button in the TableAdapter Query Configuration Wizard dialog box.

17. Save the solution. Close the MoviesDataSet.xsd window and then close the solution.

Lesson B Summary

- To query a database using SQL:

  Use the SELECT statement. The statement's syntax is shown in
  Figure 14-20.

- To limit the records you want to view:

  Use the SELECT statement's WHERE clause.

- To sort the selected records:

  Use the SELECT statement's ORDER BY clause.

- To open the DataSet Designer window:

  Right-click the name of the dataset's schema file in the Solution Explorer
  window and then click Open. The schema filename ends with .xsd.

- To start the TableAdapter Query Configuration Wizard:

  Open the DataSet Designer window and then right-click the table
  adapter's name. Point to Add on the shortcut menu and then click Query.
  If Add does not appear on the shortcut menu, click Add Query instead.

- To open the Query Builder dialog box:

  Start the TableAdapter Query Configuration Wizard. Click the Next
  button and then click the Next button again to display the Specify a SQL
  SELECT statement screen. Click the Query Builder button.

- To represent zero or more characters in the WHERE clause's condition:

  Use the % wildcard.

Lesson B Key Terms

%—a wildcard character used in the condition in a SELECT statement's
WHERE clause; represents zero or more characters

LIKE operator—an operator used along with a wildcard character in the condition in a SELECT statement's WHERE clause

ORDER BY clause—used in a SELECT statement to sort the selected records

SELECT statement—the SQL statement that allows you to specify the fields
and records to select, as well as the order in which the fields and records
appear when displayed

SQL—an acronym for Structured Query Language

Structured Query Language—SQL; a set of statements that allows you to
access and manipulate the data stored in a database

WHERE clause—used in a SELECT statement to limit the records to be
selected

Lesson B Review Questions

1. SQL stands for _____.

   a. Select Query Language

   b. Semi-Quick Language

   c. Structured Quick Language

   d. Structured Query Language

2. Which of the following SELECT statements will select the First and Last fields from the tblNames table?

   a. `SELECT First AND Last FROM tblNames`

   b. `SELECT First OR Last FROM tblNames`

   c. `SELECT First, Last FROM tblNames`

   d. `SELECT ONLY First, Last FROM tblNames`

3. Which of the following SELECT statements will select the SSN field from the tblPayInfo table, and then sort the records in descending order by the SSN field?

   a. `SELECT SSN FROM tblPayInfo DESC`

   b. `SELECT SSN FROM tblPayInfo`
      `ORDER BY SSN DESC`

   c. `SELECT SSN FROM tblPayInfo`
      `WHERE SSN DESC`

   d. `SELECT SSN FROM tblPayInfo`
      `SORT SSN DESC`

4. Which of the following SELECT statements will select only records whose Status field contains the letter A? The Status field is contained in the tblWorker table.

   a. `SELECT Id, Name, Status FROM tblWorker`
      `WHERE Status = 'A'`

   b. `SELECT Id, Name, Status FROM tblWorker`
      `ORDER BY Status = 'A'`

   c. `SELECT Id, Name, Status FROM tblWorker`
      `FOR Status = 'A'`

   d. `SELECT Id, Name, Status FROM tblWorker`
      `SELECT Status = 'A'`

5. The tblState table contains a text field named State. Which of the following SELECT statements will select the State and Capital fields from only the Kansas and Kentucky records?

    a. `SELECT State, Capital FROM tblState`
       `WHERE State LIKE 'K'`

    b. `SELECT State, Capital FROM tblState`
       `WHERE State LIKE 'K*'`

    c. `SELECT State, Capital FROM tblState`
       `WHERE State LIKE 'K%'`

    d. `SELECT State, Capital FROM tblState`
       `WHERE State LIKE 'K#'`

6. The tblState table contains a numeric field named Population. Which of the following SELECT statements will select the State and Capital fields from only states with populations that exceed 5,000,000?

    a. `SELECT State, Capital FROM tblState`
       `WHERE Population > 5000000`

    b. `SELECT State, Capital FROM tblState`
       `WHERE Population > '5000000'`

    c. `SELECT State, Capital FROM tblState`
       `WHERE Population > "5000000"`

    d. `SELECT State, Capital FROM tblState`
       `SELECT Population > 5000000`

7. In a SELECT statement, which clause is used to limit the records that will be selected?

    a. LIMIT

    b. ORDER BY

    c. ONLY

    d. WHERE

8. If a funnel symbol appears next to a field's name in the Query Builder dialog box, it indicates that the field is _____.

    a. used in an ORDER BY clause in a SELECT statement

    b. used in a WHERE clause in a SELECT statement

    c. the primary key

    d. the foreign key

9. The SQL SELECT statement performs case sensitive comparisons.

    a. True

    b. False

Lesson B Exercises

INTRODUCTORY

1. The tblMagazine table contains three fields. The Cost field is numeric. The Code and MagName fields contain text.

    a. Write a SQL SELECT statement that arranges the records in descending order by the Cost field.

    b. Write a SQL SELECT statement that selects only the MagName and Cost fields from records having a code of PG10.

    c. Write a SQL SELECT statement that selects only the MagName and Cost fields from records having a cost of $3 or more.

    d. Write a SQL SELECT statement that selects the Visual Basic record.

    e. Write a SQL SELECT statement that selects only the MagName field from records whose magazine names begin with the letter C.

    f. Open the Magazine Solution (Magazine Solution.sln) file contained in the VB2010\Chap14\Magazine Solution folder. If necessary, open the designer window. The application is connected to the Magazines database, which is stored in the Magazines.accdb file. Start the application to view the records contained in the dataset, and then stop the application. Open the DataSet Designer window and then start the TableAdapter Query Configuration Wizard. Open the Query Builder dialog box. Use the dialog box to test your SELECT statements from Steps a through e.

    g. Close the Query Builder dialog box and the TableAdapter Query Configuration Wizard dialog box. Save the solution. Close the MagazinesDataSet.xsd window and then close the solution.

INTRODUCTORY

2. The tblEmploy table contains seven fields. The Emp_Number, Rate, and Code fields are numeric. The Last_Name, First_Name, Hired, and Status fields contain text. The Status field contains either the letter F (for full-time) or the letter P (for part-time). The Code field identifies the employee's department: 1 for Accounting, 2 for Advertising, 3 for Personnel, and 4 for Inventory.

    a. Write a SQL SELECT statement that selects all of the fields and records in the table, and then sorts the records in ascending order by the Code field.

    b. Write a SQL SELECT statement that selects only the Emp_Number, Last_Name, and First_Name fields from all of the records.

    c. Write a SQL SELECT statement that selects only the records for full-time employees.

    d. Write a SQL SELECT statement that selects the Emp_Number and Rate fields for employees in the Personnel department.

    e. Write a SQL SELECT statement that selects the Emp_Number and Last_Name fields for employees having a last name of Smith.

f.　Write a SQL SELECT statement that selects the Emp_Number and Last_Name fields for employees having a last name that begins with the letter S.

g.　Write a SQL SELECT statement that selects only the first and last names for part-time employees, and then sorts the records in descending order by the Last_Name field.

h.　Open the Morgan Industries Solution (Morgan Industries Solution.sln) file contained in the Morgan Industries Solution-SQL folder. If necessary, open the designer window. The application is connected to the Employees database from Chapter 13. The database is contained in the Employees.accdb file. Start the application to view the records contained in the dataset, and then stop the application. Open the DataSet Designer window and then start the TableAdapter Query Configuration Wizard. Open the Query Builder dialog box. Which field in the table is the primary key? How can you tell that it is the primary key?

i.　Use the Query Builder dialog box to test your SELECT statements from Steps a through g.

j.　Close the Query Builder dialog box and the TableAdapter Query Configuration Wizard dialog box. Save the solution. Close the EmployeesDataSet.xsd window and then close the solution.

LESSON C

After studying Lesson C, you should be able to:

- Create a parameter query
- Save a query
- Invoke a query from code
- Add records to a dataset using the SQL INSERT statement
- Delete records from a dataset using the SQL DELETE statement

Parameter Queries

In Lesson B, you learned how to create queries that search for records meeting a specific criteria, such as `Title = 'Chicago'` and `YearWon >= 2006`. Most times, however, you will not know ahead of time the values to include in the criteria. For example, the next time the user runs the query, he or she may want to view the Gladiator record (`Title = 'Gladiator'`) rather than the Chicago record. Or, the user may want to view the movies that won the Academy Award in the year 2007 and later (`YearWon >= 2007`). When you don't know the specific value to include in the criteria, you use a parameter query. A **parameter query** is a query that uses the parameter marker in place of the criteria's value. The **parameter marker** is a question mark (**?**). Figure 14-32 shows examples of parameter queries using the tblMovies table from Lessons A and B.

Parameter queries

Example 1
```
SELECT YearWon, Title, ProductionCo FROM tblMovies
     WHERE Title = ?
```
selects all of the fields from the record whose title is represented by the parameter marker

Example 2
```
SELECT YearWon, Title, ProductionCo FROM tblMovies
     WHERE YearWon >= ?
```
selects all of the fields from records whose YearWon field contains a value that is greater than or equal to the value represented by the parameter marker

---

Figure 14-32   Examples of parameter queries

In the following set of steps, you will open the Academy Award Winners application and then use it to test the SELECT statements from Figure 14-32.

To test the SELECT statements from Figure 14-32:

START HERE

1. If necessary, start Visual Studio 2010 or Visual Basic 2010 Express. Open the Movie Awards Solution (Movie Awards Solution.sln) file contained in the VB2010\Chap14\Movie Awards Solution-Parameter Queries folder. If necessary, open the designer window. The application is already connected to the Movies database.

2. Start the application. The dataset appears in the DataGridView control. See Figure 14-33.

Figure 14-33   Records displayed in the DataGridView control

3. Click the **Exit** button to end the application. Right-click **MoviesDataSet.xsd** in the Solution Explorer window and then click **Open** to open the DataSet Designer window.

4. Right-click **tblMoviesTableAdapter** in the DataSet Designer window. Point to **Add** on the shortcut menu and then click **Query** to start the TableAdapter Query Configuration Wizard. (If Add does not appear on the shortcut menu, click Add Query instead.) Verify that the Use SQL statements radio button is selected. Click the **Next** button to display the Choose a Query Type screen. Verify that the "SELECT which returns rows" radio button is selected. Click the **Next** button to display the Specify a SQL SELECT statement screen. Click the **Query Builder** button to open the Query Builder dialog box.

5. First, you will create a query that selects only the Chicago record. In the Grid pane, click the **blank cell** in the Title field's Filter column. Type **?** and press **Enter**. The Filter column entry tells the Query Builder to include the WHERE (Title = ?) clause in the SELECT statement.

6. Click the **Execute Query** button to run the query. The Query Parameters dialog box opens. Type **Chicago** in the Value column. See Figure 14-34.

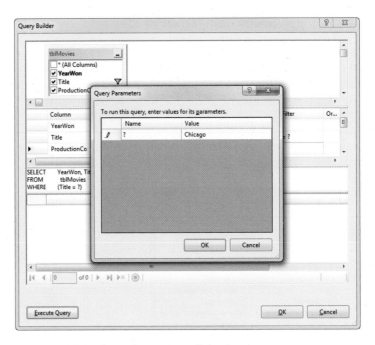

Figure 14-34   Query Parameters dialog box

7. Click the **OK** button to close the Query Parameters dialog box. The Chicago record appears in the Results pane.

8. Now, you will run the query again. This time, however, you will select the Gladiator record. Click the **Execute Query** button to run the query. Type **Gladiator** in the Value column of the Query Parameters dialog box and then click the **OK** button. The Gladiator record appears in the Results pane.

9. Next, you will create a query that selects all of the fields, but only from records for the year 2006 and later. Delete the = ? from the Title field's Filter column. Now, type >= **?** in the YearWon field's Filter column and then press **Enter**. Click the **Execute Query** button to run the query. Type **2006** in the Value column of the Query Parameters dialog box and then click the **OK** button. Three records appear in the Results pane.

10. Now, you will run the query again. This time, however, you will select records for the year 2007 and later. Click the **Execute Query** button to run the query. Type **2007** in the Value column of the Query Parameters dialog box and then click the **OK** button. Two records appear in the Results pane.

11. Click the **Cancel** button in the Query Builder dialog box and then click the **Cancel** button in the TableAdapter Query Configuration Wizard dialog box.

12. Save the solution. Close the MoviesDataSet.xsd window and then close the solution.

Saving a Query

In order for an application to use a query during run time, you will need to save the query and then invoke it from code. You save a query that contains the SELECT statement by associating the query with one or more methods. The TableAdapter Query Configuration Wizard provides an easy way of performing this task.

To use the TableAdapter Query Configuration Wizard to save a query: START HERE

1. Open the Academy Award Solution (Academy Award Solution.sln) file contained in the VB2010\Chap14\Academy Award Solution-Parameter Query folder. If necessary, open the designer window. The application is connected to the Movies database. The application allows the user to display either all of the records or only the record for the year entered in the txtYear control.

2. Save the solution and then start the application. The dataset appears in the DataGridView control. See Figure 14-35.

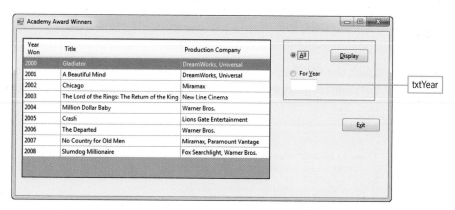

Figure 14-35   Interface for the Academy Award Winners application in Lesson C

3. Click the **Exit** button to end the application. Right-click **MoviesDataSet.xsd** in the Solution Explorer window and then click **Open** to open the DataSet Designer window.

4. Right-click **tblMoviesTableAdapter** in the DataSet Designer window. Point to **Add** on the shortcut menu and then click **Query** to start the TableAdapter Query Configuration Wizard. (If Add does not appear on the shortcut menu, click Add Query instead.) Verify that the Use SQL statements radio button is selected. Click the **Next** button to display the Choose a Query Type screen. Verify that the "SELECT which returns rows" radio button is selected. Click the **Next** button to display the Specify a SQL SELECT statement screen. The "What data should the table load?" box contains the default query, which selects all of the fields and records in the table. See Figure 14-36. You can invoke the default query using the TableAdapter object's Fill method.

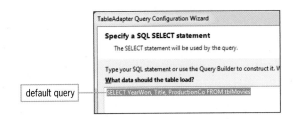

Figure 14-36   Default query in the Specify a SQL SELECT statement screen

5. Click the **Query Builder** button to open the Query Builder dialog box. Recall that the interface provides the txtYear control for the user to enter a year number. You will create a parameter query that allows the user to display the Academy Award winner for that year. In the Grid pane, click the **blank cell** in the YearWon field's Filter column. Type **?** and press **Enter**. The Query Builder adds the WHERE (YearWon = ?) clause to the SELECT statement.

6. Click the **Execute Query** button to run the query. The Query Parameters dialog box opens. Type **2004** in the Value column and then click the **OK** button to close the dialog box. The 2004 record appears in the Results pane.

7. Click the **OK** button to close the Query Builder dialog box. The parameter query appears in the "What data should the table load?" box. See Figure 14-37.

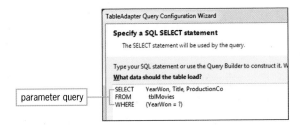

Figure 14-37   Parameter query in the Specify a SQL SELECT statement screen

8. Click the **Next** button to display the Choose Methods to Generate screen. If necessary, select the **Fill a DataTable** and **Return a DataTable** check boxes. Change the Fill a DataTable method's name from FillBy to **FillByYear**. Change the Return a DataTable method's name from GetDataBy to **GetDataByYear**. See Figure 14-38. As the figure indicates, the FillByYear and GetDataByYear methods are associated with the parameter query you created. Therefore, you can use the methods to invoke the query during run time.

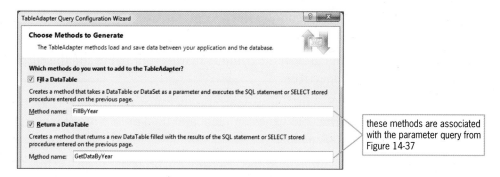

Figure 14-38 Completed Choose Methods to Generate screen

9. Click the **Next** button to display the Wizard Results screen. See Figure 14-39.

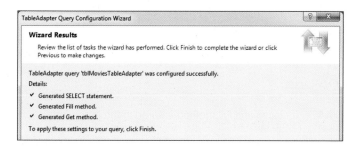

Figure 14-39 Wizard Results screen

10. Click the **Finish** button. The FillByYear and GetDataByYear methods are added to the DataSet Designer window, as shown in Figure 14-40.

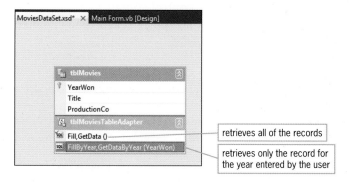

Figure 14-40 Method names included in the DataSet Designer window

11. Save the solution and then close the MoviesDataSet.xsd window.

Invoking a Query from Code

You can use the methods associated with a query to invoke the query during run time. You do this by entering the methods in a procedure. In the next set of steps, you will enter the appropriate methods in the Display button's Click event procedure.

START HERE **To code the Display button's Click event procedure:**

1. Open the Code Editor window. Replace <your name> and <current date> in the comments with your name and the current date, respectively.

2. Locate the btnDisplay control's Click event procedure. Click the **blank line** below the comment and then press **Enter** to insert another blank line.

3. If the All radio button is selected, the procedure will use the TblMoviesTableAdapter object's Fill method to select all of the records. (Recall that the form's Load event procedure also uses the Fill method.) Enter the lines of code shown in Figure 14-41.

```
Private Sub btnDisplay_Click(ByVal sender As Object, ByVal
    ' displays a specific record

    If radAll.Checked Then
        TblMoviesTableAdapter.Fill(MoviesDataSet.tblMovies)

    End If
```

enter these lines of code

Figure 14-41 If clause and Fill method entered in the procedure

4. If the All radio button is not selected, it means that the For Year radio button is selected. In that case, the procedure will use the TblMoviesTableAdapter object's FillByYear method to select the appropriate record. The record to select is the one whose YearWon field matches the year number entered in the txtYear control. First, you will determine whether the control contains a value. If it does not contain a value, you will display an appropriate message. Enter the lines of code shown in Figure 14-42.

```
    If radAll.Checked Then
        TblMoviesTableAdapter.Fill(MoviesDataSet.tblMovies)
    Else
        If txtYear.Text.Trim = String.Empty Then
            MessageBox.Show("Please enter the year.", "Year Entry",
                        MessageBoxButtons.OK,
                        MessageBoxIcon.Information)

        End If
    End If
```

enter these lines of code

Figure 14-42 Additional code entered in the procedure

5. The YearWon field is numeric, so you will need to convert the text box entry to a number. Enter the following lines of code:

Else
    Dim intYear As Integer
    Integer.TryParse(txtYear.Text, intYear)

6. Next, you will invoke the TblMoviesTableAdapter object's FillByYear method. Because the method is associated with a parameter query, you will need to include the parameter information in the method. Enter the additional lines of code shown in Figure 14-43.

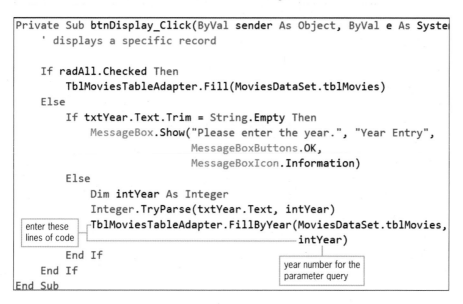

```
Private Sub btnDisplay_Click(ByVal sender As Object, ByVal e As Syste
    ' displays a specific record

    If radAll.Checked Then
        TblMoviesTableAdapter.Fill(MoviesDataSet.tblMovies)
    Else
        If txtYear.Text.Trim = String.Empty Then
            MessageBox.Show("Please enter the year.", "Year Entry",
                        MessageBoxButtons.OK,
                        MessageBoxIcon.Information)
        Else
            Dim intYear As Integer
            Integer.TryParse(txtYear.Text, intYear)
            TblMoviesTableAdapter.FillByYear(MoviesDataSet.tblMovies,
                                            intYear)
        End If
    End If
End Sub
```

enter these lines of code

year number for the parameter query

Figure 14-43   Display button's Click event procedure

7. Save the solution and then start the application. Click the **For Year** radio button and then click the **Display** button. The "Please enter the year." message appears in a message box. Close the message box.

8. Type **2005** in the text box located below the For Year radio button and then click the **Display** button. Only the 2005 record appears in the DataGridView control. See Figure 14-44.

Figure 14-44   2005 record shown in the interface

9. Click the **All** radio button and then click the **Display** button. All of the records appear in the DataGridView control.

10. Click the **Exit** button. Close the Code Editor window and then close the solution.

The INSERT and DELETE Statements

In addition to using SQL to select records, you also can use it to insert records into a database, as well as to delete records from a database. You use the **INSERT statement** to insert records, and use the **DELETE statement** to delete records. Figures 14-45 and 14-46 show the syntax and examples of the INSERT and DELETE statements, respectively.

INSERT statement

Syntax
INSERT INTO *tableName* (*fieldName1*, *fieldName2*, ..., *fieldNameN*)
        VALUES (*field1Value*, *field2Value*, ..., *fieldNValue*)

Example 1
```
INSERT INTO 'tblMovies' ('YearWon', 'Title', 'ProductionCo')
    VALUES (1997, 'Titanic', 'Paramount, 20th Century Fox')
```

Example 2
```
INSERT INTO 'tblMovies' ('YearWon', 'Title', 'ProductionCo')
    VALUES (1994, 'Forrest Gump', 'Paramount')
```

Example 3—parameter query
```
INSERT INTO 'tblMovies' ('YearWon', 'Title', 'ProductionCo')
    VALUES (?, ?, ?)
```

Figure 14-45   Syntax and examples of the SQL INSERT statement

---

DELETE statement

Syntax
DELETE FROM *tableName* **WHERE** *condition*

Example 1
```
DELETE FROM tblMovies
    WHERE YearWon = 1997
```

Example 2
```
DELETE FROM tblMovies
    WHERE Title = 'Forrest Gump'
```

Example 3—parameter query
```
DELETE FROM tblMovies
    WHERE YearWon = ?
```

Figure 14-46   Syntax and examples of the SQL DELETE statement

In the next set of steps, you will use the TableAdapter Query Configuration Wizard to create both an Insert query and a Delete query for the Movies database in the Academy Award Winners application. An **Insert query** uses the INSERT statement to add a record to a database. A **Delete query** uses the DELETE statement to delete a record from a database.

To create Insert and Delete queries in the Academy Award Winners application:

START HERE

1. Open the Academy Award Solution (Academy Award Solution.sln) file contained in the VB2010\Chap14\Academy Award Solution-InsertDelete folder. If necessary, open the designer window. The application is already connected to the Movies database. Start the application to view the records contained in the dataset. See Figure 14-47.

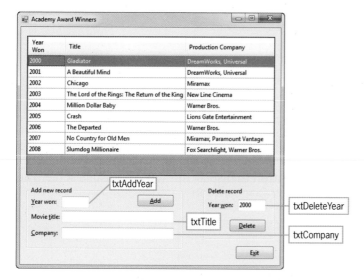

Figure 14-47   Records displayed in the TblMoviesDataGridView control

2. Click the **Exit** button to end the application. First, you will create the Insert query. Right-click **MoviesDataSet.xsd** in the Solution Explorer window and then click **Open** to open the DataSet Designer window.

3. Right-click **tblMoviesTableAdapter** in the DataSet Designer window. Point to **Add** on the shortcut menu and then click **Query** to start the TableAdapter Query Configuration Wizard. (If Add does not appear on the shortcut menu, click Add Query instead.) Verify that the Use SQL statements radio button is selected. Click the **Next** button to display the Choose a Query Type screen.

4. Click the **INSERT** radio button and then click the **Next** button to display the Specify a SQL INSERT statement screen, which contains the default INSERT statement for the tblMovies table. See Figure 14-48.

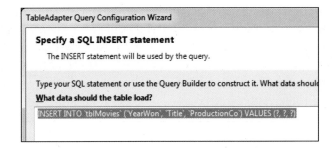

Figure 14-48   Default INSERT statement for the tblMovies table

5. Click the **Next** button to display the Choose Function Name screen. Change the function's name to **InsertRecordQuery**. See Figure 14-49.

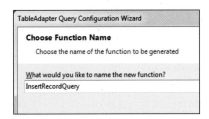

Figure 14-49   Choose Function Name screen

6. Click the **Next** button to display the Wizard Results screen. See Figure 14-50.

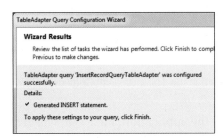

Figure 14-50   Wizard Results screen

7. Click the **Finish** button. The InsertRecordQuery function is added to the DataSet Designer window, as shown in Figure 14-51.

Figure 14-51   InsertRecordQuery function

8. Now, you will create the Delete query. Right-click **tblMoviesTableAdapter** in the DataSet Designer window. Click **Add Query** on the shortcut menu to start the TableAdapter Query Configuration Wizard. (If Add Query does not appear on the shortcut menu, point to Add and then click Query.) Verify that the Use SQL statements radio button is selected. Click the **Next** button to display the Choose a Query Type screen.

9. Click the **DELETE** radio button and then click the **Next** button to display the Specify a SQL DELETE statement screen, which contains the default DELETE statement for the tblMovies table. Click the **Query Builder** button. Change the statement in the SQL pane of the Query Builder dialog box as shown in Figure 14-52.

```
DELETE FROM tblMovies
WHERE     (YearWon = ?)
```

Figure 14-52   SQL DELETE statement

10. Click the **OK** button, and then click the **Next** button to display the Choose Function Name screen. Change the function's name to **DeleteRecordQuery**, and then click the **Next** button to display the Wizard Results screen. Click the **Finish** button to add the DeleteRecordQuery function to the DataSet Designer window. See Figure 14-53.

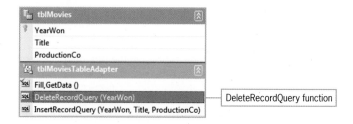

DeleteRecordQuery function

Figure 14-53   DeleteRecordQuery function

11. Save the solution and then close the MoviesDataSet.xsd window.

In the next set of steps, you will code the Click event procedures for the Add and Delete buttons. The Add button will use the InsertRecordQuery function to add a record to the Movies database. The Delete button will use the DeleteRecordQuery function to delete a record from the Movies database.

To code the Add and Delete buttons:

START HERE

1. Open the Code Editor window. Locate the btnAdd control's Click event procedure. Click the **blank line** below the comment and then press **Enter** to insert another blank line. First, you will determine whether the txtAddYear control contains data. If it doesn't, the procedure should display an appropriate message. Enter the selection structure shown in Figure 14-54.

Figure 14-54 Selection structure entered in the btnAdd control's Click event procedure

2. If the txtAddYear control contains data, you will need to convert the data to a number, because the YearWon field in the tblMovies table is numeric. Enter the following lines of code:

   Else
       Dim intYear As Integer
       Integer.TryParse(txtAddYear.Text, intYear)

3. Now, you will use the TblMoviesTableAdapter object's InsertRecordQuery function to add the record to the database. You then will use the object's Fill method to retrieve the appropriate data from the database. Enter the additional lines of code shown in Figure 14-55.

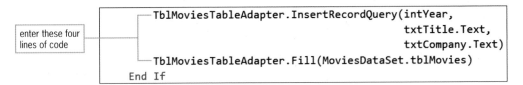

Figure 14-55 Additional lines of code entered in the btnAdd_Click procedure

4. Next, you will code the Delete button's Click event procedure. Locate the btnDelete control's Click event procedure. Click the **blank line** below the comment and then press **Enter** to insert another blank line. First, you will determine whether the txtDeleteYear control contains data. If it doesn't, the procedure should display an appropriate message. Enter the selection structure shown in Figure 14-56.

Figure 14-56 Selection structure entered in the btnDelete control's Click event procedure

5. If the txtDeleteYear control contains data, you will need to convert the data to a number, because the YearWon field in the tblMovies table is numeric. Enter the following lines of code:

Else
    Dim intYear As Integer
    Integer.TryParse(txtDeleteYear.Text, intYear)

6. Before the procedure deletes the record, it will ask the user to confirm the deletion. Enter the nested selection structure shown in Figure 14-57.

```
        If MessageBox.Show("Delete record for year " &
                    intYear.ToString & "?",
                    "Delete Confirmation",
                    MessageBoxButtons.YesNo,
                    MessageBoxIcon.Exclamation) =
                DialogResult.Yes Then

        End If
    End If
```

enter this nested selection structure

Figure 14-57 Nested selection structure entered in the procedure

7. If the user confirms the deletion, you will use the TblMoviesTableAdapter object's DeleteRecordQuery function to delete the record from the database. You then will use the object's Fill method to retrieve the appropriate data from the database. Enter the additional lines of code shown in Figure 14-58.

```
                DialogResult.Yes Then
        TblMoviesTableAdapter.DeleteRecordQuery(intYear)
        TblMoviesTableAdapter.Fill(MoviesDataSet.tblMovies)
        End If
    End If
```

enter these two lines of code

Figure 14-58 Additional lines of code entered in the btnDelete_Click procedure

Figure 14-59 shows the code entered in the Click event procedures for the btnAdd and btnDelete controls. It also shows the code entered in the form's Load event procedure.

```
Private Sub frmMain_Load(ByVal sender As System.Object,
ByVal e As System.EventArgs) Handles MyBase.Load
    'TODO: This line of code loads data into the
    'MoviesDataSet.tblMovies' table. You can move,
    or remove it, as needed.
    Me.TblMoviesTableAdapter.Fill(Me.MoviesDataSet.tblMovies)
    TblMoviesBindingSource.Sort = "YearWon"
End Sub
```

Figure 14-59 Most of the application's code *(continues)*

(continued)

```
Private Sub btnAdd_Click(ByVal sender As Object,
ByVal e As System.EventArgs) Handles btnAdd.Click
    ' add a record to the dataset

    If txtAddYear.Text.Trim = String.Empty Then
        MessageBox.Show("Please enter the year.",
                        "Add a Record",
                        MessageBoxButtons.OK,
                        MessageBoxIcon.Information)
    Else
        Dim intYear As Integer
        Integer.TryParse(txtAddYear.Text, intYear)
        TblMoviesTableAdapter.InsertRecordQuery(intYear,
                        txtTitle.Text,
                        txtCompany.Text)
        TblMoviesTableAdapter.Fill(MoviesDataSet.tblMovies)
    End If
End Sub

Private Sub btnDelete_Click(ByVal sender As Object,
ByVal e As System.EventArgs) Handles btnDelete.Click
    ' delete a record from the dataset

    If txtDeleteYear.Text.Trim = String.Empty Then
        MessageBox.Show("Please enter the year.",
                        "Delete a Record",
                        MessageBoxButtons.OK,
                        MessageBoxIcon.Information)
    Else
        Dim intYear As Integer
        Integer.TryParse(txtDeleteYear.Text, intYear)
        If MessageBox.Show("Delete record for year " &
                        intYear.ToString & "?",
                        "Delete Confirmation",
                        MessageBoxButtons.YesNo,
                        MessageBoxIcon.Exclamation) =
            DialogResult.Yes Then
            TblMoviesTableAdapter.DeleteRecordQuery(intYear)
            TblMoviesTableAdapter.Fill(MoviesDataSet.tblMovies)
        End If
    End If
End Sub
```

Figure 14-59 Most of the application's code

START HERE **To test the Add and Delete buttons:**

1. Save the solution and then start the application. Click the **Add** button. The "Please enter the year." message appears in a message box. Close the message box.

2. Now, you will add two records to the database. Click the **Year won** box in the Add new record section of the interface. Type **1990** and then press **Tab**. Type **Dances with Wolves**, press **Tab**, type **Orion**, and then click the **Add** button. The new record appears at the top of the list in the DataGridView control. This is because the form's Load event procedure

842

contains the `TblMoviesBindingSource.Sort = "YearWon"`
statement, which sorts the records in numerical order by the YearWon
field. You learned about the BindingSource object's Sort method in
Lesson A.

3. On your own, add the following record to the database: **2009**, **Forrest
   Gump**, **Paramount**. The record appears at the end of the list in the
   DataGridView control. See Figure 14-60.

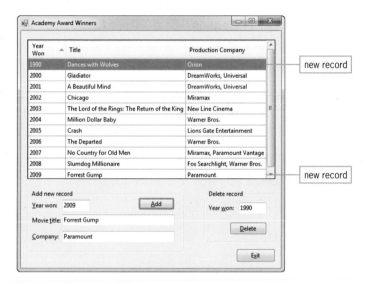

Figure 14-60 Two records added to the database

4. Click the **Exit** button to end the application, and then start the
   application again to verify that both new records appear in the
   DataGridView control.

5. Next, you will delete the record for the year 2009. Click **2009** in
   the DataGridView control. Notice that 2009 now appears in the
   txtDeleteYear control. This is because the txtDeleteYear control is
   bound to the YearWon field in the dataset. Click the **Delete** button.
   The "Delete record for year 2009?" message appears in a message box.
   Click the **Yes** button to delete the record.

6. On your own, delete the record for the year 1990.

7. Click **2005** in the DataGridView control and then click the **Delete**
   button. When the Delete Confirmation dialog box appears, click the
   No button. The record remains in the DataGridView control.

8. Click the **Exit** button to end the application, and then start the application again to verify that only the records for the years 1990 and
   2009 were deleted.

9. Click the **Exit** button to end the application. Close the Code Editor
   window and then close the solution.

Lesson C Summary

- To create a parameter query:

  Use a question mark in place of the criteria's value in the WHERE clause.

- To save a query that contains the SELECT statement:

  Use the TableAdapter Query Configuration Wizard to associate the query with one or more methods.

- To save a query that contains either the INSERT statement or the DELETE statement:

  Use the TableAdapter Query Configuration Wizard to associate the query with a function.

- To invoke a query from code:

  Enter the query's method or function in a procedure.

- To use SQL to insert records into a database:

  Use the INSERT statement.

- To use SQL to delete records from a database:

  Use the DELETE statement.

Lesson C Key Terms

?—the parameter marker in a parameter query

Delete query—a query that uses the DELETE statement to delete a record from a database

DELETE statement—the SQL statement used to delete a record from a database

Insert query—a query that uses the INSERT statement to add a record to a database

INSERT statement—the SQL statement used to insert a record into a database

Parameter marker—a question mark (?)

Parameter query—a query that uses the parameter marker (?) in place of the criteria's value

Lesson C Review Questions

1. When used in a parameter query, which of the following WHERE clauses selects the records for employees working more than 40 hours?

    a. `WHERE Hours >= 40`

    b. `WHERE Hours > ?`

    c. `WHERE Hours > #`

    d. `WHERE Hours < ?`

2. The FillByCity method is associated with a parameter query. Which of the following invokes the method, passing it the contents of the txtCity control's Text property?

    a. `TblCityTableAdapter.FillByCity(CityDataSet.tblCity, txtCity.Text)`

    b. `TblCityTableAdapter.FillByCity(txtCity.Text)`

    c. `TblCityBindingSource.FillByCity(CityDataSet.tblCity, txtCity.Text)`

    d. `CityDataSet.FillByCity(txtCity.Text)`

3. You can use the SQL _____ statement to add a record to a database.

    a. ADD

    b. ADD INTO

    c. APPEND

    d. INSERT

4. You can use the SQL _____ statement to remove a record from a database.

    a. DELETE

    b. DETACH

    c. ERASE

    d. REMOVE

Lesson C Exercises

1. In this exercise, you modify one of the Academy Award Winners applications from this lesson. Use Windows to make a copy of the Academy Award Solution-InsertDelete folder. Rename the copy Modified Academy Award-InsertDelete Solution. Open the Academy Award Solution (Academy Award Solution.sln) file contained in the Modified Academy Award Solution-InsertDelete folder. Open the

INTRODUCTORY

designer and Code Editor windows. If the user attempts to add a record that has the same year number as an existing record, a run time error will occur when the computer processes the InsertRecordQuery function in the btnAdd control's Click event procedure. Place the statement containing the function, as well as the statement containing the Fill method, in the Try block of a Try...Catch statement. The Catch block should display a message alerting the user that the record for that year already exists. Save the solution and then start the application. Test the application by attempting to add a duplicate record. Close the Code Editor window and then close the solution.

INTRODUCTORY

2. Open the JM Sales Solution (JM Sales Solution.sln) file contained in the VB2010\Chap14\JM Sales Solution folder. If necessary, open the designer window. The application is connected to the AnnualSales database. The database contains one table, which is named tblSales. The table contains two numeric fields (YearNum and Sales) and five records. The Add button's Click event procedure should allow the user to add records to the database. The Delete button's Click event procedure should allow the user to delete records from the database. Use SQL to code the procedures. Save the solution and then start and test the application. Be sure to try adding a record whose year number matches an existing year number. Stop the application. Use a Try...Catch statement to handle the run time error. (Refer to Exercise 1.) Save the solution and then start and test the application again. Close the Code Editor window and then close the solution.

INTERMEDIATE

3. Open the Addison Playhouse Solution (Addison Playhouse Solution.sln) file contained in the VB2010\Chap14\Addison Playhouse Solution folder. If necessary, open the designer window. The application is connected to the Play database. The database contains one table named tblReservations. The table has 20 records. Each record has three fields: a numeric field named Seat and two text fields named Patron and Phone. The application should allow the user to add records to the database and also delete records (by seat number) from the database. It also should allow the user to enter a seat number and then view the associated record. In addition, it should allow the user to view the records whose Patron field begins with the one or more characters the user enters. (Hint: Use LIKE ? & '%' as the filter.) The records should always appear in order by the seat number. Code the application. Save the solution and then start and test the application. Close the Code Editor window and then close the solution.

INTERMEDIATE

4. Open the Polter Solution (Polter Solution.sln) file contained in the VB2010\Chap14\Polter Solution folder. If necessary, open the designer window. The application is connected to the Products database. The database contains a table named tblProducts. The table contains 10 records, each composed of three fields. The ItemNum and ItemName fields contain text; the Price field contains numbers. The application should allow the user to view the record associated with a specific item number. It also should allow the user to enter a price and then view the records whose prices are at least that amount.

The records should appear in order by the item number when the application is started. Code the application. Save the solution and then start and test the application. Close the Code Editor window and then close the solution.

5. Open the Morgan Industries Solution (Morgan Industries Solution.sln) file contained in the Morgan Industries Solution-Advanced folder. If necessary, open the designer window. The application is connected to the Employees database. The database contains one table, which is named tblEmploy. The table contains seven fields and 14 records. The Emp_Number field is the primary key. The Status field contains the employment status, which is either the letter F (for full-time) or the letter P (for part-time). The Code field identifies the employee's department: 1 for Accounting, 2 for Advertising, 3 for Personnel, and 4 for Inventory. The records should appear in order by the employee number when the application is started. The application should allow the user to display all of the records, only the part-time records, only the full-time records, and only the records for a specific department. Code the application. Save the solution and then start and test the application. Close the Code Editor window and then close the solution.

ADVANCED

847

Locating Syntax and Logic Errors

In this appendix, you will learn how to locate and correct syntax and logic errors. You also will learn how to use the Debug menu's Step Into option, as well as how to set and remove a breakpoint.

Finding Syntax Errors

As you learned in Chapter 2, a syntax error occurs when you break one of a programming language's rules. Most syntax errors are a result of typing errors that occur when entering instructions, such as typing `Me.Clse()` instead of `Me.Close()`. The Code Editor detects most syntax errors as you enter the instructions. However, if you are not paying close attention to your computer screen, you may not notice the errors. In the following set of steps, you will observe what happens when you try to start an application that contains a syntax error.

START HERE ▶ **To debug the Total Sales Calculator application:**

1. Start Visual Studio 2010 or Visual Basic 2010 Express. Open the Total Sales Solution (Total Sales Solution.sln) file contained in the VB2010\AppA\Total Sales Solution folder. If necessary, open the designer window. The application calculates and displays the total of the sales amounts entered by the user.

2. Open the Code Editor window. Replace <your name> and <current date> in the comments with your name and the current date, respectively. Figure A-1 shows the code entered in the btnCalc control's Click event procedure. The jagged lines alert you that three lines of code contain a syntax error. However, you may fail to notice the jagged lines if you are not paying really close attention to the code.

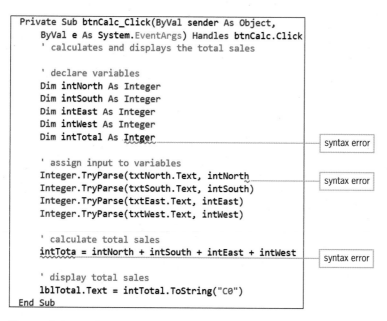

```
Private Sub btnCalc_Click(ByVal sender As Object,
    ByVal e As System.EventArgs) Handles btnCalc.Click
    ' calculates and displays the total sales

    ' declare variables
    Dim intNorth As Integer
    Dim intSouth As Integer
    Dim intEast As Integer
    Dim intWest As Integer
    Dim intTotal As Intger                          ──── syntax error

    ' assign input to variables
    Integer.TryParse(txtNorth.Text, intNorth         ──── syntax error
    Integer.TryParse(txtSouth.Text, intSouth)
    Integer.TryParse(txtEast.Text, intEast)
    Integer.TryParse(txtWest.Text, intWest)

    ' calculate total sales
    intTota = intNorth + intSouth + intEast + intWest ──── syntax error

    ' display total sales
    lblTotal.Text = intTotal.ToString("C0")
End Sub
```

Figure A-1   btnCalc control's Click event procedure

3. Start the application. If the dialog box shown in Figure A-2 appears, click the **No** button.

Figure A-2   Dialog box

4. The Error List window shown in Figure A-3 opens at the bottom of the IDE. The Error List window indicates that the code contains three errors. The window provides a description of each error and the location of each error in the code. If you want to change the size of the Error List window, position your mouse pointer on the window's top border until the mouse pointer becomes a sizing pointer. Then press and hold down the left mouse button while you drag the border either up or down.

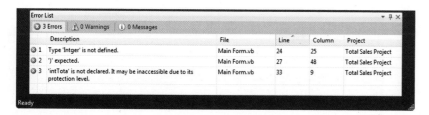

Figure A-3   Error List window

5. Double-click **the first error message** in the Error List window. A list of suggestions for fixing the error appears in a box, as shown in Figure A-4. (If the suggestion box does not appear, hover your mouse

849

pointer over the thin red box that appears below the letter r. An Error icon, which is a white exclamation point in a red circle, appears along with a down arrow. If you don't see the down arrow, hover your mouse pointer over the Error icon until the down arrow appears. Click the down arrow.)

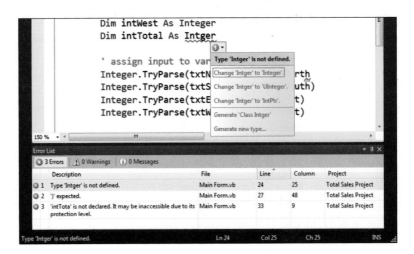

Figure A-4   Result of double-clicking the first error message

6. The first error is nothing more than a typing error. In this case, the programmer meant to type `Integer`. Click the **Change 'Intger' to 'Integer'.** suggestion. The Code Editor changes `Intger` to `Integer` in the Dim statement and then removes the error from the Error List window.

7. Double-click **')' expected.** in the Error List window. Click **Insert the missing ')'.** in the list of suggestions. The Code Editor inserts the missing parenthesis and then removes the error message from the Error List window.

8. Double-click the remaining error message in the Error List window. The Code Editor offers two suggestions for fixing the error, as shown in Figure A-5.

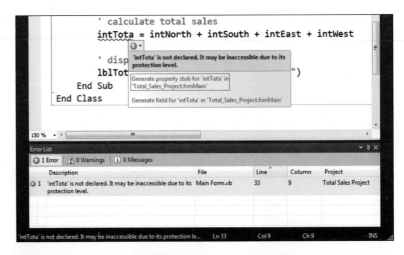

Figure A-5   Result of double-clicking the remaining error message

9. Neither suggestion shown in Figure A-5 is appropriate in this case. The error's description indicates that the Code Editor does not recognize the name `intTota`. The unrecognized name appears on the left side of an assignment statement, so it belongs to something that can store information: either the property of a control or a variable. It's not the name of either a control or a property, so it must be the name of a variable. Looking at the variable declarations at the beginning of the procedure, you will notice that the procedure declares a variable named `intTotal`. Obviously, the programmer mistyped the variable's name. Change `intTota` to `intTotal` in the assignment statement and then move the insertion point to another line in the Code Editor window. When you do this, the Code Editor removes the error message from the Error List window.

10. Close the Error List window. Save the solution and then start the application. Test the application using **2000** as the North sales, **3000** as the South sales, **1200** as the East sales, and **1800** as the West sales. Click the **Calculate** button. The total sales are $8,000. See Figure A-6.

Figure A-6   Total sales shown in the interface

11. Click the **Exit** button to end the application. Close the Code Editor window and then close the solution.

Locating Logic Errors

As you observed in the previous section, the Code Editor makes syntax errors easy to find and correct. A much more difficult type of error to locate, and one that the Code Editor cannot detect, is a logic error. A logic error can occur for a variety of reasons, such as forgetting to enter an instruction or entering the instructions in the wrong order. Some logic errors occur as a result of calculation statements that are correct syntactically, but incorrect mathematically. An example of this is the `dblRadiusSquared = dblRadius + dblRadius` statement. The statement's syntax is correct, but it is incorrect mathematically: you square a value by multiplying it by itself, not by adding it to itself. In the remainder of this appendix, you will debug two applications that contain logic errors.

To debug the Discount Calculator application:

START HERE

1. Open the Discount Solution (Discount Solution.sln) file contained in the VB2010\AppA\Discount Solution folder. If necessary, open the

designer window. The application calculates and displays three discount amounts, which are based on the price entered by the user.

2. Open the Code Editor window. Replace <your name> and <current date> in the comments with your name and the current date, respectively. Figure A-7 shows the code entered in the btnCalc control's Click event procedure.

```
Private Sub btnCalc_Click(ByVal sender As Object,
    ByVal e As System.EventArgs) Handles btnCalc.Click
    ' calculates and displays a 10%, 20%, and
    ' 30% discount on an item's price

    ' declare variables
    Dim dblPrice As Double
    Dim dblDisc10 As Double
    Dim dblDisc20 As Double
    Dim dblDisc30 As Double

    ' calculate discounts
    dblDisc10 = dblPrice * 0.1
    dblDisc20 = dblPrice * 0.2
    dblDisc30 = dblPrice * 0.3

    ' display discounts
    lblDisc10.Text = dblDisc10.ToString("N2")
    lblDisc20.Text = dblDisc20.ToString("N2")
    lblDisc30.Text = dblDisc30.ToString("N2")
End Sub
```

Figure A-7   Code entered in the btnCalc control's Click event procedure

3. Start the application. Type **100** in the Price box and then click the **Calculate** button. The interface shows that each discount is 0.00, which is incorrect. Click the **Exit** button to stop the application.

4. You'll use the Debug menu to run the Visual Basic debugger, which is a tool that helps you locate the logic errors in your code. Click **Debug** on the menu bar. The menu's Step Into option will start your application and allow you to step through your code. It does this by executing the code one statement at a time, pausing immediately before each statement is executed. Click **Step Into**. Type **100** in the Price box and then click the **Calculate** button. The debugger highlights the first instruction to be executed. In this case, it highlights the btnCalc _Click procedure header. In addition, an arrow points to the instruction (as shown in Figure A-8) and the code's execution is paused. (If the interface still appears on the screen, click the Code Editor window's title bar.)

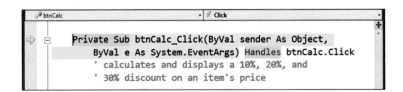

Figure A-8   Procedure header highlighted

5. To execute the highlighted instruction, you can use either the Debug menu's Step Into option or the F8 key on your keyboard. Press the **F8** key. After the computer processes the procedure header, the debugger highlights the next statement to be processed—in this case, the `dblDisc10 = dblPrice * 0.1` statement—and then pauses execution of the code. (The Dim statements are skipped over because they are not considered executable by the debugger.)

6. While the execution of a procedure's code is paused, you can view the contents of properties and variables that appear in the highlighted statement, as well as in the statements above it in the procedure. Before you view the contents of a property or variable, however, you should consider the value you expect to find. Before the `dblDisc10 = dblPrice * 0.1` statement is processed, the `dblDisc10` variable should contain its initial value, 0. (Recall that the Dim statement initializes numeric variables to 0.) Place your mouse pointer on `dblDisc10` in the highlighted statement. The variable's name and current value appear in a small box, as shown in Figure A-9. (The .0 indicates that the value's data type is Double.) At this point, the `dblDisc10` variable's value is correct.

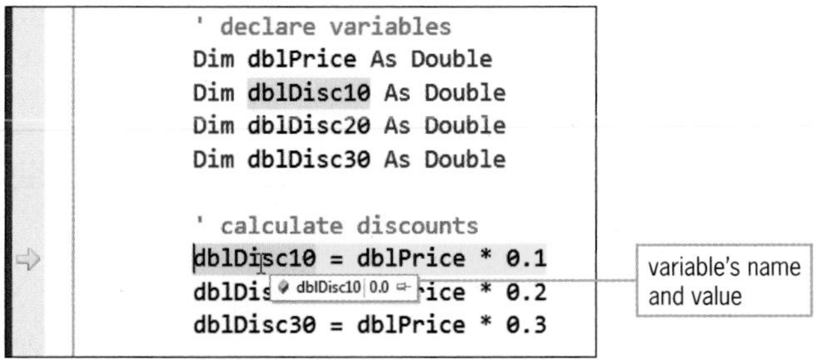

```
' declare variables
Dim dblPrice As Double
Dim dblDisc10 As Double
Dim dblDisc20 As Double
Dim dblDisc30 As Double

' calculate discounts
dblDisc10 = dblPrice * 0.1
dblDis ⬦ dblDisc10 0.0 ⬦ rice * 0.2
dblDisc30 = dblPrice * 0.3
```

variable's name and value

Figure A-9   Value stored in the `dblDisc10` variable before the highlighted statement is executed

7. Now consider the value you expect the `dblPrice` variable to contain. Before the highlighted statement is processed, the `dblPrice` variable should contain the number 100, which is the value you entered in the Price box. Place your mouse pointer on `dblPrice` in the highlighted statement. As Figure A-10 shows, the `dblPrice` variable contains 0.0, which is its initial value. Consider why the `dblPrice` variable's value is incorrect. In this case, the value is incorrect because no statement above the highlighted statement assigns the Price box's value to the variable. In other words, a statement is missing from the procedure.

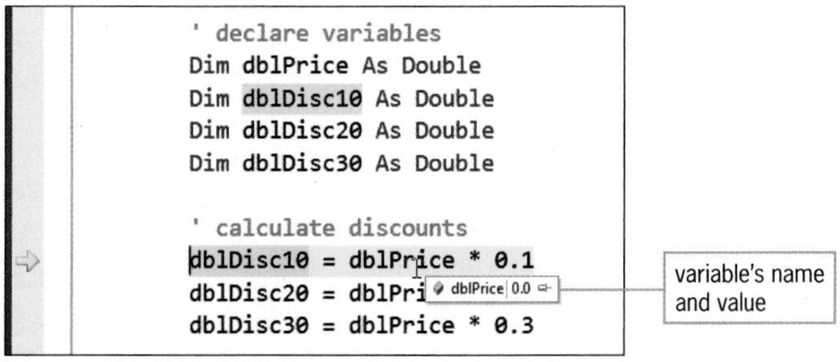

```
' declare variables
Dim dblPrice As Double
Dim dblDisc10 As Double
Dim dblDisc20 As Double
Dim dblDisc30 As Double

' calculate discounts
dblDisc10 = dblPrice * 0.1
dblDisc20 = dblPri ⬦ dblPrice 0.0 ⬦
dblDisc30 = dblPrice * 0.3
```

variable's name and value

Figure A-10   Value stored in the `dblPrice` variable before the highlighted statement is executed

8. Click **Debug** on the menu bar and then click **Stop Debugging** to stop the debugger. Click the **blank line** below the last Dim statement and then press **Enter** to insert another blank line. Enter the following comment and TryParse method:

   ' assign price to a variable
   Double.TryParse(txtPrice.Text, dblPrice)

9. Save the solution. Click **Debug** on the menu bar and then click **Step Into**. Type **100** in the Price box and then click the **Calculate** button. (If the interface still appears on the screen, click the Code Editor window's title bar.) Press **F8** to process the procedure header. The debugger highlights the statement containing the TryParse method and then pauses execution of the code.

10. Before the highlighted statement is processed, the txtPrice control's Text property should contain 100, which is the value you entered in the control. Place your mouse pointer on `txtPrice.Text` in the highlighted statement. The box shows that the Text property contains the expected value. The 100 is enclosed in quotation marks because it is considered a string.

11. The `dblPrice` variable should contain its initial value, 0.0. Place your mouse pointer on `dblPrice` in the highlighted statement. The box shows that the variable contains the expected value.

12. Press **F8** to process the TryParse method. The debugger highlights the `dblDisc10 = dblPrice * 0.1` assignment statement before pausing execution of the code. Place your mouse pointer on `dblPrice` in the TryParse method, as shown in Figure A-11. Notice that after the method is processed by the computer, the `dblPrice` variable contains the number 100.0.

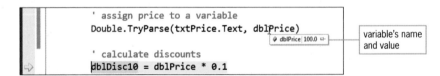

```
' assign price to a variable
Double.TryParse(txtPrice.Text, dblPrice)
                              dblPrice 100.0          variable's name
                                                      and value
' calculate discounts
dblDisc10 = dblPrice * 0.1
```

Figure A-11 Value stored in the `dblPrice` variable after the TryParse method is executed

13. Before the highlighted assignment statement is executed, the `dblDisc10` variable should contain its initial value, and the `dblPrice` variable should contain the value assigned to it by the TryParse method. Place your mouse pointer on `dblDisc10` in the highlighted statement. The box shows that the variable contains 0.0, which is correct. Place your mouse pointer on `dblPrice` in the highlighted statement. The box shows that the variable contains 100.0, which also is correct.

14. After the highlighted statement is processed, the `dblPrice` variable should still contain 100.0. However, the `dblDisc10` variable should contain 10.0, which is 10% of 100.0. Press **F8** to execute the statement, and then place your mouse pointer on `dblDisc10` in the statement. The box shows that the variable contains the expected value. On your own, verify that the `dblPrice` variable in the statement contains the appropriate value.

15. To continue program execution without the debugger, click **Debug** on the menu bar and then click **Continue**. This time, the correct discount amounts appear in the interface, as shown in Figure A-12.

Figure A-12 Discount amounts shown in the interface

16. Click the **Exit** button to end the application. Close the Code Editor window and then close the solution.

Setting Breakpoints

Stepping through code one line at a time is not the only way to search for logic errors. You also can use a breakpoint to pause execution at a specific line in the code. You will learn how to set a breakpoint in the following set of steps.

To debug the Hours Worked application:

START HERE

1. Open the Hours Worked Solution (Hours Worked Solution.sln) file contained in the VB2010\AppA\Hours Worked Solution folder. If necessary, open the designer window. The application calculates and displays the total number of hours worked during four weeks.

2. Open the Code Editor window. Replace <your name> and <current date> in the comments with your name and the current date, respectively. Figure A-13 shows the code entered in the btnCalc control's Click event procedure.

```vb
Private Sub btnCalc_Click(ByVal sender As Object,
    ByVal e As System.EventArgs) Handles btnCalc.Click
    ' displays total number of hours worked during 4 weeks

    Dim decWeek1 As Decimal
    Dim decWeek2 As Decimal
    Dim decWeek3 As Decimal
    Dim decWeek4 As Decimal
    Dim decTotal As Decimal

    ' assign input to variables
    Decimal.TryParse(txtWeek1.Text, decWeek1)
    Decimal.TryParse(txtWeek2.Text, decWeek2)
    Decimal.TryParse(txtWeek3.Text, decWeek2)
    Decimal.TryParse(txtWeek4.Text, decWeek4)

    ' calculate total hours worked
    decTotal = decWeek1 + decWeek2 + decWeek3 + decWeek4

    ' display total hours worked
    lblTotal.Text = decTotal.ToString
End Sub
```

Figure A-13 Click event procedure for the btnCalc control

855

3. Start the application. Type **4** in the Week 1 box, **1** in the Week 2 box, **5** in the Week 3 box, and **2** in the Week 4 box. Click the **Calculate** button. The interface shows that the total number of hours is 11, which is incorrect; it should be 12. Click the **Exit** button to stop the application.

4. Obviously, something is wrong with the statement that calculates the total number of hours worked. Rather than having the computer pause before processing each line of code in the procedure, you will have it pause only before processing the calculation statement. You do this by setting a breakpoint on the statement. Right-click the **calculation statement**, point to **Breakpoint**, and then click **Insert Breakpoint**. (You also can set a breakpoint by clicking the statement and then using the Toggle Breakpoint option on the Debug menu. Or, you can simply click in the gray margin next to the statement.) The debugger highlights the statement and places a circle next to it, as shown in Figure A-14.

```
' calculate total hours worked
decTotal = decWeek1 + decWeek2 + decWeek3 + decWeek4
```

Figure A-14   Breakpoint set in the procedure

5. Start the application. Type **4** in the Week 1 box, **1** in the Week 2 box, **5** in the Week 3 box, and **2** in the Week 4 box. Click the **Calculate** button. The computer begins processing the code contained in the button's Click event procedure. It stops processing when it reaches the calculation statement, which it highlights. The highlighting indicates that the statement is the next one to be processed. See Figure A-15.

```
' calculate total hours worked
decTotal = decWeek1 + decWeek2 + decWeek3 + decWeek4
```

Figure A-15   Result of the computer reaching the breakpoint

6. Before viewing the values contained in each variable in the highlighted statement, consider the values you expect to find. Before the calculation statement is processed, the decTotal variable should contain its initial value (0). The other four variables should contain the numbers you entered in each text box: 4, 1, 5, and 2. Place your mouse pointer on decTotal in the highlighted statement. The box shows that the variable's value is 0D, which is correct. (You can verify the variable's initial value by placing your mouse pointer on decTotal in its declaration statement.) Don't be concerned that 0D appears rather than 0. As you learned in Chapter 3, the letter D is one of the literal type characters in Visual Basic; it indicates that the value's data type is Decimal.

7. On your own, view the values contained in the decWeek1, decWeek2, decWeek3, and decWeek4 variables. Notice that the decWeek1 and decWeek4 variables contain the appropriate values: 4D and 2D.

However, the values in the decWeek2 and decWeek3 variables are incorrect: the decWeek2 variable contains 5D and the decWeek3 variable contains its initial value (0D).

8. Two of the TryParse methods are responsible for assigning values to the decWeek2 and decWeek3 variables. Looking closely at the TryParse methods in the procedure, you will notice that the third one is incorrect. After converting the contents of the txtWeek3 control's Text property to a number, the method should assign the number to the decWeek3 variable rather than to the decWeek2 variable. Click **Debug** on the menu bar and then click **Stop Debugging**.

9. Change decWeek2 in the third TryParse method to **decWeek3**.

10. Now you can remove the breakpoint. Right-click the **statement containing the breakpoint**, point to **Breakpoint**, and then click **Delete Breakpoint**. (Or, you can simply click the breakpoint circle.)

11. Save the solution and then start the application. Type **4** in the Week 1 box, **1** in the Week 2 box, **5** in the Week 3 box, and **2** in the Week 4 box. Click the **Calculate** button. The total number of hours is 12, as shown in Figure A-16.

Figure A-16 Total hours worked shown in the interface

12. On your own, test the application using other values for the hours worked in each week. When you are finished testing, click the **Exit** button. Close the Code Editor window and then close the solution.

GUI Design Guidelines

Chapter 1—Lesson C

FormBorderStyle, ControlBox, MaximizeBox, MinimizeBox, and StartPosition Properties

- A splash screen should not have Minimize, Maximize, or Close buttons, and its borders should not be sizable. In most cases, a splash screen's FormBorderStyle property is set to either None or FixedSingle. Its StartPosition property is set to CenterScreen.

- A form that is not a splash screen should always have a Minimize button and a Close button, but you can choose to disable the Maximize button. Typically, the FormBorderStyle property is set to Sizable; however, it also can be set to FixedSingle. Most times, the form's StartPosition property is set to CenterScreen.

Chapter 2—Lesson A

Layout and Organization of the User Interface

- Organize the user interface so that the information flows either vertically or horizontally, with the most important information always located in the upper-left corner of the screen.

- Group related controls together using either white (empty) space or one of the tools contained in the Containers section of the toolbox.

- Use a label to identify each text box in the user interface. Also use a label to identify other label controls that display program output. The label text should be meaningful. It also should be from one to three words only and appear on one line. Left-align the text within the label, and position the label either above or to the left of the control it identifies. Enter the label text using sentence capitalization, and follow the label text with a colon (:).

- Display a meaningful caption on the face of each button. The caption should indicate the action the button will perform when clicked. Enter the caption using book title capitalization. Place the caption on one line and use from one to three words only.

- When a group of buttons are positioned horizontally, each button in the group should be the same height. When a group of buttons are positioned vertically, each button in the group should be the same height and width. In a group of buttons, the most commonly used button is typically the first button in the group.

- Align the borders of the controls wherever possible to minimize the number of different margins appearing in the interface.

Chapter 2—Lesson B

Adding Graphics

- Use graphics sparingly. If the graphic is used solely for aesthetics, use a small graphic and place it in a location that will not distract the user.

Selecting Font Types, Styles, and Sizes

- Use only one font type for all of the text in the interface. Use a sans serif font, preferably the Segoe UI font.

- Use no more than two different font sizes in the interface.

- Avoid using italics and underlining, because these font styles make text difficult to read.

- Limit the use of bold text to titles, headings, and key items that you want to emphasize.

Selecting Colors

- Build the interface using black, white, and gray. Only add color if you have a good reason to do so.

- Use white, off-white, or light gray for the background. Use black for the text.

- Never use a dark color for the background or a light color for the text. A dark background is hard on the eyes, and light-colored text can appear blurry.

- Limit the number of colors in an interface to three, not including white, black, and gray. The colors you choose should complement each other.

- Never use color as the only means of identification for an element in the user interface.

Setting the BorderStyle Property of a Text Box or Label

- Keep the BorderStyle property of text boxes at the default value, Fixed3D.

- Keep the BorderStyle property of labels that identify other controls at the default value, None.

- Set to FixedSingle the BorderStyle property of labels that display program output, such as those that display the result of a calculation.

- In Windows applications, a control that contains data that the user is not allowed to edit does not usually appear three-dimensional. Therefore, avoid setting a label control's BorderStyle property to Fixed3D.

Setting the AutoSize Property of a Label

- Keep the AutoSize property of identifying labels at the default value, True.

- In most cases, change to False the AutoSize property of label controls that display program output.

Assigning Access Keys

- Assign a unique access key to each control that can accept user input.

- When assigning an access key to a control, use the first letter of the caption or identifying label, unless another letter provides a more meaningful association. If you can't use the first letter and no other letter provides a more meaningful association, then use a distinctive consonant. Lastly, use a vowel or a number.

Using the TabIndex Property to Control the Focus

- Assign a TabIndex value (starting with 0) to each control in the interface, except for controls that do not have a TabIndex property. The TabIndex values should reflect the order in which the user will want to access the controls.

- To give users keyboard access to a text box, assign an access key to the text box's identifying label. Set the identifying label's TabIndex property to a value that is one number less than the value stored in the text box's TabIndex property.

Chapter 3—Lesson B

InputBox Function's Prompt and Title Capitalization

- Use sentence capitalization for the *prompt*, but book title capitalization for the *title*.

Assigning a Default Button

- The default button should be the button that is most often selected by the user, except in cases where the tasks performed by the button are both destructive and irreversible. In most interfaces, the default button is the first button.

Chapter 4—Lesson B

Labeling a Group Box

- Use sentence capitalization for the optional identifying label, which is entered in the group box's Text property.

MessageBox.Show Method

- Use sentence capitalization for the *text* argument, but book title capitalization for the *caption* argument.

- Display either the Exclamation icon or the Question icon to alert the user that he or she must make a decision before the application can continue. You can phrase the message as a question.

- Display the Information icon along with an OK button in a message box that displays an informational message.

- Display the Stop icon to alert the user of a serious problem that must be corrected before the application can continue.

- The default button in the dialog box should be the one that represents the user's most likely action, as long as that action is not destructive.

Chapter 5—Lesson B

Radio Button Standards

- Use radio buttons to limit the user to one choice in a group of related but mutually exclusive choices.

- The minimum number of radio buttons in a group is two and the recommended maximum number is seven.

- The label in the radio button's Text property should be entered using sentence capitalization.

- Assign a unique access key to each radio button in an interface.

- Use a container (such as a group box) to create separate groups of radio buttons. Only one button in each group can be selected at any one time.

- Designate a default radio button in each group of radio buttons.

Check Box Standards

- Use check boxes to allow the user to select any number of choices from a group of one or more independent and nonexclusive choices.

- The label in the check box's Text property should be entered using sentence capitalization.

- Assign a unique access key to each check box in an interface.

Chapter 6—Lesson C

List Box Standards

- A list box should contain a minimum of three items.

- A list box should display a minimum of three items and a maximum of eight items at a time.

- Use a label control to provide keyboard access to the list box. Set the label's TabIndex property to a value that is one less than the list box's TabIndex value.

- List box items are either arranged by use, with the most used entries appearing first in the list, or sorted in ascending order.

Default List Box Item

- If a list box allows the user to make only one selection, a default item should be selected when the interface first appears. The default item should be either the item selected most frequently or the first item in the list. However, if a list box allows more than one selection at a time, you do not select a default item.

Chapter 7—Lesson B

Combo Box Standards

- Use a label control to provide keyboard access to a combo box. Set the label's TabIndex property to a value that is one less than the combo box's TabIndex value.

- Combo box items are either arranged by use, with the most used entries appearing first in the list, or sorted in ascending order.

Chapter 8—Lesson B

Menu Standards

- Menu title captions should begin with a capital letter and be one word only. Each menu title should have a unique access key.

- Menu item captions can be from one to three words. Use book title capitalization and assign a unique access key to each menu item on the same menu.

- Assign unique shortcut keys to commonly used menu items.

- If a menu item requires additional information from the user, place an ellipsis (…) at the end of the item's caption, which is entered in the item's Text property.

- Follow the Windows standards for the placement of menu titles and items.

- Use a separator bar to separate groups of related menu items.

Visual Basic Conversion Functions

Syntax	Return data type	Range for *expression*
CBool(*expression*)	Boolean	Any valid String or numeric expression
CByte(*expression*)	Byte	0 through 255 (unsigned)
CChar(*expression*)	Char	Any valid String expression; value can be 0 through 65535 (unsigned); only the first character is converted
CDate(*expression*)	Date	Any valid representation of a date and time
CDbl(*expression*)	Double	−1.79769313486231570E+308 through −4.94065645841246544E-324 for negative values; 4.94065645841246544E-324 through 1.79769313486231570E+308 for positive values
CDec(*expression*)	Decimal	+/−79,228,162,514,264,337,593,543,950,335 for zero-scaled numbers, that is, numbers with no decimal places; for numbers with 28 decimal places, the range is +/−7.9228162514264337593543950335; the smallest possible non-zero number is .0000000000000000000000000001 (+/−1E-28)
CInt(*expression*)	Integer	−2,147,483,648 through 2,147,483,647; fractional parts are rounded
CLng(*expression*)	Long	−9,223,372,036,854,775,808 through 9,223,372,036,854,775,807; fractional parts are rounded
CObj(*expression*)	Object	Any valid expression
CSByte(*expression*)	SByte (signed Byte)	−128 through 127; fractional parts are rounded
CShort(*expression*)	Short	−32,768 through 32,767; fractional parts are rounded
CSng(*expression*)	Single	−3.402823E+38 through −1.401298E-45 for negative values; 1.401298E-45 through 3.402823E+38 for positive values
CStr(*expression*)	String	Depends on the expression
CUInt(*expression*)	UInt	0 through 4,294,967,295 (unsigned)
CULng(*expression*)	ULng	0 through 18,446,744,073,709,551,615 (unsigned)
CUShort(*expression*)	UShort	0 through 65,535 (unsigned)

Index

*Appendix D is available online at *www.cengagebrain.com.*
Note: Page numbers in **boldface** indicate key terms.

% (percent sign), SQL wildcard, 823
? (question mark)
    parameter (query) marker, **844**
    in pattern-matching, 463
<asp:ListItem> tag, **729**, **734**

 tag, **732–733**, **734**
<div> tag, **722**, **734**

A
ABC Company application, 615–616,
    661–667
Academy Award Winners application,
    796–810, 831–833
Access database, connecting
    application to, 745–749
access keys, **81**, **87**
    assigning, 81–82
    GUI design guidelines, 860
accessing characters in strings, 460–462
accumulator arrays, 522–525
accumulators
    and counters, using, 339–346
    described, **339**, **356**
ActiveMdiChild property, **D-25***,
    D-35*
Add Connection dialog box, 746
Add method, **376**, **385**
adding
    adding items to DropDownList
        control, 729–730
    check boxes to interfaces, 292–294
    colors to user interfaces, 77–78
    comments to program code, 96–98
    controls to forms, 32–33
    dollar signs, 168–170
    graphics, 76–77
    group boxes to forms, 231–233
    images to Web pages, 698–700
    items to BindingNavigator control,
        777–779
    link button controls to Web pages,
        694–696
    menus to forms, 476–479

picture box controls to forms, 36–37
radio buttons to forms, 290–292
records to datasets, 799–804
splash screens to applications,
    D-4–D-6*
Start Without Debugging option,
    696–698
static text to Web pages, 691–693
text box controls to forms, 80
Web pages to Web applications,
    693–694
addition (+) operator, 222
aggregate operators
    described, **779**, **782**
    using, 779–782
algorithms
    described, **271**, **283**
    desk-checking, 271
Align option, Format menu, 35
aligning
    characters in strings, 453–454
    columns of information, 602–604
ampersand (&)
    and access key assignments, 81
    concatenation operator, **160**, **171**
And operator, 207, **208**, 222, **223**
AndAlso operator, 207, **208**, 222, **223**
apostrophes (') and code comments, 96
AppendText method, **582**, **592**
applications, **4**, **8**
    assembling the documentation,
        108–109
    connecting to Microsoft Access
        database, 745–749
    creating Visual Basic 2010
        Windows, 13–14
    with multiple forms, D-1–D-35*
    object-oriented, 63–71
    primary window, dialog boxes,
        D-6–D-8*
    running Visual Basic 2010, 5–6
    starting and ending, 38–40
    testing and debugging, 105–108

Area Calculator application, 139–141,
    672–678
arithmetic assignment operators
    described, **347**, **356**
    using, 347–348
arithmetic expressions, 98–100
Array.Reverse method, **525**, **530**
arrays, **504**, **530**
    accumulator, 522–525
    and collections, 518–522
    counter, 522–525
    elements, **506**
    one-dimensional. *See* one-
        dimensional arrays
    parallel one-dimensional, 539–543
    populating, **507**, **530**
    of structure variables, creating,
        571–575
    two-dimensional. *See*
        two-dimensional arrays
    using, 504–505
    using For Each...Next statements,
        511
Array.Sort method, **525**, **530**
As keyword, 565
ASP, **686**, **704**
ASP table control, **724**, **734**
ASP tables, using, 724–729
assigning
    access keys, 81–82
    data to existing variables, 125–131
    shortcut keys to menu items, 479–480
    values to properties during run
        time, 94–96
assignment operator (=), **94**, **110**, 125
assignment operators, arithmetic, **347**,
    356
assignment statements, **94**, **110**, 126
asterisks (*)
    on designer window's tab, 23
    in pattern-matching, 463
attributes, **617**, **645**
auto-hiding windows in IDE, 15–16

auto-implemented properties, **658**, **668**
AutoSize property controls, 78–79
AutoSizeColumnsMode property, **754**, **768**

B

BackColor property, 22–23, 78
background colors, changing text box, 78
base classes
    creating, 672–678
    described, **672**, **678**
behaviors, **617**, **645**
binary operators, 98
binding, **749**, **768**
    to existing controls, 762–766
    objects in datasets, 749–756
BindingNavigator controls, 757, 759
    described, **752**, **768**
    personalizing, 777–779
BindingSource objects, **752**, **768**
block scope, **203**, **224**
block-level variables, **203**, **224**
bold text, using, 77
book title capitalization, **70**, **72**
Boole, George, 50
Boolean data types, 122–123
Boolean values, comparing, 219–221
borders
    form, 52–53
    GUI design guidelines, 859
BorderStyle property, for controls, 78–79
bottom-driven loops, 332
bound controls
    creating, 750–753
    described, **749**, **768**
breakpoints, setting in code, 855–857
browsers, **684**, **704**
bugs, **105**, **110**
button controls, **38**, **45**
Button tool, using, 38
buttons
    designating default, 166–167
    radio. *See* radio buttons
    stacking, 76
ByRef keyword, 400, 403
ByVal keyword, 397

C

calculating
    area of circles, 140
    gross pay, 211–213
    periodic payments, 236–237
    total and average values, 512–514
Call keyword, 301
Call statements, **301**, **306**, **396–397**
camel case, **20**, **26**
Cancel property, **429**, **442**
capitalization, **70**, **72**
captions, menu title, 476
Carpet Haven application, 624–636, 632–636

Case clause in Select Case statements, 280
CD Collection application, 562–564, 598–602
cells (ASP table), **724**, **735**
cells (DataGridView control), **753**, **768**
centering label controls, 36
changing
    form files' names, 18–19
    form names, 20–21
    properties for multiple controls, 35
chapters, using this book's, 6–7
Char data types, 122–123
characters
    accessing in strings, 460–462
    aligning in strings, 453–454
    determining number in string, 449–450
    inserting in strings, 453–456
    removing from strings, 450–452
    stream of, **581**, **593**
charts, TOE. *See* TOE charts
check boxes, **292**, **306**
    adding to interfaces, 292–294
    determining whether checked, 315
    GUI design guidelines, 861
    selecting, 294
    standards, 293
child tables, **744**, **768**
circles, calculating area of, 140
Cities application, 511
City and State application, 458–459
class definitions, **20**, **26**
Class Name list box, **41**, **45**
class scope, **134**, 135, **146**
Class statement, 565, **618**, **645**
classes, **4**, **8**, 17, **617**, **645**
    See also specific class
    creating generally, 618–619
    reusing, 640–644
class-level variables, **134**, **146**
Clear method, 93
Click event, 41–42, 93–98, 155–159, 178–181
client computers, **684**, **704**
Clock application, 365–366
Close method, **584**, **592**
closing
    current solution, 23
    forms, 429
    input sequential access files, 589–591
    Web applications, 700
    windows in IDE, 15–16
code, **17**, **26**
    adding comments, 96–98
    collapsing, expanding in Code Editor window, 40–41
    error-handling, 757–760
    finding logic errors, 851–855
    finding syntax errors, 848–851
    internally documenting program, 96–98
    invoking queries from, 833–835

printing splash screen's, 54–55
    and pseudocode, 91–92
    setting breakpoints, 855–857
    testing, 281
    viewing Visual Basic, 756–757
Code Editor
    and logic errors, 105
    and syntax errors, 848–851
Code Editor window
    exploring, 40–42, 54
    and Option statements, 143–144, 154–160
    viewing code with, 756–757
Code Editor's IntelliSense feature, 662
coding, **3**, **8**
collections
    arrays and, 518–522
    described, **375**, **385**
Color dialog box, **D-7***, **D-35***
ColorDialog tool, D-35*
colors
    adding to user interfaces, 77–78
    and GUI design, 78, 859
columnar layouts, creating, 722–724
combo boxes, **419**, **424**
    GUI design guidelines, 862
    including in interfaces, 419–423
comments, adding to code, 96–98
comparing
    Boolean values, 219–221
    strings containing letters, 213–214
    strings using pattern-matching, 463–466
comparison operators, **199**, **224**
    See also specific operator
    commonly used (fig.), 200
    displaying sum or difference, 204–206
    swapping numeric values using, 201–204
component tray, IDE, **50**, **56**
compound conditions vs. nested selection structures, 272–273
computer databases, **743**, **768**
    See also databases
    overview of, 740–741
computer programs, **2**, **8**
computers, programming, 2–3
concatenating strings, 160–161
concatenation (&) operator, **160**, **171**, 222
condition
    described, **192**, **224**
    in WHERE clauses, 815
configuring Visual Studio, 12–13
Const keyword, 139
Const statement, **138**, **146**
constants
    literal, **126**, **146**
    named, 138–141, **146**
constructors, **630**, **645**
Contains method, **457**, **468**
ControlBox property, 53
ControlChars.Back constant, **249**, **254**

ControlChars.NewLine constant, **165–166, 171**
controls, **31, 45**
 See also specific control
 adding to forms, 32–33
 binding to existing, 762–766
 BorderStyle, AutoSize properties, 78–79
 changing properties for multiple, 35
 controlling tab order, 82–85
 data-aware, 749
 dragging in Source view, 727–729
 locking, 80–81, 232, 293
 organizing in interface, 69–71
 positioning on Web pages, 701–702
 selecting several, 232
 text box, adding to forms, 80
conversion functions, 130, 863
Convert class, **130–131, 146**
converting
 currency, D-29–D-34*
 strings to uppercase, lowercase, 215–218
Convert.ToDecimal method, 139
Copy to Output Directory property, **760–761, 768**
counter arrays, 522–525
counter variables, 349
counter-controlling loops, **348, 356**
counters
 and accumulators, using, 339–346
 described, **339, 356**
Country Charm Inn application, D-4–D-6*
CreateText method, **582, 592**
creating
 Academy Award Winners application, 796–810, 831–833
 arrays of structure variables, 571–575
 base classes and derived classes, 672–678
 bound controls, 750–753
 CD Collection application, 562–564, 598–602
 class that contains a parameterized constructors, 636–640
 class that contains Private variables, Public properties, and methods, 624–636
 class that contains Public variables, 620–624
 classes generally, 618–619
 classes that contains a ReadOnly property, 654–658
 classes that contains auto-implemented properties, 658–660
 columnar layouts, 722–724
 dialog boxes, D-13*
 DJ Tom application, 681–683, 721–733
 dynamic Web pages, 708–712
 GetFwt function, 432–436

GUI (graphic user interface), 16–17
Harvey Industries application, 394–395, 427–442
independent Sub procedures, 296–300
Math Practice application, 261–263, 290–295, 312–319
Monthly Payment Calculator application, 231–254, 351–354
 object-oriented applications, 63
Playtime Cellular application, 60–62, 75–80
Quarter of a Million club application, 330–332, 336–339
queries, 773–777
Random objects, 298–299
Sales Express Company application, 340–346
SDI applications, D-3–D-35*
Shoppers Haven application, 327–328, 374–384
SQL queries, 817–822
StreamWriter objects, 581–583
Treasure Gift Shop application, 502–503
variables on the fly, 141
Visual Basic 2010 Windows applications, 13–14
Web applications, 687–688
Currency Converter application, 686, 708–716, D-29–D-34*
customizing Web pages, 690–693

D
data
 aligning columns of information, 602–604
 assigning to existing variables, 125–131
 invalid, **105, 110**
 reading from sequential access files, 585–588
 valid, **105, 111**
 writing to sequential access files, 581–584
data types, **122, 146**
 promotion and demotion, 141–142
 selecting for variables, 122–123
 user-defined, **576**
data validation, **211,** 211–213, **224**
Database Explorer window, 745
database management systems (DBMSs), 743
databases
 inserting, deleting records, 836–843
 modifying records, 787–791
 overview of, 740–741
 queries, 773–777
 using SQL, 815–822
DataGridView controls, **750,** 753–756, **768**
DataSet objects, **752, 768**

datasets, **745, 768**
 adding records to, 799–804
 binding objects in, 749–756
 deleting records from, 805–810
 previewing contents of, 748–749
 sorting records in, 804–805
Date data types, 122–123
Debug menu, Start Without Debugging option, 696–698
debugging, 7, **8, 105, 110**
 applications, 105–108
 Discount Calculator application, 851–855
 Hours Worked application, 855–857
 Total Sales Calculator application, 848–851
Decimal data type, 122–123, 126
decision symbol, **195, 224,** 335
decisions, making in programs, 192–198
decrementing, **340, 356**
default button
 described, **166, 171**
 designating, 166–167
default constructors, **630, 645**
default list box item, **379, 385,** 861–862
default radio buttons, **291, 306**
Default.aspx Web pages, 689–690
Delete method, **807, 810**
Delete query, **844**
DELETE statement, **836,** 836–843, **844**
deleting
 locked controls, 80
 records from databases, 836–843
 records from datasets, 805–810
 TabIndex boxes, 84
demoted, **142, 146**
derived classes
 creating, 672–678
 described, **672, 678**
design guidelines, GUI, 858–862
desk-checking
 algorithms, 271
 described, **271, 283**
detail tables, 744
dialog boxes in applications, D-13*, D-6–D-8*
diamond (decision symbol), 195, 224, 335
digital video recorders (DVDs), programming, 2
Dim keyword, 124
Dim statements, 298–299
Discount Calculator application, debugging, 851–855
displaying
 messages, 216–218
 properties of form files, 18
 Solution Explorer window, 16
 sum or difference of numbers, 204–206
 Toolbox window, 31

division operator, 98–99, 222
DJ Tom application, 681–683, 721–733
documentation, assembling application's, 108–109
documenting program code, 96–98
dollar signs ($), adding to value, 168–170
Do...Loop statements, 332, **333**, 336, 345, **356**
   vs. For...Next statements, 354–355
   using, 333–339
dot member access operator, **20**, **26**, 566
Double data type, 122–123, 126, 128, 141–142
downloading Visual Basic 2010 Express, 4
DropDownList control, adding items to, 729–730
DropDownStyle property, **419**, **424**
dual-alternative selection structure, **192**, 196–199, 205, **224**, 264
dynamic Web pages
   described, **685–686**, **704**
   overview of, 708–712

E

earnings of computer programmers, 3
elements
   described, **506**, **530**
   determining number in arrays, 508
ellipsis (...) and menu title captions, 477
employment opportunities for computer programmers, 3–4
empty strings, **93**, **110**
encapsulates, **617**, **645**
ending applications, 38–40
endless loops, **338**, **357**
Enter event, **251**, **254**
equal sign (=)
   assignment operator (=), **110**, 125
   comparison operator, 200
error-handling in VB code, 757–760
errors
   finding logic, 851–855
   finding syntax, 848–851
   overflow, 338
event procedures, **40**, **46**
events, **40**, **46**, **617**, **645**
   associating procedures with, 182–185
   identifying application's, 67–68
   including procedures in Class statements, 618
exceptions, **757**, **768**
executable files
   described, **39**, **46**
   renaming, 39–40
Exists method, **586**, **592**
Exit...Do statements, 333
Exit...For statements, 349
exiting Visual Studio 2010, Visual Basic 2010 Express, 24

exponentiation (^) operator, 222
expressions, writing arithmetic, 98–100
extended selection structures, 275

F

false path, **192**, **224**, 264
fields, **743**, **768**
files, and Windows applications, 13
Finally block, 757
Financial.Pmt method
   described, **236**, **244**
   using, 236–237
fixed-spaced fonts, 603
flowcharts, **92**, **110**
   charting loops in, 335
   decision symbol, **195**, **224**
   dual-alternative selection structure (fig.), 205
   input/output symbol, **110**
   multiple-alternative selection structure (fig.), 276
   nested selection structure (fig.), 267, 268
   planning procedures using, 92–93
   single-alternative selection structure (fig.), 202
flowlines, **92**, **110**
focus
   and controlling tab order, 82–85, 860
   described, **82**, **87**
Focus method
   described, **87**, **110**
   using, 96
Font and Color application, D-6–D-8*
Font dialog box, **D-7***, **D-35***
Font property, Windows form, 21–22
FontDialog tool, D-35*
font-family property, **722**, **735**
fonts
   fixed-spaced, 603
   and GUI design, 77, 859
For Each...Next statements
   described, **511**, **530**
   using, 332, 511–514
foreign key, **744**, **768**
form files, 17–18
   described, **26**
   properties of, 19–22
Format function
   described, **103**, **110**
   using, 103–105
Format menu, using, 35–36
format styles, some Visual Basic predefined (table), 104
formatting
   described, **167**, **171**
   numbers using ToString method, 167–170
FormBorderStyle property, setting, 52–53
FormClosing event, **428**, **442**, 606, **D-17***

forms, **16**, **26**
   adding controls to, 32–33
   adding group boxes to, 231–233
   adding menus to, 476–479
   adding picture box controls, 36–37
   adding radio buttons to, 290–292
   adding text box controls to, 80
   applications with multiple, D-1–D-35
   check boxes on, 292
   closing, 429
   configuring properties, 21–22
   designating default button, 166–167
   FormBorderStyle property, setting, 52–53
   GUI design guidelines, 858
   locking controls on, 80–81, 232
   renaming, 20–21
   Windows. *See* Windows forms
For...Next statements, 332, **348**, **357**
   vs. Do...Loop statements, 354–355
   using, 348–354
Friend keyword, **D-14***, **D-35***
frmMain Load event procedure, 153, 164, 178
full screen view, viewing Web pages in, 692–693
Function keyword, 405
Function procedures
   described, **405**, **410**
   using, 405–409
functions, **102**, **110**, **405**, **410**
   See also specific function
   conversion, 130, 863

G

Game Show Contestants application, 582–584
General Declarations section, **97**, **110**, 141
Get block, **626**, **645**
Get statement, **628**, **645**
GetFwt function, 432–436
GetUpperBound method, **508**, **530**, 549
global variables, 131
Grade Calculator application, 654–660
graphics
   adding to user interfaces, 76–77
   GUI design guidelines, 859
Greenview Toy Store Web application, 697–698, 700–702
group box, **231**, **244**
   adding to forms, 231–233
   GUI design guidelines, 860
grouping
   radio buttons, 291–292
   variables, 504
GUI (graphic user interface), **16**, **26**
   assigning access keys, 82
   check boxes standards, 293
   combo box standards, 420
   controlling focus with TabIndex property, 85
   default list box item, 380

design guidelines, 858–862
designating default button, 167
font types, styles, sizes, 77
guidelines, 69
InputBox function, 162
labeling group boxes, 231
list box standards, 377
MessageBox.Show method, 239
radio button standards, 292
selecting colors, 78

H

halting endless loops, 338
Handled property, **249**, **255**
Handles clause, in event procedures, 182
hand-tracing, **271**, **283**
Hangman Game application, 446–448, 477–480, 483–495
Harvey Industries application, 394–395, 427–442
Hide method, **D-15***, **D-35***
hiding
    auto-hiding windows in IDE, 15–16
    code region in Code Editor window, 40–41
horizontal sizing pointer, 52
Hours Worked application, debugging, 855–857
Hungarian notation, 20, 124
hyphen (-), negation and subtraction operators, 98

I

IDE (integrated development environment), **4**, **8**, 10
    component tray, **56**
    managing windows in, 15–16
If…Then…Else statement, **198**, 201, 203, 207, **224**, 573
images
    adding to Web pages, 698–700
    downloading free, 698
implicit type conversion, **141**, 142, **146**
incrementing, **340**, **357**
independent Sub procedures
    creating, 296–300
    described, **296**, **307**
indexes, 505
IndexOf method, **457**, **468**
infinite loops, **338**, **357**
information, storing with variables, 121–125
inheritance, **672**, **678**
Inherits clause, **672**, **678**
initializing, **340**, **357**
input dialog boxes, 161–164
input files, **581**, **592**
InputBox function
    described, **161**, **171**
    using, 161–164, 860
input/output symbol, **92**, **110**
Insert method, **453**, **468**
Insert query, **844**

INSERT statement, **836**, 836–843, **844**
inserting
    characters in strings, 453–456
    records in databases, 836–843
instances, **4**, **8**, **617**, **645**
instantiated, **4**, **8**, **617**, **645**
instantiating
    label controls, 32–34
    timer controls, 50–51
Integer data type, 122–123
integer division operator (), **99**, **110**
integers, generating random, 298
integrated development environment.
        See IDE (integrated
        development environment)
integrated development environment
        (IDE), **8**
IntelliSense feature, 662
interfaces
        See also user interfaces
        including combo box in, 419–423
        printing during run time, D-11*
invalid data, **105**, **110**
Is keyword, 280–281
IsMdiContainer property, **D-23***, **D-35***
italics, using, 77
Items collection, **375**, **385**

J

Jenko Booksellers application, 550–552
JotPad application, D-22–D-29*

K

KeyChar property, **249**, **255**
KeyPress events, **255**
    coding, 248–251
    described, **248**
keywords
    with conditions, 333
    described, **41**, **46**

L

label controls, **32**, **46**
    instantiating, 32–34
    naming, 33–34
    setting Location, Text properties, 34
    using, 67, 70
Label tool, instantiating label controls
    with, 32–34
Language Integrated Query, **773**, **782**
layouts
    creating columnar, 722–724
    window, 11
lblMessage control, 153
Length property, **449**, 450, **468**, **508**, **530**, 626
lifetime
    described, **131**, **146**
    of variables, 131–136
light bulb icon, 6
Like operator, **463**, **468**, 774
LIKE operator, **816**, **823**
line, **587**, **592**

line continuation character, **165**, **171**
link button controls
    adding to Web pages, 694–696
    described, **694**, **704**
LINQ, **773**, 775–777, 779–782, **783**
list boxes, **375**, **385**
    GUI design guidelines, 861
    items, 518
    using, 377–384
literal constants, **126**, **146**
literal type character, **126**, **146**
Load event procedure, 304–305, 599–601
local scope, 132
local variables, 132
Location property, 34, 80
locking controls, 80–81, 232, 293
logic errors, **105**, **110**
    finding, 851–855
    in selection structures, 270–275
logical operators, **207**, **224**
        See also specific operator
    calculating gross pay using, 211–213
    commonly used (fig.), 207–208
    and truth tables, 209–210
    using, 207–209
Long variables, 122–123
loop body, **333**, **357**
loop exit conditions, **329**, **357**
looping condition, **329**, **357**
loops, **329**, **357**
        See also specific loop type
    priming, and update reads, 342
    and repeating program instructions, 329–332
    stopping, 338
lowercase, converting strings to, 215–218

M

Make Same Size option, Format menu, 35
master tables, 744
Math Practice application, 261–263, 290–295, 312–319
Math.exe, 262
Math.Round function, **437**, **442**
MaximizeBox property, 53
MDI, **D-1***, **D-35***
MDI applications, **D-2***, **D-35***
MdiWindowListItem property, **D-23***, **D-35***
Me.Close() instruction, 42–43, 51
member variables, **565**, **576**
memory addresses, 397
menu items
    assigning shortcut keys to, 479–480
    described, 476
menu strip controls, **476**, **481**
menus
        See also specific menu
    access keys, 81
    adding to forms, 476–479
    GUI design guidelines, 862

MenuStrip tool, 476, 477
MessageBox.Show method
    described, **238**, **244**
    using, 238–244, 860
messages, displaying, 216–218
Method Name list box, **41**, **46**
methods, **42**, **46**, **617**, **645**
    See also specific method
    other than constructors, 631–632
    overloaded, **662**, **668**
Microsoft Access, connecting
    application to database,
    745–749
MinimizeBox property, 53
modulus operator, **99**, **110**, 222
Monthly Payment Calculator
    application, 231–254, 351–354,
    367–370
Morgan Industries application,
    745–749, 760–761
Move methods, **765**, **768**
Multiline property, **340**, **357**
multiple-alternative selection
    structures
    described, **275**, **283**
    using, 275–278
multiple-document interface, **D-1***,
    D-35*
multiple-form applications, **D-4***,
    D-35*
multiplication operator, 222
MyBase, **674**, **678**

N

Name property, Windows form,
    20–21
named constants, **138**, **146**
    intrinsic constants, 165
    using, 138–141, 234
namespace
    described, **20**, **26**
    scope, 131
naming
    See also renaming
    classes, 618
    label controls, 33–34
    variables, 123–124
negation (-) operator, 98, 222
nested repetition structures, 365–366
nested selection structures, **264**, **283**
    vs. compound conditions, 272–273
    using, 264–270
    using unnecessary, 274–275
New Project dialog box, 14
Not operator, 207, **208**, 219, 222, **224**
number sign (#) in pattern-matching,
    463
numbers
    displaying sum or difference,
    204–206
    formatting using ToString method,
    167–170
    generating random, 298–300
    rounding, 437

O

Object box, Properties window, **18**, **26**
Object data types, 122–123, 141
object-oriented (OO) applications
    creating, 63
    planning, 63–71
object-oriented programming
    languages, 4, 8, **617**, **646**
object-oriented programming
    terminology, 617
objects, **4**, **8**
    See also specific object
    associating procedures with,
    182–185
    binding in datasets, 749–756
    identifying application's, 66–67
    instantiated from classes, 17
    and object-oriented programming
    terminology, 617
    Random, **298**
    random, **307**
one-dimensional arrays, **505**, **530**
    accumulator and counter arrays,
    522–525
    parallel, 539–543
    sorting, 525–529
    traversing, 509–510
    using, 505–508
OOP, **617**, **646**
OOP (object-oriented programming),
    41, **46**
opening
    databases in IDE, 745
    existing solutions, 24
    Run dialog box, 61, 119
    Web applications, 700
    windows in IDE, 15–16
OpenText method, **586**, **592**
operators
    See also specific operator
    most commonly used (table), 98
    summary of, 222
Option Explicit, Option Infer, Option
    Strict, 141–144, 154–160
Options dialog box, 13
Or operator, 207, **208**, 209, **224**
Oracle, 743
Order By clause, **773**, **783**
ORDER BY clause, **816**, **823**
order forms, 64–65
order of precedence (operators),
    98–99, 222
OrElse operator, 207, **208**, 209, 222,
    224
outer loops, 365
output files, **581**, **592**
overflow errors, 338
overloaded methods, **662**, **668**
Overridable keyword, **674**, **678**
Overrides keyword, **674**, **679**

P

PadLeft method, **454**, **468**, 602
PadRight method, **454**, **468**, 602

Paradise Bookstore application,
    740–742, 787–791
parallel arrays, **539**, **543**
parallel one-dimensional arrays,
    539–543
parameter (query) marker, **828**, **844**
parameter queries
    described, **828**, **844**
    using, 828–830
parameterized constructors, **630**,
    636–640, **646**
parameterList, 297
parameters, **248**, **255**
parent tables, **744**, **768**
parentheses (()) and expressions, 98
Pascal case, **182**, **186**, 296, 565
passing by reference, **397**, **410**
passing by value, **397**, **410**
passing structure variables to
    procedures, 567–570
passing variables, 397–405
passing variables by reference,
    400–405
passing variables by value, 397–399
pattern-matching, comparing strings
    using, 463–466
Peek method, **588**, **592**
percent sign (%), SQL wildcard, 823
PerformClick method, 303, **304**, **307**
period (.) in expressions, 94
picture box controls
    adding to forms, 36–37
    described, **36**, **46**
PictureBox tool, 36–37
Pizza Roma application, 640–644
planning procedures using flowcharts,
    92–93
Playtime Cellular application, 60–62
    building, 75–80
    testing and debugging, 105–108
    TOE charts, 65–68, 152, 178
PMT function, 237
points, **21**, **26**
populating the array, **507**, **530**
Position property, **764**, **768**
positioning controls on Web pages,
    701–702
posttest loops, **332**, **357**, 368
Prairie Auditorium application,
    518–522
precedence
    of operators, 98–99
    order of operators (table), 222
pretest loops, **331**, 332, **357**, 368
previewing
    dataset contents, 748–749
    splash screens, 10
primary key, **744**, **768**
priming read, **342**, **357**
PrintForm tool, **D-11***, **D-35***
printing
    interfaces during run time, D-11*
    splash screen interface and code,
    54–55

`Private` keyword, 124, 139, 180, 296
Private variables, 625–629
procedure footers, **41**, **46**
procedure headers, **41**, **46**
procedure scope, **132**, **146**
procedure-level variables, **132**, **146**, 312
procedures
    See also specific procedure
    associating with different objects, events, 182–185
    exceptions, 757
    function, **405**, **410**
    passing structure variables to, 567–570
    planning using flowcharts, 92–93
process symbols, **92**, **110**
Product ID application, 451–452, 465–466
programmers, **8**
    job of, 2
    training, skills, employment opportunities, 2–4
programming, **2**, **8**
programming languages, **2**, **8**
programs, **2**, **8**
    making decisions in, 192–198
    repeating program instructions, 329–332
projects, and Windows applications, 13
promoted, **141**, **146**
properties, **18**, **26**
    See also specific property
    assigning values during run time, 94–96
    auto-implemented, **658**, **668**
    changing for multiple controls, 35
    configuring form, 21–22
    setting and restoring values, 22–23
Properties list
    described, **18**, **26**
    Settings box, 27
Properties window
    described, 18–19, **26**
    Object box, **26**
Property procedure, **626**, **646**
pseudocode
    described, **91**, **110**
    planning procedures using, 91–92
pseudo-random number generators, **298**, **307**
`Public` keyword, **40**, 565
public variables, 131
Public variables, 620–624

Q

Quarter of a Million club application, 330–332, 336–339
queries, **773**, **783**
    creating, 773–777
    creating SQL, 817–822
    invoking from code, 833–835

parameter, **844**
    saving, 831–833
    using LINQ aggregate operators, 779–782
Query Builder, using, 819–822, 832
question mark (?)
    parameter (query) marker, **844**
    in pattern-matching, 463
quotation marks (")
    string literal constants, 126
    and strings, 93, 102
    and zero-length strings, 111

R

radio buttons, **290**, **307**, 375
    adding to forms, 290–292
    default, **291**, **306**
    GUI design guidelines, 861
    selecting, 294
Random numbers, generating, 298–300
Random objects, **298**, **307**
Random.Next method, **299**, **307**
ranges, specifying in Case clauses, 280–281
ReadLine method, **587**, **592**
`ReadOnly` keyword, **626**, **646**
ReadOnly property, **340**, **357**, 626, 654–658
Rearrange application, 460–462
records (database), **743**, **768**
    adding to datasets, 799–804
    arranging in database, 773
    deleting from datasets, 805–810
    inserting, or deleting from databases, 836–843
    modifying, 787–791
    sorting in datasets, 804–805
reference controls, **36**, **46**
Refresh method, **366–367**, **371**
relational databases, **743**, **768**
relational operators, **199**
Remove method, **450**, 451, 468, **605**, **610**
RemoveAt method, **605**, **610**
removing
    See also deleting
    characters from strings, 450–452
    TabIndex boxes, 84
renaming
    executable files, 39–40
    form files, 18–19
    forms, 20–21
repeating program instructions, 329–332
repetition structures
    described, **329**, **357**
    nested, 365–366
resetting windows layout in IDE, 16
restoring property values, 22–23
Return statements, **406**, **410**
reusing classes, 640–644
rounding numbers, 437
Run dialog box, 61, 119

run time, **50**, **56**
    assigning values to properties during, 94–96
    printing interfaces during, D-11*
run time errors, **521**, **530**
running Visual Basic 2010 applications, 5–6

S

Sales Express Company application, 340–346
sans serif fonts, 77
saving
    queries, 831–833
    solutions, 23
scalar variables, **504**, **530**
Schneider, Gerrit, 698
scope, **131**, **146**
    block, **203**, **224**
    of variables, 131–136
ScrollBars property, **340**, **357**
SDI, **D-1***, **D-35***
SDI applications, **D-1***, **D-35***
searching
    strings, 457–459
    two-dimensional arrays, 552–555
Select Case statements
    described, **278**, **283**
    using, 278–282
SELECT statements, **815**, **823**
    testing, 829–830
    using, 815–817
SelectAll method, **251**, **255**
SelectedIndex property, **379**, **385**
SelectedIndexChanged event, **381**, **385**
SelectedItem property, **379**, **385**, 421
SelectedValueChanged event, **381**, **385**
selecting
    controls, 232
    radio buttons, check boxes, 294
selection structures, **192**, **224**, 488
    logic errors in, 270–275
    making decisions with, 192–198
    nested, **264**, 264–270, **283**
SelectionMode property, **375**, **385**
sentence capitalization, **70**, **72**
sequential access files, **581**, **593**
    closing input, 589–591
    closing output, 584–585
    reading data from, 585–588
    writing data to, 581–584
Server Explorer window, 745
Set block, **626**, **646**
Set statement, **628**, **646**
Settings box, Properties list, **18**, **27**
Shoppers Haven application, 327–328, 374–384
Short variables, 122–123
short-circuit evaluation, **208**, **224**
shortcut keys
    assigning to menu items, 479–480
    described, **479**, **481**

Show method, **D-15***, **D-35***
ShowDialog method, D-7*
signatures, **630**, **646**
simple variables, **504**, **530**
Single data types, 122–123
single-alternative selection structure,
    192, 193–196, 198–199, 202,
    213, **224**, 264
single-document interface, **D-1***,
    D-35*
Size property, Windows form, 22
Sleep method, **366–367**, **371**
Solution Explorer window, **17–18**, **27**
    displaying, 16
    using, 14–15
solutions
    closing, 23
    opening existing, 24
    saving, 23
    and Windows applications, 13
Sort method, **804**, **810**
Sorted property, **376–377**, **385**
sorting, **525**, **530**
    one-dimensional arrays, 525–529
    records in datasets, 804–805
source files, **17**, **27**
Source view, 727–729
splash screens
    adding timer controls to, 51
    adding to applications, D-4–D-6*
    application described, 13
    previewing, 10
    printing interface and code, 54–55
SQL, **815**, **823**
SQL Server, 743
starting
    applications, 38–40
    Visual Studio, 11–12
    Web applications, 696–698
StartPosition property, Windows
    form, 21
start/stop symbol, **92**, **110**
startup forms, **38**, **46**
State application, 526–529
statement block, **198**, **224**
Static keyword, 124, 136
static text
    adding to Web pages, 691–693
    described, **691**, **704**
static variables, 181, 312
    described, **136**, **146**
    using, 136–138
static Web pages, **684**, **704**
stopping endless loops, 338
stream of characters, **581**, **593**
StreamReader object, **585**, **593**
StreamWriter object, **581**, **593**
String data types, 122–123
String.Empty, **93**, 94–95, **111**
strings, **93**, **111**
    accessing characters in, 460–462
    comparing using pattern-matching,
        463–466
    concatenating, 160–161

containing letters, comparing,
    213–214
converting to uppercase, lowercase,
    215–218
determining number of characters
    in, 449–450
empty, **93**, **110**
    inserting characters in, 453–456
    removing characters from, 450–452
    searching, 457–459
Strings.Space method, **603**, **610**
structure statements, **565**, **576**
structure variables, **566**, **576**
    creating arrays of, 571–575
    declaring, using, 566–566
    passing to procedures, 567–570
Structured Query Language
    creating queries, 817–822
    described, **815**, **823**
structures, **565**, **576**
styles
    combo box, 419–420
    and GUI design, 77
    predefined format VB (table), 104
Sub keyword, 296, 405
Sub procedures, **42**, **46**
    independent, 296–300
    using, 396–397
submenus, 476
subscripts
    described, **505**, **530**
    determining highest, 508
Substring method, **460**, **468**
subtraction (-) operator, 98, 99
Sweet Tooth Chocolate application,
    512–514
syntax, **41**, **46**, 105
syntax errors, 106–107
    described, **105**, **111**
    finding, 848–851

T

tab order, controlling, 82–85
tabbed-document interface, **D-1***,
    D-35*
TabControl tool, **D-35***, **D-29**
TabIndex property, 82–85, 293, 860
TableAdapter objects, **752**, **768**
TableAdapter Query Configuration
    Wizard, 831–833
TableAdapterManager objects, **752**,
    768
TableCell Collection Editor dialog box,
    725
TableRow Collection Editor dialog
    box, 725
tables (database)
    described, **743**, **768**
    using, 743–744
tasks, identifying application's, 64–65
TDI, **D-1***, **D-29***, **D-35***
TDI applications, **D-3***, **D-35***
testing
    applications, 105–108

code, 281
connections, 746–747
timer, 51–52
text, using italics or bold, 77
text boxes, **66**, **72**
    adding controls to forms, 80
    changing background color of, 78
    clearing contents of, 93
    controlling characters accepted by,
        248–251
    controlling tab order, 82–85
    Enter event procedures, 251–254
text files, **581**, **593**
Text property, 21, 34, 126, 421
TextBox class, 80
TextChanged events
    coding procedure, 181–185
    described, **181**, **186**
this book, using, 6–7
Tick events, 50–51
timer controls
    described, **50**, **56**
    instantiating, adding, 50–51
Timer tool, instantiating timer
    controls, 50–51
tip notes (light bulb icon), 6
To keyword, 280–281
TOE charts
    CD Collection application, 598
    Hangman Game application, 483
    Harvey Industries application, 427
    Math Practice application, 295
    Monthly Payment Calculator
        application, 232
    Playtime Cellular application,
        65–68, 152, 178
    Shoppers Haven application, 374
ToLower method, 457
    described, **215**, **224**
    using, 215–218
toolbox, **31**, **46**
Toolbox window, **31**, **46**
top-driven loops, 332
ToString method
    described, **167**, **171**
    formatting numbers using,
        167–170
Total Sales Calculator application,
    debugging, 848–851
ToUpper method, 214, 457
    described, **215**, **225**
    using, 215–218
traversing
    arrays, 509–510
    two-dimensional arrays, 549–550
Treasures Gift Shop application,
    502–503, 539–542, 552–555,
    571–575
Trim method, **450**, 451, **468**
TrimStart, TrimEnd methods, 450
true path, **192**, 202, **225**, 264
truth tables, **208**, **225**
    for logical operators (fig.), 209
    using, 210

Try...Catch statements, **757**, 758–760, **768**
TryParse method, 219–220, 344
  described, **128**, **146**
  using, 128–129, 140
two-dimensional arrays, 505, **546**, **556**
  declaring, 546–549
  searching, 552–555
  totaling values stored in, 550–552
  traversing, 549–550

U

unary operators, 98
undeclared variables, 141
unhiding code region in Code Editor window, 40–41
Unicode, **122**, **146**
Until keyword, 333
Update method, **802**, **810**
update read, **342**, **357**
updating, **340**, **357**
uppercase, converting strings to, 215–218
user input
  controlling tab order, 82–85
  designating default button, 166–167
  InputBox function, 161–164
  and MessageBox.Show method, 238–244
  using text boxes for, 66
  validating, 714–716
user interfaces, **4**, **8**
  adding check boxes to, 292–294
  adding color to, 77–78
  adding graphics to, 76–77
  building Playtime Cellular application, 75–80
  GUI design guidelines, 858–859
  layout and organization, 71
  sketching, 69–71
user-defined data types, **565**, **576**

V

Val function, **102**, 103, **111**, 153
valid data, **105**, **111**
validating user input, 714–716

validator tools, **714**, **717**
values
  calculating total and average, 512–514
  finding highest, 515–517
  sorting in one-dimensional arrays, 525–529
  totaling in two-dimensional arrays, 550–552
variables, **121**, **146**
  See also specific type
  assigning data to existing, 125–131
  with class scope, 134–135
  creating 'on the fly,' 141
  declaring, 124–125
  grouping, 504
  member, **565**, **576**
  naming, 123–124
  passing, 397–405
  with procedure scope, 132–134
  scope and lifetime of, 131
  selecting data types for, 122–123
  static. *See* static variables
  storing information using, 121–125
  undeclared, 141
viewing
  Visual Basic code, 756–757
  Web pages in full screen view, 692–693
Visible property, **315**, **319**
Visual Basic 2010
  conversion functions, 863
  demonstration of, 4–6
  overview of, 4, 11
  viewing code, 756–757
Visual Basic 2010 Express, 11
  configuring, 12–13
  exiting, 24
  starting, 11–12
Visual Studio 2010, 11
  configuring, 12–13
  exiting, 24
  starting, 11–12
Visual Web Developer 2010, configuring, 687–688
Voter Eligibility application, 264–270

W

wages of computer programmers, 3
Warren School application, 522–525
Web applications
  adding Web pages to, 693–694
  closing and opening, 700
  creating, 687–688
  overview of, 684–687
  starting, 696–698
Web pages, **684**, **704**, 708–712
  adding images to, 698–700
  adding link button controls, 694–696
  adding static text to, 691–693
  ASP, 686
  customizing, 690–693
  dynamic. *See* dynamic Web pages
  positioning controls on, 701–702
  static, **684**, **704**
  viewing in full screen view, 692–693
Web servers, **684**, **704**
Where clause, **773**, **783**
WHERE clause, **815**, **823**
While keyword, 333
Willow Pools application, 567–570, 620–624
windows
  managing in the IDE, 15–16
  resetting layout in IDE, 16
  selecting layout, 11
Windows applications, 13
Windows Form Designer window, **16–17**, **27**
Windows Form objects, **16**, **27**
Windows forms, properties of form files, 19–22
Write method, **583**, **593**
WriteLine method, **583**, **593**
WriteOnly keyword, **626**, **646**

X

Xor operator, 207, 209, 222

Z

Zappet application, D-13–D-21*
zero-length strings, **93**, **111**